John Willis

Theatre World

1990-1991 SEASON

VOLUME 47

THEATRE BOOK PUBLISHERS
211 WEST 71 STREET • NEW YORK NY • 10023

LIBRARY OF CONGRESS CATALOG CARD NO. 73-82953
ISBN 1-55783-125-4 (cloth)
ISBN: 1-55783-126-2 (paper)

T O

R O S E T T A L e N O I R E

*actress, singer, teacher, director, founder-artistic director of Off-Broadway's AMAS (you love)
Repertory Theater: an interracial organization devoted to the presentation of new musicals, the
encouragement of new musical theater talent in all facets of this perfomrming art, and to
development of new audiences for this uniquely American art form.*

CONTENTS

EDITOR: JOHN WILLIS
Assistant Editor: Tom Lynch
Assistants: Herbert Hayward, Jr., Barry Monush, Stanley Reeves, John Sala
Staff Photographers: Bert Andrews, Ronald Faucett, Michael Riordan, Michael Viade, Van Williams
Designer: Peggy Goddard

Entire cast of Neil Simon's "Lost in Yonkers" (back row) Jamie Marsh, Danny Gerard (middle row) Mercedes Ruehl, Irene Worth, (front row) Kevin Spacey, Lauren Klein, Mark Blum. Recipient of Pulitzer Prize and "Tonys" for Best Play, Leading Actress (Mercedes Ruehl), Featured Actress (Irene Worth), Featured Actor (Kevin Spacey). See page 25. *Martha Swope Photo.*

THE SEASON IN REVIEW
June 1, 1990 - May 31, 1991

This was the most dismal, depressing season in memory. Broadway had a record-setting low number of productions and a record high in ticket sales and attendance. This was partially because of the war in the Persian Gulf and the recession. The Persian Gulf War kept people glued to tv's coverage of this historic performance. It cut attendance, not only in theatres, but also in hotels and restaurants in the theater district. Some attractions raised admission to $60 each for orchestra seats, and "Miss Saigon" had an incredible $100 top ducat. In spite of increases, the League of American Theatres and Producers reported that more people attended Broadway theatres during the year than attended all the New York City sports events combined during the same period. Touring shows again had an increase over last year's receipts, and there was a significant increase in non-union touring companies.

Only 26 productions were eligible for Tonys: 14 new plays, 7 musicals, a return of last season's "Gypsy," 4 revivals, and 4 special attractions: Harry Connick, Jr., Michael Feinstein, Jackie Mason, and Penn & Teller's "Refrigerator Tour" that moved to Off Broadway. "Miss Saigon," another British import, scored the largest advance in theater history. Its opening was postponed because of the intense controversy over Equity's attempt to deny Jonathan Pryce (a white Welshman) the privilege of repeating his London success in an Eurasian role. He was finally granted permission after the producer threatened to cancel the engagement. As usual, there was a much-heated argument over the Tony nominations and winners. Nominees were not just the best of Broadway, but practically all there were on Broadway. "Lost in Yonkers" was voted Best Play with its Mercedes Ruehl as Best Actress, Irene Worth and Kevin Spacey as Best Supporting Actress and Actor in a Play. The play was honored also with the year's Pulitzer Prize. Best Actor in a Play went to Nigel Hawthorne for "Shadowlands." Jerry Zaks was voted Best Director of a Play for "Six Degrees of Separation." The play was cited as best of the season by the New York Drama Critics Circle. The Tony for Best Musical went to the "The Will Rogers Follies" that was honored also by the NY Drama Critics Circle, and additional Tonys were awarded to it for Best Score, Best Direction, Choreography, Lighting, and Costumes. "The Secret Garden" received Tonys for Best Book, Best Scenery, Best Featured Actress in a Musical (Daisy Eagan). Tonys for Best Actor, Best Actress, and Best Supporting Actor in a Musical went respectively to Jonathan Pryce, Lea Salonga, and Hinton Battle, all of "Miss Saigon." "Fiddler on the Roof" with Topol was voted Best Revival. NY Drama Critics Circle cited "Our Country's Good" for Best Foreign Play (although written by an American), and a Special Citation went to Eileen Atkins for her solo performance Off-Broadway in "A Room of One's Own."

Broadway adopted a plan to put 3 new plays in 3 unbooked Broadway theatres at prices ranging from $10 to $24. The Broadway Alliance was agreed to by theater unions, owners, producers and suppliers. This was a response to the escalating costs that have driven plays from Broadway. Unfortunately, the first 2 productions were failures: "The Speed of Darkness" and "Our Country's Good."

Broadway performers deserving mention, in addition to those noted above, are Jane Adams, Bruce Adler, Jane Alexander, June Angela, Adam Arkin, Dylan Baker, Christopher Benjamin, Mark Blum, Philip Bosco, Len Cariou, Keith Carradine, Philip Casnoff, Stockard Channing, Marcus Chong, Jack Coleman, Susan Cremin, Tyne Daly, Kathryn Erbe, Willy Falk, Alison Fraser, Peter Frechette, Danny Gerard, Jill Hennessy, Paul Hipp, Dee Hoty, Lauren Klein, LaChanze, Robert Lambert, Stephen Land, Robert Sean Leonard, Marcia Lewis, Jamie Marsh, Kathleen Rowe McAllen, Spike McClure, Tom McGowan, Liza Minnelli, Brian Mitchell, Crista Moore, Kenny Neal, Kevin Ramsey, Cathy Rigby, Eric Riley, Francis Ruivivar, Michael Rupert, John Schneider, Sam Tsoutsouvas, Tracey Ullman, Courtney B. Vance, Robert Westenberg, and Tom Wopat.

As has become customary, Off-Broadway with more than 250 productions was more prolific and exciting than "the great white way." Among the best presentations were "Absent Friends", "The American Plan", "Breaking Legs", "Cirque de Soleil", "Dougherty & Fields", "Elliot Loves", "The Kingfish", "Life during Wartime", "Lips Together, Teeth Apart",

"Lyndon", "Machinal", "Mambo Mouth", "Ninagawa Macbeth", "The Old Boy", "Red Scare on Sunset", "Sex, Drugs, Rock & Roll", "The Subject Was Roses", "The Substance of Fire", "The Sum of Us", "The Taming of the Shrew", "Township Fever"; the popular musicals were "Assassins", "Broadway Juke Box", "Falsettoland", "A Funny Thing Happened on the Way to the Forum", "I Can Get It for You Wholesale", "Love Lemmings", "Pageant", "Song of Singapore", "Yiddle with a Fiddle", and the delightfully ingenious and innovative "And the World Goes 'Round".

Off-Broadway performers deserving mention are Karen Allen, Gillian Anderson, Alison Bartlett, Christine Baranski, Brian Bedford, Brenda Blethyn, Scotty Bloch, Stephen Bogardus, Philip Bosco, Simon Brooking, Charles Busch, Joanne Camp, Erma Campbell, Peggy Cass, Stephen Collins, Joan Copeland, Lindsay Crouse, Kevin Conway, Laura Dean, Patrick Dempsey, Patrick Fitzgerald, Peter Francis-James, Morgan Freeman, Tovah Feldsuh, Lauren Gaffney, Sue Giosa, Angela Goethals, Victor Garber, Tony Goldwyn, Clark Gregg, Julie Halston, Anthony Heald, Tess Harper, Earle Hyman, Jonathan Hogan, Dana Ivey, Page Johnson, Stephen Joyce, Patti Karr, Laurie Kennedy, Swoosie Kurtz, Caroline Lagerfelt, Robert Lambert, Nathan Lane, Bethel Leslie, Audra Lindley, Emily Loesser, Lizbeth Mackay, John Mahoney, Tom Mardirosian, John McConnell, Elizabeth McGovern, Mark Metcalf, Bill Moor, Jennie Moreau, Donna Murphy, Cynthia Nixon, Ciaran O'Reilly, Evan Pappas, Anne Pitoniak, Amanda Plummer, Charlotte Ray, Dick Reynolds, Ron Rifkin, Michael Rupert, Kyra Sedgwick, Barry Sherman, Jean Stapleton, Marisa Tomei, John Turturro, Tracey Ullman, Joe Urla, Richard Venture, Jim Walton, James Whitmore, Chandra Wilson.

This season over 25 plays Off-Broadway were concerned with homosexual relationships--a record. However, the AIDS epidemic was not prominently addressed in any of them. An increasing number of audience participation productions were working hard to assure enjoyment: "Song of Singapore", "Prom Queens Unchained", "Pageant", and the long-running "Tony 'n' Tina's Wedding". There was also a proliferation of monologists/solo performers: Eileen Atkins, Eric Bogosian, Tovah Feldshuh, Spalding Gray, Julie Harris, John Leguizama, Laurence Luckinbill, John McConnell, Wallace Shawn, Red Skeleton, Tracey Ullman, and Paul Zaloom.

RANDOM NOTES: Possibly the most expensive flop in Broadway history was this season: Andrew Lloyd Weber's "Aspects of Love" that lost its entire $8 million investment...Many New York artists and organizations were rejecting endowment funds because the National Endowment for the Arts required signing an anti-obscenity pledge that violates the First Amendment rights to free speech. The Dramatists Guild of playwrights announced that it would withhold all works from the 68 League of Residential Theatres (LORT) until a contract is signed giving the author rights to contract approval...Nov. 2, 1990 Joseph Papp appointed JoAnne Akalaitis as his Artistic Associate...Nicole Williamson, the ghost of John Barrymore in "I Hate Hamlet," nightly offered advice on acting and show business, and forced one of the cast to walk out on the production after the first act...A Broadway "Walk of Stars" was inaugurated from 42nd to 59th Streets. Each star commemorates a Tony awardee and Helen Hayes was the first so honored...TV ratings for the Tony presentations rose slightly this year. It was produced by Joe Cates in the Minskoff Theatre...In December two taxi stands were inaugurated in the theater district from 10 p.m. to midnight...The 78-year-old landmark Palace Theatre, the most renowned vaudeville house in the U.S., re-opened May 1, 1991 with "The Will Rogers Follies" after a three-year and $3 million restoration to its original decor. It was achieved by selling air rights to Embassy Suites Hotel. ..."The Phantom of the Opera" celebrated its third sold-out year, "Les Miserables" its fourth, and "Cats" was beginning its 9th life...The Westside Arts Theater was beautifully renovated and re-named Westside Theater. It was originally a Dutch Reform Church...The Actors Studio Building, also a former church, gained landmark status...Owners challenged the landmark designation of 28 New York theatres, but the court dismissed the case. Thank you, State Court of Appeals.

A LITTLE NIGHT MUSIC

Music & Lyrics, Stephen Sondheim; Book, Hugh Wheeler; Suggested by Ingmar Bergman's 1956 film *Smiles of a Summer Night*; Director, Scott Ellis; Conductor, Paul Gemignani; Original Orchestrations, Jonathan Tunick; Sets, Michael Anania; Costumes, Lindsay W. Davis; Lighting, Dawn Chiang; Choreography, Susan Stroman; Sound, Abe Jacob; Press, Susan Woelzl, Dale Zeidman; Presented in repertory by the New York City Opera. Opened in the New York State Theatre on Friday, August 3, 1990.*

CAST

Mrs. Segstrom	Susanne Marsee
Mr. Lindquist	Ron Baker
Mrs. Nordstrom	Lisa Saffer
Mrs. Anderssen	Barbara Shirvis
Mr. Erlanson/Bertrand	Michael Rees Davis
Frederika Armfeldt	Danielle Ferland
Madame Armfeldt	Regina Resnik[1]
Frid	David Comstock
Henrik Egerman	Kevin P. Anderson[2]
Anne Egerman	Beverly Lambert[3]
Fredrik Egerman	George Lee Andrews[4]
Petra	Susan Terry[5]
Desirée Armfelt	Sally Ann Howes
Malla	Raven Wilkinson
Count Carl-Magnus Malcolm	Michael Maguire
Countess Charlotte Malcolm	Maureen Moore[6]
Osa	Judith Jarosz
Serving Gentlemen	Michael Cornell, Ernest Foederer, Kent A. Heacock, Ronald Kelley, Brian Michels, Brian Quirk, Christopher Sheperd, John Henry Thomas

MUSICAL NUMBERS: Overture, Night Waltz, Now/Later/Soon, Glamorous Life, Remember?, You Must Meet My Wife, Liaisons, In Praise of Women, Every Day a Little Death, Weekend in the Country, The Sun Won't Set, It Would Have Been Wonderful, Perpetual Anticipation, Send in the Clowns, Miller's Son, Finale

A new production of the musical, performed in two acts. The action takes place in turn of the century Sweden. For original production see *Theatre World* Vol. 29 .

*Closed November 7, 1990 after 11 performances in repertory. For original Broadway production, see *Theatre World* Vol. 29.

†Succeeded by: 1. Elaine Bonazzi 2. Michael Rees Davis 3. Michele McBride 4. Harlan Foss 5. Liz Larson 6. Susanne Marsee

Martha Swope/Carol Rosegg Photo

Sally Ann Howes

Sheryl Woods, Margaret Cusak in "Street Scene"

STREET SCENE

Music/Orchestrations, Kurt Weill; Lyrics, Langston Hughes; Adapted from the play by Elmer Rice; Director, Jay Lesenger; Production, Jack O'Brien; Conductor, Chris Nance; Sets, Paul Sylbert; Costumes, Marjorie McCown; Lighting, Gilbert V. Hemsley, Jr.; Choreography, Patricia Birch; Chorus Master, Joseph Colaneri; Children's Chorus, Mildred Hohner; Press, Susan Woelzl, Dale Zeidman; Presented in repertory by the New York City Opera. Opened in the New York State Theatre on Friday, September 7, 1990*

CAST

Greta Fiorentino	Rachel Rosales
Emma Jones	Joyce Castle
Olga Olsen	Susanne Marsee
Carl Olsen	Robert Ferrier
Neighborhood Woman	Lisa Jablow
Shirley Kaplan	Elinor Basescù
Abraham Kaplan	David Rae Smith
Salvation Army Girls	Deborah Williams, Kathleen Smith
Henry Davis	Eugene Perry
Willie Maurrant	Keith Cacciola-Morales
Anna Maurrant	Margaret Cusack
Sam Kaplan	Kevin P. Anderson
Daniel Buchanan	Peter Blanchet
Mrs. Buchanan	Lila Herbert
Frank Maurrant	William Parcher
George Jones	William Ledbetter
Steve Sankey	Richard Maynard
Lippo Fiorentino	Jonathan Green
Mrs. Hildebrand	Jennifer Lane
Jenny Hildebrand	Robin Tabachnik
Graduates	Alexis Martin, Karla Simmons
Charlie Hildebrand	Derek Dreyer
Mary Hildebrand	Rachel Samberg
Grace Davis	Melissa Martin
Rose Maurrant	Sheryl Woods
Harry Easter	Harlan Foss
Mae Jones	Jeanette Palmer
Dick McGann	John MacInnis
Vincent Jones	David Comstock
Dr. Wilson	Don Henderson
Officer Murphy	David Frye
Milkman	Ian D. Klapper
Joan	Allegra Victoria Forste
Myrtle	Francesca LaGuardia
Workman	Louis Perry
Eddie	Gregory Moore
Sally	Kelley Faulkner
Joe	Michael Cole
Strawberry Seller	Marty Singleton
Corn Seller	Rita Metzger
James Henry	Don Yule
Fred Cullen	Jonathan Guss
Old Clothes Man	Don Henderson
Grocery Boy	Kent A. Heacock
Ambulance Driver	Ronald Kelley
Music Student	Jane Cummins
Intern	John Henry Thomas
Furniture Movers	Glenn Rowen, Webster Latimer
Nursemaids	Lee Bellaver, Susan Ward
Policemen	Michael Putsch, Neil Eddinger
Middle-aged Couple	Harris Davis, Rita Metzger

MUSICAL NUMBERS: Ain't It Awful the Heat?, I Got a Marble and a Star, Get a Load of That, When a Woman Has a Baby, Somehow I Never Could Believe, Ice Cream, Let Things Be Like They Always Was, Wrapped in a Ribbon and Tied in a Bow, Lonely House, Wouldn't You Like To Be on Broadway?, What Good Would the Moon Be, Moon-Faced Starry-Eyed, Remember That I Care, Catch Me If You Can, There'll Be Trouble, A Boy Like You, We'll Go Away Together, The Woman Who Lived Up There, Lullaby, I Loved Her Too, Don't Forget the Lilac Bush

A new production of the musical in two acts and three scenes. The action takes place on a sidewalk in New York City during June. For original production see *Theatre World* Vol. 3.

*Closed September 29, 1990 after 6 performances in repertory.

Carol Rosegg/Martha Swope Photo

Michael Feinstein Top:Feinstein

MICHAEL FEINSTEIN IN CONCERT: PIANO AND VOICE

Production Staged and Supervised by Christopher Chadman; Musical Director, Ian Finkel; Special Material, Bruce Vilanch; Lighting, David Agress; Sound, Daryl Bornstein; General Management, David Strong Warner; Production Manager, Sam Ellis; Production Stage Manager, Peter Glazer; Presented by Ron Delsener; Press, Adrian Bryan-Brown/Kevin McAnarney, Chris Boneau, Jackie Green, Eva Patton. Opened in the John Golden Theatre on Tuesday, October 2, 1990.*

CAST

Michael Feinstein

Ian Finkel (Xylophone)	David Fink (Bass)
Martin Fischer (Drums)	Bruce Uchitel (Guitar)

An entertainment in two acts. This was Mr. Feinstein's third Broadway engagement, previously playing the Lyceum Theatre (see *Theatre World* Vol. 44) and the Booth Theatre (see *Theatre World* Vol. 45). On opening night, composer Burton Lane also performed.

*Closed October 27, 1990 after a limited engagement of 30 performances.

Marc Bryan-Brown, Joan Marcus, Chris White Photos

Jack Coleman, Marcus Chong Top: Robert Barry Fleming, Ray Oriel,
Chong, Anthony Barrile, Darrin DeWitt Henson

Marcus Chong (top), Jack Coleman

STAND-UP TRAGEDY

By Bill Cain; Director, Ron Link; Sets, Yael Pardess; Costumes, Carol Brolaski; Lighting, Michael Gilliam; Sound, Jon Gottlieb; Music, Craig Sibley; Rap Choreography, Charles Randolph-Wright; Company Manager, Marshall B. Purdy; Production Supervisor, Frank Bayer; Stage Managers, Franklin Keysar, Ruth E. Sternberg; Production Coordinator, Robert Routolo; Dramaturg, Corey Beth Madden; Wardrobe, Kia Heath; Presented by Charles B. Moss, Jr., Brent Peek, Donald Taffner, Center Theatre Group/Mark Taper Forum and Hartford Stage Company; Previewing from Tuesday, September 25, 1990. Opened in the Criterion Center Stage Right on Thursday, October 4, 1990.*

CAST

Marco Ruiz	Anthony Barrile
Lee Cortez	Marcus Chong
Father Ed Larkin	Charles Cioffi
Tom Griffin	Jack Coleman
Mitchell James	John C. Cooke
Freddy	Robert Barry Fleming
Burke Kendall	Dan Gerrity
Carlos Cruz	Darrin DeWitt Henson
Henry Rodriguez	Ray Oriel

UNDERSTUDIES/STANDBYS: Christopher Cass (Larkin/Griffin/James/Kendall), Robert Barry Fleming (Cortez/Ruiz), Darrin DeWitt Henson (Rodriguez), Marc Joseph (Cruz/Freddy)

A drama in two acts. The action takes place in a Lower East Side Catholic boys school during the 1980s.

* Closed Tuesday, October 16, 1990 after 13 performances and 12 previews.

Jay Thompson, T. Charles Erickson Photos

Darrin DeWitt Henson, Anthony Barrile, John C. Cooke, Marcus
Chong, Jack Coleman, Dan Gerrity, Robert Barry Fleming
Above: Cooke, Coleman, Charles Cioffi, Ray Oriel

THE MISER

By Molière; Translation, John Wood; Director, Stephen Porter; Sets, James Morgan; Costumes, Gail Brassard; Lighting, Mary Jo Dondlinger; Production Stage Managers, Wm. Hare, Alex Scott; Casting, Julie Hughes, Barry Moss; Company Manager, Susan Elrod; Presented by Circle in the Square Theatre (Theodore Mann, Artistic Director; Paul Libin, Producing Director); Press, Merle Debuskey/Susan Chicoine. Previewing from Friday, September 31, 1990; Opened in the Circle in the Square Uptown on Thursday, October 11, 1990.*

CAST

Dame Claude	Jennifer Roblin
Valere	Christian Baskous
Elise	Mia Dillon
Cleante	Thomas Gibson
Harpagon	Philip Bosco
La Fleche	Adam Redfield
Maitre Simon/Officer's Assistant	Bill Buell
Frosine	Carole Shelley
Maitre Jacques	John Christopher Jones
Brindavoine	Willis Sparks
La Merluche	Joseph Jamrog
Marianne	Tracy Sallows
Police Officer	Tom Brennan
Anselme	John MacKay

UNDERSTUDIES: John MacKay (Harpagon), Jennifer Roblin (Elise/Marianne), Willis Sparks (Valere/Cleante), Bill Buell (La Fleche/Simon), Joseph Jamrog (Anselme/Policeman), John Tyrrell (Brindavoine/La Merluche/Simon/Assistant), Lucy Martin (Frosine/Dame Claude).

A comedy in two acts. The action takes place in Harpagon's Paris house in 1668.

* Closed December 30, 1990 after 93 performances and 23 previews.

Martha Swope Photos

Right: Tracy Sallows, Carole Shelly, Thomas Gibson, Mia Dillon
Top: Christian Baskous, Dillon, Philip Bosco

Jackie Mason

JACKIE MASON: BRAND NEW

Executive Producer, Jyll Rosenfeld; Design/Lighting, Neil Peter Jampolis; Sound, Bruce Cameron; General Management, Joseph Harris; Company Manager, Kathleen M. Lowe; Stage Manager, Don Myers; Opening Sequence Direction, David Niles; Presented by Old Friends Group Inc. (Michael Simoff, Eric P. Ashenberg); Press, Robert M. Zarem/Jason Weinberg. Previewing from Tuesday, October 9, 1990; Opened in the Neil Simon Theatre on Wednesday, October 17, 1990.*

CAST

JACKIE MASON

An entertainment in two acts. An earlier version of this production was performed at the Public Theater in January/February 1990 (See *TheatreWorld* Vol. 46). Mr. Mason's Broadway performance, *The World According To Me*, opened at the Brooks Atkinson in December 1986 (See *TheatreWorld* Vol. 43).

*Closed June 30, 1991 after 237 performances and 7 previews.

ONCE ON THIS ISLAND

Music, Stephen Flaherty; Lyrics/Book, Lynn Ahrens; Based on novel *My Love, My Love* by Rosa Guy; Director/Choreographer, Graciela Daniele; Orchestrations, Michael Starobin; Musical Director, Steve Marzullo; Sets, Loy Arcenas; Costumes, Judy Dearing; Lighting, Allen Lee Hughes; Sound, Scott Lehrer; Associate Choreographer, Willie Rosario; Stage Managers, Leslie Loeb, Fred Tyson; Casting, Alan Filderman, Daniel Swee; Vocal & Dance Arrangements/Musical Continuity, Mr. Flaherty; Percussion Concepts, Norbert Goldberg; General Manager, James Walsh; Company Manager, Florie Seery; Wardrobe, Anita Ellis; Original Cast Recording by RCA Victor; Presented by The Shubert Organization, Capital Cities/Abc Inc., Suntory International Corp., and James Walsh, in association with Playwrights Horizons; Press, Philip Rinaldi/Tim Ray. Previewing from Tuesday, October 2, 1990;, Opened in the Booth Theatre on Thursday, October 18, 1990.*

CAST

Daniel	Jerry Dixon
Erzulie, Goddess of Love	Andrea Frierson
Mama Euralie	Sheila Gibbs
Ti Moune	LaChanze
Asaka, Mother of the Earth	Kecia Lewis-Evans†1
Little Ti Moune	Afi McClendon†2
Armand	Gerry McIntyre
Agwe, God of Water	Milton Craig Nealy
Andrea	Nikki Rene
Papa Ge, Demon of Death	Eric Riley
Tonton Julian	Ellis E. Williams

UNDERSTUDIES: Fuschia Walker (Mama/Asaka/Erzulie), PaSean Wilson (Ti Moune/Andrea), Desiree Scott (Little Ti Moune), Keith Tyrone (Daniel/Armand/Tonton/Agwe), Gerry McIntyre (Papa Ge)

MUSICAL NUMBERS: We Dance, One Small Girl, Waiting for Life, And the Gods Heard Her Prayer, Rain, Pray, Forever Yours, Sad Tale of the Beauxhommes, Ti Moune, Mama Will Provide, Some Say, The Human Heart, Some Girls, The Ball, A Part of Us, Why We Tell the Story

A musical performed without intermission. The action takes place on an island in the French Antilles during a stormy night. .

*Closed Dec. 1, 1991 after 469 performances and 19 previews. This show originated last season at Playwrights Horizons (See *Theatre World* Vol. 46)

†Succeeded by: 1. Lillias White 2. Desiree Scott

Martha Swope Photos

Left: LaChanze Top: The Company

LaChanze and Company

Jerry Dixon, LaChanze, Andrea Frierson

Gregg Burge, Kyme

Gregg Burge, Stanley Wayne Mathis, Kevin Ramsey

Tamara Tunie Bouquett, Brian Mitchell,
Angela Teek

Rae Dawn Chong, Mark Kenneth Smaltz, Ron Alexander

OH, KAY!

Music, George Gershwin; Lyrics, Ira Gershwin; Book, Guy Bolton, P.G. Wodehouse; Adaptation, James Racheff; Direction/Choreography/Concept, Dan Siretta; Musical Direction/Vocal and Additional Dance Arrangements, Tom Fay; Orchestrations, Arnold Goland; Dance Arrangements, Donald Johnston; Sets, Kenneth Foy; Costumes, Theoni V. Aldredge; Lighting, Craig Miller; Sound, Jan Nebozenko; Hairstylist, Robert DiNiro; Stage Managers, Harold Goldfaden, Tracy Crum; Wardrobe, Sharon A. Lewis; General Manager/Associate Producer, Leo K. Cohen; Executive Producer, Natalie Lloyd; Inspired by productions of Goodspeed Opera House & Birmingham Theatre; Presented by David Merrick; Press, Joshua Ellis/Susanne Tighe, John Barlow. Previewing from Tuesday, October 16, 1990; Opened in the Richard Rodgers Theatre on Thursday, November 1, 1990.*

CAST

Billy Lyles	Gregg Burge
Dolly Greene	Kyme
Duke	Stanley Wayne Mathis
Nick/Sam	David Preston Sharp
Joe	Fracaswell Hyman
Waiter/Jake	Frantz Hall
Larry Potter	Kevin Ramsey
Shorty	Helmar Augustus Cooper
B.J.	Keith Robert Bennett
Floyd	Frederick J. Boothe
Zeke	Ken Roberson
Jimmy Winter	Brian Mitchell†1
Constance Du Grasse	Tamara Tunie Bouquett
Chauffeur	Byron Easley
Kay Jones	Angela Teek†2
Janson	Mark Kenneth Smaltz
Rev. Alphonse DuGrasse	Alexander Barton
Ensemble	Keith Robert Bennett, Jacquelyn Bird, Cheryl Burr, Robert H. Fowler, Karen E. Fraction, Garry Q. Lewis, Greta Martin, Sharon Moore, Elise Neal, Allyson Tucker, Mona Wyatt

UNDERSTUDIES: Tamara Tunie Bouquett (Kay), Sharon Moore (Dolly), Karen E. Fraction (Constance), Fracaswell Hyman (Shorty/Rev./Janson), Melissa Haizlip, Ken Leigh Rogers (Swings)

MUSICAL NUMBERS: Slap That Bass (From the film *Shall We Dance?*), When Our Ship Comes Sailing In (cut from original), Dear Little Girl, Maybe, You've Got What Gets Me , Do Do Do, Clap Yo' Hands, Oh Kay, Ask Me Again (previously unpublished), Fidgety Feet, Someone to Watch Over Me, Heaven on Earth, Show Me the Town (cut from original), Sleepless Nights, Finale (*Note:* Two other interpolations, Somehow It Seldom Comes True and Where's the Boy? Here's the Girl! were heard in the preview performances.)

A musical in two acts. The action takes place in Harlem in 1926.

*Closed January 5, 1991 after 77 performances and 19 previews. Re-opened in the Lunt-Fontanne Theatre on Tuesday, April 2, 1991 and played 16 more previews only before closing April 14, 1991. The original production opened November 8, 1926 at the Imperial Theatre.

†Succeeded in re-opening by 1. Ron Richardson 2. Rae Dawn Chong

Martha Swope, Carol Rosegg Photos

BUDDY: THE BUDDY HOLLY STORY

Music/Lyrics, Buddy Holly and Various; Book, Alan Janes; Director, Rob Bettinson; Musical Director, Paul Jury; Musical Consultant, Bruce Welch; Design, Andy Walmsley; Costumes, Bill Butler, Carolyn Smith; Lighting, Graham McLusky; Sound, Rick Price; Company Manager, Mark Johnson; Production Manager, Patrick Molony; Stage Managers, Peter B. Mumford, Shirley Third, Gary M. Zabinski; Wardrobe, Michael Boncoeur; Original Cast Recording, Relativity; Executive Producer, Brian Sewel; Associate Producer, Contracts International Ltd.; Presented by Paul Elliott, Laurie Mansfield & Greg Smith and David Mirvish; Press, Adrian Bryan-Brown. Previewing from Tuesday, October 23, 1990; Opened in the Shubert Theatre on Sunday, November 4, 1990.*

CAST

Buddy Holly	Paul Hipp
Richie Valens/WWOL DJ	Philip Anthony
Vi Petty	Jo Lynn Burks
Man at Apollo/WDAS DJ	Demo Cates
Shirley/Mary Lou Sokolof	Caren Cole
Candy/Peggy Sue	Melanie Doane
Maria Elena	Russ Jolly
Jerry Allison	Paul McQuillan
Decca Engineer/English DJ/Dion	Paul McQuillan
Big Bopper/Decca Producer	David Mucci
Joe Mauldin	Bobby Prochaska
Hipockets Duncan	Fred Sanders
Apollo Performer	Jerome Smith, Jr.
Murray Deutch/Jack Daw	Steve Steiner
Maria's Aunt	Liliane Stilwell
Clear Lake MC/Decca Engineer/KPST DJ	Don Stitt
Cricket/Tommy	Ken Triwush
Norman Petty/KRWP DJ	Kurt Ziskie
Apollo Singers	Sandra Caldwell, Denese Matthews, Lorraine Scott
Ensemble	Alvin Crawford, Kevin Fox, Tom Nash, Louis Tucci, James H. Wiggins, Jr.

Members of the Company also appear as various singers, band members, boppers, photographers, etc.

UNDERSTUDIES: Ken Triwush (Buddy), Kevin Fox (Joe/Cricket), Tom Nash (Jerry/English DJ), Steve Steiner (Big Bopper/Hipockets/Various), Paul McQuillan (Richie Valens/Norman/Various), Caren Cole (Vi/Candy/Peggy Sue/Aunt), Alvin Crawford (Man & Performer at Apollo/DJ), Melanie Doane (Maria/Shirley/Mary Lou/Singer), Louis Tucci (General Understudy)

MUSICAL NUMBERS: Texas Rose, Flower of My Heart, Ready Teddy, That's All Right, That'll Be the Day, Blue Days Black Nights, Changing All These Changes, Peggy Sue, Looking for Someone to Love, Mailman Bring Me No More Blues, Maybe Baby, Everyday, Sweet Love, You Send Me, Not Fade Away, Words of Love, Oh Boy, Listen to Me, Well All Right, It's So Easy to Fall in Love, Think It Over, True Love Ways, Why Do Fools Fall in Love, Chantilly Lace, Peggy Sue Got Married, Heartbeat, La Bamba, Raining in My Heart, It Doesn't Matter Anymore, Rave On, Johnny B. Goode

A musical in two acts. The action covers the life of Buddy Holly with a re-creation of his last concert in Clear Lake, Iowa on February 2, 1959.

*Closed May 19, 1991 after 225 performances and 15 previews.

Martha Swope Photos

Paul Hipp Top: Jill Hennessy, Hipp

Philip Anthony, Jo Lynn Burks, Russ Jolly, Paul Hipp, Bobby Prochaska, Jill Hennessy

THOSE WERE THE DAYS

Concept/Continuity, Zalem Mlotek, Moishe Rosenfeld; Director/Choreographer, Eleanor Reissa; Music/Lyrics, M. Warshavsky, M. Gebirtig, A. Lebedeff, Itsik Manger, W. Younin, J. Rumshinsky, Mani Leib, Gene Raskin, Mel Tolkin, Ben Bonus, Ben Yomen, Hymie Jacobson, Chana Mlotek, Gioacchino Rossini, R. Abelson, M. Rosenfeld, Jack Yeller, Lew Pollack, Jacob Jacobs, Sholom Secunda, Sammy Cahn, Saul Chaplin, Bella Meisel, Herman Yablokoff, Nellie Casman, Samuel Steinberg; Scenes by I.L. Peretz, Sholom Aleichem and Various; Musical Director, Zalem Mlotek; Lighting, Tom Sturge; Costumes, Gail Cooper-Hecht; Sound, Jim Badrak, Alan Gregorie; General Manager, Leonard Soloway; Company Manager, Abby Evans; Production Manager, Peter Lawrence; Stage Managers, Charles Blackwell, Greta Minsky; Presented by Moe Septee in association with Victor H. Potamkin, Zalem Mlotek, Moishe Rosenfeld; Press, Max Eisen/Madelon Rosen. Previewing from Tuesday, October 23, 1990; Opened in the Edison Theatre on Wednesday, November 7, 1990.*

CAST

Bruce Adler	Mina Bern
Eleanor Reissa	Robert Abelson
Lori Wilner	

The Golden Land Klezmer Orchestra

UNDERSTUDIES: Stuart Zagnit (for Mr. Adler), Norman Atkins (for Mr. Abelson), Shifra Lerer (for Ms. Bern), Sandra Ben Dor (for Ms. Reissa/Ms. Wilner)

MUSICAL NUMBERS: Prologue, Lomir Loybn, Sha Shtil, Oyfn Pripetshik, Ver Der Ershter Vet Lahkn, Motele, Hudl Mitn Shtrudl, Di Dinst, Yosl Ber, Halevay Volt Ikh Singl Geven, Shloymele-Malkele, Mamenyu Tayere, Nokhumke Mayan Zun, Saposhkelekh, Wedding Sequence, Those Were the Days, Palace of the Czar, Shabes Shabes Shabes, Litvak/Galitsyaner, Yiddish International Radio Hour, Figaro's Aria, My Yiddishe Mame, Hootsatsa, Bei Mir Bistu Schoen, In An Orem Shtibele, A Khanzndl Oyf Shabes, Papirosn, Yosl Yosl, Rumania Rumania, Finale.

An English-Yiddish musical revue in two acts. The show celebrates the Jewish music and theatre experience from the Shtetl to Second Avenue.

*Closed February 24, 1991 after 126 performances and 18 previews.

Martha Swope, Carol Rosegg Photos

Right: Lori Wilner, Bruce Adler, Eleanor Reissa
Top: Reissa, Adler, Wilner

Bruce Adler, Eleanor Reissa, Mina Bern, Lori Wilner, Robert Abelson

SIX DEGREES OF SEPARATION

By John Guare; Director, Jerry Zaks; Set, Tony Walton; Costumes, William Ivey Long; Lighting, Paul Gallo; Sound, Aural Fixation; Hairstylist, Angela Gari; General Manager, Steven C. Callahan; Production Manager, Jeff Hamlin; Stage Managers, Steve Beckler, Sarah Manley; Wardrobe, Helen Toth; Presented by Lincoln Center Theatre (Gregory Mosher, Director; Bernard Gersten, Executive Producer); Press, Merle Debuskey, Susan Chicoine. Previewing from Tuesday, October 30; Opened in the Vivian Beaumont Lincoln Center Theater on Thursday, November 8, 1990.*

CAST

Ouisa	Stockard Channing[†1]
Flan	John Cunningham
Geoffrey	Sam Stoneburner
Paul	Courtney B. Vance[†2]
Hustler	David Eigenberg[†3]
Kitty	Kelly Bishop
Larkin	Peter Maloney
Detective	Brian Evers
Tess	Robin Morse
Woody	Gus Rogerson
Ben	Anthony Rapp
Dr. Fine	Stephen Pearlman
Doug	Evan Handler[†4]
Policeman/Eddie	Philip LeStrange
Trent	John Cameron Mitchell[†5]
Rick	Robert Duncan McNeil[†6]
Elizabeth	Mari Nelson

A comedy-drama performed without intermission. The action takes place in New York City today.

† Succeeded by 1. Kelly Bishop during vacation 2. James McDaniel during vacation 3. James DuMont 4. David Burke 5. Jon Matthews 6. Paul McCrane

*Closed Jan. 5, 1992 after 485 performances and 11 previews. Winner of New York Drama Critics Circle Award for Best Play. Winner of 1991 "Tony" for Best Direction of a play. This production originated May 16, 1990 at the smaller Newhouse Theater, off-Broadway, where it played 185 performances. During this period Kelly Bishop and Swoosie Kurtz succeeded Stockard Channing during vacation and Gregory Simmons and Courtney Vance succeeded James McDaniel in the role of Paul.

Martha Swope/Brigitte Lacombe Photos

Left: John Cameron Mitchell, James McDaniel Above: Stockard Channing, John Cunningham, Stephen Pearlman, Peter Maloney, Kelly Bishop Top Left: Channing, Courtney B. Vance

Peter Maloney (rear), Stockard Channing, Gus Rogerson, Robin Morse, Anthony Rapp, Kelly Bishop, John Cunningham

Kelly Bishop, Courtney B. Vance, John Cunningham

The Rockettes

THE CHRISTMAS SPECTACULAR

Original Conception/Production/Direction, Robert F. Jani; Director, Scott Salmon; Musical Director/Vocal Arranger, Don Pippin; Dance Music Arranger, Marvin Laird; Sets, Charles Lisanby; Lighting, Ken Billington; Costumes, Frank Spencer, Jose Lengson, Pete Menefee; Choreography, Mr. Salmon, Violet Holmes, Linda Lemac, Marianne Selbert; Orchestrations, Michael Gibson, Danny Troob, Jonathan Tunick, Jim Tyler, Bob Wheeler, Elman Anderson, Robert N. Ayars, Don Harper, Arthur Harris, Bob Krogstad, Philip J. Lang; Original Music/Lyrics, Stan Lebowsky, Fred Tobias; Production Manager, J. Greg De Felice; Stage Managers, Mimi Apfel, Travis DeCastro, Andrew Feigin, Peter Muste; General Manager, John H. Lowe; Executive Producer, David J. Nash; Press, Sandra Manley, Kevin Brockman; Opened in Radio City Music Hall on Friday, November 9, 1990.*

CAST

Narrator/Scrooge/Santa	Charles Edward Hall
Mrs. Santa/New Yorker	Marty Simpson
Bob Cratchit	David Elder
Scrooge's Nephew/New Yorker	Frank DiPasquale
First Man	Joe Bowerman
Second Man	Robert Ashford
Marley's Ghost	Scott Spahr
Ghost of Christmas Past	Pascale Faye-Williams
Ghost of Christmas Present	Tim Hamrick
Mrs. Cratchit	Karen Longwell
Belinda	Suzanne Phillips
Sarah	Laura Bundy, Christen Tassen
Peter	Sean Dooley, Joey Rigol
Tiny Tim	Joey Cee, Ari Vernon
Poultry Man	Todd Hunter
Skaters	Laurie Welch, Randy Coyne, Shelly Winters-Stein, Bruce Hurd
Jiggle	Michael Lee Gogin
Squiggle	R. Lou Carry
Wiggle	John Edward Allen
Giggle	Michael J. Gilden
Bruce	Leslie Stump
New Yorkers	Ellyn Arons, David Askler, Michael Berglund, Maria Calabrese, John Clonts, James Darrah, John Dietrich, Jane Labanz, Keith Locke, Karen Longwell, Michele Mallardi, Wendy Piper, Jennifer Smith, Mary Jane Waddell, Jim Weaver, David Wood
Other Dancers	Tina DeLeone, Christopher Gattelli, Steve Geary, Terry Lacy, Bonnie Lynn, Marty McDonough, Joan Mirabella

ALSO STARRING THE ROCKETTES

SCENES AND SONGS: Herald Trumpeters, We Need A Little Christmas, Overture, Nutcracker, Dickens' Christmas Carol, Christmas in New York, Ice Skating in the Plaza, Story of Santa Claus, They Can't Start Christmas Without Us, Parade of Wooden Soldiers, Santa's Journey, Carol of the Bells, Living Nativity, Joy To The World

A holiday entertainment presented without intermission.

*Closed January 3, 1991 after 188 performances.

Mark Kozlowski Photos

The Living Nativity Above: Santa and Elves

SHADOWLANDS

By William Nicholson; Director, Elijah Moshinsky; Design, Mark Thompson; Lighting, John Michael Deegan; Casting, Marjorie Martin; General Manager, Ralph Roseman; Stage Managers, Elliott Woodruff, Wally Peterson; Presented by Elliot Martin, James M. Nederlander, Brian Eastman, Terry Allen Kramer and Roger L. Stevens, by arrangement with Armanda Productions Ltd. and The Plymouth Theatre Royal, England; Press, Jeffrey Richards/David LeShay, Irene Gandy, Jillana Devine. Previewing from Friday, November 2, 1990; Opened in the Brooks Atkinson Theatre on Sunday, November 11, 1990.*

CAST

C.S. Lewis	Nigel Hawthorne
Christopher Riley	Paul Sparer
Rev. Harry Harrington	Robin Chadwick
Dr. Oakley/Waiter/Clerk/Priest	Hugh A. Rose
Alan Gregg/Doctor	Edmund C. Davys
Major W.H. Lewis ("Warnie")	Michael Allinson
Douglas	Jonathan Gold, Lance Robinson (alternating)
Joy Davidman	Jane Alexander
Registrar/Nurse	Mary Layne

UNDERSTUDIES: Mary Layne (Joy), Michael Allison (C.S. Lewis), Ian Sullivan (Warnie/Dr. Oakley/Waiter/Priest), Edmund C. Davys (Riley), Hugh A. Rose (Gregg/Doctor/Rev.), Jennifer Sternberg (Nurse/Registrar)

A drama in two acts. The action takes place in Oxford in the 1950s and involves the relationship of author C.S. Lewis and American poetess Joy Davidman.

*Closed April 7, 1991 after 169 performances and 11 previews. Winner of "Tony" award for Leading Actor in a Play (Nigel Hawthorne).

Martha Swope Photos

Right: Jane Alexander, Nigel Hawthorne, (Also Top)

WAITIN' IN THE WINGS:
The Night the Understudies
Take Centerstage

Conceived and Produced by William Spencer Reilly; Director, Peter Link; Musical Director, Keith Thompson; Written by Norm Bleichman; Press, Becky Flora.

CAST

Helen Hayes

Douglas Fairbanks, Jr.	Geraldine Fitzgerald
Tammy Grimes	Barnard Hughes
Dorothy Loudon	James Naughton
Milo O'Shea	Tony Randall
Vincent Sardi	Denzel Washington

and this season's understudies

PROGRAM: Songs from *The Phantom of the Opera, Gypsy, Forbidden Broadway, Oh Kay!, City of Angels, The Fantasticks, Les Miserables, Fiddler on the Roof, Grand Hotel, Once On This Island, Cats*

FIDDLER ON THE ROOF

Music, Jerry Bock; Lyrics, Sheldon Harnick; Book, Joseph Stein; Direction Reproduced by Ruth Mitchell; Choreography Reproduced by Sammy Dallas Bayes; Original Direction/Choreography, Jerome Robbins; Orchestrations, Don Walker; Musical Direction/Vocal Arrangements, Milton Greene; Sets, Boris Aronson; Costumes from Patricia Zipprodt's originals; Lighting, Ken Billington; Sound, Peter J. Fitzgerald; Hair Stylist, Robert DiNiro; Casting, Stuart Howard, Amy Schecter; Music Coordinator, John Monaco; Technical Supervisor, Arthur Siccardi; General Manager, Charlotte Wilcox, Connie Weinstein; Stage Managers, Martin Gold, David John O'Brien; Company Manager, Constance Weinstein; Wardrobe, Sydney Smith; Associate Producer, Alecia Parker; Produced in association with C. Itoh & Co., Tokyo Broadcasting System, A. Deshe Pashanel; Presented by Barry and Fran Weissler and Pace Theatrical Group; Press, Shirley Herz/Pete Sanders, Laura Matalon, Glenna Freedman, Sam Rudy, Robert Larkin, Miller Wright. Previewing from Saturday, November 3, 1990; Opened in the Gershwin Theatre on Sunday, November 18, 1990.*

CAST

Tevye	Topol†1
Golde	Marcia Lewis
Tzeitel	Sharon Lawrence
Hodel	Tia Riebling
Chava	Jennifer Prescott
Shprintze/Grandma Tzeitel	Kathy St. George
Bielke	Judy Dodd
Motel	Jack Kenny
Perchik	Gary Schwartz
Fyedka	Ron Bohmer
Lazar Wolf	Mark Zeller
Mordcha	David Masters
Nachum	Michael J. Farina
Yente	Ruth Jaroslow
Rabbi	Jerry Matz
Avram	Jerry Jarrett
Constable	Mike O'Carroll
Mendel	David Pevsner
Fiddler	Stephen Wright
Fruma-Sarah	Jeri Sager
Shandel	Panchali Null

Bottle Dancers.........Kenneth M. Daigle, David Enriquez, Craig Gahnz, Keith Keen
Russian Dancers ....Brian Arsenault, Michael Berresse, Brian Henry
Other Villagers.................................Joanne Borts, Stacy Lynn Brass, Lisa Cartmell, Todd Heughens, Marty Ross, Beth Thompson, Lou Williford

UNDERSTUDIES: Mark Zeller (Tevye), Lou Williford (Golde/Yente), Lisa Cartmell (Tzeitel), Beth Thompson (Hodel), Stacy Lynn Brass (Chava/Shprintze/Bielke), David Pevsner (Motel), Mike O'Carroll (Lazar Wolf), Keith Keen (Perchik), Brian Henry (Fyedka), David Masters (Rabbi), Marty Ross (Constable/Avram/Mordcha), Todd Heughens (Mendel), David Enriquez (Fiddler), Newton Cole (Nachum), Judy Dodd (Grandma) **SWINGS:** Chris Jamison, Newton Cole

MUSICAL NUMBERS: Tradition, Matchmaker Matchmaker, If I Were A Rich Man, Sabbath Prayer, To Life, Miracle of Miracles, The Dream, Sunrise Sunset, Wedding Dance, Now I Have Everything, Do You Love Me?, The Rumor, Far From the Home I Love, Chavaleh, Anatevka, Epilogue

A new production of the musical in two acts and seventeen scenes with prologue and epilogue. The action takes place in Anatevka, Russia in 1905. For original 1964 production, see *Theatre World* Vol. 21. For 1976 revival, see *Theatre World* Vol. 33. Topol previously appeared in the 1967 London production which was recorded by Columbia.

†Succeeded by 1. Mark Zeller during vacation

*Closed on Sunday, June 16, 1991 after 241 performances and 18 previews. Winner of "Tony" award for best revival of the season.

Carol Rosegg/Martha Swope/Robert Ragsdale Photos

Right: Jennifer Prescott, Sharon Lawrence, Tia Riebling Above: Topol

**Marcia Lewis, Ruth Jaroslaw
Top Right: Topol, Mark Zeller**

AN EVENING WITH HARRY CONNICK, JR. AND HIS ORCHESTRA

Conductor, Marc Shaiman; Director, Joe Layton; Musical Director, Benjamin Jonah Wolfe; Set, John Falabella; Lighting, Marilyn Lowey; Wardrobe, Alexander Julian; Stage Manager, Tracey Freeman, Jack Hyle; Producers, Ed Micone, Scott Sanders; Executive Producer, Ann Marie Wilkins; Presented by Radio City Music Hall Productions and James L. Nederlander. Opened in the Lunt-Fontanne Theatre on Friday, November 23, 1990.*

CAST

HARRY CONNICK, JR.

Musicians include ....Ben Wolfe, Shannon Powell, Leroy Jones, Jerry Weldon, Lucien Barbarin, Russell Malone, Craig Klein, Mark Mullins, Jeremy Davenport, Roger Ingram, Dan Miller, Ned Goold, Brad Leali, William Campbell, Dave Schumacher

A musical evening of original songs and big band standards in two parts.

*Closed December 8, 1990 after a limited engagement of 13 performances.

**Eric Chan, JoAnn M. Hunter Top Left: Lee Lobenhoffer,
Philip Casnoff, Ron Navarre**

SHOGUN: THE MUSICAL

Music, Paul Chihara; Lyrics/Book, John Driver; Based on novel by James Clavell; Director/Choreographer, Michael Smuin; Orchestrations, David Cullen, Steven Margoshes; Musical Director, Edward G. Robinson; Sets, Loren Sherman; Costumes, Patricia Zipprodt; Lighting, Natasha Katz; Hair/Wigs, Patrik D. Moreton; Sound, Tony Meola; Fights, Masahiro Kunii; Co-Choreographer, Kirk Peterson; Assistant Director, J. Steven White; Production Supervision, Jeremiah J. Harris; General Management, J. Harris, Inc.; Company Manager, Robb Lady; Stage Managers, S. Randolph Post, Deborah Clelland, Michael Pule, Donna A. Drake; Wardrobe, Barrett Hong; Casting, Julie Hughes, Barry Moss; Co-Producers, Hiroshi Sugawara, Lloyd Phillips; Presented by James Clavell, Joseph Harris, Haruki Kadokawa; Press, Shirley Herz/Sam Rudy, Miller Wright. Previewing from Thursday, November 1, 1990; Opened in the Marquis Theatre on Tuesday, November 29, 1990.*

CAST

John Blackthorne	Philip Casnoff
Roper/Ninja	Ron Navarre
Pieterzoon/Captain Ferriera/Taiko Drummer	Lee Lobenhofer
Sonk/Ninja	Terry Lehmkuhl
Father Alvito	John Herrera
Lord Buntaro	Joseph Foronda
Omi	Eric Chan
Samurai/Ninja	Tito Abeleda
Gyoko	Freda Foh Shen
Kiku	JoAnn M. Hunter
Guard/Courtier/Ninja	Darren Lee
Guard/Red Guard/Taiko Drummer/Daimyo	Marc Oka
Guard/Ninja	Owen Johnston
Lord Toranaga	Francis Ruivivar
Sazuko	Jenny Woo
Osagi/Ishido's General/Acolyte/Ninja/Taiko Drummer	Jason Ma
Lady Mariko	June Angela
Catholic Daimyo/Ninja	Cholsu Kim
Daimyo/Guard	Kenji Nakao
Lord Ishido	Alan Muraoka
Ninja/Guard	Andrew Pacho
Fujiko/Taiko Drummer	Leslie Ishii
Chimmoko	Kiki Moritsugu
Slatterns of the Hovel	Tina Horii, Linda Igarashi, Chi-En Telemaque
Red Guard	Alan Ariano
Ninja	Cheri Nakamura
Swings and Other Dancers	Ted Hewlett, Herman Sebek, Victoria Lee, Lyd-Lyd Gaston, Kathy Wilhelm, Betsy Chang, Deborah Geneviere

MUSICAL NUMBERS: Karma, Night of Screams, This Is Samurai, How Nice to See You, Impossible Eyes, He Let Me Live, Honto, Assassination, Shogun, Royal Blood, An Island, No Word for Love, Mad Rum Below/Escape, Born to Be Together, Fireflies, Sail Home, Rum Below, Pillowing, No Man, Cha-No-Yu, Absolution, Poetry Competition, Death Walk, One Candle, Ninja Raid, Winter Battle, Resolutions, Trio, Finale (*Note:* Additional numbers in Washington previews included: Crucified, Torment.)

A musical in two acts. The action takes place in Japan between April and July 1600. In the Washington, D.C. previews, The part of Blackthorne was played by Peter Karrie.

*Closed January 20, 1991 after 72 performances and 19 previews.

Martha Swope/Carol Rosegg Photos

June Angela, Philip Casnoff Above: Francis Ruivivar

John Herrera, Francis Ruivivar, June Angela

A CHRISTMAS CAROL

By Charles Dickens; Producer/Director Zoe Caldwell; Music Composed and Performed by David Amram; Consulting Producer, Robert Whitehead; Design, Ben Edwards; Costumes, Jane Greenwood; Production Supervisor, William Dodds;Graphic Art, Tom Morrow; Decoration, Robb Alverson; Press, Rebecca Lyden Mitchell. Opened in the Hudson Theatre on Monday, December 10, 1990 for one performance only.

CAST

Narrators ....Christopher Plummer, Zoe Caldwell
Ebeneezer Scrooge/Young Cratchit ....Jason Robards
Fred..David Rasche
Marley's Ghost/Fezziwig ....Eli Wallach
Ghost of Christmas Past..Hume Cronyn
Ghost of Christmas Present...Richard Kiley
First Businessman/Husband/First Man ....E.G. Marshall
Second Businessman/Second Man ....Mallory Factor
Mrs. Fezziwig.. ....Anne Jackson
Girl/Scrooge's Niece/Fan..Julie Harris
Boy...Sebastian Iervolino
Belle ....Maureen Stapleton
Mrs. Cratchit..Lindsay Crouse
Bob Cratchit ....Jack Gilpin
Tiny Tim ....Adam Amram
Cratchit Household.........................Adira Amram, Alana Amram, Katie Benincasa, Dimitri Iervolino, Willa Mamet, Amelia Rasche, Sam Whitehead
Soprano ....Anne McKenna
Tenor ....David Kellet

A holiday benefit for the Actor's Fund of America. The production also marks the return of theatre to 1902's Hudson Theatre for the first time since 1965. The building was recently renovated as part of the Hotel Macklowe.

Christopher Plummer, Maureen Stapleton, Mallory Factor, E.G. Marshall, Anne Jackson, Eli Wallach, Richard Kiley

Eli Wallach, Richard Kiley, Jason Robards, Hume Cronyn, Julie Harris

PETER PAN

Cathy Rigby

Music, Moose Charlap, Jule Styne; Lyrics, Carolyn Leigh, Betty Comden, Adolph Green; From the play by James M. Barrie; Director, Fran Soeder; Choreography, Marilyn Magness; Original Direction, Choreography and Conception by Jerome Robbins; Musical Supervision/Direction, Kevin Farrell; Flying by Foy; Costumes, Mariann Verheyen; Lighting, Natasha Katz; Sound, Peter J. Fitzgerald; Neverland Sets, James Leonard Joy; Wigs, Rick Geyer; Additional Arrangements, M. Michael Fauss, Mr. Farrell; General Management, Lonn Entertainment, Ltd.; Stage Managers, John M. Galo, Eric Insko; Company Manager, Stephen Arnold; Wardrobe, Jean Evans; A McCoy-Rigby Entertainment Production; Presented by James M. Nederlander, Arthur Rubin, Thomas P. McCoy, Keith Stava, P.P. Investments, Jon B. Platt; Press, Shirley Herz/Glenna Freedman, Sam Rudy, Pete Sanders, Robert Larkin, Miller Wright. Previewing from Tuesday, December 11, 1990; Opened in the Lunt-Fontanne Theatre on Thursday, December 13, 1990.*

CAST

Wendy Darling/Jane	Cindy Robinson
John Darling	Britt West
Michael Darling	Chad Hutchison
Liza/Indian	Anne McVey
Nana/Pirate/Indian	Bill Bateman
Mrs. Darling/Wendy Grown Up	Lauren Thompson
Mr. Darling/Captain Hook	Stephen Hanan
Peter Pan	Cathy Rigby
Never Bear	Adam Ehrenworth
Curly	Alon Williams
First Twin	Janet Kay Higgins
Second Twin	Courtney Wyn
Slightly	Christopher Ayres
Tootles	Julian Brightman
Mr. Smee	Don Potter
Cecco/Pirate/Indian	Calvin Smith
Gentleman Starkey/Pirate/Indian	Carl Packard
Noodler/Pirate/Indian/Crocodile	Barry Ramsey
Bill Jukes/Pirate/Indian	Andy Ferrara
Tiger Lily	Holly Irwin
Other Pirates and Indians	Christian Monte, Joseph Savant, Timothy Talman, David Thome, John Wilkerson

UNDERSTUDIES: Cindy Robinson (Peter), Carl Packard (Mr. Darling/Hook), Anne McVey (Mrs. Darling), Bill Bateman (Mr. Smee), Courtney Wyn (Wendy/Tiger Lily), Christopher Ayers (John), Adam Ehrenworth (Michael/Twins/Curly), Janet Kay Higgins (Tootles/Slightly), (Swing): Jim Alexander

MUSICAL NUMBERS: Tender Shepherd, I've Got to Crow, Neverland, I'm Flying, Pirate March, Princely Scheme, Indians, Wendy, Tarantella, I Won't Grow Up, Ugg-a-Wugg, Distant Melody, Hook's Waltz, Finale (*Note:* This production omits Dangerous Lady.)

A musical in three acts and seven scenes. The action takes place in England and Neverland. For original 1954 production, see *Theatre World* Vol. 11. For 1979 revival, see *Theatre World* Vol. 36.

*Closed January 20, 1991 after limited engagement of 45 performances and 3 previews.

Cathy Rigby, Cindy Robinson

Stephen Hanan, Cathy Rigby

LA BÊTE

By David Hirson; Director, Richard Jones; Sets/Costumes, Richard Hudson; Lighting, Jennifer Tipton; Sound, Peter Fitzgerald; General Management, Gatchell & Neufeld Ltd.; Technical Supervisor, Jeremiah J. Harris; Stage Managers, Bob Borod, Glen Gardali; Company Manager, Wendy Orshan; Bird Handler, Dorothy Hanrahan; Presented by Stuart Ostrow and Andrew Lloyd Webber; Press, John Springer/Gary Springer. Previewing from Tuesday, January 29, 1991; Opened in the Eugene O'Neill Theatre on Sunday, February 10, 1991.*

CAST

Elomire ....Michael Cumpsty
Bejart ....James Greene
Valere ....Tom McGowan
Dorine ....Johann Carlo
Servants ....Cheryl Gaysunas, Ellen Kohrman,
Michael McCormick, Eric Swanson
Prince Conti...Dylan Baker
Madeleine Bejart ....Patricia Kilgarriff
De Brie ....John Michael Higgins
Catherine De Brie ....Holly Felton
Rene Du Parc...William Mesnik
Marquise-Therese Du Parc..Suzie Plakson

UNDERSTUDIES: John Michael Higgins (Valere), Michael James Reed (Elomire), William Mesnik (Bejart), Ellen Kohrman (Dorine/Therese), Eric Swanson (Conti/De Brie), Michael McCormick (Du Parc), Cheryl Gaysunas (Catherine/Madeleine)

A comedy of manners in two acts. The action takes place on Prince Conti's estate in Pezenas, France.

*Closed March 2, 1991 after 24 performances and 15 previews.

James Greene, Michael Cumpsty
Top Left: Dylan Baker and Company

The Company
Above: Tom McGowan

Michael James Reed (rear), Tom McGowan, Dylan Baker
Above: Johann Carlo

Theresa Merritt, Kenny Neal

**Eric Ware, Akousa Busia, Kenny Neal Top Left: Ware, Vanessa
Williams, Allie Woods, Jr., Marilyn Coleman, Joy Lee (rear),
Mansoon Najeeullah, Neal**

**Arthur French, Eric Ware, Kenny Neal, Leonard Jackson
Above: Akousa Busia, Ware, Neal**

MULE BONE

By Langston Hughes and Zora Neale Hurston; Prologue and Epilogue by George Houston Bass; Music, Taj Mahal; Director, Michael Schultz; Sets, Edward Burbridge; Costumes, Lewis Brown; Lighting, Allen Lee Hughes; Sound, Serge Ossorguine; Music Supervision, Taj Mahal; Fights, Ron Van Clief; Dances, Dianne McIntyre; General Manager, Steven C. Callahan; Production Manager, Jeff Hamlin; Stage Managers, Maureen F. Gibson, Frederic H. Orner; Company Manager, Edward J. Nelson; Wardrobe, Celia Bryant; Poster, James McMullan; Presented by Lincoln Center Theatre (Gregory Mosher, Director; Bernard Gersten, Executive Producer); Press, Merle Debuskey/Susan Chicoine.; Previewing from Sunday, January 20, 1991; Opened in the Ethel Barrymore Theatre on Thursday, Februaury 14, 1991.*

CAST

Zora/Teets	Joy Lee
Dave Carter	Eric Ware
Jim	Kenny Neal
Daisy	Akosua Busia
Deacon Hambo	Sonny Jim Gaines
Old Man Brazzle	Clebert Ford
Lum Boger	Paul S. Eckstein
Lige Mosely	Reggie Montgomery
Robena	Pauline Meyer
Joe Lindsay	Allie Woods, Jr.
Walter Thomas	Donald Griffin
Mayor Joe Clark	Samuel E. Wright
Sister Blunt	Ebony Jo-Ann
Senator	Pee Wee Love
Bootsie	Vanessa Williams
Mattie Clark	Myra Taylor
Luther	Bron Wright
Matilda	Shareen Powlett
Willie Lewis	Robert Earl Jones
Tony Taylor	Mansoon Najeeullah
Sister Taylor	Marilyn Coleman
Rev. Simms	Leonard Jackson
Jesse/Julius	T.J. Jones
Katie Pitts	Theresa Merritt
Sister Lewis	Frances Foster
Sister Thomas	Fanni Green
Sister Hambo	Edwina Lewis
Sister Lindsay	Peggy Pettitt
Rev. Singletary	Arthur French

UNDERSTUDIES: Myra Taylor (Zora/Teets/Mambo/Lindsay), Vanessa Williams (Daisy), Guy Davis (Jim/Dave/Boger/Tony), Arthur French (Mayor), Peggy Pettitt (Blunt/Lewis), T.J. Jones (Senator), Oni Faida Lampley (Bootsie/Mattie/Thomas), Billy Ray Tyson (Brazzle/Walter/Joe), Pauline Meyer (Matilda), Shareen Powlett (Robena/Julius), Ebony Jo-Ann (Katie), Mansoor Najeeullah (Lige), Fanni Green (Taylor), Bron Wright (Jesse), Pee Wee Love (Luther), Edwina Lewis (Katie), George Lee Miles (Singletary/Hambo/Willie/Simms)

A comedy with songs in two acts, three scenes, and two prologues. The action takes place in Eatonville, Florida during the 1920's. The play, based on Hurston's short story "The Bone of Contention," was written in 1930 but never performed because of disagreements between the authors. Several of Hughes' poems were set to music by Taj Mahal for this production.

*Closed April 14, 1991 after 67 performances and 27 previews.

Bridgette Lacombe Photos

Jonathan Hogan, Christopher Benjamin,
Spike McClure Top Left: Jane Summerhays,
Benjamin, Bill Buell, McClure

ChristopherBenjamin, Bill Buell, Spike McClure, Pippa Pearthree
Top Right: Jane Summerhays, Buell, Jonathan Hogan, McClure

TAKING STEPS

by Alan Ayckbourn; Director, Alan Strachan; Sets, James Morgan; Costumes, Gail Brassard; Lighting, Mary Jo Dondlinger; Stage Managers, Wm. Hare, Alex Scott; Music John Pattison; Sound, Fox & Perla; Company Manager, Susan Elrod; Wardrobe, Claire Libin; Casting, Julie Hughes/Barry Moss; Presented by Circle in the Square (Theodore Mann, Artistic Director; Robert A. Buckley, Managing Director; Paul Lubin, Consulting Producer); Press, Merle Debuskey/Susan Chicoine. Previewing from Friday, February 1, 1991; Opened in the Circle in the Square Uptown on Wednesday, February 20, 1991.*

CAST

Elizabeth ....Jane Summerhays
Mark...Jonathan Hogan
Tristram ....Spike McClure
Roland ....Christopher Benjamin
Leslie Bainbridge ....Bill Buell
Kitty...Pippa Pearthree

UNDERSTUDIES: Connie Roderick (Elizabeth/Kitty), Mark Soper (Mark/Tristram), John Rainer (Roland/Leslie)

A farce in two acts. The action takes place in the bedrooms, lounges, linking stairs and passageways of The Pines, a decaying English mansion. The time is the present.

*Closed April 28, 1991 after 78 performances and 22 previews.

Martha Swope Photos

Jonathan Hogan, Christopher Benjamin, Spike McClure

LOST IN YONKERS

By Neil Simon; Director, Gene Saks; Sets/Costumes, Santo Loquasto; Lighting, Tharon Musser; Sound, Tom Morse; Production Supervisor, Peter Lawrence; General Manager, Leonard Soloway; Company Manager, Brian Dunbar; Stage Manager, Jim Woolley; Wardrobe, Penny Davis; Casting, Jay Binder; Presented by Emanuel Azenberg; Press, Bill Evans/Jim Randolph. Previewing from Tuesday, February 12, 1991; Opened in the Richard Rodgers Theatre on Thursday, February 21, 1991.*

CAST

Jay	Jamie Marsh
Arty	Danny Gerard
Eddie	Mark Blum
Bella	Mercedes Ruehl
Grandma Kurnitz	Irene Worth
Louie	Kevin Spacey
Gert	Lauren Klein

STANDBYS: Pauline Flanagan (Grandma), Didi Conn (Bella/Gert), David Chandler (Louie/Eddie), Justin Strock (Arty), David Neipris (Jay)

A play in two acts and eight scenes. The action takes place in a two-bedroom apartment over Kurnitz's Kandy Store in Yonkers, New York during 1942.

*Still playing May 31, 1991. Recipient of Pulitzer Prize and "Tonys" for Best Play, Leading Actress (Mercedes Ruehl), Featured Actress (Irene Worth), Featured Actor (Kevin Spacey).

Martha Swope Photos

The Company

Danny Gerard, Mark Blum, Jamie Marsh, Irene Worth
Above Left: Kevin Spacey Above Right: Mercedes Ruehl

Left: Jamie Marsh, Danny Gerard Right: Mercedes Ruehl,
Irene Worth Above: Gerard, Worth

THE SPEED OF DARKNESS

By Steve Tesich; Director, Robert Falls; Sets, Thomas Lynch; Costumes, Merrily Murray-Walsh; Lighting, Michael S. Philippi; Music/Sound, Rob Milburn; Stage Managers, William Dodds, Jay Adler; General Manager, Stuart Thompson; Company Manager, Nancy Nagel Gibbs; Wardrobe, Eileen Miller; Casting, Terry Fay; Associate Producers, Howard Platt, Sheila Henaghan, Michael Cullen, Constance Towers; Presented by Robert Whitehead and Roger L. Stevens with Robert L. Sachter and American National Theatre and Academy; Originally produced by Goodman Theatre, Chicago; Press, David Powers. Previewing from Thursday, February 14, 1991; Opened in the Belasco Theatre on Thursday, February 28, 1991.*

CAST

Joe ....Len Cariou
Anne ....Lisa Eichhorn
Mary ....Kathryn Erbe
Lou ....Stephen Lang
Eddie ....Robert Sean Leonard

UNDERSTUDIES: William Wise (Joe/Lou), Lisa Sloane (Anne), Abigael Sanders (Mary), Alan Mozes (Eddie)

A drama in two acts. The action takes place in South Dakota in the recent past. This production marks the premiere of the Broadway Alliance.

*Closed March 30, 1991 after 36 performances and 16 previews.

Martha Swope Photos

Right: Stephen Lang, Len Cariou Far Right: Cariou, Lisa Eichhorn

Kathryn Erbe, Stephen Lang, Robert Sean Leonard

THE BIG LOVE

By Brooke Allen & Jay Presson Allen; Based on the book by Florence Aadland & Tedd Thomey; Director, Jay Presson Allen; Sets/Projections, David Mitchell; Costumes, Jane Greenwood; Lighting, Ken Billington; Sound, Otts Munderloh; Original Music, Stephen Lawrence; Makeup, Kevin Haney; Stage Managers, Dianne Trulock, Jane Grey; General Manager, Stuart Thompson; Company Manager, Tom Santopietro; Wardrobe, Kate Edwards; Wig, Paul Huntley; Presented by Lewis Allen Productions, Robert Fox Ltd., Witzend Productions, Lanmark Entertainment Group and Home Box Office, Inc.; Press, Fred Nathan/Merle Frimark. Previewing from Thursday, February 21, 1991; Opened in the Plymouth Theatre on Sunday, March 3, 1991.*

CAST

Florence Aadland..Tracey Ullman

A comedy in two acts. The action takes place in Los Angeles in 1961 and relates the affair between actor Errol Flynn and 15-year-old Beverly Aadland, as seen through the eyes of her mother. A previous version was seen in 1988 at the New York Theatre Workshop with Marsha Mason. (See *Theatre World* Vol. 44.)

*Closed April 7, 1991 after 41 performances and 11 previews.

Martha Swope Photos

Right and Below: Tracey Ullman

Teller, Penn Jillette

PENN & TELLER: THE REFRIGERATOR TOUR

Sets, John Lee Beatty; Lighting, Dennis Parichy; Sound, T. Richard Fitzgerald, Craig Van Tassel; Director of Covert Activities, Robert P. Libbon; Director of Internal Affairs, Mike Wills; Stage Manager, Cathy B. Blaser; Company Manager, Kim Sellon; Associate Producer, Marc Routh; Presented by Richard Frankel, Thomas Viertel & Steven Baruch; Press, Chris Boneau/Jackie Green, Jim Sapp. Previewing from Tuesday, March 26, 1991; Opened in the Eugene O'Neill Theatre on Wednesday, April 3, 1991.*

CAST

Penn Jillette   Teller
Carol Perkins

PROGRAM: Amanao'damocles, A Card Trick, Liftoff to Love/Ripoff of Love, Two Modern Fakir Tricks, Quotation of the Day, Two Houdini Tricks, Mofo the Psychic Gorilla, By Buddha This Duck is Immortal!, Cuffed to a Creep, Burnin' Luv, Shadows, King of Animal Traps

An evening of magic and mayhem presented in two parts. Penn & Teller previously played Broadway in 1987-88 (*Theatre World* Vol. 45) and off-Broadway, starting in 1985 (*Theatre World* Vol. 42).

*Closed June 29, 1991 after 103 performances and 9 previews.

Anthony Loew Photos

LUCIFER'S CHILD

By William Luce; Based on writings of Isak Dinesen; Director, Tony Abatemarco; Incidental Music, Charles Gross; Set, Marjorie Bradley Kellogg; Costumes, Noel Taylor; Lighting, Pat Collins, Sound, T. Richard Fitzgerald; Company Manager, Charlie Willard; Stage Managers, Patrick Horrigan, Jack Doulin; Wardrobe, Debra Weber; Presented by Ronald S. Lee; Press, David Rothenberg Associates. Previewing from Saturday, March 30, 1991; Opened in the Music Box Theatre on Thursday, April 4, 1991.*

CAST

Isak Dinesen, Baroness Karen Blixen...Julie Harris

A monodrama in two acts. The action takes place in Karen Blixen's study at Rungstedlund, Denmark on New Year's Eve, 1958 and in April, 1959.

*Closed April 27, 1991 after 28 performances and 6 previews.

T. Charles Erickson Photos

Julie Harris (All Photos)

Jane Adams Top Left: Evan Handler, Adam Arkin

**Caroline Aaron, Evan Handler, Celeste Holm
Top Right: Nicol Williamson, Holm**

I HATE HAMLET

By Paul Rudnick; Director, Michael Engler; Sets, Tony Straiges; Costumes, Jane Greenwood; Lighting, Paul Gallo; Music, Kim Sherman; Sound, Scott Lehrer; Fights, B.H. Barry; Casting, John Lyons/Randy Carrig; Dance Consultant, Peter Anastos; Company Manager, Sally Campbell Morse; Stage Managers, Pat Sosnow, Eric S. Osbun; Wardrobe, W. Tony Powell; Associate Producers, 126 Second Ave. Corp., William P. Wingate; Presented by Jujamcyn Theatres, James B. Freyberg, Robert G. Perkins, Margo Lion; Press, Adrian Bryan-Brown/John Barlow, Cabrini Lepis. Previewing from Monday, March 18, 1991; Opened in the Walter Kerr Theatre on Monday, April 8, 1991.*

CAST

Felicia Dantine	Caroline Aaron
Andrew Rally	Evan Handler†1
Deirdre McDavey	Jane Adams
Lillian Troy	Celeste Holm
John Barrymore	Nicol Williamson
Gary Peter Lefkowitz	Adam Arkin

A comedy in two acts. The action takes place in Greenwich Village, in an apartment once owned by John Barrymore.

†Succeeded by 1. Andrew Mutnick on May 4th after an onstage altercation between Mr. Handler and Mr. Williamson.

*Closed June 22, 1991 after 80 performances and 20 previews.

Bob Marshack/Joan Marcus Photos

Nicol Williamson, Evan Handler

MISS SAIGON

A musical in two acts. The action takes place in Saigon, Bangkok, and the United States between 1975 and 1978.

*Still playing May 31, 1991. Winner of "Tonys" for Leading Actor in a Musical (Jonathon Pryce), Leading Actress in a Musical (Lea Salonga), and Featured Actor in a Musical (Hinton Battle).

Music, Claude-Michel Schonberg; Lyrics, Richard Maltby, Jr., Alain Boublil; Adapted from French lyrics by Mr. Boublil; Book, Mr. Boublil, Mr. Schonberg; Additional Material, Mr. Maltby, Jr.; Director, Nicholas Hytner; Musical Staging, Bob Avian; Orchestrations, William D. Brohn; Musical Supervision, David Caddick, Robert Billig; Associate Director, Mitchell Lemsky; Production Design, John Napier; Lighting, David Hersey; Costumes, Andreane Neofitou, Suzy Benzinger; Sound, Andrew Bruce; Conductor, Mr. Billig; General Manager, Alan Wasser; Company Manager, Martin Cohen; Stage Managers, Fred Hanson, Sherry Cohen, Tom Capps; Wardrobe, Adelaide Laurino; Hair Stylist, David Brown; Casting, Johnson-Liff & Zerman; Associate Producer, Martin McCallum; Executive Producers, Mitchell Lemsky, Richard Jay-Alexander; Original Cast Recording, Geffen; Presented by Cameron Mackintosh; Press, Fred Nathan/Marc Thibodeau. Previewing from Saturday, March 23, 1991; Opened in the Broadway Theatre on Thursday, April 11, 1991.*

CAST

SAIGON-1975
TheEngineer ....Jonathan Pryce
Kim ....Lea Salonga, Kam Cheng (Saturday matinee)
Gigi ....Marina Chapa
Mimi ....Sala Iwamatsu
Yvette ....Imelda De Los Reyes
Yvonne ....Joann M. Hunter
Bar Girls ....Raquel C. Brown, Annette Calud,
Mirla Criste, Jade Stice, Melanie Mariko Tojio
Chris ....Willy Falk
John ....Hinton Battle
Marines...............................Paul Dobie, Michael Gruber, Leonard Joseph,
Paul Matsumoto, Sean McDermott, Thomas James O'Leary, Gordon Owens,
Christopher Pecaro, Matthew Pedersen, Kris Phillips, W. Ellis Porter,
Alton F.White, Bruce Winant
Barmen.......................................Zar Acayan, Alan Ariano, Jason Ma
Vietnamese Customers ....Tony C. Avanti, Eric Chan, Francis J. Cruz,
Darren Lee, Ray Santos, Nephi Jay Wimmer
Thuy ....Barry K. Bernal
Embassy Workers, Saigon Inhabitants, Vendors ....Company

HO CHI MINH CITY (formerly Saigon)-APRIL 1978
Ellen ....Liz Callaway
Tam................................Brian R. Baldomero, Philip Lyle Kong
Guards...Tony C. Avanti, Francis J. Cruz
Assistant Commissar ....Eric Chan
Dragon Acrobats ....Darren Lee, Michael Gruber, Nephi Jay Wimmer
Soldiers ....Zar Acayan, Alan Ariano, Jason Ma,
Paul Matsumoto, Ray Santos, Nephi Jay Wimmer
Citizens, Refugees...Company

USA-SEPTEMBER 1978
Conference Delegates..Company

BANGKOK-OCTOBER 1978
Hustlers.....................................Zar Acayan, Jason Ma, Paul Matsumoto,
Ray Santos, Nephi Jay Wimmer
Moulin Rouge Owner...Francis J. Cruz
Inhabitants, Bar Girls, Vendors, Tourists ....Company

SAIGON - APRIL 1975
Schultz...Thomas James O'Leary
Antoine..Alton F. White
Reeves..Bruce Winant
Gibbons..Paul Dobie
Troy..Leonard Joseph
Nolen..Gordon Owens
Huston..Matthew Pedersen
Frye..Sean McDermott
Marines, Vietnamese...Comapny

BANGKOK-October 1978
Inhabitants, Moulin Rouge Customers...Company

UNDERSTUDIES: Tony C. Avanti, Paul Matsumoto (Engineer), Annette Calud, Imelda De Los Reyes, Melanie Mariko Tojio (Kim), Sean McDermott, Christopher Pecaro (Chris), Leonard Joseph, Alton F. White (John), Jane Bodle (Ellen), Zar Acayan, Jason Ma (Thuy), **SWINGS:** Sylvia Dohi, Henry Menendez, Marc Oka, Todd Zamarripa

MUSICAL NUMBERS: The Heat Is On in Saigon, Movie in My Mind, Transaction, Why God Why?, Sun and Moon, Telephone, Ceremony, Last Night of the World, Morning of the Dragon, I Still Believe, Back in Town, You Will Not Touch Him, If You Want to Die in Bed, I'd Give My Life for You, Bui-Doi, What a Waste, Please, The Guilt Inside Your Head, Room 317, Now That I've Seen Her, Confrontation, The American Dream, Little God of My Heart

The Company   Top Left: Jonathan Pryce TopRight: Lea Salonga

Hinton Battle, Jonathan Pryce, Lea Salonga Above Left: Willy Falk, Salonga Above Right: Brian R. Baldomero, Salonga

The Company   Top Left: Hinton Battle Right: Liz Callaway

Lea Salonga, Willy Falk   Above Right:Barry K. Bernal
Above Left: Jonathan Pryce

The Company (Also Above and Top Right)

LIZA MINNELLI:
STEPPING OUT AT RADIO CITY

Director, Fred Ebb; Musical Director, Bill LaVorgna; Choreography, Susan Stroman, Lisa Mordente; Special Material, John Kander & Fred Ebb; Musical Supervision, Marvin Laird, Glen Roven; Vocal Arranger, Billy Stritch; Sets, Michael Hotopp; Lighting, David Agress; Costumes, Julie Weiss; Sound, Hank Catteneo; Orchestrations, Mr. Laird, Artie Schreck, Mike Abene, Ralph Burns, Torrie Zito, Glen Roven, Russell Kassoff, Mr. Stritch, Peter Howard, Pet Shop Boys; Company Manager, Gary Labriola; Stage Manager, Arturo E. Porazzi; Ms. Minnelli's Assistant, Roni Gallion; Executive Producers, Eliot Weisman, Premiere Artists Services; Presented by Radio City Music Hall Productions (Scott Sanders & Ed Micone). Opened in Radio City Music Hall on Tuesday, April 23, 1991.*

CAST

LIZA MINNELLI

Mamie Duncan-Gibbs	Sherry Dundish	Roxanne Dundish
Ruth Gotschall	Joanne McHugh	Joanna Noble
Irma Rogers	Jessica Sheridan	Dorothy Stanley
Terri White	Monica Wemitt	Tara Young
	Jeanette Palmer	

MUSICAL NUMBERS: Overture, Nearness of You, Teach Me Tonight, Who Would Have Dreamed/Cottage for Sale, Some People, Sara Lee, Sorry I Asked, Similar Features, Le Temps, Quiet Love, What Makes a Man a Man, Sailor Boy, I'm Living Alone and I Like It, Seeing Things, Vincent Minnelli Tribute, Stepping Out, Losing My Mind, The World Goes Round, All by Myself, Hey Liza It's Me, Men Medley with Demon Divas, Natural Man, The Man I Love, Not for the Life of Me, Drum Dance, Old Friend, My Buddy, Fosse Tribute: Pack Up Your Troubles/Long Way to Tipperary/Imagine, Group Stepping Out, New York New York

A musical spectacular in two acts.

*Closed May 12, 1991 after limited engagement of 15 performances and 1 preview.

THE SECRET GARDEN

Music, Lucy Simon; Book/Lyrics, Marsha Norman; Based on novel by Frances Hodgson Burnett; Director, Susan H. Schulman; Choreography, Michael Lichtefeld; Orchestrations, William D. Brohn; Musical Direction/Vocal Arrangements, Michael Kosarin; Sets, Heidi Landesman; Costumes, Theoni V. Aldredge; Lighting, Tharon Musser; Dance Arrangements, Jeanine Levenson; Sound, Otts Munderloh; Music Coordinator, John Miller; Hair/Makeup, Robert DiNiro; Production Manager, Peter Fulbright; General Manager, David Strong Warner, Inc.; Stage Managers, Perry Cline, Francis Lombardi, Maximo Torres; Company Manager, Sandy Carlson; Wardrobe, Nancy Schaefer; Casting, Wendy Ettinger; Original Cast Recording, Columbia/Sony; Senior Associate Producer, Greg C. Mosher; Associate Producers, Rhoda Mayerson, Playhouse Square Center, Dorothy & Wendell Cherry, Margo Lion, 126 Second Ave. Corp.; Presented by Heidi Landesman, Rick Steiner, Frederick H. Mayerson, Elizabeth Williams, Jujamcyn Theatres/TV Asahi, and Dodger Productions; Press, Adrian Bryan-Brown/Cabrini Lepis, John Barlow. Previewing from Friday, April 5; Opened in the St. James Theatre on Thursday, April 25, 1991.*

CAST

Lily	Rebecca Luker
Mary Lennox	Daisy Egan, Kimberly Mahon (Wed. matinee/Thurs. evening)
Fakir	Peter Marinos
Ayah	Patricia Phillips
Rose	Kay Walbye
Capt. Albert Lennox	Michael DeVries
Lieutenant Peter Wright	Drew Taylor
Lieutenant Ian Shaw	Paul Jackel
Major Holmes	Peter Samuel
Claire	Rebecca Judd
Alice/Mrs. Winthrop	Nancy Johnston
Archibald Craven	Mandy Patinkin
Dr. Neville Craven	Robert Westenberg
Mrs. Medlock	Barbara Rosenblat
Martha	Alison Fraser
Dickon	John Cameron Mitchell
Ben	Tom Toner
Colin	John Babcock
Jane	Teresa De Zarn
William	Frank DiPasquale
Betsy	Betsy Friday
Timothy	Alec Timerman

UNDERSTUDIES: Greg Zerkle (Archibald standby), Michael DeVries, Peter Samuel (Archibald), Teresa De Zarn, Nancy Johnston (Lily), Melody Kay (Mary), Mr. DeVries, Paul Jackel (Neville), Rebecca Judd, Jane Seaman (Mrs. Medlock), Betsy Friday, Jennifer Smith (Martha/Alice), Kevin Ligon, Alec Timerman (Dickon/Fakir/Shaw), Bill Nolte, Drew Taylor (Ben), Joel B. Chaiken (Colin), Ms. De Zarn, Ms. Friday (Rose), Mr. Jackel, Mr. Zerkle (Lennox), Ms. Judd, Ms. Smith (Ayah/Mrs. Winthrop), Frank DiPasquale, Mr. Nolte (Wright/Holmes), Ms. Friday, Ms. Seaman (Claire), **SWINGS:** Kevin Ligon, Bill Nolte, Jane Seaman, Jennifer Smith

MUSICAL NUMBERS: Opening Dream, There's a Girl, House upon the Hill, I Heard Someone Crying, A Fine White Horse, A Girl in the Valley, It's a Maze, Winter's on the Wing, Show Me the Key, A Bit of Earth, Storm, Lily's Eyes, Round-Shouldered Man, Final Storm, Girl I Mean to Be, Quartet, Race You to the Top of the Morning, Wick, Come to My Garden, Come Spirit Come Charm, Disappear, Hold On, Letter Song, Where in the World, How Could I Ever Know, Finale

A musical in two acts, with eighteen scenes and a prologue. The action takes place in Colonial India and at Misselthwaite Manor, North Yorkshire, England, in 1906.

*Still playing May 31, 1991. Winner of "Tonys" for Featured Actress in a Musical (Daisy Egan), Best Book of a Musical, and Best Scenic Design.

Bob Marshak Photos

John Cameron Mitchell, Daisy Eagan

Daisy Eagan, Alison Fraser

John Babcock, Mandy Patinkin

Peter Marinos, Daisy Eagan, Alison Fraser, Rebecca Luker (top), John Babcock, John Cameron Mitchell Above: Mandy Patinkin, Eagan

33

Tyne Daly

Crista Moore
Top Right: Daly, Moore, Jonathan Hadary

Robert Lambert

GYPSY

Music, Jule Styne; Lyrics, Stephen Sondheim; Book/Direction, Arthur Laurents; Original Direction/Choreography, Jerome Robbins; Choreography Reproduction, Bonnie Walker; Orchestrations, Sid Ramin, Robert Ginzler; Musical Director, Michael Rafter; Dance Arrangements, John Kander; Sets, Kenneth Foy; Costumes, Theoni V. Aldredge; Lighting, Natasha Katz; Sound, Peter Fitzgerald; Hair/Make-up, Robert DiNiro, Alan E. Schubert; General Manager, Alecia Parker; Production Supervisor, James Pentecost; Technical Director, Arthur Siccardi; Asst. Director, Richard Sabellico; Music Coordinator, John Monaco; Stage Managers, Craig Jacobs, James Bernandi; Company Manager, Scott A. Moore; Wardrobe, Larch Miller; Original Cast Recording, Elektra Nonesuch; Presented by Barry & Fran Weissler, Kathy Levin and Barry Brown; Press, Shirley Herz/Bob Larkin, Wayne Wolfe. Previewing from Thursday, April 18; Opened in the Marquis Theatre on Sunday, April 28, 1991.*

CAST

Uncle Jocko/Kringelein	Stan Rubin
George/Mr. Goldstone	Victor Raider-Wexler
Clarence	Bobby John Carter
Balloon Girl	Jeana Haege
Baby Louise	Kristen Mahon
Baby June	Susan Cremin
Rose	Tyne Daly
Pop/Cigar	Ronn Carroll
Newsboys	Mr. Carter, Thomas Fox, Danny Cistone, Tony Yazbeck
Weber/Phil	Richard Levine
Herbie	Jonathan Hadary
Louise	Crista Moore
June	Tracy Venner
Tulsa	Robert Lambert
Yonkers	Bruce Moore
L.A.	Craig Waletzko
Kansas	Paul Geraci
Flagstaff	Kevin Petitto
St. Paul	Cory English
Cow	Ms. Moore, Barbara Folts, Robin Robinson, Mr. English, Mr. Petitto
Miss Cratchitt/Tessie	Barbara Erwin
Hollywood Blondes	Terri Furr, Ms. Folts, Michele Pigliavento, Nancy Melius, Ms. Robinson
Agnes	Lori Ann Mahl
Pastey/Bougeron-Cochon	Jeff Brooks
Mazeppa	Jana Robbins
Electra	Anna McNeely
Maid	Ginger Prince

UNDERSTUDIES/STANDBYS: Jana Robbins (Rose), Richard Levine (Herbie), Ginger Prince (Mazeppa/Tessie/Electra/Cratchitt), Victor Raider-Wexler (Pop/Cochon), Craig Waletzko (Tulsa), Teri Furr (Agnes/June), Jeana Haege (Baby June/Baby Louise), Stan Rubin (Weber/Cigar/Phil), Michele Pigliavento (Louise)

MUSICAL NUMBERS: Overture, Let Me Entertain You, Some People, Small World, Baby June & Her Newsboys, Mr. Goldstone, Little Lamb, You'll Never Get Away from Me, Dainty June & Her Farmboys, If Momma Was Married, All I Need Is the Girl, Everything's Coming Up Roses, Toreadorables, Together, You Gotta Have a Gimmick, The Strip, Rose's Turn

A return engagement of last season's production of the musical suggested by the memoirs of Gypsy Rose Lee. Performed in two acts. The action takes place in various American cities in the 1920s and 1930s. Original engagement of this production opened November 16, 1989 in the St. James Theatre and played 476 performances (See *Theatre World* Vol. 46).

*Closed July 28, 1991 after 105 performances and 12 previews.

OUR COUNTRY'S GOOD

By Timberlake Wertenbaker; Based on novel *The Playmaker* by Thomas Keneally; Director, Mark Lamos; Sets, Christopher Barreca; Costumes, Candice Donnelly; Lighting, Mimi Jordan Sherin; Sound, David Budries; General Manager, Gindi Theatrical Management; Casting, Julie Mossberg, Brian Chavanne; Stage Managers, Frederic H. Orner, Barbara Reo; Originally Produced by Royal Court Theatre, London; Presented by Frank and Woji Gero, Karl Sydow, Raymond L. Gaspard, Frederick Zollo, Diana Bliss; A Hartford Stage Co. Production; Press, Chris Boneau/Susan Tighe, Bob Fennell. Previewing from Friday, April 19; A Broadway Allliance presentation.Opened in the Nederlander Theatre on Monday, April 29, 1991.*

CAST

Captain Arthur Phillip/John Wisehammer	Richard Poe
Major Robbie Ross/Ketch Freeman	Adam LeFevre
Captain David Collins/Robert Sideway	Sam Tsoutsouvas
Captain Watkin Tench/Black Caesar/Aborigine	Gregory Wallace
Captain Jemmy Campbell/Harry Brewer/Arscott	Ron McLarty
Reverend Johnson/Liz Morden	Cherry Jones
Lieutenant George Johnston/Mary Brenham	Tracey Ellis
Lieutenant Will Dawes/Meg Long/Duckling Smith	Amelia Campbell
Second Lieutenant Ralph Clark	Peter Frechette
Second Lieutenant William Faddy/Dabby Bryant	J. Smith-Cameron
Convicts	Neville Aurelius, John Hickok

UNDERSTUDIES: Orlagh Cassidy (Dawes/Smith/Long/Johnston/Brenham/Johnson/Morden/Faddy/Bryant), Neville Aurelius (Campbell/Brewer/Arscott/Phillip/Wisehammer/Tench/Aborigine/Caesar), John Hickok (Clark/Ross/Freeman/Collins/Sideway)

A drama in two acts. The action takes place in Sydney, Australia in 1788-89.

*Closed June 8, 1991 after 48 performances and 12 previews. Recipient of New York Drama Critics Circle Award for Best Foreign Play.

Martha Swope Photos

The Company Above: Tracey Ellis, Cherry Jones, J. Smith-Cameron Top: Peter Frechette, Ellis

Keith Carradine and New Ziegfeld Girls

Cady Huffman

Dee Hoty

THE WILL ROGERS FOLLIES: A LIFE IN REVUE

Music Composition /Arrangement, Cy Coleman; Lyrics, Betty Comden and Adolph Green; Book, Peter Stone; Director/Choreographer, Tommy Tune; Orchestrations, Billy Byers; Musical Director, Eric Stern; Musical Contractor, John Miller; Sets, Tony Walton; Costumes, Willa Kim; Lighting, Jules Fisher; Sound, Peter Fitzgerald; Projection Design, Wendall K. Harrington; Wigs, Howard Leonard; General Management, Marvin A. Krauss Associates; Stage Managers, Peter von Mayrhauser, Patrick Ballard; Wardrobe, Alyce Gilbert; Associate Director, Phillip Oesterman; Associate Choreographer, Jeff Calhoun; Casting, Julie Hughes and Barry Moss, CSA; Original Cast Recording, Columbia; Presented by Pierre Cossette, Martin Richards, Sam Crothers, James M. Nederlander, Stewart F. Lane, Max Weitzenhoffer, and Japan Satellite Broadcasting; Press, Judy Jacksina/Robin Monchek, Julianne Waldheim, Penny M. Landau. Previewing from Monday, April 1; Opened in the Palace Theatre on Wednesday, May 1, 1991.*

CAST

Ziegfeld's Favorite..Cady Huffman
Will Rogers...Keith Carradine
Unicyclist/Roper...Vince Bruce
Wiley Post...Paul Ukena, Jr.
Clem Rogers...Dick Latessa
Will's Sisters/Betty's Sisters.................Roxane Barlow, Maria Calabrese,
        Colleen Dunn, Dana Moore, Wendy Waring, Leigh Zimmerman
Betty Blake...Dee Hoty
The Wild West Show/Trainers/Madcap Mutts ....Tom & Bonnie Brackney
        with B.A., Cocoa, Gigi, Rusty, Trixie and Zee
Will Rogers, Jr. ....Rick Faugno
Mary Rogers ....Tammy Minoff
James Rogers ....Lance Robinson
Freddy Rogers..Gregory Scott Carter
The Will Rogers Wranglers ....John Ganun, Troy Britton Johnson,
        Jerry Mitchell, Jason Opsahl
The New Ziegfeld Girls.......................Ms. Barlow, Ms. Calabrese, Ganine Derleth,
        Rebecca Downing, Ms. Dunn, Sally Mae Dunn, Toni Georgianna,
    Eileen Grace, Luba Gregus, Tonia Lynn, Ms. Moore, Aimee Turner, Jillana
        Urbina, Ms. Waring, Christina Youngman, Ms. Zimmerman
Voice of Mr. Ziegfeld..Gregory Peck

UNDERSTUDIES/STANDBYS: Paul Ukena, Jr. (Will), Dana Moore (Ziegfeld's Favorite), Lance Robinson (Will Jr.), Tom Flagg (Clem), Erica Dutko (Mary/James/Freddy), **SWINGS:** Mary Lee DeWitt, Jack Doyle, Angie L. Schwarer

MUSICAL NUMBERS: Let's Go Flying, Will-a-Mania, Give a Man Enough Rope, It's a Boy, So Long Pa, My Unknown Someone, We're Heading for a Wedding, The Big Time, My Big Mistake, Powder Puff Ballet, Mary Me Now/I Got You, Look Around, Favorite Son, No Man Left for Me, Presents for Mrs. Rogers, Without You, Never Met a Man I Didn't Like

A musical inspired by the words of Will and Betty Rogers in two acts and 12 scenes. The action takes place in the Palace Theatre, New York City, at present.

*Still playing May 31, 1991. Winner of "Tonys" for Best Musical, Best Direction of a Musical, Best Original Score, Best Costumes, Best Lighting, Best Choreography. Selected by the New York Drama Critics Circle as Best Musical.

The Company Center: Keith Carradine (Left), Carradine and Company (Right, also Top)

CATS

Music, Andrew Lloyd Webber; Lyrics, Adapted from *Old Possums' Book of Practical Cats* by T.S. Eliot; Additional Lyrics, Trevor Nunn, Richard Stilgoe; Director, Mr. Nunn; Choreography/Associate Direction, Gillian Lynne; Design, John Napier; Orchestrations, Mr. Webber, David Cullen; Production Musical Director, David Caddick; Musical Director, Sue Anderson; Sound, Martin Levan; Presented by Cameron Mackintosh, The Really Useful Company Ltd., David Geffen, The Shubert Organization; Executive Producers, R. Tyler Gatchell, Jr., Peter Neufeld; Casting, Johnson-Liff & Zerman; Cast-Recording, Geffen. Opened in the Winter Garden Theatre on Thursday, October 7, 1982.*

CAST

Alonzo	Scott Taylor
Bustopher/Asparagus/Growltiger	Dale Hensley
Bombalurina	Marlene Danielle†1
Cassandra	Leigh Webster
Coricopat	Johnny Anzalone
Demeter	Brenda Braxton
Grizabella	Loni Ackerman
Jellylorum/Griddlebone	Bonnie Simmons
Jennyanydots	Cindy Benson
Mistoffelees	Michael Arnold
Mungojerrie	Ray Roderick
Munkustrap	Greg Minahan
Old Deuteronomy	Larry Small
Plato/Macavity/Rumpus Cat	Randy Wojcik
Pouncival	John Joseph Festa
Rumpleteazer	Kristi Lynes
Rum Tum Tiger	Frank Mastrocola
Sillabub	Michelle Schumacher
Skimbleshanks	Eric Scott Kincaid
Tantomile	Lisa Dawn Cave
Tumblebrutus	Jay Poindexter
Victoria	Claudia Shell
Cats Chorus	Joel Briel, Jay Aubrey Jones, Susan Powers, Heidi Stallings

UNDERSTUDIES/STANDBYS: John Aller, Brian Andrews, Jack Magradey (Alonzo), Joel Briel (Bustopher/Gus/Growltiger), Rebecca Timms, Darlene Wilson (Bombalurina), Rebecca Timms, Darlene Wilson, Lily-Lee Wong (Cassandra), John Aller, Wade Laboissonniere, John Vincent Leggio, Jack Magradey (Coricopat), Lisa Dawn Cave, Rebecca Timms, Darlene Wilson (Demeter), Brenda Braxton, Heidi Stallings (Grizabella), Marcy DeGonge, Susan Powers (Jellylorum/Griddlebone), Marcy DeGonge, Susan Powers, Suzanne Viverito (Jennyanydots), Johnny Anzalone, John Joseph Festa, John Vincent Leggio (Mistoffelees), Brian Andrews, Wade Laboissonniere, John Vincent Leggio, Jack Magradey (Mungojerrie), John Aller, Jack Magradey, Scott Taylor (Munkustrap), Jay Aubrey Jones (Deuteronomy), John Aller, Brian Andrews, Scott Taylor (Plato/Macavity/Rumpus), Brian Andrews, Wade Laboissonniere, John Vincent Leggio (Pouncival), Michelle Schumacher, Suzanne Viverito, Lily-Lee Wong (Rumpleteazer), John Aller, Jack Magradey, Scott Taylor (Rum Tum), Rebecca Timms, Suzanne Viverito, Lily-Lee Wong (Sillibub), Wade Laboissonniere, Jack Magradey (Skimbleshanks), Rebecca Timms, Suzanne Viverito, Darlene Wilson, Lily-Lee Wong (Tantomile), Brian Andrews, Wade Laboissonniere, John Vincent Leggio (Tumblebrutus), Lisa Dawn Cave, Suzanne Viverito, Lily-Lee Wong (Victoria)

MUSICAL NUMBERS: Naming of Cats, Invitation to the Jellicle Ball, Old Gumbie Cat, Rum Tum Tugger, Grizabella the Glamour Cat, Bustopher Jones, Mungojerrie and Rumpleteazer, Old Deuteronomy, Awefull Battle of Pekes and Pollicles, Memory, Moments of Happiness, Gus the Theatre Cat, Growltiger's Last Stand, Skimbleshanks, Macavity, Mr. Mistoffelees, Journey to the Heaviside Layer, Ad-dressing of Cats.

A musical in two acts and twenty scenes.

*Still playing May 31, 1991. Winner of 1983 "Tonys" for Best Musical, Score, Book, Direction, Costumes, Lighting and Featured Actress in a Musical (Betty Buckley as Grizabella). For original production, see *Theatre World* Vol. 39.

† Succeeded by 1. Karen Curlee

Top Right: The Company

The Company Above: Loni Ackerman

CITY OF ANGELS

Music, Cy Coleman; Lyrics, David Zippel; Book, Larry Gelbart; Director, Michael Blakemore; Musical Staging, Walter Painter; Sets, Robin Wagner; Costumes, Florence Klotz; Lighting, Paul Gallo; Orchestrations, Billy Byers; Musical Director, Gordon Lowry Harrell; Fights, B.H. Barry; Sound, Peter Fitzgerald, Bernard Fox; Vocal Arrangements, Mr. Coleman, Yaron Gershovsky; Hair Stylist, Steve Atha; General Manager, Ralph Roseman; Stage Managers, Steven Zweigbaum, Brian Meister; Casting, Johnson-Liff & Zerman; Cast Recording, Columbia; Presented by Nick Vanoff, Roger Berlind, Jujamcyn Theatres, Suntory International Corp., and The Shubert Organization; Press, Bill Evans/Jim Randolph. Opened in the Virginia Theatre on December 11, 1989.*

Michael Rupert

MOVIE CAST

Stone	James Naughton†1
Orderlies	James Hindman, Tom Galantich
Oolie	Randy Graff†2
Alaura Kingsley	Dee Hoty†3
Big Six	Herschel Sparber
Sonny	Raymond Xifo
Jimmy Powers	Scott Waara†4
Angel City 4	Peter Davis, Amy Jane London, Gary Kahn, Jackie Presti
Munoz	Shawn Elliott
Officer Pasco	Tom Galantich
Bobbi	Kay McClelland†5
Irwin S. Irving	Rene Auberjonois†6
Peter Kingsley	Doug Tompos
Margaret	Carolee Carmello†7
Luther Kingsley	Keith Perry
Dr. Mandril	James Cahill†8
Mallory Kingsley	Rachel York†9
Mahoney	James Hindman
Yamato	Alvin Lum
Commissioner Gaines	Evan Thompson†10
Margie/Madame	Eleanor Glockner
Bootsie	Jacquey Maltby

HOLLYWOOD CAST

Stine	Greg Edelman†11
Buddy Fidler	Rene Auberjonois†6
Shoeshine	Evan Thompson†10
Gabby	Kay McClelland†5
Barber	James Cahill†8
Donna	Randy Graff†2
Anna/Masseuse	Eleanor Glockner
Jimmy Powers	Scott Waara†4
Angel City 4	Peter Davis, Amy Jane London, Gary Kahn, Jackie Presti
Carla Haywood	Dee Hoty†3
Del Dacosta	James Hindman
Pancho Vargas	Shawn Elliott
Werner Kriegler	Keith Perry
Gerald Pierce	Doug Tompos
Avril Raines	Rachel York†9
Gene	Tom Galantich
Cinematographer	Alvin Lum
Stand-In	Carolee Carmello†7
Hairdresser	Eleanor Glockner
Studio Cops	Herschel Sparber, Raymond Xifo

UNDERSTUDIES: Tom Galantich (Stone/Jimmy), James Hindman (Stine/Munoz/Buddy/Irwin/Sonny), William Linton (Irwin/Buddy/Sonny/Luther/Werner/Mandril), Jan Maxwell, Elizabeth Ward (Alaura/Carla), Jacquey Maltby (Oolie/Donna/Mallory/Avril/Madame/Masseuse/Hairdresser), Christopher Wynkoop (Luther/Werner/Mandril), Marcus Neville (Peter/Gerald/Pasco/Angel (Barber/Orderly/Mahoney/Dacosta/Gaines), William Linton (Barber/Orderly/Dacosta/ Gaines), Millie Whiteside (Margaret/Bootsie/Angel)

MUSICAL NUMBERS: Prelude, Double Talk, What You Don't Know About Women, Ya Gotta Look Out for Yourself, Buddy System, With Every Breath I Take, Tennis Song, Ev'rybody's Gotta Be Somewhere, Lost and Found, All You Have to Do Is Wait, You're Nothing Without Me, Stay With Me, You Can Always Count on Me, It Needs Work, Funny Finale

A musical in 2 acts and 37 scenes. The action takes place in Los Angeles during the late 1940s.

†Succeeded by: 1. Tom Wopat, Franc Luz, Tom Galantich, Joel Higgins 2. Susan Terry 3. Beverly Leech, Jan Maxwell, Linda Thorson 4. Bob Walton 5. Donna Bullock 6. Charles Levin 7. Elizabeth Ward 8. George Taylor 9. Karen Fineman 10. Christopher Wynkoop 11. James Hindman (during vacation), Michael Rupert

*Closed Jan. 19, 1992 after 878 performances and 24 previews. Winner of 1990 "Tonys" for Best Musical, Best Book, Best Score, Best Sets, Best Actor (Naughton), Best Featured Actress (Graff) in addition to Best Musical Awards from the New York Drama Critics Circle, Outer Critics Circle and Drama Desk.

Herechel Sparber, Raymond Xifo, Tom Wopat Above: Wopat

Chip Zien, Lynnette Perry Above: Caitlin Brown

GRAND HOTEL

Music/Lyrics, Robert Wright/George Forrest; Additional Songs, Maury Yeston; Book, Luther Davis; Based on the novel by Vicki Baum; Director/Choreographer, Tommy Tune; Sets, Tony Walton; Costumes, Santo Loquasto; Lighting, Jules Fisher; Orchestrations, Peter Matz; Musical/Vocal Director, Jack Lee; Musical Supervision/Additional Music, Wally Harper; Associate Director, Bruce Lumpkin; Sound, Otts Munderloh; Music Coordinator, John Monaco; Hair Stylist, Werner Sherer; General Manager, Joey Parnes; Production Associate, Kathleen Raitt; Company Manager, Nina Skriloff; Stage Managers, Mr. Lumpkin, Robert Kellogg, Rob Babbitt; Presented by Martin Richards, Mary Lea Johnson, Sam Crothers, Sander Jacobs, Kenneth D. Greenblatt, Paramount Pictures, Jujamcyn Theatres, Patty Grubman, and Marvin A. Krauss; Press, Judy Jacksina/Julianne Waldhelm. Opened in the Martin Beck Theatre on Sunday, November 12, 1989.*

CAST

The Doorman	Charles Mandracchia†1
Colonel Doctor Otternschlag	John Wylie
The Countess and The Gigolo	Yvonne Marceau, Pierre Dulaine
Rohna, the Grand Concierge	Rex D. Hays
Erik, Front Desk	Bob Stillman

Bellboys:
Georg Strunk	Ken Jennings
Kurt Krönenberg	Keith Crowningshield†2
Hanns Bittner	Gerrit de Beer
Willibald, Captain	J.J. Jepson

Telephone Operators:
Hildegarde Bratts	Jennifer Lee Andrews†3
Sigfriede Holzhiem	Suzanne Henderson
Wolffe Bratts	DeLee Lively Mekka†4
The Jimmys	David Jackson, Danny Strayhorn
The Chauffeur	Ben George†5
Zinnowitz, the Lawyer	Hal Robinson†6
Sandor, the Impresario	Mitchell Jason
Victor Witt, Company Manager	Michel Moinot
Madame Peepee	Kathi Moss
General Director Preysing	Timothy Jerome
Flaemmchem, the Typist	Jane Krakowski†7
Otto Kringlelein, the Bookkeeper	Michael Jeter†8
Felix Von Gaigern, the Baron	Brent Barrett†9
Raffaela, the Confidante	Karen Akers†10
Elizaveta Grushinskaya, the Ballerina	Liliane Montevecchi†11

Scullery Workers:
Gunther Gustafsson	Walter Willison
Werner Holst	David Elledge
Franz Kohl	William Ryall†12
Ernst Schmidt	Henry Grossman
Hotel Courtesan	Suzanne Henderson
Tootsie	Jennifer Lee Andrews†4
Detective	William Ryall†12
Trude, the Maid	Jennifer Lee Andrews†3

UNDERSTUDIES/STANDBYS: Walter Willison (Baron), Jerry Ball (Chauffeur/Rohna/Zinnowitz), Gerrit de Beer (Sandor), David Elledge (Chauffeur/Rohna), Niki Harris (Countess/Grushinskaya/Peepee), Eivind Harum (Chauffeur/Zinnowitz), Rex D. Hays (Doctor), Ken Jennings (Kringlelein/Witt), J.J. Jepson (Gigolo/Kringlelein/Erik), Merwin Goldsmith (Baron/Erik/Zinnowitz/Chauffeur/Preysing), Lee Lobenhofer (Preysing/Baron/Erik/Zinnowitz/Chauffeur), Meg Tolin (Flaemmchem), Eric Bohus (Erik), Ben George (Baron) **SWINGS:** Rob Babbitt, Niki Harris, Eivand Harum, Lee Lobenhofer, Glenn Turner, Eric Bohus

MUSICAL NUMBERS: The Grand Parade, As It Should Be, Some Have Some Have Not, At The Grand Hotel, Table with a View, Maybe My Baby Loves Me, Fire and Ice, Twenty-two Years, Villa on a Hill, I Want to Go to Hollywood, Everybody's Doing It, The Crooked Path, Who Wouldn't Dance with You, The Boston Merger, No Encore, Love Can't Happen, What She Needs, Bonjour Amour, Happy, We'll Take a Glass Together, I Waltz Alone, Roses at the Station, How Can I Tell Her?, The Grand Waltz

A musical in twenty scenes performed without intermission. The action takes place in Berlin's Grand Hotel in 1928.

†Succeeded by: 1. George Dudley 2. Carlos Lopez 3. Lisa Merrill, Jill Powell 4. Meg Tolin 5. Luis Perez 6. Merwin Goldsmith 7. DeLee Lively-Mekka, Lynnette Perry, Meg Tolin (during vacation) 8. J.J. Jepson, Chip Zien 9. Rex Smith, David Carroll, John Schneider, Walter Willison (during vacation) 10. Caitlin Brown 11. Rene Ceballos, Tina Paul (during illness), Zina Bethune 12. Jerry Ball

Martha Swope Photos

Top Left: Lynnette Perry, Danny Strayhorn, David Jackson
Below: John Schneider, Zina Bethune

LES MISÉRABLES

By Alain Boublil, Claude-Michel Schonberg; Based on novel by Victor Hugo; Music, Claude-Michel Schonberg; Lyrics, Herbert Kretzmer; Original French Text, Alain Boublil, Jean-Marc Natel; Additional Material, James Fenton; Orchestral Score, John Cameron; Musical Supervision/Direction, Robert Billig; Sound, Andrew Bruce/Autograph; Associate Director/Executive Producer, Richard Jay-Alexander; Executive Producer, Martin McCallum; Casting, Johnson-Liff & Zerman; General Management, Alan Wasser; Presented by Cameron Mackintosh; Director/Adaptation, Trevor Nunn, John Caird; Design, John Napier; Lighting, David Hersey; Costumes, Andreane Neofitou; Produced in association with JFK Center for the Performing Arts; Press, Fred Nathan Co./Marc Thibodeau, Merle Frimark, William Schelble, Maria Somma, Ian Rand; Opened in the Broadway Theatre on Thursday, March 12, 1987, and moved to the Imperial Theatre on October 16, 1990.*

CAST

PROLOGUE: Craig Schulman†1(Jean Valjean), Robert Westenberg†2 (Javert), J.C.Sheets, Joel Robertson, Tom Zemon, Rohn Seykell, Ed Dixon, Joe Locarro, Hugh Panaro, Bruce Kuhn, (Chain Gang), Jeffrey Clonts (Farmer), Bruce Kuhn (Laborer), Deborah Bradshaw (Innkeeper's Wife), Merwin Foard (Innkeeper), Adam Heller (Bishop of Digne), Willy Falk, Paul Avedisian (Constables)

MONTREUIL-SUR-MER 1823: Christy Baron (Fantine), Joel Robertson (Foreman), Jeffrey Clonts, Rohn Seykell, Jessica Molaskey,Olga Merediz, Cissy Rebich, Jean Fitzgibbons (Workers), Mary Gutzi (Factory Girl), Jordan Leeds, J.C. Sheets, Rohn Seykell (Sailors), Mary Gutzi, Jean Fitzgibbons, Cissy Rebich,Natalie Toro, Lisa Ann Grant, Tracy Shayne, Betsy True, Deborah Bradshaw (Whores), Jessica Molaskey (Old Woman), Adam Heller (Pimp),Tom Zemon (Bamatabois), Adam Heller (Fauchelevent)

MONTFERMEIL 1823: Marlo Landry, Eden Riegel or Tamara Robin Spiewak (Young Cosette), Evalyn Baron (Mme. Thenardier), Ed Dixon (Thenardier), Eden Riegel or Tamara Robin Spiewak (Young Eponine), Jeffrey Clonts (Drinker), Bruce Kuhn, Betsy True (Young Couple), Merwin Foard (Drunk) Paul Avedisian, Jean Fitzgibbons (Diners), Jordan Leeds (Young Man), Cissy Rebich, Lisa Ann Grant (Young Girls), Olga Merediz, Robin Seykell (Old Couple), Joel Robertson, Willy Falk (Travelers), Others: Adam Heller, Tom Zemon, J.C. Sheets, Jessica Molaskey, Deborah Bradshaw, Mary Gutzi

PARIS 1832: Alex Dezen or Joey Rigol (Gavroche), Deborah Bradshaw (Old Beggar Woman), Mary Gutzi (Young Prostitute), Merwin Foard (Pimp), Natalie Toro (Eponine), BruceKuhn (Montparnassse), Willy Falk (Babet), J.C. Sheets (Brujon), Adam Heller (Claquesous), Joel Robertson (Combeferre), Jordan Leeds (Feuilly), Jeffrey Clonts (Courfeyrac), Rohn Seykell (Joly), Paul Avedisian (Lesgles), Merwin Foard (Jean Prouvaire), Joseph Kolinsk (Enjolras), Matthew Porretta (Marius), Jacquelyn Piro (Cosette)

MUSICAL NUMBERS: Prologue, Soliloquy, At the End of the Day, I Dreamed a Dream, Lovely Ladies, Who Am I?, Come to Me, Castle on a Cloud, Master of the House, Thernardier Waltz, Look Down, Stars, Red and Black, Do You Hear the People Sing?, In My Life, A Heart Full of Love, One Day More, On My Own, A Little Fall of Rain, Drink with Me to Days Gone By, Bring Him Home, Dog Eats Dog, Javert's Soliloquy, Turning, Empty Chairs at Empty Tables, Wedding Chorale, Beggars at the Feast, Finale

A dramatic musical in two acts and four scenes with a prologue.

*Still playing May 31, 1991. Winner of 1987 "Tonys" for Best Musical, Book, Score, Featured Actor and Actress in a Musical (Michael Maguire, Frances Ruffelle), Direction, Scenic Design, Lighting.

†Succeeded by 1. J. Mark McVey 2. Robert Du Sold

The Company Center: J. Mark McVey
Top: McVey, Robert DuSold

THE PHANTOM OF THE OPERA

Music, Andrew Lloyd Webber; Lyrics, Charles Hart; Additional Lyrics, Richard Stilgoe; Book, Richard Stilgoe, Andrew Lloyd Webber; Based on novel by Gaston Leroux; Director, Harold Prince; Musical Staging/Choreographer, Gillian Lynne; Production Design, Maria Bjornson; Lighting, Andrew Bridge; Sound, Martin Levan; Musical Supervision/Direction, David Caddick; Orchestrations, David Cullen, Andrew Lloyd Webber; Casting, Johnson-Liff & Zerman; General Management, Alan Wasser; Presented by Cameron Mackintosh and the Really Useful Theatre Company; Assistant to Director, Ruth Mitchell; Production Supervisor, Mitchell Lemsky; Stage Managers, Fred Hanson, Bethe Ward, Frank Marino; Press, Fred Nathan Co./Merle Frimark, William Schelble, Marc P. Thibodeau, Ian Rand, Colleen Brown. Opened in the Majestic Theatre on Tuesday, January 26, 1988.*

CAST

The Phantom of the Opera	Steve Barton†1
Christine Daae	Rebecca Luker or Katharine Buffaloe†2
Raoul, Vicomte de Chagny	Davis Gaines†3
Carlotta Giudicelli	Marilyn Caskey
Monsieur Andre	Jeff Keller
Monsieur Firmin	George Lee Andrews
Madame Giry	Leila Martin
Ubaldo Piangi	John Horton Murray
Meg Giry	Elisa Heinsohn
Monsieur Reyer	Gary Barker
Auctioneer	Richard Warren Pugh
Porter/Marksman	David Cleveland
Monsieur Lefevre	Kenneth Waller
Joseph Buquet	Philip Steele
Don Attilio/Passarino	Thomas Sandri
Slave Master	David Loring
Flunky/Stagehand	Jeff Siebert
Policeman	Charles Rule
Page	Patrice Pickering
Porter/Fireman	William Scott Brown
Page	Elena Jeanne Batman
Wardrobe Mistress/Confidante	Mary Leigh Stahl
Princess	Raissa Katona
Madame Firmin	Dawn Leigh Stone
Innkeeper's Wife	Lorin Stein
Ballet Chorus of Opera	Tener Brown, Natasha MacAller, Alina Hernandez, Tania Philip, Dodie Pettit, Catherine Ulissey
Ballet Swing	Lori MacPherson
Swings	James Romick, Paul Laureano, Suzanne Ishee

MUSICAL NUMBERS: Think of Me, Angel of Music, Little Lotte, The Mirror, The Phantom of the Opera, The Music of the Night, I Remember, Stranger Than You Dreamt It, Magical Lasso, Notes, Prima Donna, Poor Fool He Makes Me Laugh, Why Have You Brought Me Here?, I've Been There, All I Ask of You, Masquerade, Why So Silent?, Twisted Every Way, Wishing You Were Somehow Here Again, Wandering Child, Bravo Bravo, Point of No Return, Down Once More, Track Down the Murderer

A musical in two acts and nineteen scenes with a prologue. The action takes place in the Paris Opera House.

*Still playing May 31, 1990. 1988 "Tonys" were awarded for Best Musical, Leading Actor in a Musical (Michael Crawford), Featured Actress in a Musical (Judy Kaye), Scenic Design, Lighting, Direction of a Musical.

†Succeeded by 1. Kevin Gray, Mark Jacoby 2. Karen Culliver 3. Hugh Panaro

The Company

The Company Center: Hugh Panaro, Karen Culliver
Top: Mark Jacoby

Timothy Hutton, Mary-Louise Parker

PRELUDE TO A KISS

by Craig Lucas; Director, Norman René; Sets, Loy Arcenas; Costumes, Walker Hicklin; Lighting, Debra J. Kletter; Sound, Scott Lehrer; Hair/Wigs, Bobby H. Grayson; Production Stage Manager, James Harker; Stage Manager, M.A. Howard; Company Manager, Douglas C. Baker; General Manager, David Strong Warner, Inc.; Production Supervisor, Neil Mazzella; Wardrobe, Dawn Walnut; Associate Producer, Lawrence J. Wilker; Presented by Christopher Gould, Suzanne Golden, Dodger Productions; Original Producer, South Coast Repertory with support from the National Endowment for the Arts; Produced Off-Broadway by Circle Repertory Theatre Company ; Press, Joshua Ellis/Adrian Bryan-Brown, Jackie Green, Suzanne Tighe, Tim Ray; Opened in the Helen Hayes Theatre on Tuesday, May 1, 1990.*

CAST

Peter ....Timothy Hutton†1
Rita ....Mary-Louise Parker†2
Taylor ....John Dossett†3
Tom/Jamaican Waiter...L. Peter Callendar†4
Mrs. Boyle..Debra Monk†5
Dr. Boyle..Larry Bryggman†6
Minister/Guest/Barfly/Vacationer...Craig Bockhorn
Aunt Dorothy/Leah...Joyce Reehling†7
Uncle Fred/Guest/Barfly/Vacationer...Michael Warren Powell
Old Man..Barnard Hughes†8
Party-Wedding Guests/Barflies/Vacationers.....Brian Cousins†9, Kimberly Dudwitt

A contemporary fairy tale in two acts. The action takes place in New York City, New Jersey and Jamaica.

*Closed May 19, 1991 after 440 performances and 8 previews. It previously played 57 Performances Off-Broadway at Circle Repertory Theatre.

†Succeeded by: 1. John Dossett, Steve Guttenberg 2. Ashley Crowe, Taylor Young 3. Tom Verica 4. Monte Russell 5. Mary Louise Wilson 6. Joe Ponazecki 7. Cynthia Darlow 8. John Randolph 9. Daniel Markel

Steve Guttenberg, Ashley Crow

THE FANTASTICKS

Music, Harvey Schmidt; Lyrics/Book, Tom Jones; Director, Word Baker; Original Musical Direction/Arrangements, Julian Stein; Design, Ed Wittstein; Musical Director, Dorothy Martin; Stage Managers, Kim Moore, James Cook, Steven Michael Daley, Mathew Eaton Bennett, Christopher Scott; Presented by Lore Noto; Associate Producers, Sheldon Baron, Dorothy Olim, Jules Field; Cast Recording, MGM/Polydor; Press, Ginnie Weidmann; Opened in the Sullivan Street Playhouse on Tuesday, May 3, 1960.*

CAST

The Boy ....Neil Nash†1
The Girl ....Marilyn Whitehead
The Girl's Father ....William Tost
The Boy's Father ....George Riddle
Narrator/El Gallo ....Robert Vincent Smith†2
Mute ....Steven Michael Daley†3
Old Actor ....Bryan Hull
Man Who Dies ....Earl Aaron Levine
Piano ....Dorothy Martin
Harp ....Hank Whitmire

UNDERSTUDIES: Anne Fisher, Kate Suber (Girl), Steven Michael Daley, Mathew Eaton Bennett (Boy), William Tost, George Riddle (Fathers), Neil Nash, Rex Nockengust, Kevin R. Wright, Mathew Bennett (Narrator)

MUSICAL NUMBERS: Overture, Try to Remember, Much More, Metaphor, Never Say No, It Depends on What You Pay, Soon It's Gonna Rain, Abduction Ballet, Happy Ending, This Plum Is Too Ripe, I Can See It, Plant a Radish, Round and Round, They Were You, Finale

A musical in two acts.

*Still playing May 31, 1991. The world's longest running musical has now passed 13,000 performances.

†Succeeded by: 1. Rex Nockengust, Kevin R. Wright, Mathew Eaton Bennett 2. David Brummel, Michael Licata, Kenneth Kantor, Scott Willis 3. Mathew Eaton Bennett, Christopher Scott

Steve Young Photo

Marilyn Whitehead, Kevin R. Wright

Marilyn Whitehead, Neil Nash

William Tost, George Riddle

FORBIDDEN BROADWAY

By Gerard Alessandrini; Costumes, Erika Dyson; Wigs, Bobby Pearce; Consultant, Pete Blue; Stage Manager, Jerry James; Associate Producer, Chip Quigley; Management, Kevin Dowling; Executive Director, Arthur B. Brown; Press, Shirley Herz/Glenna Freedman; Originally opened at Palssons on January 15, 1982 and moved to Theatre East on September 15, 1988.*

CAST

Suzanne Blakeslee   Herndon Lackey
Jeff Lyons   Marilyn Pasekoff
                Brad Ellis

A musical revue spoofing other shows. The '90-91 editions targeted the *Miss Saigon* controversy, Mandy Patinkin, *Aspects of Love*, Topol and many others.

*Still playing May 31, 1991.

Carol Rosegg/Martha Swope Photos

Top Left: (Clockwise from Top L) Herndon Lackey, Jeff Lyons, Susanne Blakeslee, Marilyn Pasekoff Below: Lackey

Jeff Lyons, Susanne Blakeslee, Marilyn Pasekoff, Herndon Lackey Center: Pasekoff, Lackey Top Right: Lackey, Blakeslee, Lyons

FOREVER PLAID

Written, Directed and Staged by Stuart Ross; Sets, Neil Peter Jampolis; Lighting, Jane Reisman; Costumes, Debra Stein; Casting, Judy Henderson; Assistant. Director, Larry Raben; Musical Direction/Arrangements/Continuity, James Raitt; Stage Manager, John Rainwater; Producer, Gene Wolsk, Steven Suskin; Original Cast Recording, RCA; Press, Shirley Herz/Miller Wright; Opened in Steve McGraw's on Friday, May 4, 1990.*

CAST

Jinx ....Stan Chandler
Smudge ....David Engel
Sparky ....Jason Graae†1
Francis ....Guy Stroman

UNDERSTUDIES: Drew Geraci, Larry Raben

A musical in two acts. The action takes place on a night in 1964.

*Still playing May 31, 1991.

†Succeeded by: 1. Larry Raben

Carol Rosegg/Martha Swope Photo

Left: (Clockwise from bottom) Stan Chandler, Larry Raben, Guy Stroman, David Engel

NUNSENSE

Music/Lyrics/Book/Direction by Dan Goggin; Choreography, Felton Smith; Sets, Barry Axtell; Lighting, Susan A. White; Musical Director, Michael Rice; General Manager, Roger Alan Gindi; Casting, Joseph Abaldo; Stage Managers, Paul Botchis, Nancy Wernick; Cast Recording, DRG; Presented by The Nunsense Theatrical Company in association with Joseph Hoesl, Bill Crowder & Jay Cardwell; Press, Shirley Herz/Pete Sanders, Glenna Freedman, Sam Rudy, Miller Wright, Robert Larkin. Opened in the Cherry Lane Theatre on Tuesday, December 3, 1985.*

CAST

Sister Mary Regina.............................Marilyn Farina/Nancy Carroll/Julie J. Hafner
Sister Mary Hubert.....................................Julie J. Hafner/Alvaleta Guess
Sister Robert Anne....................................Christine Anderson/Lin Tucci
Sister Mary Amnesia ....Amanda Butterbaugh/Sarah Knapp
Sister Mary Leo ....Alicia Miller

UNDERSTUDIES: Susan J. Jacks, Teri Gibson

MUSICAL NUMBERS: Nunsense is Habit-Forming, A Difficult Transition, Benedicte, Biggest Ain't the Best, Playing Second Fiddle, So You Want to Be a Nun, Turn Up the Spotlight, Lilacs Bring Back Memories, Tackle That Temptation with a Time Step, Growing Up Catholic, We've Got to Clean out the Freezer, Just a Coupl'a Sisters, Soup's On, Dying Nun Ballet, I Just Want to Be a Star, The Drive In, I Could've Gone to Nashville, Gloria in Excelsis Deo, Holier Than Thou, Finale

A musical in two acts. The action takes place in Mt. Saint Helen's School Auditorium in Hoboken, New Jersey, at the present time.

*Still playing May 31, 1991 after transferring to Circle Repertory Theatre and then to the Douglas Fairbanks Theatre.

Lin Tucci, Nancy E. Carroll, Alvaleta Guess, Alica Miller, Amanda Butterbaugh

Steven Keats, Priscilla Lopez Right: Dan Lauria

OTHER PEOPLE'S MONEY

By Jerry Sterner; Director, Gloria Muzio; Sets, David Jenkins; Costumes, Jess Goldstein; Lighting, F. Mitchell Dana; Sound, David Budries; General Management, George Elmer Productions Ltd., Associate Producers, Michael Mathis, Our Money Productions; Press, Shirley Herz/Sam Rudy, Glenna Freedman, Pete Sanders, Robert Larkin. Opened in the Minetta Lane Theatre on Tuesday, February 7, 1989.*

CAST

William Coles ....James Murtaugh
Andrew Jorgenson ....Arch Johnson[1]
Bea Sullivan ....Jacqueline Brookes[2]
Lawrence Garfinkle ....Kevin Conway[3]
Kate Sullivan ....Priscilla Lopez

A play in two acts. The action takes place in New York and Rhode Island, at present.

*Closed June 30, 1991 after 990 performances.

[†]Succeeded by: 1. James Pritchett 2. Lenka Peterson, Sloane Shelton 3. Steven Keats, Dan Lauria

Carol Rosegg, Peter Cunningham Photos

THE ROTHSCHILDS

Music, Jerry Bock; Lyrics, Sheldon Harnick; Book, Sherman Yellen; Based on book by Frederic Morton; Director, Lonny Price; Music Director, Grant Sturiale; Choreography, Michael Arnold; Sets, E. David Cosier, Jr.; Costumes, Gail Brassard; Lighting, Betsy Adams; Stage Manager, Rachel S. Levine; Associate Producers, Dana Sherman, Phil Witt; Presented by Jeff Ash/Susan Quint Gallin in association with Tommy Valando and the American Jewish Theatre (Sidney Brechner, Artistic Director). Originally opened Sunday, February 25, 1990 at the American Jewish Theatre where it played 56 performances, before moving to the Circle in the Square Downtown on Friday, April 27, 1990 where it played 379 performances before closing on March 24, 1991.

CAST

Prince William/Fouche/Herries/Metternich ....Allen Fitzpatrick
Guard/Vendor/Jacob ....Nick Corley
Mayer Rothschild ....Mike Burstyn
Urchin/Young Nathan ....Evan Ferrente
Urchin/Young Solomon...Hal Goldberg
Urchin/Young Jacob..Etan and Josh Ofrane
Gutele Rothschild...Sue Anne Gershenson
Vendor/Banker/Amshel ....David Cantor
Vendor/Kalman...Joel Malina
Budurus ....Ted Forlow
Banker/Solomon Rothschild/Sceptic..Ray Wills
Young Amshel ....Adam Paul Plotch
Nathan Rothschild ....Bob Cuccioli
Hannah Cohen ....Leslie Ellis

MUSICAL NUMBERS: Pleasure/Privilege, One Room, He Tossed a Coin, Sons, Everything, Rothschilds and Sons, Allons, Act I Finale, British Free Enterprise Auction, This Amazing London Town, They Say, I'm in Love, In My Own Lifetime, Have You Ever Seen a Prettier Little Congress?, Bonds

A Musical in two acts. The action takes place in the Frankfort Ghetto, the Hessian and Austrian Courts, London, and Aix-La-Chapelle. For the original 1970 Broadway production, see *Theatre World* Vol. 27.

Bob Cuccioli, Mike Burstyn, Sue Anne Gershenson, Allen Fitzpatrick, Leslie Ellis (seated)

TONY 'N' TINA'S WEDDING

By Artificial Intelligence (Nancy Cassaro, Artistic Director); Conception, Ms. Cassaro; Director, Larry Pellegrini; Supervisory Director, Julie Cesari; Musical Director, Debra Barsha; Choreography, Hal Simons; Design & Decor, Randall Thropp; Costumes/Hairstyle/Makeup, Juan DeArmas; General Manager, Leonard A. Mulhern; Company Manager, James Hannah; Stage Managers, K.A. Smith, Bernadette McGay; Presented by Joseph Corcoran & Daniel Corcoran; Press, David Rothenberg/Terence Womble. Opened in the Washington Square Church & Carmelita's on Saturday, February 6, 1988.*

CAST

Valentina Lynne Nunzio, the bride ....Kelly Cinnante†1
Anthony Angelo Nunzio, the groom ....Robert Cea†2
Connie Mocogni, the maid of honor...Dina Losito†3
Barry Wheeler, the best man...Bruce Kronenberg†4
Donna Marsala, bridesmaid...Lisa Casillo†5
Dominick Fabrizzi, usher ....George Schifini†6
Marina Gulino, bridesmaid ....Aida Turturro†7
Johnny Nunzio, usher and brother of groom ....James Georgiades†8
Josephine Vitale, mother of the bride...Nancy Timpanaro
Joseph Vitale, brother of the bride...Paul Spencer
Luigi Domenico, great uncle of the bride...........................Allen Lewis Rickman
Rose Domenico, aunt of the bride...Wendy Caplan
Sister Albert Maria, cousin of the bride ....Fran Gennuso
Anthony Angelo Nunzio, Sr., father of the groom ....Dan Grimaldi
Madeline Monroe, Mr. Nunzio's girlfriend ....Georgienne Millen
Grandma Nunzio, grandmother of the groom...........................Bonnie Rose Marcus
Michael Just, Tina's ex-boyfriend ....Anthony T. Lauria
Father Mark, parish priest...Gary Schneider
Vinnie Black, caterer...Tom Karlya
Loretta Black, wife of the caterer...Victoria Constan
Mick Black, brother of the caterer...Joe Bacino†9
Nikki Black, daughter of the caterer...Jodi Grant†10
Mikie Black, son of the caterer...Anthony Luongo
Pat Black, sister of the caterer ....Jody Oliver
Rick Demarco, the video man ....Marc Romeo
Sal Antonucci, the photographer ....Glenn Taranto

An environmental theatre production. The action takes place at the wedding and reception, at the present time.

*Still playing May 31, 1991 after moving to St. John's Church and Vinnie Black's Coliseum.

†Succeeded by: 1. Sharon Angela 2. Rick Pasqualone 3. Doma Villella, Susan Laurenzi 4. Keith Primi, Timothy Monagan 5. Susan Campanaro 6. Lou Martini, Jr. 7. Celeste Russi 8. Michael Creo, Ken Garito 9. Tony Palellis 10. Maria Gentile

Linda Alaniz Photos

Sharon Angela, Glenn Taranto, Rick Pasqualone

Rick Pasqualone, Sharon Angela

Sharon Angela, Rick Pasqualone

SMOKE ON THE MOUNTAIN

By Connie Ray; Director, Alan Bailey; Scenic Design, Peter Harrison; Costumes, Pamela Scofield; Lighting, Don Ehman; Stage Manager, Tom Clewell; Musical Directors, John Foley, Mike Craver; Production Manager, Clark Cameron; Musical Arrangements, Mike Craver, Mark Hardwick; General Manager, Nancy Nigel Gibbs; Press, Cromarty & Co.; Presented by Carolyn Rossi Copeland (Producing Director) and Robert de Rothschild; Opened in the Lambs Theatre on Thursday, May 10, 1990.*

CAST

Burl Sanders ....Reathel Bean
Mervin Oglethorpe..Kevin Chamberlin
Stanley ....Dan Manning†1
Vera Sanders ....Linda Kerns†2
Dennis Sanders..Robert Olsen
Denise Sanders...Jane Potter†3
June Sanders ....Connie Ray†4

MUSICAL NUMBERS: The Church in the Wildwood; A Wonderful Time Up There, Build on the Rock, Meet Mother in the Skies, No Tears in Heaven, Christian Cowboy, The Filling Station, I'll Never Die (I'll Just Change My Address), Jesus Is Mine, Blood Medley: Nothing But the Blood/There Is Power in the Blood/Are You Washed in the Blood/There Is a Fountain Filled with Blood, I'll Live a Million Years, Everyone Home But Me, I Wouldn't Take Nothing for My Journey Now, Angel Band, Bringing in the Sheaves, Whispering Hope, Inching Along, Transportational Medley: I'm Using My Bible for a Roadmap/I'll Wake Every Step of the Way/Life's Railway to Heaven, Smoke on the Mountain, I'll Fly Away, When the Roll Is Called Up Yonder

A musical in two acts. The action takes place on a Saturday night in June, 1938 at Mount Pleasant Baptist Church, Mount Pleasant, North Carolina.

†Succeeded by: 1. John Foley 2. Susan Mansur 3. Mimi Bessette, 4. Constance Shulman

*Closed June 30, 1991 after 452 performances and 11 previews.

Carol Rosegg/Martha Swope Photo

The Company

PRODUCTIONS FROM PAST SEASONS
THAT CLOSED DURING THIS SEASON

Title	Opened	Closed	Performances
Accomplice	4/26/90	6/10/90	52 + 23 previews
Aspects of Love	4/8/90	3/2/91	377 + 22 previews
Black and Blue	1/26/89	1/20/91	829
Cat on a Hot Tin Roof	3/21/90	8/1/90	149 + 7 previews
The Cemetery Club	5/15/90	6/1/90	56 + 10 previews
Closer Than Ever	11/6/89	7/1/90	288 + 24 Previews
A Few Good Men	11/15/89	1/26/91	497 + 15 previews
The Grapes of Wrath	3/22/90	9/2/90	188 + 11 previews
Gypsy	11/6/89	1/6/91	476
The Heidi Chronicles	3/9/89	9/1/90	621 + 9 previews
Jerome Robbin's Broadway	2/26/89	9/1/90	634 + 55 previews
Lettice & Lovage	3/25/90	12/23/90	284 + 13 previews
Meet Me in St. Louis	11/2/89	6/10/90	253 + 16 previews
The Piano Lesson	4/16/90	1/27/91	320 + 8 previews
The Rothschilds	2/25/90	3/24/91	435
Some Americans Abroad	5/2/90	6/17/90	62 (off-B'wy: 81)
Spunk	4/10/90	9/2/90	165
Tamara	12/14/89	7/15/90	1036
Tru	12/14/89	9/1/90	295 + 11 previews
Zoya's Apartment	5/10/90	6/17/90	45 + 13 previews

(Mitzi Newhouse Theater) Sunday, June 3, 1990 (2 limited performances) The 52nd Street Project (Willie Reale, Artistic Director) presents:
HUMAN NATURE; Erika Alexander, Linda Atkinson, June Ballinger, Charles Dumas, Karen Evans-Kandel, John Fiedler, Jack Gilpin, Greg Grove, Evan Handler, Fracaswell Hymen, Marcia Jean Kurtz, Peter MacNicol, Michaela Murphy, Paul McCrane, James McDaniel, Ann McDonough, Willie Reale, Seret Scott, Daniel Judah Sklar, Phyllis Somerville, Judy Tate, Susan Willerman, Janet Zarish

A collaboration of eight "Hell's Kitchen kids" and 25 professional theatre artists presenting eight new one-act plays written by the kids.

(South St. Theatre) Wednesday, June 6–September 2, 1990 (106 performances) The Irish Repertory Theatre Co. and One World Arts Foundation in association with South St. Theatre present:
PHILADELPHIA, HERE I COME! by Brian Friel; Director, Paul Weidner; Sets, David Raphel; Sound/Lighting, Richard Clausen; Costumes, Natalie Walker; Stage Manager, Chris A. Kelly; Hairstylist, Gary Brennan; Props, Athena Baer; Press, Chris Boneau/Eva Patton, Bob Fennell. CAST: Pauline Flanagan (Madge), Patrick Fitzgerald (Gareth O'Donnell-Public), Ciaran O'Reilly (Gareth O'Donnell-Private), W.B. Brydon (S.B. O'Donnell), Madeline Potter (Kate Doogan), Chris Carrick (Senator Doogan), Frank McCourt (Master Boyle), Paddy Croft (Lizzy Sweeney), Bernard Frawley (Con Sweeney), John William Short (Ben Burton), Colin Lane (Ned), Brian F. O'Byrne (Tom), Denis O'Neill (Joe), Dermot McNamara (Canon Mick O'Byrne). A revival of the play in two acts. The action takes place in the small village of Ballyberg, Ireland in 1962.

This production originated last season at the TADA Theatre.

(UBU Rep Theatre) Wednesday, June 6–July 1, 1990 (24 performances) Double Image Theatre (Helen Waren Mayer, Artictic Director) presents:
THE HOUSEKEEPER by Eliza Wyatt; Director/Design, Jack Chandler; Lighting, Terry A. Bennett; Costumes, Ken Mooney; Stage Manager, Steve Wildern. CAST: M. William Lettich, Ann MacMillan, Elizabeth Roby, Michael Wells, Christina Wright, Margaret Warncke.

A drama in two acts.

(Pearl Theatre) Thursday, June 7–16, 1990 (12 performances) Jay Michaels and The Kompanie Theatre Ensemble in cooperation with Richardson/Yale Property Trust (Elliot S. Blair, Administrator) presents:
DARK OF THE MOON by Howard Richardson and William Berney; Director, Jay Michaels; Sets, Tim McGraw; Musical Director, Edward Smitt; Assistant Director, Jonathan M. Smith; Dance, Teresa Casese Aubel; Technical, Helen Gary. CAST: Brian Hooks (Floyd Allen), Melissa Rendel (Dark Witch), Janice Carrell (Fair Witch), Jonathan Russo (Conjur Man), Mark Edward Lang (John), Margaret Mattic (Conjur Woman), Kurt Carley (Mr. Atkins), Tim McGraw (Burt Dinwitty), Lisa Guibord (Edna Summey), Michael O'Neill (Hank Gudger), Bill Janson (Uncle Smelicue), Madalyn McKay (Miss Metcalf), Laurie Lawrence (Mrs. Summey), Hugh Mack Dill (Mr. Summey), Paula Davis (Mrs. Allen), David S. Greulich (Mr. Allen), Claudia Lane (Barbara Allen), Jeff Zeichner (Marvin Hudgens), Christopher Smith (Preacher Haggler).

Ciaran O'Reilly, Patrick Fitzgerald in "Philadelphia..." (*Carol Rosegg*)

Claudia Lane, Mark Lang in "Dark of the Moon"

(William Redfield Theatre) Thursday, June 7-24, 1990 (12 performances) Third Step Theatre Company presents:
SANCTUARY by Andrew Young; Director, Margit Ahlin; Sets, Ketti Schoenfeld; Lighting, Amy Coomb; Costumes, Traci DiGesu. CAST: Al D'Andrea, Peter Famulari, Muriel Gould, Joyce Carol Lyons, Kevin O'Leary, Lucky Salidar

A play in two acts. The action takes place in New Jersey and involves three generations of an Italian-American family.

(Primary Stages) Friday, June 8–30, 1990 (20 performances) Primary Stages Co. Inc. (Casey Childs, Artistic Director; Janet Reed, Associate Artistic director) presents:
SWIM VISIT by Wesley Moore; Director, William Partlan; Sets, Robert Klingelhoefer; Lighting, Tina Charney; Costumes, Amanda J. Klein; Sound, Gayle Jeffrey; Fights, Jake Turner; Associate Producer, Herbert H. O'Dell; General Manager, Gordon Farrell. CAST: Caroline Lagerfelt (Izz), Alice Haining (Beth), Pirie MacDonald (Ted), Mark Metcalf (Clay)

A play in two acts. The action takes place around a pool in Charlottestown, at present.

(Nat Horne Theatre) Friday, June 8–July 9, 1990 (17 performances and 3 previews) William De Silva and Darla Productions in association with Riverside Shakespeare Co. present:
LITTLE LIES by Joseph George Caruso; from *The Magistrate* by Sir Arthur Wing Pinero; Director, Crandall Diehl; Sets/Costumes, Michael Bottari, Ronald Case; Lighting, Norman Coates; Music, Mildred Kayden; Stage Manager, Douglas Shearer; Technical, Peter Barbieri, Jr.; Hair/Makeup, Gloria Rivera; Casting, Alan Coleridge; Press, Francine L. Trevens CAST: Alison Bevan (Charlotte), Melissa Meg Davis (Beatie Tomlinson), Ian Fleet (Colonel Lukyn), Sylvia Gassell (Madame Blonde), Joseph Jamrog (Mr. Posket), Robert McFarland (Wyke), George Millenbach (Capt. Vale), Alec Murphy (Inspector Bullamy), Rex Nockengust (Cis Farringdon), Laurel Thornby (Agatha)

A comedy in three acts. The action occurs in Edwardian London in 1912. The play was performed in June, 1978 under the title *Baby Face* at Greenwich Mews.

Laurel Thornby, Rex Nockengust, Melissa Meg Davis in "Little Lies"

(Theatre Arielle) Monday, June 11–August 26, 1990 (57 performances) Eric Krebs presents:
FLORIDA GIRLS by Nancy Hasty; Director, Robert Stewart; Sets/Production Manager, E.F. Morrill; Sound, J. Bloomrosen; Stage Manager, Lloyd Davis, Jr.; Press, David Rothenberg. CAST: Nancy Hasty

An autobiographical monodrama. The action takes place in Crestview, Florida in 1965.

(Courtyard Playhouse) Thursday, June 14–November 25, 1990 (150 performances) The Glines presents:
MEN OF MANHATTAN: *Scenes of New York City Gay Life* by John Glines; Director, Charles Catanese; Sets, Lou Anne Gilleland; Costumes, Gene Lauze; Lighting, Tracy Dedrickson; Associate Producer, William Castleman; Stage Manager, Courtney Flanagan; Press, Chris Boneau/Joe D'Ambrosia. CAST: David Baird, Steven Liebhauser, Cy Orfield, T.L. Reilly, Leslie Roberts, Richard Skipper, succeeding actors: John Carhart III, Scott Zimmerman

Eleven short plays in two acts. The action takes place in New York City at present.

(Westbeth Theatre Center) Friday, June 15–July 1, 1990 resumed at Orpheum Theatre from Tuesday, August 7–September 23, 1990 (56 performances and 9 previews) The Westbeth Theatre Center and Coup De Grace Productions in association with 126 Second Ave. Corp. present:
QUIET ON THE SET by Terrell Anthony; Director, A.C. Weary; Sets, Rick Dennis; Lighting, Nancy Collings; Costumes, Colleen McFarlane; Company Manager, Richard Berg; Stage Managers, Susan Whelan, Michael Musick; Press, David Lotz/Teresa Conway, Peter Cromarty. CAST: Kate Collins (Judith Petri/Barbara Stewart), Robert Newman (Taylor Lydell/John Whittington), Cady McClain succeeded by Beth Ehlers (Tamra Lydell/Bridget Stewart), Trent Bushey (Bruce Mitchell/Bart Whittington), Matt Servitto (Director/Characters)

A comedy in two acts. The action takes place on the sound stage of *Sunset*, a television soap opera, at present.

(St. John the Divine Cathedral) Tuesday, June 19–July 1, 1990 (13 performances and 1 preview) The Flock Theatre Company presents:
ANTIGONE by Jean Anouilh; Adaptation, Lewis Galantiere; Directors, Suzanne Shepard and Lara Kritskaya; Music/Sound, Ms. Kritskaya; Press, Chris Boneau/Eva Patton, Bob Fennell. CAST: Tiffany Carr (Page), Brian Dykstra (Creon), Faith Geer (Nurse), Irene Glezos (Antigone), Carolyn Horan (Eurydice), Jed Krascella (Third Guard), David Pillard (Haemon), Michael Rains (Polynices), Danny Rose (Second Guard), Phil Soltanoff (First Guard/Jonas), Jeannie Zusy (Ismene)

A tragedy performed without intermission.

(Theatre 1010) Tuesday, June 26–July 10, 1990 (12 performances) Bandwagon (Jerry Bell, Producer) presents:
THE DAY BEFORE SPRING with Music by Frederick Loewe; Lyrics/Book, Alan Jay Lerner; Director/Choreographer, Danya Krupska; Music Direction, Steven Gross; Costumes, Pauline Kent Dennis; Sets, Jeffrey M. Glovsky; Lighting, Eric T. Haugen; Press, Audrey Ross. CAST: Rebecca Hoodwin (Katharine Townsend), Michael Harrington (Peter Townsend), Joan Crowe (May Thompkins), Chuck Muckle (Bill Thompkins), Matthew DuBois (Joe McDonald/Plato), Gerald Sell (Alex Maitland), Jeannie Abolt (Marie/Alumni), Frank Farrell (Eddie Warren), Keith Arthur Davis (Harry Scott), Nancy Setny (Lucille/Alumni), Man-Ching Tom (Susan/Alumni), Stephanie Hofeller (Josephine/Alumni), Maia Wilkins (Nancy/Alumni/Dancing Katherine), Luis Raúl Negrón (Student/Luis Paramo), Terrell Rittenhouse (George Sinclair/Student), Terrence Carey (Ted Thomas/Student), Adri-

T.L. Reilly, Steven Liebhauser in "Men of Manhattan"
(*Jonathan Slaff*)

(Clockwise from Botton L) Kate Collins, Robert Newman, Matt Servitto, Trent Bushey, Cady McClain, Terrell Anthony (playwright) in "Quiet on the Set"

ano Gonzales (Ramon Ramirez/Student), Lenny Daniel (Leonard Bradshaw/Dancing Alex), James A. Zemarel (Gerald Barker), Lisa Marie Tracy (Christopher Randolph), Charles Duval (Voltaire), Jack Drummond (Freud)
MUSICAL NUMBERS: Day before Spring. The Invitation, God's Green World, You Haven't Changed at All, My Love Is a Married Man, Katherine Receives Advice, Ballet of the Book, Friends to the End, A Jug of Wine, The Book, I Love You This Morning, Where's My Wife? This Is My Holiday, Finale

A musical in two acts. The first New York City revival of the 1945 work.

(En Garde Arts) Wednesday, June 27–July 21, 1990 (16 performances) En Garde Arts presents:
FATHER WAS A PECULIAR MAN by Reza Abdoh and Mira-Lani Oglesby; Director, Mr. Abdoh; Music, Eric Liljestrand; Sets, Kyle Chepulis; Costumes, Claudia Brown; Lighting, Brian Aldous; Choreography, Maggie Rush, Kent Roht; Production Manager, David Waggett; Stage Manager, Dan Weir; Press, Tray Batres. CAST: Banipal Babilla Ebrahim, Leyla Ebtehadj, Tom Fitzpatrick, Jan Leslie Harding, Meg Kruszewska, Irma Paule, Ken Roht, Davidson Thomson, and a cast of 60.

An environmental travelling theatrical drama performed in the meat packing district.

(Apple Corps Theatre) Tuesday, June 26–July 22, 1990 (23 performances and 9 previews) Apple Corps (John Raymond and Michael Tolan, Artistic Directors) present:
A SILENT THUNDER by Eduarda Ivan Lopez; Director, John Cappelletti; Sets, Randy Benjamin; Lighting, William J. Plachy; Costumes, MaryAnn D. Smith; Sound, Neal Arluck; Stage Manager, Ken Simmons; Press, David Rothenberg/Meg Gordean, Skip Lindsey, Terence Womble. CAST: Nestor Carbonell (Joe Santana), Suzen Murakoshi (Kimiyo)

A drama in two acts. The action takes place on Kadena Okinawa Island during the spring of 1986.

Suzen Murakoshi, Nestor Carbonelle in "A Silent Thunder" (*Austin Truett*)

(John Houseman Theatre) Friday, July 6–September 2, 1990 (53 performances and 15 previews) Eric Krebs in association with Joanne Macan and Carol Wernli present:
ED LINDERMAN'S BROADWAY JUKEBOX; Conceived and Supervised by Mr. Linderman; Director/Choreographer, Bill Guske; Sets, James Morgan; Costumes, Barbara Forbes; Lighting, Stuart Duke; Sound/Management, E.F. Morrill; Stage Manager, Michael J. Chudinski; Developed with the American Stage Co., Press, David Rothenberg. CAST: Robert Michael Baker, Susan Flynn, Beth Leavel, Gerry McIntyre, Amelia Prentice, Sal Viviano, Pianists: Ken Lundie, Mr. Linderman

MUSICAL NUMBERS (chosen from the following): Waitin' for the Evening Train, I Had a Ball, Show Me Where the Good Times Are, What Do We Do We Fly, Don't Waste the Moon, Little Old New York, Call Me Back, Harmony, Things Were Out, Love in a New Tempo, Pink Fish, Butler's Song, Home, Saturday Night at the Rose & Crown, You Mustn't Be Discouraged, We Love a Broadway Song, Pillar to Post, Philosophy, Like Yours, A Certain Girl, I'm Not Through, Feather in My Shoe, I'm All Smiles, All of My Laughter, A Girl Could Go Wacky, Broadway My Street, Unrequited Love, Useful Phases, Dance the Dark Away, Jubilee Joe, Woman and Man, Yes He's Here, Wherever He Ain't, Bobo's, Loud & Funny Song, Summertime Love, Aw Ma, Railbird, Sur Les Quais, I've Got a One Track Mind, Poor Everybody Else, Everybody Wants to Die Onstage, Soon, His Own Little Island, A Life without Her, You Have Made Me Love, I Know the Feeling, All the Time, Flowers and the Rainbow, After Love, I Won't Send Roses, Anyone Would Love You, One Promise Come True, Take the Moment, Where I Want to Be, Once Upon a Time, All at Once You Love Her, Everything Needs Something, Take Love Easy, Billy, Someone Else's Story, April Child, My True Heart, Mountain High Valley Low, Alone, I Never Know When to Say When, How Does the Wine Taste, Sing Happy, Madeleine, I Don't Want to Know, The Only Girl, Ciao Compare, Nothing More to Look Forward To, We Live for Another Day, There Are Days, Live a Little, Here's to Love, Lilas, Shall I Take My Heart and Go?, Our Time, I Never Want to See You Again, Belonging, Close upon the Hour, What Makes Me Love Him?

A musical revue in two acts focusing on great songs from shows that were commercial failures.

(Theatre Off Park) Thursday, July 5–15, 1990 (14 performances) Maya Associates presents:
TIMING IS EVERYTHING by Richard Salvatore; Director, Michael Petshaft; Sets/Lighting, Peter R. Feuche; Costumes, Ann Davis; Press, Penny M. Landau. CAST: Amy Falbaum, Jessica Hughes, Adrian Kneubuhl, Alex Leydenfrost, Noel Wilson

A realistic melodrama.

(Quaigh Theatre) Friday, July 6–22, 1990 (12 performances and 8 previews) Quaigh Theatre presents:
SUBLIME LIVES by Paul Firestone; Director, Jay E. Raphael; Sets, Josh Rothenberg; Costumes, Jan Finnell; Lighting, Deborah Matlack; Sound, Suzanne Hall; Stage Managers, Kathleen M. Nolan, Nick Plakias; Press, Francine L. Trevens/Debra Sue Keller. CAST: Matthew Loney (Richard Mansfield), Eugene J. Anthony (William Winter), Nick Plakias (Fred), Woody Dahlia (Henry Salomon), Sharon Cornell (Beatrice Cameron), Steven Dennis (Clyde Fitch), Maggie Wood (Constance Neville)

A drama in two acts. The action deals with the last years of the actor-manager era of American theatre and takes place from 1889 to 91.

Steven Dennis, Matthew Loney, Sharon Cornell in "Sublime Lives" (*Anita Shevett*)

(Clockwise from L) Beth Leavel, Ed Linderman, Gerry McIntyre, Susan Flynn, Sal Viviano, Robert Michael Baker, Ken Lundie, Amelia Prentice in "Broadway Jukebox" (*Linda Alaniz*)

Mila Burnette, Holly Baron, Kevin Conway in "Man Who Fell in Love..." (*William Gibson*)

(Quaigh Theatre) Saturday, July 28- September 1, 1990 (13 performances and 6 previews) Quaigh Theatre (Will Lieberson, Producing Artistic Director) presents:
THE MAN WHO FELL IN LOVE WITH HIS WIFE by Ted Whitehead; Directors, Will Lieberson, Kevin Conway; Production Coordinator, Marjorie Horn; Lighting/Sound, Graeme F. McDonnell; Sets, Jeff Read Freund; Costumes, V. Jane Suttell; Stage Managers, David O'Connell, Deborah Matheson; Directors' Assistant, Todd Olson; Production Associate, Joyce Korbin Bell; Press, Francine L. Trevens/Debra Sue Keller. CAST: Kevin Conway (Tom Fearon), Mila Burnette (Mary Fearon), Julia Gibson (Susy Fearon), Holly Barron (Julia)

The American premiere of a drama in two acts and three scenes. The action takes place in Liverpool over three years.

(Westbeth Theatre Center) Monday, July 30–August 16, 1990 (12 performances) Westbeth Theatre (Arnold Engelman, Producing Director) presents:
THE LIFE with Music by Cy Coleman; Lyrics, Ira Gasman; Book, Mr. Coleman, Mr. Gasman; Director/Choreographer, Joe Layton; Musical Director, Donald York; Sets, Bob Phillips; Costumes, Franne Lee; Lighting, Nancy Collings; Sound, Richard Dunning; Hair/Makeup, Michelle Bruno; Associate Choreographer, Gary Chryst; Stage Manager, Victor Lukas; Press, David Lotz. CAST: Heather Wright (Bar Maid), Mark Maharrey (Sam/Vendor/Bum), Stuart Hult (Scotty/Police), Edwin Louis Battle (Fleetwood), Stanley W. Mathis (JoJo), Jan Mussetter (April), Enrique Cruz De Jesus (Rick), Lori Fischer (Mary/Angel), Alde Lewis, Jr. (Bobby), Pamela Isaacs (Queen), Percy Cohran Hall III (Chiba), Matt Zarley (Bull), Lillas White (Sonja), Mamie Duncan-Gibbs (Taffy), Laura Berman (Frenchie), Larry Marshall (Lacy), Sharon Wilkins (ChiChi), Guylane Bouchard (Blackie), Degan Everhart (Tracy), D. Drake (Crystal), Lillian Colon (Pepa), Sachi Shimizu (Toya), Chuck Cooper (Memphis), Harold Cromer (Snickers), Peter Schankowitz (Sal/Minister), Jorge Rios (Tony), Kurt Elftman (Voyeur/Con Ed Man), Bill Buell (Harry), Allyson Pimentel (Bar Maid) Jane MacPherson (Prison Matron)

MUSICAL NUMBERS: The Street, Piece of the Action, Lovely Day to Be Outta Jail, Getting Too Old, Don't Take Much, My Body, Easy Money, Working Girls, Reefer Man, He's No Good, Hooker's Ball, Signifyin' Monkey, Mr. Greed, My Way or the Highway, Lucky Me, Someday, People Magazine, Use What You Got, I'm Leaving You, We Gotta Go, Finale

A musical in two acts. The action takes place in New York City, during summer, in the early seventies. The plot involves a hooker, her pimps, and their struggle for survival on 42nd Street.

(Illustrious Theatre) Tuesday, July 31–August 4, 1990 (5 performances) The Illustrious Theatre presents:
MOI, MOLIÈRE by Richard Morse; Staging Concept/Design, Donald L. Brooks; Music/Sound, Marc Murphy, David Gutelius; Costumes, Robert Schmidt, Bente Morse. CAST: Richard Morse, Cliff Foerster
   A recreation of the famous French playwright.

(McGuinn/Cazale Theatre) Tuesday, July 31–August 18, 1990 (24 performances) HAI Theatre Festival presents:
THE TRIAL by Guy Davis; Director, Jamal Joseph; Lighting, Douglas Cox; Producer, Max Daniels; Stage Manager, Toby Cohen. CAST: Sharon Hope (Labooda), Guy Davis (Stevie)
   A drama performed without intermission.

(Duplex) Wednesday, August 1–15, 1990 (3 performances) Village Playwrights Productions presents:
O SAPPHO, O WILDE! by Claire Olivia Moed, Karen Mullen, Carol Polcovar, Mark Castle, Al Luongo; Director, Bill Cosgriff; Musical Director, Joel Maisano; Music, Raven Hall. CAST: Lisa Goodman, Raven Hall, John Kudan, Joanna Rush, Joe Spencer White
   A comedy revue with music.

(Perry St. Theatre) Wednesday, August 8–12, 1990 (5 performances)
SWEET SONG with Music by Ricky Ian Gordon; Lyrics from the poetry of Dorothy Parker, Edna St. Vincent Millay, Emily Dickinson, e.e. cummings, Langston Hughes, Frank O'Hara, May Sarton; Director, Fabrizio Melano; Press, Jeffrey Richards/Jilliana Devine. CAST: Angelina Réaux
   A theatricalized song cycle.

(Charles Ludlam Theatre) Tuesday, August 14, 1990–March 3, 1991 (129 performances and 20 previews) The Ridiculous Theatrical Co. (Everett Quinton, Artistic Director; Steve Asher, Managing Director) presents:
CAMILLE by Charles Ludlam; Director, Everett Quinton; Costumes, Elizabeth Michal Fried; Sets, Mark Beard; Lighting, Terry Alan Smith; Hairstylist, Joseph Boggess; Jewelry, Larry Vrba; Sound, Mark Bennett; Stage Managers, James Eckerle, Mark Rizzo; Press, Judy Jacksina/Mary Lugo. CAST: H.M. Koutoukas (Baron de Varville), Stephen Pell (Nanine), Everett Quinton (Marguerite Gautier), Kevin Scullin (Joseph), Carl Clayborn (Nichette Fondue), Cheryl Reeves (Olympe de Taverne), Bobby Reed (Saint Gaudens), Eureka (Prudence Duvernoy), Jim Lamb (Gaston Roue), Georg Osterman (Armand Duval), Jean-Claude Vasseux (Duval Sr.), James Eckerle (Molnik)
   Ludlam's 1973 tearjerker in three acts. The action takes place in Paris and Auteil in 1848. A travesty on La Dame aux Camelias by Alexander Dumas Fils.

(Triplex) Wednesday, August 15–30, 1990 (10 performances)
PHANTOMS TWO-STEP by Greg Tate; Directors, Henry Fonte, Mr. Tate. CAST: Terrence Martin, Deborah Meyers, Bryan Michael McGuire, Cara O'Shea, Olinda Turturro
   Two one-act plays. *The Patch* involves a homeless woman's final refuge. *Ritual* is a tale of sexual obsession.

David McCann, David DeBeck in "Hosanna" (*Stan Sadowski*)

Arnie Kolodner, Helen Gallagher, Janet Sarno, Dolores Gray (seated), Lucille Patton, Helen Hanft, in "Money Talks" (*Carol Rosegg*)

Sharon Hope, Guy Davis in "The Trial" (*William Gibson*)

Everett Quinton in "Camille" (*Carmen Schiavone*)

Chris Fields, Roma Maffia, Welker White in "Broken English"

(Judith Anderson Theatre) Thursday, August 16–September 4, 1990 (11 performances) Redwood Productions in association with Home for Contemporary Theatre and Art present:
BROKEN ENGLISH by Gilbert Girion; Director, Tim Sanford; Sets, David Birn; Lighting, Karen Spahn; Costumes, Jonathan Green; Sound, Karen Wanamaker, Aaron Emke; Photography, Christie Mullen; Stage Manager, Jennifer Freed; Press, Douglas Grabowski. CAST: Welker White (Stevie), Christopher Fields (Richard), Roma Maffia (Lorraine), Michael Patterson (Will), Sarah Fleming (Sharon)
   A play in two acts. The action takes place in New York City.

(Actor's Playhouse) Thursday, August 16–September 30, 1990 (23 performances and 20 previews) Bill Repicci and M.D. Minichiello in association with The Performing Arts Preservation Association present:
HOSANNA by Michael Tremblay; Translation, John Van Burke, Bill Glassco; Director, Charlie Hensley; Sets, Judi Guralnick; Costumes, Constance Hoffman; Lighting, Tracy Dedrickson; Associate Producer, Pamela Ross; Stage Manager, Linda J. Heard; Press, David Rothenberg/Terence Womble, Meg Gordean. CAST: David McCann (Hosanna), David DeBeck (Cuirette)
   A drama in two acts. The action takes place in a bachelor apartment in Montreal in the mid-seventies.

(Judith Anderson Theatre) Sunday, August 19–September 5, 1990 (11 performances) Wild Bird Productions and Ravenswood Theatre present:
THREE ONE-ACT PLAYS: *Attic and Porch* by Keller Easterling; Director, Elfin Frederick Vogel; *Late Evening in the Fall* by Friedrich Durrenmatt; Director, Mihaly Kerenyi; No other information available.

(Promenade Theatre) Tuesday, August 21–September 9, 1990 (5 performances and 18 previews) Arthur Cantor presents:
MONEY TALKS by Edwin Schloss; Director, David Kaplan; Set, James Noone; Costumes, David Woolard; Lighting, Don Kotlowitz; Sound, Aural Fixation; Casting, Leonard Finger; Company Manager, Laura Heller; Press, Arthur Cantor Associates. CAST: Dolores Gray (Phyllis Stein), Helen Hanft (Vivian Newhouse), Judith Cohen (Adrienne), Janet Sarno (Irma Katzenbach), Lucille Patton (Lucille Blumenthal), Helen Gallagher (Natalie Kilroy Axelrod), Arnie Kolodner (Morty Drexler), Ted Neustadt (Allan Rothenberg), Julie Halston (Claudia Stein), Jill Wisoff (Carla Axelrod), John Braden (Cesare Rotini)
   A comedy in two acts. The action takes place in New York City, at present.

(RAPP Arts Center) Wednesday, August 22–September 16, 1990 (20 performances) RAPP Theatre Company presents:
AS YOU LIKE IT—FRESH by William Shakespeare; Conception/Direction, R. Jeffrey Cohen; Sets/Original Art, Michael Confer; Costumes, Karen Perry; Lighting, Michael Gutkin. CAST: Ami Brabson, Omar Carter, Frances DeLustro, Winston Duncan, Charles Duval, Vinnie Edgehill, Keith Glover, Charles Hall, Mark Daniel Hayes, Maria Hurtado, Kamala Lopez, Marilyn McDonald, George McGrath, Linda Powell, Michael Twaine, Michael Wells, Howard Wesson, Jeff Williams
An adaptaion set in modern day New York City and featuring the music of Ton-Loc, De La Soul, the B-52's and the Fresh Prince.

(Theatre at St. Peter's) Wednesday, September 5–October 6, 1990 (34 performances) Musical Theatre Works presents:
WHATNOT with Music and Lyrics by Dick Gallagher; Conceived and Written by Mark Waldrop and Howard Crabtree; Direction/Musical Staging, Mr. Waldrop; Musical Direction/Orchestrations/Arrangements, Mr. Gallagher; Sets, James Noone; Costumes/Special Effects, Mr. Crabtree; Lighting, Kendall Smith; Sound, One Dream; Stage Manager, Ira Mont; Production Manager, Michael Francis Moody; Press, Shirley Herz. CAST: Mark Lazore (Chuck Farley/May Holiday Buford/Henry Buford/Moth), Howard Crabtree (Lightning Bug/Bud/June Holiday Leadbetter/Lester Leadbetter), Jennifer Smith (Bernice/April Holiday/Tubb Parker/Fly), John Treacy Egan (Norman Dupe/Vivian McVanish), with special appearance by The Claude Rains Memorial Dance Troupe, and introducing Claire McVanish as herself.
MUSICAL NUMBERS: Prologue, Shine, Put It on a Whatnot Shelf, Bugs, Bernice's Showdown, Blue Flame, Hat and Cane, When I Stop the Show, Entr'acte, Bernice, Just Desserts, Teach It How to Dance, Gamblin' Heart, Variety
A musical vaudeville in two acts. The action takes place in the mythical town of Whatnot Springs, U.S.A. (Curio Cabinet Capital of the World).

(Nat Horne Theatre) Thursday, September 6, 1990– The Stillwaters Theatre Company presents:
MIDSUMMER by Paul Parente; Director, Rick Lombardo; Sets, Deborah Scott; Costumes, Michael Massee; Lighting, Franklin Meissner; Press, Jeffrey Richards/Jillana Devine. CAST: John Amedro (Oberon), Henry Tenney (Puck), James Doerr (Peter), Celia Howard (Gertrude), Colleen Quinn (Nora), Mark Weil (Serviceman), James Brill (Geordie), Maxine Taylor-Morris (Mother)
A play bringing the Shakespearean characters Oberon and Puck into the lives of a post-World War II British family.

(Primary Stages) Thursday, September 6–29, 1990 (20 performances) and reopened Thursday, May 16, 1991– Still playing May 31, 1991. Primary Stages presents:
LUSTING AFTER PIPINO'S WIFE by Sam Henry Kass; Director, Casey Childs; Sets, Ray Recht; Lighting, Deborah Constantine; Costumes, Amanda J. Klein; Sound, Gayle Jeffery; Stage Manager, Tony Luna; Press, Shirley Herz/Miller Wright. CAST: Joseph Siravo (Vinnie), Wayne Maugans (Patsy), Alexandra Gersten (Lorraine), Debra Riessen (Rita)
A comedy in two acts.

Mark Nadler (*Susan Cook*)

Lorraine Serabian, Robert Petito, Joan Nimmo in "Deathtrap"

John Treacy Egan in "Whatnot"
(*Gerry Goodstein*)

Wayne Maugans, Joseph Siravo, Alexandra Gersten, Debra Riessen in "Lusting after Pipino's Wife" (*Carol Rosegg*)

(South St. Theatre) Friday, September 7, 1990– My Father My Son Productions presents:
MY FATHER, MY SON by Ken Wolf and Henry E. Wolf; Director, Frank Trezza; Lighting, Jeff Nash; Sets/Costumes, Ina Mayhew; Music, Rodger Davidson; Choreography, Dan Hogan; Sound, David Lawson; Stage Manager, Paul A. Kochman. CAST: Steve Paris (Harry Fox), Ken Wolf (Ted)
A drama in two acts written by, and about, a father-son team.

(Village Gate) Tuesday, September 11–22, 1990 (12 performances) Joseph Holloway presents:
MARK NADLER: 7 O'CLOCK AT THE TOP OF THE GATE; Director/Choreographer, Tony Stevens; Orchestration/Arrangements, Mr. Nadler; Lighting, Bob Kneeland; Stylist, Matthew Kasten; Costumes, Mark and Tony; Host, Sidney Myer. CAST: Mark Nadler, The Swizzle Sisters: Pam Fleming (Trumpet), Martha Hyde (Sax/Clarinet), Anna Mondragon (Trombone), Kim Clarke (Bass), Barbara Kreigh (Drums)
PROGRAM: I Got You, New Orleans Louisiana Blues, Any Place I Hang My Hat, Bill Bailey, If You Want Life, Sweetest Thing, Everybody Loves My Baby, You Must Have Been a Beautiful Baby, Sweet Georgia Brown, Gigolo Medley, Mama Medley, S'Wonderful, Cake-Walkin' Babies from Home, Dream a Little Dream of Me
An evening of zany fun, performed without intermission.

(Mazur Theatre) Wednesday, September 12–29, 1990 (12 performances and 1 preview) Playwrights' Preview Productions presents:
WHO COLLECTS THE PAIN by Sean O'Connor; Director, Joe Paradise; Sets, Al Doyle; Lighting, Jeff Koger; Costumes, Traci De Gesu; Technical, E.W. Morrill; Press, Ellen White. CAST: Michael Santoro (Mickey), John Canada Turrell (Mercy), Federico Edwards (Danny), Santo Fazio (Raphael), Damon White (Jeff), Kevyn Morrow (Howard), Harry O'Reilly (Ryan), Bahni Turpin (Lorainne), Charles Demas

(Saval Theatre) Friday, September 14–October 7, 1990 (12 performances) American Ensemble Co. presents:
DEATHTRAP by Ira Levin; Director, Robert Petito; Sets, Michael Kay; Lighting, Joseph Goshert; Technical, Richard Leu; Stage Manager, Robert Dominguez CAST: Robert Petito (Sidney Bruhl), Joan Nimmo (Myra), Antonio Valente (Cliff), Lorraine Serabian (Helga), Patrick McCullough (Porter)
A mystery in two acts. The action takes place in the Bruhl study in Westport, Connecticut.

(Lucille Lortel Theatre) Friday, September 14, 1990–March 3, 1991 (161 performances and 4 previews) Maurice and Lois Rosenfield, Steven Suskin, Playwrights Horizons, and Lucille Lortel present:
FALSETTOLAND with Music and Lyrics by William Finn; Book, James Lapine, Mr. Finn; Director, Mr. Lapine; Musical Direction/Arrangements, Michael Starobin; Sets, Douglas Stein; Costumes, Franne Lee; Lighting, Nancy Schertler; Sound, Scott Lehrer; Stage Managers, Kate Riddle, Benjamin Gutkin; Original Cast Recording, DRG; Press, Shirley Herz/Pete Sanders. CAST: Lonny Price (Mendel), Michael Rupert succeeded by Scott Waara (Marvin), Danny Gerard succeeded by Jebby Handwerger (Jason), Stephen Bogardus (Whizzer), Faith Prince (Trina), Heather MacRae (Dr. Charlotte), Janet Metz (Cordelia/Caroline)
MUSICAL NUMBERS: Falsettoland, About Time, Year of the Child, Miracle of Judaism, Baseball Game, Day in Falsettoland, Planning the Bar Mitzvah, Everyone Hates His Parents, What More Can I Say?, Something Bad Is Happening, More Raquetball, Holding to the Ground, Days Like This, Cancelling the Bar Mitzvah, Unlikely Lovers, Another Miracle of Judaism, You Gotta Die Sometime, Jason's Bar Mitzvah, What Would I Do?

A musical performed without intermission. The action takes place in New York City in 1981–82. Performed earlier in the season at Playwrights Horizons.

Danny Gerard, Lonny Price, Faith Prince, Michael Rupert, Stephen Bogardus, Janet Metz, Heather MacRae in "Falsettoland" Top Right: Bogardus, Rupert (*Carol Rosegg*)

Audra Lindley, James Whitmore in "Handy Dandy" (*Martha Swope*)

(John Houseman Theatre) Saturday, September 15–November 10, 1990 (30 performances) Eric Krebs presents:
ABOUT TIME by Tom Cole; Director, Tony Giordano; Sets, Kent Dorsey; Lighting, Mr. Dorsey, Neil Peter Jampolis; Costumes, Christine Dougherty; Sound, Tom Gould; Stage Manager, Christine Michael; Executive Producer, Roger Allen Gindi; Press, David Rothenberg. CAST: James Whitmore (Old Man), Audra Lindley (Old Woman)

Performed in two acts and four scenes. The action takes place in a modern condominium. Originally produced at George St. Playhouse under the title *The Eighties*. In repertory with: Tuesday, September 18–November 11, 1990 (29 performances)
HANDY DANDY by William Gibson; Director, Mr. Giordano; Sets/Lighting, Mr. Jampolis; Costumes, Barbara Forbes. CAST: Audra Lindley (Molly Egan), James Whitmore (Henry Pulaski)

Performed in two acts and seven scenes. The action takes place in Boston at present.

(Westbeth Theatre Center) Sunday and Monday, September 16 and 17, 1990 (2 performances) Westbeth (Arnold Engelman, Producing Director) presents:
BABES IN BERLIN (WEST) by Owen Levy; Director, Dale Parry. CAST: Dominic Cuskern (Simon), Loretta Ehrhardt (Frau Hildebrandt), Christopher Hardwick (Johannes), Stan Ingram (Alton), Peter Lang (Wolfgang), Deedy Lederer (Magda), Deena Maurus (Sheila), Rodney Nugent (Fontaine), David Boldt (Stage Direction)

A reading of a new play in two acts. The action takes place in Berlin in the fall and winter of 1988–89.

(Joyce Theatre) Tuesday, September 18–22, 1990 (5 performances)
WE KEEP OUR VICTIMS READY; Written and performed by Karen Finley; Press, Susan Bloch/Ellen Zeisler, Suzanne Ford

A performance piece about the exploitation of women, the plight of the oppressed, and the consequences of male violence.

(Perry Street Theatre) Wednesday, September 19–November 4, 1990. The Perry Street TheatreCompany's Prima Artists in association with Buzzhead Productions presents:
BIG, FAT AND UGLY WITH A MOUSTACHE by Christopher Widney; Director, Stone Widney; Scenic Design, George Allison; Lighting, Michael Stiller; Costumes, Tracy Di Gesu; Sound, Scott Widney; Stage Managers, Herbert H. O'Dell, Kathleen Mary; Press, Jeffrey Richards, Jillana Devine. CAST: Alison Martin (Spike), David Beach (David), Brian Howe (Zeke), Evan O'Meara (Tyler), Jane Gabbert (Kathleen), Gordon Stanley (Frank Krutchik)

A comedy in two acts. The action takes place in the living room of David and Tyler's apartment.

Virginia Dillon, Ed Setrakian, Rick Zieff
in "The Mensch" (*Carol Rosegg*)

"Remembrance" (*William Gibson*)

Elizabeth Perry, Clement Fowler in "The Chairs" (*Carol Rosegg*)

Renee Upchurch in "Yesterdays"

(BAM Opera House) Wednesday, September 19–23. 1990 (6 performances)
COURT ART OF JAVA FROM THE KRATON OF YOGYAKARTA; Artistic Director, R.M. Soedarsono; Vice Troupe Leader, G.B.P.H. Hadiwinoto; Choreographer/Dance Master, R. Rio Saminta Mardawa; Music Director, R.M. Dinusatomo; Stage Manager, Y. Sumandiyo Hadi; Costume Mistress, G.B.R. Ay. Murywati Darmokusumo; Production Manager, Stan Presser; Company Manager, Frier McCollister
PROGRAM: Wayang Wong, Bedhaya and Golek Menak, Golek Menak, Wayang Kulit
A program of *Festival of Indonesia* in performance.

(Judith Anderson Theatre) Saturday, September 22–October 21, 1990 (23 performances) Manhattan Punch Line Theatre (Steve Kaplan, Artistic Director) and the Mensch Company present:
THE MENSCH by Steven Kronovet; Director, Joel Bassin; Sets, Vaughn Patterson; Lighting, Danianne Mizzy; Costumes, Kitty Leech; Sound, Bruce D. Cameron; Production Manager, Robert Daley; Stage Manager, Cheryl Zoldowski; Press, Shirley Herz/Miller Wright. CAST: Rick Zieff (Ronald Meyer), Ed Setrakian (Melvin Meyer), Virginia Dillon (Lorraine Goldman), Claudia Silver (Sonya Strossnakoff)
A comedy in two acts. The action takes place on the Upper East Side and Lower East Side, New York City, at present.

(Irish Arts Center) Friday, September 28, 1990–May 19, 1991 (200 performances and 7 previews) Irish Arts Center (Jim Sheridan, Artistic Director; Nye Heron, Executive Director) presents:
REMEMBRANCE by Graham Reid; Director, Terence Lamude; Sets, Duke Durfee; Lighting, John McLain; Sound, Tom Gould; Props/Scenic, Pearl Broms; Costumes, C. Jane Epperson; Technical, David Raphel; Stage Managers, Kurt Wagemann, Siobhan Kennedy; Press, Francine L. Trevens/David Lombardo. CAST: Malachy McCourt (Bert Andrews), John Finn (Victor Andrews), Aideen O'Kelly (Theresa Donaghy), Ann Dowd (Joan Donaghy), Terry Donnely (Deidre Donaghy), Ellen Tobie (Jenny)
A drama in two acts. The action takes place in Belfast at present.

(Producers Club Theatre) Monday, October 1–4, 1990 (8 performances)
SAVAGE IN LIMBO by John Patrick Shanley; Director, Stuart Warmflash; Sets/Lighting, Cynthia Dorrel; Art Direction, Vivian Barre; Stage Manager, Bill Burke; House Manager, Valora Braun; Press, Scotti Rhodes. CAST: Jeffrey Spolan (Murk), Jan Dorn (April White), Deborah Laufer (Denise Savage), Taryn Quinn (Linda Rotunda), Michael Cannis (Tony Aronica)
The action takes palce at a bar in the Bronx at present.

Sanford Meisner Theatre) Tuesday, October 2–14, 1990 (16 performances) Second Story Ensemble (Janis Powell, Artistic Director) presents:
TAKE THE WAKING SLOW by Jane Edith Wilson; Director, Janis Powell; Set/Lighting, Joel Golden; Stage Manager, John Kane; Press, Chris Boneau/Eva Patton. CAST: Elisa Anders (Ellen), Patrick White (Michael), Susan Barry (Traci), Neil Carpenter (Robert), Lee Schaefer (Marilyn)
A drama in two acts and twelve scenes. The action takes place at the present time in New York City and Chicago.

(UBU Repertory Theatre) Tuesday, October 2–28, 1990 (24 performances) UBU Repertory (Francoise Kourilsky, Artistic Director) presents:
THE CHAIRS by Eugene Ionesco; Translation, Donald Watson; Director, Francoise Kourilsky; Sets/Lighting, Watoku Ueno; Costumes, Carol Ann Pelletier; Sound, Phill Lee and Tim Pritchard; Stage Manager, Peter Muste. CAST: Clement Fowler (Old Man), Elizabeth Perry (Old Woman), Waguih Takla (Orator)

(Chelsea Stage) Wednesday, October 3–28, 1990 (28 performances) Chelsea Stage (Geoffrey Sherman, Artistic Director; Dara Hershman, Managing Director) presents:
THEME AND VARIATIONS by Samuil Alyoshin; Translation, Michael Glenny; Director, Geoffrey Sherman; Sets/Lighting, Paul Wonsek; Costumes, Marianne Powell Parker; Sound, Richard Rose; Stage Manager, Randy Lawson; Press, Jeffrey Richards/David LeShay. CAST: William Wise (Dmitry Nikolaevich), Ethan Phillips (Igor Mikhailovich), Kathleen McCall (Lyuba Sergeyevna)
A comedy in two acts. The action takes place in Moscow and Simferpol, Crimea at present.

(Village Gate/Top of the Gate) Thursday, October 4–28, 1990 (20 performances) National Black Touring Circuit (Woodie King, Producer) and Art D'Lugoff present:
YESTERDAYS: *An Evening with Billie Holiday* by Reenie Upchurch; Director, Woodie King Jr.; Stage Manager, Antoinette Tynes. CAST: Reenie Upchurch (Billie Holiday), Herb Lovelle (Drummer), Weldon Irvine (Pianist)
MUSICAL NUMBERS: Good Morning Heartache, Fooling Myself, Them There Eyes, God Bless the Child, Somebody's on My Mind, Don't Explain, Moonlight, No More, Deep Song, Pig Feet, Please Set Me Free, You've Changed, Unchained Melody, Fine and Mellow, Strange Fruit
A musical evening in two parts. The action takes place in a small New York City nightclub in May, 1959.

(Cornelia St. Cafe) Thurday, October 4–20, 1990 (16 performances)
THREE LITTLE PLAYS ABOUT SEX by Fred Kollo; Director, Robert Landau. CAST: Laura Carney, Jill Choder, Ricardo Matamoros, Christopher Mixon, Denise Pence, Amy Warner

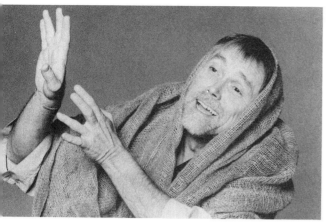

Kip Niven in "Two By Two"

Alix Korey in "Songs You Might Have Missed" (*Nick Granito*)

Neil Maffin, Tony Goldwyn in "The Sum of Us" Right: Richard Venture, Goldwyn (*Carol Rosegg*)

(Triangle/Holy Trinity) Thursday, October 4–28, 1990 (20 performances) Triangle Theatre Company presents:
TWO BY TWO with Music by Richard Rodgers; Lyrics, Martin Charnin; Book, Peter Stone; Based on *The Flowering Peach* by Clifford Odets; Director, Michael Ramach; Music Direction, Lawrence W. Hill; Lighting, Nancy Collings; Sets, Bob Phillips; Costumes, Amanda J. Klein; Stage Manager, Robert Cartwright; Press, Jim Baldassare. CAST: Kip Niven (Noah), Meredyth Rawlins (Esther), Tom Lloyd (Japheth), Jeffrey Blair Cornell (Shem), Wendy Baila (Leah), Bryan Batt (Ham), Mary Lee Marson (Rachel), Lindsey Mitchell (Goldie)
MUSICAL NUMBERS: Why Me, Put Him Away, Gitka Song, Something Somewhere, You Have Got to Have a Rudder, Something Doesn't Happen, An Old Man, Ninety Again, Two by Two, I Do Not Know a Day I Did Not Love You, When It Dries, You, The Golden Ram, Papa Knows Best, As Far As I'm Concerned, Hey Girlie, The Covenant
   The musical in two acts. The action takes place around Noah's house and Mt. Ararat. The time is before, during, and after the flood.

(Westbeth Theatre Center) Thursday, October 4–21, 1990 (16 performances) Barbara Bornmann presents:
THE DREAM CURE by Drucilla Cornell; Director, Beatrice Da Silva; Sets, Mary Blanchard; Lighting, Anna Bezzola; Costumes, Brian Pride; Sound, Vera Beren; Stage Manager, Yung Tam. CAST: Elizabeth Bove, Gerald Simon, Shirley Hedden, Tony Patellis

(Steve McGraw's) Friday, October 5–26, 1991 (4 performances) , returned Monday, March 11–April 1, 1991 (4 performances) Steve McGraw's presents:
SONGS YOU MIGHT HAVE MISSED with Music by Roger Anderson, Skip Kennon, Paul Katz, Alan Menken, David Friedman, Howard Marren, Michael Korie, William Finn, Henry Krieger; Lyrics, Lee Goldsmith, Ellen Fitzhugh, Michael Colby, Alan Menken, Muriel Robinson, Enid Futterman, Michael Korie, Howard Ashman, Robert Lorick. CAST: Alix Korey with David Friedman (piano)
PROGRAM: Get Back on the Bus, I Almost Cry, I Can Sing, Ah Men, I'm Not My Mother, Remember Today, Midnight Snack, He Comes Home Tired, I Shut the Door, If I Were Pretty, All Fall Down, Daughter of God, Stage Door
   An evening featuring songs cut from shows, songs from unproduced shows, or songs that were just overlooked.

(Cherry Lane Theatre) Friday, October 5, 1990–Augist 4, 1991 (335 performances and 14 previews) Dowling Entertainment, Duane Wilder, Gintare Seleika Everett and Chantepleure, Inc. present:
THE SUM OF US by David Stevens; Director, Kevin Dowling; Sets, John Lee Beatty; Lighting, Dennis Parichy; Costumes, Therese A. Bruck; Sound, Darren West; Associate Producers, Jay Hass, Donald R. Stoltz; Stage Manager, Larry Bussard; Company Manager, Diana L. Fairbanks; Press, Bill Evans/Jim Randolph. CAST: Tony Goldwyn succeeded by Neil Maffin/Matt Salinger (Jeff), Richard Venture succeeded by Robert Lansing/Richard Thomsen (Dad), Neil Maffin succeeded by Matthew Ryan/Daniel Baum (Greg), Phyllis Somerville (Joyce)
   An unconditional love story in two acts. The action takes place in a house and park in Footscray, an industrial suburb of Melbourne, Australia.

Barbara Bates Smith
in "Ivy Rowe" (*Carol Rosegg*)

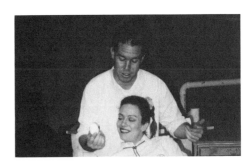

David Burke, Monika Mitchell in
"Curse of the Starving Class"

(45th St. Theatre) Wednesday, October 10–November 4, 1990 (15 performances and 5 previews) The Ivy Company presents:
I REMANE IVY ROWE; Adaptation by Barbara Smith and Mark Hunter; From the novel by Lee Smith; Director, Mr. Hunter; Sets, Barton Lee; Lighting, Ken Kaczynski; Press, Shirley Herz/Miller Wright. CAST: Barbara Bates Smith

A one-woman play spanning the life of an Appalachian mountain woman. A revised version opened April 15, 1991 at the Provincetown Playhouse.

(John Houseman Theatre) Wednesday, October 10–26, 1991 (4 performances)
IBSEN WOMEN: *Put An Eagle In Cage . . .* from the work of Henrik Ibsen; Created by Juni Dahr; Music, Chris Poole; Directing Advice, Marketta Kimmbrel, Aimée Malthe Harnes, Kristin Olsoni; Costumes, Inger Derlick, Ms. Dahr; Production Manager, Ms. Harnes; Production Assistant, Jacquline Hayes; Press, Jim Baldassare. CAST: Juni Dahr (Hilde/Hedd/Mrs. Alving/Nora/Ellida/Hjørdis)

A solo performance.

(Harold Clurman Theatre) Thursday, October 11–28, 1990 (14 performances, with a one week extension at the Samuel Beckett Theatre November 9–16 of 7 performances) Second Generation Theatre Company presents:
BLACKOUT by Gary Lennon; Directed by Ron Stetson; Sets, Ron Kurash; Lighting, Zdenek Kriz; Costumes, Clare Tattersall; Stage Manager, Sonya Smith; Graphics, Robin Reid and Susan Smiley; Press, Jim Baldassare. CAST: Sam Gray (Jim), Jill Gatsby (Kathy), William Neish (Tim), Gary Lennon (Jack), Susan Boehm (Debbie), Nancy McDoniel (Rachel), Kelly Kane (Patty), Lee Ann Martin (Becky), Jessica Bern (Carroll), Jackie Bees (Helen), Blair Tatton (Kent)

A group of alcoholics meet on Christmas Eve to share their experience, strength and hope.

(Folksbiene Theatre) Sunday, October 11, 1990–January 13, 1991 (39 performances) Folksbiene (Ben Schechter, Managing Director) presents:
FATHER'S INHERITANCE: Music/Lyrics/Adaptation, Emil Gorovets; Based on Jacob Gordin's *The Charlatan*; Director, Yevgeny Lanskoye; Musical Director, Nikolas Levinowsky; Choreography, Felix Fibich; Sets, Brian P. Kelly; Costumes, Susan Sigrist; Lighting, Thomas Goldberg, Janet Clancy; Translator, Simcha Kruger; Stage Manager, Judith Scher; Press, Max Eisen, Madelon Rosen. CAST: Zypora Spaisman (Esther-Rokhl), Semyon Grinberg (Benish-Lemakh), Julie Alexander (Oliyetchke), Shira Flam (Mendele), Emil Gorovets (Shloimke), Ira Sakolsky (Misha), Sandy Levitt (Simon Kozlin), Irina Fogelson (Golde)
MUSICAL NUMBERS: We Are 76 Years Old Today, Laugh Brother Laugh Sister, Goodbye Odessa, Angry Father, I'll Sing a Little Song, I Play Cards, My Brother Is a Fool, The Wheel of Fortune Turns, I Am a Comedian, I Don't Want to Study Anymore, I Was a Singer, It's Hard for Me Here, Love Is a Heavenly Song, I Want to Be an Aristocrat, Money Is Only Paper, At Work I Don't Sweat, Dear You Are My Comfort, Like in the Garden of Eden, Purim Is Coming, Sir Chancellor, Jews Jews, Dance Dance, Achashverush's Song, Misha Is My Child, I Can Swear by Heaven, There Are Such Daughters, Oh My Olyetchke, Stop Stop, In a Lucky Hour

A musical in two acts. The action takes place in Odessa and Tirospol.

(Space 603) Saturday, October 13–27, 1990 (16 performances) New Nine Company presents:
HALF-LIFE by Peter Hodges; Director, Michael C. Mahon; Sets, Kevin Amalia; Lighting, Marc C. Andrews. CAST: Kevin Amalia, Mary Hedahl, Bernard Hocke, Mare Kenney, Tom Verica, Susan Wisdom

A comedy-drama in three acts about an isolated family's feud over a run-down ranch.

(Colony Theatre/Taylor Hall) Wednesday, October 17–November 10, 1990 (16 performances) The Colony Theatre (Timothy Kelleher, Artistic Director) presents:
CURSE OF THE STARVING CLASS by Sam Shepard; Director, Nathaniel Kahn; Sets, Jonathan T. Cook; Producer, Barry Levy; Lighting, Than Hussey; Stage Manager, Jamie Joyce; Press, Monika Mitchell. CAST: Timothy Kelleher (Wesley), Mary Kaye Swedish (Ella), Monika Mitchell (Emma), Barry Levy (Taylor), Jonathan T. Cook (Weston), Gregg Allen Holt (Ellis), Doug Anderson (Malcolm), Than Hussey (Slatter), R.A. Waite (Emerson)

A black comedy in three acts.

(New Federal Theatre/Intar) Wednesday, October 17–November 18, 1990 and reopened (Top of the Gate) Wednesday, January 16–February 24, 1991 (36 performances) Woodie King Jr., Producer and Art D'Lugoff present:
THE WIZARD OF HIP (*Or When In Doubt Slam Dunk*) by Thomas W. Jones II; Director, Kenny Leon; Sets, Tony Loadholt; Lighting, Jeff Guzik; Score, James Pelton Jr.; Stage Manager, Lisa L. Watson; Press, Max Eisen. CAST: Thomas W. Jones II

A one man odyssey on the search for the meaning of Hip.

(Intar Theatre) Wednesday, October 17–November 25, 1990 (33 performances and 12 previews) Intar Hispanic American Arts (Max Ferra, Artistic Director; Eva Brune, Managing Director) presents:
THE LADY FROM HAVANA by Luis Santeiro; Director, Max Ferra; Sets/Costumes, Campbell Baird; Lighting, Debra Dumas; Sound, Fox/Perla Ltd. Musical Arrangements, Fernando Rivas; Hair/Makeup, Bobby Miller; Press, Peter Cromarty/David Lotz. CAST: Olga Merediz (Marita/Rosa), Xonia Benguria (Mama/Gloria), Alina Troyano (Zoila/Isabel)

A comedy in two acts. The action takes place in Miami, at present.

Garry Lennon, William Neish in "Blackout" (*Larry Cox*)

Olga Merediz, Alina Troyano, Xonia Benguira in "Lady from Havan"
(*Carol Rosegg*)

Tim Loughrin, Jim Walton, Courtenay Collins, Leon B. Flagg
in "Life on the Third Rail" (*Carol Rosegg*)

Patrick Fitzgerald, Madeline Potter in
"Playboy of the Western World" (*Carol Rosegg*)

(Actors Outlet) Friday, October 19, 1990– Tommy De Maio presents:
PRETTY FACES: *The Large & Lovely Musical* with Music/Lyrics/Book by Robert W. Cabell; Director/Choreographer, Gene Foote; Sets, Peter Rogness; Costumes, George Bergeron; Lighting, Clifton Taylor; Musical Director, Jim Mironchik; Musical Supervisor/Arranger, Arnie Gross; Stage Manager, John Frederick Sullivan; Production Manager, Dale Phelps McGowan; Press, Jeffrey Richards/David LeShay. CAST: Lynn Halverson (Monique), Ron Meier (Jimmy), Michael Winther (Carter), Kathleen Rosamond Kelly (Bobby-Joy), Amy Jo Phillips (Daphne), Heather Anne Stokes (Patricia), Amy Ryder (Pleasure), Margaret Dyer (Paulette), Liz Leisek (Deloris), Charles Mandracchia (Roger)
MUSICAL NUMBERS: Taking Chances, 42-32-42, How Do You Like Your Men, Furs Fortune Fame Glamour, Interviews, Sleep Walkers Lament, Too Plump for Prom Night, Heartbreaker, What's Missing in My Life, Pretty Faces, Daddy Doesn't Care, Solo for the Telephone, Waiting for the Curtain, Global Glamour Girls, Woman That I Am, Purple Hearted Soldiers, Song for Jesus, Are You the One, On With the Show, Tears and Tears Ago, What Is Missing in My Life, This Moment Is Mine, Finale
A musical in two acts. The action takes place at a beauty pageant at present.

(St. Peter's Church Theatre) Tuesday, October 23–November 25, 1990 (29 performances and 11 previews) Michael D. Thompson and Florence Hohenstein present:
LIFE ON THE THIRD RAIL by Mitchell Uscher; Director, Pat Carmichael; Sets, Wm. John Aupperlee; Costumes, Clifford Capone; Lighting, Vivien Leone; Sound, One Dream; Hair/Makeup, David Windsor; General Manager, Gindi Theatrical Management; Stage Manager, Crystal Huntington; Press, Becky Flora. CAST: Jim Walton (Jim Manfredi), Lee Meredith (Chi-Chi), Courtenay Collins (Sandra Donnelly), Tim Loughrin (Kenny Baxter), Leon B. Flagg (Bruce Grant), Jim Boyd (Taxi Driver/Harold Donelly), Jack Mahoney (Jacques/Teller/Dodson/Minister), Florence Hayle (Miriam)
A romantic comedy in two acts. The action takes place in Manhattan, New York City, at present.

(Pan Asian Repertory) Wednesday, October 24–December 1, 1990 (40 performances) Pan Asian Repertory (Tisa Chang, Artistic Director; Dominick Balleta, Producing Associate) presents:
LUCKY COME HAWAII by Jon Shirota; Director, Ron Nakahara; Sets, Robert Klingelhoefer; Costumes, Maggie Raywood; Sound, Ty Sanders; Lighting, Victor En Yu Tan; Stage Manager, Sue Jane Stoker; Press, Peter Cromarty. CAST: Tom Matsusaka (Ishi), Mel Duane Gionson (Tengan), Norris M. Shimabuku (Kama Gusuda), Kati Kuroda (Tsuyu), Les J.N. Mau (Ikehara-san), Ann M. Tsuji (Kimiko), James Jenner (Bob Weaver), Stan Egi (Kenyei), Joe Fiske (Specks)
A family comedy in two acts. The action takes place in Hawaii between December 6 and 15, 1941.

(Irish Repertory Theatre) Thursday, October 25–December 2, 1990 (35 performances and 5 previews) Irish Repertory Theatre presents:
THE PLAYBOY OF THE WESTERN WORLD by J.M. Synge; Director, Charlotte Moore; Sets, David Raphel; Costumes, Natalie Walker; Sound/Lighting, Richard Clausen; Fights, J. Steven White; Music, Black 47 performing Larry Kerwin's original compositions; Stage Manager, J. Andrew Burgreen. CAST: Madeleine Potter (Pegeen Mike), Ciaran O'Reilly (Shawn Keogh), Brendan Burke (Michael James Flaherty), Chris Carrick (Jimmy Farrell), Brian F. O'Byrne (Philly Cullen), Patrick Fitzgerald (Christy Mahon), Caroline Winterson (Widow Quin), Mac Orange (Susan Brady), Miriam Foley (Honor Blake), Laura Hughes (Sara Tansey), Stephen Joyce (Old Mahon), Adian O'Byrne (Crier)
A comedy in three acts. The action takes place on a wild coast in Mayo, Ireland in 1900.

(Town Hall) Wednesday, October 24–December 30, 1990 (62 performances) Raymond Ariel and Lawrence Toppall present:
YIDDLE WITH A FIDDLE with Music by Abraham Ellstein; Lyrics/Book, Isaiah Sheffer; Based on the 1936 film by Joseph Green; Director, Ran Avni; Musical Director/Orchestrations, Lanny Meyers; Choreography, Helen Butleroff; Sets, Jeffrey Schneider; Costumes, Karen Hummel; Lighting, Robert Bessoir; Sound, David Smith; Stage Manager, D.C. Rosenberg; Press, Pete Sanders/Shirly Herz. CAST: Emily Loesser (Yiddle), Robert Michael Baker (Froym), Susan Flynn (Teibele's Mother/ Channah), Mitchell Greenberg (Aryeh), Michael Ingram (Kalamutke), Patricia Ben Peterson (Teibele), Rachel Black (Helper/Musician's Assistant), Steven Fickinger (Chauffeur/Yossel), Andrea Green (Waitress/Cook/Stage Manager), Danny Rutigliano (Truck Driver/Zalmen Gold/Zinger), Steve Sterner (Tavern Keeper/Rabbi/Becker)
MUSICAL NUMBERS: Come Gather 'Round, If You Wanna Dance, Music It's a Necessity, Yiddle with a Fiddle, New Rhythm, Help Is on the Way, I'll Sing, Hard as a Nail, Man to Man, Oh Mama Am I in Love, Travelling First Class Style, Badchen's Verses, Only for a Moment, Wedding Bulgar Dance, Warsaw!, How Can the Cat Cross the Water, Stay Home Here with Me, Take It from the Top, To Tell the Truth, We'll Sing, Finale
A musical in two acts. The action takes place in Poland during the summer of 1936.

Ann M. Tsuji, Stan Egi, Norris Shimabuku
in "Lucky Come Hawaii" (*Carol Rosegg*)

Emily Loesser, Michael Ingram, Mitchell Greenberg, Robert Michael
Baker in "Yiddle with a Fiddle" (*Carol Rosegg*)

(Duo Theatre) Wednesday, October 24–November 10, 1990 (12 performances) Duo Theatre (Michael Alasa, Artistic/Executive Director) presents:
EASTERN STANDARD by Richard Greenberg; Director, B.C. Ruiz; Sets, Leon Munier; Costumes, Natalie Barth-Walker; Lighting, Jerry Kumin; Stage Manager, Mary Lisa Kinney. CAST: O.V. Vargas (Stephen Wheeler), Tony Louden (Drew Paley), Jeanette Toro (Phoebe Kidde), J. Ed Araiza (Peter Kidde), Carmen Rosario (May Logan), Laura Duncan (Ellen)

A comic drama in two acts. The action takes place in New York City and environs, at present.

(Promenade Theatre) Wednesday, October 24–November 18, 1991 (8 performances and 27 previews) The Never Or Now Company presents:
CATCH ME IF I FALL with Music/Lyrics/Book by Barbara Schottenfeld; Director, Susan Einhorn; Additional Staging, Stuart Ross; Orchestrations, Joe Gianono; Musical Supervisor/Director, Joseph Church; Sets/Costumes, G.W. Mercier; Lighting, Richard Nelson; Sound, Garry and Timmy Harris; Stage Manager, John C. McNamara; General Manager, Paul B. Berkowsky; Associate Producers, Frederick Schultz, Terry A. Johnston; Press, David Rothenberg. CAST: James Judy (Lonny Simon), David Burdick (Brian Simon), Sal Viviano (Peter Bennington), Jeanine Morick (Laurie Simon), Ronnie Farer (Godiva Harris), Laura Dean (Dominica Gruia), A.D. Cover (Andrei Gruia)
MUSICAL NUMBERS: Catch Me If I Fall, Veterinarian, Love that Came Before, Sometimes at Night, The Beach House, I Want You to Be, It's Not a Real Wedding, Home Never Leaves You, When You Live in NY, Libertate, Isn't It Strange, Timing and Lighting, Chaperone, Never or Now, Finale

A musical comedy in two acts. The action takes place in New York City during late fall of 1989.

(Triplex) Thursday, October 25–November 17, 1990 (13 performances and 3 previews) Under One Roof and Cucarache present:
FAMINE PLAYS: *A Downtown Opera* Written/Directed by Richard Caliban; Music, John Hoge; Lighting, Brian Aldous; Costumes, Mary Myers; Projections, Tony Jacobs; Sound, John Huntington; Stage Manager, J. Tori Evand; Press, Ted Killmer, Tray Batres. CAST: Hugh Palmer (Adolphe Beckh), George Tynan (Fleet), Steven Bland (Buffoon), Mark Dillahunt (Stoley), Brennan Murphy (Lester), Lia Chang (Edie), Vivian Lanko (Rosie), Glen Santiago (Mr. K), Corinne Edgerly (Mrs. K), Lauren Hamilton (Runner), David Simonds (Stub), Mollie O'Mara (Jones), Deborah Arenstein, Paul Bosco, Michael Bubrick, Dale Davidson, Thomas Davison, Miranda Hessler, Mark Leydorf, Jessica Paul, Joy Pincus, Cheryl Scaccio, Terri Towns.

A drama in two parts.

David Burdick, Laura Dean in "Catch Me if I Fall" (*Michael Romanos*)

Brennan Murphy, Lia Chan in "Famine Plays" (*M. Ambo*)

(Judith Anderson Theatre) Tuesday, October 30–November 25, 1990 (21 performances and 7 previews) The Women's Project & Productions (Julia Miles, Artistic Director) presents:
DAYTRIPS by Jo Carson; Director, Billie Allen; Sets, James Noone; Lighting, Anne Militello; Costumes, Barbara Beccio; Sound, Lia Vollack; Stage Manager, Robert Daley; Press, Fred Nathan/Merle Frimark. CAST: Linda Atkinson (Pat), Barbara Barrie (Irene/Ree), Beth Dixon (Pat), Helen Stenborg (Rose)

A drama performed without intermission. The action takes place in Upper-East Tennessee, during the recent past and at present.

(263 W. 86th) Wednesday, October 31–November 18, 1990 (14 performances) Centerfold Productions present:
ARSENIC AND OLD LACE by Joseph Kesselring; Director, Michael Miller CAST: Michael Blanc, Russ Coyne, Eric Eisenberg, Bobb Fessler, Robert Bailey, Mary Grace, Joanne Joseph, Daniel Leventritt, Peter Regan, Roger Rifkin, Barbara Schwartz, Jim Siatkowski, Mary Ann Stackpole, Yohanna Yonas

(William Redfield Theatre) Wednesday, October 31–November 25, 1990 (21 performances) The Phoenix Ensemble presents:
BALL by John Jiler; Director, Steve Stout; Sets, Jeff Vaughn; Lighting, Richard Currie; Costumes, Barbara A. Joyce. CAST: Carter Inskeep, DruAnn Chuchran; Mary Jasperson, Kim Highland, Marty Grillo, Pam Shafer, Michael Varna, Margaret Hunt

A comedy about diplomacy, romance, sex, sabotage, war, and, above all, baseball.

(Studio Theatre) Thursday, November 1–19, 1990 (18 performances) The Spuyten Duyvil Theatre Company presents:
THEM by Tom Coffey; Director, Dennis Delaney; Sets, Charles Golden; Lighting, Chris Gorzelnick; Costumes, Noel Noblett. CAST: Isabel Glasser, Clarke Gordon, Casey McDonald, Maureen MacDougall, Leslie McMahon, Rusty Owen, Joan Penn, Robert Poletick, Janelle Sperow, Robert Verlaque

A drama in three acts. The action involves a retarded small town Irish boy and his search for happiness.

(Westbeth Theatre Center) Thursday, November 1–25, 1990 (18 performances and 3 previews) Classicworks Company presents:
THE RELAPSE by Sir John Vanbrugh; Director, Anthony Naylor; Costumes, Carol Sherry; Press, Shirley Herz/Miller Wright. CAST: Russ Billingsly, Anne Lilly, Sandy Laub, Sean Hopkins, Michael Santorico, Amy Gordon

A restoration comedy set in 17th century England.

Linda Atkinson, Barbara Barrie, Helen Stenborg (front), Beth Dixon in "Daytrips" (*Martha Holmes*)

Sandra Laub, Anne Lilly, Sean Hopkins, Russ Billingsly in "The Relapse"

(Nat Horne Theatre) Saturday, November 3–17, 1990 (18 performances) Manhattan Class Company (Robert LuPone and Bernard Telsey, Executive Directors) presents:
MANHATTAN CLASS ONE-ACTS; Sets, Rob Odorisio; Costumes, Dianne Rosetti-Finn; Lighting, Howard Werner; Sound, Lia Vollack; Production Supervisor, Laura Kravets Gautier; Production Manager, Ira Mont; Press, Peter Cromarty/David Lotz, Lynne McCreary. CAST: Kent Adams, Gil Bellows, Charles Cragin, Margaret Eginton, Tony Gilbert, Sarah Knapp, Joseph Knight, John Kozeluh, Ilana Levine, Micah Lewis, Laura Linney, Ken Marks, Beth McGee-Russell, Edward Miller, Ross Mondschain, Patti Onorato, Connie Ray, Philip J. Reilly, Gregory Wolfe, Sam Zuckerman.
A Snake in the Vein by Alan Bowne; Director, Jimmy Bohr. *Forgetting Frankie* by Annie Evans; Director, Melia Bensussen. *Lonely on the Bayou* with Music by Catherine Stone; Book/Lyrics, Lynne Ginsburg; Choreography, Margaret Eginton; Director, Robert LuPone. *Research and Development* Written and Choreographed by Fay Simpson.

(Home For Contemporary Theatre and Art) Saturday, November 3–December 2, 1990 (16 performances and 4 previews) Theatre For A New Audience (Jeffrey Horowitz, Artistic/Producing Director) and Home For Contemporary Theatre and Art present:
THE MUD ANGEL by Darrah Cloud; Director, Kevin Kuhlke; Sets, Clay Snider; Lighting, Mary Louise Geiger; Costumes, Marina Draghici; Fights, David S. Leong; Sound, Scott Steidl; Stage Managers, Kristin Nieuwenhuis, Jeffrey Pajer; Press, Shirley Herz/Miller Wright. CAST: Seane Corn (Jenny), Alyssa Breshnahan (Shadow), Andrew Weems (Sonny), David Neipris (Burt), Sofia Landon (Mrs. Malvetz)
A drama set on a family farm in Sturgeon Bay, Wisconsin.

(Open Eye Theatre) Sunday, November 4–December 30, 1990 (6 performances) Open Eye presents:
A PLACE BEYOND THE CLOUDS by Sandra Biano; Director, Sharone Stacy. CAST: Joey Chavez, Steven Dominguez, Cathy Gale, Doug Jewell, Cynthia Kaplan, Valerie Williams
A play about man's eternal fascination with flight.

(Kaufman Theatre) Tuesday, November 6–December 30, 1990 (42 performances and 14 previews) Martin R. Kaufman presents:
CARNAL KNOWLEDGE by Jules Feiffer; Director, Martin Charnin; Sets, Alan Kimmel; Lighting, Ken Billington; Sound, Abe Jacob; Stage Manager, Brandon E. Doemling; General Manager, Marshall B. Purdy; Press, David Powers. CAST: Jon Cryer (Sandy), Judd Nelson (Jonathan), Justine Bateman (Susan), Karen Byers (Bobbie), Mimi Quillin (Cindy), Laura Rogers (Daisy), Arminae Azarian (Louise)
A drama in two acts. Originally produced as a film in 1971. The action spans the late 1940's to late 1960's.

Gregory Wolfe, Fay Simpson, Joseph Knight in "Manhattan Class One-Acts" (*Carol Rosegg*)

(Clockwise from Top L) Karen Byers, Judd Nelson, Justine Bateman, Jon Cryer in "Carnal Knowledge" (*Martha Swope*)

(Double Image Theatre) Tuesday, November 6, 1990–June 9, 1991 (193 performances) Double Image Theatre (John Martello, Artistic Director) presents:
DAUGHERTY & FIELD: OFF-BROADWAY; Special Material Written and Composed by Robin Field; Set, Bob Essman; Lighting, Shawn Moninger; Stage Manager, Ernie Barbarash; Technical Director, Teamdesign; Press, David Rothenberg/Meg Gordean, Terence Womble, Manny Igrejas. CAST: Bill Daugherty, Robin Field
PROGRAM: Daugherty & Field Off-Broadway, Big Bands vs. Broadway, Sing Your Own Song, Remember Radio?, Juke Box Saturday Night, South Pacific, Teamwork, Invention I, The Three B's, Tchaikovsky, Pagliacci, Kismet, An Interview, Rhapsody in Blue, Mr. Paganini
A musical comedy revue in two parts.

(New Federal Theatre) Wednesday, November 7–December 9, 1990 (30 performances) New Federal Theatre, Inc. (Woodie King, Jr., Producer) and Victory Gardens Theatre (Dennis Zacek, Producer) present:
JELLY BELLY by Charles Smith; Director, Dennis Zacek; Sets/Lighting, Richard Harmon; Costumes, Judy Dearing; Sound, Acqui Casto; Stage Manager, Jesse Wooden, Jr.; Press, Max Eisen/Madelon Rosen. CAST: Gina Torres (Barbara), Weyman Thompson (Mike), Donald Douglass (Bruce), Ramon Melindez Moses (Kenny), Tony Smith (Jelly Belly)
A drama performed without intermission. The action takes place on Mike's front porch late one Indian summer evening.

(224 Waverly Place) Thursday, November 8-25, 1990 (18 performances) Maya Associates presents:
FLYPAPER with Music/Lyrics/Book by Cheryl Paley and Larry Pellegrini; Director/Choreographer, Shari Upbin; Musical Director, Don Rebic; Sets, David P. Gordon; Lighting, Mark C. Andrew; Costumes, Goran Sparrman; Sound, Joe Gallant; Press, Penny M. Landau. CAST: Cheryl Paley, James Loren
A musical set in a Greenwich Village tavern at present.

(Sanford Meisner Theatre) Thursday, November 8–18, 1990 (12 performances) Echo Repertory presents:
RING ROUND THE MOON by Jean Anouilh; Adaptation, Christopher Fry; Directlor, Philip Burton; Lighting/Sets, Scot A. Newell; Costumes, Charlotte Yetman. CAST: Dennis Bigelow, Kate Britton, Milton Carney, Max Chalawsky, Amelia David, Charles Duval, Christopher Kearns, Julie Lloyd, Janice Orlandi, Lisa Randall, Sandra Waugh

Bill Daugherty, Robin Field

Gina Torres, Weyman Thompson in "Jelly Belly" (*Bert Andrews*)

(Chelsea Stage) Thusday, November 8–December 2, 1990 (30 performances)
Chelsea Stage (Geoffrey Sherman, Artistic Director; Dara Hershman, Managing
Director) in association with The Cleveland Playhouse presents:
THE MARCH ON RUSSIA by David Storey; Director, Josephine R. Abady;
Lighting, Marc. B. Weiss; Costumes, Linda Fisher; Sound, Jeffrey Montgomerie;
Stage Manager, Robert Bennett; Press, Jeffrey Richards. CAST: Sean Griffin
(Colin), John Carpenter (Mr. Pasmore), Bethel Leslie (Mrs. Pasmore), Carol
Locatell (Wendy), Susan Browning (Eileen)
   A drama in two acts. The action takes place in the Pasmore's retirement bunga-
low, near the Yorkshire coast, at present.

(Studio 4-A) Wednesday, November 14–December 2, 1990 (15 performances)
Acorn Productions and One World Arts Foundation present:
INDEPENDENCE by Lee Blessing; Director, Ann Bowen; Sets, Chris Pickart;
Lighting, John Sellars; Costumes, Barbara A. Bell; Sound, Bruce Ellman; Stage
Managers, Cheryl Zoldowski, Reed Clark. CAST: Mary Doyle, Susan Johanna,
Ruth A. McQuiggan, Pamela Moller

(Vineyard Theatre) Thursday, November 15, 1990– The Vineyard Theatre (Doug-
las Aibel, Artistic Director; Barbara Zinn Krieger, Executive Director) presents:
NIGHTINGALE by Elizabeth Diggs; Director, John Rubenstein; Sets, William
Barclay; Lighting, Phil Monat; Costumes, James Scott; Music, Robert Waldman;
Sound, Bruce Ellman; Musical Staging, Jane Lanier; Stage Manager, Kate Broder-
ick; Press, Shirley Herz/Sam Rudy. CAST: James A. Stephens (William Edward
Nightingale/Dr. Hall), Kathryn Pogson (Florence Nightingale), Pippa Pearthree
(Parthenope Nightingale), Sloane Shelton (Fanny Nightingale), John Curless (Sid-
ney Herbert), Robertson Carricart, Jane Lanier, Edmund Lewis, Elizabeth Logun,
Jodie Lynn McClintock, Emily Arnold McCully, Patrick O'Connell, Greg Porretta,
Diana Van Fossen
   A drama based on the life of Florence Nightingale.

(Cooper Square Theatre) Thursday, November 15–December 9, 1990 (12 perfor-
mances) Transatlantic Theatre and Cooper Square Theatre present:
HISTORICAL PRODS by Eoin West; Director/Sets, John Michael Johnson; Cos-
tumes, Alison Mullin; Lighting, Tracy Dedrickson; Producer, Charlie Dunne.
CAST: Lisa Ebeyer, Lynne Mold (Fruit Seed/Lizzie/Fruit), Marshall Lucas
(Kilty/Director/Cold Shoulders), Charlie Dunne (Spirit Invader/Charles Parnell),
Kevin McClatchy (Spirit/Invader), Michael Rains (Voice/DeVice), Kent Abbett
(Kip/Eugene/Rip), Jack Hazan (Bram/C.D./Bramley/Cee Dee), Alison Mullin
(Ellenora), John Moraitis (Luke), Jamie Callahan (George), Tinne Metcalf (Kay),
Kevin Martin (Stanley/Paul Diamond), Marty Cinis (MacMorrough), Catherine
Cullen (Katherine O'Shea), Howard Atlee (Anthony Og Mac Anthony), Scott
Striegel (Billy Ballast), Jon Michael Johnson (Butler McGuinea)
   A play in two acts. The action takes place in Ireland and spans the later stone age,
3500 B.C., to the present.

(Orpheum Theatre) Friday, November 16–25, 1990 and Friday, December 14,
1990- Jan. 6, 1991 (25 performances) Frederick Zollo and Robert Cole in associa-
tion with 126 Second Ave. Corp. and Sine/D'addario Ltd. present:
SEX, DRUGS, ROCK & ROLL by Eric Bogosian; Director, Jo Bonney; Sets,
John Arcone; Lighting; Jan Kroeze; Sound, Jan Nebozenko; Stage Manager, Pat
Sosnow; Press, Phillip Rinaldi. CAST: Eric Bogosian
   A limited return engagement of last season's exploration of American obses-
sions.

(Saval Theatre) Saturday, November 17– December 9, 1990 (12 performances)
American Ensemble Co. presents:
TONIGHT AT 8:30 by Noel Coward; Director, Judd Silverman; Sets, George A.
Allison; Lighting, Joseph Goshert; Technical, Richard Leu; Costumes, Lisa Emer-
son; Stage Manager, Angus Steele. CAST: *Red Peppers* with Thomas Connor
(George), Lorraine Serabia (Lilly), Angus Steele (Alf), John Alban Coughlan
(Bert), Ian Fleet (Edwards), Patricia Power (Mabel). *Fumed Oak* with Michael
Mauldin (Henry), Alison Brunell (Doris), Nancy Daly (Elsie), Patricia Power (Mrs.
Rockett). *Ways and Means* with Barbara Hilson (Stella), J.J. Reap (Toby), Alison
Brunell (Olive), Thomas Connor (Chaps), Patricia Power (Nanny), Ian Fleet (Mur-
doch), John Alban Coughlan (Stevens), Lorraine Serabian (Elena), Michael
Mauldin
   A program of three short plays.

(45th St. Theatre) Tuesday, November 20–December 9, 1990 (24 performances)
Frederick Douglas Creative Arts Center (Fred Hudson, Producer) presents:
TELLTALE HEARTS by Joe Barnes; Director, Dean Irby; Sets, Charles McClen-
nahan; Costumes, Terry Leong; Lighting, Ron Burns; Sound, Joel Foster; Stage
Manager, Kathleen Mahoney; Press, Howard and Barbara Atlee. CAST: Iona Mor-
ris (Janet), Tony Evans (Michael), Count Stovall (James), Petronia Paley (Char-
lene), Elain Graham (Lola), Kim Sykes (Marie), Jack Landron (Kevin), Fred
Anderson (Bob)
   A comedy in two acts. The action takes place in NYC during summer and fall.

(Village Theatre) Wednesday, November 21- December 16, 1990 (20 perfor-
mances) Village Theatre Company presents:
ARE YOU NOW OR HAVE YOU EVER BEEN by Eric Bentley; Director,
Henry Fonte; Lights, David Edwardson; Sets/Sound, Mr Fonte; Stage Manager,
Lisa Jean Lewis. CAST: Ray Atherton, Barbara Berque, Michael Berke, Michael
Curran, Milton Elliott, Wally Dunn, Randy Kelly, Terrence Martin, Rodney L.
Nugent, Dugg Smith, Howard Thorenson
   A drama about the attacks on freedom by the House Un-American Activities
Committee in the early 1950s.

**Susan Browning, John Carpenter, Carol Locatell
in "The March on Russia" (*Gerry Goodstein*)**

**Eric Bogosian in "Sex, Drugs,
Rock & Roll" (*Paula Court*)**

Count Stovall, Petronia Paley in "Telltale Hearts" (*Mel Wright*)

"Are You Now..."

(Triangle/Holy Trinity) Saturday, November 24- December. 16, 1990 (14 performances) Triangle Theatre Company presents:
THE DIARIES OF ADAM AND EVE by Mark Twain; Adapted and Edited by David Birney; Director, Lou Jacob; Original Music/Accompaniment, Gerry Giola; Lighting, Nancy Collings; Sets, Jeff Read Freund; Costumes, Amanda J. Klein; Stage Manager, Jerry Grant; Press, Jim Baldassare. CAST: Robert Emmet (Adam), Rose Stockton (Eve)
   A comedy performed without intermission. The action takes place in the Garden and elsewhere, immediately after creation.

(Marriott Marquis Ballroom) Monday, November 26, 1990 (1 limited performance) Cyma Rubin presents:
I LOVE A PIANO! with Music and Lyrics by Irving Berlin; Director/Choreography, Ray Roderick; Musical Director, Michael Berkeley; Concept/Arrangements, Mr. Roderick, Mr. Berkeley; Sets, Lenore Doxsee; Costumes, David Toser; Lighting, Ed McCarthy; Sound, Steve Kennedy; Orchestrations, Ross Konikoff, Randy Klein, Phil Reno, Mark Suozo, Ted Allen; Production Supervisor, Ron Annas; Press, Fred Nathan/Ian Rand. CAST: Loni Ackerman, James Brennan, Marcy DeGonge, Dale Hensley, Eddie Korbich, Dorothy Stanley, Jonathon Hadary, Helen Hayes, Elizabeth and Paul Michael Glaser.
   A benefit for St. Clare's Hospital celebrating the work of Irving Berlin.

(CSC Theatre) Tuesday, November 27–December 9, 1990. Ensemble International Theatre in association with Mabou Mines presents:
C.E.O. by Stig Larsson; Translation, Joe Martin; Director, Frederick Neumann. CAST: Ensemble International members
   An examination of power relations between a working class couple and the C.E.O. of the corporation for which one of them works.

(Theatre 603) Thursday, November 29–December 16, 1990 (12 performances) The Basic Theatre presents:
THE ROVER by Aphra Behn; Director, Jared Hammond; Sets, Maeve Dunn; Lighting/Technical Director, Marc D. Malamud; Costumes, Mr. Hammond, Patti Burke; Dramaturg, David Ganon. CAST: Weston Blakesley, Margaret Burnham, Sheri Delaine, Sarah Ford, Nicolas Glaeser, David Goldman, Rosemary Keogh, Nelson Simon, Tom Spivey, Neil Tadken, Loretta Toscano, Elizabeth Townsend

(ReGenesis Theatre at St. Mark's) Thursday, November 29- December 16, 1990 (15 performances) White Bird Productions, Inc. presents:
VILLAGERS by John Francis Istel; Director, Bonnie Mark
   An epic story of Greenwich Village life spanning three centuries.

(Lamb's Theatre) Tuesday, December 4–30, 1990 (32 performances) Lamb's Theatre Company presents:
THE GIFTS OF THE MAGI with Music/Lyrics by Randy Courts; Book/Lyrics, Mark St. Germain; Director, Carolyn Rossi Copeland; Musical Director/Incidental Music, Steven M. Alper; Orchestrations, Douglas Besterman; Choreography, Ricarda O'Conner; Costumes, Hope Hanafin, Kathryn Wagner; Lighting, Heather Carson; General Manager, Nancy Nagel Gibbs; Production Manager, Clark Cameron; Stage Manager, Robin Anne Joseph; Press, Peter Cromarty/David Lotz, David Katz. CAST: Richard Blake (Willy), Sarah Knapp (City Her), Gordon Stanley (City Him), Paul Jackel (Jim Dillingham), Lyn Vaux (Della Dillingham), Ron Lee Savin (Soapy Smith)
MUSICAL NUMBERS: Star of the Night, Gifts of the Magi, Jim and Della, Christmas to Blame, How Much to Buy My Dream, The Restaurant, Once More, Bum Luck, Greed, Pockets, The Same Girl, Gift of Christmas, Finale
   A musical performed without intermission. The action takes place in NYC from December 23-25, 1905. Since 1984 a Christmas perennial at the Lamb's Theatre.

(Colony Theatre/Taylor Hall) Wednesday, December 5-22, 1990 (16 performances) The Colony Theatre presents:
A LIE OF THE MIND by Sam Shepard; Director, Timothy Kelleher; Sets, Jonathan T. Cook; Technical Director, Gregg Allen Holt; Stage Manager, David Burke; Press, Monika Mitchell. CAST: Michael Griffiths (Jake), R.A. White (Frankie), Leila Gastil (Beth), Barry Levy (Mike), Helen Jean Arthur (Lorraine), Monika Mitchell (Sally), Jonathan T. Cook (Baylor), Rose Marie Norton (Meg)
   A drama in three acts.

(Sanford Meisner Theatre) Wednesday, December 5–9, 1990 (8 performances) Swimmer Productions present:
3 PLAYS BY ROBERT SHAFFRON; Sets, Robert William Ryan; Costumes, Mary McFadden; Lighting, Kristabelle Munson; Press, Judy Jacksina/Robin Monchek. CAST: Richard Rodgers, John Steber, Clarke McCarthy, Timothy Boisvert, Laurie Sanders-Smith, Mr. Shaffron, Tim Ahern, Katherine Altkeener, Richard Nahem, Sam Brent Riegel, Karen Wimmer
Plastic; Director, David Zarko
   A play about people who love themselves.
The Survival of the Species; Director, Roger Dowdeswell
   A play about people who love the wrong people.
Rube's All-Night; Director, Rebecca Taylor
   A play about a person who loves someone she invented.

Robert Emmet, Rose Stockton, in "Dairies of Adam and Eve" (*Carol Rosegg*)

Eddie Korbich, Loni Ackerman, Ray Roderick, Michael Berkeley, Cyma Rubin, Dale Hensley, Marcy DeGonge, James Brennan, Dorothy Stanley in "I Love a Piano" (*Ken Katz*)

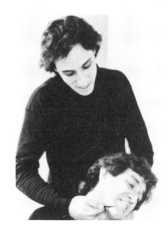

"C.E.O."

R.A.Waite, Helen Jean Arthur, Michael Griffiths, Monika Mitchell in "Lie of the Mind"

Rainn Wilson, Laurence Drozd, Stephanie Erb, Andrew Prosky in "Two Gentlemen of Verona" (*Irene Haupt*)

Diana LaMar, Mark Stewart Guin in "Romeo and Juliet" (*Irene Haupt*)

Kevin Greer, Jack Cirillo in "Voice of the Prairie" (*Gerry Goodstein*)

(RAPP Arts Center) Wednesday, December 5–30, 1990 (19 performances and 5 previews) Rapp Theatre Company (R. Jeffrey Cohen and Alexis S. Cohen, Artistic Directors) present:
THE SEAGULL: THE HAMPTONS: 1990; Adapted from Chekhov by R. Jeffrey Cohen; Director, Mr. Cohen; Sets, Alexis Siroc; Lighting, Jim Kellough; Costumes, Karen Perry; Music, Kevin Scott; Technical, Jim Kellough; Stage Manager, Rebecca Nestle; Press, Jeff Ranbom. CAST: Karen Millard (Masha), Sheridan Crist (Simon), Lucille Rivin (Paulina), John Bakos (Dr. Dorn), D.B. Sweeney (Constantine), Howard Wesson (Peter), Laura Linney (Nina), Carol Lynley (Irina), Michael Twaine (Ilya), George McGrath (Boris)
Performed in four acts. This adaptation takes place at Peter's beach house in the Hamptons. The time is now.

(29th St. Theatre) Thursday, December 6–23, 1990 (12 performances) Alexander E. Racolin and Annette Moskowitz present:
RIVERMAN by Sam Dowling; Director, Ken Lowstetter; Sets/Lighting, Randall Etheredge; Press, Howard and Barbara Atlee. CAST: Leonard Kelly-Young (Walter Greaves), Lynn McCollough (Tinnie), Eve Martinez (Elizabeth), Phil Miller (Joseph), Stephanie Silverman (Sarah), Cameron Sisk (Jennie), Russell Stevens (William Marchant), J. Kelley Salvadore (Augustus)
A play about the controversial life of British painter Walter Greaves.

(Judith Anderson Theatre) Friday, December 7–16, 1990 (8 performances) Victor Coopersmith, Beth Polish, and John Stovall present:
ROSETTA STREET by Ken Lipman; Director, Maggie da Silva; Sets, Tye Burris; Costumes, Christopher Del Coro; Lighting, Ken Posner; Press, Peter Cromarty/David B. Katz. CAST: Richard Panebianco, Holt McCallany, Victor Arnold, Ronald Bruce, Tony Gillan, Susannah Julien, Sam Rockwell, Bo Rucker
A drama dealing with a racial attack in a working-class neighborhood in Queens.

(Ensemble Studio Theatre) Friday, December 7–15, 1990 (12 performances) Ensemble Studio Theatre (Curt Dempster, Artistic Director; Dominick Balletta, Managing Director) presents:
GO TO GROUND by Stuart Spencer; Director, Matthew Penn; Sound, Andrew Bellware; Lighting, Greg MacPherson; Costumes, Lee Robin Kerkapoly; Sets, Sharon Sprague; Production Manager, David Waggett. CAST: James MacDonald (Oliver), Mary Kane (Caitlin/Celia), Salty Loeb (Joy/Mama Wojtusik), Baxter Harris (Ford/Gordon), Richard Joseph Paul (Tony/Cron), Emma Walton (Evelyn/Darly)
A drama set in New York City and Bailey, a small Eastern seaboard town, at the present time.

(Westbeth Theatre Center) Saturday, December 8–15, 1990 (10 performances) Edgar Lansbury, John Wulp, and The Shubert Organization present:
CLUB XII with Music/Lyrics by Rob Hanning, Randy Weiner and Sasha Lewis; Book, Mr. Hanning, Mr. Weiner; Director/Choreographer, Patricia Birch; Sets, Douglas Schmidt; Lighting, Jules Fisher; Costumes, Willa Kim; Press, Keith Sherman/Chris Day
A musical adaptation of Shakespeare's *Twelfth Night* set in a hot dance club.

(Triplex) Monday, December 10–15, 1990 (5 performances) The Acting Company (Margot Harley and John Houseman, Founders) presents:
TWO GENTLEMEN OF VERONA by William Shakespeare; Director, Charles Newell; Sets, Derek McLane; Costumes, Catherine Zuber; Lighting, Marcus Dilliard; Music, Kim D. Sherman; Stage Manager, George Darveris; Press, Fred Nathan/Ian Rand. CAST: Laurence Drozd (Valentine), William D. Michie (Proteus), Rainn Wilson (Speed), Diana LaMar (Julia), Trish Jenkins (Lucetta), Ethan T. Bowen (Antonio), Mark Kincaid (Panthino), Stephanie Erb (Silvia), Jeffrey Guyton (Launce), Maggie (Crab), Andrew Prosky (Thurio), John Michalski (Duke), David Eichman (Host), Matthew Edwards (Eglamour), Kathleen Mary Mulligan (Ursula), Dan Berkey, Ben Eric, Mark Stewart Guin (Outlaws)
A comedy in two acts. This adaptation takes place in the Old West.
in repertory with:
ROMEO AND JULIET by William Shakespeare; Director, Leon Rubin. CAST: Mark Stewart Guin (Romeo), Diana LaMar (Juliet), William D. Michie (Mercutio), Mark Kincaid (Tybalt), John Michalshi (Lord Capulet), Trish Jenkins (Nurse), Kathleen Mary Mulligan (Lady Capulet)

(Chelsea Stage) Wednesday, December 12–19, 1990 (3 performances and 5 previews) Chelsea Stage (Geoffrey Sherman, Artistic Director; Dara Hershman, Managing Director) presents:
THE VOICE OF THE PRAIRIE by John Olive; Director, John Daines; Sets, Randall Etheredge; Lighting, Philip Monat; Costumes, Kathryn Wagner; Sound, Richard Rose, Stuart Bernstein; Stage Manager, Randy Lawson; Press, Jeffrey Richards. CAST: Kevin Geer (Actor 1), Jack Cirillo (Actor 2), Wendy Barrie-Wilson (Actor 3)
The life of a storyteller in the early days of American radio. Unfortunately, financial difficulties forced Chelsea Stage, formerly the Hudson Guild, to suspend operations after the opening of this production.

Colin Fisher, Sean Nelson in "Gift of Winter" (*Susan Cook*)

"Landscape with Male Figures"

Marilyn Sokol in "Guilt Without Sex"

Monté Russell, Robert Jason in "Let Me Live"
(*Carol Rosegg*)

(Hartley House Theatre) Friday, December 14, 1990–January 18, 1991 (20 performances) On Stage Productions (Lee Frank, Artistic Director) presents:
STARMITES; Music/Lyrics by Barry Keating; Book, Stuart Ross, Mr. Keating; Director, Gabriel Barre; Musical Director, Wayne Blood; Choreography, Denise Webb; Sets, Josh Rothenberg; Lighting, Jason Sturm; Costumes, Marc Borders; Stage Manager, Bill Burke. CAST: Benjamin Bedenbaugh (Dazzle), Robert Belfry (Ack Ack), Ryan Bonn (Space Punk), Carol Cornicelli (Shotzi), Michele Foor (Mother/Diva), Jozie Hill (Balbraka), Randall E. Lake (Trinkulus), Allan Larkeed (Shak Graa), Susan Levine (Eleanor/Bizarbara), Hollis Lewis (Herbie), Sheryl McCallum (Maligna), Sue Lynn Yu (Cannibele)
MUSICAL NUMBERS: Prelude/Prologue, Superhero Girl, Starmites, Trink's Narration, Afraid of the Dark, Little Hero, Attack of the Banshees, The Cruelty, Hard to Be Diva, Love Duet, Dance of the Spousal Arousal, Finaletto, Bizarbara's Wedding, Milady, Beauty Within, Cruelty Stomp, Reach Right Down, Immolation, Starmites, Finale

(TADA) Friday, December 14–31 1990 (30 performances and 4 previews) TADA! presents:
THE GIFT OF WINTER; Music, David Evans; Lyrics, Faye Greenberg; Book, Michael Slade; Based on book by John Leach and Jean Rankin; Director, James Learned; Musical/Vocal Director, Jason Robert Brown; Sets, Wendy Ponte; Lighting, A.C. Hickox; Costumes, Martha Bromelmeier; Press, Chris Boneau/Bob Fennell. CAST: Colin Fisher, Sean Nelson and 22 other performers between the ages of 8 and16.
A musical offering a comic explanation of the history of snow.

(John Houseman Theatre) Saturday, December 15, 1990–January 1, 1991 (32 matinee performances) Arthur Cantor and Peter B. Baird present:
ALICE IN WONDERLAND; Music By Joe Raposo; Lyrics, Sheldon Harnick; Book, A.J. Russell; Director, Carl Harms; Sets, Howard Mandel; Conceived and Designed by Bil Baird; Production Supervision, Peter B. Baird; Stage Manager, John Pavlik. CAST: Bil Baird's Marionettes: Peter B. Baird, Pady Blackwood, Randy Carfagno, Helen Elizabeth, William Tost, Susan Wall; Singing Voices: Mary Case, George S. Irving, Sheldon Harnick, Rose Marie Jun, Ivy Austin, Margery Gray, William Tost, Bil Baird
A holiday revival of the puppet theatre.

(John Houseman Theatre) Sunday, December 16, 1990–January 1, 1991 The Shoestring Players present:
THE PEOPLE WHO COULD FLY; Conceived and Directed by Joe Hart; Press, David Rothenberg. CAST: Keith Adams, Nunzio Caccamo, Michael Calderone, Andrew Mapp, Sheila McDevitt, Victoria Noone, James O'Neill, Ev Phillip, Kristina Wright
A holiday revival of an evening of tales from around the world.

(Courtyard Playhouse/Glines) Thursday, December 27, 1990–January 20, 1991 (23 performances) re-opened in Wings Theatre Friday, January. 25–March 31, 1991 (50 performances) The Wings Theatre Company presents:
LANDSCAPE WITH MALE FIGURES by John Crabtree; Director, John Wall; Sets/Costumes, Leon Munier; Lighting, David Jensen. CAST: Martin Outzen (Sam/Harry), Rob Parker (Harry), Jimmy O'Neal, Edmond Ramage (Cupid), Michael McKinney (Sam)
A farce about the pursuit of happiness though sexual fantasies.

(Theatre Arielle) Thursday, January 3– still playing May 31, 1991. Eric Krebs presents:
GUILT WITHOUT SEX; Musical Director, Bob Goldstone; Lighting, Jonathan Shulman; Production Manager, Ed Morrill; Wardrobe, Brenda Rousseau; Consultant, Sue Lawless; Based on book by Marilyn Sokol and Ken Friedman; Press, David Rothenberg. CAST: Marilyn Sokol
A musical exposé in two parts.

(Harold Clurman Theatre) Friday, January 4, 1991–March 3, 1991 (52 performances and 4 previews) The Working Theatre presents:
LET ME LIVE by OyamO; Director, Bill Mitchelson; Music, Olu Dara; Fights, David S. Leong; Lighting, Don Holder; Sets,/Costumes, Anne C. Patterson; Sound, Serge Ossurguine; Stage Manager, James Marr; Press, Bruce Cohen. CAST: Randy Frazier (Kennedy), LeLand Gantt (Dupree), Earl Hagen (Allen), Rande Harris (Bracey), Lawrence James (Jenkins), Robert Jason (Shonuff), Mitchell Marchand (Smiley), Jasper McGruder (Davis/Jenkins), Eugene Nesmith (Clancy), Monte Russell (Angelo)
A drama in two acts. The story of Angelo V. Herndon, who was threatened with Georgia's death penalty in 1932. The action takes place in Fulton Tower Prison in Atlanta.

Marlene Goudreau, Joel Aroeste in "Narnia"
(Tim Rabb)

Laurence Luckinbill in "Lyndon"

(Haft Theatre) Monday, January 7–20, 1991 (14 performances and 1 preview) New York State Theatre Institute presents:
NARNIA; Music, Thomas Tierney; Lyrics, Ted Drachman; Book, Jules Tasca; Based on the book *The Lion, the Witch, and the Wardrobe* by C.S. Lewis; Director, Shela Xoregos; Musical Director, Gene Abrams; Orchestrations, Alasdair Mac-Neill; Sets, Stuart Wurtzel; Costumes, Patrizia von Brandenstein; Lighting, John McLain; Sound, Matt Elie; Musical Supervisor, Betsy Riley-Normile; Choreography, Raymond C. Harris; Stage Manager, Robin Horowitz; Press, Chris Boneau/Eva Patton, Bob Fennell. CAST: Joel Aroeste (Digory Kirke/Mr. Beaver), Richard Barrows (Tumnus/Panther), Daniel J. Breault (Zebra), David Bunce (Creature), Etta Caren Fink (Jadis/White Witch), Sherry Goodling (Ostrich/Pirate Witch), Marlene Goudreau (Mrs. Beaver), Shana Lynn Harris (Fox), Debra Joy (Susan Pevensie), Joseph Larrabee-Quandt (Ferris Ulf), Christian Line (Edmund Pevensie), John Thomas McGuire III (Father Christmas/Wolf-that-dies/Spectre Witch), Christina Patrick (Leopard/Ghoul), James H. Patrick (Peter Pevensie), Quency René (Mrs. Macready/She-Wolf), John Romeo (Aslan), Elizabeth Neumann Waterhouse (Lucy Pevensie), Michael John Ziccardi (Glimfeather/Eagle/Mastiff)
MUSICAL NUMBERS: Doors and Windows, Turkish Delight, Narnia, All of These, Hot and Bothered, At Last It's Christmas, Wot a Bit a' Spring Can Do, Cair Paravel, Murder Today, From the Inside Out, Deep Magic, A Field of Flowers, Catch Me if You Can, To Make the World Right Again, The Days Danced By, Finale
    A musical adaptation of the classic story in two acts. The action takes place in England in the early 1940s . . . and Narnia.

(Charles Ludlam Theatre) Tuesday, January 8–February 28, 1991 (16 performances and 8 previews) The Ridiculous Theatre Company (Everett Quinton, Artistic Director; Steve Asher, Managing Director) presents:
WHEN LIGHTNING STRIKES TWICE; Two one-act plays by H.M. Koutoukas; Director, Eureka; Sets, Tom Moore; Costumes, Daniel Boike; Lighting, Richard Currie; Props, Vicky Rabb; Jewelry, Wendy Gell; Music/Sound, Mark Bennett; Stage Manager, James Eckerle; Press, Judy Jacksina/Mary Lugo
Awful People Are Coming Over So We Must Pretend To Be Hard At Work And Hope They Will Go Away CAST: Everett Quinton (Clickety Clack), Eureka (Mrs. Trompe L'Oeil Clack)
    The action takes place on Jefferson Avenue, Endicott, New York, during the Roosevelt epoch.
Only A Countess May Dance When She's Crazy CAST: Mr. Quinton (Countess Olie Samovitch)
    The action takes place in the Tower.

(John Houseman Theatre) Thursday, January 10, 1991– Eric Krebs in association with Don Buford presents:
LYNDON by James Prideaux; Based on the book *Lyndon: An Oral Biography* by Merle Miller; Director, Richard Zavaglia; Makeup, Kevin Haney; Company Manager, Gail Bell; Production Manager, Jonathan Schulman; Press, David Rothenberg. CAST: Laurence Luckinbill (Lyndon Johnson)
    A monodrama performed without intermission. The action takes place in the White House Oval Office in 1968.

(UBU Repertory Theatre) Friday, January 11–27, 1991 (16 performances) Liberty Stage Company (Ronald Bly, Producing Director; Laurence Gewirtz, Artistic Director) presents:
THE BEAUTY PART by S.J. Perelman; Directors, Laurence Gewirtz and Ronald Bly; Choreography, Carole Schweid; Sets, R.J. Bila; Lighting, Michael David Winter; Costumes, Shelly Saltzman; Stage Manager, Michael David Winter. CAST: Georgia Boughton, Ian Cohen, Theresa Cornish, Cheri Couture, Peter Gatto, Diedre Manganaro, Vicki Meisner, Hank Neimark, Gerry Paone, Raymond Quinn, Carole Schweid
    A comedy in two acts. The action takes place in New York City and California.

(Ohio Theatre) Saturday, January 12–16, 1991 (14 performances and 2 previews) T.W.E.E.D. presents:
THE HISTORY OF PORNOGRAPHY; Conceived, Written and Directed by Kevin Malony; Music/Lyrics, Carol Lipnik; Choreography, John O'Malley; Video, Matthew Caldwell; Film, David Flanigan; Projections, Tina West, Nancy Hyland; Costumes, Kay Grunder; Sets, Jane Sablow; Sound, Tim Noble; Lighting, Beau Kennedy; Stage Manager, Craig Victor; Press, Chris Boneau/Bob Fennell. CAST: Bobbi Berger, Lisa Caraballo, Damion DaCosta, Peggy Gould, Nathan Hinkle, Jerry Kernion, Carol Lipnik, Kevin Malony, Randy Miles, Colleen O'Neill, Carlos Osorio, Sharon Port, Judy Reyes, Terry Robison, Helayne Schiff, Stephen Pell, Todd Whiteley
    A multimedia performance work.

(Wings Theatre) Tuesday, January 15–February 28, 1991 (21 performances) Wings Theatre Company presents:
WIRING ELECTRA by William Lannon; Director, Michael Hillyer; Choreography, Schellie Archbold; Lighting, Jeanne G. Koenig; Fights, Simon Brooking; Costumes, Vicki R. Davis CAST: Joseph Hillyer (Link), Peter Cohn (Trevor), Kay Bourbeil (Duchess of Malfi)
    Two related one-acts about the theatre.

Ian Cohen, Peter Gatto, Deirdre Manganaro, Georgia Boughton, Vicki Meisner in "Beauty Part" *(Joseph Bly)*

Lisa Carballo, Jerry Kernion in "History of Pornography"
(Carol Rosegg)

Donald Grody, Wesley Stevens in "Measure for Measure"
(*Martha Swope*)

Patricia R. Floyd in "A Woman Called Truth"
(*Scott Humbert*)

(Westbeth Theatre Center) Thursday, January 17–February 3, 1991 (11 performances and 1 preview) Westbeth Theatre (Arnold Engelman, Producing Director) presents:
UNDYING LOVE (L'AMOR, TOUJOURS, LA MORT) by Charles Horine; Director, George Elmer; Set, Bob Phillips; Lighting, Nancy Collings; Costumes, Connie Singer; Sound, Richard Dunning; Press, Peter Cromarty/David Lotz. CAST: George Wolf Reily, Nicola Sheara
   A comedy about two divorcées searching for the perfect relationship.

(Westbeth Theatre Center) Thursday, January 17–February 3, 1991 (24 performances and 2 previews) Shakespeare Stage Company, Ltd. presents:
MEASURE FOR MEASURE by William Shakespeare; Director, Edward Griffith; Costumes, Julie Doyle; Sets/Lighting, Donald A. Gingrasso; Musical Director, Glenn Braun; Press, David Rothenberg. CAST: Clifton Bolton (Froth/Second Gentleman), Dina Corsetti (Francisca/Julietta), William Felix (Friar/Abhorson), Brendan Ford (Claudio), Lisa Griffith (Isabella), J. Bryan McMillen (First Gentleman/Barnardine), Christopher Knott (Provost), Donald Grody (Escalus), Thom Haneline (Pompey), Tom Dale Keever (Provost), Lewis Musser (Elbow), T. Ryder Smith (Lucio), Wesley Stevens (Vincentio), Keith Suranna (Attendant/Servant), Debra Whitfield (Mariana/Mistress Overdone), Craig Wroe (Angelo)
   Performed with one intermission. The action takes place in Vienna and environs.

(Primary Stages) Friday, January 18–February 16, 1991 (20 performances and 3 previews) Primary Stages Inc. (Casey Childs, Artistic Director; Janet Reed, Associate Director) presents:
BETTER DAYS by Richard Dresser; Director, John Pynchon Holms; Sets, Ray Recht; Lighting, Steve Shelly; Costumes, Amanda J. Klein; Sound, Tom Gould; Production Manager, Jerry Goshring; Stage Manager, Randy Lawson; Press, Anne Einhorn. CAST: Daniel Ahearn (Ray), Kevin McClarnon (Arnie), Susan Greenhill (Faye), James Gleason (Phil), Ann Talman (Crystal), Larry Pine (Bill)
   A comedy in two acts. The action takes place in a dying mill town in New England at the present time.

(Open Eye Theatre) Saturday, January 19–February 17, 1991 (10 performances) Open Eye New Stagings (Amie Brockway, Artistic Director) presents:
A WOMAN CALLED TRUTH by Sandra Fenichel Asher; Director, Ernest-Johns; Musical Director, Charles S. Brown; Choreographer, Jamale Graves; Designer, Adrienne J. Brockway; Stage Manager, Nancy Caterino; Press, Shirley Herz/Sam Rudy. CAST: Patricia R. Floyd (Sojourner Truth), Kim Bey (First Woman/ Mama/Sissy/Old Woman), Jen Wolfe (Second Woman/Mrs. Neely/Maria/Mrs. Whiting), Garrett Walters (First Man/Baumfrey/Neely/Caitlin/Issac/Chip/Old Man/First. Rev.), Ricky Genaro (Second Man/Auctioneer/Dumont/Gedney/Officer/Second Rev.), Doug Jewell (Third Man/Peter/Bob/Pete/Slave Boy)
   A play with a musical score of American slave songs. The action takes place in Ulster County New York, New York City, and Ohio in the first half of the 1800s.

(Glines/CourtyardPlayhouse) Wednesday, January 23–March 3, 1991 (36 performances) The Glines presents:
CHICKEN DELIGHT by John Glines; Based on *C'est Une Femme De Monde* by Georges Feydeau and Maurice Desvallières; Director, Charles Catanese; Sets/Lighting, David Jensen; Costumes, Gene Lauze; Stage Manager, Courtney Flanagan. CAST: Bill Graber (Jesus), David Gordon (Harry), J. Clay Lawson (Splash), David Boldt (Brock), Mark Irish (Neal), John Carhart III (Randy)
   A comedy in two acts. The action takes place in New York City during summer.

(Victory Theatre) Friday, January 25, 1991– (40 performances and 7 previews) Theatre For a New Audience (Jeffrey Horowitz, Artistic/Producing Director) presents:
ROMEO AND JULIET by William Shakespeare; Director, Bill Alexander; Sets/Costumes, Fotini Dimou; Lighting, Frances Aronson; Fights, David S. Leong; Choreography, Dona Lee Kelly; Voice/Text Consultant, Robert Neff Williams; Music, Matthias Gohl; Stage Manager, Allison Sommers; Press, Shirley Herz/Miller Wright. CAST: Irwin Appel (Peter), Renée Bucciarelli (Lucia), Omar Carter (Benvolio), Jamie Cheatham (Abraham), David Deblinger (Gregory), Mark Dold (Tybalt), Drew Ebersole (Balthasar), Lynnda Ferguson (Lady Capulet), Richard Ferrone (Montague), Ken Forman (Sampson), Miriam Healy-Louie (Juliet), Max Jacobs (Capulet), Patrick (Friar Laurence), Daniel Dae Kim (Paris), John Lathen (Escalus), Paul Lima (Giorgio/Friar John), Jacie Loren (Margherita), Mark Niebuhr (Romeo), Peggy Pope (Nurse), Mary Ed Porter (Lady Montague/Helena/Apothecary), Timothy D. Stickney (Mercutio)
   Performed with one intermission. The action takes place in Verona, Italy, during mid-July of 1492.

James Gleason, Daniel Ahearn, Kevin McClarnon in "Better Days"
(*William Gibson*)

Mark Niebuhr, Miriam Healy-Louie in "Romeo and Juliet" (*Carol Rosegg*)

(Judith Anderson Theatre) Saturday, January 26–March 10, 1991 (48 performances) Manhattan Punch Line (Steve Kaplan, Artistic Director) presents:
7TH ANNUAL FESTIVAL OF ONE ACT COMEDIES; Artistic Associate, Jonathan Mintz; Sets, Vaughn Patterson; Lighting, Pat Dignan; Costumes, Sharon Lynch (A), Kitty Leech (B); Sound, Aural Fixation; Stage Managers, David Waggett (A), Cathy Tomlin (B); Press, Shirley Herz/Miller Wright
EVENING A: *Variations on the Death of Trotsky* by David Ives; Director, Jason McConnell Buzas. CAST: Daniel Hagen (Trotsky), Alison Martin (Mrs. Trotsky), Steven Rodriguez (Ramon)

The action takes place in Coyoacan.
Gorgo's Mother by Laurence Klavan; Director, Steve Kaplan. CAST: Cheryl Hulteen (Joanne), Ben Seigler (Kenny), Elaine Rinehart (Terry), Michael Aschner (Brian)

The action takes place in the park at lunchtime, at present.
Gangster Apparel by Richard Vetere; Director, Matthew Penn. CAST: Mark Lotito (Louie Falco), Richard Raynor (Joey Pugg)

The action takes place in a dingy motel room in Sunnyside, Queens, at present.
Stay Carl Stay by Peter Tolan; Director, Charles Karchmer. CAST: Christine Toy (Caroline), Chris Lutkin (Brian), Ronnie Farer (Mary Sue), Kathrin King Segal (Dr. Weiss), Daniel Hagen (Carl), David Goldman (Bingo)
The action takes place in New York at present.
EVENING B: *The Experts* by Bill Bozzone; Director, Chris Ashley. CAST: Mark Tymchyshyn (Jerry), Dan Moran (Mitch), Jay Devlin (Harold)

The action takes place in a city alley, at present.
The Staged Reading by Michael Panes; Director, David Konig. CAST: Peter Basch (Laurence C. Beagleman), Scott Klavan (Peter Yarbrow), Esther Brandice (Edna Yarbrow), Ken Martin (Tommy), Elaine Rinehart (Kathy), Brian Howe (Brian Howe)

The place is here, right now.

(Billie Holiday Theatre) Wednesday, January 30–February 24 and March 7–31, 1991 (54 performances and 12 previews) Marjorie Moon in association with Mountaintop Productions present:
CAMP LOGAN by Celeste Bedford Walker; Director, A. Yujuan Carrière-Anderson; Technical Director, Eoghan Ryan; Stage Manager, Avan. CAST: Chaz McCormack (Captain Zuelke), Kelly Lamarr (Franciscus), Darrell Hughes (Bugaloosa), Le Verne Summers (Moses), Kevin Richardson (Hardin), Alvin Walker (Gweely), Zaria Griffin (Sergeant McKinney)

A drama in two acts involving a violent racial incident outside Houston, Texas in 1917.

(Triangle/Holy Trinity) Thursday, January 31–March 3, 1991 (24 performances) The Triangle Theatre Company presents:
UNCHANGING LOVE by Romulus Linney; From *In the Hollow* by Anton Chekov; Director, John Dillon; Music Direction/Movement, Edward Morgan; Lighting, Nancy Collings; Set, Steven Perry; Costumes, Amanda J. Klein; Stage Manager, Jerry Grant; Press, Jim Baldassare. CAST: Gordon G. Jones (Elmer Musgrove), Elisabeth Lewis Corley (Annie Musgrove), Jennifer Parsons (Judy Musgrove), Tom McDermott (Benjamin Pitman), Jacqueline Knapp (Barbara Pitman), Mark Doerr (Avery Pitman), T. Cat Ford (Leena Pitman), Scott Sowers (Shelby Pitman), Fred Burrell (Crutch Holston), Cap Pryor (Oats Pyatt)

A drama in two acts. The action takes place in Maynard, North Carolina, a small mill town in the Appalachian foothills, in 1921.

Jay Brian Winnick, Terrence O'Brien, Steve Sterner, David Babbit, Trudi Posey in "Let it Ride!"

Alison Martin, Tony Carlin, Laura Dean, Robert Stanton in "7th Annual Manhattan Punch Line Festival" (*Carol Rosegg*)

Alvin Walker, LeVerne Summers in "Camp Logan" (*Jessica Katz*)

(All Souls Players) Thursday, January 31- February 17, 1991 (15 performances) All Souls Players presents:
LET IT RIDE; Music and Lyrics, Jay Livingston and Ray Evans; Libretto, Abram S. Ginnes; Based on the play *Three Men on a Horse* by John Cecil Holm and George Abbott; Director/Choreographer, Jeffrey K. Neill; Musical Direction/Arrangements, Joyce Hitchcock; Sets, Barry Girsh; Costumes, Catherine Harber; Lighting, Tim Callery; Stage Manager, Scott Will; Producers, Marie & Walter Landa, Harry Blum. CAST: David Babbitt (Erwin Trowbridge), Dan Entriken (Chief/Ralph), Robin Fernandez (Daisy/Lisa), John Golterman (Fenster/Gigolo George/Witherspoon/John Charles), Susan Hale (Girl on bus/Violet/Sadie/Alice), Teressa Hoover (Iris/Marlene), Hugh Hysell (Jack Carver), Casey Jones (Girl/Mimi/Hazel/Roz), Jerry Koenig (Nice Nose Brophy), Robert Laconi (Herbert/Hennes/Spanish Spam/Patrolman Fiori), John Lindsay (Man/Oscar/Hot Horse Herbie/Davis/McDonald), Terrence O'Brien (Charlie), Trudi Posey (Mabel), Steve Sterner (Patsy Pomeroy), Larry Stotz (Krokover/Jack O'Hearts/Cagney), William Walters (Harry the Bartender), Jay Brian Winnick (Frankie), Wendy Worth (Audrey), Bob Zanfini (Repulski)
MUSICAL NUMBERS: Run Run Run, Nicest Thing, Sweet Man, Through Children's Eyes, Best Undressed Girl in Town, Let It Ride, I'll Learn Ya, Love Let Me Know, Happy Birthday/I Wouldn't Have Had To, Everything Beautiful, It Just Didn't Happen That Way, My Own Little Island, He Needs You, Just an Honest Mistake, If Flutterby Wins, Finale

A revised version of the 1961 musical in two acts.

(Cooper Square Theatre) Thursday, January 31–February 17, 1991 (13 performances) Cow Minnie Productions in association with Cooper Square Theatre presents:
LOCKED UP by James Dean Jay Bird; Director, Lynne Mold; Sets, Evan Shapiro; Lighting, David J. Weiner; Stage Manager, Mark Duncan; Press, Howard and Barbara Atlee. *Cigarette Break* CAST: Sarah Kalidonis (Zivia), Jack Hazan (Jack) *Lucky Strike* CAST: Michael Rains (Lucky), Jon Michael Johnson (Brother Mann) *These Shoes* CAST: Jon Michael Johnson (Dad), Catherine Cullen (Daughter) *French Toast* CAST: Jack Hazan (Waiter), Michael Rains (Boy), Scott Davidson (Man)

Four short dark comedies presented with one intermission.

(Provincetown Playhouse) Friday, February 1–March 3, 1991 (24 performances and 12 previews) Cheryl L. Fluehr and Starbuck Productions, Ltd. present:

AN UNFINISHED SONG; Music/Lyrics/Book, James J. Mellon; Director, Simon Levy; Musical Director, Mark Mitchell; Musical Supervision/Arrangements, Lawrence Yurman; Sets, Scott Bradley; Costumes, Jeffrey Ullman; Lighting, Robert M. Wierzel; Sound, Raymond D. Schilke; General Manager, Marshall B. Purdy; Stage Manager, Karen Moore; Press, Chris Boneau/Joe D'Ambrosia, Bob Fennell. CAST: Aloysius Gigl (Worth), Joanna Glushak (Debbie), Robert Lambert (Brad), Ken Land (Mort), Beth Leavel (Beth)
MUSICAL NUMBERS: Things We've Collected, Balance the Plate, Crossing Boundaries, The Frying Pan, Being Left Out, As I Say Goodbye, Hobby Horses/How Could I Let You Leave Me, New Hampshire Nights, Blonde Haired Babies, Is That Love, An Unfinished Song, We Were Here
 A musical drama in two acts. The action takes place in New York City, California, and New Hampshire. The time is the present.

(Village Theatre) Wednesday, February 6–March 3, 1991 (17 performances) Village Theatre Company presents:

WHAT WOULD ESTHER WILLIAMS DO IN A SITUATION LIKE THIS?; Music/Lyrics, Jimmy Flynn; Book, Rich Werbacher and Don Werbacher; Director, Steven Yuhasz; Musical Director, Mark McLaren; Sets, Bryan Johnson; Costumes, Kate Sherman; Stage Manager, Jennifer Freed. CAST: Michael Curran, Susan Farwell, Jim Fleming, Stephen Geason, Julia McLaughlin, Keith Michl, Terrence Martin, Howard Thoresen
 A musical about three generations of a wacky Staten Island family.

(Dimson Theatre) Thursday, February 7–March 10, 1991 (31 performances) preceded by special preview performances (Samuel Beckett Theatre) Wednesday, September 19–23, 1990 (6 previews) AMAS Musical Theatre presents:

JUBA; Music, Russell Walden; Lyrics/Book, Wendy Lamb; Director, Sheldon Epps; Choreography, Mercedes Ellington; Musical Director, Ted Kociolek; Lighting, Susan White; Sets, James Leonard Joy; Costumes, Daniel Lawson; Production Manager, Christophe Pierre; Stage Manager, Bruce Greenwood; Press, Peter Cromarty/David B. Katz. CAST: James Brennan (Diamond), Katherine Buffaloe (Polly), Lawrence Clayton (Hayden), Ken Prymus (Uncle Jim), Terri White (Bella), Mark Hardy (Fogarty), Kevin Ramsey (Juba), Steve Boles (Spruce), Mark Aldrich, Evan Bell, Mark Dovey, Raymond Harris, Trent Kendall, Donna Ingram-Young, Erich Macmillan McCall, Dore Manasevit, Allison Mulrain, William Selby, Frank Walker, Lawson Walker
MUSICAL NUMBERS: Prologue, Juba, Every Step You Take, The Gift, Irish Air, No Irish Need Apply, Today Is the Day, Kick Up Your Heels, It Wouldn't Be Fair, A Long Way, Here and Now, Next Time We Meet, Listen to Me, The Eighth Wonder, Challenge Match, My Blue-Eyed Gal, Heartless, Five Points, This Isn't What I Expected, Take Heart, My Yellow Sun, He's Our Man, You Do, One Chance, Rivals, Finale
 A musical in two acts based on the life of street dancer William Henry Lane. The action takes place in New York City and Philadelphia in 1844.

Ken Land, Aloysius Gigl in "An Unfinished Song" Top Right: Joanna Glushak, Robert Lambert, Gigl, Beth Leavel (*Carol Rosegg*)

Kevin Ramsey, James Brennan in "Juba" (*Carol Rosegg*)

Angela Bullock, Margit Ahlin,
Bob Knapp, Tom Treadwell
(front) in "The Elephant Piece"
(*Jonathan Slaff*)

(Play Ground Theatre) Thursday, February 7–24, 1991 (12 performances) The Third Step Theatre Company presents:

THE ELEPHANT PIECE; Music/Lyrics/Book, Darryl Curry; Dirrector, Al D'Andrea; Sets, Watoku Ueno; Lighting, Eric Cornwell; Costumes, Natalie Barth Walker; Producer, Beate Hein Bennett; Stage Manager, Paul A. Kochman. CAST: Jay Kiman (Paul), Margit Ahlin (Iris), Angela Bullock (Chafey), Jackie Mari Roberts (Bonita), Tom Treadwell (Bones), Bob Knapp (Butch), Denise M. Kennedy (Pernicia), O.V. Vargas (Pug), George Croom (Buzz), Judy Premus (Fawn), Lee Winston (Pachy Derman), Michael J. Starita (Darlene)
MUSICAL NUMBERS: Lullaby, Akatu Akate, We Hack, You'll See, Alchemist Song, Baby, Families Continue, Gimme, I'm Smellin' Just Like a Rose, Whaddaya Want, Anthem, Finale
 A musical fable performed without intermission. The action is here, the time is now.

(Triplex) Saturday, February 9–March 3, 1991 (14 performances and 3 previews) Under One Roof in association with the Triplex presents:

THE MERMAID WAKES; Based on the book by Lora Berg, Margaret Deutsch and Canute Caliste; Music, Judy Bennett, Barington Antonio Burke-Green, Natalie Carter, Percy Pitzu, Silindile Sokutu, Elizabeth Swados; Dramaturge, Dianne Houston; Additional Material, Lora Berg; Director, Ms. Swados; Choreography, Mr. Burke-Green, Leslie Boyce, Thuli Dumakude, Dennison George, Ms. Sokutu; Sets, Beau Kennedy, Jane Sablow; Lighting, Brian Aldous, Adam Macks; Costumes, Mary Myers; Masks, Mr. Kennedy; Stage Manager, J. Tori Evans; Press, Ted Killmer/Tray Batres. CAST: Judy Bennett, Barrington Antonio Burke-Green, Leslie Arlette Boyce, Natalie Carter, Jerriese Daniel Johnson, Jesse Moore, Percy Pitzu, Silindile Sokutu, Felicia Wilson
 A musical performed without intermission. The action takes place in the Caribbean.

(One Dream Theatre) Thursday, February 14–March 4, 1991 (16 performances) Chris Van Groningen in association with One Dream Productions presents:

BEFORE WE DIE; Director, Chris Van Groningen; Sets, Robert John Andrusko; Lighting, Kristabelle Munson; Costumes, Nina Canter; Sound, David Christenberry; Stage Manager, Heather Roberts. *Everybody's Got It* by Armand Ruhlman; CAST: Cliff Weissman, Renee Sicignano. *Grandma's Play* by Mr. Van Groningen; CAST: Jen Jones, Jeff Bender
 Two one-act plays.

(Westbeth Theatre) Thursday, February 14–March 3, 1991 (16 performances) The Colossal Theatre Company presents:
THE MISANTHROPE by Molière; Translation, Rod McLucas; Director, Mr. McLucas; Sets, John Farrell; Lighting, Otis Howard; Press, Peter Cromarty/David B. Katz. CAST: Kevin Black, Julia Dean, Michele Maher, Katie MacNichol, Peter McCabe, Max Miller
   A new verse translation of the classic comedy.

(29th St. Playhouse) Thursday, February 14- March 2, 1991 (12 performances) The 29th Street Repertory Theatre (Tim Corcoran, Artistic director; Mallory Morris, Managing Director) in association with Annette Moskowitz and Alexander E. Racolin present:
KILLERS by John Olive; Director, Bern Gautier; Sets, Murphy Gigliotti; Costumes, Geff Rhian; Lighting, Stewart Wagner; Fights, Ron Piretti; Props, Anne Capron; Stage Manager, Amanda Junquera. CAST: Leo Farley, Linda Larson, David Mogentale, Kent Heacock, William Preston

(Theatre Ten Ten) Friday, February 15–March 9, 1991 (12 performances and 1 preview) Ten Ten Players (N. Thomas Pedersen, Artistic Director) presents:
WHAT THE BUTLER SAW by Joe Orton; Director, Steven Jakuboski; Costumes, Rick Guier; Sets, Alex Hutton; Lighting, David Castaneda; Stage Managers, David Alan Comstock, Jessica Murrow; Press, Audrey Ross. CAST: Joanna Daniels (Geraldine Barclay), David Beckett (Dr. Prentice), Gwendolyn Lewis ((Mrs. Prentice), Craig Archibald (Nicholas Beckett), Ryan Hilliard (Dr. Rance), George Millenbach (Sergeant Match)
   A comedy in two acts. The action takes place in a private mental clinic in the 1960s.

(Intar Theatre Two) Wednesday, February 20–March 24, 1991 (20 performances and 4 previews) Intar Hispanic American Arts Center (Max Ferra, Artistic Director) presents:
BLUE HEAT; Written, Directed and Designed by John Jesurun; Lighting, Jeffrey Nash; Production Manager, Dayton Taylor; Choreography, Richard Eric Winberg; Press, Peter Cromarty/David Lotz. CAST: Oscar de la Fe Colon, Divina Cook, Larry Tighe, Michael Tighe, Eileen Vega, Sanghi Wagner
   A multimedia piece blending theatre, video, and music.

(Rear) Michael Tighe, Sanghi Wagner, Larry Tighe, (Front) Oscar de la Fe Colon, Eileen Vega in "Blue Heat" (*Carol Rosegg*)

O.L. Duke, Ed Wheeler, Douglas Turner Ward, Helmar Augustus Cooper, Kevin Smith, Charles Weldon in "Little Tommy Parker..." (*Bert Andrews*)

Eileen Atkins in "A Room of One's Own"

(St. Peter's/Universalist Church) Wednesday, February 27–March 16, 1991 (9 performances and 3 previews) En Garde Arts presents:
OCCASIONAL GRACE by Michael Ahn, Neena Beber, Migdalia Cruz and Talvin Wilks; Music Composition/Direction, Amina Claudine Myers; Director, Bill Rauch; Producer, Anne Hamburger; Costumes, Claudia Brown; Lighting, Brian Aldous; Sound, Eric Liljestrand; Choreography, Sabrina Peck; Production Manager, Adam Kushner; Stage Manager, Paul J. Smith; Press, Ted Kilmer/Tray Batres. CAST: Christopher Adams (Demon), J. Ed Araiza (Tito), Kana Aoki (Rose), Sonnie Brown (Alice), Reg E. Cathey (P.C.), Engle Cheung (Engle Cheung), John Cheung (Gang Member), Sara Erde (Live Doris), Sea Glassman (Ruthie), Ruthanna Graves (Dead Doris), Helen Greenberg (Naomi), Brian Hertera (Demon), Andrew Ing-Kavet (June), Joel Leffert (Elijah), Carol Jean Lewis (Fannie Mae Reilly), Phillip Lin (Gang Member), Nela Wagman (Ann Harris), Peter Yoshida (Henry), and CHORUS: Adam Dyer, Robert James Gardner, Greg Jackson, Lori Leshner, Jory Levine, Hollis Lewis, Cathy Markoff, Johnny Martinez, Adelaide Mestre, Joy Lynn Pak, Drue Pennella, Tami Tyree, Cherise Villafana
MUSICAL NUMBERS: Angels, Safe, Dorises Song, Oh My God, Sinner, All Heard Your Cry, It Don't Mean Nothing, If I Walk Down the Aisle, Jesus Was a Working Man, Being Alive, I'm in Love With an Angel, Nothing But the Grace, Beautiful, Am I Wrong to Believe, House of Doris, Get Right Church, Finale
   A play with music in two acts. A site-specific event performed in churches.

(Master Theatre) Thursday, February 28–March 31, 1991 (38 performances) The Negro Ensemble Company (Douglas Turner Ward, Artistic Director/President; Susan Watson Turner, General Manager) presents:
THE LITTLE TOMMY PARKER CELEBRATED COLORED MINSTREL SHOW by Carlyle Brown; Director, Douglas Turner Ward; Sets, Michael Green; Costumes, Gregory Glenn; Lighting, William H. Grant III; Sound, Selina Dixon; Stage Manager, Pemi; Press, Howard and Barbara Atlee. CAST: Douglas Turner Ward (Henry), Helmar Augustus Cooper (Doc), O.L. Duke (Tambo), Ed Wheeler (Soloman), Kevin Smith (Archie), Charles Weldon (Percy)
   A drama in two acts depicting the lives of black performers at the turn of the century.

(Lamb's Theatre) Thursday, February 28–June 9, 1991 (98 performances) Arthur Cantor presents:
A ROOM OF ONE'S OWN from the book by Virginia Woolf; Adaptation/Direction, Patrick Garland; Set, Bruce Goodrich; Lighting, Lloyd Sobel; Production Manager, Mitchell Erickson; Company Manager, Laura Heller; Associate Producer, Alexander Racolin; Press, Mr. Cantor/Laura Heller. CAST: Eileen Atkins (Virginia Woolf)
   A monodrama recreating two historic lectures.

(Kaufman Theatre) Tuesday, March 5-23, 1991 (16 performances) The Quaigh Theatre presents:
MR. DOOM by Ward Morehouse III; Directors, Will Lieberson, Gerard J. Gentleman; Production Supervisor, Jean Dalrymple; Lighting, John Wooding; Costumes, Renee Davenport; Music, Bill Zeffiro; Stage Manager, Mr. Gentleman; Press, Philip Leshin. CAST: Steve Shoup (W.J. Allenhawk), Tom Lytel (Captain John "Jupp" Smith), Peter Gregory Thomson (Alonzo Dumas/Mr. Doom), Jennifer Ann Kelly (Billie Jo), Martha Whitehead (Opal Adderly), Lynne Wilson (Elvena Lubinoff), Paul Campana (C.A.B. Branch)
   A romantic comedy. The action takes place in a post office in Fancy Gap, Georgia in 1928.

(Westside Theatre) Tuesday, March 5, 1991 and still playing May 31, 1991. R. Tyler Gatchell, Jr., Peter Neufeld, Patrick J. Patek, Gene R. Korf in association with The McCarter Theatre present:
AND THE WORLD GOES 'ROUND: *The Songs of Kander & Ebb*; Music, John Kander; Lyrics, Fred Ebb; Conception, Scott Ellis, Susan Stroman, David Thompson; Director, Mr. Ellis; Choreography, Ms. Stroman; Sets, Bill Hoffman; Costumes, Lindsay W. Davis; Lighting, Phil Monat; Sound, Gary Stocker; Musical Direction/Vocal and Dance Arrangements, David Loud; Orchestrations, David Krane; Assistant Musical Director, Stephen Milbank; Stage Manager, Michael A. Clarke; Press, Philip Rinaldi/Tim Ray. CAST: Bob Cuccioli, Karen Mason, Brenda Pressley†1, Jim Walton†2, Karen Ziemba; STANDBYS: George Dvorsky, Andrea Green
MUSICAL NUMBERS: The World Goes 'Round, Yes, Coffee in a Cardboard Cup, Happy Time, Colored Lights, Sara Lee, Arthur in the Afternoon, My Coloring Book, I Don't Remember You, Sometimes a Day Goes By, All That Jazz, Class, Mr. Cellophane, Me and My Baby, There Goes the Ball Game, How Lucky Can You Get, The Rink, Ring Them Bells, Kiss of the Spider Woman, Only Love, Marry Me, Quiet Thing, When It All Comes True Dance, Pain, Grass Is Always Greener, We Can Make It, Maybe This Time, Isn't This Better?, Money, Cabaret, New York New York

A revue in two acts with Kander and Ebb's Broadway, cabaret and film songs.
†Succeeded by: 1. Terry Burrell. 2. Joel Blum.

Joan Marcus Photos

"And the World Goes Round" Left: Karen Ziemba, Bob Cuccioli
Right: Cuccioli, Ziemba, Jim Walton, Karen Mason, Brenda Pressley

Vladimir Mashkov in "My Big Land" (*Carol Rosegg*)

Patricia Norcia in "World of Ruth Draper" (*Bill MIller*)

(Triplex Theatre) Tuesday, March 5–10, 1991 (7 performances) The Acting Company and the Oleg Tabakov Moscow Theatre Studio present:
A TEACHER OF RUSSIAN by Aleksandr Buravshy; Director, Evgeni Kamen'kovich; Translation, Alexander Gelman; Sets, Aleksandr Borovsky; Music, Victor Apukhtin; Lighting, Efim Udler; Stage Manager, Lyudmila Ulanova; Press, Fred Nathan/Ian Rand. CAST: Aleksandr Marin (Tolya), Maria Mironova (Kozitskaya), Vladimir Mashkov (Dr. Popov), Irina Petrova (Nina)

A black comedy in two acts. The action takes place in a hospital room in a South Russian resort at present.
and
MY BIG LAND by Aleksandr Galich; Translation, Mr. Gelman; Director, Oleg Tabakov; Sets/Costumes, Mr. Borovsky; Music, Sergei Ya. Nititkin; Lighting, Mr. Udler. CAST: Vladimir Mashkov (Abraham), Aleksandr Marin (David), Marina Zudina (Tanya), Nadezhda Timokhina (Khanakh), Sergei Garazov (Meyer), Olga Blok (Rosa), Aleksandr Mokhov (Mitya), Mikhail Khomiakov (Slavka), Aleksei Zolotnitsky (Chernyshov), Aleksandra Tabakova (Lyudmila), Vadim Aleksandrov (Lapshin), Andrei Smolyakov (Odintsov), Igor Nefyodov (Zhenka), Marina Shimanskaya (Arisha)

A drama in three acts, performed without intermission.

(Mazur Theatre) Thursday, March 7–23, 1991 (14 performances and 1 preview) Playwrights' Preview Productions presents:
JEKYLL IN CHAMBER; Music, Brad Ellis; Libretto, Joann Green; Director, Ms. Green; Musical Director, Mr. Ellis; Sets, E.F. Morrill; Costumes, Ari Viera; Lighting, Judy Daitsman; Production Manager, Lysna Leon-Scriven; Stage Manager, Janet Magajna. CAST: Frank Licato (Dr. Jekyll/Mr. Hyde), Frederick Freyer (Pianist), Ian Johnson (Child), Ruth Adams (Dr. Lanyon), James Bundy (Mr. Utterson)

A music-theatre piece based on the Robert Stevenson classic. Performed without intermission.

(Weill Recital Hall) Tuesday, March 12–13, 1991 (2 limited performances)
THE WORLD OF RUTH DRAPER CAST: Patricia Norcia PROGRAM: Four Imaginary Folk Songs, In a Church in Italy, The Italian Lesson, A Scottish Immigrant at Ellis Island, Doctors and Diets, Three Women and Mr. Clifford

A solo recreation of the monologist.

(Theatre of Riverside Church) Wednesday, March 13–April 14, 1991 (30 performances) New Federal Theatre (Woodie King, Artistic Director) presents:
THE BALM YARD by Don Kinch; Director, Shauneille Perry; Musical Director, Julius Williams; Set, Robert Joel Schwartz; Costumes, Judy Dearing; Lighting, Sandra Ross; Sound, Pepsi Robinson; Choreography, Thomas Pinnock; Stage Manager, Jacqui Casto; Press, Max Eisen/Madelon Rosen. CAST: Ras Tesfa (Spirit), Nichole Thompson (Celia), Nick Smith (Batuola), Roxie Roker (Hilda), Gary Dourdan (Samson), Kim Weston Moran (Edna), Donna Manno (Daisy), Trevor Thomas (Prime Minister), Carla Williams, Irene Datcher, Mac Arthur (Spirits), Larry McDonald (Musician).
    A drama about the rise and fall of a prime minister. The action takes place in the West Indies over several years.

(Actors' Playhouse) Tuesday, March 12–April 7, 1991 (22 performances and 10 previews) East-West Theatre Productions present:
PVT. WARS by James McLure; Director, Sylvia Caminer; Sets, Michael Lalicki; Costumes, Joseph Petrollese; Lighting, Eric Thoben; Press, David Rothenberg/Meg Gordean, Manuel Igrejas, Terence Womble. CAST: Jason Werner (Woodruff Gately), Richard Werner (Silvio), Adrian Basil (Natwick).
    An expanded two-act version of the 1979 one-act drama. The action takes place in a veterans' hospital during the 1970s.

(Impact Theatre) Thursday, March 14–17, 1991 (5 performances) Yaffa Prod.II, PM Productions and The Impact Studio present:
MITOTE (WOMEN TALK) by Maisha Baton; Director, Cynthia Stokes. CAST: Linda H. Humes, Jane Galvin-Lewis, Yvonne Warden, Lorenzo
    Performed without intermission. A historically based drama that weaves the tales of three women of New Mexico.

(Victory Theatre) Thursday, March 14–31, 1991 (12 performances and 3 previews) Judy Del Giudice and "4X5 Flash" present:
STEALING SOULS (BRING YOUR CAMERA); Conceived and Written by Mira-Lani Ogelsby; Inspired by the work of Weegee; Director, Thomas Calabro; Music, Marc Ryan; Design, Steve Oglesby; Choreography, Beverly Prentice-Ryan; Stage Manager/Costumes, Mary B. Johnson; Press, Ted Killmer/Tray Batres. CAST: Sharlanda Alexander, Vincent Bandille, Anita Bernice, Robert Caccomo, Patti Chambers, Tom Coble, Sally Conners, Judy Del Giudice, Liz Evert, Burt Garza, Chris Hoffman, Mary B. Johnson, Wendy Johnson, Mike Lumer, Matte Osian, Beverly Prentice-Ryan, Marc Ryan, Halinda Ujda, Robert Keith Watson
    A vaudevillian kaleidoscope based on the work of crime photographer Weegee.

(John Houseman Theatre) Friday, March 15–April 28, 1991 (41 performances and 11 previews) Claudet & Christen Productions (Michel Claudet, Darryl K. Christen) present:
THE KINGFISH by Larry L. King and Ben Z. Grant; Director, Perry Martin; Production Design, John McConnell; Lighting, F. Mitchell Dana; Sound, Tom Gould; General Manager, George Elmer Productions; Stage Manager, Susan Whelan; Press, Peter Cromarty/David Lotz. CAST: John McConnell
    A one-man recreation of the life and times of Huey P. Long. Presented in two acts.

John McConnell in "The Kingfish"
(Carol Rosegg)

Dorrie Joiner, Patrick McNellis in
"Encanto File" (Martha Holmes)

Kim Weston-Moran, Gary Dourdan, Roxie Roxer in the
"The Balm Yard" (Bert Andrews)

"Mitote"

(Judith Anderson Theatre) Tuesday, March 19–April 14, 1991 (21 performances and 7 previews) The Women's Project & Productions (Julia Miles, Artistic Director) presents:
THE ENCANTO FILE AND OTHER SHORT PLAYS: New Work from the Women's Project Directors' Forum; Sets, Mark Fitzgibbons; Lighting, Franklin Meissner, Jr.; Costumes, Barbara Beccio; Sound, Bruce Ellman; Stage Managers, Jill Cordle, Jennifer Plate; Press, Fred Nathan/Merle Frimark
That Midnight Rodeo by Mary Sue Price; Director, Melanie Joseph. CAST: Patrick McNellis (Bo), Wendy Lawless (Cindy). The action takes place in a small farmhouse near Wheaton, Missouri on a summer morning.
but there are fires by Caridad Svich; Director, Susana Tubert. CAST: Cliff Weissman (Jeff Metzner), Dorrie Joiner (Gina Metzner), Patrick McNellis (Todd Neely)
    The action takes place in a small town in western Pennsylvania, at present.
Relativity by Marlene Meyer; Director, Melanie Joseph. CAST: Dana Bate (Carl), Divina Cook (Carmen), Faye M. Price (Lucy). Friendship and desire, intellect and emotion-everything is relative.
Pagan Day by Sally Nemeth; Director, Melanie Joseph. CAST: Wendy Lawless, Faye M. Price. A comedy on sex, power, romance, militarism, and patriarchy.
The Encanto File by Rosa Lowinger; Director, Melia Bensussen. CAST: Divina Cook (Rita), Dorrie Joiner (Natalie), Thomas Kopache (Julian). The action takes place in a small construction firm in Miami, shortly after work.

(Theatre at St. Peter's) Wednesday, March 20–April 13, 1991 (26 performances) Musical Theatre Works presents:
LOVE IN TWO COUNTRIES; Music, Thomas Z. Shepard; Libretto, Sheldon Harnick; Director, Michael Montel; Choreography, Karen Azenberg; Sets, Marie Anne Chiment; Lighting, Betsy Adams; Costumes, Amanda J. Klein; Musical Director, Albert Ahronheim; Production Manager, Hilliard Cohen; Stage Manager, Ira Mont. *That Pig of a Molette* CAST: Scott Robertson (Molette), Bill Carmichael (Rivet), Elizabeth Walsh (Henriette), SuEllen Estey (Clothilde/Mme. Molette), Lannyl Stephens (Germaine), Michael Brian (Michel/Belloncle), Tim Ewing (Jean Claude/Gendarme/Uncle) *A Question Of Faith* CAST: SuEllen estey (Mother), Scott Robertson (Father), Elizabeth Walsh (Kapitolina Nikitshina), Lannyl Stephens (Katerina Nikitshina), Caryn Kaplan (Olga Nikitshina), Michael Brian (Larion), Tim Ewing (Boris), Bill Carmichael (Father Koreisha)
    Two one-act musicals. *Molette* takes place in France in 1870. *Faith* takes place in Russia in 1870.

(Lucille Lortel Theatre) Tuesday, March 26–May 19, 1991 (54 performances and 10 previews) John Nassivera and Don Schneider by Special Arrangement with Lucille Lortel present:
ADVICE FROM A CATERPILLAR by Douglas Carter Beane; Director, Edgar Lansbury; Sets, Rick Dennis; Costumes, Jonathan Bixby; Lighting, Brian Nason; Music, David Abir; General Management, Brent Peek, Allen Merritt; Company Manager, Marshall B. Purdy; Stage Managers, Robert Bennett, Gretchen Krich. CAST: Dennis Christopher (Spaz), Ally Sheedy (Missy), Harley Venton (Suit), David Lansbury (Brat), Gretchen Krich (Voice of Linda Lee)
A post-modern romantic comedy in two acts. The action takes place in the East Village, Soho, and Old Chatham, New York.

(Naked Angels Theatre) Monday, April 1–19, 1991 (16 performances) Naked Angels presents:
NEBRASKA by Keith Reddin; Director, Joe Mantello; Sets, George Xenos; Lighting, Brian MacDevitt; Costumes, Laura Cunningham; Sound, Charles Bugbee III; Producers, Beth Emelson, Christie Wagner; Stage Manager, Damond Gallagher; Press, Jeffrey Richards/David LeShay. CAST: Tim Ransom (Dean Swift), Susan Batten (Julie Swift), Keith Langsdale (Jack Gurney), Leslie Lyles (Carol Gurney), Merrill Holtzman (Henry Feilding), Kenneth Longergan (Ted Barnes), Moira Driscoll (Kim Newman)
A drama exploring the lives of men on an Air Force base, and their families and relationships.

(Theatre Row Theatre/formerly South St. Theatre) Tuesday, April 2–28, 1991 (24 performances) A. James Keeler and Thomas Palumbo present:
PALS by Stephen Mantin; Director, Martin Shakar; Sets, Edward Gianfrancesco; Lighting, Frances Aronson; Costumes, Natalie Barth Walker; Press, Jeffrey Richards/David LeShay. CAST: Anthony Spina, Ivan Kronefeld, Sam Coppola, Victor Arnold
A sinister comedy about the perfect crime.

(Irish Repertory Theatre) Tuesday, April 2–30, 1991 (29 performances) Irish Repertory presents:
MAKING HISTORY by Brian Friel; Director, Charlotte Moore; Sets, David Raphel; Costumes, Natalie Walker; Sound/Lighting, Richard Clausen; Stage Managers, Mary E. Lawson, Athena Baer. CAST: Ray Fitzgerald (Harry Hoveden), Robert Murch (Hugh O'Neill), Ciaran O'Reilly (Hugh O'Donnell), W.B. Brydon (Peter Lombard), Miriam Foley (Mabel), Angela Cooper Scowen (Mary)
A drama in two acts. The action takes place in Dungannon, Ireland in August, 1591 and Rome, twenty years later. The story of an Irish national hero.

(Harold Clurman Theatre) Wednesday, April 3–21, 1991 (17 performances) The Directors Company (Artistic/Producing Director, Michael Parva; Artistic/Managing Director, Victoria Lanman Chesshire) in association with TRG Productions (Associate Producer, Marvin Kahan) present:
OF BLESSED MEMORY by George Rattner; Director, David McKenna; Sets, Richard Meyer; Lighting, Stephen J. Backo; Costumes, Niomi Kaiz; Sound, Hector Milia; Stage Manager, Russell Marisak; Press, Chris Boneau/Bob Fennell. CAST: Jose Zuniga (Jesse Rodriguez), T. Ryder Smith (Aaron Greenwald), Julian Fleisher (Lazar), Nicolette Vajtay (Maria), Richard Anthony Petrocelli (Willie Cruz), Scott Sowers (Detective Vincenzo)
A drama in two acts. The action takes place in Aaron's Paint Store, Williamsburg, Brooklyn, at the present time.

John Daggett, Steve Ahern, Helen Greenberg, Becky Borczon
in "Love Lemmings"

Harley Venton, Ally Sheedy, Dennis Christopher, David Lansbury
in "Advice from a Caterpillar" (*Carol Rosegg*)

Robert Murch, Miriam Foley in "Making History"

(Village Gate/Top of the Gate) Wednesday, April 3–August 4, 1991 (101 performances and 13 previews) Fireball Entertainment in association with Mark May presents:
LOVE LEMMINGS: *A Comic Leap into the Dating Abyss* by Joe DiPietro; Director, Melia Bensussen; Music, Eric Thoroman; Lyrics, Mr. DiPietro and Mr. Thoroman; Sets, Rob Odoristo; Lighting, Anne Chesney; Stage Manager, Sergio Cruz; Press, Philip Leshin. CAST: Steve Ahern, Becky Borczon succeeded by Kathryn Rosseter, John Daggett, Helen Greenberg
PROGRAM: Messed Up for the Rest of My Life, Men Who Don't Call and the Women Who Wait for Them, It's 3 a.m. Do You Know Where Your Condom Is?, On and On and On, Basic Dating, Not Tonight I'm Busy Busy Busy, Jacoby & Meyers, What He Wants, Where Have All the Pirates Gone?, Very First Date of Martha Mitz, Scared Straight, We Don't Need Your Stinkin' Baggage, More Than One Way, Whatever Happened to Baby's Parents?, Magazines, She's Out of My Life Again, First a Clock Then, Single Bars Single People, Possession, Nat'l Organization of Single Women Seminar for Men, Beat Your Biological Clock, Love's a Bitch
A revue performed without intermission.

(Theatre at 224 Waverly Place) Wednesday, April 3–May 26, 1991 (56 performances) P.I.A. Productions present:
HOMOSEXUAL ACTS; Director, Rich Rubin; Sets, Jamie Leo; Lighting, Glenn J. Powell; Costumes, Gregory Melendrez; Press, David Rothenberg Associates. CAST: Kristina Keefe, Andrew Marvel, Leslie Roberts, Tony Salas, Ted Senecal, Kevin Weiler; *Ludwig & Wagner, The Family Bar, The Way We War* by Robert Patrick; *S&M, Celebrities in Hell, One Man's Opinion* by David Curzon; *Annunciation, Fairy Fuck-In or a Call to the States* by Carl Morse; *Somebody's Little Boy* by Robert Chesley; *Show* by Victor Bumbalo; *Mother Father Lover Man* by Bill Wright; *That Al Pacino Look* by Rich Rubin
Twelve short plays.

(Courtyard Playhouse) Wednesday, April 3–June 9, 1991 (60 performances) The Glines presents:
HIGH STRUNG QUARTET by Evan Bridenstine; Director, Leslie Irons; Sets, David Jensen; Lighting, Tracy Dedrickson; Costumes, Ina Raye. CAST: John Cathcart III, Suzanne Cryer, Dane Hall, Mark Leydorf
A comedy about three men and a woman, each in pursuit of the wrong person.

(Practical Cats Theatre) Thursday, April 4–28, 1991 (18 performances and 2 previews) The Practical Cats Theatre Company presents:
GIANT ON THE CEILING by Alice Eve Cohen; Director, Alma Becker; Sets/Costumes, Connie Singer; Lighting, Steven Petrilli; Press, Shirley Herz/Miller Wright. CAST: Charlotte Colavin, Brian Kosnik, Paula Prizzi, Stephen Nisbet, Lorey Hayes, Alice Eve Cohen
   A collection of short plays about contemporary life.

(Henry Street Settlement) Thursday, April 4–21, 1991 (11 performances and 4 previews) The New York Street Theatre Caravan presents:
BLUES IN RAGS; Written and Directed by Marketa Kimbrell; Music, Nick Cosco; Sets, Remy Tessler; Choreography, Marcia Donalds; Press, Peter Cromarty/Robert Schmerler. CAST: Ariel Joseph, Marcia Donalds, Jennifer Johnson
   A musical theatre piece utilizing pantomime, skits, and song.

(One Dream Theatre) Friday, April 5–21, 1991 (16 performances) Echo Repertory presents:
THE TRIANGLE PROJECT by Daniel Rietz and Barbara Wiechmann; Director, Richard Corley; Sets, Sarah Edkins; Lighting, Warren Karp; Costumes, Patricia Sarnataro; Stage Manager, Herbert W. Miller. CAST: Amelia David, Frank Deal, Cherry Madole, Christine Mourad, Kerry Muir, Janice Orlandi, Lisa Randall, Robin Francis Robinson
   A play about the 1911 fire at the Triangle Shirtwaist factory in New York City.

(Joyce Theatre) Tuesday, April 9–21 (16 performances)
AMERICAN BALLROOM THEATRE; Choreography by Patricia Birch, John Roudis, Peter DiFalco, Gary Pierce, Graciela Daniele. COMPANY: Danny Carter and Gay Bowidas, Stanley McCalla and Jennifer Ford, Helmut Salas and Candace Langhoff, Jeff and Donna Shelley, Victor Kanevsky and Dee Quinones, William Wayne and Lori Brizzi PROGRAM A: Posin, The Rainbow Room, Tango & Waltz PROGRAM B: It Takes Two, Presley Pieces, Tango & Waltz

(Ubu Repertory Theatre) Wednesday, April 10, 1991– Ubu Repertory (Francoise Kourilsky, Artistic Director) presents:
GRAND FINALE by Copi; Translation, Michael Feingold; Director, Andre Ernotte; Sets, William Barclay; Lighting, Phil Monat; Costumes, Carol Ann Pelletier; Stage Manager, Elise-Ann Konstantin; Press, Jeffrey Richards/David LeShay. CAST: Keith McDermott (Cyril), Margo Skinner (Nurse), David Pursley (Hubert), Jack Koenig (Reporter), Delphi Harrington (Regina Morti), Robertson Carricart (Dr. Backsleider)
   A farce about AIDS. The last play by the late French-Argentinian Author.

Keith McDermott, Margot Skinner in "Grand Finale" (*Carol Rosegg*)

Lynndawn Couch, Ilvi Dulack in "The Catalyst" (*Gerry Goldstein*)

(Theatre Arielle) Wednesday, April 10, 1991– Phyle Productions presents:
DON'T GET ME STARTED by Tina Smith; Director, Kathy Najimy. CAST: Tina Smith
   A one-woman show comprised of a gallery on unrelated women.

(29th St. Playhouse) Thursday, April 11–28, 1991 (15 performances) Annette Moskowitz and Alexander E. Racolin present:
THE CATALYST by Ronald Duncan; Director, Stephen Jobes; Set, Mitch J. Christenson; Lighting, Jason Livingston; Costumes, Liz Elkins; Stage Manager, Barry Cote; General Manager, Tim Corcoran; Press, Max Eisen/Madelon Rosen. CAST: Lynndawn Couch (Thererse), William Charlton (Charles), Ilvi Dulack (Leone)
   A comedy in two acts. The play was banned by the Lord Chamberlain in 1957 for dealing with abnormal relations—a *ménage à trois*. This is the American premiere. The action takes place in London in 1957.

(Battery Park City) Thursday, April 11–June 2, 1991
CIRQUE DU SOLEIL: NOUVELLE EXPERIENCE; Artistic director, Franco Dragone; Creative Director, Gilles Ste-Croix; Sets, Michel Crete; Costumes, Dominique Lemieux; Music/Score, Rene Dupere; Lighting, Luc Lafortune; Choreography, Debra Brown; Press, Susan Bloch/Ellen Zeisler, Kevin P. McAnarney. CAST: Brian Dewhurst, Vladimir Kekhaial, France LaBonte, Anne Lepage, David Shiner
   A new program from the theatrical circus. Performed with one intermission.

(Triangle/Holy Trinity) Thursday, April 11–May 5, 1991 (16 performances) The Triangle Theatre Company presents:
REUNION and **DARK PONY** by David Mamet; Director, Michael Ramach; Costumes, Amanda J. Klein; Lighting, Nancy Collings; Sets, Miles Ray; Stage Manager, Jerry Grant; Press, Jim Baldassare. *Reunion* CAST: Mel Boudrot (Bernie), Allyson Rice-Taylor (Carol) The action takes place in Bernie's apartment in early March, 1973. *Dark Pony* CAST: Mr. Boudrot (Father), Ms. Rice-Taylor (Daughter)
   The action takes place in an automobile at night, 1950.

(Westside Theatre/Downstairs) Friday, April 12–June 30, 1991 (83 performances and 7 previews) Rollins & Joffe and Radio City Music Hall Productions in association with Showtime Networks, Inc. present:
RICK REYNOLDS: ONLY THE TRUTH IS FUNNY; Written by Mr. Reynolds; Director, Mr. Reynolds; Lighting, Wendall S. Hinkle; Sound, Tom Morse; General Manager, Fremont Associates; Executive Producers, Jack Rollins, Charles Joffe, Scott Sanders, Ed Micone; Manager, Sally Campbell Morse; Press, PMK/Leslie Dart, Randi Wershba; Radio City/Kevin Brockman, Sandra Manley. CAST: Rick Reynolds
   Performed with one intermission.

Allyson Rice-Taylor, Mel Boudrot in "Dark Pony" (*Carol Rosegg*)

Rick Reynolds in "Only the Truth *Is* Funny" (*Carol Rosegg*)

(Atlantic Theatre/Formerly Apple Corps Theatre) Friday, April 12–May 4, 1991 (20 performances) Atlantic Theatre presents:
THREE SISTERS by Anton Chekhov; Adaptation, David Mamet from literal translation by Vlada Chernomordik; Director, W.H. Macy; Sets, James Wolk; Costumes, Laura Cunningham; Lighting, Howard Werner; Music, Robin Spielberg; Production Manager, Sarah Pickett; Stage Manager, Matthew Silver; Press, Jim Baldassare. CAST: Melissa Bruder (Olga), Mary McCann (Irina), Elizabeth McGovern (Masha), Herbert DuVal (Ivan), Todd Weeks (Nikolai), Robert Bella (Vassily), Jen Jones (Anfisa), Nesbitt Blaisdell (Ferapont), Jordan Lage (Alexandr), Neil Pepe (Andrei), Steven Goldstein (Fyodor), Sarah Eckhardt (Natalya), David Valcin (Alexei), Scott Zigler (Vladimir), Robin Spielberg (Maid)
   Performed in 4 acts.

(Provincetown Playhouse) Monday, April 15–May 26, 1991 (42 performances and 7 previews) The Ivy Company presents:
IVY ROWE; Adaptation, Mark Hunter and Barbara Bates Smith; Based on *Fair and Tender Ladies* by Lee Smith; Director, Mark Hunter; Sets, James Morgan; Costumes, Vicki S. Holden; Lighting, Ken Kaczynski; General Manager, Steven Warnick; Stage Manager, Suzanne V. Beerman; Press, Peter Cromarty/David Katz. CAST: Barbara Bates Smith
   A monodrama in two acts. The action takes place in Southwest Virginia between 1912 and 1974.

(Westbeth Theatre Center) Friday, April 19–28, 1991 (12 performances) Sandra Hochman, Marsha Singer, and Sybil Wong, in association with The Risk Company present:
CUSTODY; Music, Marsha Singer; Lyrics/Book, Sandra Hochman; Based on a portion of the novel *Walking Papers* by Ms. Hochman; Director, Mina Yakim; Musical Director/Arranger, Jim Mironchik; Choreography, Darryl Quinton; Sets, Pat Sutton; Lighting, Jason Sturm; Press, John & Gary Springer. CAST: Martin Austin (Patrick), Lea Barron (Dr. Purdy), Robin Boudreau (Diana/Narrator), Terrence Clowe (Bernie), Joel Goodness (Coach Brennon), H.E. Greer (Nick), Mark C. Healey (Skip), Rachel Hillman (Alice), John-Michael Lander (Al), Lenny Mandel (Mr. Balooka), Amanda Miller (Laurie), Barbara Mills (Mrs. Balooka), Elan Rivera (Pee Wee), Tara Sands (Diana Balooka), Emily Schulman (Fat Face), Scott Taylor (Roger), Colleen Ward (Leslie)
MUSICAL NUMBERS: Dance of Custody, Risk, Throwaway Kid, We Have to Love Each Other, Cherry Lawn, Boys/Girls on My Mind, Watercolor Girl, Doin' It, It Hurts Like a Razor Strap, Missing You, Stargazers, Friendship Is the Most Important Thing, Ugly Song, Rap Song, Blessings 'n' Bruises, There Was Something Wrong with Your Head, Sum of My Dreams, Finale
A musical in two acts. The action takes place during the early 1950s in a Connecticut boarding school for girls.

**Everett Quinton (top), Hapi Phace
in "Hunchback of Notre Dame"
(*Anita Shevett*)**

**Matthew Dixon, Frank Licato
in "New Voice One-Act Festival"**

**Melissa Bruder, Elizabeth McGovern, Mary McCann
in "Three Sisters" (*Carol Rosegg*)**

**(Clockwise from center) J.T. Cromwell,
Dick Scanlan, Joe Joyce, David Drake in
"Pageant" (*Scott Humbert*)**

(Blue Angel) Tuesday, April 23– still playing May 31, 1991. Jonathan Scharer presents:
PAGEANT; Music, Albert Evans; Lyrics/Book, Bill Russell and Frank Kelly; Conception/Direction/Choreography, Robert Longbottom; Musical Direction/Orchestration/Arrangemnents/Supervision, James Raitt; Co-Choreographer, Tony Parise; Sets, Daniel Ettinger; Costumes, Gregg Barnes; Lighting, Timothy Hunter; Hairstylist, Lazaro Arencibia; Associate Producer, Chip Quigley; General Manager, Dowling Entertainment/Ken Dowling, Gwen Cassel; Stage Manager, Debora Porazzi; Press, Shirley Herz/Glenna Freedman. CAST: Randl Ash (Miss Bible Belt), David Drake (Miss Deep South), Russell Garrett (Miss Texas), Joe Joyce (Miss Industrial Northeast), John Salvatore (Miss West Coast), Dick Scanlan (Miss Great Plains), J.T. Cromwell (Frankie Cavalier)
MUSICAL NUMBERS: Natural Born Females, Something Extra, The Talent Competition, It's Gotta Be Venus, Girl Power, Good Bye Miss Glamouresse
   A musical beauty contest with the winner selected by a panel from the audience.

(Charles Ludlam Theatre) Wednesday, April 24– June 23, 1991 (54 performances) The Ridiculous Theatrical Company (Everett Quinton, Artistic Director; Steve Asher, Managing Director) presents:
THE HUNCHBACK OF NOTRE DAME by Everett Quinton; Freely adapted from the novel by Victor Hugo; Music, Mark Bennett; Lyrics, Mr. Quinton, Mr. Bennett; Director, Mr. Quinton; Sets, Tom Moore; Lighting, Richard Currie; Costumes, Mr. Quinton; Props, Jeffrey Rebelo; Stage Manager, Karen Ott; Press, Judy Jacksina/Penny Landau. CAST: Everett Quinton (Archdeacon Frollo), Eureka (Passerby/Sister Gudule/Dame Aloise), Noelle Kalom (Heidi), Robert Lanier (Ruthie), Therese McIntyre (Cripple), Sophie Maletsky (Pierre Gringoire), Gary Mink (Jehan Frollo), Stephen Pell (Gracie St. Paul), Hapi Phace (Quasimodo), Bobby Reed (Master Florian Poussypain), Cheryl Reeves (Esmeralda), Robert Vellani (Phoebus de Chateaupers), Christine Weiss (Edna/Fleur de Lys), Mark Bennett (Eustache)
   A "quasimusical" in two acts.

(Harold Clurman Theatre) Wednesday, April 24–May 19, 1991 (22 performances) New Voice Theatre Company presents:
NEW VOICE: 2ND ANNUAL SPRING ONE-ACT FESTIVAL CAST: Sara Bragaw, Kathleen Cullen, Matthew Dixon, Genevieve Dinovart, Brian Dykstra, Tim Harris, Becky Jones, Dennis Jordan, David Devine, Frank Licato, Lawrence Mason, Carolyn M. McCarthy, Gabrielle Shannon, Kyle Shannon, Susan Sharkey, Eton O'Malley, Joseph Verhauz.
SERIES A: *My Type* by Debbie Jones; Director, Kathleen Cullen; *Rex* by Arden Lewis; Director, Gary C. Walter; *Lot's Wife* by Brian Dykstra; Director, Mr. Dykstra; *Herders* by Michael Schwartz; Director, Jason Fogelson
SERIES B: *Shall We Dance?* by Marilyn Sevens; Director, Scott Schneider; *Blackout* by Matthew Dixon; Director, Gary C. Walter; *Migrations* by Michael Oaks and Jennifer Wells; Director, Debbie Jones

(William Redfield Theatre) Thursday, April 25–May 4, 1991 (8 performances) Qwirk Productions present:
RUMOR OF GLORY by James Bosley; Director, Peter Dalto. CAST: Richard Psarros, Molly McKenna, Jennifer Jay Stewart, David Blackman, Simon Brooking, Daniel J. Leventritt, William Preston, Diane Shore, Laurence Addeo, Chris Tolliver, Alfred Preisser
   The story of Achilles and live coverage of the Trojan War.

(One Dream Theatre) Thursday, April 25–May 18, 1991 (16 performances) Purgatorio Ink presents:
THE TRUE STORY OF A WOMAN BORN IN IRAN AND RAISED TO HEAVEN IN MANHATTAN; Written and Directed by Assurbanipal Babilla; Sets, Sonia Balassanian; Lighting, Kristabelle Munson; Costumes, Dennis Lang; Press, Ted Killmer/Tray Batres. CAST: Assurbanipal Babilla, Leyla Ebtehadj, Donna Linderman, Jessie Marquez, Tom Pearl
An "autobiographical comedy."

(Promenade Theatre) Saturday, April 27– still playing May 31, 1991. Elliot Martin, Bud Yorkin, James and Maureen O'Sullivan Cushing present:
BREAKING LEGS by Tom Dulack; Director, John Tillinger; Sets, James Noone; Costumes, David C. Woolard; Lighting, Ken Billington; General Manager, Ralph Roseman; Stage Manager, Elliott Woodruff; Press, Jeffrey Richards. CAST: Vincent Gardenia (Lou Graziano), Sue Giosa (Angie), Nicolas Surovy (Terence O'Keefe), Philip Bosco (Mike Fransisco), Victor Argo (Tino De Felice), Larry Storch (Frankie Salvucci)
   A comedy in two acts. The action takes place in a restaurant in a New England university town at present.

Sue Giosa, Vincent Gardenia in "Breaking Legs"
(Peter Cunningham)

Vincent Gardenia, Philip Bosco in "Breaking Legs"
(Peter Cunningham)

(Village Theatre) Wednesday, May 1–26, 1991 (28 performances) The Village Theatre Company presents:
ANGEL & DRAGON by Sally Netzel; Director, Gigi Rivkin; Sets, Michael Blasberg; Costumes, Ismael Hernandez, Jillian Maslow; Stage Manager, Susan Kelleher. CAST: Barbara Bercu, Michelle Berke, Susan Farwell
FRONTIERS by Meir Z. Ribalow; Director, Henry Fonte; Sets, Mr. Fonte; Costumes, Marj Feenan; Stage Manager, Lisa Lewis. CAST: Wally Dunn, Denise Dalfo, Stephen Gleason, Randy Kelly, Terrence Martin, Bryan Michael McGuire
   Angel is a love story about two women artists. *Frontiers* is two related one-acts, *Sundance* and *Moondance*.

(St. Peter's) Friday, May 3–19, 1991 (28 performances) Musical Theatre Works (Anthony Stimac, Artistic Director; Mike Teele, Managing Director) presents:
COLETTE COLLAGE: *Two Musicals about Colette* with Music by Harvey Schmidt; Lyrics/Book, Tom Jones; Direction, Jones and Schmidt; Choreography/Musical Staging, Janet Watson and Scott Harris; Musical Director, Norman Weiss; Sets/Costumes, Ed Wittstein; Lighting, Mary Jo Dondlinger; Production Supervisor/Associate Director, Dan Shaheen; Production Manager, Hilliard Cohen; Stage Manager, Ira Mont. CAST: Betsy Joslyn (Colette), Joanne Beretta (Sido), Kenneth Kantor (Willy), Ralston Hill (Jacques), James J. Mellon (Maurice), Paul Blankenship, John Bransdorf, Jaime Zee Eisner, Hilary James, Mary Setrakian, Craig Wells
MUSICAL NUMBERS: *Willy* Joy, Come to Life, Simple Country Wedding, Do It for Willy, Willy Will Grow Cold, The Claudines, Why Can't I Walk Through That Door?, Music Hall, Dream of Egypt, I Miss You, La Vagabonde, Love Is Not a Sentiment Worthy of Respect, Now I Must Walk Through That Door; *Maurice* Autumn Afternoon, Riviera Nights, Ooh-La-La, Something for the Summer, Madame Colette, You Could Hurt Me, Be My Lady, The Room Is Filled with You, Growing Older, Finale
   The latest incarnation of a project that was presented on the road in 1982 and revised at the York Theatre in 1983. *Willy* involves Colette's marriage to Henry Gauthier-Villars. *Maurice* involves her marriage to Maurice Goudeket.

(Pan Asian Repertory) Tuesday, May 7–June 1, 1991 (28 performances) Pan Asian Repertory (Tisa Chang, Artistic director; Dominick Balleta, Producing Associate) presents:
LETTERS TO A STUDENT REVOLUTIONARY by Elizabeth Wong; Director, Ernest Abuba; Sets, Kyung Won Chang; Historical Consultant, David Jiang; Slides, Corky Lee; Costumes, Maggie Raywood; Sound, Ty Sanders; Lighting, Anne Somogye; Stage Manager, Sue Jane Stoker. CAST: Caryn Ann Chow (Bibi), Karen Tsen Lee (Karen), Andrew Ingkavet (Charlie/Jonathan/Brother/Chorus 1), Keenan Shimizu (Cat/Lu Yan/Father/Chorus 2), Christen Villamor (Boss/Ins Officer/Soldier/Chorus 3), Mary Lum (Sweeper/Mexican Lady/Mother/Chorus 4)
   A drama performed without intermission. The action takes place in Beijing, China and in the U.S.A. between spring 1979 and June 1989.

(Stageworks) Tuesday, May 7–18, 1991 (16 performances) New York City Stageworks presents:
PRELUDES, FUGES & RIFTS by Terrence McNally
   A collection of unpublished theatre pieces by McNally.

Caryn Ann Chow, Karen Tsen Lee in "Letter to a Student Revolutionary" *(Carol Rosegg)*

(17 Irving Place) Tuesday, May 7– still playing May 31, 1991. Steven Baruch, Richard Frankel, Thomas Viertel in association with Allen Spivak and Larry Magid present:

SONG OF SINGAPORE with Music/Lyrics by Erik Frandsen, Robert Hipkens, Michael Garin, Paula Lockheart; Book, Alan Katz, Mr. Fransen, Mr. Hipkens, Mr. Garin, Ms. Lockheart; Director, A.J. Antoon; Orchestrations, John Carlini; Musical Supervision, Art Baron; Sets, John Lee Beatty; Costumes, Frank Krenz; Lighting, Peter Kaczorowski; Sound, Stuart J. Allyn; Vocal Arrangements, Yaron Gershovsky; Jazzaturg, Paula Lockheart; Associate Producer, Marc Routh; Production Manager, Miriam Schapiro; Stage Manager, Ron Nash; Press, Chris Boneau/Jackie Green, Jim Sapp. CAST: Erik Frandsen (Spike Spauldeen), Michael Garin (Freddy S. Lyme), Robert Hipkens (Hans van der Last), Donna Murphy (Rose), Cathy Foy (Chah Li), Francis Kane (Inspector Marvin Kurland et al), Oliver Jackson, Jr. (Kenya Ratamacue), Earl C. May (Taqsim Arco), Jon Gordon (Zoot DeFumee), Art Baron (T-Bone Kahanamoku)

MUSICAL NUMBERS: Song of Singapore, Inexpensive Tango, I Miss My Home in Haarlem, You Gotta Do What You Gotta Do, Rose of Rangoon, Necrology, Sunrise, Never Pay Musicians What They're Worth, Harbour of Love, I Can't Remember, I Want to Get Offa This Island, Foolish Geese, Serve It Up, Fly Away Rose, I Remember, Shake Shake Shake, We're Rich, Finale

A musical comedy in two acts recreating the sights and sounds of a Singapore nightclub in 1941. The performers play their own underscoring.

Michael Garin, Donna Murphy, Erik Frandsen in "Song of Singapore"
Top Right: Garin, Murphy (*Carol Rosegg*)

(Duo Theatre) Wednesday, May 8–25, 1991 (12 performances) Duo Theatre Presents:

BORN TO RUMBA with music by Michael Alasá and David Welch; Lyrics/Book/Direction, Mr. Alasá; Choreography, Michael Louis; Lighting, Jeremy Kumin; Costumes, Natalie Barth-Walker; Sets, Design Associates. CAST: Blanca Camacho (Colette), Catherine Lippencott (Marie), Elisa De La Roche (Marisol), Georgina Corbo (Maribel), Al D. Rodriguez (Marijuana), Laura Duncan (Maria Elena), Tony Ruiz (Mario), Tony Louden (Antonio), Al Roffe (Al)

MUSICAL NUMBERS: Roses, No You Can't, At the Rivoli, Santiago, The Warning, Poison, Dark Perfect Stranger, Sir, Loving for Sale, Gonna Catch Me a Dream, Antonio, Rumba, Off to Hollywood, Strange Times, Havana, Dreamers

(Mazur Theatre) Wednesday, May 8–25, 1991 (15 performances) Playwrights' Preview Productions presents:

POKEY: *Confessions of An Inconsequential Man*; Written and Directed by Paul Dervis. CAST: Michael Santoro, Amy Stiller, Kathleen Gati, Tara Dolan, Sandy Moore, Diane Cossa, Julie Alexander, Karen Marek

A play about a man's wild odyssey across America.

(Broome St. Theatre) Wednesday, May 8–26, 1991 (21 performances and 2 previews) Under One Roof & High Noon Productions present:

SONGS OF ADDICTION; Text, Robert Douglas Walters; Music, Dave Hall; Sets, Michael E. Downs; Lighting, Jeffrey Zeidman; Projections, Richard Madigan; Costumes, Faith Fisher; Sound, Anise Richey; Additional Text, Daniel O'Brien; Director, Cheryl Katz; Stage Manager, Felicia Caplan; Producer, Eric Gulotty; Press, Ted Killmer/Tray Batres. CAST: Richard Gillman, Lisa Lyons, Marcia Mintz, Bruce Taylor Robinson, Patricia Thorndike, Cathy Diane Tomlin

An evening of poetry, music, and humor on the conditions of addictions.

(Theatre 603) Thursday, May 9–19, 1991 (8 performances) The Basic Theatre presents:

ZASTROZZI by George F. Walker; Director, Jared Hammond; Sets/Lighting, Marc D. Malamud; Fights, John Edmond Morgan; Costumes, Mr. Hammond. CAST: Andrew Borba, Eric Brandenburg, Sheri Delaine, David Goldman, Mindi L. Lyons, John Edward Morgan

A revenge comedy.

(CB's 313 Gallery) Thursday, May 9–June 19, 1991 (12 performances) Hilly Kristal and Artists International Representatives present:

THE COOL CLUB by Michael Small; Director, B.T. McNicholl; Lighting, Jill Proctor, Laura E. Glover; Stage Managers, Brooke Taylor, Meilyn Soto. CAST: Jim Barry, Melissa Christopher, Kyle Clementson, Amy Edlin, David Hagman, Carrena Lukas

A comedy taking place in an East Village living room turned nightclub in New York City.

Tim Corcoran, Bruce Haggerty in "Necktie Breakfast" *(Phillip Wong)*

(Alliance Francaise/Florence Gould Hall) Thursday, May 9–12, 1991 (4 performances) The French Institute in association with Evans Haile presents:
FIFTY MILLION FRENCHMEN: *A Musical Comedy Tour of Paris in Concert;* Music/Lyrics, Cole Porter; Book, Herbert Fields; Conductor, Evans Haile; Director, Larry Carpenter; Adaptor, Tommy Krasker; Lighting, Stuart Duke; Choreography, Mike Phillips; Orchestrations, Robert Russell Bennett, Hans Spialek, F. Henri Klickmann; Stage Manager, David Waggett; Press, Shirley Herz/Glenna Freedman. CAST: Jean LeClerc (Louis Parnasse), Peggy Cass (Gladys Carroll), James Harder (Emmit Carroll), Karen Ziemba (Joyce Wheeler), Scott Waara (Billy Baxter), Jason Graae (Michael Cummins), Susan Powell (Looloo Carroll), Howard McGillin (Peter Forbes), J.Q. & the Bandits (Quartet), Kay McClelland (Violet Hildegarde), Kim Criswell (Mary DeVere), Orchestra New England
MUSICAL NUMBERS: Overture, You Do Something to Me, The American Express, You've Got That Thing, Find Me a Primitive Man, I Worship You, Do You Want to See Paris?, Where Would You Get Your Coat?, I'm in Love, Please Don't Make Me Be Good, You Don't Know Paris, Entr'acte, Queen of Terre Haute, Let's Step Out, Tale of the Oyster, I'm Unlucky at Gambling, Why Shouldn't I Have You, Paree What Did You Do to Me?
A concert version of the 1929 musical in two acts with original orchestrations.

(Theatre Ten Ten) Friday, May 10–June 2, 1991 (14 performances) Ten Ten Players present:
COWARDY CUSTARD; Music/Lyrics by Noel Coward; Devised by Gerald Frow, Alan Strachan and Wendy Toye; Director, David Dunn Bauer; Musical Director, N. Thomas Pedersen; Choreography, Hal Simons; Press, Audrey Ross. CAST: Anne Gartlan, Judith Jarosz, Jeanette Landis, Karol Richter, Kenneth Garner, Mark L. Greenberg, Richard Bret Miller, Michael Milton, Christopher Scott
A revue originally presented in London in 1972.

(Judith Anderson Theatre) Tuesday, May 14–June 9, 1991 (21 performances and 7 previews) The Women's Project and Productions (Julia Miles, Artistic Director) present:
NIGHT SKY by Susan Yankowitz; Director, Joseph Chaikin; Sets, George Xenos; Lighting, Beverly Emmons; Costumes, Mary Brecht; Sound, Mark Bennett; Stage Manager, Ruth Kreshka; Press, Fred Nathan/Merle Frimark. CAST: Edward Baran (Daniel), Tom Cayler (Bill), Joan MacIntosh (Anna), Aleta Mitchell, Paul Zimet, Lizabeth Zindel
A drama about an astronomer who suffers an injury that leaves her aphasic.

(Clockwise from L) John Turner, Michael Kennard, Debby Tidy in "Mump&Smoot in 'Caged with Wog'"

(29th St. Repertory Theatre) Wednesday, May 15–June 2, 1991 (13 performances and 2 previews) Annette Moskowitz, Alexander E. Racolin and the 29th St. Repertory present:
NECKTIE BREAKFAST by Bill Nave; Director, Vera Beren; Sets, Murphy Gigliotti; Lighting, Stewart Wagner; Costumes, La Berensteinas of NY, Chris Nieder; Music, Ms. Beren, Barry Coté; Press, Chris Boneau/Bob Fennell. CAST: Linda June Larson (Ellie Midkiff), Bruce Haggerty (Franklin Midkiff), Lois Raebeck (Mammy Mac), Leo Farley (Lee Jim Bobbet), Dana Lyons (Jenny Riddle), Charles Willey (Wade Savoye/Captain of Guards), Mallory Morris (Helen Maude Mudd), Tim Corcoran (Fish Frye), Suzette Breibart (Miss Queenie DeVane), Paula Ewin (Lydia Turner), David Sitler (Raleigh Ray Turner), David Mogentale (Red Joe Williams/Hobie the Hangman), Robert J. Yocum (Woodrow Martin), Richard Sachar (FBI/Mr. Moore), Bruce Goldberg (Grave Digger/W.P. Whitehead), Kent Heacock (Priest/Minister/Fortune Teller)
A drama in two acts. The action takes place in Smothers, Kentucky in 1936 and involves the last public hanging in the United States.

(Vineyard 26th St.) Thursday, May 16–18, 1991 (4 performances) The Womens's Project and Productions (Julia Miles, Artistic Director) presents:
MAGGIE AND MISHA by Gail Sheehy; Director, Julianne Boyd; Press, Fred Nathan/Merle Frimark. CAST: Carole Shelley (Maggie), George Morfogen (Misha), Victor Steinbach (Boris Yelpsin), Ching Valdes/Aran
A comedy based on East-West relations in the past decade.

(Vineyard 15th St.) Thursday, May 16–June 16, 1991. The Vineyard Theatre presents:
FOOD AND SHELTER by Jane Anderson; Director, André Ernotte; Sets, Ann Sheffield; Lighting, Donald Holder; Costumes, Muriel Stockdale; Sound/Music, Aural Fixation; Stage Manager, Crystal Huntington. CAST: Philip Seymour Hoffman (Earl), Kelly Coffield (Lois), T-F Walker (Chrissie), John Speredakos (Police/Clerk), Isiah Whitlock Jr. (Lamar), Virginia Wing (Librarian)

(Astor Place Theatre) Tuesday, May 21–June 9, 1991 (13 performances and 7 previews) Arthur Cantor and Hollywood Canada Productions, Inc. present:
MUMP & SMOOT IN "CAGED" . . . WITH WOG; Written and Created by Michael Kennard and John Turner; Director, Karen Hines; Lighting, Michael Charbonneau; Art Direction, John Dawson; Music/Sound, David Hines; General Manager, Laura Heller; Press, Mr. Cantor. CAST: Michael Kennard (Mump), John Turner (Smoot), Debbie Tidy (Wog)
Performed without intermission. An evening with Canada's clowns of horror.

Biff McGuire, John Heard in "The Last Yankee"

William Wise, David Rasche in "A Way with Words"

Kellie Overbey, Sam Rockwell in "Face Divided"

Evan Handler, Gus Rogerson in "Big Al"

Charles Weldon, Mansoor Najeeullah, Ramone Moses
in "Salaam Huey Newtown...."

(Ensemble Studio Theatre) Wednesday, May 15–26, 1991 (14 performances)
Ensemble Studio Theatre (Curt Dempster, Artistic Director; Dominick Balletta, Managing Director) presents:
MARATHON 1991 SERIES A; Sets, Ann Waugh; Lighting, Greg MacPherson; Sound, One Dream; Costumes, Deborah Rooney; Production Supervisor, Paul E. King; Stage Manager, Carol Avery; Producer, Kate Baggott; Associate Producer, Margaret Mancinelli
Where Were You When It Went Down? by David Mamet; Director, Billy Hopkins; Stage Manager, Brian Rohan. CAST: Steve Goldstein (B), Victor Slezak (A)
Naomi in the Living Room; Written and Directed by Christopher Durang; Stage Manager, Robert Daley. CAST: Sherry Anderson (Naomi), John Augustine (John), Ilene Kristen (Johnna)
Intimacy; From a short story by Raymond Carver; Adaptation/Direction, Harris Yulin; Stage Manager, Richard Lollo. CAST: Deborah Hedwall (Woman), Paul McIsaac (Man)
You Can't Trust the Male by Randy Noojin; Director, Melodie Somers; Stage Manager, Mark E. Cole. CAST: Garrett M. Brown (Harvey Kessel), Lynn Ritchie (Laura Spivey)
A Way with Words by Frank D. Gilroy; Director, Christopher A. Smith; Stage Manager, Eric Eligator. CAST: Melinda Mullins (Louise), David Rasche (Fred), William Wise (Artie)
Wednesday, May 29–June 6, 1991 (14 performances)
SERIES B; Sets, David K. Gallo; Costumes, David E. Sawaryn; Lighting, Greg MacPherson
Practice by Leslie Ayvazian; Director, Elinor Renfield. CAST: Leslie Ayvazian (Maggie), Karen Rizzo (Eve)
Face Divided by Edward Allan Baker; Director, Risa Bramon Garcia. CAST: Trazana Beverley (Nurse Sue Wilcox), Kellie Overbey (Debbie Irons), Sam Rockwell (Freddie Irons)
Over Texas by Michael John LaChiusa; Director, Kirsten Sanderson; Musical Director, David Loud. CAST: Gloria Bogin (Lady Bird Johnson), Mary Beth Peil (Evelyn Lincoln), Debra Stricklin (Mary Gallager), Anthony Sandkamp (Aide), Julie White (First Lady)
Rapid Eye Movement by Susan Kim; Director, Margaret Mancinelli. CAST: Heather Lupton (Celia), Anne O'Sullivan (Lorraine), Ethan Phillips (Warren), Michael Wells (Teddy)
Can Can by Romulus Linney; Director, David Shookhoff. CAST: Hope Davis (French Girl), T. Cat Ford (Housewife), Cass Morgan (Country Woman), Scott Sowers (Ex-G.I.)
Wednesday, June 12–23, 1991 (14 performances)
SERIES C; Sets, Anne Waugh; Lighting, Greg MacPherson; Costumes, Patricia Sarnutaro; Production Supervisor, Craig T. Raisner
The World at Absolute Zero by Sherry Kramer; Director, Jason McConnell Buzas; Stage Manager, Mark Cole. CAST: Debra Cole (Didi), Michael Countryman (Fred)
Salaam, Huey Newton, Salaam by Ed Bullins; Director, Woodie King, Jr.; Stage Manager, Elizabeth Brady Davis. CAST: Ramon Melindez Moses (Younger Brother), Mansoor Najeeullah (Marvin), Charles Weldon (Huey Newton)
The Last Yankee by Arthur Miller; Director, Gordon Edelstein; Stage Manager, Sara Gormley Plass. CAST: John Heard (Leroy), Biff McGuire (Frick)
Big Al by Brian Gobuloff; Director, Peter Maloney; Stage Manager, Sabrina B. Leuning. CAST: Evan Handler (Leo), Gus Rogerson (Ricky)

Carol Rosegg Photos

(Perry St. Theatre) Thursday, May 23–June 9, 1991 (16 performances) Merry Enterprises Theatre and the Perry Street Theatre's Prima Artists present:
THE GOAT by Ben Morse; Director, Beatrice Winde; Sets, Don Jensen; Lighting, David Neville; Costumes, Traci di Gesu; Stage Manager, Elizabeth Larson; Press, Jeffrey Richards/Philip Thurston. CAST: Joyce Blint (Gloria), Marc Wolf (Richie), Erma Campbell (Coley), Gregory Henderson (Arthur), Louis D. Giovanetti (Dominic), Guy Davis (Leroy), Willi Burke (Beatrice)

A comedy in two acts. The action takes place in Coley's Brooklyn home, at the present time.

(Avalon Repertory Theatre) Thursday, May 23–June 2, 1991 (12 performances) The Zena Group Theatre presents:
MOMENTARY LAPSES: Eight New Ten Minute Plays From Actors Theatre of Louisville; Producers, Jeremy Gold, Josh Liveright, Bruce Marshall Romans; Stage Manager, Kate Splaine *Valentine's Day* by Kathleen Chopin; Director, Kate Cummings. CAST: Kate Splaine (Annie), Matt Kozlowski (Barry), Jeremy Gold (Rick), Arthur Halpern (Mutt) *What She Found There* by John Glore; Director, Libba Harmon. CAST: Belinda Morgan (Celia), Bruce Marshall Romans (Louis) *Out The Window* by Neal Bell; Director, Tracy Brigden. CAST: Matt Kozlowski (Jake), Diane Casey (Andy) *Mixed Emotions* by Bob Krakower; Director, Rod Lachlan. CAST: Belinda Morgan (Deb), Arthur Halpern (Michael), Josh Liveright (Ed), Bruce Marshall Romans (Jack), Kara Flannery (Laura) *Really Bizarre Rituals* by Reid Davis; Director, Jameel Khaja; Music, Max Risenhoover. CAST: Josh Liveright (Stan), Kara Flannery (Val), Jeremy Gold (Hallie) *After You* by Steven Dietz; Director, Alex Aron. CAST: Margaret Howard (Amy), Arthur Halpern (Ben) *The Problem Solver* by Michael Bigelow Dixon and Valerie Smith; Director, Kate Cummings. CAST: Matt Kozlowski (Phil), Matra Johnson (Megan), Diane Casey (Tina), Kate Splaine (Kathy), Jeremy Gold (Jer) *The Last Supper* by Reid Davis; Director, Libba Harmon. CAST: Margaret Howard (Bucky), Bruce Marshall Romans (Phil), Josh Liveright (Bob)

Beatrice Winde, Ben Morse, Erma Campbell in "The Goat"
Top Left: Gregory Henderson, Campbell (*Alex Rupert*)

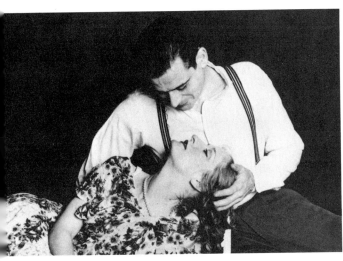

Theo Polites, Kathryn Chilson in "Full Circle" (*Michael Ian*)

Michael McLernon, Christopher Howatt in "Troubadour" (*Carol Rosegg*)

(Harold Clurman Theatre) Saturday, May 25–June 9, 1991 (19 performances) Artemis Associates Inc. presents:
FULL CIRCLE by Erich Maria Remarque; Adaptation, Peter Stone; Director, Murray Changar; Sets, Roger Hanna; Lighting, Kathryn A. Eader; Producer, Terry Ann Bennett. CAST: Kathryn Chilson (Anna), John Di Benedetto (Schmidt), Russell Leib (Katz), Theo Polites (Rohde), Ronald Rand (Koerner), Katherine Schroeder (Grete), Robert Skehan (Mack/Soviet Soldier), Peter Toran (Captain), Eric Vogt (Maurer/Sergeant)

Remarque's only play. The action takes place in war-ravaged Berlin, 1945.

(Ubu Rpertory) Saturday, May 25–August 3, 1991. Beech Knight Productions in association with Ubu Repertory Theatre presents:
TROUBADOUR; Music, Bert Draesel; Lyrics, John Martin; Book, Mr. Martin and Mr. Draesel; Director/Musical Director, D.J. Maloney; Choreographer, Tom Ribbink; Sets, Tom Cariello; Lighting, Curt Ostermann; Costumes, Daniele Hollywood; Stage Manager, Barry Ravitch; Press, David Rothenberg. CAST: Christopher Howatt (Francesco), Steve Gilden (Leo), William R. Park (Bernardo), Michael McLernon (Elias), Sarah Downs (Clare), Keith Douglas Heimpel (Juniper), Jack O'Reilly (Cardinal Ugolino), David Harryman (Pietro/Pope Innocent III), Randy Mulder (Signor Faverone/Sultan/Crusader), Pressley Sutherland (Merchant/Saracen/Beggar/Crusader/Bologna Scholar), Byron Allen (Pope's Secretary/Crusader/Scholar), Ann Schlafley (Leper/Nun)
MUSICAL NUMBERS: On Behalf of the Maker, The Troubadour, Dance, A Father's Dream, Who Can Benefit You Most?, Change, Listen to the Voice, Soliloquy, There Must Be Something More, You Can't Have Me, The Earth Is the Lord's, The Rule, Called to the Simple Life, An Unusual Normal, There Is a Mystery, Patching, Brother Mountain, There Is a Time, This Is the Man, Every Day, Jerusalem, Soon, I Wonder I Wonder, And We Were One, It Was Magnificent, The Order, It's Glorious, Let There Be Books, Where Is That Vision Now?, Praised Be My Lord, Finale

A musical in two acts. The action takes place in Italy in the early 1200s.

(Space 603) Monday, May 27–June 8, 1991 (12 performances) 10 Penny Productions present:
THE SLAB BOYS by John Byrne; Director, Elizabeth Greenberg; Sets, Peter R. Feuche; Costumes, Joseph Cigliano; Lighting, Edward Fasbender. CAST: Karl P. Carrigan, Willie DiMartino, Bart Fasbender, Peter R. Feuche, Judette Jones, Robert Maschio, E.F. Morrill, Emily Wachtel

A comedy in two acts. The action takes place in Scotland in 1957.

(Atlantic Theatre) Tuesday, May 28–June 8, 1991 (11 performances) Atlantic Theatre Company presents:
THE VIRGIN MOLLY by Quincy Long; Director, Sarah Eckhardt; Sets, Jack O'Reilly; Costumes, Cyndi Lee; Lighting, Howard Werner; Stage Manager, Matthew Silver; Fights, Rick Sordelet; Press, Jim Baldassare. CAST: Robert Bella (Private Molly Petersen), Christopher McCann (Corporal), Todd Weeks (Civilian), Ray Anthony Thomas (Jones), Neil Pepe (Captain), Jordan Lage (Harmon)

A drama performed without intermission. The action takes place in the "Queerhouse" of a Marine boot camp.

Robert Maschio, Peter R. Feuche, Karl P. Carrigan in "Slab Boys"

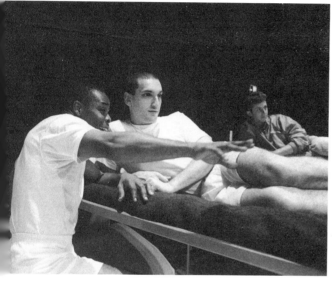

Ray Anthony Thomas, Robert Bella, Todd Weeks in
"The Virgin Molly" (*Jeff Harris*)

Geoffrey Nauffts, Marisa Tomei in "Summer Nights" (*Jay Strauss*)

(Naked Angels) Wednesday, May 29–June 15, 1991 (16 performances) Naked Angels presents:
THE SUMMER WINDS by Frank Pugliese; Director, Gareth Williams; Sets, Rick Sobel; Lighting, John-Paul Szczepanski; Sound, Ray Schilke; Costumes, Lorraine Anderson, Lauren Press; Musical Director, Steve Alper; Stage Manager, Jennifer Freed; Press, Jeffrey Richards. CAST: Ashley Crow (Ann), Lisa Eichhorn (Mary), Geoffrey Nauffts (Lou), Timothy Britten Parker (Pinky), Barry Sherman (Rick), Marisa Tomei (Janie), Gareth Williams (Joe), Jeff Williams (Sam), Kelly Wolf (Joanne)

A romantic drama where love songs become love stories. The action takes place on the hottest night of the summer.

(Intar Theatre) Wednesday, May 29–June 30, 1991 (30 performances) Intar Hispanic American Arts Center (Max Ferrá, Artistic Director; Eva Bruné, Managing Director) presents:
THE HAVE-LITTLE by Migdalia Cruz; Director, Nilo Cruz; Sets, Donald Eastman; Costumes, Gabriel Berry; Lighting, Kenneth Posner; Sound, Fox and Perla, Ltd.; Stage Manager, Michael Garces; Press, Peter Cromarty/David Lotz. CAST: Divina Cook (Carmen Rivera), David Roya (Jose Rivera), Marisol Massey (Lillian Rivera), Gabriella Diaz Farrar (Michi Rodriguez)

A drama performed without intermission. The action takes place in the South Bronx between 1974 and 1976.

(AMAS Theatre) Thursday, May 30–June 21, 1991 (24 performances) AMAS Musical Theatre (Rosetta LeNoire, Founder/Artistic Director; Jeffrey Solis, Producing Director) presents:
ECHOES; Music, James Campodonico; Lyrics/Book, Bryan D. Leys; Director, Mark S. Herko

Gabriella Diaz Farrar, Marisol Massey
in "The Have-Little" (*Carol Rosegg*)

AMERICAN JEWISH THEATRE

Seventeenth Season

Artistic Director, Stanley Brechner; Associate Artistic Director, Lonny Price; Counsel, Walter Gidaly, Howard I. Golden; Development, Norman Golden; Special Programs, Evanne Christian; Press, Jeffrey Richards Associates/Gary D. Bramnick
 Saturday, October 27–November 25, 1990 (31 performances)
I OUGHT TO BE IN PICTURES by Neil Simon; Director, Stanley Brechner; Sets, James Wolk; Lighting, David Holcomb; Costumes, Pamela Schofield. CAST: David Baily, Betsy Friday, Jenn Thompson

Saturday, January 12–February 10, 1991 (31 performances)
GROWN UPS by Jules Feiffer; Director, Lonny Price; Sets, John Falabella; Costumes, Gail Brassard; Lighting, David Holcomb; Stage Manager, Eric Eligator. CAST: Rosemary Prinz (Helen), Len Stanger (Jack), Barbara Niles (Marilyn), Barry Craig Friedman (Jake), Lisa Emery (Louise), Lauren Gaffney (Edie)
 A bitter comedy in three acts. The action takes place in New Rochelle, New York and New York City, at the present time.

Saturday, April 27–May 26, 1991 (31 performances)
FAYEBIRD by Diane Amsterdam; Director, Elinor Renfield; Sets, Judy Gailen; Costumes, Barbara Beccio; Lighting, Brian McDevitt. CAST: Janet Sarno, Rochelle Oliver succeeded by Elinor Basescu
 A comedy about two sisters.

Betsy Friday, Jenn Thompson, David Baily in "I Ought to Be in Pictures"

Carolee Carmello, Richard Levine, Patti Karr, Evan Pappas, Alix Korey, Jim Bracchitta in "I Can Get It For You Wholesale"

Saturday, February 23–April 21, 1991 (59 performances)
I CAN GET IT FOR YOU WHOLESALE; Music/Lyrics, Harold Rome; Book, Jerome Weidman, based on his novel; Director/Choreographer, Richard Sabellico; Musical Director, Jonny Bowden; Sets, David Sumner; Costumes, Gail Baldoni; Lighting, Tom Sturge; Hairstylist, Kristian Kraai; Stage Manager, Sandra M. Bloom. CAST: Vicki Lewis (Miss Marmelstein), Joel Brooks (Maurice Pulvermacher/Eddie), Richard Levine (Meyer Bushkin/Ramon), Evan Pappas (Harry), Jim Bracchitta (Tootsie Maltz/Teddy Asch), Carolee Carmello (Ruthie Rifkin), Patti Karr (Mrs. Bogen), Deborah Carlson (Martha Mills), Alix Korey (Blanche Bushkin), Sam Brent Riegel (Delivery Boy/Sheldon Bushkin)
MUSICAL NUMBERS: The Way Things Are, When Gemini Meets Capricorn, Momma Momma, Sound of Money, Family Way, Too Soon, Who Knows, Have I Told You Lately?, Ballad of the Garment Trade, Gift for Today, Miss Marmelstein, On My Way to Love, What's in It for Me?, What Are They Doing to Us Now?, Eat a Little Something, Finale
 A revision of the 1962 musical performed in two acts. The action takes place in New York City during the late 1930s.

Rosemary Prinz, Barry Craig Friedman in "Grown Ups"

Vicki Lewis in "...Wholesale"

Evan Pappas, Patti Karr in "...Wholesale"
Carol Rosegg/Martha Swope Photos

AMERICAN PLACE THEATRE

Twenty-seventh Season

Director, Wynn Handman; General Manager, Dara Hershman; Marketing/Development Director, Donna Moreau-Cupp; Production Manager, Andrew Meyer; Technical Director, Gregory Erbach; Resident Stage Manager, Lloyd Davis, Jr.; Press, David Rothenberg/Terrence Womble, Meg Gordean, Manuel Igrejas

Thursday, October 11–28, 1990 (11 performances and 3 previews)
CALVIN TRILLIN'S WORDS, NO MUSIC; Written and Performed by Calvin Trillin; Director, Wynn Handman; Design, Bill Stabile; Lighting, Andrew James Meyer; Stage Manager, Lloyd Davis, Jr.

A new show from the humorist.

Thursday, November 8, 1990–April 28, 1991, reopened at the Orpheum Theatre on Tuesday, June 4, 1991 (107 performances)
MAMBO MOUTH by John Leguizamo; Director, Peter Askin; Sets, Philipp Jung; Lighting, Graeme F. McDonnell; Sound, Bruce Ellman; Production Manager, Andrew Meyer; Stage Managers, Joseph A. Onorato, Michael Robin. CAST: John Leguizamo (Agememnon/Angel Garcia/Loco Louie/Pepe/Manny the Fanny/Inca God/Crossover King)

A solo theatre piece performed without intermission.

Calvin Trillin

John Leguizamo in "Mambo Mouth"

Sunday, November 11, 1990–
I STAND BEFORE YOU NAKED by Joyce Carol Oates; Director, Wynn Handman; Design, Bill Stabile; Lighting, Andrew James Meyer; Costumes, Sally J. Lesser; Stage Manager, Lloyd Davis, Jr. CAST: Bronwen Booth (Little Blood Button/Orange), Marguerite Kuhn (Wife of/Good Morning Good Afternoon), Penny Templeton (The Boy/Slow Motion), Nancy Barrett (Wealthy Lady/Nuclear Holocaust), Annie McGreevey (Darling I'm Telling You-Angel Eyes), Elizabeth Alley (Pregnant)

Ten monologues performed by women.

Tuesday, March 19–April 7, 1991 (18 performances)
STRUCK DUMB by Jean-Claude van Itallie and Joseph Chaikin and **THE WAR IN HEAVEN** by Joseph Chaikin and Sam Shepard; Director, Nancy Gabor; Sets, Jun Maeda; Lighting, Beverly Emmons; Costumes, Mary Brecht; Dramaturg, Bill Coco; Stage Manager, Lloyd Davis, Jr. CAST: Joseph Chaikin

Two one-act plays exploring Mr. Chaikin's illness and the healing process.

Joseph Chaikin in "War in Heaven"

Tuesday, April 30-June 2, 1991 (35 performances)
STATES OF SHOCK by Sam Shepard; Director, Bill Hart; Sets, Bill Stabile; Costumes, Gabriel Berry; Lighting, Pat Dignan, Anne Militello; Composer/Sound, J.A. Deane; Production Manager, Andrew Meyer; Stage Manager, Lloyd Davis, Jr. CAST: John Malkovich (Colonel), Erica Gimpel (Glory Bee), Isa Thomas (White Woman), Steve Nelson (White Man), Michael Wincott (Stubbs), Richard Dworkin, Joseph Sabella (Percussion)

A drama performed without intermission. The action takes place in a family restaurant in America.

John Malkovich in "States of Shock"
Martha Holems, David Hughes Photos

BROOKLYN ACADEMY OF MUSIC

President/Executive Producer, Harvey Lichtenstein; Executive Vice-President, Karen Brooks Hopkins; Marketing/Promotion, Douglas W. Allan; Finance/Administration, Jacques Brunswick; General Manager, James D. Nomikos; Next Wave Festival, Liz Thompson; Press, Peter Carzasty

(Majestic) October 2–14, 1990 (14 performances)
ENDANGERED SPECIES; Conception/Direction, Martha Clarke; Created with the Company; Text: *Leaves of Grass* by Walt Whitman; Adaptation, Robert Coe; Sound, Richard Peaslee, Stanley Walden; Sets/Costumes, Robert Israel; Lighting, Paul Gallo; Stage Manager, Steven Ehrenberg; Presented with Music Theatre Group (Lyn Austin, Producing Director; Diane Wondisford, Managing Director) in association with Circus Flora (Ivor David Balding, Artistic Director/Producer)
COMPANY: Michael J. Anderson, Flora Baldini (African Elephant), Bert (Miniature Goat), Felix Blaska, Bluey (Irish Cobb Horse), Alistair Butler, Courtney Earl, Lisa Giobbi, David Grausman, Mr. Grey (Percheron Horse), Paul Guilfoyle, Valarie Eileen Henry, Jack (Clydesdale Horse), Judy Kuhn, Peter McRobbie, Mike (Miniature Horse), Frank Raiter, Tony (Capuchin Monkey)
   A music-theatre piece performed without intermission. The work explores the bond between man, animals and nature, performed by actors, dancers and animals.

(Opera House) Friday, October 19–26, 1990 (10 performances)
NINAGAWA MACBETH by William Shakespeare; Translation, Yushi Odashima; Director, Yukio Ninagawa; Sets, Kappa Senoh; Lighting, Sumio Yoshii; Music, Masato Kai; Sound, Akira Honma; Choreography, Kinnosuke Hanayagi; Fights, Masahiro Kunii; Costumes, Jusaburo Tsujimura; Producer, Tadao Nakane.
CAST: Mizuho Suzuki (Duncan), Norihiro Inoue (Malcolm), Eiichi Seike (Donalbain), Masane Tsukayama (Macbeth), Kazuhisa Seshimo (Banquo), Haruhiko Joh (Macduff), Masafumi Seno (Ross), Tomoyuki Yamada (Fleance), Tatsumi Aoyama (Siward/Old Man), Komaki Kurihara (Lady Macbeth), Hitomi Kageyama (Lady Macduff), Tokusaburo Arashi, Goro Daimon, Matanosuke Nakamura (Witches)
   A drama performed in two acts by Japan's Ninagawa Company.

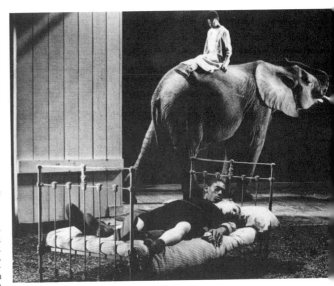

"Endangered Species"

"Ninagawa Macbeth"

"Township Fever"

(BAM/Majestic Theatre) Friday, November 23, 1990–January 20, 1991 (39 performances and 30 previews)
TOWNSHIP FEVER; Music, Lyrics and Book, Mbongeni Ngema; Conceived, Choreographed and Directed by Mr. Ngema; Sets/Costumes, Sarah Roberts; Lighting, Mannie Manim; Sound, Mark Malherbe, Rick Rowe; Arrangements/Orchestrations, Mr. Ngema; Horn Arrangements, Brian Thusi, Eric Norgate; General Manager, Steven C. Callahan; Production Manager, Jeff Hamlin. CAST: Brian Mazibuko (Jazz Mngadi), Sindiswa Dlathu (Tonko Mnisi), Bhoyi Ngema (Sibisi), Bheki Mqadi (Bra Cobra), Faca Khulu, Mabonga Khumalo, Sbusiso Ngema (Hostel Workers), John Lata (Phillidelphia), David Manqele (Priest), Mamthandi Zulu (Mrs. Mngadi), Themba Mbonani (American Molefe), Dieketseng Mnisi (Manyewu Mnisi), Mike Motsogi (Dzehwe), Sduduzo Mthethwa (Fireman), Sphamandla Ngcamu (M.C.), Siphiwe Nkosi (Kiriman), Clara Reyes (News Presenter/Pregnant Woman), Mabonga Khumalo (Police)
MUSICAL NUMBERS: One Blood, Ngatheth 'Amacala, Hear My Prayer, Township Fever, Blazing Like Fire, Amasendenduna, Isiglino, U'Mandela U' Thithlome, Ekufikeni, Isidudla, Beautiful Little Mamas, Church Amen Song, Xolisinhliziyo, Entr'acte, Ngamiwamina, Mtubatuba, Wasiqoqela Ndawonye, Times of War, Oliver Tambo, Nduna Ngibolekinduku, Ngobamakhosi, Corruption, Ize Lakithi, E South Africa, Mathambo Kababa, Mandela, Freedom Charter
   A musical in two acts. The action takes place in South Africa in 1987.

(BAM/Lepercq Space) Tuesday, October 23–28, 1990 (6 performances)
POLYGRAPH; Written by Marie Brassard and Robert Lepage; Music, Pierre Brousseau and Yves Chamberland; Director, Mr. Lepage; Sets, Mr. Lepage; Translation, Gyllian Raby; Lighting, Eric Fauque, Mr. Lepage; Props, Steve Lucas; Stage Manager, Mr. Fauque; Slides, Dave Lepage. CAST: Pierre Auger, Marc Beland, Marie Brassard
   A metaphysical detective story performed without intermission. A presentation of Canada's La Theatre Repere.

Robert Lepage, Marie Brassard, Pierre-Philippe Guay in "Polygraph"
Robert Laliberté, Ruphin Coudyzer Photos

CIRCLE REPERTORY COMPANY

Twenty-second Season

Artistic Director, Tanya Berezin; Managing Director, Terrence Dwyer; Associate Artistic Director, Mark Ramont; Lab Director, Michael Warren Powell; Literary Manager, Adrienne Hiegel; Development Director, Virginia Finn Lenhardt; Production Manager, Jody Boese; Press, Gary Murphy

Wednesday, October 3–November 11, 1990 (47 performances)
THE COLORADO CATECHISM by Vincent J. Cardinal; Director, Mark Ramont; Sets, James Youmans; Costumes, David C. Woolard; Lighting, Pat Dignan; Sound, Stewart Werner, Chuck London; Stage Manager, Denise Yaney. CAST: Becky Ann Baker (Donna), Kevin James O'Connor (Ty)

A drama in two acts. The action takes place in a painting studio and the Roger Goodman Drug and Alcohol Clinic in Cripple Creek, Colorado, in the not-too-distant past.

Wednesday, December 5, 1990–January 31, 1991 (47 performances)
LOVE DIATRIBE by Harry Kondoleon; Director, Jorge Cacheiro; Sets, G.W. Mercier; Costumes, Walker Hicklin; Lighting, Dennis Parichy; Sound, Scott Lehrer; Stage Manager, Fred Reinglas. CAST: Martha Gehman (Frieda), Barry Sherman (Orin), Amy Aquino (Sandy), Jane Cronin (Mrs. Anderson), Edward Seamon (Dennis), Michael Rispoli (Mike), Lynn Cohen (Gerry)

A comedy performed without intermission. The action takes place in the family room of a suburban house, at present.

Kevin James O'Connor, Becky Ann Baker
in "The Colorado Catechism"

Michael Rispoli, Amy Aquino, Barry Sherman in "Love Diatribe"

Amy Aquino, Sandra Santiago, Jon Polito,
Peter Riegert in "Road to Nirvana"

Ashley Gardner, Christopher Shaw
in "Walking the Dead"

Wednesday, February 13–March 31, 1991 (54 performances)
ROAD TO NIRVANA by Arthur Kopit; Director, Jim Simpson; Sets, Andrew Jackness; Costumes, Ann Roth; Lighting, Scott Zielinski; Sound, Stewart Werner, Chuck London; Hair/Wigs, Bobby H. Grayson; Stage Manager, Fred Reinglas. CAST: Jon Polito (Al), Saundra Santiago (Lou), Peter Rigert (Jerry), James Puig (Ramon), Amy Aquino (Nirvana)

A comedy in two acts. The action takes place in Hollywood, at present.

Wednesday, April 24–June 2, 1991 (48 performances)
WALKING THE DEAD by Keith Curran; Director, Mark Ramont; Sets, Tom Kamm; Costumes, Toni-Leslie James; Lighting, Kenneth Posner; Sound, Scott Lehrer; Fights, Rick Sordelet; Hairstylist, Bobby H. Grayson; Stage Manager, Denise Yaney. CAST: Ashley Gardner (Veronica Tass), Scotty Bloch (Dottie Tass), Myra Taylor (Maya Deboats), Christopher Shaw (Chess Wysynsky), Cotter Smith (Bobby Brax), Tyrone Wilson (Dr. Drum), Joe Mantello (Stan)

A drama about a disparate group of friends gathering for a murdered companion's memorial service.

Wednesday, June 16-July 28, 1991 (48 performances)
THE BALCONY SCENE by Wil Calhoun; Director, Michael Warren Powell; Set, Kevin Joseph Roach; Costumes, Thomas L. Keller; Lighting, Dennis Parichy; Sound, Chuck London, Stewart Werner; Fights, Rick Sordelet; Stage Manager, Fred Reinglas. CAST: William Fichtner (Paul), Cynthia Nixon (Karen), Jonathan Hogan (Alvin)

A comedy performed without intermission. The action takes place on adjoining balconies of a Chicago apartment building, at the present time.

Jonathan Hogan, Cynthia Nixon in "The Balcony Scene"
Gerry Goodstein Photos

85

CLASSIC STAGE COMPANY
CSC REPERTORY, LTD.

Twenty-fourth Season

Charlotte Rae in "Happy Days"

Artistic Director, Carey Perloff; Managing Director, Patricia Taylor; Development, Catherine Pagès; Production Manager, Jeffrey Berzon; Conservatory, Rebecca Guy; Company Manager, Kelley Voorhees; Press, Peter Cromarty/David Katz, David Lotz

Tuesday, October 2–November 11, 1990 (42 performances and 8 previews)
HAPPY DAYS by Samuel Beckett; Director, Carey Perloff; Sets, David Eastman; Costumes, Julie Weiss; Lighting, Frances Aronson; Stage Manager, Carol Dawes. CAST: Charlotte Rae (Winnie), Bill Moor (Willie)

Performed in two acts.

Tuesday, February 26–April 7, 1991 (48 performances)
THE LEARNED LADIES by Molière; Translation/Adaptation, Freyda Thomas; Additional Material, Richard Seyd and Ms. Thomas; Director, Mr. Seyd; Sets, Richard Hoover; Costumes, Beaver Bauer; Lighting, Mary Louise Geiger; Composer, Gina Leishman; Stage Manager, Carol Dawes. CAST: Georgine Hall (Belise), Julia Gibson (Henriette), Alice Haining (Armande), Peter Francis-James (Clitandre), Frank Raiter (Ariste), Martin B. Nathan (Ariste's Assistant), Merwin Goldsmith (Chrysale), Michael Reilly (Belise's Suitors), Amy Brenneman (Martine), Jean Stapleton (Philamente), Michael R. Wilson (Lepine), Nestor Serrano (Trissotin), Peter Bartlett (Vadius/Judge)

A comedy in two acts.

Tuesday, April 23-June 9, 1991 (42 performances and 13 previews)
THE RESISTIBLE RISE OF ARTURO UI by Bertolt Brecht; Translation, Ralph Manheim; Director, Carey Perloff; Sets, Douglas Stein; Costumes, Donna Zakowska; Lighting, Stephen Strawbridge; Composer, David Lang; Sound, Daniel Moses Schreier; Music Director, Catherine Reid; Fights, Jason Kuschner; Stage Manager, Richard Hester; CAST: Larry Joshua (Flake/ Defense Counsel), Michael McCormick (Butler/Judge/Pastor's Voice), Miguel Perez (Mulberry/O'Casey/Hook), Keith R. Smith (Caruther/Greenwool/Goodwill), Richard Ziman (Clark/Actor/Fish), Ron Faber (Sheet/Gaffles/Prosecutor/Dullfeet), Sam Gray (Dogsborough), Nicholas Turturro (Young Dogsborough/Ted Ragg/ Inna), Michael Reilly (Bowl), John Turturro (Arturo Ui), Olek Krupa (Ernesto Roma), Katherine Borowitz (Dockdaisy/Wounded Woman/Betty Dullfeet), Zach Grenier (Emanuele Giri), Michael R. Wilson (Butler), David Patrick Kelly (Giuseppe Givola), Tom Delling (Physician), Ani Apardian, Elizabeth Beirne, Charles Campbell, Katherine Cohen, Dimitrius Conly, Mary Beth Kilkelly, Ethan Mintz, Martin B. Nathan, Catherine Pagès, Katherine Puma, Gwynne Rivers, Suzanne Robertson, Julina Tatlock

A drama in two acts. This adaptation sets the action in Chicago.

Jay Thompson, Paula Court Photos

Jean Stapleton, Georgine Hall in "The Learned Ladies"

Zach Grenier, John Turturro, Olek Krupa, David Patrick Kelly in "Arturo Ui"

Stephen Mailer, Michael Lombard in "What's Wrong with This Picture?"

Ronald Guttman (Top), Will Scheffer in "Modigliani"

Pamela Burrell, Diego Matamoros in "Spinoza"

Tovah Feldsuh in "A Fierce Attachment"

JEWISH REPERTORY THEATRE

Seventeenth Season

Artistic Director, Ran Avni; Associate Director, Edward M. Cohen; Development, Bruce Fagin; Playwrights-in-Residence, Dan Ellentuck, Brenda Shoshanna Lukeman, Donald Margulies, Bob Morris, Gordon Rayfield, David Rush, Susan Sandler, Nahma Sandrow, Richard Schotter, Michael Taav; Composers-in-Residence, Raphael Crystal, Margaret Rachlin Pine; Press, Shirly Herz/Pete Sanders, Glenna Freedman, Robert Larkin, Sam Rudy.

Saturday, June 9–August 5, 1990 (44 performances)
WHAT'S WRONG WITH THIS PICTURE? by Donald Margulies; Director, Larry Arrick; Sets, Ray Recht; Costumes, Jeffrey Ullman; Lights, Brian Nason; Stage Manager, Nina Heller. CAST: Stephen Mailer (Artie), Michael Lombard (Mort), Dolores Sutton (Bella), Salem Ludwig (Sid), Barbara Spiegel (Ceil), Lauren Klein (Shirley)

A comedy in two acts. The action takes place in a middle-class Brooklyn apartment at present. An earlier version of this play was presented at Manhattan Theater Club in 1985.

Saturday, October 20–November 13, 1990 (20 performances)
SPINOZA by Dimitre Frenkel Frank; Translation, Martin Cleaver; Director, Robert Kalfin; Sets, Richard Hoover; Costumes, Gail Cooper-Hecht; Lighting, John Gisondi; Composer, John Clifton, Stage Manager, Nina Heller. CAST: Salem Ludwig (Rabbi Morteira), Jeffrey Logan (Zacuto), Diego Matamoros (Spinoza), W.B. Brydon (Rembrandt), Karen McLaughlin (Hendrickje), Pamela Burrell (Countess), William Duff-Griggin (Magistrate), Funda Duyal (Polish Girl)

A drama in two acts. The action takes place in Amsterdam in 1656.

Saturday, December 15, 1990–January 13, 1991 (20 performances)
TAKING STOCK by Richard Schotter; Director, Marilyn Chris; Sets, Ray Recht; Costumes, Gail Cooper-Hecht; Lights, Najla Hanson; Composer, Ronnie Breines; Stage Manager, Nina Heller. CAST: Lee Wallace (Alvi), George Guidall (Sam), Stephen Singer (Howie)

A comedy in two acts. The action takes place at Sam and Alvi's Sports Shop on the Upper West Side of Manhattan in New York City. The time is now.

Saturday, February 16–March 17, 1991 (20 performances)
A FIERCE ATTACHMENT based on the book *Fierce Attachments* by Vivian Gornick; Adapted/Directed by Edward M. Cohen; Sets, Ray Recht; Costumes, Carrie Robbins; Lighting, Brian Nason; Stage Manager, Geraldine Teagarden. CAST: Tovah Feldshuh (The Daughter)

A monodrama in two acts. Based on the memoirs of journalist Vivian Gornick. The action takes place in a Manhattan apartment, at present.

Saturday, April 13–May 12, 1991 (20 performances)
MODIGLIANI by Dennis McIntyre; Director, Bryna Wortman; Sets, Scott Bradley; Costumes, Barbara A. Bell; Lighting, Brian Nason; Sound, Aural Fixation; Stage Manager, D.C. Rosenberg. CAST: Ronald Guttman (Modigliani), Karen Sillas (Beatrice), Martin Rudy (Art Dealer), David Beach, Daniel James, Dane Knell, Will Scheffer

Saturday, June 1–30, 1991 (25 performances)
ENCORE; Conceived by Ran Avni and Raphael Crystal; Director, Mr. Avni; Music Director, Andrew Howard; Music Supervision, Mr. Crystal; Choreography, Helen Butleroff; Sets, Jeffrey Schneider; Costumes, Gail Cooper-Hecht; Lights, Brian Nason; Stage Manager, D.C. Rosenberg. CAST: Adam Heller, Michele Ragusa, Susan Friedman Schrott, Steve Sterner, Stuart Zagnit
MUSICAL NUMBERS: All of That Made for Me, It's Just Like I Was You, Welcome to the Family, Another April, My Heart Is in the East, Stars of the Morning, What Happened What?, You'll Have to Change, I'll Talk to Her, The Boy Is Perfect, Matchmaker's Daughter, What's My Name?, Lovesongs and Lullabies, Be Fruitful and Multiply, Living in America, Watch Your Step, My Greenhorn Cousin, She's Missing the Cherry on the Top, Raisins and Almonds, Columbus You Done Okay By Me, My Terms, What's So Special About a Special?, What Will People Think?, I'll Be Here Tomorrow, We're Almost There, Less and Less, I Think I Think, You I Like, Encore

A revue of highlights from musicals presented at JRT through the years. Shows include: *Up From Paradise, My Heart Is in the East, Chu Chem, Kuni-Leml, Vagabond Stars, Sophie, The Special, The Grand Tour*

Left: Adam Heller, Michele Ragusa, Steve Sterner, Susan Friedman Schrott, Stuart Zagnit in "Encore!"
Carol Rosegg/Martha Swope Photos

LA MAMA E.T.C.

Director, Ellen Stewart; Business Manager, James W. Moore; Associate Director, Meryl Vladimer; Development Director, Maurice McClelland; Archivist, Doris Pettijohn; Art Director, Susan Haskins; Technical Director, Brad Phillips; Resident Set Designer, Jun Maeda; Resident Lighting Designer, Howard Thies; Resident Costume Designer, Gabriel Berry; Press, Jonathan Slaff

WHITESTONES by William J. Boesky; Director, Toni Kotite; Sets, Allen Moyer; Lighting, Valerie LauKee; Costumes, James Scott; Music Director, Will McKenna; Stage Manager/Props, Michelle McIntyre. CAST: Brian Jennings (Old and Young Teddy), Douglas Whitely-Weston (Jonah), Fred Fehrmann (Sam), Cynthia Crumlish (Mother), Marisol Massey (Jennifer), Joseph McKenna (Roach), John Dee (Teddy and Jonah vocals), Sarah Jane Symons (Mother vocals), Greta C. Lauran (Jennifer vocals), Max Baxter (Guitar), Will McKenna (Bass), Benny Kay (Percussion)

Folk rock theatre in two acts. The action takes place in Teddy's darkroom and places in his memory. The time is 2010 (present) and 1991 (past).

Sarah Simons, Douglas Whitely Weston, Greta C. Lauren in "White Stones"

Thursday, January 31–February 9, 1991 (6 performances)
AN AMERICAN GRIOT: *(A Jazz Autobiography)* by Iris Ackamoor and Ed Bullins; Directorial Assistance, Rhodessa Jones and Brian Freeman; Lighting, Stephanie Johnson, Howard Thies; Costumes, Pat Stewart; Sets, Kemit Amenophis; Music mostly by Mr. Ackamoor.
An homage to the practitioners of jazz.

Wednesday, February 13–24, 1991 (12 performances)
SAINT TOUS with Music by André DeShields and Thaddeus Pinkston; Book/Lyrics/Conception/Direction, Mr. DeShields; Musical Direction/Vocal Arrangements, Mr. Pinkston; Lighting, Don Coleman; Costumes, Lauren Press; Choreography, Fletcher L. Nickerson; Stage Manager, Isaac Ho; Graphics, Junanne Peck; Percussion, Dan W. Al-Mateen; Technical, Rande Harris; Scenic Design, Mark Forsythe. CAST: Cheryl Alexander (Queen Gou-Guinou), Reggie Bruce Ashanti (Henri Christophe), André DeShields (Toussaint L'Ouverture), Ellia English (Oldest Living Person in the Universe), Drew Kahn (General Charles Leclerc), Mary Elizabeth McGlynn (Mulatto), Nicky Paraiso (Napoleon Bonaparte), Syd Rushing (Jean Jacques Dessalines), Susan Riley Stevens (Pauline Leclerc)
MUSICAL NUMBERS: The Trouble in Saint Domingue, Challenge of a Dream, Voodoo Babble, Shine On, Tragic Mulatto, Cum Sancto Spiritu, Alleluia Deo Gratias, Gloria, Emperor's Anthem, B-U-Wit-Me?, Measure of Life, Mercy Saint Tous
A music-theatre piece based on the life of Haiti's revolutionary hero, Toussaint L'Ouverture.

Andre De Shields in "Saint Tous"

Saturday, February 16–March 3, 1991 (12 performances)
ANCIENT BOYS by Jean-Claude van Itallie; Director, Gregory Keller; Design, Jun Maeda; Music, Tony Scheitinger; Movement, John Goodwin; Lighting, Michael Smith; Costumes, Mary Brecht; Stage Manager, Marybeth Ward. CAST: Tom Bozell (Luke), Preston Dyar (Danny), Wayne Maugans (Chris), Michael Ornstein (Ruben), Rosemary Quinn (Sherry)
A drama exploring the relationship between individual disease, planetary disease, and art.

Wayne Maughans, Rosemary Quinn, Preston Dyar, Michael Ornstein (front) in "Ancient Boys"

Friday, March 1–17, 1991 (13 performances); re-opened at Actors' Playhouse) Friday, April 19, 1991 and still playing May 31, 1991. La MaMa E.T.C. and Lawrence Lane present:
THE HAUNTED HOST by Robert Patrick; Director, Eric Concklin; Sets, David Adams; Lighting, Tracy Dedrickson; Associate Producers, Steven J. Korwatch, Wayne Hamilton; Stage Manager, Joe McGuire; Press, Shirley Herz/Sam Rudy. CAST: Harvey Fierstein (Jay Astor-The Host), Jason Workman (Frank-The Guest)
A comedy performed without intermission. The action takes place in Jay's apartment on Christopher St., Greenwich Village, New York City. The time is 1964.
with:
POUF POSITIVE by Robert Patrick. CAST: Harvey Fierstein (Robin Wood)
A monologue. The action takes place on a Sunday morning, at the present time. This piece was added after the production moved to Actors' Playhouse.
On June 5th it was replaced with:
SAFE SEX by Harvey Fierstein. The playwright and Jason Workman were the cast.

Wednesday, April 3–28, 1991 (20 performances)
EDDIE GOES TO POETRY CITY: PART 2; Written/Directed/Designed by Richard Foreman; Lighting, Heather Carson; Costumes, Donna Zakowska; Technical Director, Mike Taylor; Sound, Tim Schellenbaum. CAST: Rebeca Ellens (Estelle), Henry Stram (Eddie), Brian Delate (Doctor), Kyle deCamp (Marie), Colin Hodgson (Figure)
A parable performed without intermission.

Right: Jason Workman, Harvey Fierstein in "The Haunted Host"
Jonathan Slaff, Sara Krulwich Photos

LINCOLN CENTER THEATER

Sixth Season

Director, Gregory Mosher; Executive Producer, Bernard Gersten; General Manager, Steven C. Callahan; Production Manager, Jeff Hamlin; Development, Hattie K. Jutagir; Finance Director, David S. Brown; Marketing Director, Thomas Cott; Company Dramaturg, Anne Cattaneo; Casting, Risa Bramon, Billy Hopkins; Press; Merle Debuskey/Susan Chicoine

(Newhouse) Wednesday, May 16–October 28, 1990 (185 performances) then transferred to (Beaumont) Tuesday, October 30-
SIX DEGREES OF SEPARATION (See Broadway Calendar)

(Newhouse) Friday, November 2, 1990–January 29, 1991 (68 performances) then transferred to (Beaumont) Monday, February 4–25, 1991 (7 performances) and Sunday, May 12–27, 1991 (5 performances)
MONSTER IN A BOX by Spalding Gray; Director, Renee Shafransky. CAST: Spalding Gray
 The thirteenth autobiographical monologue by Mr. Gray concerns interruptions that happen while trying to write an autobiographical novel.

(Ethel Barrymore) Sunday, January 20-April 14, 1991
MULE BONE (See Broadway Calendar)

(Newhouse) Friday, May 10–July 28, 1991 (55 performances and 35 previews)
MR. GOGOL AND MR. PREEN by Elaine May; Director, Gregory Mosher; Sets, John Lee Beatty; Costumes, Jane Greenwood; Lighting, Kevin Rigdon; Sound, Serge Ossorguine; General Manager, Steven J. Callahan; Production Manager, Jeff Hamlin; Stage Manager, Michael F. Ritchie. CAST: Mike Nussbaum (Mr. Gogol), Willim H. Macy (Mr. Preen), Zohra Lampert (The Woman)
 A comedy in two acts. The action takes place in an Upper West Side apartment, at the present time.

Brigitte Lacombe, Paula Court Photos

**Top Right: Courteney B. Vance (top), Swoosie Kurtz,
John Cunningham in "Six Degrees of Separation"**

Spalding Gray in "Monster in a Box"

**Mike Nussbaum, William H. Macy in
"Mr. Gogol and Mr. Preen", Also above**

MANHATTAN THEATRE CLUB

Nineteenth Season

Artistic Director, Lynne Meadow; Managing Director, Barry Grove; General Manager, Victoria Bailey; Artistic Associates, Michael Bush, Jonathan Alper; Casting, Donna Isaacson; Script Department, Kate Loewald; Writers in Performance Series, Alice Gordan; Development, Janet Harris; Press, Helene Davis, Stephen Hancock

(Stage I) Thursday, October 4–November 25, 1990 (52 performances)
ABUNDANCE by Beth Henley; Director, Ron Lagomarsino; Sets, Adrienne Lobel; Costumes, Robert Wojewodski; Lighting, Paulie Jenkins; Music/Sound, Michael Roth; Fights, J. Allen Suddeth; Stage Managers, Ruth Kreshka, Buzz Cohen. CAST: Amanda Plummer (Bess Johnson), Tess Harper (Macon Hill), Michael Rooker (Jack Flan), Lanny Flaherty (William Curtis), Keith Reddin (Prof. Elmore Crome)

A comedy in two acts. The action takes place in Wyoming Territory and later in St. Louis, starting in the late 1860s and spanning 25 years.

Amanda Plummer, Tess Harper in "Abundance"

(Stage II) Tuesday, October 23–November 18, 1990 (32 performances)
THE WASH by Philip Kan Gotanda; Director, Sharon Ott; Sets, Marshall Factora; Costumes, Lydia Tanji; Lighting, Dan Kotlowitz; Music/Sound, Stephen Le Grand; Stage Manager, Renee Lutz. CAST: Sab Shimono (Nobu Matsumoto), Nobu McCarthy (Masi Matsumoto), Diane Takei (Marsha Matsumoto), Jody Long, (Judy Adams), Shizuko Hoshi (Kiyoko Hasegawa), Marshall Factora (Blackie), George Takei (Sadao Nakasato), Carol A. Honda (Chiyo Froelich)

A drama in two acts. The action takes place in San Jose, California at present.

Tuesday, December 4, 1990–January 18, 1991 (52 performances)
THE AMERICAN PLAN by Richard Greenberg; Director, Evan Yionoulis; Sets, James Youmans; Costumes, Jess Goldstein; Lighting, Donald Holder; Sound/Original Music, Thomas Cabaniss; Stage Manager, Richard Hester. CAST: D.W. Moffett (Nick Lockridge), Wendy Makkena (Lili Adler), Joan Copeland (Eva Adler), Yvette Hawkins (Olivia Shaw), Jonathan Walker (Gil Harbison)

A drama in two acts. The action takes place in the Catskills during the summer of 1960, and on Central Park West ten years later.

George Takei, Nobu McCarthy in "The Wash"

Tuesday, January 29–March 15, 1991 (64 performances)
ABSENT FRIENDS by Alan Ayckbourn; Director, Lynne Meadow; Sets, John Lee Beatty; Costumes, Jane Greenwood; Lighting, Ken Billington; Stage Manager, Pamela Singer. CAST: Gillian Anderson (Evelyn), Brenda Blethyn (Diana), Ellen Parker (Marge), David Purdham (Paul), John Curless (John), Peter Frechette (Colin)

A comedy in two acts. The action takes place in the living room of Paul and Diana's home on Saturday, about 3 p.m.

(Stage II) Tuesday, February 19–March 17, 1991 (32 performances)
LIFE DURING WARTIME by Keith Reddin; Director, Les Waters; Set, James Noone; Costumes, David C. Woolard; Lighting, Michael R. Moody; Original Music/Sound, John Kilgore; Stage Manager, Tom Aberger. CAST: Bruce Norris (Tommy), W.H. Macy (Heinrich), Leslie Lyles (Gale), Welker White (Sally/Mrs. Fielding/Megan), Matt McGrath (Howard/Waiter/Richie/Delivery Boy), James Rebhorn (John Calvin/Fielding/Lieutenant Waters/DeVries)

A dark comedy in two acts. The action takes place here and now.

Gerry Goodstein Photos

Wendy Makkena (top), Joan Copeland, D.W. Moffett in "The American Plan"

W.H. Macy, Bruce Norris in "Life During Wartime"

John Curless, Gillian Anderson, David Purdham (top), Ellen Parker, Peter Frechette, Brenda Blethyn in "Absent Friends"

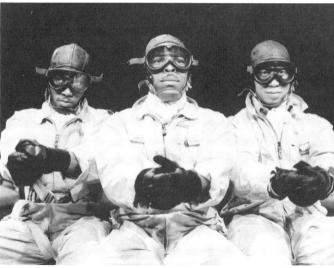

Scott Whitehurst, Raymond Anthony Thomas,
David Rainey in "Black Eagles"

Lindsay Crouse, Julie White
in "The Stick Wife"

Tuesday, April 2–May 19, 1991 (56 performances)
BLACK EAGLES by Leslie Lee; Conception/Direction, Ricardo Khan; Sets,\
Charles McClennahan; Costumes, Beth A. Ribblett; Lighting, Natasha Katz; Chore-
ography; Hope Clark; Fights, Rick Sordelet; Sound, Rob Gorton; Music Coordina-
tion, Robert LaPierre; "Julius' Theme" by Damien Leake; Ventriloquy Consultant,
Robert Aberdeen; Stage Manager, Cassandra Scott; Produced in association with
Crossroads Theatre Co. CAST: Lawrence James (Elder Clarkie), Robinson Frank
Adu (Elder Nolan), Graham Brown (Elder Leon), Michael Barry Greer (General
Lucas), Raymond Anthony Thomas (Clarkie), L. Peter Callender (Roscoe), Scott
Whitehurst (Nolan), Reggie Montgomery (Buddy), David Rainey (Leon), Brian
Evaret Chandler (Othel), Laura Sametz (Pia), Larry Green (Dave Whitson), Milton
Elliott (Roy Truman)
A drama in two acts about America's first black fighter pilots. The action takes
place in Italy during 1944 and Washington, D.C., 1989.

Monday, April 8, 1991 (1 performance only)
REASSURANCE: *Stories by Allan Gurganus*; Arranged by Lynne Meadow;
Lighting, Michael R. Moody.
PROGRAM: *It Had Wings* CAST: Allan Gurganus
A Body Tends to Shine CAST: Colleen Dewhurst
Reassurance CAST: Dylan Baker (Soldier), Victor Garber (Walt Whitman),
Colleen Dewhurst (Mother)

(Stage II) Tuesday, April 23–May 19, 1991 (32 performances)
THE STICK WIFE by Darrah Cloud; Director, David Warren; Sets, James
Youmans; Costumes, David C. Woolard; Lighting, Donald Holder; Sound, John
Kilgore; Fights, J. Allen Suddeth; Stage Manager, Christine Michael. CAST: Lind-
say Crouse (Jessie Bliss), Murphy Guyer (Ed Bliss), Julie White (Marguerite Pul-
let), Lanny Flaherty (Big Albert Connor), Margo Martindale (Betty Connor),
Michael Countryman (Tom Pullet)
A drama in two acts. The action takes place in Birmingham, Alabama in 1963.

Tuesday, May 28– still playing May 31, 1991
LIPS TOGETHER, TEETH APART by Terrence McNally; Director, John Tillin-
ger; Sets, John Lee Beatty; Costumes, Jane Greenwood; Lighting, Ken Billington;
Sound, Stewart Werner; Fights, Jerry Mitchell; Stage Manager, Pamela Singer.
CAST: Christine Baranski succeeded by Deborah Rush (Chloe Haddock), Nathan
Lane (Sam Truman), Anthony Heald (John Haddock), Swoosie Kurtz succeeded by
Roxanne Hart (Sally Truman)
A play in three acts. The action takes place in a Fire Island beach house over a
Fourth of July weekend at the present time.

Nathan Lane, Swoosie Kurtz, Christine Baranski, Anthony Heald in
"Lips Together, Teeth Apart" *Gerry Goodstein Photos*

NEW YORK SHAKESPEARE FESTIVAL

Twenty-fourth Season

Producer, Joseph Papp; Associate Producer, Jason Steven Cohen; Artistic Staff, David Greenspan, Michael Greif, George C. Wolfe, Joanne Akalaitis; General Manager, Bob McDonald; Associate General Manager, Susan Sampliner; Development, Gail Merrifield; Casting, Rosemarie Tichler; Development Director, Steve Dennin; Associate Director, Betsy Heer; Education Program, Stuart Vaughn; Executive Assistant, Barbara Carroll; Archives, Serge Mogilat; Production Manager, Andrew Mihoi; Technical Director, Mervyn Haines, Jr.; Press, Richard Kornberg/Barbara Carroll, Reva Cooper, Carol Fineman, David Josephberg

(Delacorte Theater/Central Park) Friday, June 22–July 22, 1990 (27 performances)

THE TAMING OF THE SHREW by William Shakespeare; Director, A.J. Antoon; Sets, John Lee Beatty; Costumes, Lindsay W. Davis; Lighting, Peter Kaczorowski; Music, Claude White; Fights, B.H. Barry; Stage Managers, Ron Nash, Lisa Buxbaum. CAST: Graham Winton (Lucentio), Robert Joy (Tranio), George Guidall (Baptista Minola), Tracey Ullman (Katherine), Helen Hunt (Bianca), Mark Hammer (Gremio), Tom Mardirosian (Hortensio), Peter Appel (Biondello), Morgan Freeman (Petruchio), Jose Perez (Grumio), Royal E. Miller (Bartender), Michael Gaston (Curtis), Joe Zaloom (Nathaniel), Wade Williams (Joe Bobb), Timothy Perez (Walter), Timothy D. Stickney (Sugarsop), Peter Ryan (Beau), William Duff-Griffin (Travelling Actor), Norris M. Shimabuku (Tailor), Thomas Barbour (Vincentio), Leah Maddrie (Widow)

The comedy performed in two acts. This version sets the action in the American wild west, circa 1890. This production is #14 in the Shakespeare Marathon.

Wednesday, August 1-31, 1990
FESTIVAL LATINO; The fourteenth annual celebration of Latin American music, theatre and dance. Theatrical productions included:
Mondo Mambo by Adal Maldonado and Pedro Pirtri; *Cronica De Una Muerte Anuncida* by Gabriel Garcia Marquez; Director, Salvador Tavora; *La Misma Sangre* by Carlos Velis; Director, Emilio Carballido; *De Donde?* by Mary Gallagher; Director, Sam Blackwell; *Los Rayos Gamma*; *Sin Testigos*; Director, Inda Ledesma; *El Palomar* by Carlos Catania, Director, Alfredo Catania; *Andar Por La Gente* by Inda Ledesma; *Voices of Steel*; Director, Alvan Colon Lespier; *O Doente Imaginaro*; Adaptor/Director, Caca Rosset; Music, Marc Antoine Charpentier; *La Secreta Obscenidad De Cada Dia* & *Matatangos* by Marc Antonio de la Parra

Morgan Freeman, Tracey Ullman in "Taming of the Shrew"

Ruth Maleczech, Frederick Neumann in "Through the Leaves"

**Denzel Washington, Nancy Palk
in "Richard III"**

(Delacorte Theater/Central Park) Friday, August 3–September 2, 1990 (27 performances)

THE TRAGEDY OF KING RICHARD III by William Shakespeare; Director, Robin Philipps; Scenery/Costumes, Elis Y. Lam; Lighting, Louise Guinard; Music, Louis Applebaum; Fights, Martino N. Pistone; Stage Managers, Susie Cordon, Allison Sommers. CAST: Mary Alice (Queen Margaret), Lisa Arrindell (Second Citizen/Ensemble), David Aaron Baker (Dorset/Ensemble), Jesse Bernstein (Duke of York), Rafeal Clements, Todd Eastland, Steve Graham, Robert Harryman, Richard Roy (Ensemble), Tracey Copeland (First Citizen/Ensemble), Daniel Davis, (Duke of Buckingham), Chris DeBari (Sir Walter Herbert/Ensemble), Virginia Downing (Duchess of York), Jonathan Fried (Sir Richard Ratcliffe), Seth Gilliam (Prince Edward/Ensemble), Ben Hammer (Earl of Derby), Tom Hewitt (Archbishop of Canterbury/Third Citizen/Ensemble), Richard Holmes (Lord Grey/Ensemble), Curt Hostetter (Archbishop of York/Francis, Lord Lovell), Bruce Katzman (Duke of Norfolk), Reese Madigan (Edward Plantagenet/Ensemble), Michael McElroy (Guard/Messenger/Ensemble), Peter McRobbie (Sir James Tyrrel/Lord Mayor), Royal E. Miller (Oxford/Tressel/Father John/Soldier), John Miskulin (Berkeley/Christopher Urswick/Messenger/Ensemble), Philip Moon (Lord Rivers/Ensemble), Jean-Paul Moreau (Earl of Surrey/Ensemble), William Moses (Sir Thomas Vaughan/Ensemble), Tim Nelson (Second Murderer/Ensemble), John Newton (Sir Robert Brakenbury/Bishop of Ely), Jenny Nichols (Margaret Plantagenet/Ensemble), Jeffrey Nordling (William, Lord Hastings), Erin J. O'Brien (Jane Shore/Ensemble), Nancy Palk (Queen Elizabeth), Brett Rickaby (Sheriff/Messenger/Ensemble), Armand Schultz (Earl of Richmond), Justin Thompson (Halberdier/Messenger/Ensemble), Sam Tsoutsouvas (King Edward IV), Denzel Washington (Richard, Duke of Gloucester), Sharon Washington (Lady Anne), Jake Weber (Sir William Catesby), Wade Williams (Sir James Blunt/First Murderer/Ensemble), Joseph Ziegler (George, Duke of Clarence)

Production #15 in the New York Shakespeare Festival Marathon.

(Public/Shiva) Wednesday, August 22-September 9, 1990 (18 performances and 6 previews)

INDECENT MATERIALS, two one-act plays adapted for the stage by Edward Hunt and Jeff Storer; Director, Mr. Storer; Choreographer, Barbara Dickinson; Photographic Design, Alan Dehmer; a production of the Manbites Dog Theatre Company. CAST: Patricia Esperson, David Ring, Rebecca Hutchins.
Indecent Materials; Text, Senator Jesse Helms (R-NC)
Report from the Holocaust; Adapted from material in the book *Report from the Holocaust: The Making of an AIDS Activist* by Larry Kramer

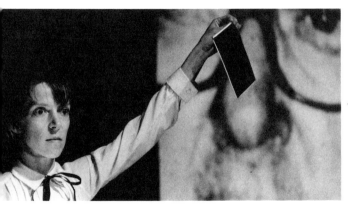

Rebecca Hutchins in "Indecent Materials"
Martha Swope, Joseph Schuyler Photos

(Delacorte Theater/CentralPark) Tuesday, September 11–16, 1990 (6 performances)

ROMEO AND JULIET by William Shakespeare; Indigenous version Adapted, Designed, and Directed by Maria Martinez Medrano; Translation, Martin Perez Ozul, Carlos Yocupicio; Music, Guillermo Briseno. CAST: Octavio Cervantes (Romeo), Lesvi Vazquez (Juliet), Roman Cota (Benvolio), Toribio Flores (Tybalt), Luz Emilia Vazquez (Nurse), Victor Bacasehua (Mercutio) and 72 members of Mexico's Laboratorio de Teatro Campesino y Indigena.

Shakespeare's tragedy in Mayan and Mayon. The action takes place in southeastern Mexico in 1910.

(Public/Newman) Friday, September 14–October 14, 1990 (33 performances and 4 previews)

THROUGH THE LEAVES by Franz Xaver Kroetz; Translation, Roger Downey; Director, Jo Anne Akalaitis; Sets, Douglas Stein; Lighting, Frances Aronson; Costumes, Teresa Snider-Stein; Sound, L.B. Dallas; Stage Manager, Jack Doulin; Technical, Richard Meyer; A co-production with Interart Theatre and Mabou Mines; Press, Ellen Jacobs. CAST: Ruth Maleczech (Annette), Frederick Neumann (Victor)

Twentieth anniversary production. Performed without intermission. The action takes place in Queens, at present.

(Public/LuEsther) Tuesday, September 25–November 25, 1990 (47 performances and 24 previews)

MACHINAL by Sophie Treadwell; Director, Michael Greif; Sets, David Gallo; Costumes, Sharon Lynch; Lighting, Kenneth Posner; Original Music/Sound, John Gromada; Stage Managers, Jess Lynn, Allison Sommers. CAST: Timothy Britten Parker (Announcer/Bellboy/Defense Attorney/Jailer), Ralph Marrero (Adding Clerk/Prosecuting Attorney/Barber), Omar Carter (Clerk/Neighbor/Boy/Reporter), Linda Marie Larson (Stenographer/Neighbor/Nurse/Speakeasy Woman/Reporter), Kristine Nielsen (Telephone Girl/Neighbor/Court Stenographer), John Seitz (Husband), Jodie Markell (Young Woman), Marge Redmond (Mother), Darby Rowe (Singer/Neighbor), Christopher Fields (Doctor/Salesman/Neighbor/Reporter/Barber), William Fichtner (Lover), Rocco Sisto (Speakeasy Man/Priest/Neighbor), Regina Taylor (Speakeasy Woman/Neighbor/Matron), Gareth Williams (Speakeasy Man/Neighbor/Bailiff/Reporter/Guard), Michael Mandell (Judge/Speakeasy Man/Convict)

A 1928 drama performed without intermision. Based on the 1927 trial of Ruth Snyder, the first woman executed by electric chair.

(Public/Shiva) Tuesday, October 9–November 4, 1990 (15 performances and 17 previews)

GONZA THE LANCER by Chikamatsu Monzaemon; Translation, Donald Keene; Director, David Greenspan; Sets, William Kennon; Costumes, Elsa Ward; Lighting, David Bergstein; Fights, B.H.Barry; Stage Managers, Diane C. Hartdagen, Mark McMahon. CAST: Ron Bagden (Kawazura Bannojo/Kakuske/Asaka Ichinoshin), Fanni Green (Iwaki Chutabei/Okiku), Koji Okamura (Sasano Gonza), Tim Perez (Governess/Narrator B), Keenan Shimizu (Oyuki/Torajiro/Min/Sugi/Namisuke/Osute/Servant/Boatman), Mary Schultz (Osai/Mother), Ching Valdes/Aran (Narrator A/Iwaki Jimbei)

A domestic tragedy in two acts and five scenes. Chikamatsu wrote the play in the 18th century, but this version was transported to the 20th century.

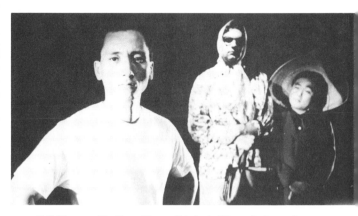

John Seitz, Jodie Markell in "Machinal"

Koji Okamura, Tim Perez, Keenan Shimizu in "Gonza the Lancer"

(Public/Martinson) Tuesday, November 13–December 23, 1990 (25 performances and 22 previews)

THE CAUCASIAN CHALK CIRCLE by Bertold Brecht; Adaptation, Thulani Davis; From translation by William R. Speigelberger; Director, George C. Wolfe; Choreography, Hope Clark; Music/Vocal Arrangements, Kweyao Agyapon; Additional Vocal Arrangements, Carol Maillard; Sets, Loy Arcenas; Costumes, Toni-Leslie James; Lighting, Don Holder; Masks/Puppets, Barbara Pollitt and Stephen Kaplin. CAST: Peter Callender (Casbeque/Corporal/Laurent/Landlord/Old Couple), Fanni Green (Nurse/Trader/Mother-in-Law/Shauva), Kevin Jackson (Simon/Landlord/Shadow Puppeteer/Fugitive/Lame Man), Cynthia Martells, Tonya Pinkins (Doctor/Architect/Chambermaid/Younger Lady/Trader/Blackshirt/Ludo/Lawyer), Patrick P. Mathieu (Messenger/Fire/Blackshirt/Michel Abasville Puppeteer/Hired Hand), Reggie Montgomery (Azdak), Novella Nelson (Storyteller/Woman Cook/Mon Oncle/Servant), Luis A. Ramos (Doctor/Architect/Elderly Lady/Trader/Blackshirt/Invalid/Enrique/Lawyer), M.W. Reid (Aide-de-Camp/Blackshirt/Jussup/Extortionist/Rich Peasant), Raymond Anthony Thomas (Man/Cook/Blackshirt/Monk/Casbeque's Nephew/Doctor Old Woman), Sharon Washington (Madame Le Gouverneur/Peasant/Anique), Charlayne Woodard (Grusha)

Performed in two acts. This production sets the action on L'Ile Antillais de Gonave in the Caribbean, at present.

(Public/Shiva) Saturday, November 17–December 1, 1990 (12 performances), reopened at Second Stage Monday, February 18–March 3, 1991 and March 4–10, 1991 (19 performances), moved to La Mama Thursday, March 21–31, 1991 (8 performances)

THE FEVER; Written and performed by Wallace Shawn

A monologue from the point of view of a privileged traveler.

(Public/Anspacher) Tuesday, November 20–December 16, 1990 (8 performances and 23 previews)

THE BIG FUNK; Written and Directed by John Patrick Shanley; Sets, Nancy Winters; Costumes, Lindsay W. Davis; Lighting, Arden Fingerhut; Sound, John Gromada; Stage Manager, Pamela Singer. CAST: Jeanne Tripplehorn (Jill), Jayne Haynes (Fifi), Graham Beckel (Omar), Jake Weber (Austin), Skip Sudduth (Gregory)

A play about grease, water, nudity, and a good mirror in two acts. The action takes place here. The time is now.

Graham Beckel, Jayne Haynes, Sipp Sudduth, Jeanne Tripplehorn, Jake Weber in "The Big Funk" *Martha Swope Photos*

(Public/LuEsther Hall) Thursday, December 13, 1990–January 20, 1991 (46 performances)
A BRIGHT ROOM CALLED DAY by Tony Kushner; Director, Michael Greif; Sets, John Arcone; Costumes, Walker Hicklin; Lighting, Frances Aronson; Sound, John Gromada; Projections, Jan Hartley. CAST: Reno (Zillah Katz), Frances Conroy (Agnes Eggling), Joan MacIntosh (Annabella Gotchling), Ellen McLaughlin (Paulinka Erdnuss), Olek Krupa (Vealtninc Husz), Henry Stram (Gregor Bazwald), Marian Seldes (Die Alte), Kenneth L. Marks (Roland/Marks), Angie Phillips (Rosa Malek), Frank Raiter (Gottfried Swetts)

A drama in two acts. The action takes place in an apartment in Berlin in 1990, and in 1932-33.

(Public/Shiva) Tuesday, January 8–February 10, 1991 (16 performances and 24 previews)
DEAD MOTHER *or Shirley Not All In Vain*; Written and Directed by David Greenspan; Sets, William Kennon; Costumes, Elsa Ward; Lighting, David Bergstein; Stage Manager, Diane Hartdagen. CAST: David Greenspan (Character1-Harold), Ben Bodé (Character 2-Daniel), Terra Vandergaw (Character 3-Sylvia), Mary Shultz (Character 4-Maxine), Ron Bagden (Character 5-Uncle Saul), Steve Mellor (Character 6-Melvin)

A comedy in 5 acts, performed with one intermission.

David Greenspan, Mary Shultz in "Dead Mother..."

(Public/Newman) Tuesday, January 22-March 21, 1991 (43 performances)
HENRY IV PART I by William Shakespeare; Director, JoAnne Akalaitis, Sets, George Tsypin; Costumes, Gabriel Berry, Lighting, Jennifer Tipton; Original Music, Philip Glass; Music Director, Alan Johnson; Sound, John Gromada; Hair/Makeup, Bobby Miller; Projections, John Boesche; Fights, David S. Leong; Stage Manager, Lisa Buxbaum. CAST: Larry Bryggman (King Henry IV), Thomas Gibson (Prince Hal), Arnold Molina (John), Roger Bart (Thomas/Francis), Reese Madigan (Humphrey), Norris Shimabuku (Earl of Westmoreland), Richard Russell Ramos (Lord Chief Justice), Kelly C. Morgan (Blunt), Miguel Perez (Percy), Jared Harris (Hotspur), Lisa Gay Hamilton (Kate), Daniel Oreskes (Thomas), Traber Burns (Owen), Mark Deakins (Mortimer), Moon Hi Hanson (Lady Mortimer), John Wojda (Earl of Douglas), Mel Duane Gionson (Vernon), Rodney Scott Hudson (Archbishop of York), Richard Spore (Brother Michael), Tom Nelis (Morton), Louis Zorich (Falstaff), David Manis (Bardolph), David J. Steinberg (Peto), Tim Perez (Gadshill), René Rivera (Ned Poins), Ruth Maleczech (Mistress Quickly), J. David Brimmer (Vintner), William Duell (Carrier), Susan Wands (Chamberlain), Kent Gash, Rafeal Clements (Guards), Caris Corfman, Peter Schmitz, Mia Sneden, Jason S. Woliner

Performed with one intermission. The action takes place in 1400. Production #16 in the New York Shakespeare Festival Marathon.

Thomas Gibson, Louis Zorich in "Henry IV"

(Public/Newman) Wednesday, January 23–March 21, 1991 (37 performances)
HENRY IV PART II by William Shakespeare; Director, JoAnne Akalaitis; All credits same as *Part I*. CAST: Caris Corfman (Rumor/Lady Northumberland), Larry Bryggman (King Henry IV), Thomas Gibson (Prince Hal), Arnold Molina (John/Wart), Roger Bart (Thomas/Francis), Reese Madigan (Humphrey), Norris Shimabuku (Earl of Westmoreland), Richard Russell Ramos (Lord Chief Justice), Kelly C. Morgan (Harcourt), Miguel Perez (Percy/Bullcalf), Lisa Gay Hamilton (Lady Percy), Rodney Scott Hudson (Archbishop of York), Richard Spore (Brother Michael/Silence), Daniel Oreskes (Lord Bardolph), Tom Nelis (Morton/Shadow), Kent Gash (Travers/Guard), Traber Burns (Hastings), Mark Deakins (Mowbray), John Wojda (Coleville), Louis Zorich (Falstaff), Jason S. Wolinger (Page), David Manis (Bardolph), David J. Steinberg (Peto), Jared Harris (Pistol/Feeble), René Rivera (Ned Poins), Ruth Maleczech (Mistress Quickly), Susan Wands (Doll Tearsheet), Tim Perez (Fang/Mouldy), J. David Brimmer (Snare), William Duell (Shallow), Peter Schmitz (Davy), Rafeal Clements (Guard), Mel Duane Gionson, Moon Hi Hanson, Mia Sneden

Performed with one intermission. The action takes place in 1403. Production #17 in the New York Shakespeare Festival Marathon.

John Seitz, Lani Pai, Ethan Hawke in "Casanova"
Martha Swope Photos

Jayne Atkinson, André Braugher in "Way of the World"

(Public/Shiva) Tuesday, April 30–June 2, 1991 (40 performances)
THE WAY OF THE WORLD by William Congreve; Director, David Greenspan; Sets, William Kennon; Costumes, Elsa Ward; Lighting, David Bergstein; Choreography, James Cunningham; Stage Manager, Diane Hartagen. CAST: René Rivera (Fainall), André Braugher (Mirabell), Joe Urla (Witwoud), Burke Moses (Petulant), Joseph Costa (Sir Wilfull Witwoud), James Lally (Waitwell), John Elsen (Servant/Messenger/Coachman/Footman), Ruth Maleczech (Lady Wishfort), Jayne Atkinson (Mrs. Millamant), Caris Corfman (Mrs. Marawood), Mary Schultz (Mrs. Fainall), Angie Phillips (Foible), Terra Vandergaw (Mincing), Ami Brabson (Betty/Peg/Mrs. Hodgson)

A modern dress version of the comedy in five acts. The action takes place in a chocolate-house, St. James Park, and Lady Wishfort's house.

(Public/Martinson) Tuesday, May 7–June 2, 1991 (31 performances)
CASANOVA by Constance Congdon; Director, Michael Greif; Sets, John Arcone; Costumes, Gabriel Berry; Lighting, Frances Aronson; Music/Sound, John Gromada; Musical Director, Jill Jaffe; Choreography, James Cunningham; Stage Manager, Jess Lynn. CAST: Ethan Hawke (Young Casanova), John Seitz (Giacomo Casanova), Erika Alexander (Rousseau's Girl/Uta/Charpillon), Marylouise Burke (Grandmama/Sorceress/Laura/Madame d'Urfé), Margaret Gibson (Therese), Kailani Lee (Sophie), James Noah (Monsignor/Mariucci's Husband/DaPonte/Julien), Liana Pai (Girl Sophie/Caterina/Jacomine), LaTanya Richardson (Zanetta/Marina/Marcoline/Mariucci), Robert Stanton (Priest/Dancing Master/Paris-Duverny), Jack Stehlin (Old Count/Salembini/DeBernis/Traveler #1), Martha Thompson (Bellino/Boy Bobo/Guillelmine), Jeff Weiss (Bobo)

A drama in two acts. The action spans several European cities, 1725-98.

94

NEW YORK THEATRE WORKSHOP

Artistic Director, James C. Nicola; Managing Director, Nancy Kassak Diekmann; Artistic Associate, Christopher Grabowski; Literary Associate, Christopher Ashley; General Manager, Esther Cohen; Development, Glen Knapp; Marketing, Carla Forbes-Kelly; Production Manager, George Xenos; Press, Gary Murphy

(Perry St. Theatre) Friday, November 23–December 30, 1990 (36 performances)
LOVE AND ANGER by George F. Walker; Directors, James C. Nicola and Christopher Grabowski; Sets, James Schuette; Costumes, Gabriel Berry; Lighting, Christopher Akerlind; Fights, David Leong; Music/Sound, Adam Guettel and Mark Bennett; Stage Manager, Liz Small. CAST: Saul Rubinek (Peter Maxwell), Tonia Rowe (Gail Jones), Kristine Nielsen (Eleanor Downey), Arthur Hanket (John Connor), Steve Ryan (Sean Harris), Deirdre O'Connell (Sarah Downey)

American premiere of a comedy about a lawyer whose near fatal stroke awakens his dormant soul.

Friday, February 1–March 10, 1991 (39 performances)
LIGHT SHINING IN BUCKINGHAMSHIRE by Caryl Churchill; Director, Lisa Peterson; Sets, Bill Clarke; Costumes, Michael Krass; Lighting, Brian MacDevitt; Dialects, Elizabeth Smith; Music/Sound, Mark Bennett; Stage Manager, Liz Small. CAST: Bill Camp, Philip Goodwin, Steve Hofvendahl, Cherry Jones, Shona Tucker, Gregory Wallace

The American premiere of a 1976 drama in two acts. The action takes place in England, during the Civil War and after, 1642-60.

Thursday, March 21–May 11, 1991 (37 performances)
JEFFREY ESSMANN'S ARTIFICIAL REALITY; Written by Mr. Essmann; Director, David Warren; Music Composed and Performed by Michael John LaChiusa; Sets, George Xenos; Costumes, David C. Woolard; Lighting, Pat Dignan; Sound, Mark Bennett; Stage Manager, Liz Small; Press, Jim Baldassare. CAST: Jeffrey Essmann
PROGRAM: The Passion of Patsy, Stan M, Jean-Louis DeBris, Scott Thornton, Barbie Night Club, Sturm & Drang Songbook, Raye, Clive Lord Thatch-Hewitt, Sister Bernice

An evening of character comedy. Performed with one intermission.

Thursday, March 28–April 25, 1991 (18 performances)
EVE'S DIARY and **THE STORY OF A TIGER** by Dario Fo; Translations, Ron Jenkins, Christina Nutrizio; Director, Christopher Ashley; Sets, George Xenos; Costumes, David C. Woolard; Lighting, Pat Dignan; Sound, Mark Bennett; Stage Manager, Thom Widmann. CAST: Jane Kaczmarek, Ricco Sisto

Two plays by Italy's social satirist.

Gerry Goodstein, Roy Blakey, Bob Marshak Photos

"Jeffrey Essmann's Artificial Reality"

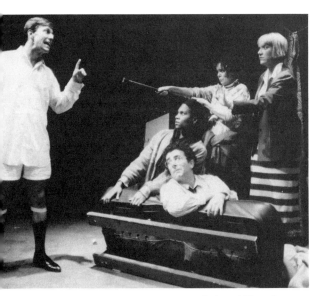

**Arthur Hanket, Tonia Rowe, Saul Rubinek, Deirdre O'Connell,
Kristine Nielsen in "Love and Anger"**

**Steve Hofvendahl, Cherry Jones, Shona Tucker, Gregory Wallace in
"Light Shining in Buckinghamshire"**

Frank Geraci, Robin Leslie Brown in "Major Barbara"

Stuart Lerch, Joanne Camp in "Measure for Measure"

Donnah Welby in "Fine Art of Finesse"

Richard Fancy, Joanne Camp in "Dance of Death"

Joanne Camp in "Countess Mitzi"
Carol Rosegg/Martha Swope Photos

PEARL THEATRE COMPANY

Seventh Season

Artistic Director, Shepard Sobel; General Manager, Mary L. Harpster; Development Director, Ivan Polley; Artistic Associate, Joanne Camp; Dramaturge, Dale Ramsey; Resident Costumes, Barbara A. Bell; Resident Lighting, Stephen Petrilli; Resident Sets, Robert Joel Schwartz; Press, Elizabeth L. Henry, James van Maanen
    Saturday, October 6–November 3, 1990 (24 performances)
MEASURE FOR MEASURE by William Shakespeare; Director, Shepard Sobel; Lighting, Richard A. Kendrick; Costumes, Tracy L. Christensen; Sound, Arthur C. Mortensen; Stage Manager, Mary Ethel Schmidt. CAST: William Verderber (Vincentio), John Newton (Escalus), Frank Geraci (Angelo), Stuart Lerch (Lucio), Patrick Frederic (First Gentleman/Friar/Abhorson), Alex Leydenfrost (Second Gentleman/Barnardine), Rhianna Jean Waters (Mistress Overdone/Mariana), Anthony Giaimo (Pompey), Arnie Burton (Claudio), Bob Ari (Provost), Joanne Camp (Isabella), Diane Paulus (Francisca/Juliette), Buddy Saunders (Elbow), Hank Wagner (Froth/Attendant)

    Sunday, November 10–December 8, 1991 (24 performances)
MAJOR BARBARA by George Bernard Shaw; Director, Anthony Cornish; Sets, Robert Joel Schwartz; Lighting, Stephen Petrilli; Costumes, Barbara A. Bell; Sound, Arthur C. Mortensen; Stage Manager, Lynn Bogarde. CAST: Stuart Lerch (Stephen Undershaft/Snobby Prince), Margaret Hilton (Lady Undershaft/Rummy Mitchens), Robin Leslie Brown (Major Barbara Undershaft), Laura Rathgeb (Sarah/Jenny), Tom Bloom (Adolphus), Arnie Burton (Charles Lomax/Bill Walker), Woody Sempliner (Morrison/Peter/Bilton), Frank Geraci (Andrew Undershaft), Sylvia Davis (Mrs. Baines)
    A social comedy in three acts.

    Saturday, December 15, 1990–January 12, 1991 (24 performances)
THE FINE ART OF FINESSE by Marivaux; Translation, Alex Szogyi; Director, Richard Morse; Sets, Robert Joel Schwartz; Lighting, Richard A. Kendrick; Costumes, Barbara A. Bell; Sound, John Wise; Stage Manager, Ernest L. Williams. CAST: Ahvi Spindell (Dorante), Frank Geraci (Blaise), Stuart Lerch (Harlequin), Matthew Loney (The Chevalier), Laura Rathgeb (Lisette), Robin Leslie Brown (Countess), Donnah Welby (Marquise), Hank Wagner (Frontin), Christopher Cook (Lackey/Notary)
    A comedy in two acts. The action takes place in the Countess' home.

    Saturday, January 19–February 16, 1991 (24 performances)
DANCE OF DEATH: Part One by August Strindberg; Translation, Harry G. Carlson; Director, Shepard Sobel; Sets, Robert Joel Schwartz; Lighting, Stephen Petrilli; Costumes, Shelly Saltzman; Sound, Arthur C. Mortensen; Choreography, Alice Teirstein; Sequencer Arrangements, Stephen J. Schaffer. CAST: Richard Fancy (Edgar), Joanne Camp (Alice), Janet Kingsley (Jenny/Woman), Paul O'Brien (Kurt)
    A drama in two acts. The action takes place in autumn.

    Saturday, February 23–March 23, 1991 (24 performances)
TWO PLAYS by Arthur Schnitzler; Sets, Robert Joel Schwartz; Costumes, Barbara A. Bell; Lighting, Stephen Petrilli; Sound, Arthur C. Mortensen; Stage Manager, Norma Dunkelberger
The Farewell Supper; Director, Frank Geraci. CAST: Stuart Lerch (Max), Arnie Burton (Anatol), Robin Leslie Brown (Annie), Hank Wagner (Waiter)
    The action takes place at a Separee at the Hotel Sacher in 1938.
Countess Mitzi; Director, Tom Bloom. CAST: Arnie Burton (Valet), Richard Seff (Count Arpad Pazmandy), Joanne Camp (Countess Mitzi), Frank Geraci (Gardener/Wasner), Richard Bourg (Prince Egon Ravenstein), Hank Wagner (Philip), Robin Leslie Brown (Lolo Langhuber), Stuart Lerch (Professor Windhofer)
    The action takes place in the garden of Count Arpad, near Vienna.

Chip Zien, Heather MacRae, Janet Metz, Danny Gerard, Michael Rupert, Stephen Bogardus in "Falsettoland"

Monique Cintron, Divina Cook in "Miriam's Flowers"

PLAYWRIGHTS HORIZONS

Twentieth Season

Artistic Director, Andre Bishop; Executive Director, Paul S. Daniels; Production Manager, Tom Aberger; Development Director, Ruth Cohen; Controller, Margaret Wade; Casting Director, Daniel Swee; Musical Theatre Program, Ira Weitzman; Literary Manager, Tim Sanford; Press, Philip Rinaldi, Shirley Herz/ Sam Rudy

Friday, June 8–August 12, 1990 (77 performances)
FALSETTOLAND; Music and Lyrics, William Finn; Director, James Lapine; Musical Director/Arrangements, Michael Starobin; Sets, Douglas Stein; Costumes, Franne Lee; Lighting, Nancy Schertler; Sound, Scott Lehrer; Stage Managers, Kate Riddle, Benjamin Gutkin; Associate Music Director, James Kowal; Original Cast Recording, DRG. CAST: Chip Zien (Mendel), Michael Rupert (Marvin), Danny Gerard (Jason), Stephen Bogardus (Whizzer), Faith Prince (Trina), Heather MacRae (Dr. Charlotte), Janet Metz (Cordelia)

MUSICAL NUMBERS: Falsettoland, About Time, Year of the Child, Miracle of Judaism, Baseball Game, Day in Falsettoland, Planning the Bar Mitzvah, Everyone Hates His Parents, What More Can I Say? Something Bad Is Happening, More Raquetball, Holding to the Ground, Days Like This, Cancelling the Bar Mitzvah, Unlikely Lovers, Another Miracle of Judaism, You Gotta Die Sometime, Jason's Bar Bitzvah, What Would I Do?

A musical performed without intermission. The action takes place in New York City in 1981-82. This is the third part of the Marvin Trilogy, following *In Trousers* (1978) and *March of the Falsettos* (1981). The production re-opened at the Lortel Theatre on September 14, 1990.

Wednesday, June 13–24, 1990 (14 performances)
MIRIAM'S FLOWERS by Migdalia Cruz; Director, Roberta Levitow; Sets, Tom Kamm; Costumes, Mary Myers; Lighting, Kenneth Posner; Sound, John Bowden; Stage Manager, Eric Osbun. CAST: Monique Cintron (Miriam), Divina Cook (Delfina), Ralph Marrero (Nando), Alex Caicedo (Puli), Peter Jay Fernandez (Enrique)

A drama performed without intermission. The action takes place in the South Bronx, at present.

Saturday, September 15–October 6, 1990
THE 1990 YOUNG PLAYWRIGHTS FESTIVAL; Producing Director, Nancy Quinn; Managing Director, Sheri M. Goldhirsch; Sets, Allen Moyer; Costumes, Claudia Stephens; Lighting, Pat Dignan; Sound, Janet Kalas; Production Manager, Tom Aberger; Production Stage Manager, James FitzSimmons; Presented by the Foundation of the Dramatists Guild

Mutterschaft by Gregory Clayman; Director, Michael Mayer; Dramaturg, Morgan Jenness; Stage Manager, Cathy Diane Tomlin. CAST: Leslie Lyles (Mom), Jane Adams (Opal), Harold Perrineau (Evan), Victor Slezak (Klaus)

Believing by Allison Birch; Director, Clinton Turner Davis; Fights, B.H. Barry; Dramaturg, Karen Jones-Meadows; Stage Manager, Liz Small. CAST: Marjorie Johnson, Rosanna Carter (Miss Agnes), Cynthia Martells (Thelma), Tonya Pinkins (Lawna), Kevin Jackson (Martin), Sasha Mujica (Sharon), Zakee Howze (David), Chandra Wilson (Leater), Michael Rogers (Frank), Wendell Pierce, Ramon Moses (Boysie)

Psychoneurotic Phantasies by Gilbert David Feke; Director, Gloria Muzio; Dramaturg, Victoria Abrash; Stage Manager, Liz Small. CAST: Jane Adams (Elaine), Christopher Shaw (Joshua), Walter Bobbie (Freud), Mia Korf, Leslie Lyles, Bruce MacVittie, Wendell Pierce, Ramon Moses, Angela Pietropinto, Tonya Pinkins, Kevin Rock, Victor Slezak, Jill Tasker, Lenny Venito

Hey Little Walter by Carla D. Alleyne; Director, Mark Brokow; Dramaturg, OyamO; Stage Manager, Cathy Diane Tomlin. CAST: Harold Perrineau (Walter), Seth Gilliam (Rakim), Cynthia Martells (Mama), Merlin Santana (Albert), Natalia Harris (Latoya), Lisa Carson (Nicky), Sean Nelson (Treybag)

The annual festival featuring plays by writers under the age of 19. This year's selection committee included Stephen Sondheim, Christopher Durang, David Henry Hwang, Wendy Wasserstein, André Bishop, Marsha Norman, Nancy Quinn, Mary Rogers, Albert Innaurato, Carol Hall and Ruth Goetz.

Friday, October 19–December 9, 1990 (60 performances)
SUBFERTILE by Tom Mardirosian; Director, John Ferraro; Sets, Rick Dennis; Costumes, Abigail Murray; Lighting, Brian McDevitt; Sound, Frederick Wessler; Stage Manager, Karen Armstrong. CAST: Tom Mardirosian, Richard Council, Frederica Meister, Susan Knight, Kitty Crooks

A comedy performed without intermission. The action takes place in the American Museum of Natural History at present.

Left: Susan Knight, Tom Mardirosian in "Subfertile"
Gerry Goodstein, Paula Court Photos

Jonathan Hadary, Victor Garber, Terrence Mann in "Assassins"

**Patrick Breen, Jon Tenney, Ron Rifkin, Sarah Jessica Parker
in "Substance of Fire"**

Tuesday, December 18, 1990–February 16, 1991 (71 performances)
ASSASSINS; Music and Lyrics, Stephen Sondheim; Book, John Weidman; Director, Jerry Zaks; Choreography, D.J. Giagni; Musical Director, Paul Gemignani; Sets, Loren Sherman; Costumes, William Ivey Long; Lighting, Paul Gallo; Sound, Scott Lehrer; Hairstylist, Angela Gari; Stage Manager, Clifford Schwartz; Production Supervisor, Paul E. King; Cast Recording, RCA. CAST: Jace Alexander (Lee Harvey Oswald), Patrick Cassidy (Balladeer), Joy Franz (Benjamin's Mother), Victor Garber (John Wilkes Booth), Greg Germann (John Hinckley), Annie Golden (Lynette "Squeaky" Fromme), Lyn Greene (Emma Goldman), Jonathan Hadary (Charles Guiteau), John Jellison (James Blaine), Eddie Korbich (Guiseppe Zangara), Terrence Mann (Leon Czolgosz), Debra Monk (Sara Jane Moore), Marcus Olson (David Herold), William Parry (Proprietor/James Garfield/Gerald Ford), Michael Shulman (Benjamin/Billy), Lee Wilkof (Samuel Byck).
A musical using elements of revue, vaudeville, folksong, historical pageant, and musical comedy, revealing the story of the men and women who attempted presidential assassinations. Performed without intermission.

Friday, March 1–June 30, 1991 (140 performances)
THE SUBSTANCE OF FIRE by Jon Robin Baitz; Director, Daniel Sullivan; Sets, John Lee Beatty; Costumes, Jess Goldstein; Lighting, Arden Fingerhut; Sound, Scott Lehrer, Stage Manager, Roy Harris. CAST: Sarah Jessica Parker (Sarah Geldhart), Patrick Breen (Martin Geldhart), Ron Rifkin (Isaac Geldhart), Jon Tenney (Aaron Geldhart), Maria Tucci (Marge Hackett)
A drama in two acts. The action takes place in the offices of Kreeger/Geldhart Publishers and in a Gramercy Park apartment, New York City. The time spans spring 1987 to present.

Friday, April 5–June 2, 1991 (41 performances and 35 previews)
THE OLD BOY by A.R. Gurney; Director, John Rubinstein; Sets, Nancy Winters; Costumes, Jane Greenwood; Lighting, Nancy Schertler; Sound, Bruce Ellman; Stage Manager, Michael Pule. CAST: Richard Woods (Dexter), Clark Gregg (Bud), Stephen Collins (Sam), Nan Martin (Harriet), Matt McGrath (Perry), Lizbeth Mackay (Alison)
A play in two acts. The action takes place in a private boarding school in New England. The time is graduation weekend in the early 1990s.

Left: Lizbeth Mackay in "The Old Boy"
Martha Swope, Peter Cunningham, Joan Marcus Photos

Adriano Gonzalez, Emma Mio, Jose Rey in
"English Only Restaurant"

Graciela Mas, Orlando George, Emilio Del Pozo in
"In Miami as It Is in Heaven"

Cordelia Gonzalez, Nancy Walsh in "Sabina and Lucrecia"

PUERTO RICAN TRAVELING THEATRE

Twenty-forth Season

Artistic Director, Miriam Colon Valle; Managing Director, Patricia Baldwin; Development, Vera Ryan; Community Coordinator, Lissette Montolio; Assistant Coordinator, Margarita Morales; Press, Max Eisen, Madelon Rosen
Thursday, July 19–August 26, 1990
THE ENGLISH ONLY RESTAURANT; Music and Lyrics, Sergio Garcia Marruz, Saul Spangenberg; Book, Silvio Martinez Palau; Director, Susana Tubert; Musical Directors, Mr. Marruz, Mr. Spangenberg; Sets/Costumes, Michael Sharp; Lighting, Rachel Budin; Choreography, Ron Brown; Stage Manager, Roger Franklin; Technical Director, James E. Fuller, Jr. CAST: Alberto Guzman (Mr. Martinezz), Al D. Rodriguez (Henry), Miguel Antonio Sierra (Johnny Garcia/Jorg), Jose Rey (Mr. Table/Language Police), Emma Mio (Eugenica Heads/News Reporter), Hal Blankenship (Mr. Peters), Sheila Kay (Mrs. Peters), Adriano Gonzalez (Henryque/Language Police), David Seatter (Mr. Fartley), Jeanette Toro (Patricia)
MUSICAL NUMBERS: English Only Restaurant, Money Tree, Conjugate/VCR, Brown-Eyed Blues, Connoisseurs Must Have Panache, Blue-eyed Knight, So Ama Speaking Espanol, Police Raid, Martinezz Lament, Finale
A musical farce. The action takes place in Queens in the future, when Spanish is forbidden by law.

Wednesday, January 16–February 24, 1991
IN MIAMI AS IT IS IN HEAVEN by Raúl de Cárdenas; Translation, Asa Zatz; Director, Alba Oms; Sets, Michael Sharp; Lighting, Rachel Budin; Costumes, Mary Marsicano; Stage Manager, Lisa Ledwich. CAST: Emilio Del Pozo (Primitivo), Suzanne Costallos (Lola-English performances), Graciela Mas (Lola-Spanish performances), Cari Gorostiza (Maruja), Eileen Galindo (Vivian), Orlando George (Mario)
A drama in two acts. The action takes place in the "Florida Room" of a prosperous Cuban-American home in Miami at the present time.

Wednesday, March 13–April 21, 1991
SABINA AND LUCRECIA by Alberto Adellach; Translation, Jack Agüeros; Director, Alba Oms; Sets, Edward Gianfrancesco; Lighting, Rick Butler; Costumes, Mary Marsicano; Stage Manager, Lisa Ledwich. CAST: Cordelia Gonzales (Lucrecia), Tatiana Vecino (Sabina-Spanish performances), Nancy Wlash (Sabina-English performances)
A drama based on a true story. Performed in two acts. The action takes place in a large city slum at the present time.

Wednesday, May 15–June 23, 1991
CHARGE IT, PLEASE; Music/Lyrics/Book, Carlos Gorbea; Spanish Translation, Walter Krochmal; Director, William Martin; Co-Director/Associate Producer, Alba Oms; Sets/Lighting, Rick Butler; Costumes, Mary Marsicano; Sound, Sergio Garcia Marruz; Music Director, David Wolfson; Choreography, Dennis Dennehy; Mural Design, Marc Lida; Stage Manager, Jana Llynn. CAST: Mel Gorham (Juanita Ramirez-English performances), Jeanette Toro (Juanita-Spanish Performances), Iraida Polanco (Antonia Gonzales), Alberto Guzman (Manuel Perez/Lechoso), Joan Jaffe (Americana), Fred Barrows (Americano)
MUSICAL NUMBERS: Dance a Bomba at Funeral Time, Love and No Dinero, Listen to My Little Song, Manhattan Shines, Show That Card, Entr'acte, Shall We Take a Cruise, Love's in Full Bloom, Dear Love, A Locco Finale
A musical comedy in two acts. The action takes place in New York City and the capitals of Europe, at present.

Carol Rosegg, Martha Swope, Peter Krupenye Photos

Joan Jaffe, Mel Gorham in "Charge It, Please"

RIVERSIDE SHAKESPEARE COMPANY

Fourteenth Season

Artistic Directors, Gus Kaikkonen, Timothy W. Oman; Managing Director, Steve Vetrano; Operations Director, Wyatt Obeid; Academy Director, Laura Fine; Co-Founders, W. Stuart McDowell, Gloria Skurski; Development, Jeannie Dobie; Marketing, Anne Vaughan; Press, Jane Badgers, Douglas Tuchman, Chris Boneau
(Playhouse 91) Thursday, October 11–November 25, 1990 (47 performances)
TWELFTH NIGHT by William Shakespeare; Director, Stuart Vaughan; Sets, David P. Gordon; Lighting, Mark C. Andrew; Costumes, Judy Kahn. CAST: Kathryn Meisle (Viola), James Goodwin (Orsino), Robert Murch (Malvolio), Johanna Leister (Maria), John Fitzgibbon (Feste), Angela Roberts (Olivia), Dan Daily (Sir Andrew Aguecheek), Robert Mooney (Sir Toby), Jody Barrett (Lady-in-Waiting), Olivia Charles (Lady-in-Waiting), John Elejalde (Sailor/Officer), Suzanne Graff (Lady-in-Waiting), James Haskins (Sailor/Officer), Robert Parks Johnson (Captain), David Lockhart (Curio/Priest), Robert Sedgwick (Sebastian), Bryan Webster (Antonio), David Cole Wheeler (Valentine)

Thursday, November 29, 1990–January 27, 1991 (61 performances)
ROMEO and JULIET by William Shakespeare; Director, Charles Keating; Sets, David P. Gordon; Lighting, Sam Scripps; Costumes, Martha Hally; Music, James Keating; Fights, J. Allen Suddeth; Stage Manager, Paul A. Kochman. CAST: Robert Sean Leonard (Romeo), Gerit Quealy (Juliet), Stephen Schnetzer (Mercutio), Beth Fowler (Nurse), Wendy Allegaert (Flute), Brian Byrnes (Gregory), Michael Connor (Balthasar), Margot Dionne (Lady Capulet), Debra England (Lady Montague), Jeremy Johnson (Capulet), Lynellen Kagen (Page), Youssif Kamal (Abram/Friar John), Cuivan Kelly (Watch), Tom Kelly (Peter), Herb Klinger (Montague), John Leighton (Escalus/Apothecary), Joanne Lessner (Page), Brian Mulligan (Paris' Page), Andrew Palmer (Sampson/Chief Watch), Gary Piquer (Tybalt), John Plumpis (Benvolio), Will Rhys (Friar Laurence), James Ryan (Watch), Ian Stuart (Paris), Andy Taylor (Cello)
A tragedy in two acts.

Saturday, February 9–April 21, 1991 (73 performances)
CANDIDA by George Bernard Shaw; Director, Gus Kaikkonen; Sets, Bob Barnett; Costumes, Steven F. Graver; Lighting, Stephen J. Backo; Music, Ellen Mandel; Stage Manager, Matthew G. Marholin. CAST: Alice White (Prosperpine Garnett), Guy Paul (Rev. James Mavor Morell), Christopher Mixon (Rev. Alexander Mill), Victor Raider-Wexler (Mr. Burgess), Laurie Kennedy (Candida Morell), Don Reilly (Eugene Marchbanks)
Presented in three acts. The action takes place in London, during October 1894.

Friday, May 3–June 23, 1991 (53 performances)
FRIDAYS by Andrew Johns; Director, Gus Kaikkonen; Sets, Bob Barnett; Costumes, Steven F. Graver; Lighting, Stephen J. Backo; Stage Manager, Matthew G. Marholin. CAST: John Peakes (Holly Crawford), Henderson Forsythe (George Herrick), Kent Adams (Chuck Hart), Stephanie Madden (Gail Herrick), David Edward Jones (Douglas Herrick), Alice White (Kay Strong)
A comedy-drama evolving from a Friday night poker game.

Guy Paul, Laurie Kennedy, Don Reilly in "Candida"

Stephen Schnetzer, Robert Sean Leonard in "Romeo and Juliet"
Carol Rosegg/Martha Swope Photos

ROUNDABOUT THEATRE COMPANY

Twenty-fifth Season

Founding Director, Gene Feist; Producing Director, Todd Haimes; General Manager, Ellen Richard; Development Director, Julia C. Levy; Marketing Director, Virginia Louloudes; Ensemble Company Director, Janet McCall; Business Manager, Ellen Scrimger Gordon; Subscriptions, Martin S. Herstein; Archivist, Andrea J. Nouryeh; Press, Joshua Ellis/Susanne Tighe, John Barlow

Friday, August 1–September 23, 1990 (41 performances and 21 previews)
LIGHT UP THE SKY by Moss Hart; Director, Larry Carpenter; Sets, Andrew Jackness; Costumes, Martin Pakledinaz; Lighting, Dennis Parichy; Sound, Philip Campanella; Stage Managers, Roy W. Backes, Kathy J. Faul. CAST: Elaine Bromka (Miss Lowell), Charles Keating (Carleton Fitzgerald), Betsy Joslyn (Frances Black), Humbert Allen Astredo (Owen Turner), Peggy Cass (Stella Livingston), John Bolger (Peter Sloan), Bruce Weitz succeeded by Jason Alexander (Sidney Black), Paul Niesen (Sven), Linda Carlson (Irene Livingston), John C. Vennema (Tyler Rayburn), Max Robinson (Max), Bill McCutcheon (William H. Gallegher), Peter Robinson (Cop/Shriner)

A comedy in three acts. The action takes place in the Ritz-Carlton Hotel, Boston, in 1950.

Friday, October 19–December 16, 1990 (37 performances and 31 previews)
KING LEAR by William Shakespeare; Director, Gerald Freedman; Sets, John Ezell; Costumes, Robert Wojewodski; Lighting, Thomas R. Skelton; Music, John Morris; Sound, Tom Mardikes; Fights, Robert L. Behrens; Stage Manager, Kathy J. Faul. CAST: Hal Holbrook (King Lear), Peter Aylward (Curan/Lear at student shows), Gloria Biegler (Cordelia), Andrew Boyer (Duke of Cornwall), Simon Brooking (King of France/Ensemble), John Buck, Jr. (Duke of Albany), Suzy Hunt (Goneril), John Hutton (Edmund), Michael James-Reed (Edgar), Richard Long (Ensemble), Christopher McCann (Lear's Fool), Kevin McCarty (Lear's Knight), Patrick Mulcahy (Duke of Burgundy/Ensemble), Margery Murray (Regan), Eric Nolan (Officer/Ensemble), Ron Randell (Earl of Gloucester), Stephan Roselin (Ensemble), David Ruckman (Messenger/Ensemble), Andrew M. Segal (Captain/Ensemble), Gary Sloan (Oswald), Darrell Starnik (Servant/Ensemble), Justin Thompson (Servant/Ensemble), Eric Vogt (Messenger/Ensemble), William Wilson (Herald/Ensemble), John Woodson (Earl of Kent)

Performed with one intermission. The action takes place in an ancient time.

Peggy Cass, Linda Carlson, Charles Keating, Betsy Joslyn, John C. Vennema, Bruce Weitz in "Light Up the Sky"

Hal Holbrook in "King Lear"

Charles Keating, Madeline Potter, Anthony Heald, Earle Hyman, Anne Pitoniak in "Pygmalion"

Paul McCrane, Karen Allen,
David Rasche in "The Country Girl"

Wednesday, December 26, 1990–February 10, 1991 (37 performances and 18 previews)
THE COUNTRY GIRL by Clifford Odets; Director, Kenneth Frankel; Sets, Hugh Landwehr; Costumes, David Murin; Lighting, Stephen Strawbridge; Sound, Philip Campanella; Stage Manager, Roy W. Backes. CAST: Paul McCrane (Bernie Dodd), Stephen Mendillo (Larry), George Morfogen (Phil Cook), Jim Abele (Paul Unger), Geraldine Leer (Nancy Stoddard), David Rasche (Frank Elgin), Karen Allen (Georgie Elgin), Henry LeBlanc (Ralph)

A drama in two acts. The action takes place in New York City and Boston.

Wednesday, March 6–April 28, 1991 (64 performances)
PYGMALION by George Bernard Shaw; Director, Paul Weidner; Sets, John Conklin; Costumes, Martin Pakledinaz; Lighting, Natasha Katz; Sound, Philip Campanella; General Manager, Ellen Richard; Stage Manager, Kathy J. Faul. CAST: Pamala Tyson (Clara Eynsford-Hill), Annie Murray (Mrs. Eynsford-Hill), Edwin J. McDonough (Bystander), Willis Spark (Freddy Eynsford-Hill), Madeleine Potter (Eliza Doolittle), Earle Hyman (Colonel Pickering), Anthony Heald (Henry Higgins), Joyce Worsley (Mrs. Pearce), Charles Keating (Alfred Doolittle), Anne Pitoniak (Mrs. Higgins), Page Clements (Parlormaid), Lester Chit-Man Chan, Daniel Tedlie, Henry Traeger, Angela Schreiber, Michael Schwendemann

A comedy performed with one intermission.

Wednesday, May 15–July 7, 1991
THE SUBJECT WAS ROSES by Frank D. Gilroy; Director, Jack Hofsiss; Sets, David Jenkins; Costumes, Michael Krass; Lighting, Beverly Emmons; Sound, Philip Campanella; General Manager, Ellen Richard; Stage Manager, Kathy J. Faul. CAST: John Mahoney (John Cleary), Dana Ivey (Nettie Cleary), Patrick Dempsey (Timmy Cleary)

A drama in two acts. The action takes place in an apartment in the Bronx, New York City, in May 1946. Winner of the Pulitzer Prize in 1965 for the original production.

John Mahoney, Patrick Dempsey, Dana Ivey in "Subject Was Roses"
Peter Cunningham, Martha Swope, Roger Mastroianni Photos

Eddie Castrodad, Alison Bartlett in "Jersey City"

SECOND STAGE

Twelfth Season

Artistic Directors, Robyn Goodman, Carole Rothman; Managing Director, Dorothy J. Maffei; Development Director, Robin L. Drummond; Dramaturg, Jim Lewis; Casting, Simon & Kumin; Production Manager, Carol Fishman; Marketing Director, Savannah Whaley; Press, Richard Kornberg

Tuesday, June 19–July 22, 1990 (11 performances and 23 previews)
JERSEY CITY by Wendy Hammond; Director, Risa Bramon; Sets, James Youmans; Lighting, Anne Militello; Costumes, Sharon Sprague; Sound, Bruce Ellman; Hairstylist, Antonio Soddu; Fights, Robert Goodwin; Stage Managers, Liz Small, Elise-Ann Konstantin. CAST: Alison Bartlet (Magaly), Jude Ciccolella (Pa), Adina Porter (Esther), Eddie Castrodad

A drama in two acts. The action takes place in Brooklyn and Jersey City at present.

Saturday, November 3–December 22, 1990 (22 performances and 28 previews)
LAKE NO BOTTOM by Michael Weller; Director, Carole Rothman; Sets, Adrienne Lobel; Lighting, Kevin Rigdon; Costumes, Jess Goldstein; Sound, Mark Bennett; Hairstylist, Antonio Soddu; Stage Managers, Pamela Edington, Elise-Ann Konstantin. CAST: Marsha Mason (Petra), Robert Knepper (Will), Daniel Davis (Rubin)

A black comedy in two acts. The action takes place in a country house, at present.

Thursday, January 17–February 24, 1991 (21 performances and 21 previews)
EARTH AND SKY by Douglas Post; Director, Andre Ernotte; Set, William Barclay; Lighting, Phil Monat; Costumes, Deborah Shaw; Sound, Bruce Ellman; Hairstylist, Antonio Soddu; Stage Managers, Crystal Huntington, J. Courtney Pollard. CAST: Jennifer Van Dyck (Sara McKeon), Ted Marcoux (David Ames), Ron Nakahara (Sergeant Al Kersnowski), Justin Deas (Detective H.E. Weber), Lisa Arrindell (Joyce Lazlo), Michael Genet (Billy Hart), Evan Thompson (Carl Eisenstadt), Lisa Beth Miller (Marie Defaria), Paul Kandel (Julius Gatz)

A mystery thriller performed without intermission. The action takes place in Chicago during August.

Tuesday, March 26–June 23, 1991 (106 performances)
THE GOOD TIMES ARE KILLING ME by Lynda Barry; Director, Mark Brokaw; Sets, Rusty Smith; Lighting, Don Holder; Costumes, Ellen McCartney; Sound, Janet Kalas; Hairstylist, Antonio Soddu, Musical Director, Steve Sandberg; Choreography, Don Philpott; Stage Managers, James Fitzsimmons, Lori Lundquist. CAST: Angela Goethals (Edna Arkins), Lauren Gaffney (Lucy Arkins), Holly Felton (Mom/Mrs. Doucette), Ellia English (Aunt Martha/Bonita), Wendell Pierce (Mr. Willis), Kim Staunton (Mrs. Willis), Ruth Williamson (Aunt Margaret), John Lathan (Earl Stelly/Preacher/Marcus), Jennie Moreau (Cousin Ellen/Mrs. Hosey/Mrs. Mercer), Kathleen Dennehy (Sharon/Therese Doucette), Ray DeMattis (Uncle Jim), Peter Appel (Dad/Cousin Steve), Chandra Wilson (Bonna Willis), Brandon Mayo (Elvin Willis)

A play with music in two acts. The action takes place in a working class neighborhood in the mid-1960s.

Susan Cook Photos

Robert Knepper, Marsha Mason, Daniel Davis in "Lake No Bottom"

**Jennifer Van Dyck, Ted Marcoux
in "Earth and Sky"**

**Angela Goethals, Chandra Wilson in
"The Good Times Are Killing Me"**

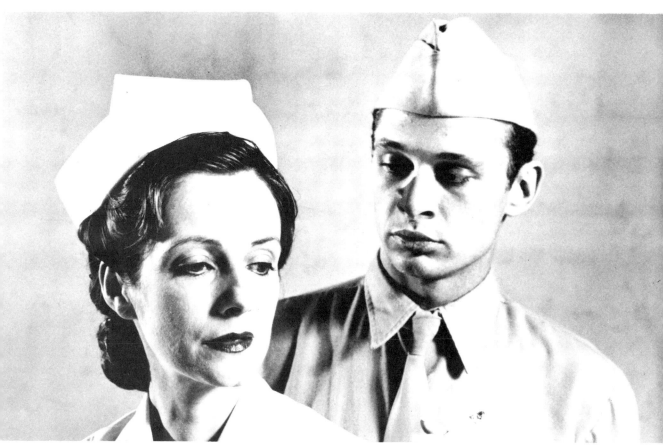

Susanna Frazer, Brett Rickaby in "Yokohama Duty"

SOHO REPERTORY

Sixteenth Season

Artistic Directors, Marlene Swartz, Julian Webber; Administrative Director, Michael Rosenberg; Play Development, Peter Hays; Press, Jonathan Slaff
(Alma Shapiro Theatre) Friday, July 6–29, 1990 (28 performances)
HANGING THE PRESIDENT by Michele Celeste; Director, Julian Webber; Sets, Stephan Olson; Costumes, Patricia Sarnataro; Lighting, Donald Holder; Sound, Eric Liljestrand; Fights, Jim Manley; Production Manager, David Waggett; Dialects, Nora Dunfee; Stage Manager, Barbara Lynn Rice. CAST: Dan Moran (Warder), Peter Drew Marshall (Nak van der Merwe), Peter Crombie (Le Grange), Thomas Ntinga (Zwanini)
A drama performed without intermission. The action takes place in a Pretorian prison cell.

Thursday, April 11–May 5, 1991 (19 performances)
NATIVE SPEECH by Eric Overmyer; Director, John Pynchon Holms; Sets, Kyle Chepulis; Costumes, Patricia Sarnataro; Lighting, Steve Shelly; Sound, Tom Gould; Stage Manager, Randy Lawson. CAST: Kario Salem (Hungry Mother), Deborah Mansy (Loud Speaker/Freddy Navajo), Iona Morris (Free Lance), Fracaswell Hyman (Belly Up), Allan Tung (Charlie Samoa), Sixto Ramos (Johnnie Sucrose), James Encinas (Jimmy Shillelagh/Crazy Joe), Jennifer Parsons (Janis), SáMi Chester (Mook), J. Reuben Silverbird (Hoover)
A drama in two acts. The action involves the world of a post-apocalyptic disc jockey.

Friday, May 17–June 9, 1991 (18 performances)
YOKOHAMA DUTY by Quincy Long; Director, Julian Webber; Sets, Stephan Olson; Costumes, Patricia Sarnataro; Lighting, Donald Holder; Stage Manager, Monty Hicks. CAST: Nesbitt Blaisdell (Priest), Preston Keith Smith (Red), Bruce Katzman (Clerk/Bob), Brett Rickaby (Joe), Susanna Frazer (Frankie), Cheri Nakamura (Suo), Peter Yoshida (Jap), Michael Cullen (Jack)
A comedy in two acts. The action takes place in and around Yokohama in 1945.

Deborah Mansey, Jay Silverbird, Kario Salem
(front) in "Native Speech"

Jonathan Slaff Photos

103

Kyra Sedgwick, Laila Robins , Elizabeth McGovern in "Maids of Honor"

WPA THEATRE

Fourteenth Season

Workshop of the Players Art: Artistic Director, Kyle Renick; Managing Director, Donna Lieberman; General Manager, Lori Sherman; Resident Designer, Edward T. Gianfrancesco; Resident Lighting, Craig Evans; Production Manager, Gordon W. Brown; Press, Jeffrey Richards/Jillana Devine, David LeShay.

Friday, June 8-July 8, 1990 (31 performances)
MAIDS OF HONOR by Joan Casademont; Director, Max Mayer; Sets, Edward T. Gianfrancesco; Lighting, Craig Evans; Costumes, Mimi Maxmen; Sound, Aural Fixation; Stage Manager, Denise Laffer; Production Manager, Stephen Jones; Props, Catherine Policella. CAST: Elizabeth McGovern (Isabelle Bowlin), Kyra Sedgwick (Annie Bowlin), Laila Robins (Monica Bowlin), Kristine Nielsen (Pat Weinhardt), John Michael Higgins (Harry Hobson), Jake Weber (Joel Silverman), Joe Urla (Roger Dowling)

A comedy in two acts. The action takes place in Marblehead, Massachusetts at present.

Kathryn Erbe, Lewis J. Stadlen in "The My House Play"

Tuesday, October 30–December 2, 1990 (35 performances)
GROTESQUE LOVE SONGS by Don Nigro; Director, Kenneth Elliot; Sets, Edward T. Gianfrancesco; Costumes, Debra Tennenbaum; Sound, Aural Fixation; Stage Manager, Paul Mills Holmes. CAST: Felicity Huffman (Romy), Ted Marcoux (Pete), Sally Kirkland succeeded by Suzanne Collins (Louise), Stephen Mendillo (Dan), Chad Lowe (John)

A drama in two acts. The action takes place in Terre Haute, Indiana in 1980.

Thursday, January 17, 1991–
THE MY HOUSE PLAY by Wendy MacLeod; Director, Rob Greenberg; Set, James Schuette; Lighting, Craig Evans; Costumes, Candice Donnelly; Sound, John Huntington; Stage Manager, Denise Laffer. CAST: Leslie Lyles (Frances Battaglia), Kathryn Erbe (Fiona Battaglia), Jayce Bartok (Sid), Lewis J. Stadlen (Ernie Battaglia), Welker White (Charisse Battaglia), David Eigenberg (Buzz)

A comedy in two acts. The action takes place in Arlington, Virginia during summer. The time is the early 1980s.

Tuesday, March 19–May 5, 1991
RED SCARE ON SUNSET by Charles Busch; Director, Kenneth Elliott; Set, B.T. Whitehill; Lighting, Vivien Leone; Costumes, Debra Tennenbaum; Sound, Aural Fixation; Wigs, Elizabeth Katherine Carr; Stage Manager, T.L. Boston. CAST: Mark Hamilton (Ralph Barnes/Sales Girl/R.G. Benson/Granny Lou), Roy Cockrum (Harold/Bertram Barker), Julie Halston (Pat Pilford), Arnie Kolodner (Frank Taggart), Charles Busch (Mary Dale), Andy Halliday (Malcolm/Old Lady), Judith Hansen (Marta Towers), Ralph Buckley (Mitchell Drake)

A comedy in two acts. The action takes place in Hollywood in 1951.

Charles Busch in "Red Scare on Sunset"
Blanche Mackey, Carol Rosegg, T.L. Boston Photos

THE YORK THEATRE COMPANY

Twenty-second Season

Producing Director, Janet Hayes Walker; Managing Director, Molly Pickering Grose; Artistic Advisors, John Newton, James Morgan; House Managers, Suzanne Fabricant, Jerry Fisher, Luisa M. Walker; Audience Development, Brendi Drosnes; Press, Keith Sherman/Tony Origlio, Chris Day

Friday, September 28–October 21, 1990 (17 performances)
EAST TEXAS by Jan Buttram; Director, Alex Dmitriev; Sets, Jim Morgan; Costumes, Holly Hynes; Lighting, Mary Jo Dondlinger; Sound, David Oberon; Technical, Matt Goldin; Stage Manager, Mary Ellen Allison. CAST: Venida Evans (Naomi Ludlam), Peter Brouwer (Billy Swagger), Susanne Marley (Joan Ann Buford Percy), Dorothy Lancaster (Lucy Buford), Page Johnson (Sly Rubins)
   A comedy in two acts. The action takes place in a small East Texas town.

Wednesday, November 28–December 16, 1990 (18 performances)
THE LUNATIC, THE LOVER & THE POET; Compiled, Directed and Performed by Brian Bedford
   A one-man Shakespeare festival. This edition featured excerpts from *Romeo and Juliet*, *Hamlet*, *A Midsummer Night's Dream*, *Richard II*, *King Lear*, and others.

Friday, January 11–February 3, 1991 (23 performances)
PHILEMON; Music, Harvey Schmidt; Lyrics, Tom Jones; Director, Fran Soeder; Musical Director, Norman Weiss; Sets, James Leonard Joy; Costumes, Mariann Verheyen; Lighting, Natasha Katz; Technical, Matt Goldin; Stage Manager, Michael J. Chudinski. CAST: Michael Tucci (Cockian), Kenneth Kantor (Marcus), Tony Floyd (Servillus), Joel Malina (Andos), Jean Tafler (Kiki), Kim Crosby (Marsyas), Kathryn McAteer (Woman)
MUSICAL NUMBERS: Within This Empty Space, Streets of Antioch Stink, Gimme a Good Digestion, Don't Kiki Me, I'd Do Most Anything to Get Out of Here and Go Home, He's Coming/Antioch Prison, Name:Cockian, I Love Order, My Secret Dream, I Love His Face, Sometimes/Protest, The Nightmare, The Greatest of These, The Confrontation: How Free I Feel, How Easy to Be Scornful, Come with Me, The Vision: I See a Light, Finale
   The 1975 musical in two acts. The action takes place in the Roman city of Antioch in 287 A.D.

Friday, March 22–April 28, 1991 (26 performances)
A FUNNY THING HAPPENED ON THE WAY TO THE FORUM; Music and Lyrics, Stephen Sondheim; Book, Burt Shevelove and Larry Gelbart; Director/Choreographer, Pamela Hunt; Musical Director, Lynn Crigler; Associate Choreographer, Michelle Yarashko; Sets, James Morgan; Costumes, Beba Shamash; Lighting, Mary Jo Dondlinger; Technical, Matt Goldin; Stage Manager, Mary Ellen Allison. CAST: Jack Cirillo (Prologus/Pseudolus), John Remme (Senex), Chris Callen (Domina), Jeffrey Herbst (Hero), Jason Graae (Hysterium), Jim Harder (Erronius), Ken Parks (Miles Gloriosus), Tony Aylward (Lycus), Hope Harris (Tintinabula), Denise Ledonne, Isabel Rose (The Geminae), Valerie Macklin (Vibrata), Sloan Wilding (Gymnasia), Deborah Graham (Philia), John Dietrich, Mark DiNoia, Barry Finkel (The Proteans)
   A musical in two acts. The action takes place in Rome, two hundred years before the Christian era.

Carol Rosegg/Martha Swope Photos **Right: Brian Bedford
in "The Lunatic, The Lover & The Poet"**

Susanne Marley, Page Johnson in "East Texas"

Ken Kantor, Michael Tucci, Tony Floyd in "Philemon"

**John Remme, Jack Cirillo, Jason Graae in
"Funny Thing Happened…"**

BYE BYE BIRDIE

Music, Charles Strouse; Lyrics, Lee Adams; Book, Michael Stewart; Director, Gene Saks; Choreography, Edmond Kresley; Music Director, Michael Biagi; Sets, Peter Larkin; Costumes, Robert Mackintosh; Lighting, Peggy Eisenhauer; Sound, Peter Fitzgerald; Hairstylist, Robert DiNiro; Casting, Stuart Howard, Amy Schecter; General Manager, Barbara Darwall, Alecia Parker; Production Supervisor, Craig Jacobs; Technical Supervisor, Arthur Siccardi; Company Manager, Jim Brandeberry; Stage Managers, David Wolfe, Thomas Bartlett; Presented by Barry and Fran Weissler and Pace Theatrical Group; Press, Judy Jacksina/Anita Dionak, Penny M. Landau. Opened May 9, 1991 in Long Beach, California after previous St. Louis engagement, and still touring May 31, 1991.

CAST

Rose Alvarez ....Anne Reinking
Albert Peterson ....Tommy Tune
Ursula Merkle ....Jessica Stone
Kim MacAfee ....Susan Egan
Doris MacAfee ....Belle Calaway
Harry MacAfee ....Dale O'Brien
Randolph MacAfee..Joey Hannon
Mae Peterson ....Marilyn Cooper
Conrad Birdie ....Marc Kudisch
Hugo Peabody ....Steve Zahn
Deborah Sue ....Robyn Peterman
Suzie ....Jane Labanz
Mayor ....J. Lee Flynn
Mayor's Wife ....Kristine Nevins
Mrs. Merkle ....Mary Kilpatrick
Gloria Rasputin ....Belle Calaway
TV Stage Manager...Martin Coles
Charles F. Maude...J. Lee Flynn
Harvey Johnson ....Paul Castree

ENSEMBLE: Paul Castree, Martin Coles, Vincent D'Elia, Michael Duran, Kim Frankenfeld, Simone Gee, Elizabeth Green, Peter Gregus, Vanessa Handrick, Jorinda Junius, Brian Loeffler, Brian-Paul Mendoza, Elizabeth O'Neill, Robyn Peterman, Tracy Rosten, H. Hyland Scott II, Tara Sobeck, Wendy Springer, Shaver Tillitt

UNDERSTUDIES/STANDBYS: Belle Calaway (Rose), Dennis Daniels (Albert/Birdie), Tracy Rosten (Mae), Vincent D'Elia (Birdie), J. Lee Flynn (Harry), Mary Kilpatrick (Doris/Gloria), Jane Labanz (Kim), Wendy Springer (Randolph), Paul Castree (Hugo), Elizabeth Green (Ursula), Brian-Paul Mendoza (Harvey)

MUSICAL NUMBERS: An English Teacher, Telephone Hour, How Lovely to Be a Woman, Put on a Happy Face, Normal American Boy, One Boy, Honestly Sincere, Hymn for a Sunday Evening, One Last Kiss, What Did I Ever See In Him?, A Lot of Livin' to Do, Kids, Baby Talk to Me, Shriner's Ballet, A Giant Step (new song), He's Mine (new song), Rosie

A musical in two acts. The action takes place in New York and Ohio, 1959.

Marc Kudisch (center)

Robyn Peterman, Susan Egan, Jane Labanz, Steve Zahn

Tommy Tune, Ann Reinking

A CHORUS LINE

Originally Conceived, Choreographed, and Directed by Michael Bennett; Music, Marvin Hamlisch; Lyrics, Edward Kleban; Book, James Kirkwood, Nicholas Dante; Restaged by Baayork Lee; Musical Director, Joseph Klein; Lighting, Richard Winkler; Sound, Abe Jacob; Assistant Director, Jim Litten; General Manager, Robert V. Straus; Stage Manager, Joseph Sheridan; Presented by Robert L. Young, Richard Martini, and Albert Nocciolino; Press, Molly Smyth

CAST

Frank	Jim Athens
Al	Buddy Balou
Richie	Philip Michael Baskerville
Shelia	Gail Benedict
Connie	Melinda Cartwright
Judy	Janie Casserly
Butch	Kevin Chinn
Zach	Randy Clements
Don	Michael Danek
Roy	Morris Freed
Cassie	Laurie Gamache
Diana	Deborah Geneviere
Bobby	Michael Gorman
Val	Julie Graves
Tricia	Julia Gregory
Tom	Darrell Hankey
Kristine	Melissa Johnson
Greg	Bradley Jones
Vicki	Diana Kavilis
Maggie	Julie Pappas
Paul	Porfirio
Larry	Danny Rounds
Mike	Mark Santillano
Mark	John Scott
Lois	Anna Simonelli
Bebe	Beth Swearingen

UNDERSTUDIES: Jim Litten (Mike/Larry/Al), Julia Gregory (Maggie/Bebe/Kristine/Diana), Kevin Chinn (Richie/Paul), Anna Simonelli (Connie/Diana/Bebe), Jim Athens (Bobby/Greg/Paul), Morris Freed (Larry/Mark), Darrell Hankey (Don/Al/Greg), Diana Kavilis (Val/Judy/Kristine/Cassie), Michael Danek (Zach), Janie Casserly (Shelia), Buddy Balou (Zach/Bobby), Danny Rounds (Mark/Mike/Don), Beth Swearingen (Cassie), Karis Christensen (Don/Zach/Al), Mindy Hull (Judy/Shelia)

A musical performed without intermission. The action takes place during an audition, circa 1975.

The Company performs the finale.

Gerry Vichi, Neil Nash, Glory Crampton, Ralston Hill,
Robert Goulet (center)

THE FANTASTICKS

Music, Harvey Schmidt; Lyrics/Book, Tom Jones; Directors, Mr. Jones and Mr. Schmidt; New Orchestrations, Jack Elliott; New Sets/Costumes, Ed Wittstein; Presented by Robert L. Young and Chris Manos in association with Richard Martini; Press, Molly Smyth. Opened in the Des Moines, Iowa, Civic Center on Monday, June 18, 1990 and closed December 9, 1990 in Rochester, New York.

CAST

El Gallo/Narrator	Robert Goulet
The Mute	Rudy Hogenmiller
Hucklebee	Ralston Hill
Bellomy	Gerry Vichi
Luisa	Glory Crampton
Matt	Neil Nash
Old Actor	James Valentine
Man Who Dies	James Cook

and Terry Baughan, Paul Blankenship, Marie-Laurence Danvers, Jaime Zee Eisner, James Harms, Dale O'Brien, Scott Willis. SWINGS: Susan Bachman, Dan Shaheen

UNDERSTUDIES: Scott Willis (El Gallo), Marie-Laurence Danvers (Luisa), Paul Blankenship (Matt/Mute), James Harms (Bellomy/Henry), Dale O'Brien (Hucklebee/Mortimer)

A musical in two acts suggested by Edmond Rostand's 1894 play *Les Romanesques*. For original 1960 production see *Theatre World* Vol. 16. This production employed a full orchestration and chorus instead of the original combo arrangement.

GRAND HOTEL

Songs, Robert Wright, George Forrest; Additional Music and Lyrics, Maury Yeston; Book, Luther Davis; Based on Vicki Baum's *Grand Hotel*; Director/Choreographer, Tommy Tune; Setting Design, Tony Walton; Costumes, Santo Loquasto; Lighting, Jules Fisher; Sound, Otts Munderloh; Associate Director, Bruce Lumpkin; Associate Choreographer, Niki Harris; Musical Director, Michael Biagi; Orchestrations, Peter Matz; Original Music Direction/Vocal Arrangements, Jack Lee; Music Supervision/Additional Music, Wally Harper; Musical Coordinator, John Monaco; Casting, Julie Hughes, Barry Moss; Stage Manager, Mark Krause; Hair Design, Werner Sherer; General Manager, Joey Parnes; Press, Judy Jacksina; Tour Direction, Irving Siders/CAMI; Presented by Columbia Artists Management, Concert Productions International, James M. Nederlander, Pace Theatrical Group (Inc.). For original Broadway production see *Theatre World* Vol. 46. Opened November 27, 1990 in the Tampa Bay Performing Arts Center and still touring May 31, 1991.

CAST

Grushinskaya..Liliane Montevecchi
Flaemmchen...DeLee Lively-Mekka
Director Preysing..K.C. Wilson
Baron Von Gaigern ....Brent Barrett
Otto Kringelein..Mark Baker
Doctor Otternschlag...Anthony Franciosa
Eric...Dirk Lumbard
Zinnowitz ....Erick Devine
Chauffeur..David Dollase
Raffaela..Debbie de Coudreaux
and Bernie Passeltiner, Arte Phillips, Victoria Regan, David Rogers, Martin Van Treuren, Sterling Clark, Dan Conroy, Keith Crowningshield, Mark Enis, Nathan Gibson, Scott Hayward, Carrie-Ellen Heikkila, Rachel Jones, Barbara Marineau, Corinne Melancon, Marc Mouchet, Doug Nagy, Reggie Phoenix, Abe Reybold, William Ryall, Rick Stockwell, Vincent Vogt, David Andrew White, Susan Wood

Martha Swope Photos

Liliane Montevecchi

Brent Barrett, DeLee Lively

Mark Baker, DeLee Lively

Arte Phillips, Victoria Regan

Elaine Hausman, Amy Ryan, Maggie Baird,
Stephanie Dunnam, Mimi Lieber

Mark Harelik, Stephanie Dunnam

Robert Curtis-Brown, Stephanie Dunnam,
Elaine Hausman, Mark Harelik

THE HEIDI CHRONICLES

By Wendy Wasserstein; Director, Daniel Sullivan; Sets, Thomas Lynch; Costumes, Jennifer von Mayrhauser; Lighting, Pat Collins; Sound, Scott Lehrer; Production Design, Wendell Harrington; a Center Theatre Group/Ahmanson Theatre, the Shubert Organization, Suntory International and James Walsh in association with Playwrights Horizons presentation; for the original Broadway production see *Theatre World* Vol. 45; Press, Fred Nathan/Marc P. Thibodeau. Opened October 12, 1990 in the Doolittle Theatre, Hollywood, California and closed April 28, 1991 in Washington, D.C.

CAST

Heidi Holland	Amy Irving†1
Susan Johnston	Mimi Lieber
Chris Boxer/Mark/TV Attendant/Waiter/Ray	Michael Sandels
Peter Patrone	Robert Curtis-Brown
Scoop Rosenbaum	Mark Harelik
Jill/Debbie/Lisa	Maggie Baird
Fran/Molly/Betsy/April	Elaine Hausman
Becky/Clara/Denise	Amy Ryan

†1. Succeeded by Stephanie Dunnam

A play in two acts and eleven scenes. The action takes place from 1965 to 1989 at various locations.

Mark Harelik, Stephanie Dunnam
Jay Thompson Photos

Scott Wise (center) and cast

JEROME ROBBINS' BROADWAY

By James M. Barrie, Irving Berlin, Leonard Bernstein, Jerry Bock, Sammy Cahn, Moose Charlap, Betty Comden, Larry Gelbart, Morton Gould, Adolph Green, Oscar Hammerstein II, Sheldon Harnick, Arthur Laurents, Carolyn Leigh, Stephen Longstreet, Hugh Martin, Jerome Robbins, Richard Rodgers, Burt Shevelove, Stephen Sondheim, Joseph Stein, Jule Styne; Director/Choreographer, Jerome Robbins; Assistant to the Choreographer, Cynthia Onrubia, Victor Castelli, George Russell; Music Director, Paul Gemignani; Scenery, Boris Aronson, Jo Mielziner, Oliver Smith, Robin Wagner, Tony Walton; Costumes, Joseph G. Aulisi, Alvin Colt, Raoul Pene du Bois, Irene Sharaff, Tony Walton, Miles White, Patricia Zipprodt; Orchestrations, Sid Ramin, William D. Brohn; Musical Continuity, Scott Frankel; Conductor, Carl Hermanns, Sound, Otts Munderloh; Hair/Makeup, J. Roy Helland; Casting, Jay Binder; Production Supervisor, Beverly Randolph; Press, William Schelble; The Shubert Organization and Suntory International Corporation presentation of The Shubert Organization, Roger Berlind, Suntory International Corporation, Byron Goldman and Emanuel Azenberg production; for original Broadway production see *Theatre World* Vol. 45. Opened October 10, 1990 in the Shubert Theatre, Los Angeles, and still touring May 31, 1991

CAST

Tony Roberts, Debbie Shapiro, Scott Wise, Jennifer Allen, Cleve Asbury, John Baker, Harrison Beal, Jim Borstelmann, Bill Burns, Tony Caligagan, Lisa Dawn Cave, Christine DeVito, Donna Marie Elio, Jeffrey Hankinson, Ned Hannah, Suzanne Harrer, Alexia Hess, Naoko Katakami, Annie Kelly, David Koch, Michael Kubala, Jeff Lander, David Lowenstein, Mary MacLeod, Carol Lee Meadows, Julio Monge, Maria Neenan, Steve Ochosa, Michael O'Donnell, Valerie Perri, Stephen Reed, James Rivera, Erin Robbins, Mary Rotella, Greg Shanuel, Beth Swearingen, Linda Talcott, John Norman Thomas, Nancy Ticotin, Lynn Torgove, Leslie Trayer, Jerome Vivona, Robert Weber, Kayoko Yoshioka, Karen Ziemba
MUSICAL NUMBERS: New York New York, Sailors on the Town, Ya Got Me, Charleston, Comedy Tonight, I Still Get Jealous, Suite of Dances from *West Side Story*, The Small House of Uncle Thomas, You Gotta Have a Gimmick, I'm Flying, On a Sunday by the Sea, Mr. Monotony, Fiddler on the Roof, Some Other Time, Finale

Debbie Shapiro

Karen Ziemba, Jeffrey Elsass
Martha Swope Photos

LEND ME A TENOR

By Ken Ludwig; Director, Jerry Zaks; Setting, Tony Walton; Costumes, William Ivey Long; Lighting, Paul Gallo; Sound, Gary Stocker; Casting, Stuart Howard, Amy Schecter; Hairstylist, Angela Gari; Executive Producer, George MacPherson; Production Supervisor, Steven Beckler; Production Stage Manager, Allen McMullen; Tour Direction, American Theatre Productions, Inc.; a Pace Theatrical Group and Tom Mallow presentation; Press, Laura Matalon; for original Broadway production see *Theatre World* Vol. 45. Opened September 11, 1990 at the Shubert Theatre, New Haven, Connecticut.

CAST

Maggie	Valerie Leonard
Max	Michael Waldron
Saunders	Barry Nelson
Tito Merelli	Ron Holgate
Maria	D'Jamin Bartlett
Bellhop	Patrick Garner
Diana	Kate Skinner
Julia	Justine Johnston

The action takes place in a hotel suite in Cleveland, Ohio in 1934.

Barry Nelson, Justine Johnston

D'Jamin Bartlett, Ron Holgate
Martha Swope Photos

111

LES MISÉRABLES

For original creative credits and Musical Numbers, see Broadway Calendar; Musical Director, Dale Rieling; Company Manager, David Musselman; Stage Managers, Liza C. Stein, David Hansen, Steve Marquette; Press, Fred Nathan/Marc Thibodeau. First National Company opened Tuesday, December 15, 1987 in Boston's Shubert Theatre and was still touring on May 31, 1991; for original 1987 Broadway production see *Theatre World* Vol. 43.

CAST

Gary Morris succeeded by Mark McKerracher (Jean Valjean), Richard Kinsey (Javert), Daniel C. Cooney, Drew Eshelman, Andy Gale, Peter Gunther, Daniel Guzman, Gordon Paddison, Richard Poole, Todd Thurston, Christopher Yates (Chain Gang), Christopher Carothers (Farmer), Daniel Guzman (Laborer), Ann Arvia (Innkeeper's Wife), J.C. Montgomery (Innkeeper), Stephen Frugoli (Bishop), RayFrewen, Frank Mastrone (Constables), Diane Frantantoni, Ann Crumb, Hollis Resnik, Kathy Taylor, Susan Dawn Carson, Laurie Beechman, Susan Gilmour, Anne Runolfsson (Fantine), Todd Thurston (Foreman), Mr. Carothers, Mr. Cooney (Workers), Eydie Alyson, Kay Elise Kleinerman, Regina O'Malley, Sandy Rosenberg (Workers), Jeanne Croft (Factory Girl), Mr. Cooney, Mr. Gale, Mr. Poole (Sailors), Ms. Arvia, Kimberly Behlmann, Christa Justus, Gretchen Kingsley, Ms. Kleinerman, Ms. Rosenberg, Sandy Tilson (Whores), Ms. O'Malley (Old Woman), Ms. Alyson (Crone), Mr. Mastrone (Pimp), Gordon Paddison (Bamatabois), Mr. Mastrone (Fauchelevent), Natalie Berg, Raegan Kotz, Lee Alison Marino (Young Cosette), Rosalyn Rahn (Madame Thénardier), Drew Eshelman (Thénardier), Ms. Berg, Ms. Kotz, Ms. Marino (Young Eponine), Mr. Carothers, Ms. Arvia, Mr. Mastrone, Ms. O'Malley, Mr. Paddison, Mr. Poole (Drinkers), Ms. Kingsley, Mr. Guzman (Couple), Mr. Montgomery (Drunk), Mr. Frugoli, Ms. Rosenberg (Diners), Mr. Gale (Young Man), Ms. Justus, Ms. Kleinerman (Girls), Ms. Alyson, Mr. Cooney (Old Couple), Mr. Frewen, Mr. Thurston (Travelers), Joey Morano (Gavroche), Ms. O'Malley (Beggar), Ms. Croft (Young Prostitute), Mr. Montgomery (Pimp), Susan Tilson (Eponine), Mr. Guzman (Montparnasse), Mr. Frewen (Babet), Mr. Poole (Brujon), Mr. Mastrone (Claquesous), Christopher Yates (Enjolras), Peter Gunther (Marius), Kimberly Behlmann (Cosette), Mr. Thurston (Combeferre), Mr. Gale (Feuilly), Mr. Carothers (Courfeyrac), Mr. Cooney (Joly), Mr. Paddison (Grantaire), Mr. Frugoli (Lesgles), Mr. Montgomery (Prouvaire)

A musical in two acts. The action takes place in Digne, Montreuil-Sur-Mer, Montfermeil, and Paris, 1815-32.

Susan Tilson

Mark McKerracher

The Company in the Act I finale.

Jerry Chistakos (center)

Brian Lynch

Marian Murphy, Gilles Chaisson

Lisa Vroman

LES MISÉRABLES

For original creative credits and Musical Numbers, see Broadway Calendar; Musical Director, Robert S. Gustafson; Associate Director/Executive Producer, Richard Jay-Alexander; Production Supervisor, Sam Stickler; Company Manager, Daryl T. Dodson; Stage Manager, Michael John Egan; Press, Fred Nathan; for original 1987 Broadway production see *Theatre World* Vol. 43.

CAST

Richard Poole succeeded by Brian Lynch (Jean Valjean), David Jordan (Javert), Lisa Vroman (Fantine), Aloysius Gigle succeeded by Jerry Christakos (Enjolras), Gilles Chiasson (Marius), Marian Murphy (Cosette), Candese Marchese (Eponine), J.P. Dougherty (Thénardier), Diana Rogers (Mme. Thénardier), Craig Bennett (Combeferre), Kelly Briggs (Lesgles), Jennifer Elaine Davis, Talaria Haast (Young Cosette/Young Eponine), Jarrod Emick (Prouvaire), Joshua Finkel (Claquesous), Taylor John (Gavroche), Bryant Lanier (Montparnasse), Ron LaRosa (Joly), Cary Lovett (Brujon), Kirk Mouser (Babet), Alan Osburn (Bamatabois/Grantaire), Ron Sharpe (Feuilly), Buddy Smith (Gavroche), Douglas Webster (Courfeyrac), and Mercedes Perez, Tina Paradiso, Judy Malloy, Scott Logsdon, Christina M. LaGreca, Trisha Gooch, Jeffra Cook, Mary Chesterman, Jim Charles, Ruthann Bigley, Jeanne Bennett, Jennifer Rae Beck

UNDERSTUDIES: Douglas Webster (Valjean), Bryant Lanier, Alan Osburn (Javert), Jeanne Bennett, Trisha Gooch, Mercedes Perez (Fantine), Mary Chesterman, Jeffra Cook (Mme. Thénardier), Craig Bennett, Joshua Finkel (Thénardier), Jennifer Rae Beck, Ruthann Bigley (Eponine/Cosette), Kirk Mouser, Ron Sharpe (Marius), Jim Charles, Jarrod Emick (Enjolras), SWINGS: Jim Charles, Christina M. LaGreca, Ron LaRosa, Scott Logsdon, Tina Paradiso

Taylor John
Joan Marcus Photos

Kevin Gray, Teri Bibb

Keith Buterbaugh, Teri Bibb

David Huneryager, Patricia Hurd, Rick Hilsabeck
Joan Marcus Photos

THE PHANTOM OF THE OPERA

For original creative credits and Musical Numbers, see Broadway Calendar; Musical Director, Jack Gaughan; General Manager, Alan Wasser; Company Manager, Barbara Nunn; Stage Manager, Steve McCorkle; Press, Fred Nathan/Merle Frimark; For original 1988 Broadway production see *Theatre World* Vol. 44. This company played Chicago, Fort Lauderdale and was still playing Washington, D.C. as of May 31, 1991

CAST

Phantom of the Opera	Mark Jacoby succeeded by Kevin Gray
Christine Daaé	Karen Culliver succeeded by Teri Bibb
	Sarah Pfisterer (Alternate)
Raoul	Keith Buterbaugh
Carlotta Guidicelli	Patricia Hurd
Monsieur Firmin	David Huneryager
Monsieur André	Rick Hilsabeck
Madame Giry	Olga Talyn
Ubaldo Piangi	Donn Cook
Meg Giry	Patricia Ward
Monsieur Reyer	Richard L. Reardon
Auctioneer	Lawson Skala
Porter/Marksman	Charles Bergell
Monsieur Lèfevre	Robert Hildreth
Joseph Buquet	Brad Keating
Don Attilo/Passarino	Lawson Skala
Slave Master	Douglas Graham
Flunkies/Porters/Stagehands	Travis L. Wright, Stephen Gould
Policeman	William Lynn Dixon
Pages	Valerie DeBartolo, Patti Davidson-Gorbea
Lion Man	James R. Guthrie
Wardrobe Mistress/Confidante	Dorothy Byrne
Princess	Dodie Pettit
Madame Firmin	Lisa Faletto
Innkeeper's Wife	Virginia Croskery
Ballet Chorus	Diane Anastasio, Nicole Chelini, Candice Peterson
	Tait Runnfeldt, Susan Zaguirre

UNDERSTUDIES/SWINGS: Keith Buterbaugh, Randal Keith (Phantom), Dodie Pettit (Christine), Steven Douglas Blair, Randal Keith (Raoul), Lawson Skala, William Lynn Dixon (Firmin), Richard L. Reardon, Charles Bergell (André), Lisa Faletto, Virginia Croskery (Carlotta), Patti Davidson-Gorbea, Valerie DeBartolo, Dorothy Byrne (Giry), Stephen Gould, James R. Guthrie (Piangi), Susan Zaguirre, Teresa DeRose (Meg) SWINGS: Ms. DeRose, Steven Douglas Blair, Mr. Keith, Lisa Kristina

A musical in two acts. The action takes place in and around the Paris Opera House, 1881-1911.

THE PLAYBOY OF THE WESTERN WORLD

By John Millington Synge; Director, Vincent Dowling; Set, Noel Sheridan; Costumes, Anne Cave, Rachel Pigot-Judd; Lighting, Tony Wakefield; U.S. Tour Design Supervisor, Geraldine O'Malley; U.S. Tour Lighting Supervisor, Ken Billington; Exclusive Tour Direction, American Theatre Productions, Inc.; Press, Patt Dale Associates, Philip Thurston; a Kennedy Center presentation. Opened September 13, 1990 in the Eisenhower Theatre, Washington, D.C.

CAST

Pegeen Mike ....Roma Downey
Shawn Keogh ....Macdara O'Fatharta
Michael James ....John Cowley
Philly Cullen ....Niall O'Brien
Jimmy Farrell ....Peadar Lamb
Christopher Mahon ....Frank McCusker
Widow Quin ....Nuala Hayes
Susan Brady ....Miriam Kelly
Nelly ....Margaret Fegan
Honor Blake ....Sarah Jane Scaife
Sara Tansey ....Maire Ni Ghrainne
Old Mahon ....David Kelly
Bellman ....David Carey
Townsman..Kevin Reynolds
Townswoman ....Miriam Coleman

The action takes place near a village, on a wild coast of Mayo, on an Autumn evening and the following day.

Martha Swope Photos

Macdara O'Fatharta, Roma Downey, Frank McCusker

Frank McCusker, Macdara O'Fatharta, John Cowley, Roma Downey

Roma Downey, Frank McCusker

Margaret Fegan, Miriam Kelly, Sarah Jane Scaife,
Maire Ni Ghrainne, Nuala Hayes, Frank McCusker

115

ALLENBERRY PLAYHOUSE

Boiling Springs, Pennsylvania.
June 13, 1990-June 9, 1991

Producer, John J. Heinze; Managing Director, Michael Rothaar; Production Stage Manager/Lighting Design/Director, Richard J. Frost; Production Coordinator, Cate Van Wickler; Sets, Robert Klingelhoefer; Costumes, Rose Parent; Technical Director, Rob Murtoff; Master Carpenter, Doug Van Wickler; Master Electrician, Gretchen Knowlton; Property Manager, Richard Adams; Costume Assistant, Jeanette Lewis; Public Relations, Cathy Stone

PRODUCTIONS AND CASTS

SOUTH PACIFIC; Music, Richard Rodgers; Lyrics, Oscar Hammerstein II; Book, Oscar Hammerstein II and Joshua Logan; Director, Richard J. Frost; Musical Direction, Robert Feldstein; Choreography, Patti D'Beck; Production Stage Manager, Cate Van Wickler; Sceneic Design, Robert Klingelhoefer; Lighting Design, Linda Ifert; Costume Design, Rose Parent; Production Coordinator, Cate Van Wickler. CAST: David Brubaker (Capt. Brackett), Randy Bettis (Abner), Debbie Lee Jones (Ensign Murphy), William R. Monnen (Lt. Cable), Myrna Paris (Bloody Mary), Julie Pasqual (Ensign Jeager), Len Pfluger (Stewpot), Elizabeth Ward (Ensign Nellie Forbush), Jay Willoughby (Emile), Ron Wisniski (Luther Billis), Richard Adams (Lt. Commander Harbison), Kim Araki (Liat), Adrian Bethea (Yeoman Quayle), Joseph Brier (Jerome), Michelle Carano (Ensign McGregor), Frank Castrina (Seaman O'Brien), Jill Christenson (Ensign MacRae), Kristen Copenhaver (Ensign Pitt), Kevin Dean (Cpl. Steeves), Terri Green (Ensign Noonan), Ed Hammond (Professor), Renee Hoffman (Ngana), James Jaeger (Seabee Wise/Lt. Adams), Gretchen Knowlton (Henry), Marisa Paley (Ensign Whitmore), Matthew Solari (Radio Operator)

ANYTHING GOES; Book, Guy Bolton, P.G. Wodehouse, Howard Lindsay and Russell Crouse; Music/Lyrics, Cole Porter; Director, Michael Rothaar; Musical Direction, Robert Feldstein; Choreography, Glenn Leslie; Production Stage Manager, Richard J. Frost; Scenic Design, Robert Klingelhoefer; Lighting Design, Lynnette Watley; Costume Design, Rose Parent; Production Coordinator, Cate Van Wickler. CAST: Ellen Arthur (Virtue), Randy Bettis (2nd Sailor), Kathleen Conry (Reno Sweeney), Debbie Lee Jones (Bonnie), William R. Monnen (Billy Crocker), Michael Nostrand (Moonface Martin), Nick Olcott (Sir Evelyn), Julie Pasqual (Chastity), Len Pfluger (1st Sailor), Debra Segal (Hope Harcourt), Kim Araki (Charity), Adrian Bethea (Steward), Michelle Carano (Purity), Kristen Copenhaver (Girl/Passenger), Kevin Dean (Bishop/Sailor/Drunk), Terri Green (Ling/Passenger), Ed Hammond (Purser), James Jaeger (Reporter/Captain), Gretchen Knowlton (Girl/Passenger), Marisa Paley (Photographer/Girl), Matthew Solari (Ching/Sailor/Passenger), Bob Tron (Elisha Whitney), Jeanne Tron (Mrs. Harcourt).

CABARET; Book, Joe Masterhoff; Music, John Kander; Lyrics, Fred Ebb; Director, Michael Rothaar; Musical Direction, Robert Felstein; Choreography, Rebecca Timms; Production Stage Manager, Richard J. Frost; Sceneic Design, Robert Klingelhoefer; Costume Design, Rose Parent; Lighting Design, Richard J. Frost; Production Coordinator, Cate Van Wickler. CAST: Hayden Adams (Clifford Bradshaw), Ellen Arthur (Kit Kat Girl), Eddie Buffum (1st Sailor), Kathleen Conry (Sally Bowles), Debbie Lee Jones (Fraulein Kost), Michael Nostrand (The M.C.), Nick Olcott (Herr Schultz), Myrna Paris (Fraulein Schneider), Julie Pasqual (Kit Kat Girl), Len Pfluger (2nd Sailor/Gorilla), Adrian Bethea (Waiter), Michelle Carano (Kit Kat Girl), Kevin Dean (Tenor Solo/Waiter), Terri Green (Kit Kat Girl), Tina Guice (Kit Kat Girl), Ed Hammond (Waiter/Brown Shirt), James Jaeger (Ernst Ludwig), Gretchen Knowlton (Kit Kat Girl), Marisa Paley (Kit Kat Girl), Matthew Solari (Waiter/Brown Shirt), Bob Tron (Customs Officer/Max).

Kathleen Conry, Nancy Linehan in "A Murder Is Announced"

POOLS PARADISE by Philip King; Director, Michael Rothaar; Production Stage Manager, Richard J. Frost; Scenic Design, T. Owen Baumgartner; Lighting Design, Lynette Watley; Costume Design, Jeanette Lewis; Production Coordinator, Cate Van Wickler. CAST: Hayden Adams (Rev. Lionel Toop), David Brubaker (Bishop Lax), Kathleen Conry (Penelope Toop), Debbie Lee Jones (Miss Skillon), Gretchen Knowlton (Ida), Steven Smyser (Willie Briggs), Matthew Solari (Rev. Humphrey).

A MURDER IS ANNOUNCED adapted from Agatha Christie by Leslie Darbon; Director, Michael Rothhaar; Production Stage Manager, Richard J. Frost; Scenic Design, Robert Klingelhoefer; Lighting Design, Richard J. Frost; Costume Design, Rose Parent; Production Coordinator, Cate Van Wickler. CAST: Hayden Adams (Edmund Swetenham), Richard Adams (Patrick Simmons), Kathleen Conry (Letitia Blacklock), Debbie Lee Jones (Mitzi), Nancy Linehan (Miss Marple), Syd Rushing (Inspector Craddock), Catherine Blaine (Mrs. Swetenham), Terri Green (Phillipa Haymes), Gretchen Knowlton (Julia Simmons), Matthew Solari (Rudi Scherz), Steven Smyser (Sgt. Mellors), Jeanne Tron (Dora Bunner).

DRIVING MISS DAISY by Alfred Uhry; Director, Michael Rothhaar; Production Stage Manager, Richard J. Frost; Sceneic Design, Robert Klingelhoefer; Lighting Design, Richard J. Frost; Costume Design, Rose Parent; Music, Robert Waldman; Production Coordinator, Cate Van Wickler. CAST: Michael Haney (Boolie Werthan), Nancy Linehan (Daisy Werthan), Syd Rushing (Hoke Coleburn).

ON GOLDEN POND by Ernest Thompson; Director, Michael Rothhaar; Production Stage Manager, Richard J. Frost; Sceneic Design, Robert Klingelhoefer; Lighting Design, Richard J. Frost; Costume Design, Rose Parent; Production Coordinator, Cate Van Wickler. CAST: David Brubaker (Norman Thayer, Jr.), Richert Easley (Charlie Martin), Nancy Linehan (Ethel Thayer), Amy Warner (Chelsea), James Hayney (Bill Ray), Jason Voight (Billy Ray).

RUMORS by Neil Simon; Director, Michael Rothhaar; Production Stage Manager, Richard J. Frost; Sceneic Design, Robert Klingelhoefer; Lighting Design, Richard J. Frost; Costume Design, Rose Parent; Production Coordinator, Cate Van Wickler. CAST: Richard Adams (Glenn Cooper), Richert Easley (Lenny Ganz), Debbie Lee Jones (Chris Gorman), Nancy Linehan (Claire Ganz), Amy Warner (Cassie Cooper), Catherine Blaine (Cookie Cusack), Patt Giblin (Ken Gorman), James Hayney (Ernie Cusack), Selena Nelson (Pudney), Steven Smyser (Welch).

THE MOUSETRAP by Agatha Christie; Director, Michael Nostrand; Production Stage Manager, Richard J. Frost; Sceneic Design, Robert Klingelhoefer; Lighting Design, Richard J. Frost; Costume Design, Jeanette Lewis; Production Coordinator, Cate Van Wickler. CAST: Richert Easley (Mr. Paravicini), Michael Haney (Detective Sgt. Trotter), Nancy Linehan (Miss Casewell), Amy Warner (Molly Ralston), James Allen (Christopher Wren), Steven Smyser (Giles Ralston), Bob Tron (Major Metcalf), Jeanne Tron (Mrs. Boyle).

Michael Nostrand and cast in "Cabaret"

ARENA STAGE

Washington, D.C.
Fortieth Season
September 4, 1990-June 23, 1991

Producing Director, Zelda Fichandler; Associate Producing Director, Douglas C. Wager; Executive Director, Stephen Richard; General Manager, Guy Bergquist; Artistic Associate, Tazewell Thompson; Production Manager, Martha Knight; Technical Director, David M. Glenn; Administrative Director, JoAnn M. Overholt; Communications, Regan Byrne; Development, Elspeth Udvarhelyi; Living Stage Directors, Robert A. Alexander, Catherine Irwin; Press Director, Sara Hope Franks. RESIDENT COMPANY: Richard Bauer, Teagle F. Bougere, Ralph Cosham, Terrence Currier, Gail Grate, Margo Hall, M.E. Hart, Tana Hicken, Michael W. Howell, Julian Hughes, David Marks, Pamela Nyberg, Henry Strozier, Jeffrey V. Thompson, John Leonard Thompson, Halo Wines.

PRODUCTIONS AND CASTS

CLOSER THAN EVER with Music by David Shire, Lyrics, Richard Maltby, Jr.; Director, Mr. Maltby; Sets, Philipp Jung; Costumes, Jess Goldstein; Lighting, Joshua Starbuck. CAST: Meg Bussert, Sally Mayes, Louis Padilla, Craig Wells.
CAUCASIAN CHALK CIRCLE by Brecht; Translation, Ralph Manheim; Director, Tazewell Thompson; Music, Fabian V. Obispo, Jr.; Sets, Loy Arcenas; Costumes, Paul Tazewell; Lighting, Nancy Schertler. CAST: Terrence Currier, Ralph Cosham, Richard Charles Lowe, Henry Strozier, Halo Wines, Teagle F. Bougere, Gail Grate, Tana Hicken, Jarlath Conrot, Jane White, James Brown-Orleans, Jennifer Collins, George Fulginiti-Shakar, Wendy Lanxner, Namu Lwanga, Pedro Porro, Brian Rha, Nia Harris, Ryan S. Richmond, Zhalisa Lila Clarke, Thomas Ikeda, Jurian Hughes, Saul Stein, Jeffrey V. Thompson, Anna Bergman, Jennifer Collins, Helen Hedman, Lona Alias, Socorro Santiago, James Brown-Orleans, Tom Simpson, Richie Porter, Michael W. Howell, Raphael Angelo Clarke, Langston Wood Shaw, Nicholas Crain, Lewis J. Stadlen, Tony Carlin.
CERCEAU by Viktor Slavkin; Translation, Fritz Brun and Laurence Maslon; Director/Design, Liviu Ciulei; Costumes, Majorie Sliaman; Lighting, Nancy Schertler. CAST: Charles Geyer (Rooster), Randy Danson (Valyusha), Jed Diamond (Vladimir), John Leonard Thompson (Lars), Pamela Nyberg (Nadya), David Marks (Pasha), Richard Bauer (Koka).
OUR TOWN by Thornton Wilder; Director, Douglas C. Wager; Sets, Thomas Lynch; Costumes, Marjorie Sliaman. CAST: Robert Prosky (Stage Manager), M.E. Hart, Julian Hughes, Drew Kahl, Eric E. Oleson (Asst. Managers), Halo Wines (Mrs. Gibbs), Tana Hicken (Mrs. Webb), Jaime Sanchez (Dr. Gibbs), John Prosky (Crowell), Jeffrey V. Thompson (Howie), Margo Hall (Rebecca), David Aaron Baker (George), Christina Moore (Emily), Teagle F. Bougere (Wally), Terrence Currier (Willard/Stoddard), Henry Strozier (Mr. Webb), Jarlath Conroy (Simon), Dorothea Hammond (Mrs. Soames), Ralph Cosham (Constable), Michael W. Howell (Sam), Jay Hillmer, Irving Jacobs, Gail Grate, Lee Holzaphel, Keith Johnson, Faith Potts, Julian Hughes (Townspeople, Dead, etc.).

Sally Mayes, Louis Padilla, Meg Bussert, Craig Wells
in "Closer Than Ever"

Robert Prosky, David Aaron Baker, Christina Moore in "Our Town"

PYGMALION by George Bernard Shaw; Director, Douglas C. Wager; Sets, Michael Yeargan; Costumes, Barbra Kravitz; Lighting, Mark McCullough. CAST: Jennifer Mendenhall (Clara), Tana Hicken (Mrs. Eynsford Hill), Conrad Feineinger (Bystander), Michael Chaban (Freddy), Gail Grate (Eliza), Terrence Currier (Pickering), Richard Bauer (Higgins), Michael W. Howell (Sarcastic Man), June Hansen (Mrs. Pearce), Charles Dumas (Doolittle), Tammy Grimes (Mrs. Higgins), Desiree Marie, John Elko, Louise Reynolds, Godfrey L. Simmons, Jr.
MY CHILDREN! MY AFRICA by Athol Fugard; Director, Max Mayer; Sets, David M. Glenn; Costumes, Crystal Walker; Lighting, Christopher Townsend. CAST: Herb Downer (Mr. M), Robin Morse (Isabel), Teagle F. Bougere (Thami)
SHE STOOPS TO CONQUER by Oliver Goldsmith; Director, Joe Dowling; Sets, F. Hallinan Flood; Costumes, Marjorie Sliaman; Lighting, Allen Lee Hughes. CAST: Halo Wines (Mrs. Hardcastle), Mark Hammer (Hardcastle), David Marks (Tony), Kathryn Meisle (Miss Hardcastle), Julian Hughes (Miss Neville), Jake Weber (Young Marlowe), Jeffrey Wright (Hastings), John William Cook (Sir Charles), Keith Fulwood, Hugh Nees, Jefferson Cronin, Brad Waller, M.E. Hart, Pedro Porro, Jane Pesci-Townsend, Jarlath Conroy.
BORN GUILTY by Ari Roth; Based on the book by Peter Sichrovsky; Director, Zelda Fichandler; Sets, Douglas Stein; Costumes, Noel Borden; Lighting, Nancy Schertler. CAST: Henry Strozier, Pamela Nyberg, Marissa Copeland, Helen Carey, Ralph Cosham, David Marks, Jed Diamond, Harold Perrineau, Jr., Halo Wines, John Leonard Thompson.
BEFORE IT HITS HOME by Cheryl West; Director, Tazewell Thompson; Sets, Douglas Stein; Costumes, Helen Qizhi Huang; Lighting, Nacy Schertler. CAST: Michael Jace (Wendal), Cynthia Martells (Simone), Keith Randolph Smith (Douglass), Trazana Beverley (Reba), Ms. Martells (Mrs. Peterson) Mercedes Herrero (Nurse), Sandra Reaves-Phillips (Maybelle), Julian Hughes (Doctor), Wally Taylor (Bailey), Ryan Richmond (Dwayne), Lee Simon, Jr. (Junior).
VIVISECTIONS FROM THE BLOWN MIND by Alonzo D. Lamont, Jr.; Director, Clinton Turner Davis; Sets, Michael Franklin-White; Lighting, Christopher V. Lewton. CAST: Lee Simon, Jr. (Castro), Katrina Van Duyn (Angelique), M.E. Hart (Dusty), Vincent Brown (Goliath).
FROM THE MISSISSIPPI DELTA by Dr. Endesha Ida Mae Holland; Director, Jonathan Wilson; Sets, Michael S. Phillippi; Costumes, Jeffrey Kelly; Lighting, Chris Phillips. CAST: Sybil Walker, Jacqueline Williams, Cheryl Lynn Bruce.
THE SEAGULL by Anton Chekhov; Director, Douglas C. Wager; Sets, Ming Cho Lee; Lighting, Arden Fingerhut; Costumes, Marjorie Sliaman. CAST: Francois Giroday, Nancy Grosshans, Johanna Rodriguez, Richard Bauer, Teagle F. Bougere, Tana Hicken, Michael W. Howell, Julian Hughes, David Marks, Pamela Nyberg, Henry Strozier, John Leonard Thompson, Halo Wines.

Joan Marcus Photos

Cynthia Martells, Michael Jayce, Keith Randolph Smith
in "Before It Hits Home"

Terrence Currier, Jane Hansen, Gail Grate,
Richard Bauer in "Pygmalion"

ARIZONA THEATRE COMPANY

Tucson and Phoenix, Arizona.
Fortieth Season
October 6, 1990-June 1, 1991

Artistic Director, Gary Gisselman; Managing Director, Robert Alpaugh; Stage Manager, Elizabeth Lohr; Production Assistants, Amy McPherson, Rob Cannon; Special Projects, Greg Lucas; Development, Don Haskell, Douglas Richards; Production Manager, Kent Conrad; Technical Director, Scott Haun; Public Relations, Prindle Gorman-Oomens.

PRODUCTION AND CASTS

AMADEUS by Peter Shaffer; Director, Gary Gisselman; Sets, Greg Lucas; Costumes, David Kay; Lighting, Don Darnutzer. CAST: George Morofogen (Salieri), Andrew Dolan, Richard Farrell (Venticelli), David Orley (Valet/Major Domo), Paul Secrest (Cook/Giuseppe Bonno/Teresa), William Roesch (Joseph II), Edwin Van Woert (von Stack), Benjamin Stewart (Count), Oliver Cliff (Baron), Bryce McDermot (Priest), Nicole Taylor (Katherina), Suzanne Bouchard (Constanze), Garry Briggle (Mozart), Maedell Dixon, Lee Gossage, Lillie Richardson.
THE PRICE by Arthur Miller; Director, Matthew Wiener; Sets, Michael Miller; Lighting, Don Darnutzer; Costumes, Sigrid Insull. CAST: Joseph Costa (Victor), Judith Roberts (Esther), David Hurst (Gregory), Tom Fuccello (Walter).
SCHOOL FOR WIVES by Moliere; Translation, Richard Wilbur; Director, Gary Gisselman; Sets, Greg Lucas; Lighting, Don Darnutzer; Costumes, Sigrid Insull. CAST: Benjamin Stewart (Chysalde), Randall Duk Kim (Arnolphe), Paul Klein (Alain), Kathy Fitzgerald (Georgette), Rana Haugen (Agnes), Geoff Elliott (Horace), Jason Kenny (Enrique/Steward), Oliver Cliff (Oronte/Notary), Digger (Le Chien).
LOOT by Joe Orton; Director, Gary Gisselman; Sets, Greg Lucas; Costumes, David Kay Mickelsen; Lighting, Don Darnutzer. CAST: Robert Cornthwaite (McLeavy), Suzanne Bouchard (Fay), Andrew Dolan (Hal), Paul Klein (Dennis), Benjamin Stewart (Truscott), Paul Secrest (Meadows).
THE HOLY TERROR (WORLD PREMIERE) by Simon Gray; Director, Mr. Gray; Sets, David Jenkins; Costumes, David Murin; Lighting, Dennis Parichy. CAST: Daniel Gerroll (Mark Melon), George Hall (Gladstone), Tracy Sallows (Samantha), Anthony Fusco (Michael/Jacob/Rupert/Graeme), Noel Derecki (Josh Melon), Julie Boyd (Gladys Powers), Rebecca Nelson (Kate Melon).
OTHER PEOPLE'S MONEY by Jerry Sterner; Director, David Ira Goldstein; Sets, Jeff Thompson; Lighting, Tracy Odishaw; Costumes, David Kay Mickelsen. CAST: Bob Morrisey (William), Clayton Corzatte (Andrew), Joe Minjares (Lawrence), Susan Corzatte (Bea), Suzanne Bouchard (Kate).

Tim Fuller Photos

**Daniel Gerroll in
"The Holy Terror"**

Randall Duk Kim, Kathy Fitzgerald in "School for Wives"

ASOLO THEATRE COMPANY

Sarasota, Florida
Fifteenth Season
November 1, 1990-June 30, 1991

PRODUCTIONS AND CASTS

THE COCKTAIL HOUR by A.R. Gurney; Director, Jamie Brown; Sets, Kevin Lock; Costumes, Vicki S. Holden; Lighting, Martin Petlock. CAST: Alan Mixon (Bradley), Seth Jones (John), Martha Randall (Ann), Kimberly King (Nina).
DRIVING MISS DAISY by Alfred Uhry; Director, John Gulley; Sets, Jeffrey W. Dean; Costumes, Howard Tsvi Kaplan; Lighting, Martin Petlock. CAST: Sally Parrish (Daisy), Gil Glasgow (Boolie), Herb Lovelle (Hoke).
A TALE OF TWO CITIES by Charles Dickens; Adaptation, Larry Carpenter; Director, Larry Arrick; Score/Music Director, John Franceschina; Sets, Kevin Lock; Costumes, Howard Tsvi Kaplan; Lighting, Martin Petlock. CAST: David Berman, Jeff Blumenkrantz, Jerry Grayson, Don Howard, Carolyn Hurlburt, Mark Hymen, James Prichett, Anne Sheldon, Alex Wipf, Sam Zapp.
ONLY KIDDING by Jim Geoghan; Director, Larry Arrick; Sets, Jeffrey W. Dean; Costumes, Howard Tsvi Kaplan; Lighting, Martin Petlock. CAST: Jerry Grayson (Jackie), Jeff Blumenkrantz (Sheldon), Don Howard (Tom), Mark Hymen (Jerry), Sam Zapp (Sal), Charlie Cronk (Voice of Buddy).
OTHER PEOPLE'S MONEY by Jerry Sterner; Director, William Gregg; Sets, Kevin Lock; Costumes, Howard Tsvi Kaplan; Lighting, Martin Petlock. CAST: Alex Wipf (William), Daivd Berman (Larry), James Pritchett (Andrew), Anne Sheldon (Bea), Carolyn Hurlburt (Kate).
MASTER HAROLD . . . AND THE BOYS by Athol Fugard; Director, Jamie Brown; Design, Lewis Folden; Costumes, Rebecca Keightley; Lighting, Phil Monat. CAST: Daryl Edwards (Sam), Todd Anthony-Jackson (Willie), Jack Boslet (Hally).
BEDROOM FARCE by Alan Ayckbourn; Director, John Going; Sets, Kevin Lock; Costumes, Howard Tsvi Kaplan; Lighting, Martin Petlock. CAST: John Gilbert (Ernest), Margaret Hilton (Delia), Jane Gabbert (Jan), P.J. Benjamin (Nick), Catherine Christianson (Kate), David Parkes (Malcolm), Malachy Cleary (Trevor), Charlotte Booker (Susannah).
THE HEIDI CHRONICLES by Wendy Wasserstein; Director, Amy Saltz; Sets, Michael Miller; Costumes, Howard Tsvi Kaplan; Lighting, Anne G. Wrightson. CAST: Susan Knight (Heidi), Judith Hawking (Susan), Lennie Loftin (Peter), Murray Rubenstein (Scoop), Daniel Pardo, Marceline Hugot, Julia Glander, Dina Spybey.

Lawrence C. Vaughn Photos

**Todd Anthony-Jackson, Jack Boslet, Daryl Edwards
in "Master Harold..."**

Mark Hymen, Sam Zap, Don Howard in "Only Kidding"

CALDWELL THEATRE COMPANY

Boca Raton, Florida
Fifteenth Season
October 2, 1990-May 19, 1991

Artistic/Managing Director, Michael Hall; Resident Scenic Designer, Frank Bennett; Company Manager, Patricia Burdett; Public Relations, Joe Gillie; Marketing, Kathy Walton; Press/Photographer, Paul Perone; Stage Manager, Bob Carter; Resident Costume Designer, Bridget Bartlett; Resident Lighting Designer, Mary Jo Dondlinger; Administrative Assistant, Noreen Petruff; Accountant, Helen Mavromatis; Technical Director, Chip Latimer; Assistant House Manager, Hank Allen; Assistant Company Manager, Nick Skoulaxenos; Master Electrician, Ken Melvin; Costume Supervisor, Joan Duffin; Props, George Sproul.

PRODUCTIONS AND CASTS

THE RAINMAKER by N. Richard Nash; Theatre for Schools pre-season production; Director, Kenneth Kay; Scenic Design, Frank Bennett; Costumes, Bridget Bartlett; Lighting, Russ Swift; Scenic Artist, Joe Gillie; Stage Manager, Bob Carter; Rehearsal Stage Manager, Chip Latimer. CAST: David Carpenter (File), Joseph Culliton (Starbuck), Gary Goodson (Sheriff Thomas), Michael Hartman (H. C. Curry), Nancy Ringham (Lizzie Curry), Tyson Stephenson (Noah Curry), Scott Treadway (Jimmy Curry).

THE HEIDI CHRONICLES by Wendy Wasserstein; Director, Michael Hall; Scenic Design, James Morgan; Costumes, Bridget Bartlett; Lighting, Kenneth Posner; Stage Manager, Bob Carter; Rehearsal Stage Manager, Chip Latimer. CAST: Vicki Boyle (Fran/Molly/Betsy/April), Kate Colburn (Becky/Clara/Denise), Kim Cozort (Jill/Debbie/Lisa), Susan Hatfield (Heidi Holland), Gary Jackson (Peter Patrone), Pat Nesbit (Susan), Dan Perry (Scoop Rosenbaum), Tom Wahl (Chris Boxer/Mark/TV Attendant/Waiter/Ray).

SEE HOW THEY RUN by Philip King; Director, Michael Hall; Scenic Design, Frank Bennett; Costumes, Bridget Bartlett; Lighting, Mary Jo Dondlinger; Stage Manager, Bob Carter; Rehearsal Stage Manager, Chip Latimer. CAST: Daniel Chapman (The Intruder), Kim Cozort (Penelope Toop), Denise Du Maurier (Miss Skillon), John Felix (The Rev. Arthur Humphrey), John Gardiner (The Bishop of Lax), John G. Preston (The Rev. Lionel Toop), Jamieson K. Price (Sergeant Towers), Tom Wahl (Corporal Clive Winton), Amelia White (Ida).

OTHER PEOPLE'S MONEY by Jerry Sterner; Director, Kenneth Kay; Scenic Design, James Morgan; Costumes, Bridget Bartlett; Lighting, Mary Jo Dondlinger; Stage Manager, Bob Carter; Rehearsal Stage Manager, Chip Latimer. CAST: Harold Bergman (Andrew Jorgenson), Gary Nathanson (Lawrence Garfinkel), Pat Nesbit (Kate Sullivan), June Prud'homme (Bea Sullivan), Geoffrey Wade (William Coles).

THE ROYAL FAMILY by George S. Kaufman and Edna Ferber; Director, Michael Hall; Scenic Design, Frank Bennett; Costumes, Bridget Bartlett; Lighting, Mary Jo Dondlinger; Scenic Artist, R. L. Markham; Stage Manager, Bob Carter; Rehearsal Stage Manager, Chip Latimer. CAST: Beth Fowler (Julie Cavendish), Denise Du Maurier (Fanny Cavendish), John Gardiner (Herbert Dean), Hal Gross (Jo), Michael Lasswell (Perry Stewart), Gary Nathanson (Oscar Wolfe), Amanda Naughton (Gwen), Pat Nesbit (Kitty Dean), Anthony Newfield (Anthony Cavendish), Jamieson K. Price (McDermott), Richard Rossomme (Gilbert Marshall), Sharon Shah (Della), A.J. Dasher (Hallboy), Bernadette Mackey (Miss Peake), Greg Wagner (Hallboy).

Paul Perone Photos

Amanda Naughton, Beth Fowler in "Royal Family"

Susan Hatfield, Gary Jackson in "Heidi Chronicles"

CAPITAL REPERTORY COMPANY

Albany, New York
October 3, 1990-June 2, 1991

Artistic Director, Bruce Bouchard; Managing Director, Robert Holley; Marketing/Public Relations, Susan Phillips; Development, Patrick Smith; Christian Conroy; Business Manager, Beth Brandt; Production Manager, Julie A. Fife; Stage Manager, Michael Samal; Technical, William Knapp; Costumes, Lynda Salsbury; Outreach Director, Mark Dalton.

PRODUCTIONS AND CASTS

THE SCANDALOUS ADVENTURES OF SIR TOBY TROLLOPE by Ron House and Alan Shearman; Director, Steven Rothman. CAST: Tony Papenfuss, Doug Kaye, Ron House, Howard Samuelsohn, Becky London, Leslie Scarlett Mason.

THE CHERRY ORCHARD by Chekhov; Director, Rene Buch. CAST: Michael Hume, Erin Ta Tavin, Bill Leone, David Walker, Martin Rudy, Tara Hugo, Susan Coon, Virginia Rambal, Josie DeGuzman, Richard Maynard, Nick Plakias, Quentin O'Brien, Steve Pelletier.

OTHER PEOPLE'S MONEY by Jerry Sterner; Director, Bruce Bouchard. CAST: Michael Arkin, Kate Kelly, Richard Maynard, Frank Latimore, Peg Small.

LAUGHING WILD by Christopher Durang; Director, Michael Hume. CAST: Eliza Ventura, Tom Riis Farrell.

BELMONT AVENUE SOCIAL CLUB by Bruce Graham; Director, James Christy. CAST: Roger Serbagi, Rik Colitti, Paul O'Brien, Barry Mulholland, James Doerr.

FENCES by August Wilson; Director, Seret Scott. CAST: John Amos, David Wolos-Fonteno, Madeline McCray, Keith Glover, Rony Clanton, Isiah Washington, Monee McAdoo, Tiana Morris.

Joseph Schuyler Photos

Rik Colitti, Paul O'Brien, Barry Mulholland, Roger Serbagi (front) in "Belmont Ave. Social Club"

Frank Muller in "Lost Electra"

CINCINNATI PLAYHOUSE IN THE PARK

Cincinnati, Ohio

Artistic Director, Worth Gardner; Managing Director, Kathleen Norris; Artistic Assistant, Lauren Campolongo; Managing Assistant, Gayle Barksdale; Literary Manager, Susan Banks; Development, Cynthia Colebrook, Kris Killen; Business Manager, Gail Lawrence; Stage Managers, Tom Lawson, Bruce E. Coyle, Candace Lofrumento; Lighting, Kirk Bookman; Marketing Director, Kimberly Cooper; Public Relations, Peter M. Robinson, Laura Cleavinger.

PRODUCTIONS AND CASTS

LOOT by Joe Orton; Director, Margaret Booker; Sets, Patricia Woodbridge; Costumes, D. Bartlett Blair. CAST: Philip Pleasants (McLeavy), Tessie Hogan (Fay), Marko Maglich (Hal), Arthur Hanket (Dennis), David Sabin (Truscott), Howard Kaye (Meadows).

BURN THIS by Lanford Wilson; Director, Jay E. Raphael; Sets, Joseph P. Tilford; Costumes, Cindy Witherspoon. CAST: Jacquelyn Riggs (Anna), Stuart Rider (Burton), Michael Babin (Larry), Michael Hammond (Pale).

THE WIZARD OF OZ by L. Frank Baum; Adaptaion, Frank Gabrielson; With MGM Score by Arlen and Harburg; Additional Songs, Worth Gardner; Director/Choreography, Mr. Gardner; Sets/Costumes, Paul Shortt. CAST: William Brown (Baum), Suzanne Bedford (Dorothy), Darren Matthias (Witch), Robert E. Fitch (Scarecrow), Howard Kaye (Tin Man), Bob Arnold (Lion), Timothy Booth, Desmon Zachary Dent, Bill E. Dietrich, Mark Douglas-Jones, Rebecca Hirsch, Martha M. Kelly, Patricia Linhart, Michael McCauley, Michael Pappa, Wendy Perelman, Kathi Ridley, Michael N. Shapiro, Clarence Snow.

EDUCATING RITA by Willy Russell; Director, Dorothy Marie Robinson; Sets, Jay Depenbrock; Costumes, Jo Wimer. CAST: Dana Bate (Frank), Catherine Moore (Rita).

A SHAYNA MAIDEL by Barbara Lebow; Director, Charles Richter; Sets, Joseph P. Tilford; Costumes, Eduardo Sicangco. CAST: Lindsey Margo Smith (Rose), Michael Marcus (Mordechai Weiss), Tessie Hogan (Luisa), David Breithbarth (Duvid), Martha M. Kelly (Hanna), Shelly Wald (Mama).

STAND-UP TRAGEDY by Bill Cain; Director, Jay E. Raphael; Sets, Linda Carmichael; Costumes, Fay Comway. CAST: Keith Robert Bennett (Henry), Ross Bickell (Larkin), Bill Bowers (Burke), Jeffrey Dreisbach (Mitchell), Trevor Jackson (Freddy), Enrique Munoz (Lee), Charles Sanchez (Marco), Renoly Santiago (Carlos), John Scherer (Tom).

OTHER PEOPLE'S MONEY by Jerry Sterner; Director, Worth Gardner; Sets/Costumes, Eduardo Sicangco. CAST: Tracy Griswold (William), Addison Powell (Andrew), Sylvia Cardwell (Bea), Tony Hoty (Garfinkle), Shannon Cochran (Kate).

LOST ELECTRA (WORLD PREMIERE) by Bruce L. Rodgers; Director, Margaret Booker; Sets, Joseph P. Tilford; Costumes, Scott Chambliss. CAST: Frank Muller (Mike Toller), Brian David Price (Alan Toller), Jacqueline Knapp (Sylvia Toller), Kathleen Marsh (Amelia Earhart), Paul Hebron (George Palmer Putnam).

THE MESMERIST by Ara Watson; Director, Worth Gardner; Sets, Majorie Bradley Kellogg; Costumes, Laura Crow. CAST: Shirin Devrim (Helena), Betty Miller (Emma), A.D. Cover (Olcott), Harsh Nayyar (Damodar), Steven Crossley (Richard), Alan Muraoka.

Sandy Underwood Photos

"Stand-Up Tragedy"

Howard Kaye, Robert E. Fitch, Suzanne Bedford in "Wizard of Oz"

**Robert Curtis-Brown, Amy Irving, Michael Sandels
in "Heidi Chronicles"**

Rupert Everett, Stephanie Beacham in "The Vortex"

CENTER THEATRE GROUP/ AHMANSON THEATRE
UCLA James A. Doolittle Theatre

Los Angeles, California
Fifteenth Season

Producing Director, Gordon Davidson; General Manager, Daouglas C. Baker; Press, Tony Sherwood, Joyce Friedmann, Julie Geiser; Staff Liason to Mr. Davidson, Susan Obrow; Audience Development Director, Robert Schlosser; Casting Director, Stanley Soble C.S.A.;Development Director, Christine Fiedler; Technical director, Robert Routolo; Central Services Director, Faith Raiguel.

PRODUCTIONS AND CASTS:

THE HEIDI CHRONICLES by Wendy Wasserstein; Director, Daniel Sullivan; Set Design, Thomas Lynch; Costume Design, Jennifer Von Mayrhauser; Lighting Design, Pat Collins; Sound Design, Scott Lehrer; Projection Design, Wendall Harrington; Casting, Daniel Swee, Pagano/Bialy-Mary Margiotta; General Manager, James Walsh; Company Manager, Alexander Holt; Production Stage Manager, Warren Crane; Stage Manager, Mary Hunter; Presented by Center Theatre Group/Ahmanson Theatre and The Schubert Organization, Suntory International Corporation and James Walsh in association with Playwrights Horizons. CAST: Amy Irving† (Heidi Holland), Mark Harelik (Scoop Rosenbaum); Robert Curtis-Brown (Peter Patrone), Mimi Lieber (Susan Johnson), Elaine Hausman (Fran/Molly/Betsy/April), Maggie Baird (Jill/Debbie/Lisa), Amy Ryan (Becky/Clara/Denise), Michael Sandels (TV Attendant/Waiter/Ray), Catherine Butterfield, Jessica Hecht, Jeff Sugarman.
†Succeeded by Stephanie Dunham.

THE VORTEX by Noel Coward; Director, Robert allan ackerman; Set Supervisor, Hugh Landwehr; Costume supervisor, Robert Wojewodski; Lighting, Arden Fingerhut; Sound, Jon Gottlieb; Production Stage Manager, Tami Toon; Stage Manager, Kathy Ogilvie. Philip Prowse directed and designed the Citizens Theatre production of *The Vortex* in Glasgow in 1988. Presented in association with Josephine Hart Productions, Ltd. and Stagescreen Productions, Ltd. CAST: Stephanie Beacham (Florence Lancaster), Rupert Everett (Nicky Lancaster), Suzanne Bertish (Helen Saville), Ian Abercrombie (Pauncefort Quentin), Milly Hagen (Bunty Mainwaring), George Innes (David Lancaster), Erica Rogers (Clara Hibbert), Simon Templeman (Tom Veryan), Julian Barnes (Bruce Fairlight), Babbie Green (Preston), Brian Wallace (Barker), Maria Hayden, Robert Petkoff.

A LITTLE NIGHT MUSIC; Music and Lyrics by Stephen Sondheim; Book, Hugh Wheeler; Director, Gordon Davidson; Choreography, Onna White; Vocal Staging, David Craig; Musical direction, Arthur B. Rubenstein; Original Orchestrations, Jonatthan Tunick; Scenery, Robert Israel; Costumes, Noel Taylor; Lighting, Paulie Jenkins; Sound, Jon Gottlieb; Casting, Stanley Soble C.S.A.; Production Stage Manager, Mark Wright; Stage Managers, James T. McDermott, Elsbeth M. Collins. CAST: Lois Nettleton (Desiree Armfeld), John McMartin (Frederick Egerman), Glynis Johns (Madame Armfeld), Franc D'Ambrosio (Henrik Egerman), Kathleen Rowe McAllen (Petra), Jeff McCarthy (Count Carl-Magnus), Marcia Mitzman (Countess Charlotte), Michelle Nicastro (Anne Egerman), Rita Baretta (Mrs. Segstrom), Ray Benson (Mr. Erlanson), Robert E. Lauder Jr. (Mr. Lindquist), Marnie Mosiman (Mrs. Nordstrom), Sarah Tattersall† (Mrs. Anderson), Joe E. Chrest (Frid), Patricia Fraser (Malla), Polly Heard (Fredrika), Stephen McDonough (Bertrand/Page), Kelli Rabke (Osa), Roger Castellano (Olof), Dan Collins (Gustav), Marjorie Mann (Ulla), Kevin McMahon (Par), Pamela Dayton, George McDaniel, Karon Kearney, Teri Ralston, Robert Yacko.
†Succeeded by Karon Kearney.

SARAFINA! Book/Music/Lyrics by Mbongeni Ngema; Conceived/Choreographed/Directed by Mbongeni Ngema; Additional Songs, Hugh Masekela; Musical Arrangements, Mbongeni Ngema and Hugh Masekela; Set/Costumes, Sarah Roberts; Set Design Supervisor, Ray Recht; Lighting, Mannie Manim; Lighting Supervisor, Robert W. Rosentel; Conductor, Ray Molefe; Sound Design, Tom Sorce; General Manager, Leonard Soloway; Associate General Manager, Brian Dunbar; Production Manager, Peter Lawrence; Company Manager, Laura Green; Production Supervisor, Bruce A. Hoover; Production Stage Manager, John Brigleb; Stage Manager, David Horton Black. Center Theatre Group presents the Lincoln Center Theatre/Committed Artists production. Produced by Emanuel Azenberg, Matthew Bronfman, Robert S. Malina and Wayne Rogers; Associate Producers: Irene Gandy, Alma Viator, Voza Rivers, Duma Ndlovu. COMPANY: Joseph Baloyi, Baby Cele, Dumisani Dlamini, Lindiwe Dlamini, Ntomb'khona Dlamini, Conga Hadebe, Thamsanqa Hltywayo, Lindiwe Hlengwa, Tim Hunter, Leleti Khumalo, Siboniso Khumalo, Mhlathi Khuzwayo, Lebo M., Kwazi Manzi, Master Mathibe, Thandani Mavimbela, Michael McElroy, Linda Mchunu, Pat Mlaba, Douglas Mnisi, Mubi Mofokeng, Bruce Mwandla, Nandi Ndlovu, Nhlanhla Ngema, Thandekile Nhlanhla, S'Manga Nhlebela, Mduduzi Nzuza, Valerie Jerusha Rochon, Kipizane Skweyiya, Thandi Zulu.

Jay Thompson Photos

Left: Lois Nettleton, John McMartin in "A Little Night Music"

CENTER THEATER GROUP/ MARK TAPER FORUM

Los Angeles, California
Twenty-fourth Season
September 27, 1990-September 8, 1991

Artistic Director/Producer, Gordon Davidson; Managing Director, Stephen J. Albert; Associate Artistic Director, Robert Egan; Resident Director, Oskar Eustis; Managers, Karen S. Wood, Michael Solomon; Staff Director for ITP, Peter C. Brosius; Staff Producer, Corey Beth Madden; Literary Administrator, Jeremy Lawrence; Development, Christine Fiedler; Technical Director/CTG, Robert Routolo; Production Supervisor, Frank Bayer; Production Administrator, Jonathan Barlow Lee; Casting Director, Stanley Soble C.S.A.; Press, Nancy Hereford, Phyllis Moberly, Evelyn Kiyomi Emi, Ken Werther; Audience Development Director, Robert J. Schlosser.

PRODUCTIONS AND CASTS

HOPE OF THE HEART; Adapted and directed by Robert Penn Warren from the writings of Robert Penn Warren (*Cass Mastern's Wedding Ring* and *Brother to Dragons*); World Premiere; Set Design, Eugene Lee; Costume Design, Dona Granata; Lighting Design, Natasha Katz, Eugene Lee; Composer/Musical Director, Nathan Birnbaum; Choreography/Fight Staging, Gary Mascaro; Associate Producer, Karen S. Wood; Dramaturg, Oskar Eustis; Casting, Stanley Soble C.S.A.; Production Stage Manager, Mary Michele Miner; Stage Manager, Tami Toon; Production Assistant, Diana Blazer. CAST: Vaughn Armstrong (Duncan Trice/Greek Figure/Ensemble), Casey Biggs (Jack Burden/Mr. Boyle/Banjo Player/Ensemble), Sherritta Durán Burns (Footman/Phoebe/Ensemble), Russell Curry (Footman/Frenchman/John/Ensemble), Clifford David (Mr. Simms/Jefferson Davis/Ensemble), Doug Hutchinson (Roomate 1/Isham Lewis/Ensemble), Jeff Jeffcoat (Musical Minstrel/Ensemble), Jeffrey King (Gilbert Mastern/Meriwether Lewis/Ensemble), Richard Kneeland (RPW), Charles McCaughan (Roomate 2/Minotaur/Liburne Lewis/Ensemble), Patrick McCollum (Dan Tucker/Footman/Ensemble), John Morrison (Librarian/Ellis Burden/Charles Lewis/Ensemble), James Ellis Reynolds (Cass Mastern/Ensemble), Margo Skinner (Mrs. Burden/Annabelle Trice/Lucy Jefferson Lewis/Ensemble), Emilie Talbot (Pasiphae/Sudie/Ensemble), Rose Weaver (Singer/Footman/Mrs. Miller/Aunt Cat/Ensemble), Nance Williamson (Anne Stanton/Ensemble).

THE LISBON TRAVIATA by Terrence McNally; Manhattan Theatre Club Production/West Coast Premiere Production at the Taper, presented in association with Carole Shorenstein Hays; Director, John Tillinger; Set Design, Phillip Jung; Costume Design, Jane Greenwood; Lighting Design, Sen Billington; Sound Design, Gary and Timmy Harris; Additional Sound Design, Jon Gottlieb; Fight Staging, Anthony DeLongis; Casting, Stanley Soble C.S.A.; Production Stage Manager, James T. McDermott; Stage Manager, Craig Palanker; Production Assistants, Diana Blazer, Richard Force. CAST: Richard Thomas (Stephen), Nathan Lane (Mendy), Dan Butler (Mike), Sean O'Bryan (Paul), Eileen Heckart (Voice of Stephen's Mother), Craig Palanker (Voice of Larry Newman), Dominic Cuskern (Voice of Allan Weeks). UNDERSTUDIES: Tom Flynn, Wayne Scherzer, Tom Astor.

THE WASH by Philip Kan Gotanda; Director, Sharon Ott; Set Design, James Youmans; Costume Design, Lydia Tanji; Lighting Design, Paulie Jenkins; Music/Sound Design, Stephen LeGrand, Eric Drew Feldman; Hair Design, Jeffrey Sacino; Hair/Makeup, Richard Arias; Casting, Stanley Soble C.S.A., Lisa Zarowin; Production Stage Manager, Cari Norton; Stage Manager, Dana Axelrod; Production Assistant, Diana Blazer. CAST: Carol A. Honda (Chiyo Froelich), Shizuko Hoshi (Kiyoko Hasegawa), Jody Long (Judy Adams), Nobu McCarthy (Masi Masumoto), James Saito (Blackie Sakata), Sab Shimono (Nobu Matsumoto), Diane Takei (Marsha Matsumoto), George Takei (Sadao Nakasato). UNDERSTUDIES: Aki Aleong, Judy Hoy, Emily Kuroda, Jerry Tondo.

(Clockwise from center) Obba Babatundé, Leilani Jones, Freda Payne, Karole Foreman, Tonya Pinkins in "Jelly's Last Jam"

JELLY'S LAST JAM; Book by George C. Wolfe; World Premiere, produced in association with Margo Lion and Pamela Koslow-Hines; Music, Jelly Roll Morton; Musical Adaptation/Additional Composition, Luther Henderson; Lyrics, Susan Birkenhead; Director, George C. Wolfe; Musical Director, Linda Twine; Choreography, Hope Clarke; Set Design, George Tsypin; Costume Design, Toni-Leslie James; Lighting Design, James F. Ingalls; Sound Design, Jon Gottlieb; Wig Design, Rick Geyer; Casting, Stanley Soble C.S.A.; Production Stage Manager, Mary K. Klinger; Stage Managers, James T. McDermott, Lani Ball; Associate Producer, Corey Beth Madden; Production Assistant, Diana Blazer. CAST: Obba Babatundé (Jelly Roll Morton), Keith David (Chimney Man), Phyliss Bailey (Hunnie/Viola), Patty Holley (Hunnie/Amede/Grieving Widow), Regina Le Vert (Hunnie/Hick woman), Karole Foreman (Maman/Crowd), Freda Payne (Gran Mimi/Crowd), Tonya Pinkins (Anita/Crowd), Leilani Jones (Mabel), Robert Barry Fleming (Young Jelly/Crowd), Peggy Blow (Eulalie/Crowd), Timothy Smith (Ancestor/Melrose Brother/Agent/Ganster/Crowd), Mary Bond Davis (Ancestor/Blues Singer/Crowd), Gil Pritchett III (Ancestor/Three Finger Jake/Hick Man/Crowd), Deborah L. Sharpe (Too Tight Nora/Crowd), Stanley Wayne Mathis (Jack the Bear/Crowd), Jerry M. Hawkins (Dead Man/Melrose Brother/Agent/Gangster/Crowd), Patrick McCollum (Pool Player/Ancestor/Crowd), Ruben Santiago-Hudson (Buddy Bolden/Crowd), Loose Lil and the Jungle Inn Jammers: Linda Twine (Loose Lil), Garnett Brown (Li'l Moe), Richard Grant (Hot Daddy), Jeffrey Clayton (Too Sharp), Quentin Dennard (Left Foot), Carl Vincent (Joe).

JULIUS CAESAR by William Shakespeare; Directed by Oskar Eustis; Set Design, Yael Pardess; Costume Design, Jeffrey Struckman; Lighting Design, Tom Ruzika; Video Design, Ken Kobland; Composer, Mel Marvin; Sound Design, Jon Gottlieb; Fight Choreography, Anthony DeLongis; Casting, Stanley Soble C.S.A., Lisa Zarowin; Hair/Makeup Design, Dale Johnson; Special Effects Makeup, Michael Key; Production Administrator, John Barlow Lee; Assistant Director, Lisa Greenman; Production Stage Manager, Cari Norton; Stage Manager, Ann C. Dippel; Associate Producer, Robert Egan. CAST: Barry Michlin (Flavius/Publius/Dardanius), Diane Robinson (Marullus/Antony's Servant/Flavia), Bruce Beatty (Soothsayer/Titinius), Stephen Weingartner (Cobbler/Caius Ligarius/Varro), Kenny Ransom (Carpenter/Cinna/Clitus), Stephen Markle (Julius Caesar), Lise Hilboldt (Calpurnia/Volumnia), Casey Biggs (Marc Antony), Dakin Matthews (Marcus Brutus), Lisa Banes (Potrtia/Lucilla), Delroy Lindo (Caius Cassius), Richard Frank (Casca), Kimberly Scott (Decia Brutus), Vaughn Armstrong (Cicero/Trebonius/Messala), Doug Hutchison (Lucius), Dierk Torsek (Metellus Cimber/Lepidus), David Drummond (Bodyguard to Caesar), Christopher Grove (Artemidorus), Marcus Chong (Popilius Lena/Cinna/Pindarus), Robert Petkoff (Octavius' Servant/Strato), James Jean Parks (Octavius Caesar), Marie Chambers (Claudia).

WIDOWS by Ariel Dorfman; World Premiere; Directed by Robert Egan.

Richard Thomas, Nathan Lane in "Lisbon Traviata"

SPECIAL EVENTS

THE DRAGONS' TRILOGY; A Théâtre Repère Production, presented in association with the Los Angeles Festival and UCLA; Written by Marie Brassard, Jean Casault, Lorraine Côté, Marie Gignac, Robert Lepage, Marie Michaud; Director, Robert Lepage; Set Design, Jean-François, Couture, Gilles Dubé; Lighting Design, Louis-Marie Lavoie, Robert Lepage, Lucie Bazzo; Music, Robert Caux. CAST: Robert Bellefuille, Norman Bissonette, Marie Brassard, Lorraine Coté, Richard Fréchette, Marie Gignac, Gaston Hubert, Yves-Erik Maries, Marie Michaud. Performed at UCLA.

SEX, DRUGS, ROCK & ROLL; Written and Performed by Eric Bogosian. West Coast Premiere, presented in association with Frederick Zollo and Robert Cole. Directed by Jo Bonney. Performed on the Taper mainstage.

TAPER, TOO

DON JUAN: A MEDITATION; Text by Moliere, Simone de Beauvoir, Blaise Pascal, and others; Director, Travis Preston; Dramaturg, Royston Coppenger; Set/Costume Design, Mark Wendland; Lighting Design, Richard Hoyes; Sound Design, Nathan Birnbaum; Casting, Stanley Soble C.S.A., Lisa Zarowin; Associate Producer, Robin McKee; Stage Manager, Jill Ragaway; Assistant Director, Nicole Arbusto; Production Assistant, Susie Walsh. CAST/ENSEMBLE: John Gould Rubin, Marissa Chibas, Nancy Allison Wolfe, Elina Löwensohn, Tamlyn Tomita, Diane Defoe.

THE WEDDING by Bertolt Brecht; Translation, Michael Henry Hein, Vladimir Strnisko; Director, Vladimir Strnisko; Set Design, Richard Hoover; Costume Design, Csilla Marki; Lighting Design, Monique L'Heureux; Producer, Corey Beth Madden; Production Stage Manager, Cari Norton; Stage Manager, Susie Walsh; Production Interpreter, Magda Ferl; Dramaturg, Frank Dwyer; Assistant Director, Liz Carlin; Production Assistant, Corky Dominguez; Fight Choreography, Anthony DeLongis. CAST: Shelly DeSai (Father), June Kyoto Lu (Mother), O-Lan Jones (Bride), Annie LaRussa (Sister), Chris Karchmar (Groom), Larry Cox (Friend), Marek Johnson (Wife), Jeremy Lawrence (Husband), Marc Epstein (Young Man).

THE TASK by Heiner Müller; Translated by Carl Weber; Director, L. Kenneth Richardson; Set Design, Edward E. Haynes Jr.; Costume Design, Lance Kenton; Lighting Design, R.S. Hoyes; Original Music/Sound Design, Jan A.P. Kaczmarek; Stage Managers, Susie Walsh, Jay Jackson; Associate Producer, Roy Conli; Dramaturg, Kathleen Dimmick; Assistant Director, Homeselle Joy; Choreography, Sloane Robinson; Production Assistants, Gabe Carrasco, Jason Jacobs. CAST: Ron Canada (Galloudec), Willie C. Carpenter (Sailor/Ensemble), John Dewey-Carter (Antoine/Ensemble), Michele Shay (First Love/Ensemble), Homeselle Joy (Angel of Despair/Ensemble), Roger Guenveur Smith (Debuisson/Priest), Glenn Plummer (Sasportas), Sloan Robinson (Treason/Ensemble), Brian R. Cheatham (Slave in Cage/Ensemble).

IMPROVISATIONAL THEATRE PROJECT

FREEDOM SONG by Peter Mattei; World Premiere; Director, Peter C. Brosius; Choreography, Gary Mascaro; Set Design, Victoria Petrovich; Costume Design, Lydia Tanji; Lighting Design, Tom Dennison; Additional Lighting Design, Brenda Berry; Casting, Lisa Zarowin; Shadow Effects/Design, Larry Reed; Original Music Composed and Performed by Udan Arum: Maria Bodmann, Cliff DeArment; Assistant Director, Patricia Pretzinger; Stage Manager, Maura J. Murphy; Assistant Stage Manager, Jaime Vasquez; Production Assistants, Ian Porter, Patricia Sawyer; Producer, Josephine Ramirez. CAST: Jorge Galvan (Ocie), Joyce Guy (Aunt D), Ivan G'Vara (Pimo), Karen Maruyama (Imogene), Patrick Roman Miller (Uncle Snoo), Rick Perkins (The Mayor). UNDERSTUDIES: Ian Porter, Patricia A. Sawyer.

George Takei, Nobu McCarthy in "The Wash"

Marcus Chong, Delroy Lindo, Bruce Beatty in "Julius Caesar"

SUNDAYS AT THE ITCHEY FOOT

THE PARTY by Virginia Woolf; Director, David Esbjornson; Adapted by Ellen McLaughlin; Lighting Design, Garth Hemphill; Managers, Michael Solomon, Karen S. Wood; Producer, Corey Beth Madden; Casting, Stanley Soble C.S.A.; Production Manager, Roy Conli. CAST: Kathleen Chalfant.

FROM THE MISSISSIPPI DELTA by Dr. Endesha Ida Mae Holland; Director, Shirley Jo Finney; Musical Direction, Delbert Taylor; Managers, Michael Solomon, Karen S. Wood; Lighting Design, Jane Lloyd; Producer, Corey Beth Madden; Casting, Stanley Soble C.S.A.; Production Manager, Roy Conli. CAST: L. Scott Caldwell, Cyndi James Gossett, Roxanne Reese.

A CHRISTMAS MEMORY and **ONE CHRISTMAS** by Truman Capote; Director, Michael Peretzian; Adapted by Michael Peretzian, Madeline Puzo; Costume Design, Kitty Murphy; Lighting Design, Monique L'Heureux; Manager, Michael Solomon; Producer, Corey Beth Madden; Casting, Stanley Soble C.S.A.; Production Manager, Roy Conli. CAST: Michael Tulin (Narrator), Jay Louden (Narrator/Father/Billy Bob), Mary Carver (Cousin Sook/Mother), David Johnson (Composer/Musician).

CABARET VERBOTEN by Jeremy Lawrence with Peter Jelavich and John Willett; World Premiere; Adaptaion/Additional Material, Jeremy Lawrence; Translations, Lawrence Selenick, John Willett; Director, Steven Albrezzi; Musical Directions/Arrangements, Nathan Birnbaum; Musical Stagings, Charles Randolph-Wright; Set Design, Michael LeValley; Costume Design, Todd Roehrman; Lighting Design, Craig Pierce; Managers, Michael Solomon, Karen S. Wood; Producers, Corey Beth Madden, Jeremy Lawrence; Casting, Stanley Soble C.S.A., Lisa Zarowin; Production Manager, Roy Conli; Stage Manager, Jill Ragaway; Production Stage Manager, Johnathan Baker. CAST: Paul Kreppel, Bebe Neuwirth, Roger Rees, Nathan Birnbaum, Richard Martinez. UNDERSTUDIES: Jonathan Baker, Linda Kerns. Produced in association with the Los Angeles County Museum of Art in Tandem with the Exhibition *Degenerate Art: The Fate of the Avant-Garde in Nazi Germany*.

SHIPWRECK by Julian Barnes; Adapted/Directed by Edward Parone; Producer, Corey Beth Madden; Managers, Michael Solomon, Karen S. Wood; Production Manager, Roy Conli; Slide Design, Daniel Carter, Christopher Komuro. CAST: David Dukes (Narrator). Produced in cooperation with the J. Paul Getty Museum and performed at the Getty Museum.

THE FEVER; Written and Performed by Wallace Shawn. Presented in association with The Museum of Contemporary Art and performed at MOCA.

Jay Thompson Photos

COCONUT GROVE PLAYHOUSE

Miami, Florida
October 9, 1990-June 30, 1991

Producing Artistic Director, Arnold Mittelman; Associate Producer, Lynne Peyser; Education Director, Judith Delgado; Institutional Advancement Director, Jordan Bock; Financial/Operations Director, Vicki Grayson; Marketing/Sales Director, Mark D. Sylvester; Public Relations, Lee Zimmerman.

PRODUCTIONS AND CASTS

CHITA RIVERA IN THE GROVE; Written by Fred Ebb; Special Material, Kander and Ebb; Director, Wayne Cilento; Choreography, Ron Field, Alan Johnson, Mr. Cilento, Chris Chadman; Musical Director, Louis St. Louis; Lighting, Rick Pettit. CAST: Chita Rivera, Robert Montano, Tony Stevens.
THE BIG LOVE (WORLD PREMIERE) by Brooke Allen and Jay Presson Allen; Adapted from the book by Florence Aadland as told to Tedd Thomey; Director, Jay Presson Allen; Sets/Projections, David Mitchell; Costumes, Jane Greenwood. CAST: Tracey Ullman.
SHIRLEY VALENTINE by Willy Russell; Direction, Jeff Lee; Sets/Lights, James Tilton; Costumes, Ellis Tillman. CAST: Loretta Swit.
ONCE UPON A SONG with Music by Anthony Newley; Lyrics, Mr. Newley; Leslie Bricusse, Herbert Kretzmer, Ian Fraser, Stanley Ralph Ross; Director, Arnold Mittelman; Conception, Mr. Newley, Mr. Mittelman; Choreography, Tony Stevens; Music Direction/Vocal/Dance Arrangements, Louis St. Louis; Orchestrations, Michael Gibson; Sets, Kevin Rupnik; Lighting, Pat Collins; Costumes, Ellis Tillman. CAST: Anthony Newley (Father), Bertilla Baker (Mother), Tracy Venner (Daughter), Sean Dooley (Son).
The World Premiere of a new piece using old and new Newley material.
DRIVING MISS DAISY by Alfred Uhry; Director, Luke Yankee; Sets/Lighting, James Tilton; Costumes, Ellis Tillman. CAST: Eileen Heckart (Daisy), Anderson Matthews (Boolie), George Merritt (Hoke).
OTHER PEOPLE'S MONEY by Jerry Sterner; Director, Robert Kalfin; Sets/Lighting, James Tilton; Costumes, Ellis Tillman. CAST: Mitchell McGuire (Coles), James Pritchett (Jorgenson), Howard Samuelsohn (Garfinkle), Peg Small (Bea), Rinnie Farer (Kate).

ENCORE ROOM SERIES

AT WIT'S END by Joel Kimmel; Director, Barbara Karp; Lighting, Todd Wren; Costumes, Ellis Tillman. CAST: Stan Freeman (Oscar Levant).
JUST DESERTS (WORLD PREMIERE) by Tom Dulack; Director, Arnold Mittelman; Sets, Stephen Lambert; Lighting, Todd Wren; Costumes, Ellis Tillman. CAST: Lewis J. Stadlen (Tyrone Cross), Steeve Arlen (Whitney Van Loon), Lynne Peyser (News Anchor).

Lenny Cohen, Andrew Mellick, Luis Castañeda Photos

(rear) Bertilla Baker, Anthony Newley, (front) Sean Dooley, Tracy Venner in "Once Upon a Song"

Tracey Ullman in "Big Love"

Loretta Swit in "Shirley Valentine"

Anderson Matthews, George Merritt, Eileen Heckart
in "Driving Miss Daisy"

DELAWARE THEATRE COMPANY

Wilmington, Delaware
Twelfth Season
July 12, 1990-April 20, 1991

Artistic Director, Cleveland Morris; Acting Artistic Director, Maureen Heffernan; Managing Director, Robert A. Gillman; Assistant to the Artistic Director, Danny Peak; Business Manager, Donna Pody; Director of Development, Ann G. Schenck; Marketing Director, Donna-Marie King; Administrative Assistant, Sheri M. Johnson; Student Outreach Coordinator, Charles J. Conway; Graphic Designer, Suzanne M. Green; Group Sales, Marcia B. Spivack; Artistic Associate, Julie A. Schanke; Box Office Manager, Lori A. Cartwright; Box Office Assistants, Chris Sosnowski, M. Lynne Wieneke; Production Stage Manager, Patricia Christian; Sets, Eric Schaeffer, Lewis Folden, Sarah Baptist, Dan Gray; Costumes, Marla Jurglanis, Kathleen Egan; Lighting, Bruce K. Morriss; Asisstant to the Lighting Designer, Adrienne Shulman, Jim Zufelt; Assistant to the Director, Danny Peak; Assistant Stage Manager, James Darkey, Paul Taylor; Props, Paul Taylor; Sound, George Stewart, Tom Gould; Costume Assistants, Melody Holton, Judith Chang; Master Carpenter, Charles O'Lone; Shop, Ginger Diamond, Mike Oosterum, Russ Johnson, Cynthia Curley.

PRODUCTIONS AND CASTS

AIN'T MISBEHAVIN': The New Fats Waller Musical Show; based on an idea by Murray Horowitz and Richard Maltby, Jr.; Director/Choreographer, Derek Wolshonak; Musical Director/Piano, LaTerry Butler. MUSICIANS: Harvey Price (Percussion), Alan Hamant (Trumpet), Charles Salinger (Clarinet), Norman Marks (Bass). CAST: James Alexander, Rufus Bonds Jr., Barbara D. Mills, Gamalia Pharms, Melodee Savage.

TO KILL A MOCKINGBIRD (WORLD PREMIERE) adapted by Christopher Sergel from Harper Lee's Pulitzer Prize-winning novel; Director, Cleveland Morris. CAST: Nicola Sheara (Miss Maudie), Finley Kipp (Scout Finch), Carol London (Calpurnia), Karen Hurley (Miss Stephanie), Drew Hanson (Judge Taylor), David C. Wyeth (Sheriff Heck Tate), Joan Chestnut (Mrs. Dubose), Chris Saenger (Jem Finch), Maurice R. Sims (Reverend Sykes), Kit Jones (Mayella Ewell), Steve Cowie (Bob Ewell), Michael Schneider (Dill Harris), Will Stutts (Atticus Finch), Matt Walker (Walter Cunningham), Paul Morella (Mr. Gilmer), Ken LaRon (Tom robinson), Nick Santoro (Boo Radley). ENSEMBLE: Bob Balick, Susie Barnes, Douglas Barney, Michael P. Cartwright, Lori Cline, Darryl V. Cox, Rita Devlin, David W. Dooley, Wendy P. Fariss, Piper Harrell, John Heffron, John R. Hoffecker, Lynn Hyatt, Danielle Johnson, Doris S. Johnson, Tina Jones, Brian Kerr, Sharon Kirby, Lawrence Laravela, Aline Lathrop, C.A. Mellinger, Erin Murray, Gemma Pagliei, Gary Peterson, Kevin Pruden, Chris Roberts, Christina Marie Schlegel, Jerome Simpson, Kelli Stich, Barbara Strawley, Marina VanRenssen, Teresa Williams, Carol S. Wooley, Tamani Wooley.

OIL CITY SYMPHONY by Mike Craver, Debra Monk, Mary Hardwick, Mary Murfitt; Director, Maureen Heffernan; Musical Director, Kathy Beaver; CAST: Robert Polenz (Mark), Kathy Beaver (Mary), Michele Horman (Debra), George Tenegal (Mike).

CROSSIN' THE LINE by Phil Bosakowski; Director, Danny Peak; CAST: Susie Barnes (Ellie Burke), Matt Walker (Richie/Therapist/Sergeant Martin), Kit Jones (Trudee/Bette), John Heffron (Mitch Kohler), Chris Roberts (Hayden Doyle).

A SHAYNA MAIDEL by Barbara Lebow; Director, Alex Dmitriev; CAST: Denise Bessette (Rose Weiss), Herman O. Arbeit (Mordechai Weiss), Maureen Siliman (Luisa Weiss Pechenik), Jean Korey (Mama), Kit Jones (Hanna), Andrew Borba (Duvid Pechenik).

A WALK IN THE WOODS by Lee Blessing; Director, Terence Lamude. CAST: Thomas Carson (Andrey Botvinnik), Daren Kelly (John Honeyman).

WHAT THE BUTLER SAW by Joe Orton; Director, Maureen Heffernan. CAST: Will Rhys (Dr. Prentice), Paige Alenius (Geraldine Barclay), Marion McCorry (Mrs. Prentice), Michael Kelly Boone (Nicholas Beckett), John Tillotson (Dr. Rance), Ray Collins (Sergeant Match).

Richard C. Carter Photos

**Right: Will Stutts and cast in "To Kill a Mockingbird" Center:
Maureen Silliman, Denise Bessette in "A Shayna Maidel"
Top: Gamalia Pharms, James Alexander, Melodee Savage,
Rufus Bonds, Jr., Barbara D. Mills in "Ain't Misbehavin'"**

Eli Wallach, Anne Jackson in "Sparky and the Fitz"

Estelle Parsons in "Forgiving Typhoid Mary"

GEORGE STREET PLAYHOUSE

New Bruswick, New Jersey
October 2, 1990-April 28, 1991

Producing Artistic Director, Gregory S. Hurst; Managing director, David Edelman; Associate Artistic director, Wendy Liscow; Press/Public Relations Director, Heidi W. Giovine; Marketing director, Diane-Gail Claussen; Business Manager, Karen S. Price; Development Director, Sylvia R. Wolf; Outreach Director/Resident Director, Susan Kerner; Resident Scenic Designer/Production Manager, Deborah Jasien; Resident Costume Designer, Barbara Forbes; Rsident Lighting Designer, Donald Holder; Resident Fight Director, Rick Sordelet; Technical Director, Mark Collino; Publications, Rick Engler.

PRODUCTIONS AND CASTS

GREETINGS (WORLD PREMIERE) by Tom Dudznick; Director, Gregory S. Hurst; Sets, Atkin Pace; Costumes, Barbara Forbes; Lighting, Donald Holder; stage Manager, Thomas L. Clewell. CAST: Mark Shannon (Andy Gorski), Barbara Gulan (Randi Stein), Beth Fowler (Emily Gorski), John Ramsey (Phil Gorski), Patrick Kerr (Michael Gorski).
DRIVING MISS DAISY by Alfred Uhry; Director, Susan Kerner; Sets, Deborah Jasien; Costumes, Barbara Forbes; Lighting, Harry Feiner; Stage Manager, Michael Suenkel. CAST: Maggie Burke (Daisy), Terry Layman (Boolie), Norman Matlock (Hoke).
OIL CITY SYMPHONY by Mike Craver, Mark Hardwick, Debra Monk, Mary Murfitt; Director, Wendy Liscow; Music Director, Shawn Stengel; Sets, James Medved; Costumes, Deborah Jasien, Barbara S. Reich; Lighting, David Lincecum; Sound, Richard Dunning; Stage Manager, Michael Suenkel. CAST: Amy Herzberg (Debbie), Emily Mikesell (Mary), Joel Spineti (Mike), Shawn Stengel (Mark).
PENDRAGON (WORLD PREMIERE) by Laurie H. Hutzler; Director, Wendy Liscow; Sets, Deborah Jasien; Costumes, Barbara Forbes; Lighting, David Neville; Music, Scott Killian; Stage Manager, Michael Suenkel. CAST: Socorro Santiago (Morgana), Ernest Abuba (Arthur), Luis A. Ramos (Lancelot), Catherine Christianson (Guinevere), Michael O'Shea (Garth/Gareth), Enrique Munoz (Mordred), Jay Duckwork (Page).
SPARKY AND THE FITZ (WORLD PREMIERE) by Craig Volk; Director, Stephen Rothman; Sets, Deborah Jasien; Costumes, Barbara Forbes; Lighting, Donald Holder; Stage Manager, Michael Suenkel. CAST: Eli Wallach (Sparky), Anne Jackson (Fitz), Ben Hammer (Rudy).
FORGIVING TYPHOID MARY by Mark St. Germain; Director, Gregory S. Hurst; Sets, Atkin Pace; Costumes, Barbara Forbes; Lighting, Donald Holder; Music/Sound, Randy Courts; Stage Manager, Michael Suenkel. CAST: Estelle Parsons (Mary Mallon), Meghan Andrews (Sarah), Jack Davidson (Dr. Mills), Harriet Harris (Dr. Saltzer), Michael Louden (Fr. McKuen), James Morgan (Intern/Martin Frazier).
THE ROOT (WORLD PREMIERE) by Gary Richards; Director, Matthew Penn; Sets, Deborah Jasien; Costumes, Barbara Forbes; Lighting, Donald Holder; Stage Manager, Christine M. Terchek. CAST: Jesse Moore (Willie), John Shepard (Vinnie), Jude Ciccolella (Jerry), Larry Block (Chick).

Miguel Pagliere Photos

John Shepard, Jude Ciccolella in "The Root"

Beth Fowler, Mark Shannon, Barbara Gulan in "Greetings"

126

THE GOODMAN THEATRE

Chicago, Illinois
September 14, 1990-August 4, 1991

Artistic Director,Robert Falls; Producing Director, Roche Schulfer.

PRODUCTION AND CASTS

THE ICEMAN COMETH by Eugene O'Neill; Director, Robert Falls; Sets, John Conklin; Costumes, Merrily Murray-Walsh; Lighting. James F. Ingalls. CAST: Brian Dennehy (Hickey), Jerome Kilty (Harry Hope), Bill Visteen (Ed Mosher), Ron Dean (Rocky Pioggi), Peter Siragusa (Chuck Morello), Brice M. Fischer (General), Derek Murcott (Captain), Larry McCauley (Jummy Tommorrow), Ernest Perry Jr. (Joe Mott), James Cromwell (Larry Slade), Dennis Kennesy (Hugo Kalmar), Denis O'Hare (Willie Oban), Jim True (Don Parritt),Rengin Altay (Pearl), Hope Davis (Margie), Kate Buddeke (Cora), Dev Kennedy (Moran), Tom Webb (Lieb).

A CHRISTMAS CAROL by Charles Dickens; Adaptation, Tom Creamer; Director, Steve Scott; Music, Larry Schanker; Sets, Joseph Nieminski; Costumes, Julie Jackson; Lighting, Robert Christen. CAST: William J. Norris (Scrooge), Robert Scogin (Cratchit), David E. Chadderdon, Paul Henry Thompson (Businessmen), Terence Gallagher (Fred), Steve Pickering (Marley's Ghost/Joe), Shannon Cochran (Ghost Christmas Past/Guest), RJ Coleman (Schoolmaster/Undertaker), Ismael Brito (Boy Scrooge/Turkey Boy), Bridgett Ane Lawrence (Fan/Belinda), Ray Chapman (Young Man Scrooge), James Sie (Wilkins/Guest/Man), Dennis Kennedy (Fezziwig/Businessman), E. Faye Butler (Mrs. Fezziwig/Mrs. Dilber), Ellen Jane Smith (Belle/Woman), Marty Higginbotham (Fiddler/Guest), Ernest Perry Jr. (Ghost Christmas Present), Ora Jones (Mrs. Cratchit), Tanya Suesuntisook (Martha), Nikkieli Lewis (Peter), Patrick Coffey (Tim), Johanna McKay (Abby), Paula Newsome (Philomena/Charwoman), Eddie Jemison (Topper), Denisha V. Powell (Want), Lewis A. Affetto (Ignorance), Ray Chapman, Terence Gallagher, Marty Higginbotham (Ghost Christmas To Come).

JOE TURNER'S COME AND GONE by August Wilson; Director, Jonathan Wilson; Sets, Michael S. Philippi; Costumes, Claudia Boddy; Lighting, Robert Christen. CAST: Jaye Tyrone Stewart (Seth), Pat Bowie (Bertha), Norman Matlock (Bynum), Dick Sasso (Rutherford), Danny Johnson (Jeremy), Johnny Lee Davenport (Herald), Jené Marie Culp (Zonia), Susan Diane Payne (Mattie), Dwight Golden (Reuben), Glenda Starr Kelly (Molly), Linda Marie Bright (Martha).

A MIDSUMMER NIGHT'S DREAM by William Shakespeare; Director, Michael Maggio; Co-Director, Steve Scott; Sets, John Conklin; Costumes, Susan Hilferty; Lighting, Pat Collins. CAST: David Darlow (Thesus/Oberon), Barbara E. Robertson (Hippolyta), Jeffrey Sams (Lysander), Thomas Anthony Quinn (Demetrius), Ellen Jane Smith (Hermia), Joan Cusak (Helena), Richard Fire (Egeus/Quince), Steve Pickering (Philostrate/Puck), Barbara E. Robertson (Titania), Teria Gartelos (Fairy), Treva Tegtmeier (Cobweb), JoNell Kennedy (Peaseblossom), Shira Piven (Mustardseed), Laurie Flanigan (Moth), Peter Siragusa (Bottom), Jerry Saslow (Flute), David Sinaiko (Snout), Johnny Lee Davenport (Snug), John Möhrlein (Starveling).

THE VISIT by Friedrich Duerrenmatt; Adaptaion, Maurice Valency; Director, David Petrarca; Sets, Paul Steinberg; Costumes, Virgil Charles Johnson; Lighting, James F. Ingalls; Music, Rob Milburn, Larry Schanker. CAST: Rosalind Cash (Claire), Maury Cooper (Boby), Michael Raimondi (Pedro/Cameraman), David Connelly (Max), Warren Davis (Mike), Tim Monsion (Koby/TV Commentator), Dan Frick (Loby/Reporter), Josef Sommer (Anton), Linda Stephens (Mrs. Schill), Laura Eason (Otilie), Charley Sherman (Karl), Colin Stinton (Mayor), Michael Krawic (Pastor), Jeffrey Hutchinson (Teacher), Bob O'Donnell (Doctor), Steve Pickering (Police), John Gegenhuber (Painter), Tony Smith (Man), Christopher Pieczynski (Man), Steve Pink (Athlete), Kate Buddeke (Woman), Shanesia Davis (Woman Reporter), Marney MacAdam (Mayor's Wife), Evan Lionel (Stationmaster), Danny Johnson (Conductor/Reporter).

BOOK OF THE NIGHT (WORLD PREMIERE) by Louis Rosen and Thom Bishop; Director, Robert Falls.

STUDIO SERIES

MONSTER IN A BOX and **TERRORS OF PLEASURE**: Two monologues by Spaulding Gray; Director, Renee Shafransky. CAST: Spaulding Gray.
FROM THE MISSISSIPPI DELTA by Dr. Endesha Ida Mae Holland; Director, Jonathan Wilson; Sets, Michael S. Philippi; Costumes, Jeffrey Kelly; Lighting, Chris Phillips. CAST: Vikki J. Barrett, Jacqueline Williams, Pat Bowie.
DEEP IN A DREAM OF YOU (WORLD PREMIERE) by David Cale; Music, Roy Nathanson; Dirtector, David Petrarca; Design, Linda Buchanan. ENSEMBLE: David Cale, Roy Nathanson, Bradley Jones, Laura Blanchet, Sara Wollan, E.J. Rodriguez. PROGRAM: Swimming in the Dark, Dolphins, Warden Hills, Fire, Ellis, Your New Thrill, I Wish I'd Have Met You Before He Did, Big Kiss, 40 Winks Motel/Deep in a Dream of You, Sweater Made of Eye-Lashes, Remember, Blue Fir Trees.

Sara Hoskins, Hali Breindel Photos

**Right: Sam Butler, Jr., Martin Jacox, Terrence A. Carson
in "Gospel at Colonus"**

Kate Buddeke, Brian Dennehy in "Iceman Cometh"

Jeffrey Sams, Ellen Jane Smith, Joan Cusack,
Thomas Anthony Quinn in "Midsummer Night's Dream"

Rosalind Cash, David Connelly in "The Visit"

GOODSPEED OPERA HOUSE

East Haddam, Connecticut
Twenty-eighth Season
April 18-December 16, 1990

Executive director, Michael C. Price; Associate Artistic Director, Dan Siretta; Theatre Manager, Edward C. Blaschik; New York Representative, Warren Pincus; Technical Director, Adam J. Witko; Wardrobe Master, John Riccucci; Press, Kay McGrath, Max Eisen; Development Director, Kathy Mead; Library Advisory Panel, Ken Bloom, Lynn Crigler, Stanley Green, Mary Henderson, David Hummel, Robert Kimball, Frank C.P. McGlinn, Alfred Simon, Frank E. Tuit II; Associate Producer, Sue Frost.

PRODUCTIONS AND CASTS

THE CHOCOLATE SOLDIER with Music by Oscar Straus; Original Lyrics/Book, Stanislaus Stange; Based on play *Arms and the Man* by George Bernard Shaw; Musical Adaptation, Albin Konopka; New Lyrics, Ted Drachman; New Book/Direction, Larry Carpenter; Choreography, Danil Pelzig; Music director, Mr. Konopka; Orchestrations, Larry Moore; Sets, James Leonard Joy; Costumes, John Falabella; Lighting, Craig Miller. CAST: Victoria Clark (Raina), Susan Cella (Catherine), Joanna Glushak (Masha), Anna Bess Lank (Louka), Paul Ukena Jr. (Bluntschli), Richard Malone (Capt. Massakroff), Robert Torres (Stephen), Kurt Knudson (Petkoff), Max Robinson (Sergius), Jonathan Cerullo, Kelly Corken, Richard Costa, Pamela Dayton, Peter Flynn, Deborah Geneviere, J. Kathleen Lamb, Rose McGuire, Glenn Sneed, Stephen Lloyd Webber, Leigh-Anne Wencker. MUSICAL NUMBERS: Overture, We Are Marching Through the Night, We Too Are Lonely, We Are Hunting Down the Foe, When You Haven't Got a Man, Melodrama, Say Good Night, My Hero, Chocolate Soldier, Sympathy, Seek the Spy, Tiralala, Entr'acte, Our Heroes Come, Thank the Lord the War is Over, Never Was There Such a Lover, Tale of a Coat, Bluntschli's Prayer, Bulgarian Ballet, Falling in Love, Letter Song, Finale.

PAL JOEY with Music by Richard Rodgers; Lyrics, Lorenz Hart; Book, John O'Hara; Director/Choreography, Dan Siretta; Musical Director, Tim Stella; Additional Orchestrations, Mr. Stella, Tom Fay; Sets, Kenneth Foy; Costumes, Jose Lengson; Lighting, Kirk Bookman. CAST: Anne Allgood (Linda English), David Arthur (Ernest), Valerie Dowd (Melba), Jerry Grayson (Ludlow), Michael Hayward-Jones (Louis/O'Brien), Kurt Knudson (Mike), Florence Lacey (Vera), Kari Nicolaisen (Gladys Bumps), Peter Reardon (Joey Evans), Quin Baird, Keith Robert Bennett, Maria Calabrese, Kelly Crafton, Jan Downs, Jack Eldon, Tim Foster, Pam Klinger, Tom Kosis, Elizabeth Palmer, Jane Sonderman, Susan Trainor. MUSICAL NUMBERS: A Great Big Town, You Mustn't Kick It Around, I Could Write a Book, That Terrific Rainbow, Do It the Hard Way, What Is a Man?, Happy Hunting Horn, Bewitched Bothered and Bewildered, What Do I Care for a Dame, Ballet, Flower Garden of My Heart, Zip, Plant You Now Dig You Later, Den of Iniquity, He Was Too Good to Me, I'm Talkin' to My Pal, Finale

BELLS ARE RINGING with Music by Jules Styne; Lyrics/Book, Betty Comden and Adolph Green; Director, Sue Lawless; Choreography, Rob Marshall; Music Director, Don Jones; Additional Orchestrations, Don Jones, Wendy E. Bobbitt; Sets, James Noone; Costumes, Bradford Wood, Gregory A. Poplyk; Lighting, Kirk Bookman. CAST: Anthony Cummings (Jeff), David Gurland (Francis), David Middleton (Larry), Gabor Morea (Dr. Kitchell), Liz Otto (Sue), Lew Resseguie (Barnes), Celeste Simone (Gwynne), Lynne Wintersteller (Ella Peterson), Ron Wisniski (Sandor), Daniel Baum, John Ganun, Leslie Guy, Donald Ives, Joe Joyce, Marjorie McGovern, Casey Nicholaw, Kelly Patterson, Gayle Samuels, Conny Lee Sasfai, David Serko, Malinda Shaffer.

**Lynne Wintersteller, Anthony Cummings
in "Bells Are Ringing"**

Lauren Gaffney, Sandy in "Annie 2"

Peter Reardon, Florence Lacey in "Pal Joey"

NORMA TERRIS THEATRE

ANNIE 2 with Music by Charles Strouse; Lyrics, Martin Charnin; Book, Thomas Meehan; Director, Mr. Charnin; Choreography, Peter Gennaro; Musical Director, Steven M. Alper; Evelyn Sakash; Costumes, Theoni V. Aldredge; Lighting, Ken Billington. CAST: Lauren Gaffney (Annie), Chelsea (Sandy), Scott Robertson (Drake/FBI/Harry Winkowski), Julie Jirousek (Marie/Phyllis Wardlow/Movie Miranda), Mary-Pat Green (Mrs. Pugh/Gert Bixby/Mitzi/FBI), Sarah Knapp (Grace Farrell), Harve Presnell (Oliver Warbucks), Laurent Giroux (Henry Drummond/Houseman/Charlie/Aide/Guest/Judge), Karen Murphy (Aide/Miss Sherman/Abigail Dabney/FBI), Paula Leggett (Aide/Cecille/Glenda/Guest), Jack Doyle (Accountant/Fred Bixby/Fletcher/Markowitz/Marine/Guest/Capt.), Abe Reybold (Accountant/Steve McCall), Marian Seldes (Commissioner Margaret G. Stark), Karen L. Byers (Miss Richards/Flo Winkowski/FBI/Guest), Moriah "Shining Dove" Snyder (Molly), Lisa Molina (Tessie), Natalia Harris (Peaches), Jennifer Beth Glick (July), Blaze Berdahl (Kate Maguire), Helen Gallagher (Franes Riley), D. Rector (Announcer/Gariel Heater's Voice/Movie Priest), Raymond Thorne (FDR/Movie Tim), Todd Ellison (Pianist). MUSICAL NUMBERS: He'll Be Here, When You Smile, Changes, Perfect Kid, That's the Kind of Woman, A Younger Man, But You Go On, Rich Girls, Annie Two, He Doesn't Know, If I Wasn't Around, I Can Do No Wrong, Live a Long Long Time, All Dolled Up, Cortez, Tenement Lullaby, Isn't This the Way To Go, My Daddy, Finale.

BLANCO! with Music/Lyrics by Skip Kennon; Additional Lyrics, Michael Korie; Book, Willy Holtzman; Director, Joe Billone; Musical Director, David Evans; Sets, Linda Hacker; Costumes, Thom. J. Peterson; Lighting, John Hastings. CAST: Danile Ahearn (Slim), Gabriel Barre (Nueces), Matt Bogart (Floyd/Red), Catherine Fox (Feemy Evans), Barry Finkel (Nestor), James Gleason (Rev. P. Stone), John Horton (Kemp), Jim Morlino (Strapper), William Parry (Blanco Posnet), Joey Quenqua (Boston), Benjamin H. Salinas (Gomes), Jane Seaman (Babsy), Maureen Silliman (Emma/Rainbow Woman), Jane Smulyan (Lottie). MUSICAL NUMBERS: Ballad of Progress, Dancin' in the Middle, My Stagecoach is a-Comin' in Real Soon, It's a Bad Bad World, A Place of Your Own, Loose Ends, I Know What You Need, Noble, I Know a Town, Let it Be Him, I Done Good, Rub-a-Dub-Dub, It's Only Business, Prayer of Guidance, 'N That's Nice, Poor House, In the Eyes of a Child, Straight and Narrow Trail, No Good at Bein' Bad.

Diane Sobolewski Photos

Vicki Lewis in "Lady from Maxim's"

Jack Davidson, Jennifer Harmon, Elizabeth Franz, Nan Martin in "Dividing the Estate"

Hal Holbrook in "King Lear"

GREAT LAKES THEATRE FESTIVAL

Cleveland, Ohio
May 9-December 30, 1990

Artistic Director, Gerald Freedman; Managing Director, Mary Bill; Associate Directors, Bill Rudman, Victoria Bussert; Associate Artistic Director, John Ezell; Guest Director, Amy Saltz; Stage Managers, Richard Constabile, Deidre Fudge.

PRODUCTIONS AND CASTS

KING LEAR by William Shakespeare; Director, Gerald Freedman; Sets, John Ezell; Costumes, Robert Wojewodski; Lighting, Thomas Skelton; Music, John Morris. CAST: Hal Holbrook, Peter Aylward, Brian M. Bartels, Gloria Biegler, Andrew Boyer, John Buck Jr., Daniel P. Ensel, Eric Fisher, Suzy Hunt, John Hutton, Michael James-Reed, James Kall, Christopher McCann, Kevin McCarthy, James Moore, Margery Murray, Ron Randell, Stephan Roselin, Andrew M. Segal, Gary Sloane, Solomon Smith, Darrell Starnick, Troy Tinker, Gregory Violand, Eric Vogt, T. Patrick Walsh, John Woodson.
A DELICATE BALANCE by Edward Albee; Director, Amy Saltz; Sets, G.W. Mercier; Costumes, Alfred Kohout; Lighting, Joseph A. Futral. CAST: John Franklyn-Robbins, Suzanna Hay, Stan Lachow, Patricia O'Connell, Sally Parrish, Joan Potter.
THE LADY FROM MAXIM'S by Georges Feydeau; Translation, John Mortimer; director, Gerald Freedman; Sets, John Ezell; Costumes, James Scott; Lighting, Mary Jo Dondlinger. CAST: Elizabeth Atkeson, Simon Brooking, John Buck Jr., Edward Conery, Marji Dodrill, A. Eric Fisher, Sheila Heyman, Michael James-Reed, William Leach, Vicki Lewis, David Manis, Christiane McKenna, Ron Randell, Steve Routman, David Ruckman, Noble Shropshire, Susan Sweeney, Judith Tillman.
LA RONDE by Arthur Schnitzler; Translation, John Barton; director, Victoria Bussert; Sets, G.W. Mercier; Costumes, Al Kohout; Lighting, Mary Jo Dondlinger. CAST: Simon Brooking, Juliette Kurth, William Leach, Susan Sweeney.
DIVIDING THE ESTATE by Horton Foote; Director, Gerald Freedman; Sets, John Ezell; Costumes, Al Kohout; Lighting, Mary Jo Dondlinger. CAST: Elizabeth Atkeson, Erma Campbell, Bellary Darden, Jack Davidson, Elizabeth Franz, Jennifer Harmon, Annalee Jeffries, Brian Keeler, Nan Martin, Logan Ramsey, Christine Segal, W. Benson Terry, Lucinda Underwood.
A CHRISTMAS CAROL by Charles Dickens; Adaptaion/Direction, Gerald Freedman; Staging, Victoria Bussert; Sets, John Ezell, Gene Emerson Friedman; Costumes, James Scott; Lighting, Mary Jo Dondlinger; Music, Robert Waldman; Musical Director, Joseph Thalken; Dances, David Shimotakahara. CAST: J. Michael Brennan, John Buck Jr., Amanda Chubb, Jennifer Curfman, Molly Daw, Donna English, Robert Haley, Jason Kimes, Michael Krawic, Anna Bess Lank, William Leach, Pauline Lepor, Danielle Long, Robert Meksin, Adam Moeller, Rex Nockengust, Billy Radin, Eric Radin, Steve Routman, Paula Smith, P.J. Smith, Troy Tinker, Lucinda Underwood, Gregory Violand, Helene Weinberg, Joseph Woodside.

Roger Mastroianni Photos

Simon Brooking, Juliette Kurth in "La Ronde"

HARTFORD STAGE COMPANY

Hartford, Connecticut
Twenty-eighth Season
September 29, 1990-June 16, 1991

Artistic Director, Mark Lamos; Managing Director, David Hawkanson; Associate Artistic Director/Dramaturg, Greg Leaming; Public Relations Director, Howard Sherman; Marketing Director, David Hough; Business Manager, Michael Ross; Production Manager, Candice Chirgotis; Technical Director, Jim Keller; Costumes Director, Barbara Joyce; Properties Director, Jerry Gardner; Master Electrician, Bette Regan; Audio Department, Frank Pavlich; Casting, Brian Chavanne, Julie Mossberg.

PRODUCTIONS AND CASTS

OUR COUNTRY'S GOOD by Timberlake Wertenbaker; Director, Mark Lamos; Sets, Christopher Barreca; Costumes, Candice Donnelly; Lighting, Mimi Jordan Sherin. CAST: Amelia Campbell (Duckling Smith/MegLong), Helen Carey (Liz Morden/Lt. Will Dawes), Michael Cumpsty (2nd Lt. Ralph Clark), Herb Downer (John Arscott/Rev. Johnson/Aborigine), Tracey Ellis (Mary Brenham/Lt. George Johnston), Adam LeFevre (Ketch Freeman/Major Robbie Ross), Richard Poe (John Wisehammer/Capt. Arthur Phillip), Stephen Rowe (Harry Brewer/Jemmy Campbell), J. Smith Cameron (Dabby Bryant/2nd Lt. William Faddy), Sam Tsoutsouvas (Robert Sideway/Capt. David Collins), Gregory Wallace (Black Caesar/Watkin Tench).

MARVIN'S ROOM by Scott McPherson; Director, David Petrarca; Sets, Linda Buchanan; Costumes, Claudia Boddy; Lighting, Robert Christen; Music/Sound, Rob Milburn. CAST: Marylouise Burke (Ruth), Laura Esterman (Bessie), Peter J. Ludwig (Bob), Karl Maschek (Charlie), Aleta Mitchell (Dr. Charlotte/Retirement Director), Tim Monsion (Dr. Wally), Mark Rosenthal (Hank), Janet Zarish (Lee).

THE MASTER BUILDER by Ibsen; Translation, Gerry Bamman, Irene B. Berman; Director, Mark Lamos; Sets, Marjorie Bradley Kellog; Costumes, Jess Goldstein; Lighting, Pat Collins. CAST: Jack Bittner (Knut Brovik), Veronica Cartwright (Aline Solness), Denise Joughin Casey, Claire Cousineau, Tracey Ellis (Kaja Fosli), Peggy Johnson, Mark Nelson (Ragnar Brovik), Frederick Neumann (Dr. Herdal), Cynthia Nixon (Hilde Wangel), Pauline Bruce Thompson, Sam Waterston (Halvard Solness).

This was a world premiere of a new translation.

THE SNOW BALL (WORLD PREMIERE) by A.R. Gurney; Director, Jack O'Brien; Choreography, Graciela Daniel; Sets, Douglas Schmidt; Costumes, Steven Rubin; Lighting, David F. Segal; Co-Produced with the Old Globe Theatre. CAST: Mary R. Barnett, Terrence Caza, Kandis Chappell (Lucy Dunbar), Susan J. Coon (Young Kitty), Brian John Driscoll, Rita Gardner (Kitty Price), Cynthia D. Hanson, Tom Lacy (Van Dam/Baldwin Hall), Katherine McGrath (Liz Jones), Robert Phalen (Saul Radner), Mimi Quillin, Deborah Taylor (Joan Daley), John Thomas Waite, Donald Wayne (Jack Daley), Christopher Wells (Young Jack), James R. Winkler (Cooper Jones).

JULIUS CAESAR by William Shakespeare; Director, Mark Lamos; Sets, Michael Yeargan; Costumes, Catherine Zuber; Lighting, Christopher Akerlind; Music, Mel Mn Jacob Albert, Keith Baxter (Cassius), Lynda M. Berg, Donald Buka (Caesar), Sheridan Chist (Octavius Caesar), Robertson Dean (Decius Brutus/Pindarus), Justin Deas (Brutus), Stevin Dennis (Lucius), Bill Fennelly, Elain Graham (Potia), Jonathan Grey (Flavius/Popilius Lena), Tom Hewitt (Mark Antony), Curt Hostsetter (Metellus Cimber/Messala), Michael J. Hume (Cinna), Peter Husovsky (Trbonius), Charles Ioirio, James Vincent Langer, Charles Losacco, Tim Loughrin (Caius Ligarius/Cinna the Poet/Titinius), Patrick Mulcahy (Soothsayer/Lucilius), Jonathan Nichols (Marullus/Young Cato), Giulia Pagano (Calpurnia), Sarah Paulding, Patrick Tull (Casca), Michael Wallace.

FROM THE MISSISSIPPI DELTA by Dr. Endesha Ida Mae Holland; Director, Jonathan Wilson; Sets/Costumes, Eduardo Sicangco; Lighting, Allen Lee Hughes. CAST: Cheryl Lynn Bruce, Sybil Walker, Jacqueline Williams.

T. Charles Erickson Photos

Sam Waterston, Cynthia Nixon in "Master Builder"

Laura Esterman, Mark Rosenthal in "Marvin's Room"

Tracey Ellis, Richard Poe in "Our Country's Good"

Cheryl Lynn Bruce, Sybil Walker, Jacqueline Williams in "From the Mississippi Delta"

Robert Phalen, Terrence Caza, Christopher Wells, Brian John Driscoll, James R. Winker in "The Snow Ball"

130

Kate Burton, John Christopher Jones, Michael O'Gorman,
Kate Goehring in "Aristocrats"

Chuck Patterson, Al White, Jonathan Earl Peck
in "Two Trains Running"

HUNTINGTON THEATRE COMPANY

Boston, Massachusetts
Ninth Season
September 21, 1990-June 16, 1991

Producing Director, Peter Altman; Managing Director, Michael Maso; Marketing/Public Relations Director, William P. Prenevost; Education Director, Pamela Hill; Production Manager, Roger Meeker; Controller, Mary Kiely.

PRODUCTIONS AND CASTS

H.M.S. PINAFORE by W.S. Gilbert and Arthur Sullivan; Director, Larry Carpenter; Sets, James Leonard Joy; Costumes, Mariann Verheyen; Lighting, Stuart Duke; Music Director, Lynn Crigler; Choreography, Daniel Pelzig. CAST: Brooks Almy (Buttercup), Rebecca Baxter (Josephine), Michael Brian (Rackstraw), James Coelho (Becket), Denis Holmes (Sir Joseph Porter), James Javore (Corcoran), Roxann Parker (Hebe), Richard Pruitt (Bobstay), Paul Schoeffler (Dick Deadeye), Robert Towne, Lisa Anne Barrett, Glenn Sneed, Barbara Scanlon, Russ Jones, Joel Imbody, Stephen Brice, Dennis Bender, Peggy Bayer.
TWO TRAINS RUNNING by August Wilson; Director, Lloyd Richards; Sets, Tony Fanning; Costumes, Christi Karvonides; Lighting, Geoff Korf. CAST: Al White (Memphis), Anthony Chisholm (Wolf), Ella Joyce (Risa), Ed Hall (Holloway), Sullivan Walker (Hambone), Jonathan Earl Peck (Sterling), Chuck Patterson (West).
ARISTOCRATS by Brian Friel; Director, Kyle Donnelly; Sets, Kate Edmunds; Costumes, Erin Quigley; Lighting, Rita Pietraszek. CAST: Richard Bekins (Tom), Michael McCormick (Willie), Frank Groseclose (Uncle George), John Christopher Jones (Casimir), Kate Burton (Alice), Kate Goehring (Claire), Michael O'Gorman (Eamon), Linda Stephens (Judith), Vincent Dowling (Father), Lizza Riley (Anna's Voice).
IPHIGENIA by Euripides; Translation, W.S. Merwin, George E. Dimcock Jr., Wittner Bynner; Director, Tazewell Thompson; Sets, Donald Eastman; Costumes, Paul Tazewell; Lighting, Nancy Schertler; Music/Sound, Fabian V. Obispo Jr. CAST: Karen Evans-Kandel (Iphigenia in Tauris), Kevin Gardner (Old Man/Herdsman), David Patrick Kelly (Orestes), Matthew Loney (Achilles/Pylades), Lizan Mitchell (Clytemnestra/Athena), Jonathan Peck (Menelaos/Soldier), Joseph W. Rodriquez (Attendant/Soldier/Herdsman), Francis Ruivivar (Agamemnon), Shari Simpson (Iphigenia at Aulis), Tom Spackman (Messenger/Thoas), Christopher Charron (Soldier/Herdsman), Adam Weinberg (Soldier/Herdsman), Stephanie Clayman, Robin Miles, Suzen Murakoshi, Karen Ryker, Donna Sorbello, Lisa Tejero.

Richard Feldman Photos

Right: "H.M.S Pinafore"

Karen Evans-Kandel, David
Patrick Kelly in "Iphigenia"

JOHN F. KENNEDY CENTER FOR THE PERFORMING ARTS

Washington, D.C.
June 5, 1990-May 5, 1991

OPERA HOUSE

STARLIGHT EXPRESS with Music by Andrew Lloyd Webber; Lyrics, Richard Stilgoe; Musical Director, Paul Bogaev; Director/Choreography, Arlene Phillips. CAST: Mary Louise Bentley, Steven Cates, Renee Lynette Chambers, Dawn Marie Church, Eric Clausell, Dennis Courney, Ron DeVito, Steven K. Dry, Lori Flynn, Ronald Garza, Kimberly A. Gladman, Jamie, Steve Kadel, Todd Lester, Peter Liciaga, Jimmy Lockett, Bobby Love, Anthony Marciona, Sean McDermott, Rick Mujica, Raymond Patterson, Nicole Picard, Meera Popkin, Angela Pupello, Rachelle Rak, Reva Rice, Steven M. Schultz, Jeanna Schweppe, Glenn Shiroma, Fred Tallalsen, Matt Terry, Dwight Toppin, Angel Vargas, Scott Westmoreland, Chera Wilson, Nelson Yee.

SHOGUN (WORLD PREMIERE) with Music by Paul Chihara; Lyrics/Book, John Driver; Director/Choreography, Michael Smulin. CAST: Peter Karrie, June Angela, Francis Ruivivar. For complete credits, see *Broadway Calendar*.

GRAND HOTEL with Music/Lyrics by Robert Wright and George Forrest, Maury Yeston;Book, Luther Davis; Director/Choreography, Tommy Tune. CAST: Liliane Montevecchi, Brent Barrett, Mark Baker, Anthony Franciosa, Debbie deCoudreaux, Erick Devine, David Dollase, DeLee Lively-Mekka, Dirk Lumbard, Bernie Passeltiner, Arte Phillips, Victoria Regan, David Rogers, Martin Van Treuren, K.C. Wilson, Sterling Clark, Dan Conroy, Keith Crowningshield, Mark Enis, Nathan Gibson, Scott Hayward, Carrie-Ellen Heikkila, Rachel Jines, Barbara Marineau, Corinne Melacon, Marc Mouchet, Doug Nagy, Reggie Phoenix, Abe Reybold, William Ryall, Rick Stockwell, Vincent Vogt, David Andrew White, Susan Wood.

THE PHANTOM OF THE OPERA with Music by Andrew Lloyd Webber; Lyrics, Charles Hart, Richard Stilgoe; Book, Mr. Stilgoe and Mr. Webber; Director, Harold Prince. CAST: Kevin Gray, Terri Bibb, Keith Buterbaugh, Rick Hilsabeck, David Huneryager, Patricia Hurd, Olga Talyn, Donn Cook, Patricia Ward, Sarah Pfisterer.

Right: "Starlight Express" Top: Gary Yeats, William King in "Project!"

Valerie Leonard, Michael Waldron, Barry Nelson, Patrick Garner, Ron Holgate (front) in "Lend Me a Tenor"

Roma Downey, Frank McCusker in "Playboy of the Western World"

EISENHOWER THEATRE

PROJECT: A Musical Documentary; Conception/Original Direction, Patrick Henry; Director/Choreography, Donald Douglass; Music, Doug Lofstrom; Lyrics, Tricia Alexander, Mr. Henry; Additional Songs, T. Alexander, C. Brown, L. Dean, J. Dorman, C. Harris, C. Stephens, A. Stewart; Sets, Rob Hamilton; Lighting, Marc Shellist; A Free Street Theatre Production.
SHE ALWAYS SAID, PABLO; Conception/Direction, Frank Galati; Words, Gertrude Stein; Music, Virgil Thompson, Igor Stravinsky; Images, Pablo Picasso; Design, John Paoletti, Geoffrey Bushor, Mary Griswold; Musical Director, Edward Zelnis; Choreography, Peter Amster.
THE PLAYBOY OF THE WESTERN WORLD by John Millington Synge; Director, Vincent Dowling; Sets, Noel Sheridan; Costumes, Anne Cave, Rachel Pigot-Judd; Lighting, Tony Wakefield. CAST: The National Theatre of Ireland featuring David Carey, Miriam Colefield, John Cowley, Roma Downey, Magaret Fegan, Nuala Hayes, David Kelly, Miriam Kelly, Peadar Lamb, Frank McCusker, Maire Ni Ghrainne, Niall O'Brien, Macdara O Fatharta, Kevin Reynolds, Sarah Jane Scaife.
LEND ME A TENOR by Ken Ludwig; /Director, Jerry Zaks; Sets, Tony Walton; Costumes, William Ivey Long; Lighting, Paul Gallo. CAST: Barry Nelson, Ron Holgate, D'Jamin Bartlett, Patrick Garner, Justine Johnston, Valerie Leonard, Kate Skinner, Michael Waldron.
AMAHL AND THE NIGHT VISITORS by Gian Carlo Menotti; Director, Mr. Menotti; Conductor, Stephen Crout; Choreography, Mimi Legat; Sets/Costumes, Zack Brown; Lighting, John McLain. CAST: Gregory Lofts, Stephen Lofts, Derek West (Amahl), Suzanna Guzman, Roberta Laws, Rebecca Russell (Mother), Howard Ralph Carr, Joseph Myering (King Kaspar), Gary Aldrich, Christopher Trakas (King Melchior), Moses Braxton, Alvy Powell (King Baltahzar), James Shaffran (Page).
LUCIFER'S CHILD by William Luce; Director, Tony Abatemarco. CAST: Julie Harris. For complete credits, see *Broadway Calendar*.
THE HEIDI CHRONICLES by Wendy Wasserstein; Director, Daniel Sullivan; Sets, Thomas Lynch; Costumes, Jannifer Von Mayrhauser; Lighting, Pat Collins. CAST: Stephanie Dunnam, Mark Harelik, Robert Curtis-Brown, Mimi Lieber, Elaine Hausman, Maggie Baird, Amy Ryan, Michael Sandels.
GREATER TUNA by Jaston Williams, Joe Sears and Ed Howard; Director, Mr. Howard; Sets, Kevin Rupnik; Costumes, Linda Fisher; Lighting, Judy Rasmuson. CAST: Joe Sears, Jaston Williams.

TERRACE THEATRE

A TUNA CHRISTMAS by Jaston Williams, Joe Sears and Ed Howard; Director, Mr. Howard; Sets, Brad Braune, Loren Sherman; Costumes, Linda Fisher; Lighting, Judy Rasmuson. CAST: Joe Sears, Jaston Williams.
KILLER-OF-ENEMIES: THE DIVINE HERO; Script/Choreography, Erick Hawkins; Music, Alan Hovhaness; Design/Costumes, Ralph Lee; Sets, Ralph Dorazio; Lighting, Robert Engstrom. CAST: Erick Hawkins Dance Company featuring Robert Engstrom, Jeff Kensmoe, Erick Hawkins, Michael Moses, Gloria McLean, Cynthia Reynolds, Frank Roth, Othello Johns, Douglas Andresen, Laura Pettibone, Joseph Mills, Catherine Tharin, Brenda Connors, Renata Celichowska, Kathy Ortiz.
THE BOY WHO WANTED TO TALK TO WHALES AND OTHER STORIES by The Robert Minden Ensemble; Technical Director, Chris Pearce; Design, Nancy Walker. CAST: Carla Hallett, Robert Minden, Andrea Minden, Dewi Minden.

THEATRE LAB

SHEAR MADNESS by Paul Portner; Director/Design, Bruce Jordan; Sets, Kim Peter Kovac; Lighting, Daniel McLean Wagner. CAST: David J. Brockman, Tom Brooks, Mark Frawley, Francie Glick, Betsy Hughes, Ted McAdams.
 Continuing an open end run.

Ken Howard, Martha Swope, Joan Marcus, Jay Thompson, David Fullard Photos

Jaston Williams, Joe Sears in "Greater Tuna"

Robin Baxter, Betsy Highes, Bobby Lohmann in "Shear Madness"

ILLINOIS THEATRE CENTER

Park Forest, Illinois
Fifteenth Season
October 5, 1990-May 5, 1991

Artistic Director, Steve S. Billig; Managing Director, Etel Billig; Resident Choreographer, Gordon McClure; Artistic Associate, Wayne Adams; Resident Stage Manager, Jonathan Roark; Dramaturg, Barbara Mitchell; Public Relations, Maggie Evans.

PRODUCTIONS AND CASTS

FLORA THE RED MENACE by Kander and Ebb; Director, Steve S. Billig; Musical Director, Jonathan Roark; Set Design, Archway Scenic; Costume Design, Stephen E. Moore. CAST: Laura Novak Mead, Philip Seward, Anne C. Melby, Thomas Colby, Ed Kross, Cynthia Suarez, John D. Boss, Howard Hahn, Laura McDonough.
EXCLUSIVE CIRCLES by Kendrew Lascelles; Director, Steve S. Billig; Sets, Jonathan Roark, Costumes, Pat Decker. CAST: Rebecca Borter, Valerie D. Robinson, Wayne Adams, Shelley Crosby, George Matthew.
DEAR WORLD; Music/Lyrics by Jerry Herman; Book, Jerome Lawrence, Robert E. Lee; Based on Giradeaux's *The Madwoman of Chaillot*; Director, Steve S. Billig;Musical Director, Jonathan Roark; Costume Design, Stephen E. Moore; Sets, Archway Scenic; Choreography, Gordon McClure. CAST: Susan Doherty, Laura McDonough, Ed Kross, Thomas Colby, Laura Novak Mead, Wayne Adams, August Ziemann, John B. Boss, Miles Phillips, Philip Seward, Judy McLaughlin, Steve S. Billig, Shelley Crosby, Etel Billig
NAKED DANCING by John Banach; Director, Etel Billig; Sets, Jonathan Roark, Costumes, Pat Decker. CAST: Marlene DuBois, Alan Westbrook, Don McGrew, Karen Blackful.
ACCOMPLICE by Rupert Holmes; Director, Steve S. Billig, Sets, Jonathan Roark; Costumes, Pat Decker. CAST: Arlene Lencioni, David Six, Miles Phillips, Cynthia Huse, Daniel Meyer
WINTERSET by Maxwell Anderson; Director, Steve S. Billig; Sets, Jonathan Roark; Costumes, Pat Decker. CAST: David Six, John B. Boss, Don McGrew, Laura Collins, Wayne Adams, Laura McDonough, Steve S. Billig, Daniel Meyer, Lisa Fontana, Jennifer Lien, Glenn Fahlstrom, Michael Shannon, Joe Romanov, Dean Scalzitti.
BLUES IN THE NIGHT; Conceived by Sheldon Epps; Director, Steve S. Billig; Set Design, Wayne Adams; Costumes, Pat Decker; Musical Direction, Jonathan Roark; Choreography, Gordon McClure. CAST: Aisha DeHaas, Gordon McClure, Laura Collins, Karen Wheeler.

Glenn Davidson Photos

Laura McDonough, Michael Shannon, David Six, John B. Boss in "Winterset"

Alan Westbrook, Marlene DuBois in "Naked Dancing"

LONG ISLAND STAGE

Rockville Centre, New York
September 4, 1990-June 9, 1991

Artistic Director, Clinton J. Atkinson; Managing Director, Thomas M. Madden; Chairman of the Board, Gerard F. Scavelli; Priduction Stage Manager, David Wahl; Technical Director, John Whitford; Property Master, Laura L. Sheets; Casting Directors, Wendy Dana, Tina-Marie Marquis; Lighting, John Hickey, Kenneth R. Farley, Douglas O'Flaherty; Sets, Phillip Baldwin, Dan Conway, Steve Perry; Costumes, Don Newcomb, Marcella Beckwith, Muriel Stockdale; Music Consultant, Steve Liebman; Stage Managers, Ted Bouton, Jan Wahl.
COMPANY: Peter Bartlett, William J. Marshall, Daniel Hagen, Steve Liebman, David Konig, Donald Christopher, Kathrin King Segal, Susan Orem, P.J. Barry, Sharon Scott, La Terry Butler, Ron Brice, Jed Dickson, Sharon Hope, John Newton, C.J. Jarmon, Roxanna Stuart, Paul Malloy, Michells O'Steen, John Kozeluh, Ginger Price, Dennis Parlato, James Congdon, Pamela Burrell, John Corey, Reathal Bean, Edwin C. Owens, Harry Bennett, Scott Greer, Jim Hillgartner, Mary McCann, Robin Miles.
GUEST ARTISTS: Steven Kaplan, Richard Hopkins.
PRODUCTIONS: *The Boys Next Door* by Tom Griffin, *In White America* by Martin B. Duberman, *The Deal* by Matthew Witten, *Widowers' Houses* by Bernard Shaw.

WORLD PREMIERES: *Hi-Hat Hattie!* by Larry Parr, *After the Dancing in Jeircho* by P.J. Barry.

Deborah Raven, Oak Atkinson, Brian W. Ballweg Photos

Michelle O'Steen, John Kozeluh in "After the Dancing in Jericho"

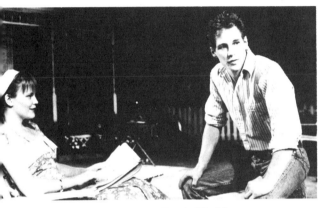

Boyd Gaines, James Noble in "Voysey Inheritance"

LONG WHARF THEATRE

New Haven, Connecticut
Twenty-sixth Season
October 4, 1990-June 23, 1991

Artistic Director, Arvin Brown; Executive Director, M. Edgar Rosenblum; Literary Consultant, John Tillinger; Associate Artistic Director, Gordon Edelstein; Artistic Administrator, Janice Muirhead; Production Coordinator, Anne Keefe; General Manager, John K. Conte; Development, Pamela Tatge, Ana Silfer; Technical Director, Ellis Benjamin Baker; Props, David Fletcher; Wardrobe, Jean Routt; Production Electrician, Jay Strevey; Press, David Mayhew, Jeff Fickes.

PRODUCTIONS AND CASTS

THE VOYSEY INHERITANCE (U.S. Premiere) by Harley Granville Barker; Director, Arvin Brown; Sets, John Lee Beatty; Costumes, David Murin; Lighting, Arden Fingerhut; Stage Manager, Anne Keefe. CAST: Caris Corfman (Alice Maitland), T. Scott Cunningham (Denis Tregoning), Joyce Ebert (Mrs. Voysey), Boyd Gaines (Edward Voysey), Michael R. Gill (Hugh Voysey), Tom Hewitt (Trenchard Voysey), Ann McDonough (Beatrice), Rebecca Nelson (Emily Voysey), James Noble (Voysey Sr.), William Prince (George Booth), Louise Roberts (Ethel Voysey), Jody Rowell (Phoebe), Jeanne Ruskin (Honor Voysey), Doug Stender (Major Booth Voysey), William Swetland (Evans Colpus), Ashley Voos (Mary), Ralph Williams (Peacey).

VALUED FRIENDS (U.S. Premiere) by Stephen Jeffreys; Director, Robin Lefevre; Sets/Costumes, Sue Plummer; Lighting, Marc B. Weiss; Stage Manager, Tammy Taylor. CAST: Bill Camp (Howard), John Benjamin Hickey (Paul), Liann Pattison (Marion), Joll Tasker (Sherry), Ian Trigger (Stewart), Mark Vietor (Scott).

BETRAYAL by Harold Pinter; Director, John Tillinger; Sets, John Lee Beatty; Costumes, Jane Greenwood; Lighting, Richard Nelson; Stage Manager, Janet Friedman. CAST: Maureen Anderman (Emma), Edmond Genest (Robert), Michael Goodwin (Jerry), Bernard Jaffe (Waiter), James O'Neill (Bartender).

THE BABY DANCE by Jane Anderson; Director, Jenny Sullivan; Sets, Marjorie Bradley Kellogg; Costumes, David Murin; Lighting, Kirk Bookman; Stage Manager, Tammy Taylor. CAST: Richard Lineback (Al), John Bennett Perry (Ron), Joel Polis (Richard), Linda Purl (Wanda), Stephanie Zimbalist (Rachel).

PICNIC by William Inge; Director, Arvin Brown; Sets, Michael Yeargin; Costumes, Jess Goldstein; Lighting, Richard Nelson; Stage Manager, Anne Keefe. CAST: Lance Ball (Bomber), Shannon Bradley (Madge), Jack Davidson (Howard Bevans), Joyce Ebert (Rosemary Sidney), Mary Fogarty (Helen Potts), Prudence Wright Holmes (Christine), Brad Hunt (Hal Carter), Sean O'Bryan (Alan Seymour), Pamela Payton-Wright (Flo Owens), Sharon Ullrick (Irma Kronkite), Margaret Welsh (Millie Owens).

GENERATIONS OF THE DEAD IN THE ABYSS OF CONEY ISLAND MADNESS (World Premiere) by Michael Henry Brown; Director, L. Kenneth Richardson; Sets, Donald Eastman; Costumes, Judy Dearing; Lighting, Anne Militello; Sound, Rob Gorton; Fight Director, David Leong; Stage Manager, Ruth M. Feldman. CAST: Jerome Preston Bates succeeded by L. Kenneth Richardson (The Butterman), Lorey Hayes (Lenore), William Jay Marshall (Job), Petie Trigg Seale (Marlenen Cooper), Kimi'Sung (Lena), Isaiah Washington (Reed), Jeff Caldwell Williams (Cody Cooper).

HOW DO YOU LIKE YOUR MEAT? (World Premiere) by Joyce Carol Oates; Director, Gordon Edelstein; Sets, Hugh Landwehr; Costumes, David Murin; Lighting, Arden Fingerhut; Sound, John Gromada; Stage Manager, Denise Winetr, Ruth M. Feldman. CAST: Michael Dolan (Son), Elisabeth Fay (Child/Daughter), Lou Ferguson (Driver), Julia Gibson (Stacey), Ribert Kerbeck (Bin/Hillard), Lily Knight (Sandy/Chloe/Dancer), Rob Kramer (Limousine Driver/Polo), Christopher Scott Mazur (Son), Gary McCleery (Limousine Driver/Luther/Man's Voice), Ann McDonough (Mother/Woman).

TEMPORARY HELP by David Wiltse; Director, Gordon Edelstein; Sets, Hugh Landwehr; Stage Manager, Denise Winter. CAST: James Andreassi (Vincent Castelnuovo-Tedesco), Eric Conger (Ron Stucker), Thomas Kopache (Karl Streber), Pamela Payton-Wright (Faye Steber).

OUT THERE WITHOUT A PRAYER by Reno; Director, Gordon Edelstein; Sets, Hugh Landwehr; Stage Manager, C.A. Clark, Ruth M. Feldman. CAST: Reno.

DEARLY DEPARTED by David Bottrell and Jessie Jones; Director, Gloria Muzio; Sets, Hugh Landwehr; Stage Manager, C.A. Clark. CAST: Brad Bellamy (Junior), Leo Burmester (Ray-Bud), Ronn Carroll (Rev. Hooker/Norval/Clyde), Mary Fogarty (Raynelle), Susan Greenhill (Suzanne), William Hill (Royce), Jessie Jones (Lucille), Karen MacDonald (Juanita/Veda), Sloane Shelton (Marguerite), Kimberly Squires (Delightful/Nadine).

T. Charles Erickson Photos

Margaret Walsh, Brad Hunt in "Picnic"

Left: Julia Gibson, Robert Kerbeck, Lily Knight, Rob Kramer, Gary McCleery in "How Do You Like Your Meat?" Above: Kimi 'Sung, Isaiah Washington in "Generations of the Dead..."

LOS ANGELES THEATRE CENTER

Los Angeles, California
Seventh Season
July 12, 1990-July 21, 1991

Artistic Director, Bill Bushnell; Producing Director, Diane White; Consulting Director, Alan Mandell; General Manager, Lee Sweet; Design Director, Timian Alsaker; Production Coordinator, Jay D. Smith; Technical Director, David McMurty; Casting, Karen Kalensky; Resident Sound Director, Jon Gottlieb; Resident Designer, Douglas D. Smith; Latino Theatre Lab Director, Jose Luis Valenzuela; Press/Public Relations Director, Dawn Setzer; Development/Marketing Director, Lynne D. Guggenheim; Education Director, Karen Goldberg; Consulting Director/Young Conservatory, Maureen O'Toole.

PRODUCTIONS AND CASTS

THE WILD DUCK (World Premiere) by Henrik Ibsen; Translation by Gerry Bamman and Irene B. Berman; Director, Stein Winge; Producer, Diane White; Sets/Costumes, Pavel Dobrosky; Lighting, Douglas D. Smith; Sound, Jon Gottlieb; Music, Jan Garbarek; Hair, Jeffrey Sacino; Stage Manager, Danny Lewin; Produced in the Tom Bradley Theatre. CAST: Thomas Newman, Anthony Geary, Stefan Gierasch, David Morse, Camilla Carr, Mary Dixie Carter, Sharon Barr, Shabaka, Ron Campbell, Lou Robb, Geoff Hoff, Philip Irwin, Mark Laska, Timothy Omundson.

THE MISSION by Culture Clash; Presented in association with LATC's Latino Theatre Lab, Artistic Director, Jose Luis Valenzuela; Director, Señor Valenzuela; Sets, Gronk; Lighting, Jose Lopez; Costumes, Herbert Siguenza; Sound, Richard Montoya, Richard Salinas; Video, Culture Clash; Stage Managers, David S. Franklin, John Paul Melfi; Produced in Theatre 3. CAST: Richard Montoya, Ricardo Salinas, Herbert Siguenza.

AUGUST 29 (World Premiere); presented in association with LATC's Latino Theatre Lab, Artistic Director, Jose Luis Valenzuela; Director, Señor Valenzuela; Sets/Projections, Gronk, Douglas D. Smith; Lighting, Mr. Smith; Costumes, Gronk; Sound, Mark Friedman; Original Music, Marcos Loya; Choreography, Rene Olivas Gubernick; Dramaturg, Binnur Karaevli; Stage Manager, Cari Norton; Produced in Theatre 2. CAST: E.J. Castillo, Evelina Fernandez, Abel Franco, Mike Gomez, Sal Lopez, Tony Maggio, Vanessa Marquez, Angela Moya, Lupe Ontiveros, Olga M. Perez.

THE CRUCIBLE by Arthur Miller; Director, Bill Bushnell; Producer, Diane White; Sets/Lighting, D. Martyn Bookwalter; Costumes, Timian Alsaker; Sound, Jon Gottlieb; Stage Manager, Nancy Ann Adler; Produced in the Tom Bradley Theatre. CAST:Ilsa Anna, Jennifer Bullock, Anne Gee Byrd, Karole Lynn Foreman, Heather Graham, Philip Baker Hall, Ann Heard, Maury Hillstrom, William Dennis Hunt, Page Leong, Beatrice Manley, Mya Maury, Barry Michlin, Valente Rodriguez, Tom Rosqui, David Selby, Kevin Symons, Barnara Tarbuck, Gregory Wagrowski.

THE JONI MITCHELL PROJECT (World Premiere); Songs by Joni Mitchell; Devised by Henry Edwards and David Schweizer; Director, Mr. Schweizer; Assistant Director, Randee Trabitz; Music Direction/Arrangements, Richard Bronskill; Assistant Music Director, Donna Debreceni; Sets/Lights, Timian Alsaker; Costumes, Donna Barrier; Sound, Mark Friedman; Projections, Donald Krieger; Stage Manager, David S. Franklin; Produced in Theatre 3. CAST: Hinton Battle, Noreen Hennessy, Philip Littel, Lisa Harlow Stark, Ren Woods. MUSICIANS: Eric Cunningham, Donna Debreceni, Ritt Henn, Lisa Maxwell, Alicia Siegall.

BLUES IN THE NIGHT (West Coast Premiere); Conceived and Directed by Sheldon Epps; Sets/Lights, Douglas D. Smith; Costumes, Marianna Elliott; Musical Direction, Perry Hart; Choreography, Patricia Wilcox; Sound, Jon Gottlieb; Stage Manager, Danny Lewin; Produced in the Tom Bradley Theatre. CAST: Obba Babatunde, Joanne Jackson, Leilani Jones, Freda Payne. MUSICIANS: Rahl Coleman (Piano/Conductor), Charles M. Owens (Reeds), Raymond Pounds (Drums); Fernando Pullum (Trumpet), Louie Spears (Bass).

Freda Payne, Obba Babatundé, Joanne Jackson,
Leilani Jones In "Blues in the Night"

Fisher Stevens, Elizabeth Berridge in "Venus and Thumbtacks"

THE HIP-HOP WALTZ OF EURYDICE (World Premiere); Created and Directed by Reza Abdoh; Producer, Diane White; Sets/Costumes, Timian Alsaker; Lighting, Rand Ryan; Sound, Erik Blank, Raul Vincent Enriquez; Vodeo, Adam Soch; Assistant Director, Sidney Montz; Dramaturgy, Morgan Jenness; Stage Manager, Susan Slagle; Produced in Theatre 2. CAST: Borracha, Tom Fitzpatrick, Alan Mandell, Julia Mengers, Joselito Amen Santo.

VEINS AND THUMBTACKS by Jonathan Marc Sherman; Director, David Saint; Producer, Diane White; Sets, David Gallo; Lights, Kenneth Posner; Costumes, Marianna Elliott; Sound, Jon Gottlieb; Stage Manager, Nancy Ann Adler; Produced in Theatre 3. CAST: Elizabeth Berridge, Bruce Mac Vittie, Beatrice Manley, William Marquez, Mercedes McNab, Noelle Parker, Fisher Stevens.

MY CHILDREN! MY AFRICA! Written and Directed by Athol Fugard; A La Jolla Playhouse production presented in association with Richard E. Pardy and Vidal Sassoon; Sets, Douglas Stein, Susan Hilferty; Costumes, Ms. Hilferty; Lights, Dennis Parichy; Sound, James LeBrecht; Associate Director, Ms. Hilferty; Stage Manager, Sandra Lea Williams; Produced in the Tom Bradley Theatre. CAST: Brock Peters, Melora Hardin, Sterling Macer, Jr.

ABSALOM'S SONG (World Premiere) by Salaelo Maredi; Director, Ann Bowen; Sets/Costumes, Timian Alsaker; Lights, Douglas D. Smith; Sound, Jon Gottlieb; Stage Manager, Danny Lewin; Produced in Theatre 2. CAST: Sam Mataoana Phillips, Maggie Soboil.

LIFE IS A DREAM by Pedro Calderon de la Barca; Adaptation of the Engish translation by Edwin Honig;Additional Text from *The Tower* by Hugo von Hofmannsthal, English translation by Michael Hamburger; Direction, Bill Bushnell, Sidney Montz; Producer, Diane White; Sets, Allison Koterbash; Lights/Costumes, Timian Alsaker; Sound, Jon Gottlieb; Original Music, Nathan Wang; Hair/Makeup, Elena Maluchin Breckenridge; Stage Manager, Susan Slagle; Produced in the Tom Bradley Theatre. CAST: Brad Brock, Ron Campbell, Maury Efrems, Tom Fitzpatrick, Richmond Hoxie, Colette Kilroy, Mark Christopher Lawrence, Julia Mengers, Time Winters.

THE RABBIT FOOT (West Coast Premiere) by Leslie Lee; Presented in association with LATC's Black Theatre Artists Workshop; Director, Shabaka; Lights/Sets, Douglas D. Smith; Costumes, Marianna Elliott; Sound, Mark Friedman; Musical Direction, Michael Skloff; Choreography, Joyce Guy; Arrangements, Rick Hozza, Robert La Pierre; Musical Consultant, Mr. La Pierre; Hair/Makeup, Elena Maluchin Breckenridge; Stage Manager, Michael F. Wolf; Produced in Theatre 3. CAST: Ethel Ayler, Loretta Devine, Thomas Mikal Ford, April Grace, John Marshall Jones, Esther Scott, Rick Fitts, Shabaka. MUSICIANS: Mykal Ali (Bass), Kevin Moore (Guitar/Banjo).

DAY OF HOPE (U.S. Premiere) by Birgir Sigurdsson; American Adaptation, Patrick Tovatt, from the English translation by Jill Brooke; Director, Bill Bushnell; Assistant Director, Alyson Campbell; Sets, Timian Alsaker; Lights, Douglas D. Smith; Costumes, Marianna Elliott; Sound, Jon Gottlieb; Original Music, Stephen Tobolwsky; Stage Manager, Nancy Ann Adler; Produced in Theatre 2. CAST: Gregory Wagrowski, Ann Hearn, Salome Jens, Julianna McCarthy, Richard Ortega, Kyle Secor.

A BOWL OF BEINGS by Culture Clash; Presented in association with LATC's Latino Theatre Lab, Artistic director, Jose Luis Valenzuela; Directed by Señor Valenzuela; Sets, Gronk; Lights, Jose Lopez; Sound, Mark Friedman; Choreography, Lettie Ibarra; Stage Manager, David S. Franklin; Produced in the Tom Bradley theatre. CAST: Richard Montoya, Ricardo Salinas, Herbert Siguenza; featuring Lettie Ibarra.

MONSTER IN A BOX (West Coast Premiere) by Spalding Gray; Director, Renee Shafransky; Produced in Theatre 3. Featuring Spalding Gray.

Craig Schwartz, Penina Meisels, Nechelle Wong,
R. Kaufman, Davis Barber Photos

Marcia Gay Harden, Anthony LaPaglia in "Those the River Keeps"

**Judy Kuhn, Shirley Knight
in "Glass Menagerie"**

McCARTER THEATRE

Princeton, New Jersey
December 8, 1990-June 2, 1991

Artistic Director, Emily Mann; Interim Executive Director, William P. Wingate; Associate Executive Director, Abby Evans; General Manager, Timothy J. Shields; Design Associate, Sandy Struth; Literary Manager, Evangeline Morphos; Development Director, Susan Reeves; Acting Communications Director, Michalann Hobson; Publicity Director, Daniel Y. Bauer; Production Manager, David York; Production Stage Manager, Susie Cordon.

PRODUCTIONS AND CASTS

A CHRISTMAS CAROL by Charles Dickens; Adaptaion, Nagle Jackson; Director, Francis X. Kuhn; Composer, Larry Delinger; Dances, Sharon Halley; Sets, Brian Martin; Costumes, Elizabeth Covey; Lighting, Richard Moore. CAST: Jeff Weiss (Scrooge), Roger Bechtel (Wilkins/Tooper), Robert Colston (Fezziwig/Christmas Present), Shelly Delaney (Christmas Past/Martha), James Doerr (Old Joe), Christopher Grossett (Citizen), Marceline Hugot (Mrs. Cratchit), Henson Keys (Marley/Nutley), Raye Lankford (Fan/Fred's Wife), Edwina Lewis (Mrs. Fezziwig/Mrs. Dilber), Ladonna Mabry (Emily/Caroline), Graeme Malcolm (1st Narrator), Don Mayo (2nd Narrator), Chistopher McHale (Cratchit), Paola Renzi (Citizen), Mark Roth (Christmas to Come), Lori Shearer (Belle), Ray Virta (Fred), David Whalen (Young Scrooge), Cheryl Whitney-Marcuard (Citizen), Andrew Ross "Drew" Beresford (Ned), Jonathan Edward "Teddy" Bersford (Tiny Tim), Leslie Ann Haines (Want), Megan Livingston (Citizen), Mark Populus (Tiny Tim), Amanda D. Squitieri (Belinda) True Star Nager-Urian (Ignorance), Mira Wilczek (Dorrit), Gregory C. Wu (Citizen), Nathaiel "Nate" Zeitz (Peter).

THE GLASS MENAGERIE by Tennessee Williams; Director, Emily Mann; Sets, Ming Cho Lee; Costumes, Jennifer von Mayrhauser; Lighting, Robert Wierzel; Music, Mel Marvin; Stage Manager, Susie Cordon. CAST: Shirley Knight (Amanda), Dylan McDermott (Tom), Judy Kuhn (Laura), Jeff Weatherford (Jim).

THOSE THE RIVER KEEPS (WORLD PREMIERE) by David Rabe; Director, Mr. Rabe; Sets, Loren Sherman; Costumes, Sharon Sprague; Lighting, Michael Lincoln; Fights, B. H. Bary; Stage Manager, Mary Michele Miner. CAST: Marcia Gay Harden (Susie), Anthony LaPaglia (Phil), Burt Young (Sal), Debra Cole (Janice).

BETSY BROWN with Music by Baikida Carroll; Lyrics, Ntozake Shange, Emily Mann, Mr. Carroll; Book, Ms. Shange, Ms. Mann; Based on idea by Ms. Shange; Director, Ms. Mann; Choreography, George Faison; Sets/Projections, David Mitchell; Costumes, Jennifer von Mayrhauser; Lighting, Pat Collins; Musical Director,/Vocal Arranger, Daryl Waters; Stage Manager, Susie Cordon. CAST: Harold Perrineau, Jr. (Eugene), Tichina Arnold (Regina), Ted L. Levy (Roscoe), Marc Joseph (Charlie), Kecia Lewis-Evans (Carrie), Eugene Fleming (Mr. Jeff), Pamela Isaacs (Jane), Tommy Hollis (Greer), Mesha Millington (Margot), Amir Jamal Williams (Allard), Ann Duquesnay (Vida), Raquel Herring (Betsy Brown). MUSICAL NUMBERS: Livin' In Your Love, Please Don't Forget About Me, Morning Jump, Vida's Rag, Stick With Me, What's Fast, Schollyard Taunt, Souls of Black Folk, Kiss Song, Carrie, I Callt Her Out, Love Is, Contemplate Your High Points, I Sho' Do Like to Grow Things, He Will Never Let You Down, This is Our House, Jesus Must Have a Telephone, Beside You, Enough, I Need You Both, Regina's Lament, Runaway, Don't Leave Me, Finale.

THE FILM SOCIETY by Jon Robin Baitz; Director, Douglas Hughes; Sets, Thomas Lynch; Costumes/Lighting, Nancy Schertler; Stage Manager, Peter C. Cook. CAST: Mark Nelson (Jonathon), William Duff-Griffin (Hamish), Bill Moor (Neville), Randy Danson (Nan), John Slattery (Terry), Angela Thornton (Sylvia).

T. Charles Erickson Photos

**Mesha Millington, Tommy Hollis, Pamela Isaacs, Raquel Herring,
Marc Joseph, Amir Williams, Ann Duquesnay in "Betsy Brown"**

William Duff-Griffin, Bill Moor, Mark Nelson in "Film Society"

Donna Kane in "Cabaret"

MEADOW BROOK THEATRE

Rochester, Michigan
Twenty-fifth Season
October 4, 1990-May 19, 1991

Artistic director, Terence Kilburn; Managing Director, James P. Spittle; Community Relations Director, Jane Mosher; Finance Manager, John K. Fischer; Public Relations Director, Sylvia Coughlin Porter; Box Office Manager, Sue Day; Resident Designer, Peter W. Hicks; Technical/Production Director, Daniel M. Jaffe; Scenic Artist, Elaine Sutherland; Master Electrician/Resident Lighting Design, Reid G. Johnson; Costume Coordinator, Barbara Jenks; Audio Engineer, Robert Campbell; Head Stage Technician, Scot B. Cleaveland; Stage Managers, Terry W. Carpenter, Robert Herrle.

PRODUCTIONS AND CASTS

CABARET by Kander, Ebb and Masteroff; Director, Carl Schurr; Musical Director, John Lehr Opfar; Choreography, Mary Jane Houdina. CAST: Michael Nostrand (MC), Paul LeBoy (Cliff), Dennis T. Kleinsmith (Ernst), Paul Hopper (Customs), Dorothy Stinnette (Fraulein Schneider), Dinah Lynch (Fraulein Kost), Wil Love (Schultz), Donna Kane (Sally Bowles), Jane Bassesett (Greta), Sylvia Dohi (Lulu), Debra Miller (Frenchie), Holly Raye (Texas), Ericka Sinclair (Olga), Tish Wiliamson (Fritzie), Tom Emmott (Max), Susan Berg Diebolt, Eddie Buffum, Richard Costa, Reinhard Michaels, Trevor Rutkowski, John Seibert, Zdzislawa Gumul, Paul Hopper, Nancy J. Kolton, David Leidholt, Stephen Lloyd Webber.

THE MOUSETRAP by Agatha Christie; Director, Terence Kilburn. CAST: Terry Heck (Mollie), Paul DeBoy (Giles), Alexamder Webb (Chistopher), Juliet Randall (Mrs. Boyle), Phillip Locker (Metcalf), Dinah Lynch (Miss Casewell), Paul Hopper (Paravicini), John Seibert (Trotter).

A CHRISTMAS CAROL by Charles Dickens; Adaptation, Charles Nolte; Director, Mr. Nolte. CAST: Booth Colman (Scrooge), Paul DeBoy, Terry Heck, Paul Hopper, Shirley Ann Kaladjian, Phillip Locker, Dinah Lynch, Glen Allen Pruett, Joseph Reed, John Seibert, Alexander Webb, Matthew Dippell, Adrianne Kriewall, Joshua Mardigan, Sean Patrick Jonaitis, Dennis T. Kleinsmith, Fred Buchalter, Adam Carpenter, Barbara C. Coven, Colin Gray, Zdzislawa Gumul, Rebecca Hyke, Mary K. Nigohosian, Denise A. Nowak, Richard A. Schrot, Joseph Seibert, Gregory Wilson.

WHAT I DID LAST SUMMER by A.R. Gurney, Jr.; Director, Terence Kilburn. CAST: John Seibert (Charlie), Alexander Webb (Ted), Jane Lowry (Grace), Traci Lyn Thomas (Elsie), Shirleyann Kaladjian (Bonny), Jeanne Arnold (Anna).

A MIDSUMMER NIGHT'S DREAM by Shakespeare; Director, John Ulmer. CAST: James Anthony (Theseus/Oberon), Kathryn Grant (Hippolyta/Titania), R. Ward Duffy (Lysander), Richard A. Schrot (Demetrius), Mary Proctor (Hermia), Sue Kenny (Helena), Joseph Reed (Egeus), Ricky Wright (Puck), Parry B. Stewart (Quince), Eric Tavares (Bottom), Randall Godwin (Flute), Roy K. Dennison (Snout), LeRoy Mitchell Jr. (Snug), Thomas D. Mahard (Starveling), Fred Buchalter, Jodilyn Takacs, Michelle Rose Walli.

BAREFOOT IN THE PARK by Neil Simon; Director, Terence Kilburn. CAST: Shirleyann Kaladjian (Corie), Joseph Reed (Telephone Man), Paul Hopper (Delivery Man), Alexander Webb (Paul), Jane Houdyshell (Mother/Mrs. Banks), Eric Tavares (Victor).

SLEUTH by Anthony Shaffer; Director, Charles Nolte. CAST: Arthur J. Beer (Andrew Wyke), Alexander Webb (Milo Tindle), Samuel A. Jacobs (Inspector Doppler), Halsey Taylor (Sgt. Tarrant), Thomas Tierney (Constable Higgs).

PUMP BOYS AND DINETTES by Foley, Harwick, Monk, Morgan, Schimmel and Wann; Director, William S. Morris. CAST: Kim Story (Jackson), Shawn Stengel (L.M.), Meghan Cary (Prudie), Joellyn Young (Rhetta), Stephen Rust (Eddie), Ollie O'Shea (Jim).

Alexander Webb, John Seibert in "What I Did Last Summer"

Meghan Cary, Shawn Stengel, Joellyn Young in "Pump Boys and Dinettes"

Eric Tavares, Thomas Mahard, LeRoy Mitchell, Jr. (front) in "Midsummer Night's Dream"

Larry Gates, Melinda McCrary, Philip Lehl in "Our Town"

Benjamin Evett in "Billy Bishop..."

MISSOURI REPERTORY THEATRE

Kansas City, Missouri
August 29, 1990-May 19, 1991

Artistic Director, George Keathley; Executive Director, James Costin; Associate Artistic Director, Mary C. Guaraldi; Operations Manager/Tour Director, Robert Thatch; Production Manager, Ronald Schaeffer; Resident Set Designer, John Ezell; Technical Director, Bruce Bacon; Publicity Manager, Kent Politsch.

PRODUCTIONS AND CASTS

OUR TOWN by Thornton Wilder; Director, George Keathley; Sets, John Ezell; Lighting, Peggy Eisenhauer; Costumes, Vincent Scassellati. CAST: Larry Gates (Stage Manager), Gary Neal Johnson (Dr. Gibbs), Joshua Baker (Joe), Stewart Skelton (Howie), Kathleen Warfel (Mrs. Gibbs), Peggy Friesen (Mrs. Webb), Philip Lehl (Goerge), Natalie Sullivan (Rebecca), John John (Wally), Melinda McCrary (Emily), Kevin Brief (Willard/Dead Man), Gary Holcombe (Mr. Webb), Elaine Flicker (Balcony Woman/Dead Woman), C. Andrew Garrson (Man), Jane Stoub (Lady in Box/Dead Woman), K.C. Helmeid (Simon), Dodie Brown (Mrs. Soames), Gordon G. Jones (Warren), Michael Smith (Si), Kevin Doyle (Sam), Charles Oldfather (Joe), George Spratt (McCarthy), James Stone, Jeffrey Cookson, Daniel Dachroeden, David White.

A MOON FOR THE MISBEGOTTEN by Eugene O'Neill; Director, William Woodman; Sets, Joseph Nieminski; Lighting, Robert Christen; Costumes, Baker S. Smith. CAST: Lyn Greene (Josie), Mark McCarthy (Mike), Robert Elliott (Phil), Richard McWilliams (James Tyrone, Jr.), David Fritts (T. Stedman Harder).

WOODY GUTHRIE'S AMERICAN SONG; From Guthrie's songs and writings; Conception/Adaptation, Peter Glazer; Direction, Mr. Glazer; Orchestrations/Vocal Arrangements/Musical Supervision, Jeff Waxman; Sets, Phillip Jung; Lighting, David Noling; Costumes, Baker S. Smith. CAST: Brian Gunter, Susan Moniz, Kate Phelan, James J. Stein Jr., Christopher Walz.

A CHRISTMAS CAROL by Dickens; Adaptation, Barbara Field; Staging, Ross Freese; Sets, John Ezell; Lighting, Joseph Appelt; Costumes, Baker S. Smith. CAST: Gary Neal Johnson (Dickens), Terrence Markovich (Scrooge), Richard James-Greene, Bruce Roach, C. Andrew Garrison, Susan K. Selvey, Natalie Sullivan, Samantha Biggs, Chariese A. Hudson, Brian Cutler, Peggy Friesen, Andrew Gilchrist, Robert Gibby Brand, Melinda McCrary, Scott Cordes, Michael Linsley Rapport, Valeen Ogzewalla, Michele Williams, Janie L. Ohmes, Jeffrey Lehr, Margaret Knapp, Ted Shonka, Chariese Glaze, Kathleen Warfel, Danny Cox, Cara Coffman, Michael Lee Sanders, Hollis McCarthy, Brendan McCurdy, Elizabeth Robbins, Sidonie Garrett, Stephanie Moore, Alison Marian, Mark Robbins, Tucker Slough, Rebecca Manring.

BILLY BISHOP GOES TO WAR by John Gray and Eric Peterson; Director, Dennis Rosa; Sets, E. David Cosier; Lighting, Jeff Davis; Costumes, Vincent Scassellati. CAST: Michael Deep (Present Billy), Benjamin Evett (Past Billy).

FENCES by August Wilson; Director, Claude Purdy; Sets, James Sandefur; Lighting, Phil Monat; Costumes, Martha Hally. CAST: John Henry Redwood (Troy), Willis Burks II (Jim), Delores Mitchell (Rose), Noble Lee Lester (Lyons), Marion McClinton (Gabriel), Gregory Simmons (Cory), Darlene Myrtil, Robin Perry (Raynell).

KING RICHARD III by Shakespeare; Director, George Keathley; Sets, John Ezell; Lighting, Jackie Manassee; Costumes, Virgil Johnson. CAST: Gary Holcombe (Edward IV/Earl), Richard McWilliams (George), Marco Barricilli (Richard, Duke of Gloucester), Tucker Slough (Edward), Brendan McCurdy (Richard, Duke of York), Pat Vern-Harris (Duchess), Juliet Randall (Margaret), Angela Yannon (Anne), Ted Shonka (Tressel/Sir James), Jay Karnes (Berkley/Henry Tudor), Peggy Friesen (Queen Elizabeth), Kelli Edwards (Elizabeth), Joel Carlton (Lord Grey), Joseph Golden (Dorset), James Shelby (Woodville), Theodore Swetz (Hastings), Terrence Markovich (Buckingham), Michael Linsley Rapport (Mayor/Sheriff/Brackenbury), Richard Bowden (Stanley), John A. Horner (Cardinal), George Spratt (Morton), Tom Overmyer (Shaa), Erik Soell (Penker), Larry Greer (Catesby), Geoffrey Beauchamp (Ratcliffe), Gary Neal Johnson (Murderer/Norfolk), David Fritts (Murderer), Margaret Knapp (Jane), Martin English (George Stanley/Walter Herbert), Brendan Cody (Sir Vaughn), Ward Wright, Michael Moseby, Jeffrey Lehr, Rich Linden, John A. Horner.

THE BOYS NEXT DOOR by Tom Griffin; Director, Mary G. Guraldi; Sets, Allen Cornell; Lighting, Robert Murphy; Costumes, Michele Siler. CAST: Richard Esvang (Arnold), William Jay Marshall (Lucien), Gary Holcombe (Jack), Cary Miller (Norman), David Fritts (Barry), David Coxwell (Hedges/Corbin/Clarke), Jeannine Hutchings (Clara/Fremus/Mrs. Warren), Susan K.Selvey (Sheila), Dan Putnam (Klemper).

Larry Pape Photos

Left: John Henry Redwood, Delores Mitchell in "Fences"

John Beasley, Charles H. Clyburn, Ora Jones in "Fences"

NEW AMERICAN THEATRE

Rockford, Illinois
September 13, 1990-June 23, 1991

Producing Director, J.R. Sullivan; Managing Director, Sharon L. Hensley; Drama School Instructors, Linda Abronski, Darcy Hill, Lou Ann McKinney, Bern Sundstedt; Costumes, Jon R. Accardo; Wardrobe, Jan Bacino; Props, J. Kenneth Barnett III; Development Director, Pat Bauerlein; Production Stage Manager, William D. Carey; Marketing Director, Jacqueline M. Goetz; Technical Director, Daniel Janssen; Box Office, Joan Jirak; Dramaturgist, Charlyne Blatcher Martin; Subscriptions, Carla Peavy; Production Manager, William R. Phillip; Associate Director, Stephen F. Vrtol III.

PRODUCTIONS AND CASTS

ARSENIC AND OLD LACE byJoseph Kesselring; Director, Fontaine Syer. CAST: Marge Henning (Abby), Dick Peterson (Rev. Harper), G. Michael Johnson (Teddy), Jamie Button (Brophy), Richard Orman (Klein), Pat Bauerlein (Martha), Cheridah A. Best (Elaine), J.R. Sullivan (Mortimer), Larry Ball (Gibbs), Bern Sundstedt (Johnathan), Frederic Stone (Einstein), Stephen F. Vrtol III (O'Hara), Charles H. Clyburn (Rooney), Stephen W. McCarty (Witherspoon).
OUR COUNTRY'S GOOD by Timberlake Wertenbaker. CAST: Frederic Stone (Phillip/Wisehammer), Daniel Scott (Ross/Freeman), Stephen F. Vrtol III (Collins/Sideway), Anthony Brown (Tench/Aboriginal Australian/Black Caesar), Bern Sundstedt (Campbell/Brewer/Arscott), Jan Bacino (Rev. Johnson/Long), Cheridah A. Best (Johnston/Smith), Linda Abronski (Dawes/Morden), Mark Ulrich (Clark), Bernadette Quigley (Faddy/Bryant), Mary MacDonald Kerr (Mary).
A CHRISTMAS CAROL by Dickens; Adaptation, Amlin Gray. CAST: Bern Sundstedt (Scrooge), Richard Raether, Andrew J. Turner, William R. Phillip, John R. Webb, Tim Maculan, Seth Marantz, Stephen F. Vrtol III, Natasha Leggero, Linda Abronski, Steven J. Wargo, Richard Orman, Larry Ball, George A. Condie, Kate Romano, Mark Ulrich, Cheridah A. Best, G. Michael Johnson, Claire E. Quandt, Heather Lane, Todd Ball, Janet Magnuson, Max Rettig, Olivia Johnson, Andrew Brearley, Carolyn Jansen, Jared S. Jensen, Theresa Cummings, Min Taber, Christopher Carter, Stephanie Gallenz, A. Scattergood.
FENCES by August Wilson; Director, Donald Douglass. CAST: John Beasley (Troy), Charles H. Clyburn (Jim), Ora Jones (Rose), Robert W. Barnett (Lyons), Larry Rucker (Gabriel), Tab Baker (Cory), Amy Byrd, Rachael Thompson, Stepenie Tennle Williams (Raynell).
THE SNEEZE by Chekhov; Adaptation, Michael Frayn; Director, Allan Carlsen. CAST: Linda Abronski, Stephen Hemming, Mark Lazar, Susan Mele, Caspar Roos, Bern Sundstedt, Stephen F. Vrtol III.
YOU NEVER CAN TELL by George Bernard Shaw. CAST: Julie Walker (Dolly), Bill McCallum (Valentine), Janet Magnuson (Parlor Maid), Jeremy Tow (Philip), Pat Bauerlein (Mrs. Clandon), Bern Sundstedt (Crampton), Jack Sydow (Waiter), Kermit Brown (Finch), Andrew C. Osen (Another Waiter), Peter H. MacKenzie (Cook), Stephen F. Vrtol III (Bohun).
MARRY ME A LITTLE by Sondheim and Lucas; Director, Allan Carlsen. No other info.

Johnna Davenport, Jon McGinty Photos

OLD GLOBE THEATRE

San Diego, California
June 22, 1990-June 16, 1991

Executive Producer, Craig Noel; Artistic Director, Jack O'Brien; Managing Director, Thomas Hall; Play Development, Mark Hofflund; Education Director, Diane Sinor; Finance Director, Derek Harrison Hurd; Development Director, Domenick Ietto; Marketing Director, Joe Kobryner; Operations Director, Ken Denison; Stage Managers, Douglas Pagliotti, Karen L. Carpenter, Robert Drake, Peter Van Dyke; Technical Director, Loren Schreiber; Publications, Charlene Baldridge; Public Relations, William B. Eaton, Mark Hiss.

PRODUCTIONS AND CASTS

REMEMBRANCE by Graham Reid; Director, Andrew J. Traister; Sets, Nick Reid; Costumes, Lewis Brown; Lighting, John B. Forbes. CAST: Jack Aranson (Bert), William Anton (Victor), Victoria Boothby (Theresa), Susan Barnes (Joan), Robin Pearson Rose (Deirdre), Lynne Griffin (Jenny).
THE SNOW BALL (WORLD PREMIERE) by A.R. Gurney; Director, Jack O'Brien; Choreogrphy, Graciela Daniele; Sets, Douglas Schmidt; Costumes, Steven Rubin; Lighting, David F. Segal. CAST: James R. Winker (Cooper Jones), Kandis Chappel (Lucy Dunbar), Katherine McGrath (Liz Jones), Tom Lacy (Van Dam), Christopher Wells (Young Jack), Susan J. Coon (Young Kitty), Robert Phalen (Saul Radner), Deborah Taylor (Joan Daley), Tom Lacy (Baldwin Hall), Donald Wayne (Jack Daley), Rita Gardner (Kitty Price), Terrence Caza, Cynthia D. Hanson, Mimi Quillin, John Thomas Waite, Brian John Driscoll, Sandra Ellis-Troy.
A joint **World Premiere** presented with the Hartford Stage.
TWO TRAINS RUNNING by August Wilson; Director, Lloyd Richards; Sets, Tony Fanning; Costumes, Christi Karvonides; Lighting, Geoff Korf. CAST: Al White (Memphis), Anthony Chisholm (Wolf), Ella Joyce (Risa), Ed Hall (Holloway), Sullivan Walker (Hambone), Larry Fishburne (Sterling), Chuck Patterson (West).
SUN BEARING DOWN (WORLD PREMIERE) by Larry Ketron; Director, Stephen Metcalfe; Sets, Robert Brill; Costumes, Robert Wojewodski; Lighting, Ashley York Kennedy. CAST: Bill Geisslinger (Forester), Annette O'Toole (Price), Adam Philipson (Mallory), James Harper (Cawhill).
THE WHITE ROSE (WORLD PREMIERE) by Lillian Garrett; Director, Craig Noel; Sets, Ralph Funicello; Costumes, Steven Rubin; Lighting, David F. Segal. CAST: Jonathan McMurtry (Robert Mohr), J. Kenneth Campbell (Anton Mahler), John K. Linton (Hans Scholl), Natalija Nogulich (Sophie Scholl), Tim Donoghue (Bauer), Steven Culp (Alexander Schmrell), Bray Poor (Christoph Probst), Will Crawford (Wilhelm Graf), Sandra Lindberg (Nurse/Matron), Jesus Ontiveros, Triney Sandoval (Guards).
OTHER PEOPLE'S MONEY by Jerry Sterner; Director, Milton Katselas; Sets, Cliff Faulkner; Costumes, Shigeru Yaji; Lighting, Barth Ballard. CAST: Allen Williams (Coles), Richard Herd (Jorgenson), Sarah Marshall (Bea), Robert Walden (Garfinkle), Laura Johnson (Kate).
LOVE LETTERS by A.R. Gurney; Director, Jack O'Brien; Lighting, Barth Ballard. CAST: Elizabeth Mongomery and Robert Foxworth, Beth Howland and Charles Kimbrough, Sada Thompson and Kevin McCarthy, Michael Learned and Jack O'Brien, Margaret Avery and Paul Winfield, Barbara Rush and Harold Gould.

Christopher Wells, Susan J. Coon in "The Snow Ball"

Dave Florek, Peter Zapp in
"White Man Dancing"

Pippa Pearthree, Charley Lang
in "As You Like It"

WHITE MEN DANCING (WORLD PREMIERE) by Stephen Metcalfe; Director, Thomas Allan Bullard; Sets/Lighting, Kent Dorsey; Costumes, Robert Wojewodski. CAST: Dave Florek (Dell), Peter Zapp (Stuart).

OUR TOWN by Thornton Wilder; Director, Edward Payson Call; Sets, Ralph Funicello; Costumes, Lewis Brown; Lighting, Peter Maradudin. CAST: Jerry Hardin (Stage Manager), Robert LaPorta, Arthur Morton (Assistants), Mitchell Edmonds (Mr. Gibb), Jill André (Mrs. Gibbs), Shad Willingham (George), Roya Shanks (Rebecca), Nicholas Pryor (Mr. Webb), Teri Ralston (Mrs. Webb), Cynthia Nixon (Emily), Sean Sedgewick (Wally), Luther Hanson (Howie), Ryan Conner (Joe), Robert Phalen (Simon), Larry Corodemus (Warren), Mary Benson (Mrs. Soames), Ryan Conner (Si), Sheldon Gero (Stoddard), David S. Cohen (McCarthy), Tavis Ross (Mr. Carter/Willard), Georgia Martin, Sue Ann Morrow, M. Susan Peck, Triney Sandoval, Therese Walden, Mark Hofflund.

HAMLET by William Shakespeare; Director, Jack O'Brien; Sets, Ralph Funicello; Costumes, Lewis Brown; Lighting, Peter Maradudin; Composer, Bob James. CAST: Campbell Scott (Hamlet), Richard Easton (Ghost of Hamlet's Father/Claudius), Katherine McGrath (Gertrude), Jonathan McMurtry (Polonius), Jonathan Walker (Laertes), Jennifer Van Dyke (Ophelia), Nicholas Martin (Reynaldo/Osric/Player), Peter Cook (Horatio), Will Crawford (Voltemand/Player), Joe Hulser (Cornelius/Captain), Jonathan Nichols (Rosencrantz), Marc Wong (Francisco/Attendants), Bray Poor (Bernardo/Attendant), Blaise Messinger (Marcellus/Priest), Tom Lacy (1st Gravedigger/Player King), Jesus Ontiveros (2nd Gravedigger/Major-domo/Player), Henry Godinez (Fortinbras/Player), Mary Kay Wulf (Player Queen), Sandra Lindberg (Player), Andres Monreal (Attendants), Al Wexo (Attendant/Sailor), James Kiernan (Player/Attendant).

AS YOU LIKE IT by William Shakespeare; Director, Julianne Boyd; Sets, David Jenkins; Costumes, Robert Wojewodski; Lighting, Peter Maradudin; Composer, Conrad Susa. CAST: Robert Phalen (Duke Senior/Duke Frederick), Eric Ferguson (Amiens/Lord), Richard Kneeland (Jaques), Nicholas Martin (Le Beau/Martext), Aldo Billingslea (Charles), Jonathan Nichols (Oliver), Blaise Messinger (Jaques, Michel R. Gill (Orlando), Jonathan McMurtry (Adam), Triney Sandoval (Dennis), Richard Easton (Touchstone), Ed Hall (Corin), Charley Lang (Silvius), Bray Poor (William), Jayne Atkinson (Rosalind), Pippa Pearthree (Phebe), M. Susan Peck (Audrey), Mickey Manley (Nymph/Hymen), Arthur Morton, Damien Valleta (Pages), Mary Kay Wulf (Hispera), Therese Walden (Lady in Waiting), Will Crawford, Joe Hulser, Sandra Lindberg, Sue-Ann Morrow, Jesus Ontiveros, Martha Perantoni, Shad Willingham.

HEARTBEATS; Created by Amanda McBroom and Bill Castellino; Lyrics, Ms. McBroom; Music, Ms. McBroom, Jerry Sternbach, Michele Brourman, Tom Snow; Director/Choreography, Mr. Castellino; Musical Director, Jerry Sternbach; Sets/Lighting, Kent dorsey; Costumes, Christina Haatainen. CAST: George Ball, Mary Bond Davis, Richard Hilton, Hilary James, Lee Lucas, Amanda McBroom, Daniel McDonald.

COBB by Lee Blessing; Director, Lloyd Richards; Sets, Rob Greenberg; Costume Designer, Joel O. Thayer; Lighting, Ashley York Kennedy. CAST: William Newman (Mr. Cobb), James E. Reynolds (Peach), George Gerdes (Ty), Dan Martin (Oscar).

Gerry Goodstein, Will Gullette, T. Charles Erickson Photos

Larry Fishburne, Ella Joyce in "Two Trains Running"

Shad Willingham, Nicholas Pryor in "Our Town"

PAPER MILL PLAYHOUSE

Millburn, New Jersey
Fifty-first Season
September 12, 1990-June 30, 1991

Executive Producer, Angelo Del Rossi; Artistic Director, Robert Johanson; General Manager, Geoffrey Cohen; Company Manager, Wade Miller; Staff Consultant, Allen J. Hegarty; Assistant to Artistic Director, Larry Grey; Literary Advisor, Maryan F. Stephens; Development Director, John McEwen; Marketing Director, Debra A. Waxman; Resident Set Design, Michael Analia; Stage Managers, Peggie Imbrie, Andrew Neal, Alan Coats; Public Relations Director, Albertina Reilly.

PRODUCTIONS AND CASTS

ME AND MY GIRL with Music by Noel Gay; Lyrics/Book, L. Arthur Rose and Douglas Furber; Revisions, Stephen Fry, Mike Ockrent; Sets, Michael Anania; Lighting, Phil Monat; Costumes, Guy Geoly and José M. Rivera; Director/Chroegraphy, Tony Parise; Musical Director, Tom Helm. CAST: Susan Cella (Lady Jacqueline), Stephen Temperly (Bolingbroke), John Jellison (Parchester), Leo Leyden (Tring), Jane Connell (Maria), Thomas Toner (Tremayne), Michael Mulheren (Butler), James Brennan (Bill Snibson), Judy Blazer (Sally Smith), Betty Winsett (Mrs. Brown), Brian Quinn (Pianist), Deborah Collins (Mrs. Worthington-Worthington), Betty Winsett (Lady Brighton), Leslie Feagan (Barking), Jeff Stone (Constable).

THE ROAR OF THE GREASEPAINT-THE SMELL OF THE CROWD with Music/Lyrics/Book by Leslie Bricusse and Anthony Newley; Directors, Robert Johanson and Larry Grey; Choreography, Susan Stroman; Musical Director, Tom Helm; Sets, Michael Anaia; Costumes, Gregg Barnes; Lighting, Mark Stanley. CAST: George S. Irving (Sir), Robert Johanson (Cocky), Denise Nolin (The Kid), Mia Malm (The Girl), Ron Richardson (The Stranger), Richard Wyzykowski (The Bully), Ribin Boudreau, Bill Brassea, Kelly Burnette, Mirla Criste, Pamela Denning, Don Johanson, Karyn Lee, Julie Pasqual, Sheryl Rifas, Paula Marie Seniors, Whitney Webster, Matt Zaeley.

LEND ME A TENOR by Ken Ludwig; Director, Steven Beckler; Sets, Ron Kadri; Lighting, Michael Lincoln; Costumes, Jennifer Arnold. CAST: Patrick Quinn (Max), Kathryn Meisle (Maggie), David Sabin (Saunders), Bob Cuccioli (Tito), Judy Blazer (Maria), Jeff Brooks (Bellhop), Marsha Waterbury (Diana), Marian Haraldson (Julia).

TO KILL A MOCKINGBIRD; Adaptation, Christopher Sergel from the novel by Harper Lee; Director, Robert Johanson; Sets, Michael Anania; Costumes, Gregg Barnes; Lighting, Mark Stanley; Music, Phil Hall. CAST: Tiffany Kriessler (Scout Finch), Marjorie Johnson (Calpurnia), Katharine Houghton (Miss Maudie), Elizabeth Owens (Miss Stephanie), Doris Brent (Mrs. Dubose), Jesse Bernstein (Jem Finch), Alexander Barton (Rev. Sykes), Dale Dickey (Mayella Ewell), Paul Albe (Bob Ewell), Daniel Reifsnyder (Dill), David Smtih (Nathan Radley), George Grizzard (Atticus Finch), Don Brennan (Mr. Cunningham), Edward James Hyland (Heck Tate), Jack Bittner (Judge Taylor), Page Johnson (Mr. Gilmer), James Cronin (Clerk), Michael White (Tom Robinson), Harriett D. Foy (Helen Robinson), David Flynn (Boo Radley), Jerry Barron, Sharon Eisen, Kurt Faunce, Millie Heckmann, Jerry Kamen, Emily Ridgway, Spencer Rowe, Mary Vining.

THE MERRY WIDOW by Franz Lehar (New English Adaptation); Original Book, Victor Leon, Leo Stein; New Book, Robert Johanson; Lyrics, Albert Evans; Director, Mr. Johanson; Musical Director, Jim Coleman; Choreography, Sharon Halley; Sets, Michael Anania; Costumes, Gregg Barnes; Lighting, Mark Stanley. CAST: Judy Kaye (Hanna), Richard White (Danilo), Merwin Goldsmith (Zeta), Hallie Neill (Valencienne), Mark Janicello (Camille) Peter Bartlett (Njegus), Grant Walden (Bogdanovich), Georgia Bibeau (Sylvanie), Donald Norris (Kromov), Sarah Rice (Olga), Joseph Mahowald (Cascada), John Clonts (Raoul), Robert Ashford, Brett Barsky, Jeffrey Lee Broadhurst, Diana Brownstone, Randy Charleville, Erik Chechak, Marcos Dinnerstein, Alyssa Epstein, Ashley Freiberger, Debbi Fuhrman, Mai Goda, Randall Graham, Alan Gray, Kristin Hennessy, Sean Hennessy, Grace Hyndman, Peter Kapetan, Julietta Marcelli, Marty McDonough, Joan Mirabella, Todd Murray, Joel Newman, Wendy Piper, Robert Randle, Catherine Ruivivar, Barbara Scanlon, Marguerite Shannon, Cynthia Thole, Blythe Turmer, Gib Twitchell.

A CHORUS LINE with Music by Marvin Hamlisch; Lyrics, Edward Kleban; Book, James Kirkwood and Nocholas Dante; Restaged by Baayork Lee from Michael Bennett's original; Sets, Michael Anania; Lighting, Marilyn Rennagel; Costumes, José M. Rivera; Musical Direction, Albin Konopka. CAST: Canuto (Jared), Michele Chase (Kristine), Philip Clayton (Greg), Mindy Cooper (Bebe), Scott Coppola (Tom), Rieka Roberta Cruz (Ruby), Michael Danek (Zach), Kriss Dias (Val), Linda Gabler (Vivki), Lyd-Lyd Gaston (Connie), Aldrin Gonzals (Mark), Kelly Groninger (Judy), Jan Leigh Herndon (Sheila), Gib Jones (Don), Frank Kosik (Al), Tom Kosis (Larry), David La Duca (Roy), Jane Lanier (Cassie), Paula Leggett (Lois), Robert Longbottom (Bobby), Du'quon Mack (Butch), Mary Jo Mahaffey (Maggie), Michelle Mallardi (Diana), Joanne McHugh (Tricia), Eric Paeper (Paul), Michael Paternostro (Frank), Darnell Pritchard (Richie), Matt Zarley (Mike).

Jerry Dalia, Gerry Goodstein Photos

**Right: Judy Kaye, Richard White, Mark Janicello,
Hallie Neill in "Merry Widow"**

Judy Blazer, James Brennan in "Me and My Girl"

**Kathryn Meisle, Patrick Quinn, Marsha Waterbury
in "Lend Me a Tenor"**

**Daniel Reifsnyder, Tiffany Kriessler, George Grizzard,
Jesse Bernstein in "To Kill a Mockingbird"**

Darlene Bel Grayson, Michele Ragusa, Tia Speros in "Nunsense"

Steven Dennis, Martin La Platney in
"Pennultimate Problem of Sherlock Holmes"

PENNSYLVANIA STAGE COMPANY

Allentown, Pennsylvania
Eighth Season
October 10, 1990-June 16, 1991

Producing Director, Peter Wrenn-Meleck; General Manager, Elisabeth Stewart; Associate Artistic Director, Scott Edmiston; Stage Directors, Gavin Cameon-Webb, Scott Edmiston, Maureen Heffernon, Charlie Hensley, Peter Wrenn-Meleck; Sets, Bennet Averyt, Sarah Baptist, Curtis Dretsch, Rob Odorisio; Costumes, Gail Brassard, David Brooks, Kathleen Egan, Barbra Kravitz, Charlotte M. Yetman; Lights, Benet Averyt, Curtis Dretsch, Mark Evancho, Harry Feiner, Spencer Mosse; Stage Managers, Thomas M. Kauffman, Robert L. Young; Technical Director, William M. Kreider; Press, Michael Traupman. RESIDENT COMPANY: Bill Crouch, Jason Hale, Jeanne Hansell, Jane Wellington.

PRODUCTIONS AND CASTS

THE PENULTIMATE PROBLEM OF SHERLOCK HOLMES by John Nassivera; with Martin La Platney, Jonathan Bustle, Rica Martens, Jerry Perna, Kathleen L. Warner, Steven McCloskey, Jane Wellington, Robert Hock, Steven Dennis.
NUNSENSE by Dan Goggin; with Kathy Robinson, Lynn Eldredge, Darlene Bel Grayson, Tia Speros, Michele Ragusa.
SPEED-THE-PLOW by David Mamet; with Michael Hammond, Bruce Nozick, Carmen Thomas.
KURU (WORLD PREMIERE) by Josh Manheimer; with Brad Bellamy, Michael Haney, Sue Brady, Kathi Kennedy.
A WALK IN THE WOODS by Lee Blessing; with Michael Marcus, Richard Maynard.
THE RAINMAKER by N. Richard Nash; with John Ramsey, Kevin Jeffries, Bill Crouch, Kim Barber, Tim Halligan, Gerald Richards, Christopher Durham.
DRIVING MISS DAISY by Alfred Uhry; with Frances Helm, Nick Smith, Terry Layman.

Gregory M. Fota Photos

Right: Michael Hammond, Bruce Nozick in "Speed-the-Plow"
Center: Kim Barber, Christopher Durham in "The Rainmaker"

Michael Mastrototaro, Shareen J. Mitchell
in "the dreamer examines...."

Patricia Mauceri, Michael Patterson in "The Undoing"

PENGUIN REPERTORY COMPANY

Stony Point, New York
June 15, 1990-May 12, 1991

Artistic Director, Joe Brancato; Executive Director/Producer, Andrew M. Horn; Stage Managers, Sandra M. Bloom, Karen T. Federing, April Adams.

PRODUCTIONS AND CASTS

the dreamer examines his pillow by John Patrick Shanley; Director, Joe Brancato; Sets/Costumes, Michael Sharp; Lighting, Dennis W. Moyes. CAST: Jonathan Lutz (Dad), Michael Mastrototaro (Tommy), Shareen J. Mitchell (Donna).

THE UNDOING by William Mastrosimone; Director, Joe Brancato; Sets/Costumes, Michael Sharp; Lighting, David Neville. CAST: Funda Duyal (Lorr), Patricia Mauceri (Lorraine), Michael Patterson (Berk), Angela Scorese (Mrs. Mosca), Angela Trotta (Mrs. Corvo).

DEAR LIAR by Jerome Kilty; Director, Joe Brancato; Costumes, Wm. Pesce, Michael Sharp; Lighting, Dennis W. Moyes. CAST; Arlene Dahl (Mrs. Patrick Campbell), Robert Stattel (George Bernard Shaw).

WORD FAIL ME (WORLD PREMIERE) with music by Michael Leonard; Lyrics, Herbert Martin, Carolyn Leigh, Annie Lebeaux, Dorthea Joyce, Barbara James, Russell George, Sheila Davis, Marshall Barer; Monologues, Deborah Laufer and David Friedlander; Concption/Direction, Joe Brancato; Musical Director, Stever Sterner; Choreography, Robyn Gardenhire; Lighting, Dennis W. Moyes; Costumes, Benjamin Soencksen.

LADY DAY AT EMERSON'S BAR AND GRILL by Lanie Robertson; Director, Joe Brancato; Misical Director, Miche Braden; Sets, Lloyd Rothschild; Lighting, David Neville. CAST: Miche Braden (Billie Holiday), Neal Tate (Piano), Sir Hildred Humphries (Sax), Regina Carter (Violin).

Kerwin McCarthy Photos

Left: Cheryl Freeman, Michael DiGioia in "Words Fail Me" Center: Robert Stattel, Arlene Dahl in "Dear Liar"

PITTSBURGH PUBLIC THEATRE

Pittsburgh, Pennsylvania
Sixteenth Season
May 24, 1990-July 7, 1991

Producing Director, William T. Gardner; Managing Director, Dan Fallon.

PRODUCTIONS AND CASTS

ELEANOR (WORLD PREMIERE); Book by Jonathan Bolt; Music, Thomas Tierney; Lyrics, John Forster; Director, Mel Shapiro; Music Director, Keith Lockhart; Choreographer, Rob Marshall; Production Stage Manager, Jane Rothman; Scenic Design, Kerl Eigsti; Costume Designer, Laura Crow; Lighting Designer, Roger Morgan; Sound Designer, James Capenos. CAST: Kelly Aquino, Barbara Broughton, Ted Brunetti, Catherine Campbell, Anthony Cummings, Linda Gabler, Mary Jay, Tamara Jenkins, Joe Joyce, Ann Kittredge, Michael McCormick, James McCrum, Karyn Quackenbush, Dale Sandish, Allan Stevens, Ty Taylor, William Thunhurst.

THE NIGHT OF THE IGUANA by Tennessee Williams; Director, Claude Purdy; Production Stage Manager, Jane Rothman; Scenic Designer, James Sandefur; Costume Designer, Martha Hally; Lighting Designer, Phil Monat; Sound Designer, James Capenos. CAST: Yancey Arias, Amanda Charlton, Scott Foster, John Hall, Ruth Lesko, Larry John Myers, Clea Montville, Helena Ruoti, Scott Schweiger, Marco St. John, John Straub, Sheridan Thomas, William Thunhurst, Olivia Williams.

OUR TOWN by Thornton Wilder; Director, Robert William Ackerman; Production Stage Manager, Fred Noel; Scenic Designer, David Sackeroff; Costume Designer, Bob Wojewodski; Lighting Designer, Brian McDevitt; Sound Designer, James Capenos. CAST: Olivia Birkelund, Harry Bouvy, Donald Christopher, Gretchen Cleevely, Willard Crosby, Bill Dalzell III, Burt Edwards, Carol Ferguson, Mac Fleischmann, John Hall, Stephen Hanna, Ruby Holbrook, J.R. Horne, Celia Howard, Eric Kramer, Ken Milchick, Lowry Miller, John Haymes Newton, Emmett O'Sullivan-Moore, Myrna Paris, Eugenia Rawls, Michael Shelle, Eric Woodall.

SPEED-THE-PLOW by David Mamet; Director, Mel Shapiro; Production Stage Manager, Jane Rothman; Scenic/Costume Designer, Karl Eigsti; Lighting Designer, Andrew David Ostrowski; Sound Designer, James Capenos. CAST: David Butler, James Anthony Shanta, Ming-Na Wen.

MY CHILDREN! MY AFRICA! by Athol Fugard; Director, Peter Bennett; Production Stage Manager, Fred Noel; Scenic Designer, Gary English; Costume Designer, Jeffrey Ullman; Lighting Designer, Brian McDevitt; Sound Designer, James Capenos. CAST: Demitri Corbin, William Jay Marshall, Sabrina Reeves.

THE LAY OF THE LAND (WORLD PREMIERE) by Mel Shapiro; Director, Lee Grant; Production Stage Manager, Jane Rothman; Scenic Designer, Karl Eigsti; Costume Designer, Laura Crow; Lighting Designer, Dennis Parichy; Sound Designer, James Capenos. CAST: Greg Mullavey, Lisa Richards.

Ric Evans, Mark Portland Photos

"Eleanor"

Demitri Corbin, Sabrina Reeves in "My Children! My Africa!"

(Front) David Butler, James Anthony Shanta in "Speed-the-Plow"

PLAYMAKERS REPERTORY COMPANY

Chapel Hill, North Carolina
September 15, 1990-May 12, 1991

Executive Producer, Milly S. Barranger; Artistic Director, David Hammond; Managing Director, Regina F. Lickteig; Production Manager, Tom Neville, Sets/Costumes, McKay Coble; Lighting, Robert Wierzel; Stage Managers, Binnie J. Baggesen, Robert Russo; Voice Coach, Nancy Lane; Movement Coach, Craig Turner; Dramaturg, Adam Versenyi; Development, Gary Gambrell; Press/Marketing, Sharon Broom; Business Manager, Peter S. Kernan; Company Manager, Mary Robin Wells.

RESIDENT COMPANY: Timothy Altmeyer, Pat Barnett, Aaron Carlos, Dede Corvinus, Ray Dooley, Eve Eaton, Thomas Gunning, Stephen Haggerty, Pilar Herrera, Aaron James Knight, Daniel Krell, Emily Newman, Sam Potter, Susanna Rinehart, Blake Robison, Jeff West.

GUEST ARTISTS: Tobias Andersen, Peter Bradbury, Edmund Coulter, William Griffis, Annie Murray, Ken Strong, Craig Wroe.

PRODUCTIONS: *YOU NEVER CAN TELL* by George Bernard Shaw; Director, David Hammond. *NOTHING SACRED* by George F. Walker; Director, Eugene Lesser. *THE NUTCRACKER* by David Hammond from the stories of E.T.A. Hoffmann; Director, David Hammond. *THE MISER* by Moliere; Translated by Sara O'Connor; Director, William Woodman. *SCENES FROM AMERICAN LIFE* by A.R. Gurney, Jr.; Director, Bill Gile. *PERICLES* by William Shakespeare; Director, David Hammond.

Kevin Keister Photos

**Pilar Herrera, Ray Dooley
in "The Miser"**

**Tobias Anderson, Pilar Herrera
in "Nothing Sacred"**

Edmund Coulter, William Griffis in "You Never Can Tell"

**(front) Aaron Carlos, Aaron James Knight, Dede Corvinus,
(back) Susanna Rinehart, Pilar Herrera, Carol Anderson,
Jeffery West in "Scenes from American Life"**

**Connan Morrissey, Timothy Altmeyer
in "Nutcracker"**

Bruce Norris in "Making of Ashenden"

Amy Morton, Glenda Starr Kelley, Martha Lavey in "Jack"

REMAINS THEATRE

Chicago, Illinois

Director, Larry Sloane; General Manager, Janis Post; Ensemble Co-Directors, Amy Morton, William Peterson; Operations/Special Events Director, Chris Peterson; Development Director, Laura Samson; Public Relations Director, Jennifer Boznos.
RESIDENT COMPANY: Gerry Becker, Lucy Childs, Holly Fulger, Kevin Hurley, Ted Levine, Mary McAuliffe, Lindsay McGee, D.W. Moffett, Amy Morton, David Alan Novak, Chris Petersen, William Petersen, Natalie West.
GUEST ARTISTS: Tom Aulino, Larry Brandenburg, Maripat Donovan, Louise Freistadt, Bruce Norris, Susan Nussbaum, David Pasquesi, John Rubano, Glenda Starr Kelly, Liz Tannenbaum Greco, Willie Williams, Kathleen Winter, Will Zahrn.
DIRECTORS: Mary Zimmerman, Neel Keller, Larry Sloan, Jeff Michalski, Mike Nussbaum. MUSICIANS: Lloyd Brodnax King, Nicholas Kitsos, Johnse Holt, Paul Mertens, Rokko Jans, June Shellene. DESIGNERS: Steve Pickering, Davod Csicsko, Kevin Snow, Frances Maggio, Laura Cunningham, Hudson Fair.
PRODUCTIONS: *Jack* by David Greenspan; Director, Mary Zimmerman; *Rameau's Nephew* by Diderot; Adaptation, Andrei Belgrader, Shelly Berc; Director, Neel Keller; *American Buffalo* by David Mamet; Director, Mike Nussbaum.
WORLD PREMIERES: *The Making Of Ashenden* by Stanley Elkin; Adaptor/Director, Larry Sloan; *The Plucky and Spunky Show* by Susan Nussbaum and Mike Ervin; Director, Jeff Michalski.

Steve Leonard Photos

**Larry Brandenburg, William Petersen, Kevin Hurley
in "American Buffalo"**

Kevin Hurley, Bruce Norris in "Rameau's Nephew"

David Harum, Bruce Longworth in "Our Country's Good"

**Brenda Denmark, Laurine Towler, June Saunders Duell
in "From the Mississippi Delta"**

Carol Dilley, Tom Flagg in "Hollywood/Ukraine"

REPERTORY THEATRE OF ST. LOUIS

St. Louis, Missouri
September 5, 1990-April 13, 1991

Artistic Director, Steven Woolf; Managing Director, Mark D. Bernstein.

PRODUCTIONS AND CASTS

OUR COUNTRY'S GOOD by Timberlake Wertenbaker; Director, Edward Stern; Sets, Andrew Jackness; Costumes, Candice Donnelly; Lighting, Peter Kaczorowski; Stage Managers, Glen Dunn, Julia P. Jones. CAST: David Harum (Clark), David Schechter (Wisehammer/Phillip), Hubert Baron Kelly (Aboriginal Autralian/Tench/Black Caesar), Bruce Longworth (Collins/Sideway), Christopher McHale (Brewer/Campbell/Arscott), Kathleen Mahony-Bennett (Long/Brenham/Dawes), Carol Schultz (Bryant/Faddy), Lorraine Lanigan (Morden/Rev. Johnson), James Andreassi (Ross/Freeman), Leah Maddrie (Johnston/Smith).

THE HEIDI CHRONICLES by Wendy Wasserstein; Director, Jim O'Connor; Sets, Michael S. Philippi; Costumes, Dorothy L. Marshall; Lighting, Peter Sargent; Stage Managers, T.R. Martin, David S. Stewart. CAST: Marsha Waterbury (Heidi), Kathryn Rossetter (Susan), Christopher Reilly (Chris/Hippie/Shopper /Mark/Steve/Waiter/Ray), Murray Rubenstein (Scoop), Molly Price (Fran/Protester/Molly/Betsy/April), Kari Ely (Jill/Debbie/Lisa), Carmen Thomas (Becky/Clara/Denise).

A DAY IN HOLLYWOOD A NIGHT IN THE UKRAINE with Music by Frank Lazarus, Jerry Herman; Lyrics/Book, Dick Vosburgh; Director/Choreography, Pamela Hunt; Musical Director, Byron Grant; Sets, John Roslevich Jr.; Costumes, Dorothy L. Marshall; Lighting, Peter E. Sargent; Stage Managers, Glenn Dunn, Julia P. Jones. CAST: Celia Tackaberry (Mrs. Pavlenko), Tom Flagg (Carlo), Caro Dilley) (Gino), Michael McGrath (Serge B. Samovar), Peggy Taphorn (Nina), Michael Watson (Constantine), Jan Leigh Herndon (Masha), Kelly Williams (Sascha).

TERRA NOVA by Ted Tally; Director, Steven Woolf; Sets, Carolyn Ross; Costumes, John Carver Sullivan; Lighting, Max De Volder; Stgae Managers, T.R. Martin, David S. Stewart. CAST: Thomas Schall (Scott), Keith Jochim (Amundsen), Sherry Skinker (Kathleen), Joneal Joplin (Wilson), Richard Victor Esvang (Bowers), Whit Reichert (Oates), Jeff Herbst (Evans).

HENRY IV PART I by William Shakespeare; Director, Martin Platt; Sets, John Ezell; Costumes, Alan Armstrong; Lighting, Peter Maradudin; Fights, David Harum; Stage Managers, Glenn Dunn, Julia P. Jones. CAST: John Henry Cox (King Henry IV), David Harum (Henry, Prince of Wales), Eric Cole (Prince John), Robert Browning (Ralph Neville/Sheriff), Donald Christopher (Northumberland/Archbishop of York), Steven Gefroh (Hotspur), Leah Maddrie (Lady Percy), Ian Stuart (Worcester), Alan Clarey (Vernon/Gadshill), Ian Christopher (Servant), William Metzo (Blunt), Keith Jochim (Falstaff), David Heuvelman (Poins/Sir Michael), Jodie Lynne McClintock (Mistress Quickly), Ian Trigger (Bardolph), Roldan Lopez (Peto), Nathaniel Sanders (Frncis), Chistopher Reilly (March), A.D. Cover (Glendower), Jennifer Holmes (Lady Mortimer), Lachlan Maclelas), Bill Church, Chris Geiger, Chad Harris, Danny McCarthy, Randle Roper, Jana Ellis, Sara Zahendra.

DRIVING MISS DAISY by Alfred Uhry; Director, Susan Gregg; Sets, Joe Fontaine; Costumes, Holly Poe Durbin; Lighting, Max De Volder; Stage Managers, T.R. Martin, David S. Stewart. CAST: Darrie Lawrence (Daisy), Whit Reichert (Boolie), William Hall Jr. (Hoke).

STUDIO THEATRE

THE LAST SONG OF JOHN PROFFIT (WORLD PREMIERE) by Tommy Thompson; Director, Susan Gregg; Musical Director, Jack S. Herrick; Sets/Lighting, Dale F. Jordan; Costumes, Carole Tucker; Stage Manager, Champe Leary. CAST: Tommy Thompson (John Proffit), Clay Buckner (Fiddler).

FROM THE MISSISSIPPI DELTA by Dr. Endesha Ida Mae Holland; Director, Edward G. Smith; Sets, Jim Burwinkle; Costumes, Arthur Ridley; Lighting, Glenn Dunn; Stage Manager, Champe Leary. CAST: Laurine Towler, Brenda Denmark, June L. Saunders Duell.

DAYTRIPS by Jo Carson; Director, Tom Martin; Sets, William F. Schmiel; Costumes, Elizabeth Eisloeffel; Lighting, Joseph W. Clapper; Stage Manager, Champe Leary. CAST: Mickey Hartnett (Ree/Irene), Alexandra O' Karma (Pat), Cynthia Hayden (Narrator), Billie Lou Watt (Rose).

TOURING COMPANY: IMAGINARY THEATRE

COMPANY: Patricia Pierre-Antoine, Tracy Arnold, KellyAnn Corcoran, Christian Malmin.
PRODUCTIONS: *A Thousand Cranes* by Kathryn Schultz Miller; Director, Jeffrey Matthews; *Alice in Wonderland* by Susie Bradley; Director, Jeffrey Matthews; *A Holiday Garland of Tales* by Kim Allen Bozar; Director, Tom Martin.

Judy Andrews Photos

Left: Patricia Pierre-Antoine (back), Kelly Ann Corcoran, Tracy Arnold, Christian Malmin in "A Thousand Cranes"

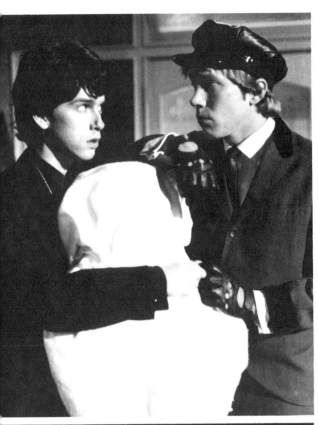

SAN DIEGO REPERTORY THEATRE

San Diego, California
June 1, 1990–February 17, 1991

Producing Director, Sam Woodhouse; Artistic director, Douglas Jacobs; Managing Director, Adrian Stewart; Artistic Associate, Todd Salovey; Production Manager, John Redman; General Manager, Michael Murphy; Communications/Development Director, Kirsten Brandt; Marketing Director, Keith Davis.

PRODUCTIONS AND CASTS

LATINS ANONYMOUS; Written and Performed by Luisa Leschin, Armando Molina, Rick Najera, Dianne Rodriguez; Director, Miguel Delgado, Jose Cruz Gonzales; Sets, Victoria Petrovich; Lighting, Brenda Barry; Costumes/Props, Patssi Valdez, Jim Reva; Arrangements, David Torres; Sound, Adam Wartnik, Nathan Stein; Stage Manager, Ronn Goswick.

LOOT by Joe Orton; Director, Walter Schoen; Sets, Thomas Buderwitz; Costumes, Emelle Holmes; Lighting, Dianne Boomer; Sound, Lawrence Czoka; Stage Manager, Julie Moore. CAST: Maury Cooper, Diana Castle, Jon Matthews, Bruce McKensie, Tom Oleniacz, Paul James Kruse, Suanne Schefke.

A LOVELY SUNDAY FOR CREVE COEUR by Tennessee Williams; Director, Douglas Jacobs; Sets, Neil Patel; Costumes, Mary Gibson; Lighting, Brenda Berry; Sound, Lawrence Czoka; Stage Manager, Julie A. Moore. CAST: Darla Cash, Diana Castle, Rosina Widdowson-Reynolds, Kim Porter.

BURN THIS by Lanford Wilson; Director, Sam Woodhouse; Sets, Robert Brill; Costumes, Christine Dougherty; Lighting, Ashly York Kennedy; Sound, Lawrence Czoka; Fights, Martin Katz; Stage Manager, Julie A. Moore. CAST: Deborah Van Valkenburgh, Andrew Barnicle, Jon Matthews, Robert Duncan.

CYMBELINE by William Shakespeare; Director, Douglas Jacobs, Sets/Lighting, Brenda Berry; Costumes, Catherine Meacham Hunt; Music, Johnathan Sacks; Sound, Will Parsons; Stage Manager, Jerome J. Sheeman. CAST: Damon Bryant, Darla Cash, Bill Dunnam, John Joseph Freeman, Eric Grischkat, Bruce McKenzie, Johathan McMurtry, Thom Murray, Ian Ross, J. Michael Ross, Terres Unsoeld, Rosina Widdowson-Reynolds.

A CHRISTMAS CAROL by Charles Dickens; Adaptation, Douglas Jacobs; Directors, Mr. Jacobs, Travis Ross; Sets, Thomas Buderwitz; Costumes, Mary Larson; Lighting, John B. Forbes; Sound, Malcolm Lowe; Composer/Arranger, Linda Vickermans; Choreography, Bruce Nelson; Stage Manager, Julie A. Moore. CAST: Kory Abosada, Richard Allen, Osayande Baruti, Beth Bayless, Paul James Kruse, Helen Reed Lehman, Olga Macias, Bruce Nelson, Lance E. Nichols, Richard Ortega, Dana Pere, Tavis Ross, Leon Singer, Alyce Smith-Cooper, Christina Soria, Mary Kay Wulf.

MAN OF THE FLESH/EL LADRON DE CORAZONES by Octavio Solis; Directors, Sam Woodhouse, Jorge Huerta; Sound/Music, Frederick B. Lanuza; Sets/Costumes, Victoria Petrovich; Lighting, Brenda Berry; Choreography, Miguel De Jerome J. Sheehan. CAST: Hector Correa, Gonzalo Madurga, Alma Martinez, Andres Monreal, Javi Mulero, Giselle Rubino, Jeanette Sepulveda, Cristina Soria.

THE LIFE AND LIFE OF BUMPY JOHNSON (WORLD PREMIERE) by Amiri Baruka; Music, Max Roach; Director, George Ferencz; Sets, Bill Stabile; Costumes, Sally J. Lesser; Lighting, Ashley York Kennedy; Stage Manager, Julie A. Moore. CAST: Babidiyi Abernathy, Osayande Baruti, Ronnel Bey, Jason Booker, Damon Bryant, Robert Duncan, Damon Eskridge, Tracy Hughes, Antonio Johnson, David Kirkwood, Carol Maillard, Bruce McKenzie, Lance Roberts, Louis Seitchik, Drew Trombello, Kevin Flournoy.

Ken Jacques Photos

Left: Terres Unsoeld, Bruce McKenzie in "Cymbeline"
Top: Jon Matthews, Bruce McKenzie in "Loot"

SEATTLE REPERTORY THEATRE

Seattle, Washington
October 10, 1990-May 18, 1991

PRODUCTIONS AND CASTS

MUCH ADO ABOUT NOTHING by William Shakespeare; Director, Stan Wojewodski Jr.; Scenic designer, Derek McLane; Costume Designer, Catherine Zuber; Lighting Designer, Stephen Strawbridge; Sound Designer, Steven M. Klein; Vocal Coach, Deborah Hecht; Dramaturg, Mark Bly. CAST: John Aylward, John Boylan, Jeannie Carson, Mark Chamberlin, Mark Gallagher, Stephen Godwin, Lou Hetler, Byron Jennings, David S. Klein, Leslie Law, Blayn Lemke, Mark Lien, Carolyn McCormick, William Biff McGuire, David Mong, Victor Morris, Marianne Owen, Tony Soper, Amy Thone, Rick Tutor, William Westenberg, R. Hamilton Wright.

THE HOUSE OF BLUE LEAVES by John Guare; Director, Douglas Hughes; Scenic Designer, Tim Sternow; Costume Designer, Rose Pederson; Lighting Designer, Pat Collins; Sound Designer, Steven J. Klein; CAST: John Aylward, Jane Galloway, Jody Aryn Hahn, Torrey Hanson, Blayn Lemke, Amy Mack, Marianne Owen, Susy Schneider, Amy Thone, Rick Tutor, William Westenberg.

TWO TRAINS RUNNING by August Wilson; Director, Lloyd Richards; Scenic Designer, Tony Fanning; Costume Designer, Chris Karvonides; Lighting Designer, Geoff Korf; Sound Consultant, Michael Holten. CAST: Anthony Chisholm, Larry Fishburne, Ed Hall, Ella Joyce, Chuck Patterson, Sullivan Walker, Al White.

SIX CHARACTERS IN SEARCH OF AN AUTHOR by Luigi Pirandello; English Version by Robert Cornthwaite; Director, Liviu Ciulei; Scenic Designer, Liviu Ciulie; Costume Designer, Smaranda Branescu; Lighting Designer, Alan Lee Hughes; Sound Designer, Steven M. Klein; Dramaturg, Mark Bly; Additional Dialog, Lloyd Rose. CAST: Ann Buchanan, Jeannie Carson, T. Scott Cunningham, Ted D'Arms, Rosemary DeAngelis, Funda Duyal, Woddy Eney, Natalya Eyzaguirre, Katie Forgette, Lou Hetler, Laura Kenny, William Biff McGuire, Majorie Nelson, Marianne Owen, Ken Ruta, Tom Spiller, Rick Tutor, R. Hamilton Wright, Wendell Wright, Claire Zimmerman.

THE MISER by Moliere; New Englih version by Douglas Hughes; Director, Mr. Hughes; Scenic Designer, Hugh Landwehr; Costume Designer, Catherine Zuber; Lighting Designer, Peter Maradudin; Sound Designer, Steven M. Klein; Dramaturg, Mark Bly. CAST: John Aylward, Ann Buchanan, T. Scott Cunningham, Woody Eney, Katie Forgette, Rex McDowell, Marianne Owen, Tom Spiller, Rick Tutor, R. Hamilton Wright, Wendell Wright.

CONVERSATIONS WITH MY FATHER (WORLD PREMIERE) by Herb Gardner; Director, Daniel Sullivan; Scenic Designer, Tony Walton; Costume Designer, Robert Wojewodshi; Lighting Designer, Pat Collins; Sound Designer, Michael Holten; Movement Consultant, Gwen Verdon; Dramaturg, Mark Bly. CAST: Jason M. Biggs, June Gable, Benny Grant, Sean G. Griffin, Judd Hirsch, William Biff McGuire, John Procaccino, Gordana Rashovich, Lee Richardson, Rick Schatz, Tony Shalhoub, Jack Wallace.

Tony Shalhoub, Gordana Rashovich, Judd Hirsch
in "Conversations with My Father"

Kenneth L. Marks, Kitty Crooks in "Elliot Loves"

STAGE 2 SEASON; THE PONCHO FORUM

LONG DAY'S JOURNEY INTO NIGHT by Eugene O'Neill; Director, Michael Engler; Scenic Designer, Andrew Jackness; Costume Designer, Rose Pederson; Lighting Designer, Peter Maradudin; Sound Designer, Steven M. Klein. CAST: Patrick Breen, Katie Forgette, William Biff McGuire, John Procaccino, Marion Ross.

HOME AND AWAY (WORLD PREMIERE) by Kevin Kling; Director, Kenneth Washington; Scenic Designer, Tim Sternow; Lighting Designer, Marcus F. Dillard; Sound Designer, Steven M. Klein; Dramaturg, Mark Bly. CAST: Kevin Kling.

ELLIOT LOVES by Jules Feiffer; Director, John Ferraro; Scenic Designer, Rick Dennis; Costume Designer, Rose Pederson; Lighting Designer, Richard Moore; Sound Designer, Steven M. Klein. CAST: Kitty Crooks, Kenneth L. Marks, Aleta Mitchell, Bob Morrisey, Gary Roberts, Mark Smaltz.

Chris Bennion Photos

R. Hamilton Wright, Wendell Wright, Ken Ruta in "Six Characters..."

STUDIO ARENA THEATRE

Buffalo, New York
Twenty-sixth Season

Artistic Director, David Frank; Executive Director, Raymond Bonnard; Development Director, Anne E. Hayes; Marketing Director, Courtney J. Walsh; Operations Manager, Jonathan L. White; Production Manager, Randy Engels; Education Director, Deborah Nitzberg; Controller, James J. Gumulak; Press, Jean Whitchen.

PRODUCTIONS AND CASTS

A FLEA IN HER EAR by Georges Feydeau; Adaptation, David Frank; Translation, Abbott Chrisman; Director, Mr. Frank; Sets/Costumes, Philipp Jung; Lighting, Michael Chybowski; Fights, Martino N. Pistone; Stage Manager, Glenn Bruner. CAST: Joseph Fuqua (Camille), Barbara Wydysh (Antoinette), David Cromwell (Etienne), Robert Spencer (Finache), Lorna C. Hill (Lucienne), Anne Newhall (Raymonde), John Rainer (Victor), David Hyde-Lamb (Romain), Martino N. Pistone (Carlos), Diane DiBernardo (Euginie), Brian LaTulip (Augustin), Gerald Finnegan (Olympe/LaRou/Baptistin), John Kiouses (Trautman), John Rainer (Poche), Ellen Opiela, Keith Carcich.
JANE EYRE with Music By David Clark; Lyrics/Book/Direction, Ted Davis; Based on the novel by Charlotte Bronte; Sets/Slides, Bob Barnett; Costumes, Pamela Scofield; Lighting, F. Mitchell Dana; Sound, Rick Menke; Musical Director, Corinne Aquilina; Orchestrations, Eric Allaman; Movement, Jim Hoskins; Stage Manager, Sally Ann Wood. CAST: Amanda Becker (Adele), Becky Lord (Adele), Melissa Gallagher (Georgiana/Miss Temple/Grace/Rosamond), Jayne Houdyshell (Bessie/Mrs. Fairfax/Hannah), Matthew Kimbrough (Reed/Butler/Wood), Joel Leffert (Mason/Doctor/Servant/Coachman), Cecile Mann (Mrs. Reed/Leah/Bertha/Mary), Charles Pistone (Rochester), Maryann Plunkett (Charlotte/Jane Eyre), David Pursley (Brocklehurst/Briggs/Old John), Maureen Sadusk (Mrs. Ingram/Miss Scatcherd), Jean Tafler (Eliza/Helen/Blanche/Diana), Greg Zerkle (Lloyd/Clerk/Carter/St. John Rivers).
A CHRISTMAS CAROL by Charles Dickens; Adaptation, Amlin Gray; Director, David Frank; Sets/Lighting, Paul Wonsek; Costumes, Mary Ann Powell; Choreography, Linda H. Swiniuch; Sound, Rick Menke; Stage Manager, Glenn Bruner. CAST: Robert Spencer (Scrooge), Brad Bellamy (Philanthropist/Fezziwig/Flipfield/Businessman), Aaron Cabell (Wilkins/Topper/Ghost of Time to Come), Nora Cole (Shopper/Mrs. Cratchit/Vagrant), Kevin Donovan (Cratchit/Throttle/Businessman), Meghan Rose Krank (Belle/Holly/Sissy), Jane Macfie (Christmas Past/Shopper/Maria), Peter Toran (Fred/Young Scrooge/Shopper), William Verderber (Philanthropist/Stepfather/Christmas Prsent), Arn Weiner (Marley/Mrs. Fezziwig/Old Joe), Margot Albert, Nadia Grabiner (Harriet), Christopher Battaglia, Ali Raza (Boy Scrooge/Urchin), Andrea Cinq-Mars, Rachel Williams (Martha), Gwendolyn Frank (Belinda/Urchin), Maureen Jones (Belinda/Urchin), Justin Jarosz, Jay Yeagle (Frederick), Philip Jarosz, Sebastian Nicholas Pratt (Peter/Turkey Boy), Sara Sansone, Ashley Wahl (Tiny Tim), Thane Schulz, Ron Veiders (Caroler), Susan Braen, John Kiouses.
BIRDSEND by Keith Huff; Director, Kathryn Long; Sets, Tom Kamm; Costumes, David C. Wollard; Lighting, Peter Kaczorowski; Sound, Rick Menke; Fights, Steven Vaughn; Music, Robert Volkman; Stage Manager, Sally Ann Wood. CAST: Richard Hicks (Pantomime), Donald Berman (Bird), Susan Batten (Margie), Nora Cole (Cathy), Richard Hicks (Ig), Walt MacPherson (Albert), John-David Wilder (Ben), Taylor Howard (Jules), Mary O'Brady (Josephine).
DRIVING MISS DAISY by Alfred Uhry; Director, William Gregg; Sets, James Fenhagen; Costumes, Susan E. Mickey; Lighting, F. Mitchell Dana; Music, Robert Waldman; Stage Manager, Glenn Bruner. CAST: Glynis Bell (Daisy), Marcial Howard (Hoke), Grover Zucker (Boolie).

Ray Virta, Nancy Marchand, Katherine Leask in "Children"

Charles Pistone, Maryann Plunkett in "Jane Eyre"

THE CAUCASIAN CHALK CIRCLE by Bertolt Brecht; Director, Kathryn Long; Sets, Anne Donnelly; Lighting, Nancy Schertler; Sound, Rick Menke; Music/Music Direction, Donald Rebic; Movement, Tom Ralabate; Stage Manager, Sally Ann Wood. CAST: Mark Bottita (Ironshirt), Laverne Clay (Eldest Architect/Farmer/Divorcing Man), Mark W. Conklin (Aide-de-Camp/Ironshirt/Doctor), Mary Craig (Nina/Farmer/Divorcing Wife), Andre De Shields (Story Teller), Jason Fitz-Gerald (Soldier/Simon/Lame Man), Verna Hampton (Goat Herder/Cook/Adpoting Farmer's Wife), Mary Helena (Agronomist/Masha/Aniko), Stephen McKinley Henderson (Expert/Doctor/Azdak), Patrick Herwood (Ironshirt), Jack Landron (Fat Prince/Lavrenti/Irakli/Lawyer), Roma Maffia (Governor's Wife/Peddler/Ludovika), Don Mayo (Rice Grower/Doctor/Grand Duke/Father-in Law), Jasper McGruder (Stable Man/Milk Man/Trial Farmer), Michael Nostrand (Governor/Peddler/Yussuip/Shauva), Ascanio Sharpe (Rice Grower/Maro/Mother-in-Law/St. Banditus Woman), Robert Spencer (Goat Herder/Corporal/Drunk/Invalid), Teresina (Tractor Driver/Grusha), Chistopher Verel (Architect/Irionshirt), Brian M. Ward (Ironshirt), Kevin Ward (Serving Man/Ironshirt/Nephew/Junior Lawyer), Tim White (Ironshirt/Peddler/Hired Hand), Fattaah Taarig Dinaan, Juba Jabulani Lomotey (Biggest Boy), Michael Bannerman-Martin, Justin Brocato (2nd Boy), Hope Olani Dove, Angel Steele (Girl), Joseph Koehn, Jessica Lynn Pratt (Michael).
CHILDREN by A.R. Gurney; Director, Paul Sparer; Sets, John Lee Beatty; Costumes, Mary Ann Powell; Lighting, Dennis Parichy; Sound, Rick Menke; Stage Manager, Glenn Bruner. CAST: Katherine Leask (Barbara), Ray Virta (Randy), Nancy Marchand (Mother), Katie Sparer (Jane), Gabriel Armstrong, Nathaniel Armstrong, Jillian Barnett, Darick Corbett, Justin Fuller, Alexis Page, Elizabeth slater, Jay Slater.

Irene Haupt, Gelfand-Piper Photos

Martino N. Pistone, Lorna C. Hill, David Hyde-Lamb, Robert Spencer, Brian LaTulip, Anne Newhall, (floor) John Rainer in "Flea in Her Ear"

SYRACUSE STAGE

Syracuse, New York
Eighteenth Season
October 2, 1990-May 5, 1991

Producing Artistic Director, Arthur Storch; Managing Director, James A. Clark; Business Manager, Diana Coles; Development, Shirley Lockwood; Marketing, Barbara Beckos; Press, Barbara Haas; Company Manager, Peter Sandwall; Stage Manager, Don Buschmann; Literary Coordinator, Howard Kerner; Production Manager, Kerro Knox 3; Technical Director, William S. Tiesi; Lighting Coordinator, Sandra Schilling; Sound Designer, James Wildman; Properties Coordinator, Dana Baker; Costumer, Maria Marrero.

PRODUCTIONS AND CASTS

THREE SISTERS by Anton Chekhov; Director, John Going; Translated by Michael Henry Heim; Sets, James Wolk; Costumes, Pamela Scofield; Lighting, Phil Monat; Musical Director, Terry Runnels. CAST: Jack Aranson (Chebutykin), Gil Cates Jr. (Rodet), Robert Cenedella (Ferapont), Edith Fisher (Anfisa), Daryll Heysham (Solyony), Bill Kux (Andrei), Peter Kybart (Kulygin), Devora Millman (Natasha), Pat Nesbit (Olga), Michael Rego (Fedotik), Guilia Pagano (Masha), Tisha Roth (Irina), Steve Routman (Tusenbach), Ken Ruta (Vershinin).

THE COCKTAIL HOUR by A.R. Gurney; Director, William Woodman; Set, Gary May; Costumes, Maria Marrero; Lighting, Harry Feiner; Sound, James Wildman. CAST: Daren Kelly (John), Edmund Lyndeck (Bradley), Robin Moseley (Nina), Dolores Sutton (Ann).

AS YOU LIKE IT by William Shakespeare; Director, Libby Appel; Sets, Michael Miller; Costumes, Nanzi Adzima; Lighting, Phil Monat; Sound, James Wildman; Musical Staging, Andrew Grose; Musical Direction, Louis Goldberg. CAST: Susan Appel (Rosalind), Michael Bartoli (Dennis/Jaques de Boys); Ray Chambers (Orlando), Kymberlly Dakin (Phebe), J. Michael Flynn (LeBeau/Jaques), Malcolm Ingram (Walter/Corin); Tim Johnson (Hymen), Erik Knutsen (Oliver), Peter Kybart (Duke Frederick/Duke Senior), Peter Moller (Adam), Karen O'Connell (Audrey), Erik Onate (Charles/William), David Ponting (Sir Oliver Martext), Michael Rego (Silvius), Tisha Roth (Celia), Howard Samuelsohn (Touchstone), Jacque Tara Wahington (Amiens).

THE MYSTERY OF IRMA VEP by Charles Ludlam; Director, Robert Fuhrmann; Set, Dan Conway; Costumes, Dan Newcomb; Lighting, Phil Monat; Sound, James Wildman; Music, Peter Golub. CAST: P.J. Benjamin (Nicodemus/Lady Enid/Alcazar), Davis Hall (Lord Edgar/Jane Twisden).

FENCES by August Wilson; Director, Clause Purdy; Set, Jim Sandefur; Costumes, Martha Hally; Lighting, Phil Monat; Sound, Tom Mardikes. CAST: Willis Burks II (Bono), Jar'La Evans (Raynell), Noble Lee Lester (Lyons), Marion McClinton (Gabriel), Delores Mitchell (Rose), Patrice Peterson (Raynell), John Henry Redwood (Troy Maxson).

ROUGH CROSSING by Tom Stoppard; Music, Andre Previn; Director, Arthur Storch; Sets/Costumes, Timothy Averill; Lighting, Kerro Knox 3; Sound, James Wildman; Musical Staging, Andrew Grose; Musical direction, Louis goldberg. CAST: Allison Briner (Natasha), Edward Conery (Turai), MichaelJohn McGann (Gal), Steve Routman (Dvornichek), Peter Shawn (Ivor), Bill Ullman (Adam).

Lawrence Mason, Jr. Photos

(top) Davis Hall, P.J. Benjamin in "The Mystery of Irma Vep"

Darren Kelly, Edmund Lyndeck in "The Cocktail Hour"

Kendall Hailey, Paul Linke in
"Joanna's Husband and David's Wife"

Pat Dwyer, Bill Jenkins in "Eastern Standard"

THEATRE THREE

Dallas, Texas
Twenty-ninth Season
June 23, 1990-March 23, 1991

Artistic Director/Founder, Norma Young; Executive Producer/Director, Jac Alder; Associate Producer, Laurence O'Dwyer; Associate Producer, Cheryl Denson; Production Stage Manager, Terry Tittle Holman; Musical Director, Terry Dobson; Costumer, Diana Figueroa Story; Technical Director, Tristan Wilson; Administration Director, Chris Harsdorff; Publicist, Gary Yawn.

PRODUCTIONS AND CASTS

JOANNA'S HUSBAND AND DAVID'S WIFE by Elizabeth Forsythe Hailey; Director, Charles Nelson Reilly; Sets, Jac Alder, Cheryl Denson; Lighting, Linda Blase. CAST: Kendall Hailey, Paul Linke.
EASTERN STANDARD by Richard Greenberg; Director, Cheryl Denson; Sets, Wade J. Giampa; Lighting, Linda Blase; Sound, Tristan Wilson. CAST: Tamara Adams, John S. Davies, Pat Dwyer, Patti Heider, Bill Jenkins, Cheryl Norris.
LONDON ASSURANCE by Dion Bouciault; Director, Jac Alder; Sets, Harland Wright; Costumes, Diana Figueroa Story; Lighting, Linda Blase. CAST: Georgia Clinton, Eric Galatas, Lynn Mathis, Ryland Merkey, Laurence O'Dwyer, Thomas Owen, Elaine Pfleiderer, Blair Sams, Malcolm Simpson, Terry Vandivort, Trey Walpole, Chris Westfall.
ACCOMPLICE by Rupert Holmes; Director, Cheryl Denson; Sets, Wade J. Giampa; Costumes, Diana Figueroa Story; Lighting, Linda Blase. CAST: Jennifer Griffin, Bill Jenkins, L. Gregg Loso, Brenda Westbrook.
JOE TURNER'S COME AND GONE by August Wilson; Director, Margie Johnson Reese. CAST: Sherry R. Boyd, Aldo Billingslea, Grover Coulson Jr., Lenikka Hardman, Jonathan Norton, Myra Joyce Nowlin, Laurence O'Dwyer, Jim Ponds, Terrence Charles Rodgers, Summer Selby, Vickie Washington.
WEILL WOMEN with Music by Kurt Weill; Lyrics, Maxwell Anderson, Bertolt Brecht, Jean Cocteau, Lion Feuchtwager, Ira Gershwin, Oscar Hammerstein, Langston Hughes, Georg Kaiser, Alan Jay Lerner, Maurice Magre, Ogden Nash, Walt Whitman; Director/Devised by Jac Alder; Musical Director, Terry Dobson; Sets, Harland Wright; Costumes, Diana Figueroa Story; Lighting, Linda Blase, Sound, Tristan Wilson. CAST: Sherry R. Boyd, Sharon Bunn, Connie Coit, Naomi Hatsfelt.

Linda Blase, Susan Kandell Photos

Right: Eric Galatas, Chris Westfall, Elaine Pfleiderer in "London Assurance" Center: Connie Nelson, Denise Le Brut, Naomi Hatsfelt, Sharon Bunn, Connie Coit, Sherry R. Boyd in "Weill Women"

Dawn Didawick, Harry Groener
in "Born Yesterday"

Carl Schurr, Wil Love, Jan Puffer in "Dial M for Murder"

Jayne Houdyshell, Curtis Armstrong in "Charley's Aunt"

Susie Wall, David Holt
in "Voice of the Prairie"

TOTEM POLE PLAYHOUSE

Fayetteville, Pennsylvania
June 2, 1990-December 23, 1990

Producing Artistic Director, Carl Schurr; Managing Director, Sue Kocek; Associate Artistic Directors, Wil Love, Robert Spencer; Resident Set Designer, James Fouchard; Resident Costume Designer, Patricia M. Risser; Resident Lighting Designer, Dave Brown; Production Stage Managers, Bryan Burch, Cosmo P. Hanson; Resident Composer, Terrence Sherman; Guest Director, Steve Woolf; Technical Director, Eugene Lee Moxley.

PRODUCTIONS AND CASTS

THE VOICE OF THE PRAIRIE by John Olive; Director, Steve Woolf; Sets, James Fouchard; Costumes, Dorothy L. Marshall; Lighting, Dave Brown. CAST: Joneal Joplin (Poppy/David Quinn/Frankie's Father/Watermelon Man), David Holt (Davey/Leon Schwab/James/Jailer), Susie Wall (Frankie/Susie/Frances Reed).
DIAL "M" FOR MURDER by Frederick Knott; Director, Robert Spencer; Set; James Fouchard; Costumes, Patricia M. Risser; Lights, Dave Brown. CAST: Jan Puffer (Margot Wendice), Paul DeBoy (Max Halliday), Carl Schurr (Tony Wendice), Richert Easley (Captain Lesgate), Wil Love (Inspector Hubbard), Robert Sean Fri (Thompson), Kip Veasey (Williams).
BORN YESTERDAY by Garson Kanin; Director, Carl Schurr; Set; James Fouchard; Costumes, Patricia M. Risser; Lights, Dave Brown. CAST: Jan Puffer (Helen), Harry Groener (Paul Verrall), Robert Sean Fri (A Bellhop), Nicholas Webster (Another Bellhop/A Bootblack/A Waiter)), Robert Spencer (Eddie Brock), Paul DeBoy (Assistant Manager), Bob Ari (Harry Brock), Dawn Didawick (Billie Dawn), Wil Love (Ed Devery), Kip Veasey (A Barber), Bronwyn Dodsn (A Manicurist), Richert Easley (Senator Norval Hedges), Jayne Houdyshell (Mrs. Hedges).
CHARLEY'S AUNT by Brandon Thomas; Director, Wil Love; Set, James Fouchard; Costumes, Patricia M. Risser; Lights, Dave Brown; Original Score, Terrence Sherman. CAST: Paul DeBoy (Jack Chesney), Richert Easley (Brassett), Alexander Webb (Charles Wyckham), Curtis Armstrong (Lord Fancourt Babberley), Jan Puffer (Kitty Verdun), Shirleyann Kaladjian (Amy Spettigue), Carl Schurr (Col. Sir Francis Chesney), Robert Spencer (Stephen Spettigue), Jayne Houdyshell (Donna Lucia D'Alvadorez), Bronwyn Dodson (Ela Delahjay).
BAREFOOT IN THE PARK by Neil Simon; Director, Carl Schurr; Set, John Ovington; Costumes, Patricia M. Risser; Lights, Dave Brown. CAST: Shirleyann Kaladjian (Corie Bratter), Robert Spencer (Telephone Repair Man), Bob Harrison (Delivery Man), Alexander Webb (Paul Bratter), Jayne Houdyshell (Mrs. Banks); Wil Love (Victor Velasco).
DRIVING MISS DAISY by Alfred Uhry; Director, Robert Spencer; Set, James Fouchard; Costumes, Patricia M. Risser; Lights, Dave Brown. CAST: Linde Hayen (Daisy Werthan), Wil Love (Boolie Werthan), Keith Johnson (Hoke Coleburn).
A CHRISTMAS CAROL by Charles Dickens; Adapted by Wil Love and Carl Schurr; Director, Mr. Schurr; Assistants to Mr. Schurr, Jan Puffer and Kay Yaukey; Set, James Fouchard; Costumes, Patricia M. Risser; Lights, Dave Brown; Music, Terrence Sherman. CAST: Wil Love (Ebenezer Scrooge), Laurence Overmire (Bob Cratchit), Francis Parkman (Fred/Christmas Future), Jeanne Tron (Charity Lady), Bob Tron (Charity Man/Old Joe); Christopher Tickner (Marley); Jan Puffer (Christmas Past), Richert Easley (Christmas Present/Mr. Fezziwig); Richard Adams (Young Scrooge), Susan Duvall (Mrs. Fezziwig/Mrs. Dilber); Helen Hedman (Belle/Laundress), Carl Schurr (Belle's Husband), Johanna Ezell (Mrs. Cratchit), Kay Yaukey (Fred's Wife), Sandra Sorenson (Fred's Guest); Lee Merriman, Gregory Walker, Chris Russo, Charles Mills, William Cramer, Annie Cramer, Cory Hummer, Emily Zullinger, Jacqueline Michael Rebok, Joseph L. Brener, Katrina Yaukey, Kevin Zullinger.

Cellar Studio Photos

154

TRINITY REPERTORY COMPANY

Providence, Rhode Island
Twenty-seventh Season
October 2, 1990-June 9, 1991

Artistic Director, Richard Jenkins; Assistant to Director, Neal Baron; Resident Designer, Eugene Lee; Set Design, Robert Soule; Resident Costume Designer, William Lane; Assistant Costume Designer, Marilyn Salvatore; Lighting Design, John F. Custer, Michael Giannitti; Properties Master, Randy Savoy; Audio Design, Anthony PM Ricci; Stage Managers, Dennis A. Blackledge, Shannon Giannitti, David Glynn; General Manager, Dennis Conway; Press, Lynn Kelly.

RESIDENT COMPANY: William Damkoehler, Howard London, Andrew Mutnick, Allen Oliver, Fred Sullivan, Nanette Van Wright, Daniel von Bargen, Dan Welch, Patricia McGuire, Anne Scurria, Jerome Davis, Peter Gerety, Timothy Crowe, Ed Shea, Anne Gerety, Janice Duclos, Brian McEleney, Cynthia Strickland, Jonathan Fried, Stephen Berenson, David Kennett, Barbara Orson, Barbara Meek, Ed Hall, Rochel Coleman.

GUEST ACTORS: Darryl Alladice, Mark Breland, Dee Hennigan, Gustave Johnson, Lindsay Crouse, Barry Press, Dee Pelletier, Jack Willis, Ralph Waite.

OTHER GUEST ARTISTS: David Wheeler, Leonard Foglia, Lee Shalit, Judith Swift, Natasha Katz, John Gromada.

PRODUCTIONS: *Golden Boy*, *Juno and the Paycock*, *Christmas Carol*, *School for Wives*, *Frankie and Johnny*, *Reckless*, *The Stick Wife*, *Other People's Money*.

WORLD PREMIERE: *The Water Principle* by Eliza Anderson.

Mark Morelli Photos

Left: Timothy Crowe, Patricia McGuire in "School for Wives"
Top: Cynthia Strickland, Peter Gerety in "Frankie and Johnny..."

Anne Scurria, Lindsay Crouse in "Reckless"

YALE REPERTORY THEATRE

New Haven, Connecticut
September 18, 1990-May 25, 1991

PRODUCTIONS AND CASTS

IVANOV by Anton Chekhov; Translated by Robert W. Corrigan; Adapted/Directed, Oleg Yefremov; Setting, David Borovsky; Costumes, Jess Goldstein; Lighting, Geoff Korf; Sound, Jamie Anderson; Associate Director, Victor Steinbach. CAST: Leo Burmester, Frances Conroy, Malcolm Gets, William Hurt, Ann Hutchinson, Zeljko Ivanek, Bernard Jaffe, Ruth Jaffe, Martha Johnson, Susan Kellerman, Sarah Long, Carol Lowrance, Mary Mara, Tom McGowan, William Mesnik, Bill Nesta, Austin Pendleton, Anne Pitoniak, Lee Richardson, Maggie Robert, Liev Schreiber, Kimberly Squires, Jayce Van Patten, Tom Whyte.

LARGO DESOLATO by Vaclav Havel, English version by Tom Stoppard; Director, Gitta Honegger; Setting, Allison Koturbash; Costumes, Elizabeth Hope Clancy; Lighting, Mark L. McCullough; Sound, Jon Newstrom. CAST: Ludmila Bokievsky, Matthew Burnett, Jordan Charney, Kristin Flanders, Matthew Locricchio, Reg Rogers, Victor Steinbach, Paul Stolarsky, Jan Triska, Julie White.

SEARCH AND DESTROY by Howard Korder; Director, David Chambers; Setting, Christopher Barreca; Costumes, Dunya Ramicova; Lighting, Chris Parry; Sound, David Budries; Production Photography, Joel Greenberg. CAST: Christopher Bauer, Robert Beatty Jr., Claudia Feldstein, Anthony Forkush, Michael Manuel, William Francis McGuire, Jarion Monroe, Amy Povich, Thom Sesma, Keith Szarabaika, Joe Urla, Welker White, Jeffrey Wright, José Zuniga.

William Hurt, Frances Conroy in "Ivanov"

Welker White, Joe Urla in "Search and Destroy"

Jan Triska in "Largo Desolato"

Frances McDormand, David Strathairn
in "Moon for the Misbegotten"

Simi Junior, Michael Early
in "Ohio State Murders"

WINTERFEST 11:
Eleventh annual festival of four new plays in rotating repertory.

BRICKLAYERS (WORLD PREMIERE) by Elvira J. DiPaolo; Director, Walter Dalls; Set, Michael Yeargan; Costumes, Susan Branch; Lighting, Mark L. McCullough; Sound, Evan Gelick. CAST: Rob Campbell, Kadina deElejalde, Joshua Fardon, Robert Katims, Jon Manfrellotti, Patricia Mauceri, Vince Viverito.
TIES THAT BIND (WORLD PREMIERE) by Walter Allen Bennett Jr.; Director, Jordan Corngold; Set, Debra Booth; Costumes, Jess Goldstein; Lighting, Karen TenEyck, Sound, Jim van Bergen. CAST: Robert Beatty Jr., Linda Maurel, Michael Potts, Seret Scott, Bahni Turpin.
OHIO STATE MURDERS (WORLD PREMIERE) by Adrienne Kennedy; Director, Gerald Freedman; Set/Costumes, Tom Broecker; Lighting, Mark L. McCullough; Sound, Stan Kozak; Projections, Kurt Sharp. CAST: Telia Anderson, Mekah-el Ben Israel, Allan Byrne, Olivia Cole, Michael Early, Simi Junior, Mary Louise.
THE SIZE OF THE WORLD (WORLD PREMIERE) by Charles Evered; Director, Walton Jones; Set, Elizabeth Hope Clancy; Costumes, Helen C. Ju; Lighting, Rick Martin. CAST: Mary Fogarty, Conrad McLaren, Liev Schreiber.

UNDERGROUND (WORLD PREMIERE) by Joshua Sobol; English adaptaion, Ron Jenkins; Director, Adrian Hall; Set, Andrew W. Broughton; Costumes, Azan Kung; Lighting, Glen Fasman; Music Composed/Arranged/Directed, Barbara Damashek. CAST: Rob Campbell, Thomas Derrah, William J.Devany, Kristin Flanders, Ruth Jaffe, Paul Kielar, Richard Kneeland, Howard London, Derek Meader, Marty New, Barbara Orson, Ford Rainey, Martin Rayner, Liev Schreiber, Priscilla Shanks, Bennet Stephens, John Watson, Jack Willis, Zoey Zimmerman.
SCAPIN by Moliere; Translated/Adapted by Shelley Berc and Andrei Belgrader; Director, Mr. Belgrader; Set, Karen TenEyck; Costumes, Christine McDowell; Lighting, Rick Martin; Original Music/Lyrics, Rusty Magee. CAST: Martin A. Blanco, Ken Cheeseman, Alexander Draper, Joshua Fardon, Claudia Feldstein, Walker Jones, Michael McCormick,Rusty Magee, Kevin Meredith, Mary Testa, Stanley Tucci, Sarah McCord Williams.
A MOON FOR THE MISBEGOTTEN by Eugene O'Neill; Director, Lloyd Richards; Set, Debra Booth; Costumes, Helen C. Ju; Lighting, Jennifer Tipton; Sound, Rob Gorton. CAST: Roy Cooper, Jay Goede, John Jellison, Frances McDormand, David Strathairn.

Gerry Goodstein Photos

Right: Seret Scott, Linda Maurel in "Ties That Bind"
Center: Joshua Fardon, Walker Jones in "Scapin"

COLORADO SHAKESPEARE FESTIVAL

Boulder, Colorado
Thirty-third Season
June 29, 1990-August 18, 1990

Producing Artistic Director, Daniel S.P. Yang; Producing Director, Richard Devin.
RESIDENT COMPANY: Susan Appel, Jennifer Blagen, Laura Puilio, Kurt Bernhardt, Andrew Brhel, Dannis Elkins, Jim Iorio, Jeff Jeffcoat, Paul Hindman, Bruce Orendorf, Ron Statler, Steve Wilson, Darryl Robinson.
GUEST ARTISTS: Barry Kraft, Dudley Knight, Sean Hennigan, Nance Williamson, Sean Kelly.
PRODUCTIONS: *As You Like It*; Director, Jack Clay; Sets, Bill Eckart; Music, John Morris; *Romeo and Juliet*; Director, Tony Church; Sets, David Mickelsen; Costumes, Vicki Smith; Music, Peter Barbieri; *Much Ado About Nothing*; Director, Joel G. Fink; Sets, Randy McMullen; Costumes, Bruce McInroy; Music, Rick Thomas.

Stacey Keach, Franchelle Stewart Dorn in "Richard III"

Quentin O'Brien, Josie De Guzman in "Fuente Ovejuna"

FOLGER SHAKESPEARE FESTIVAL

Washington, D.C.
September 11, 1990-July 7, 1991

Artistic Director, Michael Kahn; Managing Director, Jessica L. Andrews; Business Manager, Sam Sweet; Development Director, Brian H. Marcus; Public Relations/Marketing Director, Beth Hauptle; Education Director, Stephen Welch; Production Manager, John W. Kingsbury.
RESIDENT COMPANY: Emery Battis, Franchelle Stewart Dorn, Edward Gero, Floyd King, Ted van Griethuysen, Rebecca Thompson.

PRODUCTIONS AND CASTS

RICHARD III by William Shakespeare; Director, Michael Kahn; Sets, Derek McLane; Costumes, Merrily Murray-Walsh; Lighting, Howell Binkley; Stage Manager, Anne S. King. CAST: Floyd King (Edward IV/Scrivener), Edward Gero (Duke of Clarence), Stacy Keach (Richard), Matt Jones (Prince of Wales), Dan Cameron Lowe (Duke of York), Heidi Guthrie (Elizabeth), Rebecca Thompson (Duchess of York), John Patrick Rice (Henry VI/Henry Tudor), Rosemary Murphy (Queen Margaret), Lynnda Ferguson (Lady Anne), Franchelle Stewart Dorn (Queen Elizabeth), Carter Reardon (Woodville), Gregory L. Williams (Lord Grey/Blunt), José Luzarraga (Marquess of Dorset), K. Lype O'Dell (Hastings), Ted van Griethuysen (Buckingham), Emery Battis (Stanley), Robert Sams (Bishop), Bill Grimmette (Lord Mayor/Brakenbury), Michael Gaston (Catesby), A. Bernard Cummings (Ratcliffe), Richard Pelzman (Tyrrel/Herbert), George Altman (Murderer), Ronnie Jenkins (Murderer), Robin W. Edwards (Mistress Jane), Todd Dellinger (George Stanley), Stephen DeRosa, Barry Price, Kevin Roach, Karine Rosenthal, Erinn White.
OTHELLO by William Shakespeare; Director, Harold Scott; Sets, John Ezell; Costumes, Daniel L. Lawson; Lighting, Nancy Schertler; Music, Lawrence L. "Butch" Morris; Fights, Nels Hennum; Stage Manager, James Latus. CAST: Avery Brooks (Othello), Emery Battis (Brabantio), Graham Winton (Cassio), André Braugher (Iago), Floyd King (Roderigo), Ted van Griethuysen (Duke of Venice), Sean Cullen (Lodovico), K. Lype O'Dell (Gratiano), Michael Gaston (Montano), Jordan Baker (Desdemona), Franchelle Stewart Dorn (Emilia), Gayle Finer (Bianca), George Altman, Stephen DeRosa, Robin Edwards, Heidi Guthrie, Troy Jeman, Ronnie Jenkins, José Luzarraga, Richard Pelzman, Erinn White, Gregory L. Williams.
FUENTE OVEJUNA by Lope de Vega; Translation, Adrian Mitchell; Director, René Buch; Design, Robert Weber Federico; Composer, Peter Golub; Stage Manager, Linda Harris. CAST: Rebecca Thompson (Queen Isabella), Ted van Griethuysen (King Ferdinand), David Walker (Rodrigo), Edward Gero (Fernando), Michael Gaston (Flores), Richard Pelzman (Ortuno), Emery Battis (Esteban), Curtis Shumaker (Alonso), James Slaughter (Don Manrique), Josie de Guzmán (Laurencia), Diana Volpe (Jacinta), Gayle Finer (Pascuala), Carlos Juan González (Juan), Quentin O'Brien (Frondoso), Edward Morgan (Barrildo), Bill Leone (Mengo), José Luzarraga (Leonelo), Rafael Padron (Cimbranos), Stephen DeRosa (Alderman), George Altman (Alderman), Robin Edwards, Heidi Guthrie, Ronnie Jenkins, Jemal McNeil, Kevin D. Roach.
KING LEAR by William Shakespeare; Director, Michael Kahn; Sets, Thomas Lynch; Costumes, Martin Pakledinaz; Lighting, Howell Binkley; Fights, David Leong; Music, Anthony Stark; Stage Manager, James Latus. CAST: Fritz Weaver (Lear), Mary Lou Rosato (Goneril), Kate Skinner (Regan), Sabrina Le Beauf (Cordelia), Ralph Cosham (Albany), Edward Gero (Cornwall), Philip Goodwin (Fool), Richard Thompson (King of France), Todd Dellinger (Burgundy), Ted van Griethuysen (Gloucester), Gary Sloan (Edgar), Daniel Southern (Edmund), Jack Ryland (Earl of Kent), Michael Santo (Oswald), James Slaughter (Old Man), Emery Battis (Doctor), Richard Pelzman (Gentleman), Richard A. Hontz, José Luzarraga, David Martin, Jon Radulovic, Kevin Roach, Curtis Shumaker.

Joan Marcus Photos

NEW JERSEY SHAKESPEARE FESTIVAL

Madison, New Jersey
June 27, 1990-December 8, 1990

Artistic Director/Director of all Productions, Paul Barry; Producing Director, Ellen Barry; Production Stage Manager, Drew Martorella; Stage Managers, Patricia Flynn; Stephen Petrilli, Richard M. Rose; Sets, James A. Bazewicz, Mark Evancho; Lighting, Stephen Petrilli; Costumes, Julie Ables Chevan, Steven F. Graver, Constance Hoffman, Ann Waugh; Sound, Richard M. Rose; Musical Director, Deborah Martin; Mime Director, Craig Babcock; Choreography, Jozia Mieszkowski; General Manager, Jana Mack; Public Relations/Education Director, Mary Godinho.

ADMINISTRATIVE/TECHNICAL STAFF: Nick Boyle, Carolyn Dascher, Martin Kennedy Foys, Cory Fuller, Susan A. Hammon, Elliot J. Kahn, Eleanor Kennedy, Francine Matagrano, Delmar L. Rinehart Jr., Jodi Ginniver Rovere, Ken Rus Schmoll, Paul Tazewell, James Vreeland, Dawn Williams, John Wojacek, Susanne Wood.

ACTOR'S EQUITY (PROFESSIONAL) COMPANY: Ellen Barry, Kevin Barry, Paul Barry, Victoria Boothby, Peter Bradbury, Robert Branch, Thomas Carson, David Connell, Kevin Hogan, J.C. Hoyt, Rory Kelly, Christopher Martin, Robert Lee Martini, David New, Maureen Pedala, Don Perkins, Margery Shaw, Ennis Smith, Geddeth Smith, T. Ryder Smith, Eric Tavares, Kelly Walters, Cheryl Williams.

SUPPORTING COMPANY(EQUITY MEMBERSHIP CANDIDATES/INTERNS): Elise Allen, Shannon Barry, David A. Basche, Abigail Bailey, Nicole Bernadette, Clint Betz, Helen P. Coxe, Richard Damour, Valerie L. Doran, Kevin Elden, Martha Ellen, Tony Fross, Deidre A. Gilmartin, Allegra Growdon, Graig Guggenheim, Courtney Halliday, Margeaux Hasker, Carol Haunton, John P. Herring, Miles Holt, Kristen Hornlein, Ira J. Jaffe, Christopher C. Knall, Richard Kuranda, Mikki Le Moine, Tiffany Marshall, James S. McClure, Ellen M. McLaughlin, J. Bryan McMillen, Mary Frances Miller, Michael S. Miller, Ann Marie Morelli, Holmes Morrison, Richard M. Rose, Alexandria Sage, M. Alexei Sage, Sarah Ann Standing, Dan Teachout, Robin Trigg, Katrin Van Dam, Nicholas Viselli, Miriam Yucht, Lisa Zerbo.

PRODUCTIONS: *Romeo and Juliet* by William Shakespeare; *Measure for Measure* by William Shakespeare; *King John* by William Shakespeare. Playing straight runs: *A Life in the Theatre* by David Mamet; *Death of a Salesman* by Arthur Miller.

Specialized Photodesign Photos

Andre Braugher, Avery Brooks in "Othello"

Sabrina Le Beauf, Fritz Weaver in "King Lear"

Maureen Pedala, David New in "Romeo and Juliet"

T. Ryder Smith, Eric Tavares in "Life in the Theatre"

STRATFORD FESTIVAL

Stratford, Ontario, Canada
April 30, 1990-November 11, 1990

Artistic Director, David William; General Manager, Gary Thomas; Producer, Colleen Blake; Head of Design, Debra Hanson; Music Director, Berthold Carrière; Communications Director, Ellen T. Cole; Development, Diana Reitberger; Production Manager, Paul Shaw; Literary Manager, Elliott Hayes; Technical Director, Ron Kresky; Resident Lighting Designer, Michael J. Whitfield; Archivist, Lisa Brant; Stage Managers, Peter McGuire, Margaret Palmer, Nora Polley, Catherine Russell, Ann Stuart, The. John Gray, Marylu Moyer, Janine Ralph, Catherine Russell, Hilary Graham, Brenda Henderson.

ACTING COMPANY: Andrew Akman, Edward Atienza, Shaun Austin-Olsen, Marie Baron, Hume Baugh, Brian Bedford, James Binkley, Mervyn Blake, James Blendick, Mary Hitch Blendick, Barbara Bryne, Diana Cartwight, Douglas Chamberlain, Juan Chioran, Antoni Cimolino, Patricia Conolly, Richard Curnock, John Devorski, Keith Dinicol, Andrew Dolha, Peter Donaldson, William Dunlop, Karen K. Edissi, Peter Farbridge, Colm Feore, Nancy Ferguson, Adam Fleck, Lorraine Foreman, Pat Galloway, Peter Gaudreault, Brenda Gorlick, Kevin Gudahl, Michael Halberstam, Ron Hastings, Larry Herbert, Roland Hewgill, Sean Hewitt, Chris Heyerdahl, Roger Honeywell, Neil Ingram, Andrew Jackson, Melanie Janzen, Nolan Jennings, Alan Jordan, Debora Joy, Robert King, Tim Koetting, Gary Krawford, Adam Large, Shannon Lawson, Janice Luey, Larry Mannell, Marti Maraden, Roberta Maxwell, Geoff McBride, Tim McDonald, Dale Mieske, Paul Miller, Michèle Muzzi, William Needles, Vickie Papavs, Lucy Peacock, Ted Pearson, Nicholas Pennell, David Petrie, Leon Pownall, Douglas Rain, Claire Rankin, Lyndsay Richardson, Bradley C. Rudy, Fernando Santos, Ronn Sarosiak, Sal Scozzari, Goldie Semple, Joe-Norman Shaw, Joseph Shaw, Brain Smegal, Julia Smith, Donna Starnes, John Stead, Gérard Théorêt, Brian Tree, Kerri Lyn Wasylik, Ian Watson, Scott Wentworth, Ian White, Jim White, David William, Julia Winder, Anne Wright, Susan Wright, Cavan Young, Victor A. Young, Pat Armstrong, Shirley Douglas.

PRODUCTIONS: FESTIVAL THEATRE: *Guys and Dolls* by Frank Loesser, Jo Swerling and Abe Burrows; Director/Choreography, Brian McDonald; Musical Director, Berthold Carrière; *As You Like It* by William Shakespeare; Director, Richard Monette; *Macbeth* by William Shakespeare; Directors, David William, Robert Beard; *Julius Caesar* by William Shakespeare; Director, Richard Monette.

AVON THEATRE: *The Merry Wives of Windsor* by William Shakespeare; Director, Bernard Hopkins; *Love for Love* by William Congreve; Director, David William; *Home* by David Storey; Director, Marti Maraden; *Ah, Wilderness* by Eugene O'Neill; Director, Vivian Matalon; *One Tiger to a Hill* by Sharon Pollock; Director, John Wood.

THIRD STAGE: *Forever Yours, Marie-Lou* by Michel Tremblay; Translation, John Van Burek, Bill Glassco; Director, Lorne Kennedy; *Memoir* by John Murrell; Director, Albert Millaire; *Phaedra* by Jean Racine; Translation, Richard Wilbur; Director, Brian Bedford; *The Knight of the Burning Pestle* by Francis Beaumont; Adaptation, Elliott Hayes; Directors, Bernard Hopkins, Pat Galloway; *The Grand Inquisitor* by Fyodar M. Dostoevsky; English Adaptation, Ronald Mavor; Director, Jeannette Lambermont; *Swan Song* by Anton Chekhov; Translation, Michael Frayn; Director, Ms. Lambermont.

David Cooper Photos

Joseph Shaw, Keith Dinicol in "Merry Wives of Windsor"

Michael Halberstam (top), Geoff McBride, Claire Rankin, Paul Miller, Antoni Cimolino, Andrew Akman, Larry Herbert in "Knight of the Burning Pestle"

Roland Hewgill, Barbara Bryne, Susan Wright, Michele Muzzi, (Front) Andrew Dolha, Douglas Rain in "Ah, Wilderness!"

"Guys and Dolls"

1991 THEATRE WORLD AWARD RECIPIENTS
(OUSTANDING NEW TALENT)

JANE ADAMS
of "I Hate Hamlet"

ADAM ARKIN
of "I Hate Hamlet"

MARCUS CHONG
of "Stand-up Tragedy"

GILLIAN ANDERSON
of "Absent Friends"

PAUL HIPP
of "Buddy"

LACHANZE
of "Once on This Island"

LEA SALONGA
of "Miss Saigon"

KENNY NEAL
of "Mule Bone"

KEVIN RAMSEY
of "Oh, Kay!"

TRACEY ULLMAN
of "The Big Love" and "Taming of the Shrew"

CHANDRA WILSON
of "The Good Times Are Killing Me"

FRANCIS RUIVIVAR
of "Shogun"

Not Pictured: BRENDA BLETHYNE of
"Absent Friends"

THEATRE WORLD AWARDS presented Thursday, May 16, 1991 in the Equitable Auditorium.
Top: Presenters (all former recipients): Gloria Foster, Dorothy Loudon, Estelle
Parsons, Harvey Fierstein, Tommy Hollis, Joanna Gleason, William Hurt; John
Rubinstein, Catherine Burns, Alan Arkin, Michael Rupert, Tovah Feldshuh, Carol
Channing, Jonathan Pryce Below: Jonathan Pryce, Lea Salonga, John Rubinstein;
Paul Hipp, Carol Channing; Adam and Alan Arkin; Bottom Row: Dorothy Loudon,
William Hurt, LaChanze: Michael Rupert, Tovah Feldshuh Above: Francis Ruivivar,
Harvey Fierstein; Chandra Wilson; Kenny Neal, Estelle Parsons
Photos by Michael Riordan, Michael Viade, Van Williams

Top: (L-R) Tommy Hollis, Meryl Vladimer accepting for Ellen Stewart, Producer
Jay Presson Allen accepting for Tracey Ullman, Gloria Foster, Playwright Bill
Cain accepting for Marcus Chong, Gillian Anderson Below: Kevin Ramsey, Paul Hipp;
Lynne Meadow accepting for Brenda Blethyne, Lea Salonga, Jane Adams, Catherine
Burns Bottom Row: Robert Lambert, Crista Moore; Francis Ruivivar, Philip Casnoff;
LaChanze, Kevin Ramsey Above: Harvey Fierstein, Jason Workman; Dorothy Loudon,
Lee Roy Reams, Carol Channing; Adam Arkin, Jane Adams

Photos by Michael Riordan, Michael Viade, Van Williams

165

**Warren
Beatty**

**Annette
Bening**

**Matthew
Broderick**

PREVIOUS THEATRE WORLD AWARD RECIPIENTS

1944-45: Betty Comden, Richard Davis, Richard Hart, Judy Holliday, Charles Lang, Bambi Linn, John Lund, Donald Murphy, Nancy Noland, Margaret Phillips, John Raitt

1945-46: Barbara Bel Geddes, Marlon Brando, Bill Callahan, Wendell Corey, Paul Douglas, Mary James, Burt Lancaster, Patricia Marshall, Beatrice Pearson

1946-47: Keith Andes, Marion Bell, Peter Cookson, Ann Crowley, Ellen Hanley, John Jordan, George Keane, Dorothea MacFarland, James Mitchell, Patricia Neal, David Wayne

1947-48: Valerie Bettis, Edward Bryce, Whitfield Connor, Mark Dawson, June Lockhart, Estelle Loring, Peggy Maley, Ralph Meeker, Meg Mundy, Douglass Watson, James Whitmore, Patrice Wymore

1948-49: Tod Andrews, Doe Avedon, Jean Carson, Carol Channing, Richard Derr, Julie Harris, Mary McCarty, Allyn Ann McLerie, Cameron Mitchell, Gene Nelson, Byron Palmer, Bob Scheerer

1949-50: Nancy Andrews, Phil Arthur, Barbara Brady, Lydia Clarke, Priscilla Gillette, Don Hanmer, Marcia Henderson, Charlton Heston, Rick Jason, Grace Kelly, Charles Nolte, Roger Price

1950-51: Barbara Ashley, Isabel Bigley, Martin Brooks, Richard Burton, Pat Crowley, James Daley, Cloris Leachman, Russell Nype, Jack Palance, William Smithers, Maureen Stapleton, Marcia Van Dyke, Eli Wallach

1951-52: Tony Bavaar, Patricia Benoit, Peter Conlow, Virginia de Luce, Ronny Graham, Audrey Hepburn, Diana Herbert, Conrad Janis, Dick Kallman, Charles Proctor, Eric Sinclair, Kim Stanley, Marian Winters, Helen Wood

1952-53: Edie Adams, Rosemary Harris, Eileen Heckart, Peter Kelley, John Kerr, Richard Kiley, Gloria Marlowe, Penelope Munday, Paul Newman, Sheree North, Geraldine Page, John Stewart, Ray Stricklyn, Gwen Verdon

1953-54: Orson Bean, Harry Belafonte, James Dean, Joan Diener, Ben Gazzara, Carol Haney, Jonathan Lucas, Kay Medford, Scott Merrill, Elizabeth Montgomery, Leo Penn, Eva Marie Saint

1954-55: Julie Andrews, Jacqueline Brookes, Shirl Conway, Barbara Cook, David Daniels, Mary Fickett, Page Johnson, Loretta Leversee, Jack Lord, Dennis Patrick, Anthony Perkins, Christopher Plummer

1955-56: Diane Cilento, Dick Davalos, Anthony Franciosa, Andy Griffith, Laurence Harvey, David Hedison, Earle Hyman, Susan Johnson, John Michael King, Jayne Mansfield, Sara Marshall, Gaby Rodgers, Susan Strasberg, Fritz Weaver

1956-57: Peggy Cass, Sydney Chaplin, Sylvia Daneel, Bradford Dillman, Peter Donat, George Grizzard, Carol Lynley, Peter Palmer, Jason Robards, Cliff Robertson, Pippa Scott, Inga Swenson

1957-58: Anne Bancroft, Warren Berlinger, Colleen Dewhurst, Richard Easton, Tim Everett, Eddie Hodges, Joan Hovis, Carol Lawrence, Jacqueline McKeever, Wynne Miller, Robert Morse, George C. Scott

1958-59: Lou Antonio, Ina Balin, Richard Cross, Tammy Grimes, Larry Hagman, Dolores Hart, Roger Mollien, France Nuyen, Susan Oliver, Ben Piazza, Paul Roebling, William Shatner, Pat Suzuki, Rip Torn

1959-60: Warren Beatty, Eileen Brennan, Carol Burnett, Patty Duke, Jane Fonda, Anita Gillette, Donald Madden, George Maharis, John McMartin, Lauri Peters, Dick Van Dyke

1960-61: Joyce Bulifant, Dennis Cooney, Sandy Dennis, Nancy Dussault, Robert Goulet, Joan Hackett, June Harding, Ron Husmann, James MacArthur, Bruce Yarnell

1961-62: Elizabeth Ashley, Keith Baxter, Peter Fonda, Don Galloway, Sean Garrison, Barbara Harris, James Earl Jones, Janet Margolin, Karen Morrow, Robert Redford, John Stride, Brenda Vaccaro

1962-63: Alan Arkin, Stuart Damon, Melinda Dillon, Robert Drivas, Bob Gentry, Dorothy Loudon, Brandon Maggart, Julienne Marie, Liza Minnelli, Estelle Parsons, Diana Sands, Swen Swenson

1963-64: Alan Alda, Gloria Bleezarde, Imelda De Martin, Claude Giraud, Ketty Lester, Barbara Loden, Lawrence Pressman, Gilbert Price, Philip Proctor, John Tracy, Jennifer West

1964-65: Carolyn Coates, Joyce Jillson, Linda Lavin, Luba Lisa, Michael O'Sullivan, Joanna Pettet, Beah Richards, Jaime Sanchez, Victor Spinetti, Nicolas Surovy, Robert Walker, Clarence Williams III

1965-66: Zoe Caldwell, David Carradine, John Cullum, John Davidson, Faye Dunaway, Gloria Foster, Robert Hooks, Jerry Lanning, Richard Mulligan, April Shawhan, Sandra Smith, Leslie Ann Warren

1966-67: Bonnie Bedelia, Richard Benjamin, Dustin Hoffman, Terry Kiser, Reva Rose, Robert Salvio, Sheila Smith, Connie Stevens, Pamela Tiffin, Leslie Uggams, Jon Voight, Christopher Walken

1967-68: David Birney, Pamela Burrell, Jordan Christopher, Jack Crowder (Thalmus Rasulala), Sandy Duncan, Julie Gregg, Stephen Joyce, Bernadette Peters, Alice Playten, Michael Rupert, Brenda Smiley, Russ Thacker

**Stephen
Geoffreys**

**Whoopi
Goldberg**

**James Earl
Jones**

Carol
Channing

Timothy
Daly

Faye
Dunaway

1968-69: Jane Alexander, David Cryer, Blythe Danner, Ed Evanko, Ken Howard, Lauren Jones, Ron Leibman, Marian Mercer, Jill O'Hara, Ron O'Neal, Al Pacino, Marlene Warfield

1969-70: Susan Browning, Donny Burks, Catherine Burns, Len Cariou, Bonnie Franklin, David Holliday, Katharine Houghton, Melba Moore, David Rounds, Lewis J. Stadlen, Kristoffer Tabori, Fredricka Weber

1970-71: Clifton Davis, Michael Douglas, Julie Garfield, Martha Henry, James Naughton, Tricia O'Neil, Kipp Osborne, Roger Rathburn, Ayn Ruymen, Jennifer Salt, Joan Van Ark, Walter Willison

1971-72: Jonelle Allen, Maureen Anderman, William Atherton, Richard Backus, Adrienne Barbeau, Cara Duff-MacCormick, Robert Foxworth, Elaine Joyce, Jess Richards, Ben Vereen, Beatrice Winde, James Woods

1972-73: D'Jamin Bartlett, Patricia Elliott, James Farentino, Brian Farrell, Victor Garber, Kelly Garrett, Mari Gorman, Laurence Guittard, Trish Hawkins, Monte Markham, John Rubinstein, Jennifer Warren, Alexander H. Cohen (Special Award)

1973-74: Mark Baker, Maureen Brennan, Ralph Carter, Thom Christopher, John Driver, Conchata Ferrell, Ernestine Jackson, Michael Moriarty, Joe Morton, Ann Reinking, Janie Sell, Mary Woronov, Sammy Cahn (Special Award)

1974-75: Peter Burnell, Zan Charisse, Lola Falana, Peter Firth, Dorian Harewood, Joel Higgins, Marcia McClain, Linda Miller, Marti Rolph, John Sheridan, Scott Stevensen, Donna Theodore, Equity Library Theatre (Special Award)

1975-76: Danny Aiello, Christine Andreas, Dixie Carter, Tovah Feldshuh, Chip Garnett, Richard Kelton, Vivian Reed, Charles Repole, Virginia Seidel, Daniel Seltzer, John V. Shea, Meryl Streep, A Chorus Line (Special Award)

1976-77: Trazana Beverley, Michael Cristofer, Joe Fields, Joanna Gleason, Cecilia Hart, John Heard, Gloria Hodes, Juliette Koka, Andrea McArdle, Ken Page, Jonathan Pryce, Chick Vennera, Eva LeGallienne (Special Award)

1977-78: Vasili Bogazianos, Nell Carter, Carlin Glynn, Christopher Goutman, William Hurt, Judy Kaye, Florence Lacy, Armelia McQueen, Gordana Rashovich, Bo Rucker, Richard Seer, Colin Stinton, Joseph Papp (Special Award)

1978-79: Philip Anglim, Lucie Arnaz, Gregory Hines, Ken Jennings, Michael Jeter, Laurie Kennedy, Susan Kingsley, Christine Lahti, Edward James Olmos, Kathleen Quinlan, Sarah Rice, Max Wright, Marshall W. Mason (Special Award)

1979-80: Maxwell Caulfield, Leslie Denniston, Boyd Gaines, Richard Gere, Harry Groener, Stephen James, Susan Kellermann, Dinah Manoff, Lonny Price, Marianne Tatum, Anne Twomey, Dianne Wiest, Mickey Rooney (Special Award)

1980-81: Brian Backer, Lisa Banes, Meg Bussert, Michael Allen Davis, Giancarlo Esposito, Daniel Gerroll, Phyllis Hyman, Cynthia Nixon, Amanda Plummer, Adam Redfield, Wanda Richert, Rex Smith, Elizabeth Taylor (Special Award)

1981-82: Karen Akers, Laurie Beechman, Danny Glover, David Alan Grier, Jennifer Holliday, Anthony Heald, Lizbeth Mackay, Peter MacNicol, Elizabeth McGovern, Ann Morrison, Michael O'Keefe, James Widdoes, Manhattan Theatre Club (Special Award)

1982-83: Karen Allen, Suzanne Bertish, Matthew Broderick, Kate Burton, Joanne Camp, Harvey Fierstein, Peter Gallagher, John Malkovich, Anne Pitoniak, James Russo, Brian Tarantina, Linda Thorson, Natalia Makarova (Special Award)

1983-84: Martine Allard, Joan Allen, Kathy Whitton Baker, Mark Capri, Laura Dean, Stephen Geoffreys, Tod Graff, Glenne Headly, J.J. Johnston, Bonnie Koloc, Calvin Levels, Robert Westenberg, Ron Moody (Special Award)

1984-85: Kevin Anderson, Richard Chaves, Patti Cohenour, Charles S. Dutton, Nancy Giles, Whoopi Goldberg, Leilani Jones, John Mahoney, Laurie Metcalf, Barry Miller, John Turturro, Amelia White, Lucille Lortel (Special Award)

1985-86: Suzy Amis, Alec Baldwin, Aled Davies, Faye Grant, Julie Hagerty, Ed Harris, Mark Jacoby, Donna Kane, Cleo Laine, Howard McGillin, Marisa Tomei, Joe Urla, Ensemble Studio Theatre (Special Award)

1986-87: Annette Bening, Timothy Daly, Lindsay Duncan, Frank Ferrante, Robert Lindsay, Amy Madigan, Michael Maguire, Demi Moore, Molly Ringwald, Frances Ruffelle, Courtney B. Vance, Colm Wilkinson, Robert DeNiro (Special Award)

1987-88: Yvonne Bryceland, Philip Casnoff, Danielle Ferland, Melissa Gilbert, Linda Hart, Linzi Hately, Brian Kerwin, Brian Mitchell, Mary Murfitt, Aidan Quinn, Eric Roberts, B.D. Wong

1988-89: Dylan Baker, Joan Cusack, Loren Dean, Peter Frechette, Sally Mayes, Sharon McNight, Jennie Moreau, Paul Provenza, Kyra Sedgwick, Howard Spiegel, Eric Stoltz, Joanne WhalleyKilmer, Special Awards: Pauline Collins, Mikhail Baryshnikov

1989-90: Denise Burse-Mickelbury, Erma Campbell, Rocky Carroll, Megan Gallagher, Tommy Hollis, Robert Lambert, Kathleen Row McAllen, Michael McKean, Crista Moore, Mary-Louise Parker, Daniel von Bargen, Jason Workman, Special Awards: Stewart Granger, Kathleen Turner

Dorothy
Loudon

Eric
Stoltz

Mary
Woronov

PULITZER PRIZE PRODUCTIONS

1918-Why Marry?, **1919-**No award, **1920-**Beyond the Horizon, **1921-**Miss Lulu Bett, **1922-**Anna Christie, **1923-**Icebound, **1924-**Hell-Bent fer Heaven, **1925-**They Knew What They Wanted, **1926-**Craig's Wife, **1927-**In Abraham's Bosom, **1928-**Strange Interlude, **1929-**Street Scene, **1930-**The Green Pastures, **1931-**Alison's House, **1932-**Of Thee I Sing, **1933-**Both Your Houses, **1934-**Men in White, **1935-**The Old Maid, **1936-**Idiot's Delight, **1937-**You Can't Take It with You, **1938-**Our Town, **1939-**Abe Lincoln in Illinois, **1940-**The Time of Your Life, **1941-**There Shall Be No Night, **1942-**No award, **1943-**The Skin of Our Teeth, **1944-**No award, **1945-**Harvey, **1946-**State of the Union, **1947-**No award, **1948-**A Streetcar Named Desire, **1949-**Death of a Salesman, **1950-**South Pacific, **1951-**No award, **1952-**The Shrike, **1953-**Picnic, **1954-**The Teahouse of the August Moon, **1955-**Cat on a Hot Tin Roof, **1956-**The Diary of Anne Frank, **1957-**Long Day's Journey into Night, **1958-**Look Homeward, Angel, **1959-**J.B., **1960-**Fiorello!, **1961-**All the Way Home, **1962-**How to Succeed in Business without Really Trying, **1963-**No award, **1964-**No award, **1965-**The Subject Was Roses, **1966-**No award, **1967-**A Delicate Balance, **1968-**No award, **1969-**The Great White Hope, **1970-**No Place to Be Somebody, **1971-**The Effect of Gamma Rays on Man-in-the-Moon Marigolds, **1972-**No award, **1973-**That Championship Season, **1974-**No award, **1975-**Seascape, **1976-**A Chorus Line, **1977-**The Shadow Box, **1978-**The Gin Game, **1979-**Buried Child, **1980-**Talley's Folly, **1981-**Crimes of the Heart, **1982-**A Soldier's Play, **1983-**'night, Mother, **1984-**Glengarry Glen Ross, **1985-**Sunday in the Park with George, **1986-**No award, **1987-**Fences, **1988-**Driving Miss Daisy, **1989-**The Heidi Chronicles, **1990-**The Piano Lesson, **1991-**Lost in Yonkers

NEW YORK DRAMA CRITICS CIRCLE AWARDS

1936-Winterset, **1937-**High Tor, **1938-**Of Mice and Men, Shadow and Substance, **1939-**The White Steed, **1940-**The Time of Your Life, **1941-**Watch on the Rhine, The Corn Is Green, **1942-**Blithe Spirit, **1943-**The Patriots, **1944-**Jacobowsky and the Colonel, **1945-**The Glass Menagerie, **1946-**Carousel, **1947-**All My Sons, No Exit, Brigadoon, **1948-**A Streetcar Named Desire, The Winslow Boy, **1949-**Death of a Salesman, TheMadwoman of Chaillot, South Pacific, **1950-**The Member of the Wedding, The Cocktail Party, The Consul, **1951-**Darkness at Noon, The Lady's Not for Burning, Guys and Dolls, **1952-**I Am a Camera, Venus Observed, Pal Joey, **1953-**Picnic, The Love of Four Colonels, Wonderful Town, **1954-**Teahouse of the August Moon, Ondine, The Golden Apple, **1955-**Cat on a Hot Tin Roof, Witness for the Prosecution, The Saint of Bleecker Street, **1956-**The Diary of Anne Frank, Tiger at the Gates, My Fair Lady, **1957-**Long Day's Journey into Night, The Waltz of the Toreadors, The Most Happy Fella, **1958-**Look Homeward Angel, Look Back in Anger, The Music Man, **1959-**A Raisin in the Sun, The Visit, La Plume de Ma Tante, **1960-**Toys in the Attic, Five Finger Exercise, Fiorello!, **1961-**All the Way Home, A Taste of Honey, Carnival, **1962-**Night of the Iguana, A Man for All Seasons, How to Succeed in Business without Really Trying, **1963-**Who's Afraid of Virginia Woolf?, **1964-**Luther, Hello Dolly!, **1965-**The Subject Was Roses, Fiddler on the Roof, **1966-**The Persecution and Assassination of Marat as Performed by the Inmates of the Asylum of Charenton under the Direction of the Marquis de Sade, Man of La Mancha, **1967-**The Homecoming, Cabaret, **1968-**Rosencrantz and Guildenstern Are Dead, Your Own Thing, **1969-**The Great White Hope, 1776, **1970-**The Effect of Gamma Rays on Man-in-the-Moon Marigolds, Borstal Boy, Company, **1971-**Home, Follies, The House of Blue Leaves, **1972-**That Championship Season, Two Gentlemen of Verona, **1973-**The Hot l Baltimore, The Changing Room, A Little Night Music, **1974-**The Contractor, Short Eyes, Candide, **1975-**Equus, The Taking of Miss Janie, A Chorus Line, **1976-**Travesties, Streamers, Pacific Overtures, **1977-**Otherwise Engaged, American Buffalo, Annie, **1978-**Da, Ain't Misbehavin', **1979-**The Elephant Man, Sweeney Todd, **1980-**Talley's Folley, Evita, Betrayal, **1981-**Crimes of the Heart, A Lesson from Aloes, Special Citation to Lena Horne, The Pirates of Penzance, **1982-**The Life and Adventures of Nicholas Nickleby, A Soldier's Play (no musical honored), **1983-**Brighton Beach Memoirs, Plenty, Little Shop of Horrors, **1984-**The Real Thing, Glengarry Glen Ross, Sunday in the Park with George, **1985-**Ma Rainey's Black Bottom (no musical), **1986-**A Lie of the Mind, Benefactors, (no musical), Special Citation to Lily Tomlin and Jane Wagner, **1987-**Fences, Les Liaisons Dangereuses, Les Misérables, **1988-**Joe Turner's Come and Gone, The Road to Mecca, Into the Woods, **1989-**The Heidi Chronicles, Aristocrats, Largely New York (Special), (no musical), **1990-**The Piano Lesson, City of Angels, Privates on Parade, **1991-**Six Degrees of Separation, The Will Rogers Follies, Our Country's Good, Special Citation to Eileen Atkins

AMERICAN THEATRE WING ANTOINETTE PERRY (TONY) AWARD PRODUCTIONS

1948-Mister Roberts, **1949-**Death of a Salesman, Kiss Me, Kate, **1950-**The Cocktail Party, South Pacific, **1951-**The Rose Tattoo, Guys and Dolls, **1952-**The Fourposter, The King and I, **1953-**The Crucible, Wonderful Town, **1954-**The Teahouse of the August Moon, Kismet, **1955-**The Desperate Hours, The Pajama Game, **1956-**The Diary of Anne Frank, Damn Yankees, **1957-**Long Day's Journey into Night, My Fair Lady, **1958-**Sunrise at Campbello, The Music Man, **1959-**J.B., Redhead, **1960-**The Miracle Worker, Fiorello! tied with The Sound of Music, **1961-**Becket, Bye Bye Birdie, **1962-**A Man for All Seasons, How to Succeed in Business without Really Trying, **1963-**Who's Afraid of Virginia Woolf?, A Funny Thing Happened on the Way to the Forum, **1964-**Luther, Hello Dolly!, **1965-**The Subject Was Roses, Fiddler on the Roof, **1966-**The Persecution and Assassination of Marat as Performed by the Inmates of the Asylum of Charenton under the Direction of the Marquis de Sade, Man of La Mancha, **1967-**The Homecoming, Cabaret, **1968-**Rosencrantz and Guildenstern Are Dead, Hallelujah Baby!, **1969-**The Great White Hope, 1776, **1970-**Borstal Boy, Applause, **1971-**Sleuth, Company, **1972-**Sticks and Bones, Two Gentlemen of Verona, **1973-**That Championship Season, A Little Night Music, **1974-**The River Niger, Raisin, **1975-**Equus, The Wiz, **1976-**Travesties, A Chorus Line, **1977-**The Shadow Box, Annie, **1978-**Da, Ain't Misbehavin', Dracula, **1979-**The Elephant Man, Sweeney Todd, **1980-**Children of a Lesser God, Evita, Morning's at Seven, **1981-**Amadeus, 42nd Street, The Pirates of Penzance, **1982-**The Life and Adventures of Nicholas Nickleby, Nine, Othello, **1983-**Torch Song Trilogy, Cats, On Your Toes, **1984-**The Real Thing, La Cage aux Folles, **1985-**Biloxi Blues, Big River, Joe Egg, **1986-**I'm Not Rappaport, The Mystery of Edwin Drood, Sweet Charity, **1987-**Fences, Les Misérables, All My Sons, **1988-**M. Butterfly, The Phantom of the Opera, **1989-**The Heidi Chronicles, Jerome Robbins' Broadway, Our Town, Anything Goes, **1990-**The Grapes of Wrath, City of Angels, Gypsy, **1991-**Lost in Yonkers, The Will Rogers' Follies, Fiddler on the Roof

| Jim
Abele | Betty
Aberlin | Bruce
Adler | Margit
Ahlin | Fred
Anderson | June
Angela |

BIOGRAPHICAL DATA ON
THIS SEASON'S CASTS

(June 1, 1990–May 31, 1991)

AARON, CAROLINE. Born Aug. 7, 1954 in Richmond, VA. Graduate Catholic U. Bdwy debut 1982 in *Come Back to the 5 & Dime, Jimmy Dean*, followed by *The Iceman Cometh, Social Security, I Hate Hamlet*, OB in *Flying Blind, Last Summer at Bluefish Cove, Territorial Rites, Good Bargains, The House of Bernarda Alba, Tribute, Frankie and Johnny in the Clair de Lune, Marathon '89.*

ABELE, JIM. Born Nov. 14, 1960 in Syracuse, NY. Graduate Ithaca Col. Debut 1984 OB in *Shepardsets*, followed by *The Cabbagehead, The Country Girl.*

ABERLIN, BETTY. Born Dec. 40, 1942 in NYC. Graduate Bennington Col. Debut 1954 OB in *Sandhog*, followed by *Upstairs at the Downstairs, I'm Getting My Act Together, Alice in Concert, Yours Anne, 5 Women in a Chapel*, Bdwy in *Cafe Crown* (1964).

ABUBA, ERNEST. Born Aug. 25, 1947 in Honolulu, HI. Attended Southwestern Col. Bdwy debut 1976 in *Pacific Overtures*, followed by *Loose Ends, Zoya's Apartment*, OB in *Sunrise, Monkey Music, Station J., Yellow Fever, Pacific Overtures, Empress of China, The Man Who Turned into a Stick, Shogun Macbeth, Three Sisters, Song of Shim Chung.*

ACKERMAN, LONI. Born Apr. 10, 1949 in NYC. Attended New School. Bdwy debut 1968 in *George M!*, followed by *No, No Nanette, So Long 174th Street, The Magic Show, Evita, Cats*, OB in *Dames at Sea, Starting Here Starting Now, Roberta in Concert, Brownstone, Diamonds.*

ADAMS, JANE. Born Apr. 1, 1965 in Washington, DC. Juilliard graduate. Debut 1986 OB in *The Nice and the Nasty*, followed by Young Playwrights Festival, Bdwy in *I Hate Hamlet* for which she received a Theatre World Award.

ADLER, BRUCE. Born Nov. 27, 1944 in NYC. Attended NYU. Debut 1957 OB in *It's a Funny World*, followed by *Hard to Be a Jew, Big Winner, The Golden Land, The Stranger's Return, The Rise of David Levinsky, On Second Avenue*, Bdwy in *A Teaspoon Every Four Hours* (1971), *Oklahoma!* (1979), *Oh, Brother!, Sunday in the Park with George, Broadway, Those Were the Days.*

AHEARN, DANIEL. Born Aug. 7, 1948 in Washington, DC. Attended Carnegie Mellon. Debut OB 1981 in *Woyzek*, followed by *Brontosaurus Rex, Billy Liar, Second Prize Two Months in Leningrad, No Time Flat, Hollywood Scheherazade, Better Days.*

A'HEARN, PATRICK. Born Sept. 4, 1957 in Cortland, NY. Graduate Syracuse U. Debut 1985 OB in *Pirates of Penzance*, followed by *Forbidden Broadway*, followed by Bdwy in *Les Misérables* (1987).

AHLIN, MARGIT. Born Feb. 23, 19 60 in Chappaqua, NY. Graduate NYU, AMDA. Debut 1982 OB in *Romeo and Juliet*, followed by *Social Event, Vanities, Standing on the Cheese Line, Company, Onlyman, In Available Light, The Elephant Piece.*

AKERS, KAREN. Born Oct. 13, 1945 in NYC. Graduate Hunter Col. Bdwy debut 1982 in *Nine* for which she received a Theatre World Award, followed by *Jacques Brel Is Alive and Well and Living in New York, Grand Hotel.*

ALEXANDER, JACE. Born Apr. 7, 1964 in NYC. Attended NYU. Bdwy debut 1983 in *The Caine Mutiny Court Martial*, OB in *I'm Not Rappaport*, followed by *Wasted, The Good Coach, Heart of a Dog, Price of Fame, Assassins.*

ALEXANDER, JANE. Born Oct. 28, 1939 in Boston, MA. Attended Sarah Lawrence Col., U. Edinburgh. Bdwy debut 1968 in *The Great White Hope*, for which she received a Theatre World Award, followed by *6 Rms Riv Vu, Find Your Way Home, Hamlet* (LC), *The Heiress, First Monday in October, Goodbye Fidel, Monday after the Miracle, Shadowlands*, OB in *Losing Time, Approaching Zanzibar.*

ALEXANDER, JASON. Born Sept 23, 1959 in Irvington, NJ. Attended Boston U. Bdwy debut 1981 in *Merrily We Roll Along*, followed by *The Rink, Broadway Bound, Jerome Robbins' Broadway, Accomplice*, OB in *Forbidden Broadway, Stop the World …, D., Personals, Light up the Sky.*

ALICE, MARY. Born Dec. 3, 1941 in Indianola, MS. Debut 1967 OB in *Trials of Brother Jero*, followed by *The Strong Breed, Duplex, Thoughts, Miss Julie, House Party, Terraces, Heaven and Hell's Agreement, In the Deepest Part of Sleep, Cockfight, Julius Caesar, Nongogo, Second Thoughts, Spell #7, Zooman and the Sign, Glasshouse, The Ditch, Take Me Along, Departures, Marathon '80, Richard III*, Bdwy in *No Place to Somebody* (1971), *Fences.*

ALLEN, KAREN. Born Oct. 5, 1951 in Carrollton, IL. Attended Geo. Wash. U., U. Md. Bdwy debut 1982 in *Monday after the Miracle* for which she received a Theatre World Award, OB in *Extremities, The Miracle Worker, The Country Girl.*

ALLINSON, MICHAEL. Born in London, Eng. Attended RADA. Bdwy debut 1960 in *My Fair Lady*, followed by *Hostile Witness, Come Live with Me, Coco, Angel Street, My Fair Lady* (1981), *Oliver!, Shadoplay*, OB in *The Importance of Being Earnest, Staircase, Loud Bang on June 1st, Good and Faithful Servant.*

ALMY, BROOKS. Born July 15 in Fort Belvoir, VA. Attended U. Hawaii. Bdwy debut 1981 in *The Little Prince and the Aviator*, followed by NYC Opera's *Music Man, Candide, Sweeney Todd* and *Pajama Game, A Change in the Heir*, OB in *Shylock, Nunsense.*

ANDERSON, CHRISTINE. Born Aug. 6 in Utica, NY. Graduate U. Wis. Bdwy debut in *I Love My Wife* (1980), OB in *I Can't Keep Running in Place, On the Swing Shift, Red, Hot and Blue, A Night at Texas Guinan's, Nunsense.*

ANDERSON, FRED. Born July 11, 1964 in Memphis, TN. Attended NC Sch. of Arts, Joffrey Ballet Sch. Debut 1988 OB in *Lost in the Stars*, followed by *Telltale Hearts.*

ANDERSON, GILLIAN. Born Aug. 9, 1968 in Chicago, IL. Graduate Goodman Th. Sch. Debut 1991 OB in *Absent Friends* for which she received a Theatre World Award.

ANDERSON, KEVIN P. Born Jan. 5, 1960 in Peoria, IL. Attended U. WY, N. TX State. Debut 1990 in NYC Opera's *A Little Night Music*, followed by *Street Scene.*

ANDREWS, GEORGE LEE. Born Oct. 13, 1942 in Milwaukee, WI. Debut OB in *Jacques Brel Is Alive and Well …*, followed by *Starting Here Starting Now, Vamps and Rideouts, The Fantasticks*, Bdwy in *A Little Night Music* (1973), *On the 20th Century, Merlin, The Phantom of the Opera, A Little Night Music* (NYCO).

ANGELA, JUNE. Born Aug. 18, 1959 in NYC. Bdwy debut 1970 in *Lovely Ladies, Kind Gentlemen*, followed by *The King and I* (1977), *Shogun: The Musical*, OB in *Kitamura, Aldersgate '88, Song of Shim Chung.*

ANTON, SUSAN. Born Oct. 12, 1950 in Yucaipa, CA. Attended Bernardino Col. Bdwy debut 1985 in *Hurlyburly*, followed by OB's *Xmas a Go-Go.*

APPEL, PETER. Born Oct. 19, 1959 in New York City. Graduate Brandeis U. Debut 1987 OB in *Richard II*, followed by *Henry IV Part 1, A Midsummer Night's Dream, Saved from Obscurity, Titus Andronicus, The Taming of the Shrew, The Good Times Are Killing Me.*

AQUINO, AMY. Born Mar. 20, 1957 in Teaneck, NJ. Graduate Radcliffe, Yale. Debut 1988 OB in *Cold Sweat*, followed by *Right Behind the Flag, Love Diatribe, Road to Nirvana*, Bdwy 1989 in *The Heidi Chronicles.*

ARCARO, ROBERT (a.k.a. Bob). Born Aug. 9, 1952 in Brooklyn, NY. Graduate Wesleyan U. Debut 1977 OB in *New York City Street Show*, followed by *Working Theatre Festival, Man with a Raincoat, Working One-Acts, Henry Lumpur, Special Interests, Measure for Measure.*

ARNOLD, VICTOR. Born July 1, 1936 in Herkimer, NY. Graduate NYU. OB in *Shadows of Heroes, Merchant of Venice, 3 x 3, Lovey, Fortune and Men's Eyes, Time for Bed/Take Me to Bed, Emperor of Late Night Radio, Macbeth, Sign in Sidney Brustein's Window, Cacciotore, Maiden Stakes, My Prince My King, Faithful Brethern of Pitt Street, Rosetta Street, Pals*, Bdwy in *The Deputy* (1964), *Malcolm, We Bombed in New Haven, Fun City*.

ARRINDELL, LISA. Born Mar. 24, 1969 in the Bronx, NY. Juilliard graduate. Debut 1990 in *Richard III*, followed by *Earth and Sky*.

ARKIN, ADAM. Born Aug. 19, 1956 in Brooklyn, NY. Bdwy debut 1991 in *I Hate Hamlet* for which he received a Theatre World Award.

ASH, RANDL. Born Oct. 15, 1959 in Elmhurst, IL. Attended Central CT State Col. Debut 1977 OB in *The Comic Strip*, followed by *Elegies for Angels, Punks and Raging Queens, Pageant*.

ASHFORD, ROBERT. Born Nov. 19, 1959 in Orlando, FL. Attended Washington & Lee U. Bdwy debut 1987 in *Anything Goes*, followed by *Radio City Music Hall Christmas Spectacular*.

ASTREDO, HUMBERT ALLEN. Born in San Francisco, CA. Attended San Francisco U. Debut 1967 OB in *Arms and the Man*, followed by *Fragments, Murderous Angels, Beach Children, Breakfast Conversations in Miami, December 7th, Epic Proportions, End of Summer, Knuckle, Grand Magic, Big and Little, Jail Diary of Albie Sachs, Light Up the Sky*, Bdwy in *Les Blancs* (1970), *An Evening with Richard Nixon ..., The Little Foxes* (1981).

ATKINS, EILEEN. Born June 16, 1934 in London, Eng. Attended Guildhall Schl. Bdwy debut 1966 in *The Killing of Sister George*, followed by *The Promise, Viva! Vivat Regina!, The Night of the Tribades*, OB in *Prin, A Room of One's Own*.

ATKINSON, JAYNE. Born Feb. 18, 1959 in Bournemouth, Engl. Graduate Northwestern U., Yale. Debut 1986 OB in *Bloody Poetry*, followed by *Terminal Bar, Return of Pinocchio, The Art of Success, The Way of the World*, Bdwy in *All My Sons* (1987).

ATLEE, HOWARD. Born May 14, 1926 in Bucyrus, OH. Graduate Emerson Col. Debut 1990 OB in *Historical Prods*, followed by *The 15th Ward*.

AUBERJONOIS, RENE. Born June 1, 1940 in NYC. Graduate Carnegie Inst. With LCRep in *A Cry of Players, King Lear*, and *Twelfth Night*, Bdwy in *Fire* (1969), *Coco, Tricks, The Good Doctor, Break a Leg, Every Good Boy Deserves Favor, Big River, Metamorphosis, City of Angels*, BAM Co. in *The New York Idea, Three Sisters, The Play's the Thing, and Julius Caesar*.

AUGUSTINE, JOHN. Born Mar. 5, 1960 in Canton, OH. Attended Baldwin-White Col. Debut 1988 OB in *Young Playwrights Festival '88*, followed by *Insatiable/Temporary People, A Walk on Lake Erie, Marathon '91*.

AYLWARD, PETER. Born May 20, 1952 in London, Eng. Attended Rockford Col., Penn State U. Debut 1981 OB in *Love's Labour's Lost*, followed by *King Lear*.

AYLWARD, TONY. Born May 30 in New York City. Attended Hunter Col. Debut 1960 OB in *Gay Divorce*, followed by *Babes in Arms, Class Act, A Hole in the Wall, Corkscrews, Gingerbread Lady, A Funny Thing Happened on the Way to the Forum*.

BABBITT, ROB. Born July 28, 1954 in Olean, NY. Attended N. Texas State U. Debut 1980 OB in *Blues in the Night*, Bdwy in *Stepping Out, Grand Hotel*.

BAGDEN, RONALD. Born Dec. 26, 1953 in Philadelphia, PA. Graduate Temple U., RADA. Debut 1977 OB in *Oedipus Rex*, followed by *Oh! What a Lovely War, Jack, Gonza the Lancer, Dead Mother*, Bdwy in *Amadeus* (1980).

BAILA, WENDY. Born Apr. 5, 1961 in New York City. Graduate SUNY/Binghamton. Debut 1986 OB in *Hot Sake*, followed by *The Rise of David Levinsky,Two by Two*.

BAKER, DYLAN. Born in Lackey, VA. Graduate Wm. & Mary, Yale. Debut 1985 OB in *Not about Heroes*, followed by *Two Gentlemen of Verona, The Common Pursuit, Much Ado about Nothing, Eastern Standard, Wolf-Man*, Bdwy (1989) in *Eastern Standard* for which he received a Theatre World Award, *La Bete*.

BAKER, BECKY ANN (formerly Gelke). Born Feb. 17, 1953 in Ft. Knox, KY. Graduate W. KY U. Bdwy debut 1978 in *The Best Little Whorehouse in Texas*, followed by *A Streetcar Named Desire* (1988), OB in *Altitude Sickness, John Brown's Body, Chamber Music, To Whom It May Concern, Two Gentlemen of Verona, Bob's Guns, Buzzsaw Berkeley, Colorado Catechism*.

BAKER, ROBERT MICHAEL. Born Feb. 28, 1954 in Boston MA. Graduate AADA. Debut 1987 OB in *Company*, followed by *Broadway Jukebox, Yiddle with a Fiddle*.

BALL, JERRY. Born Dec. 16, 1956 in New Lexington, OH. Graduate Capitol U., NYU. Bdwy debut 1990 in *Grand Hotel*.

BALL, MICHAEL. Born during July 1963 in Stratford-on-Avon, Eng. Bdwy debut 1990 in *Aspects of Love*.

BARAN, EDWARD. Born May 18, 1950 in Minneapolis, MN. Graduate Williams Col. Debut 1984 OB in *Fool's Errand*, followed by *The Wonder Years, The Sneaker Factory, Cezanne Syndrome, The Year of the Baby, Night Sky*.

BARANSKI, CHRISTINE. Born May 2, 1952 in Buffalo, NY. Graduate Juilliard. Debut OB 1978 in *One Crack Out*, followed by *Says I Says He, The Trouble with Europe, Coming Attractions, Operation Midnight Climax, Sally and Marsha, A Midsummer Night's Dream, It's Only a Play, Marathon '86, Elliot Loves, Lips Together Teeth Apart*, Bdwy in *Hide and Seek* (1980), *The Real Thing, Hurlyburly, House of Blue Leaves, Rumors*.

BARBOUR, THOMAS. Born July 25, 1921 in New York City. Graduate Princeton, Harvard. Bdwy debut 1968 in *Portrait of a Queen*, followed by *The Great White Hope, Scratch, Lincoln Mask, Kingdoms*, OB in *Twelfth Night, Merchant of Venice, Admirable Bashful, The Lady's Not for Burning, The Enchanted, Antony and Cleopatra, The Saintliness of Margery Kemp, Dr. Willy Nilly, Under the Sycamore Tree, Epitaph for George Dillon, Thracian Horses, Old Glory, Sgt. Musgrave's Dance, Nestless Bird, The Seagull, Wayside Motor Inn, Arthur, The Grinding Machine, Mr. Simian, Sorrows of Frederick, Terrorists, Dark Ages, Royal Bob, Relatively Speaking, Aristocrats, The Taming of the Shrew*.

BARON, EVALYN. Born Apr. 21, 1948 in Atlanta, GA. Graduate Northwestern U., U. Min. Debut 1979 OB in *Scrambled Feet*, followed by *Hijinks, I Can't Keep Running in Place, Jerry's Girls, Harvest of Strangers, Quilters*, Bdwy in *Fearless Frank* (1980), *Big River, Rags, Social Security, Les Misérables*.

BARRIE-WILSON, WENDY. Born June 9 in Loveland, OH. Graduate Denison, UNC. Bdwy debut 1987 in *All My Sons*, OB in *The Voice of the Prairie*.

BARRON, HOLLY. Born Feb. 1, 1947 in Oakland, CA. Graduate UC/Berkeley. Debut 1977 OB in *Cracks*, followed by *Mecca, Last Summer at Bluefish Cove, The Man Who Fell in Love with His Wife*, Bdwy in *Design for Living* (1984).

BART, ROGER. Born Sept. 29, 1962 in Norwalk, CT. Graduate Rutgers U. Debut 1984 OB in *A Second Wind*, followed by *Lessons, Up Against It, Henry IV Parts 1 and 2*, Bdwy in *Big River* (1987).

BARTENIEFF, GEORGE. Born Jan. 24, 1933 in Berlin, Ger. Bdwy debut 1947 in *The Whole World Over*, followed by *Venus Is, All's Well That Ends Well, Quotations from Chairman Mao Tse-Tung, The Death of Bessie Smith, Cop-Out, Room Service, Unlikely Heroes*, OB in *Walking to Waldheim, Memorandum, The Increased Difficulty of Concentration, Trelawny of the Wells, Charley Chestnut Rides the IRT, Radio (Wisdom): Sophia Part I, Images of the Dead, Dead End Kids, The Blonde Leading the Blonde, The Dispossessed, Growing Up Gothic, Rosetti's Apologies, On the Lam, Samuel Beckett Trilogy, Quartet, Help Wanted, A Matter of Life and Death, The Heart That Eats Itself, Coney Island Kid, Cymbeline, Better People*.

BARTLETT, ALISON. Born in Massachusetts July 14, 1971. Debut 1984 OB in *Landscape of the Body*, followed by *Jersey City*.

BARTLETT, PETER. Born Aug. 28, 1942 in Chicago, IL. Attended Loyala U., LAMBDA. Bdwy debut 1969 in *A Patriot for Me*, followed by *Gloria and Esperanza*, OB in *Boom Boom Boom, I Remember the House Where I Was Born, Crazy Locomotive, A Thurber Carnival, Hamlet, Buzzsaw Berkeley, Learned Ladies*.

BARTLETT, ROBIN. Born Apr. 22, 1951 in New York City. Graduate Boston U. Bdwy debut 1975 in *Yentl*, followed by *The World of Sholem Aleichem*, OB in *Agamemnon, Fathers and Sons, No End of Blame, Living Quarters, After the Fall, Cheapside, The Early Girl, Reckless*.

BARTOK, JAYCE. Born July 31, 1972 in Pittsburgh, PA. Debut 1989 OB in *Dalton's Back* followed by *The My House Play*.

BARTON, STEVE. Born in Arkansas. Graduate U. Texas. Bdwy debut 1988 in *Phantom of the Opera*.

BASCH, PETER. Born May 11, 1956 in New York City. Graduate Columbia Col, UC/Berkeley. Debut 1984 in *Hackers*, followed by *Festival of 1-Act Comedies*.

BATEMAN, BILL. Born Dec. 10 in Rock Island, IL. Graduate Augustana Col. Debut 1974 OB in *Anything Goes*, followed by Bdwy in *Hello Dolly* (1978), *Bring Back Birdie, Peter Pan* (1990).

BATTLE, HINTON. Born Nov. 29, 1956 in Neubraecke, Ger. Joined DanceTheatre of Harlem before making Bdwy debut in *The Wiz* (1975), followed by *Dancin', Sophisticated Ladies, Dreamgirls, The Tap Dance Kid, Miss Saigon*.

BAUM, DANIEL. Born Mar. 19, 1961 in Omaha, NE. Attended Regis Col. Debut 1988 OB in *The Blitzstein Project*, followed by *The Sum of Us*.

BEAN, REATHEL. Born Aug. 24, 1942 in Missouri. Graduate Drake U. OB in *America Hurrah, San Francisco's Burning, Love Cure, Henry IV, In Circles, Peace, Journey of Snow White, Wanted, The Faggot, Lovers, Not Back with the Elephants, The Art of Coarse Acting, The Trip Back Down, Hunting Cockroaches, Smoke on the Mountain*, Bdwy in *Doonesbury* (1983), *Big River*.

BEECHMAN, LAURIE. Born Apr. 4, 1954 in Philadelphia, PA. Attended NYU. Bdwy debut 1977 in *Annie*, followed by *Pirates of Penzance, Joseph and the Amazing Technicolor Dreamcoat* for which she received a Theatre World Award, *Cats, Les Misérables*, OB in *Some Enchanted Evening. Pal Joey in Concert*.

BELMONTE, VICKI. Born Jan. 20, 1947 in U.S. A. Bdwy debut 1960 in *Bye Bye Birdie*, followed by *Subways Are for Sleeping, All American, Annie Get Your Gun* (LC), OB in *Nunsense*.

BENDER, JEFF. Born May 20, 1962 in Oakland, CA. Attended Pacific Consv, NYU. Debut 1985 OB in *Second Hurricane*, followed by *Alvrone, Twelfth Night, Angel City, The Odyssey, Bradley and Beth, Carbondale Dreams, Grandma's Play*.

BENSON, CINDY. Born Oct. 2, 1951 in Attleboro, MA, Graduate St. Leo Col, U. IL. Debut 1981 OB in *Some Like It Cole*, followed by Bdwy *Les Misérables* (1987).

BENTLEY, MARY DENISE. Born Dec. 28 in Indianapolis, IN. Graduate Ind. U. Bdwy debut 1983 in *Dreamgirls*, OB in *Little Shop of Horrors* (1987), followed by *Forbidden Broadway*.

BERETTA, JOANNE. Born Nov. 14 in San Francisco, CA. Attended SF State Col. Bdwy debut in *New Faces of 1962*, OB in *The Club, Dementos, Colette Collage*.

BERQUE, BARBARA. Born Aug. 31, 1953. OB in El Salvador, followed by *The Wonder Years, What Does a Blind Leopard See?, The Enclave, Measure for Measure, The Hot l Baltimore, You Never Can Tell, Are You Now or Have You Ever Been*.

BERRESSE, MICHAEL. Born Aug. 15, 1964 in Holyoke, MA. Bdwy debut 1990 in *Fiddler on the Roof*.

BEVAN, ALISON. Born Nov. 20, 1959 in Cincinnati, OH. Attended NYU. Debut 1980 in *Trixie True Teen Detective*, followed by *Brigadoon* (LC), *Little Lies*.

BEVERLEY, TRAZANA. Born Aug. 9, 1945 in Baltimore, MD. Graduate NYU. Debut 1969 OB in *Rules for Running*, followed by *Les Femmes Noires, Geronimo, Antigone, The Brothers, God's Trombones, Marathon '91*, Bdwy in *My Sister My Sister, For Colored Girls Who Have Considered Suicide* for which she received a Theatre World Award, *Death and the King's Horseman* (LC).

BICKELL, ROSS. Born Jan. 14, 1947 in Hackensack, NJ. Graduate Boston U. Debut 1971 OB in *The Sweetshop Myrium*, followed by *Privates on Parade*, Bdwy in *A Few Good Men* (1990).

BIRKELUND, OLIVIA. Born Apr. 26, 1963 in New York City. Graduate Brown U. Debut 1990 OB in *Othello*.

BISHOP, KELLY (formerly Carole). Born Feb. 28, 1944 in Colorado Springs, CO. Bdwy debut 1967 in *Golden Rainbow*, followed by *Promises Promises, On the Town, Rachel Lily Rosenbloom, A Chorus Line, Six Degrees of Separation*, OB in *Piano Bar, Changes, The Blessing, Going to New England, Six Degrees of Separation*.

BLAIR, PAMELA. Born Dec. 5, 1949 in Arlington, VT. Attended Ntl. Acad. of Ballet. Bdwy debut 1972 in *Promises Promises*, followed by *Sugar, Seesaw, Of Mice and Men, Wild and Wonderful, A Chorus Line, The Best Little Whorehouse in Texas, King of Hearts, The Nerd, A Few Good Men*, OB in *Ballad of Boris K, Split, Real Life Funnies, Double Feature, Hit Parade, 1-2-3-4-5*.

BLAISDELL, NESBITT. Born Dec. 6, 1928 in New York City. Graduate Amherst, Columbia. Debut 1978 OB in *Old Man Joseph and His Family*, followed by *Molière in Spite of Himself, Guests of the Nation, Chekhov Sketch Book, Elba, Ballad of Soapy Smith, Custom of the Country, A Cup of Coffee, The Immigrant, Yokohama Duty*, Bdwy in *Cat on a Hot Tin Roof* (1990).

BLETHYN, BRENDA. Born in Ramsgate, Kent, Eng. NY debut 1991 OB in *Absent Friends* for which she received a Theatre World Award.

Jayne
Atkinson

Rene
Auberjonois

Becky Ann
Baker

Dylan
Baker

Wendy
Barrie-Wilson

George
Bartenieff

Peter
Bartlett

Robin
Bartlett

Peter
Basch

Laurie
Beechman

Michael
Berresse

Alison
Bevan

Olivia
Birkelund

Nesbitt
Blaisdell

Joyce
Blint

Joel
Blum

Jane
Bodle

Eric
Bogosian

Jim
Bracchitta

Stacy Lynn
Brass

James
Brennan

Suzanne
Briar

Julian
Brightman

Fran
Brill

Elaine
Bromka

Simon
Brooking

Katherine
Buffaloe

James
Bundy

Pamela
Burrell

Mike
Burstyn

BLINT, JOYCE. Born Mar. 3, 1957 in Brooklyn, NY. Attended Kingsborough Col. Debut 1983 OB in *The Cherry Orchard*, followed by *Two Small Bodies, Mascara, The Goat.*
BLOCK, SCOTTY. Born Jan. 28 in New Rochelle, NY. Attended AADA. Debut 1945 OB in *Craig's Wife*, followed by *Lemon Sky, Battering Ram, Richard III, In Celebration, An Act of Kindness, The Price, Grace, Neon Psalms, Other People's Money, Walking the Dead*, Bdwy in *Children of a Lesser God* (1980).
BLOOM, TOM. Born Nov. 1, 1944 in Washington, DC. Graduate Western MD Col., Emerson Col. Debut 1989 OB in *The Widow's Blind Date*, followed by *A Cup of Coffee, Major Barbara, A Perfect Diamond.*
BLUM, JOEL. Born May 19, 1952 in San Francisco, CA. Attended Marin Col., NYU. Bdwy debut 1976 in *Debbie Reynolds on Broadway*, followed by *42nd Street, Stardust*, OB in *And the World Goes Round.*
BLUM, MARK. Born May 14, 1950 in Newark, NJ. Graduate U. PA, U. MN. Debut 1976 OB in *The Cherry Orchard*, followed by *Green Julia, Say Goodnight, Gracie, Table Settings, Key Exchange, Loving Reno, Messiah, It's Only a Play, Little Footsteps, Cave of Life, Gus & Al, Bdwy in Lost in Yonkers* (1991).
BOBBIE, WALTER. Born Nov. 18, 1945 in Scranton, PA. Graduate U. Scranton, Catholic U. Bdwy debut 1971 in *Frank Merriwell*, followed by *The Grass Harp, Grease, Tricks, Going Up, History of the American Film, Anything Goes*, OB in *Drat!, She Loves Me, Up from Paradise, Goodbye Freddy, Cafe Crown, Young Playwrights '90.*
BODLE, JANE. Born Nov. 12 in Lawrence, KS. Attended U. Utah. Bdwy debut 1983 in *Cats*, followed by *Les Misérables, Miss Saigon.*
BOGARDUS, STEPHEN. Born Mar. 11, 1954 in Norfolk, VA. Princeton graduate. Bdwy debut 1980 in *West Side Story*, followed by *Les Misérables*, OB in *March of the Falsettos, Feathertop, No Way to Treat a Lady, Look on the Bright Side, Falsettoland.*
BOGOSIAN, ERIC. Born Apr. 24, 1953 in Woburn, MA. Graduate Oberlin Col. Debut 1982 OB in *Men Inside/Voices of America*, followed by *Funhouse, Drinking in America, Talk Radio, Sex Drugs Rock & Roll.*
BOROWITZ, KATHERINE. Born in Chicago, IL. Graduate Yale, Harvard. Debut 1982 OB in *Cloud 9*, followed by *Lennon, Before the Dawn, Arturo Ui.*
BORTS, JOANNE. Born June 12, 1961 in Syosset, NY. Graduate SUNY/Binghamton. Debut 1985 in *The Golden Land*, followed by *On Second Avenue*, Bdwy in *Fiddler on the Roof* (1990).
BOSCO, PHILIP. Born Sept. 26, 1930 in Jersey City, NJ. Graduate Catholic U. Credits: *Auntie Mame, Rape of the Belt, Ticket of Leave Man, Donnybrook, A Man for All Seasons, Mrs. Warren's Profession*, with LCRep in *A Great Career, In the Matter of J. Robert Oppenheimer, The Miser, The Time of Your Life, Camino Real, Operation Sidewinder, Amphitryon, Enemy of the People, Playboy of the Western World, Good Woman of Setzuan, Antigone, Mary Stuart, Narrow Road to the Deep North, The Crucible, Twelfth Night, Enemies, Plough and the Stars, Merchant of Venice, A Streetcar Named Desire, Henry V, Threepenny Opera, Streamers, Stages, St. Joan, The Biko Inquest, Man and Superman, Whose Life Is It Anyway?, Major Barbara, A Month in the Country, Bacchae, Hedda Gabler, Don Juan in Hell, Inadmissible Evidence, Eminent Domain, Misalliance, Learned Ladies, Some Men Need Help, Ah, Wilderness!, The Caine Mutiny Court Martial, Heartbreak House, Come Back Little Sheba, Loves of Anatol, Be Happy For Me, Master Class, You Never Can Tell, A Man for All Seasons, Devil's Disciple, Lend Me a Tenor, The Miser, Breaking Legs.*
BOUDREAU, ROBIN. Born Nov. 7 in Pittsburgh, PA. Graduate NYU. Bdwy debut 1981 in *Pirates of Penzance*, followed by OB in *To Whom It May Concern, Custody.*
BOVE, ELIZABETH. Born Sept. 30 in Melbourne, Australia. Graduate U. Tex. Debut 1986 OB in *Witness for the Prosecution*, followed by *House of Bernarda Alba, The Country Girl, The Maids, Round & Peakheads, The Dream Cure.*
BRACCHITTA, JIM. Born Feb. 27, 1960 in Brooklyn, NY. Graduate NYU. Bdwy debut 1989 in *Gypsy*, OB in *The Tenants of 3-R, Merchant of Venice, Rapunzel, Mock Doctor/Euridice, I Can Get It for You Wholesale.*
BRASS, STACEY LYNN. Born Aug. 31, 1968 in New York City. Attended NYU. Bdwy debut 1978 in *Annie*, followed by *Fiddler on the Roof* (1990), OB in *Romance in Hard Times.*
BREEN, J. PATRICK. Born Oct. 26, 1960 in Brooklyn, NY. NYU graduate. Debut 1982 OB in *Epiphanyu*, followed by *Little Murders, Blood Sports, Class 1 Acts, Baba Goya, Chelsea Walls, The Substance of Fire, Bdwy in Brighton Beach Memoirs* (1983).
BRENNAN, JAMES. Born Oct. 31, 1950 in Newark, NJ. Bdwy debut 1974 in *Good News*, followed by *Rodgers and Hart, So Long, 174th Street, Little Me, I Love My Wife, Singin' in the Rain, 42nd Street, Me and My Girl*, OB in *Juba.*
BRENNAN, NORA. Born Dec. 1, 1953 in East Chicago, IN. Graduate Purdue U. Bdwy debut 1980 in *Camelot*, followed by *Cats.*
BRENNAN, TOM. Born Apr. 16, 1926 in Cleveland, OH. Graduate Oberlin, Western Reserve U. Debut 1958 OB in *Synge Trilogy*, followed by *Between Two Thieves, East, All in Love, Under Milk Wood, An Evening with James Purdy, The Golden Six, Pullman Car Hiawatha, Are You Now or Have You Ever, The Diary of Anne Frank, Milk of Paradise, Transcendental Love, The Beaver Coat, The Overcoat, Summer, Asian Shade, Inheritors, Paradise Lost, Madwoman of Chaillot, The Time of Your Life, Bdwy in Play Memory, Our Town, The Miser.*
BRIAN, MICHAEL. Born Nov. 14, 1958 in Utica, NY. Attended Boston Consv. Debut 1979 OB in *Kennedy's Children*, followed by *Street Scene, The Death of Von Richthofen as Witnessed from Earth, Lenny and the Heartbreakers, Gift of the Magi, Next Please!, Love in Two Countries, Bdwy in Baby* (1984), *Big River.*
BRIAR, SUZANNE. Born Feb. 8, 1946 in Washington, DC. Graduate U. Syracuse. Debut 1985 OB in *Tatterdemalion*, followed by *Princess Pat, The Red Mill, Oh, Boy!, No No Nanette, Can't Help Singing Kern*, Bdwy in *Chess* (1988), *Aspects of Love.*
BRIGHTMAN, JULIAN. Born Mar. 5, 1954 in Philadelphia, PA. Graduate U. PA. Debut 1987 OB in *1984* followed by *Critic, Leaves of Grass*, Bdwy in *Peter Pan* (1990)
BRIGHTMAN, SARAH. Born in London, Eng., in 1959. Bdwy debut 1988 in *The Phantom of the Opera*, followed by *Aspects of Love* (1990).
BRILL, FRAN. Born Sept. 30 in PA. Attended Boston U. Bdwy debut 1969 in *Red, White and Maddox*, OB in *What Every Woman Knows, Scribes, Naked, Look Back in Anger, Knuckle, Skirmishes, Baby with the Bathwater, Holding Patterns, Festival of One Acts, Taking Steps, Young Playwrights Festival, Claptrap, Hyde in Hollywood, Good Grief.*
BRODERICK, MATTHEW. Born Mar. 21, 1963 in New York City. Debut 1981 OB in *Torch Song Trilogy*, followed by *The Widow Claire*, Bdwy 1983 in *Brighton Beach Memoirs* for which he received a Theatre World Award, followed by *Biloxi Blues, A Christmas Carol.*
BROMKA, ELAINE. Born Jan. 6 in Rochester, NY. Graduate Smith Col. Debut 1975 OB in *The Dybbuk*, followed by *Naked, Museum, The Son, Inadmissible Evidence, The Double Game, Cloud 9, Light Up the Sky*, Bdwy in *Macbeth* (1982).
BROOKING, SIMON. Born Dec. 23, 1960 in Edinburgh, Scot. Graduate SUNY/Fredonix, U. Wash. Debut 1989 OB in *American Bagpipes*, followed by *The Mortality Project, Prelude & Liebestod, Rough Crossing, Rumor of Glory, King Lear.*
BROOKS, JEFF. Born Apr. 7, 1950 in Vancouver, Can. Attended Portland State U. Debut 1976 OB in *Titanic*, followed by *Fat Chances, Nature and Purpose of the Universe, Actor's Nightmare, Sister Mary Ignatius Explains It All, Marathon 84, The Foreigner, Talk Radio, Washington Heights*, Bdwy in *A History of the American Film* (1978), *Lend Me A Tenor, Gypsy.*
BROWN, CAITLIN. Born Jan. 27, 1961 in Marin, CA. Attended Sacramento State U. Bdwy debut 1990 in *Grand Hotel.*
BROWN, GARRETT M. Born Nov. 7, 1948 in Battle Creek, MI. Graduate Amherst Col. OB in *Noon, Where Has Tommy Flowers Gone?, Of Mice and Men, Touch Black, Two Hotdogs with Everything, The Longest Walk, Bloodletters, Marathon '91*, Bdwy in *Whoopee!* (1979)
BROWN, GRAHAM. Born Oct. 24 in New York City. Graduate Howard U. OB in *Widower's Houses* (1959), *The Emperor's Clothes, Time of Storm, Major Barbara, Land Beyond the River, The Blacks, Firebugs, God Is a (Guess Who?), Evening of 1 Acts, Man Better Man, Behold! Cometh the Vanderkellans, Ride a Black Horse, The Great MacDaddy, Eden, Nevis Mountain Dew, Season Unravel, The Devil's Tear, Sons and Fathers of Sons, Abercrombie Apocalypse, Ceremonies in Dark Old Men, Eyes of the American, Richard II, The Taming of the Shrew, Winter's Tale, Black Eagles*, Bdwy in *Weekend* (1968), *Man in the Glass Booth, River Niger, Pericles, Black Picture Show, Kings, Lifetimes, Burners' Frolic, Jonquil, Talented Tenth.*
BROWN, ROBIN LESLIE. Born Jan. 18, in Canandaigua, NY. Graduate LIU. Debut 1980 OB in *The Mother of Us All*, followed by *Yours Truly, Two Gentlemen of Verona, Taming of the Shrew, The Mollusc, The Contrast, Pericles, Andromache, Macbeth, Electra, She Stoops to Conquer, Berenice, Hedda Gabler, A Midsummer Night's Dream, Three Sisters, Major Barbara, The Fine Art of Finesse, 2 Schnitzler One-Acts.*
BROWN, WILLIAM SCOTT. Born Mar. 27, 1959 in Seattle, WA. Attended U. Wash. Debut 1986 OB in *Juba*, Bdwy in *Phantom of the Opera* (1988).
BROWNING, SUSAN. Born Feb. 25, 1941 in Baldwin, NY. Graduate Penn. State. Bdwy debut 1963 in *Love and Kisses*, followed by *Company* for which she received a Theatre World Award, *Shelter, Goodtime Charley, Big River*, OB in *Jo, Dime a Dozen, Seventeen, The Boys from Syracuse, Collision Course, Whiskey, As You Like It, Removalists, Africanis Instructus, The March on Russia.*
BRYANT, DAVID. Born May 26, 1936 in Nashville, TN. Attended Tenn. State U. Bdwy debut 1972 in *Don't Play Us Cheap*, followed by *Bubbling Brown Sugar, Amadeus, Les Misérables*, OB in *Up in Central Park, Elizabeth and Essex, Appear and Show Cause.*
BRYDON, W.B. Born Sept. 20, 1933 in Newcastle, Eng. Debut 1962 OB in *The Long the Short and the Tall*, followed by *Live Like Pigs, Sgt. Musgrave's Dance, The Kitchen, Come Slowly, Eden, The Unknown Soldier and His Wife, Moon for the Misbegotten, The Orphan, Possession, Total Abandon, Madwoman of Chaillot, The Circle, Romeo and Juliet, Philadelphia Here I Come, Making History, Spinoza*, Bdwy in *The Lincoln Mask, Ulysses in Nighttown, The Father.*
BRYGGMAN, LARRY. Born Dec. 21, 1938 in Concord, GA. Attended CCSF, Am. Th. Wing. Debut 1962 OB in *A Pair of Pairs*, followed by *Live Like Pigs, Stop, You're Killing Me, Mod Donna, Waiting for Godot, Ballymurphy, Marco Polo Sings a Solo, Brownsville Raid, Two Small Bodies, Museum, Winter Dancers, Resurrection of Lady Lester, Royal Bob, Modern Ladies of Guanabacoa, Rum and Coke, Bodies, Rest and Motion, Blood Sports, Class 1 Acts, Spoils of War, Coriolanus, Prelude to a Kiss, Macbeth, Henry IV Parts 1 and 2*, Bdwy in *Ulysses in Nighttown* (1974), *Checking Out, Basic Training of Pavlo Hummel, Richard III, Prelude to a Kiss.*
BUCK, JOHN, JR. Born Oct. 2, 1938 in Madison, WI. Graduate U. Wis., Northwestern U. Debut 1966 OB in *Elizabeth the Queen*, followed by *King Lear.*
BUELL, BILL. Born Sept. 21, 1952 in Paipai, Taiwan. Attended Portland State U. Debut 1972 OB in *Crazy Now*, followed by *Declassee, Lorenzaccio, Promenade, The Common Pursuit, Coyote Ugly, Alias Jimmy Valentine, Kiss Me Quick, Bad Habits*, Bdwy in *Once a Catholic* (1979), *The First, Welcome to the Club, The Miser, Taking Steps.*
BUFFALOE, KATHARINE. Born Nov. 7, 1953 in Greenville, SC. Graduate NC Schl. of Arts. Bdwy debut 1981 in *Copperfield*, followed by *Joseph and the Amazing Technicolor Dreamcoat*, OB in *Non Pasquale, Charley's Tale, Mary S., Alias Jimmy Valentine, Juba.*
BUNDY, JAMES. Born May 8, 1959 in Boston, MA. Graudate Harvard, LAMDA. Debut OB 1991 in *Jekyll in Chamber.*
BURGE, GREGG. Born in New York City in 1959. Juilliard graduate. Bdwy debut 1975 in *The Wiz*, followed by *Sophisticated Ladies, Song and Dance, Oh Kay!*
BURK, TERENCE. Born Aug. 11, 1947 in Lebanon, IL. Graduate S. Ill. U. Bdwy debut 1976 in *Equus*, OB in *Religion, The Future, Sacred and Profane Love, Crime and Punishment.*
BURNETT, ROBERT. Born Feb. 28, 1960 in Goshen, NY. Attended HB Studio. Bdwy debut 1985 in *Cats.*
BURRELL, FRED. Born Sept. 18, 1936. Graduate UNC, RADA. Bdwy debut 1964 in *Never Too Late*, followed by *Illya Darling*, OB in *The Memorandum, Throckmorton, Texas, Voices in the Head, Chili Queen, The Queen's Knight, In Pursuit of the Song of Hydrogen, Unchanging Love.*
BURRELL, PAMELA. Born Aug. 4, 1945 in Tacoma, WA. Bdwy debut 1966 in *Funny Girl*, followed by *Where's Charley?, Strider, Sunday in the Park with George*, OB in *Arms and the Man* for which she received a Theatre World Award, *Berkeley Square, The Boss, Biography: A Game, Strider: Story of a Horse, A Little Madness, Spinoza.*
BURSE-MICKELBURY, DENISE. Born Jan. 13 in Atlanta, GA. Graduate Spellman Col., Atlanta U. Debut 1990 OB in *Ground People* for which she received a Theatre World Award.
BURSTYN, MIKE (formerly Burstein). Born July 1, 1945 in the Bronx, NY. Bdwy debut 1968 in *The Megilla of Itzak Manger*, followed by *Inquest, Barnum, OB in Wedding in Shtetl, Prisoner of Second Avenue, The Rothschilds.*
BURTON, ARNIE. Born Sept. 22, 1958 in Emmett, ID. Graduate U. Ariz. Bdwy debut 1983 in *Amadeus*, OB in *Measure for Measure, Major Barbara, Schnitzler One Acts.*
BUSCH, CHARLES. Born Aug. 23, 1954 in New York City. Graduate Northwestern U. Debut OB 1985 in *Vampire Lesbians of Sodom*, followed by *Times Square Angel, Psycho Beach Party, The Lady in Question, Red Scare on Sunset*, all of which he wrote.

BUSFIELD, TIMOTHY. Born June 12, 1957 in Lansing, MI. Graduate East Tenn State U. OB in *Richard II, Young Playwrights Festival, A Tale Told, Mass Appeal, The Tempest*, Bdwy in *A Few Good Men* (1990).

BUSSERT, MEG. Born Oct. 21, 1949 in Chicago, IL. Attended U. Ill. Bdwy debut 1980 in *The Music Man* for which she received a Theatre World Award, followed by *Brigadoon, Camelot, New Moon, The Firefly*, OB in *Lola, Professionally Speaking, Mexican Hayride, An Evening with Loesser and Sondheim.*

BUTLER, BRUCE. Born Mar. 11, 1954 in Clanton, NC. Graduate NC Central U. Debut 1983 OB in *Street Scene*, followed by *Freedom Days, Just a Night Out.*

BUTT, JENNIFER. Born May 17, 1958 in Valparaiso, IN. Stephens Col. graduate. Debut 1983 OB in *The Robber Bridegroom*, followed by *Into the Closet*, Bdwy in *Les Misérables* (1987).

CAHILL, JAMES. Born May 31, 1940 in Brooklyn, NY. Bdwy debut 1967 in *Marat/deSade*, followed by *Break a Leg, The Marriage of Figaro, City of Angels*, OB in *The Hostage, The Alchemist, Johnny Johnson, Peer Gynt, Timon of Athens, An Evening for Merlin Finch, The Disintegration of James Cherry, Crimes of Passion, Rain, Screens, Total Eclipse, Entertaining Mr. Sloane, Hamlet, Othello, The Trouble with Europe, Lydie Breeze, Don Juan, Bathroom Plays, Wild Life, Uncle Vanya, Twelfth Night.*

CALABRESE, MARIA. Born Dec. 7, 1967 in Secone, PA. Bdwy debut 1991 in *The Will Rogers Follies.*

CALLAWAY, LIZ. Born Apr. 13, 1961 in Chicago, IL. Debut 1980 OB in *Godspell*, followed by *The Matinee Kids, Brownstone, No Way to Treat a Lady, Marry Me a Little, 1-2-3-4-5*, Bdwy in *Merrily We Roll Along* (1981), *Baby, The Three Musketeers, Miss Saigon.*

CALLEN, CHRIS. Born July 14 in Fresno, CA. Graduate San Fran. U. Bdwy debut in *Brigadoon* (1968/CC), followed by *Someone Else's Sandals, 1776, Desert Song, Over Here, Rodgers and Hart, Truckload, Coolest Cat in Town, Fiddler on the Roof* (1977), *Prince of Central Park, Lend Me a Tenor, A Funny Thing Happened on the Way to the Forum.*

CAMACHO, BLANCA. Born Nov. 19, 1956 in New York City. Graduate NYU. Debut 1984 in *Sarita*, followed by *Maggie Magalita, Salon, You Can Come Back. Belle Monde, Danny and the Deep Blue Sea, Born to Rumba!*

CAMERON, HOPE. Born Feb. 21, 1920 in Hartford, CT. Attended AADA. Bdwy debut 1947 in *All My Sons*, followed by *Death of a Salesman*, OB in *The Strindberg Brothers, The Last Days of Lincoln, Grace, Skirmishes, Big Maggie, Re-Po, Marathon '90.*

CAMP, JOANNE. Born Apr. 4, 1951 in Atlanta, GA. Graduate Fl. Atlantic U., Geo Wash. U. Debut 1981 OB in *The Dry Martini*, followed by *Geniuses* for which she received a Theatre World Award, *June Moon, Painting Churches, Merchant of Venice, Lady from the Sea, The Contrast, Coastal Disturbances, The Rivals, Andromache, Electra, Uncle Vanya, She Stoops to Conquer, Hedda Gabler, The Heidi Chronicles, Importance of Being Earnest, Medea, Three Sisters, A Midsummer Night's Dream, School for Wives, Measure for Measure, Dance of Death, Two Schnitzler One-Acts*, Bdwy in *The Heidi Chronicles* (1989).

CAMPBELL, AMELIA. Born Aug. 4, 1965 in Montreal, Can. Graduate Syracuse U. Debut 1988 OB in *Fun*, followed by *Member of the Wedding*, Bdwy in *Our Country's Good* (1991)

CAMPBELL, ERMA. Born Aug. 14, 1940 in New York City. Attended Hunter Col. Debut 1990 in *Ground People* for which she received a Theatre World Award, followed by *The Goat.*

CARIOU, LEN. Born Sept. 30, 1939 in Winnipeg, Can. Bdwy debut 1968 in *House of Atreus*, followed by *Henry V, Applause* for which he received a Theatre World Award, *Night Watch, A Little Night Music, Cold Storage, Sweeney Todd, Dance a Little Closer, Teddy and Alice, The Speed of Darkness*, OB in *A Sorrow Beyond Dreams, Up from Paradise, Master Class, Day Six, Measure for Measure, Mountain.*

CARLO, JOHANN. Born May 21, 1957 in Buffalo, NY. Attended Weber-Douglas Acad. Debut 1978 in *Grand Magic*, followed by *Artichoke, Don Juan Comes Back from the War, The Arbor, Cinders, Rich Relations, Life or Death*, Bdwy in *Plenty* (1983), *La Bete.*

CARLSON, DEBORAH. Born Dec. 21, 1952 in Bridgeport, CT. Graduate U. Conn. Debut 1988 OB in *Movie Buff*, followed by *Olympus on My Mind, I Can Get It for You Wholesale*, Bdwy in *Can-Can* (1981), *Into the Light.*

CARMICHAEL, BILL. Born June 18, 1954 in Oceanside, CA. Graduate U. Conn. Bdwy debut 1980 in *Peter Pan*, OB in *Pirates of Penzance, La Bohème, Love of Two Countries.*

CARNELIA, CRAIG. Born Aug. 13, 1949 in Queens, NY. Attended Hofstra U. Debut 1969 OB in *The Fantasticks*, followed by *Lend an Ear, Three Postcards, Pictures in the Hall.*

CARRADINE, KEITH. Born Aug. 8, 1949 in San Mateo, CA. Attended Col. State U. Bdwy debut 1969 in *Hair*, followed by *Foxfire, The Will Rogers Follies*, OB in *Wake Up It's Time to Go to Bed.*

CARROLL, DAVID (formerly David-James). Born July 30, 1950 in Rockville Centre, NY. Graduate Dartmouth Col. Debut 1975 OB in *A Matter of Time*, followed by *Joseph and the Amazing Technicolor Dreamcoat, New Tunes, La Bohème, Company, Café Crown*, Bdwy in Rodgers and Hart (1975), *Where's Charley, Oh Brother!, 7 Brides for 7 Brothers, Roberta in Concert, Wind in the Willows, Chess, Café Crown, Grand Hotel.*

CARROLL, ROCKY. Born July 9, 1963 in Cincinnati, OH. Graduate Webster U. Debut 1986 OB in *Macbeth*, followed by *As You Like It, Romeo and Juliet, Henry IV, Richard II*, Bdwy in *The Piano Lesson* (1990) for which he received a Theatre World Award.

CARTER, ROSANNA. Born Sept. 20 in Rolle Town, Bahamas. Bdwy debut 1980 in *The American Clock*, followed by *Inacent Black*, OB in *Lament of Tasti Fari, Gurghers of Callais, Scottsboro Boys, Les Femmes Noires, Killings on the Last Line, Under Heaven's Eye, Marathon '86, Ma Rose, Young Playwrights '90.*

CARTMEL, LISA. Born Feb. 11, 1964 in Iowa City, IA. Graduate Skidmore Col. Bdwy debut 1990 in *Fiddler on the Roof.*

CASNOFF, PHILIP. Born Aug. 3, 1953 in Philadelphia, PA. Graduate Wesleyan U. Debut 1978 OB in *Gimme Shelter*, followed by *Chincilla, King of Schnorrers, Mary Stuart, Henry IV, Marathon '89, Up Against It*, Bdwy in *Grease* (1973), *Chess* for which he received a Theatre World Award, *Devil's Disciple, Shogun.*

CASS, PEGGY. Born May 21, 1926 in Boston, MA. Attended Wyndham Schl. Credits include *Touch and Go, Live Wire, Bernardine, Othello, Henry V, Auntie Mame* for which she received a Theatre World Award, *A Thurber Carnival, Children from Their Games, Don't Drink the Water, Front Page, Plaza Suite, Once a Catholic, 42nd Street, The Octette Bridge Club*, OB in *Phoenix '55, Are You Now or Have You Ever Been?, One Touch of Venus, George White's Scandals, Light Up the Sky, 50 Million Frenchmen.*

CASSIDY, PATRICK. Born Jan. 4, 1961 in Los Angeles, CA. Bdwy debut 1982 in *Pirates of Penzance*, followed by *Leader of the Pack*, OB in *Assassins.*

CAVISE, JOE ANTONY. Born Jan. 7, 1958 in Syracuse, NY. Graduate Clark U. Debut 1981 OB in *Street Scene*, followed by Bdwy 1984 in *Cats.*

CEBALLOS, RENE M. Born Apr. 7, 1953 in Boston, MA. Attended San Fran. U. Bdwy debut 1977 in *A Chorus Line*, followed by *Dancin', Cats, Dangerous Games, Grand Hotel*, OB in *Tango Apasionado.*

CHAIKIN, JOSEPH. Born Sept. 16, 1935 in Brooklyn, NY. Credits OB include *Man Is Man, Victims of Duty, The Exception and the Rule, The War in Heaven, Is This Real?, Struck Dumb.*

CHAIKIN, SHAMI. Born Apr. 21, 1938 in New York City. Debut 1966 OB in *America Hurrah*, followed by *Serpent, Terminal, Mutation Show, Viet Rock, Mystery Play, Electra, The Dybbuk, Endgame, Bag Lady, The Haggadah, Antigone, Loving Reno, Early Warnings, Uncle Vanya, Mr. Universe, 5 Women in a Chapel.*

CHALAWSKY, MAX. Born Feb. 26, 1956 in Brooklyn, NY. Graduate Brooklyn Col. Debut 1980 OB in *D*, followed by *I Am a Camera, Hard to Be a Jew, Danton's Death, White Liars, Ring Round the Moon.*

CHAMBERLIN, KEVIN. Born Nov. 25, 1963 in Baltimore, MD. Graduate Rutgers U. Debut 1990 OB in *Neddy*, followed by *Smoke on the Mountain.*

CHANNING, STOCKARD. Born Feb. 13, 1944 in NYC. Attended Radcliffe Col. Debut 1970 in *Adaptation/Next*, followed by *The Lady and the Clarinet, The Golden Age, Woman in Mind, Six Degrees of Separation*, Bdwy in *Two Gentlemen of Verona, They're Playing Our Song, The Rink, Joe Egg, House of Blue Leaves, Six Degrees of Separation.*

CHARLES, WALTER. Born Apr. 4, 1945 in East Stroudsburg, PA. Graduate Boston U. Bdwy debut 1973 in *Grease*, followed by *1600 Pennsylvania Avenue, Knickerbocker Holiday, Sweeney Todd, Cats, La Cage aux Folles, Aspects of Love, Me and My Girl.*

CHARLTON, WILLIAM. Born in Vilenza, Italy. Graduate U. Col., LAMBDA. Debut 1989 OB in *Third Time Lucky*, followed by *Pericles, The Catalyst.*

CHENG, KAM. Born Mar. 28, 1969 in Hong kong. Attended Muhlenberg Col. Bdwy debut 1991 in *Miss Saigon.*

CHILSON, KATHRYN. Born Jan. 31, 1955 in Louisiana, MO. Graduate Webster U. Debut 1982 in *The Cherry Orchard*, followed by *The Constant Wife, Full Circle.*

CHODER, JILL. Born Dec. 14, 1948 in Pittsburgh, PA. Attended NYU. Bdwy debut 1962 in *Bye Bye Birdie*, followed by *Stop the World I Want to Get Off, The Roar of the Greasepaint*, OB in *Best Foot Forward*, (1963), *Your Own Thing, Boccaccio, Festival of One Acts, 3 Little Plays about Sex.*

CHONG, MARCUS. Born July 8, 1967 in Seattle, WA. Attended Santa Monica City Col. Bdwy debut 1990 in *Stand-Up Tragedy* for which he received a Theatre World Award.

CHOW, CARYN ANN. Born Dec. 13, 1957 in New York City. Bdwy debut 1968 in *The King and I*, followed by OB in *My Own Little Things, Snow in June, Letters to a Student Revolutionary.*

CHRISTOPHER, DENNIS. Born Dec. 2, 1954 in Philadelphia, PA. Attended Temple U. Debut 1974 OB in *Yentl the Yeshiva Boy*, followed by *Advice from a Caterpillar*, Bdwy in *The Little Foxes* (1981), *Brothers.*

CIOFFI, CHARLES. Born Oct. 31, 1935 in New York City. Graduate U. Minn. OB in *A Cry of Players*, followed by *King Lear, In the Matter of J. Robert Oppenheimer, Antigone, A Whistle in the Dark, Hamlet, Self Defense, Real Estate*, Bdwy in *Stand-up Tragedy* (1990).

CISTONE, DANNY. Born Apr. 10, 1974 in Philadelphia, PA. Bdwy debut 1989 in *Gypsy.*

CLARK, DANNY ROBINSON. Born Jul. 14, 1937 in Jonestown, MS. Attended U. Min. Bdwy debut 1990 in *The Piano Lesson.*

CLAYTON, LAWRENCE. Born Oct. 10, 1956 in Mocksville, NC. Attended NC Central U. Debut 1980 in *Tambourines to Glory*, followed by *Skyline, Across the Universe, Two by Two, Romance in Hard Times, Juba*, Bdwy in *Dreamgirls* (1984).

CLAYTON, PHILIP. Born June 4, 1954 in Billings, MT. Attended U. Utah. Bdwy debut 1987 in *Starlight Express*, followed by *Aspects of Love.*

COCHRAN, RAY. Born Sept. 4, 1964 in Lebanon, KY. Debut 1989 OB in *Young Playwrights Festival*, followed by *Down the Stream, Six Degrees of Separation* (also Bdwy).

COCKRUM, ROY. Born June 29, 1956 in Knoxville, TN. Graduate Northwestern U. Debut 1991 OB in *The Broken Pitcher*, followed by *Vampire Lesbians of Sodom, Red Scare on Sunset.*

COHEN, IAN. Born in Brooklyn, NY. Debut 1991 OB in *The Beauty Part.*

COHEN, JAMIE. Born Apr. 20, 1959 in Peoria, IL. Bdwy debut 1989 in *Jerome Robbins' Broadway.*

COHEN, LYNN. Born Aug. 10 in Kansas City, MO. Graduate Northwestern U. Debut 1979 OB in *Don Juan Comes Back from the Wars*, followed by *Getting Out, The Arbor, The Cat and the Canary, Suddenly Last Summer, Bella Figura, The Smash, Chinese Viewing Pavilion, Isn't It Romantic, Total Eclipse, Angelo's Wedding, Hamlet, Love Diatribe*, Bdwy in *Orpheus Descending* (1989).

COHEN, MARGERY. Born June 24, 1947 in Chicago, IL. Attended U. Wis., U. Chicago. Bdwy debut 1968 in *Fiddler on the Roof*, followed by *Jacques Brel Is Alive ...*, OB in *Berlin to Broadway*, Bdwy *Bernstein, Starting Here Starting Now, Unsung Cole, Paris Lights, Pere Gorio.*

COHENOUR, PATTI. Born Oct. 17, 1952 in Albuquerque, NM. Attended U. NM. Bdwy debut 1982 in *A Doll's Life*, followed by *Pirates of Penzance, Big River, The Mystery of Edwin Drood. Phantom of the Opera*, OB in *La Bohème* for which she received a Theatre World Award.

COLE, DEBRA. Born Oct. 27, 1962 in Buffalo, NY. Graduate NYU. Debut 1984 in *Fables for Friends*, followed by *Daughters, Bunker Reveries, Marathon '91*, Bdwy in *House of Blue Leaves* (1986).

COLEMAN, JACK. Born in 1958 in Easton, PA. Graduate Duke U. Debut 1987 OB in *The Common Pursuit*, Bdwy in *Stand-up Tragedy* (1990).

COLLINS, KATE. Born May 6, 1959 in Boston, MA. Graduate Northwestern U. Debut 1984 OB in *The Danube*, followed by *Quiet on the Set*, Bdwy in *Doubles* (1985).

COLLINS, STEPHEN. Born Oct. 1, 1947 in Des Moines, IA. Graduate Amherst Col. Bdwy debut 1972 in *Moonchildren*, followed by *No Sex Please We're British, The Ritz, Censored Scenes from King Kong, Loves of Anatol*, OB in *Twelfth Night, More Than You Deserve, Macbeth, Last Days of British Honduras*, BAM Co.'s *New York Idea, Three Sisters and The Play's the Thing, Beyond Therapy, One of the Guys, The Old Boy.*

COLLINS, SUZANNE. Born in San Francisco, CA. Graduate U. San Francisco. Debut 1975 OB in *Trelawney of the Wells*, followed by *The Cherry Orchard, The Art of Dining, Put Them All Together, Grotesque Love Songs.*

James
Cahill

Maria
Calabrese

Len
Cariou

Johann
Carlo

Bill
Carmichael

Rosanna
Carter

Lisa
Cartmell

Philip
Casnoff

Shami
Chaikin

Walter
Charles

Kam
Cheng

Dennis
Christopher

Danny
Cistone

Patti
Cohenour

Kevin
Conway

Georgina M.
Corbo

Bill
Corsair

Lynndawn
Couch

Kim
Criswell

Anthony
Crivello

Lindsay
Crouse

Keene
Curtis

Tyne
Daly

Bill
Daugherty

Edmund C.
Davys

Laura
Dean

Gerrit
de Beer

Marcy
DeGonge

Emilio
Del Pozo

Sheri
Delaine

CONNICK, HARRY, JR. Born 1967 in New Orleans, LA. Bdwy debut 1990 in *An Evening with Harry Connick, Jr.*

CONROY, FRANCES. Born in 1953 in Monroe, GA. Attended Dickinson Col., Juilliard, Neighborhood Playhouse. Debut 1978 OB with the Acting Co. in *Mother Courage, King Lear*, and *The Other Half*, followed by *All's Well That Ends Well, Othello, Sorrows of Stephen, Girls Girls Girls, Zastrozzi, Painting Churches, Uncle Vanya, Romance Language, To Gillian on Her 37th Birthday, Man and Superman, Zero Positive, Secret Rapture, Some Americans Abroad, Bright Room Called Day*, Bdwy in *The Lady from Dubuque* (1980), *Our Town* (1989), *The Secret Rapture, Some Americans Abroad.*

CONWAY, KEVIN. Born May 29, 1942 in New York City. Debut 1968 in *Muzeeka*, followed by *Saved, The Plough and the Stars, One Flew Over the Cuckoo's Nest, When You Comin' Back, Red Ryder?, Long Day's Journey Into Night, Other Places, King John, Other People's Money, The Man Who Fell in Love with His Wife*, Bdwy in *Indians* (1969), *Moonchildren, Of Mice and Men, The Elephant Man.*

COPPOLA, SAM. Born Jul. 31, 1935 in New Jersey. Attended Actors Studio. Debut 1968 OB in *A Present from Your Old Man*, followed by *Things That Almost Happen Detective Story, Jungle of Cities, Pals*, Bdwy in *The Caine Mutiny Court Martial* (1983).

CORBO, GEORGINA M. Born Sept. 21, 1965 in Havana, Cuba. Attended SUNY/Purchase. Debut 1988 OB in *Ariano*, followed by *Born to Rumba!*

CORFMAN, CARIS. Born May 18, 1955 in Boston, MA. Graduate Fla. St. U., Yale. Debut 1978 OB in *Wings*, followed by *Fish Riding Bikes, Filthy Rich, Dry Land, All This and Moonlight, Cezanne Syndrome, Tea with Mommy and Jack, Equal Wrights, Mi Vida Loca, The Way of the the World, Henry IV Parts 1 and 2*, Bdwy in *Amadeus* (1980).

CORSAIR, BILL. Born Sept. 5, 1940 in Providence, RI. Debut 1984 OB in *Ernie and Arnie*, followed by *In the Boom Boom Room, The Constituent.*

COSTA, JOSEPH. Born June 8, 1946 in Ithaca, NY. Graduate Gettysburg Col, Yale. Debut 1978 OB in *The Show Off*, followed by *The Tempest, The Changeling, A Map of the World, Julius Caesar, Titus Andronicus, Love's Labour's Lost, Macbeth, The Crucible, The Way of the World.*

COSTALLOS, SUZANNE. Born Apr. 3, 1933 in New York City. Attended NYU, Boston Consv., Juilliard. Debut 1977 OB in *Play and Other Play by Beckett*, followed by *Elizabeth I, The White Devil, Hunting Scenes from Lower Bavaria, Selma, In Miami as It Is in Heaven*, Bdwy in *Zorba* (1983).

COUCH, LYNNDAWN. Born Dec. 15 in Coeburn, VA. Graduate Emory & Henry Col, UVA. Debut 1982 OB in *Augustus Does His Bit*, followed by *Man of Destiny, Grindhouse, The Catalyst.*

COUNTRYMAN, MICHAEL. Born Sept. 15, 1955 in St. Paul, MN. Graduate Trinity Col., AADA. Debut 1983 OB in *Changing Palettes*, followed by *June Moon, Terra Nova, Out!, Claptrap, The Common Pursuit, Woman in Mind, Making Movies, The Tempest, Tales of the Lost Formicans, Marathon '91, The Stick Wife*, Bdwy in *A Few Good Men* (1990).

COUSINS, BRIAN. Born May 9, 1959 in Portland, ME. Graduate Tulane, U. Wash. Debut 1987 OB in *Death of a Buick*, followed by *Taming of the Shrew, Enrico IV, Richard III, Prelude to a Kiss*, Bdwy in *Artist Descending a Staircase* (1989), *Prelude to a Kiss.*

COVER, A.D. Born in 1928 in Stamford, CT. Attended Wesleyan, Yale, U. Vermont, AADA. Debut 1985 OB in *The Importance of Being Earnest*, followed by *Catch Me If I Fall.*

CRABTEE, HOWARD E. Born Nov. 5, 1954 in Excelsior Springs, MO. Attended Maplewood Col. Debut 1987 OB in *Howard and Drew Meet the Invisible Man*, followed by *WhatNot.*

CRAWFORD, MICHAEL. Born Jan. 19, 1942 in Salisbury, Wiltshire, Eng. Bdwy debut 1967 in *Black Comedy*, followed by *Phantom of the Opera* (1988).

CRIST, SHERIDAN. Born Dec. 5, 1957 in Los Angeles, CA. Graduate Redlands U., Rutgers U. Debut 1984 OB in *Oresteia*, followed by *The Underpants, Frankenstein, George Dandin, The Seagull: The Hamptons.*

CRISWELL, KIM. Born July 19, 1957 in Hampton, VA. Graduate U. Cin. Bdwy debut 1981 in *The First*, followed by *Nine, Baby, Stardust, 3 Penny Opera*, OB in *Sitting Pretty, 50 Million Frenchmen.*

CRIVELLO, ANTHONY. Born Aug. 2, 1955 in Milwaukee, WI. Bdwy debut 1982 in *Evita*, followed by *The News, Les Misérables*, OB in *The Juniper Tree.*

CROMWELL, J.T. Born March 4, 1935 in Ann Arbor, MI. Graduate U. Cinn. Bdwy debut 1965 in *Half a Sixpence*, followed by *Jacques Brel Is Alive ..., 1600 Pennsylvania Avenue*, OB in *Pageant.*

CRONIN, JANE. Born Apr. 4, 1936 in Boston, MA. Bdwy debut 1965 in *Postmark Zero*, OB in *The Bald Soprano, One Flew over the Cuckoo's Nest, Hot l Baltimore, The Gathering, Catsplay, The Violano Virtuoso, Afternoons in Vegas, The Frequency, A Month in the Country, The Trading Post, Booth, Love Diatribe.*

CRONYN, HUME. Born July 18, 1911 in London, Can. Bdwy debut 1934 in *Hipper's Holiday*, followed by *Boy Meets Girl, High Tor, Room Service, There's Always a Breeze, Escape This Night, Off to Buffalo, Three Sisters, Weak Link, Retreat to Pleasure, Mr. Big, Survivors, The Fourposter, The Honeys, A Day by the Sea, Man in Dog Suit, Triple Play, Big Fish, Little Fish, Hamlet, The Physicists, A Delicate Balance, Hadrian VII, Promenade All, Noel Coward in Two Keys, The Gin Game, Foxfire, The Petition, A Christmas Carol*, OB in *Krapp's Last Tape, Madam Will You Walk, Happy Days, Act without Words.*

CROSBY, KIM. Born July 11, 1960 in Fort Smith, AR. Attended SMU, Man. Schl. Music. Bdwy debut 1985 in *Jerry's Girls*, followed by *Into the Woods*, OB in *Philemon.*

CROUSE, LINDSAY. Born May 12, 1948 in New York City. Graduate Radcliffe Col. Bdwy debut 1972 in *Much Ado about Nothing*, followed by *A Christmas Carol*, OB in *The Foursome, Fishing, Long Day's Journey into Night, Total Recall, Father's Day, Hamlet, Reunion, Twelfth Night, Childe Byron, Richard II, Serenading Louie, Prairie/Shawl, The Stick Wife.*

CROWNINGSHIELD, KEITH. Born Aug. 26, 1964 in Syracuse, NY. Graduate St. Lawrence U. Debut 1987 OB in *Starmites*, Bdwy in *Grand Hotel* (1989).

CRUZ, FRANCIS J. Born Oct. 4, 1954 in Long Beach, CA. Attended F.I.D.M. Bdwy debut 1991 in *Miss Saigon.*

CRYER, DAVID. Born March 8, 1936 in Evanston, IL. Attended DePauw U. OB in *The Fantasticks, Streets of New York, Now Is the Time for All Good Men, Whispers in the Wind, The Making of Americans, Portfolio Revue, Paradise Lost, The Inheritors, Rain, Ghosts, The Madwoman of Chaillot, Clarence, Mlle. Colombe, A Little Night Music, Follies*, Bdwy in *110 in the Shade, Come Summer* for which he received a Theatre World Award, *1776, Ari, Leonard Bernstein's Mass, The Desert Song, Evita, Chess, The Devil's Disciple.*

CUCCIOLI, BOB. Born May 3, 1958 in Hempstead, NY. Graduate St. John's U. Debut 1982 OB in *H.M.S. Pinafore*, followed by *Señor Discretion, Gigi, The Rothschilds, And the World Goes 'Round.*

CULLUM, JOHN. Born Mar. 2, 1930 in Knoxville, TN. Graduate U. Tenn. Bdwy debut 1960 in *Camelot*, followed by *Infidel Caesar, The Rehearsal, Hamlet, On a Clear Day You Can See Forever* for which he received a Theatre World Award, *Man of La Mancha, 1776, Vivat! Vivat Regina!, Shenandoah* (1975/1989), *Kings, The Trip Back Down, On the 20th Century, Deathtrap, Doubles, You Never Can Tell, The Boys in Autumn, Aspects of Love*, OB in *3 Hand Reel, The Elizabethans, Carousel, In the Voodoo Parlor of Marie Leveau, The King and I, Whistler.*

CUNNINGHAM, JOHN. Born June 22, 1932 in Auburn, NY. Graduate Yale, Dartmouth U. OB in *Love Me a Little, Pimpernel, The Fantasticks, Love and Let Love, The Bone Room, Dancing in the Dark, Father's Day, Snapshot, Head over Heels, Quartermaine's Terms, Wednesday, On Approval, Miami, Perfect Party, Birds of Paradise, Six Degrees of Separation*, Bdwy in *Hot Spot* (1963), *Zorba, Company, 1776, Rose, The Devil's Disciple, Six Degrees of Separation.*

CURLESS, JOHN. Born Sept. 16 in Wigan, Eng. Attended Central Schl. of Speech. NY debut 1982 OB in *The Entertainer*, followed by *Sus, Up 'n' Under, Progress, Prin, Nightingale, Absent Friends.*

CURTIS, KEENE. Born Feb. 15, 1925 in Salt Lake City, UT. Graduate U. Utah. Bdwy debut 1949 in *Shop at Sly Corner*, with APA in *School for Scandal, The Tavern, Anatole, Scapin, Right You Are, Importance of Being Earnest, Twelfth Night, King Lear, Seagull, Lower Depths, Man and Superman, Judith, War and Peace, You Can't Take It with You, Pantaglieze, Cherry Orchard, Misanthrope, Cocktail Party, Cock-a-Doodle Dandy, and Hamlet, A Patriot for Me, The Rothschilds, Night Watch, Via Galactica, Annie, Division Street, La Cage Aux Folles*, OB in *Colette, Ride Across Lake Constance, The Cocktail Hour.*

DALY, TYNE. Born Feb. 21, 1947 in Madison, WI. Attended Brandeis U., AMDA. Debut 1966 OB in *The Butter and Egg Man*, Bdwy in *That Summer That Fall* (1967), *Gypsy* (1989).

DANNER, BRADEN. Born in 1976 in Indianapolis, IN. Bdwy debut 1984 in *Nine*, followed by *Oliver!, Starlight Express, Les Misérables*, OB in *Genesis.*

DARLOW, CYNTHIA. Born June 13, 1949 in Detroit, MI. Attended NC Schl. of Arts, Penn. State U. Debut 1974 OB in *This Property Is Condemned*, followed by *Portrait of a Madonna, Clytemnestra, Unexpurgated Memoirs of Bernard Morgandigler, Actors Nightmare, Sister Mary Ignatius ..., Fables for Friends, That's It,' Folks!, Baby with the Bathwater, Dandy Dick, Prelude to a Kiss*, Bdwy in *Grease* (1976), *Rumors, Prelude to a Kiss.*

DAUGHERTY, BILL. Born Apr. 5, 1961 in St. Louis, MO. Graduate Webster U. Debut 1990 OB in *Daugherty & Field Off Broadway.*

DAVID, AMELIA. Born Aug. 3, 1958 in NYC. Graduate NYU. Debut 1984 OB in *Couple of the Year*, followed by *The Lost Art, The Triangle Project, Ring Round the Moon.*

DAVIS, SYLVIA. Born Apr. 10, 1910 in Philadelphia, PA. Attended Temple U., Am. Th. Wing. Debut 1949 OB in *Blood Wedding*, followed by *Tobacco Road, Orpheus Descending, Autumn Garden, Madwoman of Chaillot, House of Bernarda Alba, My Old Friends Max, Pahokee Beach, Mademoiselle, Hot l Baltimore, Hedda Gabler, Three Sisters, Medea.* Bdwy in *Nathan Weinstein, Mystic, CT* (1966), *Xmas in Las Vegas, Major Barbara.*

DAVYS, EDMUND C. Born Jan. 21, 1947 in Nashua, NH. Graduate Oberlin Col. Debut 1977 OB in *Othello*, Bdwy in *Crucifer of Blood* (1979), *Shadowlands.*

DEAKINS, MARK. Born Nov. 30, 1962 in Spokane, WA. Graudate Brigham Young U., U Cal/San Diego. Bdwy debut 1990 in *The Grapes of Wrath*, followed by OB *Henry IV Parts 1 & 2.*

DEAL, FRANK. Born Oct. 7, 1958 in Birmingham, AL. Attended Duke U. Debut 1982 OB in *The American Princess*, followed by *Richard III, Ruffian on the Stair, A Midsummer Night's Dream, We Shall Not All Sleep, The Legend of Sleepy Hollow, Three Sisters, The Triangle Project.*

DEAN, LAURA. Born May 27, 1963 in Smithtown, NY. Debut 1973 OB in *The Secret Life of Walter Mitty*, followed by *A Village Romeo and Juliet, Carousel, Hey Rube, Landscape of the Body, American Passion, Feathertop, Personals, Godspell, Festival of One-Acts, Catch Me If I Fall*, Bdwy in *Doonesbury* (1983) for which she received a Theatre World Award.

deBEER, GERRIT. Born June 17, 1935 in Amsterdam, Neth. Bdwy debut 1965 in *Pickwick*, followed by *Illya Darling, Zorba, Pajama Game, All Over Town, Grand Hotel.*

deGANON, CAMILLE. Born in Springfield, OH. Appeared with several dance companies before making her Bdwy debut in 1986 in *The Mystery of Edwin Drood*, followed by *Jerome Robbins' Broadway.*

DeGONGE, MARCY. Born May 4, 1957 in Newark, NJ. Graduate Hart Col. Bdwy debut 1989 in *Cats.*

DEL POZO, EMILIO. Born Aug. 6, 1948 in Havana, Cuba. Attended AMDA. Debut 1983 OB in *Union City Thanksgiving*, followed by *El Grande de Coca Cola, Senorita from Tacna, Twelfth Night, The Wonderful Ice Cream Suit, In Miami as It Is in Heaven.*

DELAINE, SHERI. Born Sept. 15, 1953 in Ironwood, MI. Graduate U. Wis. Debut 1988 OB in *Tartuffe*, followed by *French Gray, Pericles, The Rover, Zastrozzi.*

DeLAURENTIS, SEMINA. Born Jan 21 in Waterbury, CT. Graduate Southern CT State Col. Debut 1985 OB in *Nunsense*, followed by *Have I Got a Girl for You.*

DELLA PIAZZA, DIANE. Born Sept. 3, 1962 in Pittsburgh, PA. Graduate Cincinnati Consv. Bdwy debut 1987 in *Les Misérables.*

DeMATTIS, RAY. Born June 1, 1945 in New Haven, CT. Graduate Catholic U. Bdwy debut 1974 in *Grease*, followed by OB in *El Bravo!, Talk Radio, Flora the Red Menace, Good Tmes Are Killing Me.*

DEMPSEY, PATRICK. Born Jan. 13, 1966 in Turner, ME. Debut 1983 OB in *Torch Song Trilogy*, followed by *The Subject Was Roses*, Bdwy in *Brighton Beach Memoirs* (1984)

DeSHIELDS, ANDRE. Born Jan 12, 1946 in Baltimore, MD. Graduate U. Wis. Bdwy debut 1973 in *Warp*, followed by *Rachel Lily Rosenbloom, The Wiz, Ain't Misbehavin'* (1978/1988), *Haarlem Nocturne, Just So, Stardust*, OB in *2008½, Jazzbo Brown, The Soldier's Tale, The Little Prince, Haarlem Nocturne, Sovereign State of Boogedy Boogedy, Kiss Me When It's Over, Saint Tous.*

DEUTSCH, KURT. Born Jul. 26, 1966 in St. Louis, MO. Attended Syracuse U. Bdwy debut in *Broadway Bound* (1988), followed by *A Few Good Men*, OB in *Hyde in Hollywood, Making Movies.*

DEVLIN, JAY. Born May 8, 1929 in Ft. Dodge, IA. OB in *The Mad Show, Little Murders, Unfair to Goliath, Ballymurphy, Front Page, Fasnacht Day, Bugles at Dawn, A Good Year for the Roses, Crossing the Bar, Murder of Crows, Festival of 1-Acts*, Bdwy in *King of Hearts* (1978)

DeVRIES, MICHAEL. Born Jan. 15, 1951 in Grand Rapids, MI. Graduate U. Wash. Debut 1987 OB in *Ready or Not*, Bdwy in *Grand Hotel* (1989), *The Secret Garden*.

DEWAR, JOHN. Born Jan. 24, 1953 in Evanston, IL. Graduate U. Minn. Bdwy debut 1987 in *Les Misérables*, followed by *Aspects of Love*.

DEWHURST, COLLEEN. Born June 3, 1926 in Montreal, Can. Attended Downer Col., AADA. Bdwy debut 1952 in *Desire under the Elms*, followed by *Tamburlaine the Great, The Country Wife, Caligula, All the Way Home, Great Day in the Morning, Ballad of the Sad Café, More Stately Mansions, All Over, Mourning Becomes Electra, Moon for the Misbegotten, Who's Afraid of Virginia Woolf?, An Almost Perfect Person, The Queen and the Rebels, You Can't Take It with You, Ah Wilderness, Long Day's Journey into Night* (1988) OB in *The Taming of the Shrew, The Eagle Has Two Heads, Camille, Macbeth, Children of Darkness* for which she received a 1958 Theatre World Award, *Antony and Cleopatra, Hello and Goodbye, Good Woman of Setzuan, Hamlet, Are You Now or Have You Ever ...?, Taken in Marriage, My Gene, Love Letters*.

DIETRICH, JOHN. Born Aug. 27, 1960 in Milwaukee, WI. Graduate U. Wis. Debut 1989 in *Radio City Christmas Spectacular*, followed by OB in *A Funny Thing Happened on the Way to the Forum*.

DILLON, MIA. Born July 9, 1955 in Colorado Springs, CO. Graduate Penn State U. Bdwy debut 1977 in *Equus*, followed by *Da, Once a Catholic, Crimes of the Heart, The Corn Is Green, Hay Fever, The Miser*, OB in *The Crucible, Summer, Waiting for the Parade, Crimes of the Heart, Fables for Friends, Scenes from La Vie de Bohème, Three Sisters, Wednesday, Roberta in Concert, Come Back Little Sheba, Vienna Notes, George White's Scandals, Lady Moonsong, Mr. Monsoon, Almost Perfect, The Aunts*.

DiMEO, DONNA. Born Mar. 6, 1964 in Brooklyn, NY. Bdwy debut 1989 in *Jerome Robbins' Broadway*.

DiPASQUALE, FRANK. Born Jul. 15, 1955 in Whitestone, NY. Graduate USC. Bdwy debut in *La Cage aux Folles* (1983), followed by *Radio City Christmas Spectacular 1990, The Secret Garden*.

DIXON, ED. Born Sept. 2, 1948 in Oklahoma. Attended U. Okla. Bdwy in *The Student Prince*, followed by *No No Nanette, Rosalie in Concert, The Three Musketeers, Les Misérables*, OB in *By Bernstein, King of the Schnorrers, Rabboni, Moby Dick, Shylock, Johnny Pye and the Foolkiller*.

DOHI, SYLVIA. Born Feb. 2, 1965 in Hollywood, CA. Attended UCLA, Portland CC. Bdwy debut 1991 in *Miss Saigon*.

DOLAN, MICHAEL. Born June 21, 1965 in Oklahoma City, OK. Debut 1984 OB in *Coming of Age in Soho*, followed by Bdwy in *Breaking the Code* (1987), *A Few Good Men*.

DOMINGUEZ, STEVEN. Born Oct. 17, 1961 in New York City. Graduate CCNY, AADA. Debut 1988 OB in *King John*, followed by *Oedipus Rex, The Albanian Softshoe, Strangers*, Bdwy in *A Few Good Men*.

DORN, JAN. Born Mar. 12, 1954 in Jackson, TN. Graduate UCLA. Debut 1977 OB in *Hagar's Children*, followed by *Savage in Limbo*.

DOUGLAS, ILLEANA. Born Jul. 25, 1965 in Connecticut. Attended Neighborhood Playhouse. Debut OB in *Squaring the Circle*, followed by *Owl's Breath, New Vaudeville, Black Eagles*.

DOWNING, REBECCA. Born Nov. 30, 1962 in Birmingham, AL. Graduate Oklahoma City U. Debut 1989 OB in *Wonderful Town*, Bdwy in *The Will Rogers Follies* (1991).

DOWNING, VIRGINIA. Born Mar. 7 in Washington, DC. Attended Bryn Mawr. Bdwy debut 1937 in *Father Malachy's Miracle*, followed by *Forward the Heart, The Cradle Will Rock, A Gift of Time, We Have Always Lived in a Castle, Arsenic and Old Lace*, OB in *Juno and the Paycock, Man with the Golden Arm, Palm Tree in a Rose Garden, Play with a Tiger, The Wives, The Idiot, Medea, Mrs. Warren's Profession, Mercy Street, Thuder Rock, Pygmalion, First Week in Bogota, Rimers of Eldritch, Les Blancs, Shadow of a Gunman, All the Way Home, A Winter's Tale, Billy Liar, Shadow and Substance, Silent Catastrophe, Ernest in Love, Night Games, A Frog in His Throat, All That Fall, Richard III*.

DOYLE, JACK. Born June 7, 1954 in Brooklyn, NY. Graduate Adelphi U. Debut OB in *New Faces of 1952*, followed by *Tomfoolery*, Bdwy in *The Will Rogers Follies* (1991).

DRAKE, DAVID. Born June 27, 1963 in Baltimore, MD. Attended Essex Col., Peabody Consv. Debut 1984 in *Street Theater*, followed by *Pretty Boy, Vampire Lesbians of Sodom, The Life, The Night Larry Kramer Kissed Me, Pageant*.

DREISBACH, JEFFREY. Born Apr. 19, 1956 in Dowagiac. MI. Graduate Wayne State U. Bdwy debut 1989 in *A Few Good Men*.

DRISCOLL, MOIRA. Born Oct. 11, 1962 in Boston, MA. Graduate Amherst Col. Debut 1991 OB in *Nebraska*.

DuCLOS, DANIELLE. Born Sept. 29, 1974 in Warwick, NY. Debut 1988 OB in *Rimers of Eldritch*, followed by *Asleep on the Wind, Working One Acts*, Bdwy in *Aspects of Love* (1990)

DuCLOS, DEANNA. Born Apr. 18, 1979 in New York City. Debut 1987 OB in 1984, followed by Bdwy in *Aspects of Love* (1990)

DUDLEY, CRAIG. Born Jan. 22, 1945 in Sheepshead Bay, NY. Graduate AADA, Am. Th. Wing. Debut 1970 OB in *Macbeth*, followed by *Zou, I Have Always Believed in Ghosts, Othello, War and Peace, Dial 'M' for Murder, Misalliance*.

DUDLEY, GEORGE. Born Apr. 6, 1958 in Santa Monica, CA. Graduate Humboldt State U. Bdwy debut 1990 in *Grand Hotel*.

DUDWITT, KIMBERLY. Born Aug. 19, 1963 in Wilmington, DE. Graduate U. Del. Debut 1990 off and on Bdwy in *Prelude to a Kiss*.

DUELL, WILLIAM. Born Aug. 30, 1923 in Corinth, NY. Attended Ill. Wesleyan, Yale. OB in *Portrait of the Artist ..., Barroom Monks, A Midsummer Night's Dream, Henry IV, Taming of the Shrew, The Memorandum, Threepenny Opera, Loves of Cass McGuire, Romance Language, Hamlet, Henry IV Parts 1 and 2*, Bdwy in *A Cook for Mr. General, Ballad of the Sad Café, Ilya, Darling, 1776, Kings, Stages, The Inspector General, The Marriage of Figaro, Our Town*.

DuMONT, JAMES. Born Aug. 12, 1965 in Chicago, IL. Attended Boston U. Debut 1988 OB in *Tony 'n' Tina's Wedding*, followed by *Waiting for Lefty, Not Me, American Buffalo, Special Interests, Down and Out*, Bdwy in *Six Degrees of Separation* (1990).

DUNCAN, LAURA (formerly Delano). Born Jul. 10, 1958 in San Juan, PR. Graduate Goucher Col. Debut 1983 in *Blood Wedding* (1983), followed by *A Little Something to Ease the Pain, Dona Rosita, Born to Rumba!, Eastern Standard*.

DuSOLD, ROBERT. Born June 7, 1959 in Waukesha, WI. Attended U. Cinn. Consv. Bdwy debut in *Les Misérables* (1991).

DUTTON, CHARLES S. Born Jan. 30, 1951 in Baltimore, MD. Graduate Yale. Debut 1983 OB in *Richard III*, followed by *Pantomime, Fried Chicken and Invisibility, Splendid Mummer*, Bdwy in *Ma Rainey's Black Bottom* (1984) for which he received a Theatre World Award, *The Piano Lesson*.

DYER, MARGARET. Born May 28, 1968 in Key West, FL. Graduate Ithaca Col. Debut 1990 OB in *Pretty Faces*.**EAGAN, DAISY.** Born Nov. 4, 1979 in Brooklyn, NY. Attended Neihborhood Playhouse. Debut 1988 OB in *Tiny Tim's Christmas Carol*, Bdwy in *Les Misérables* (1989), followed by *The Secret Garden*.

EASTLEY, KEELY. Born Feb. 18, 1957 in New Albany, IN. Attended U. Nev. Debut 1981 OB in *The Lesson*, followed by *I Am a Camera, Flesh Flash and Frank Harris, Journal of Albion Moonlight, Split, Walking the Blonde*.

EDELMAN, GREGG. Born Sept. 12, 1958 in Chicago, IL. Graduate Northwestern U. Bdwy debut 1982 in *Evita*, followed by *Oliver!, Cats, Cabaret, City of Angels*, OB in *Weekend, Shop on Main Street, Forbidden Broadway, She Loves Me, Babes in Arms*.

EDMEAD, WENDY. Born Jul. 6, 1956 in New York City. Graduate NYCU. Bdwy debut 1974 in *The Wiz*, followed by *Stop the World ..., America, Dancin', Encore, Cats*.

EICHHORN, LISA. Born Feb. 4, 1952 in Reading, PA. Attended Queens Ontario U., RADA. Debut 1987 OB in *The Common Pursuit*, followed by *The Summer Winds*, Bdwy in *The Speed of Darkness*.

EIGENBERG, DAVID M. Born May 17, 1964 in Manhasset, NY. Graduate AADA. Debut 1989 OB in Young Playwright's Festival/*Finnagan's Funeral Parlor & Ice Cream Shop*, followed by *Six Degrees of Separation, The My House Play*, Bdwy in *Six Degrees of Separation* (1990).

ELDARD, RON. Born in 1964 in New York City. Attended HS Performing Arts. Bdwy debut 1986 in *Biloxi Blues*, OB in *Tony 'n' Tina's Wedding*.

ELIO, DONNA MARIE. Born Oct. 30, 1962 in Paterson, NJ. Bdwy debut 1974 in *Gypsy*, followed by *Merrily We Roll Along, Smile, Jerome Robbins' Broadway*.

ELIOT, DREW. Born in Neward, NJ. Graduate Columbia, RADA. OB in *The Fairy Garden, Dr. Faustus, Servant of Two Masters, Henry V, Stephen D., Sjt. Musgrave's Dance, Deadly Game, Taming of the Shrew, Appear and Show Cause, The Visit, White Collar*, Bdwy in *Elizabeth the Queen, The Physicists, Romulus*.

ELLEDGE, DAVID. Born Jul. 27, 1957 in Omak, WA. Graduate U. Utah. Debut 1984 OB in *Clarence*, followed by *Cole Cuts*, Bdwy in *Grand Hotel* (1989).

ELLENS, REBECCA. Born Apr. 24, 1959 in Bad Kreuznach, Ger. Graduate Calvin Col. Debut 1985 *Green Fields*, followed by *Eddie Goes to Poetry City*.

ELLIOTT, KENNETH. Born June 15, 1955 in Indianapolis, IN. Graduate Northwestern U. Debut 1985 OB in *Vampire Lesbians of Sodom*, followed by *Psycho Beach Party, Zero Positive, Times Square Angel, The Lady in Question*.

ELLIS, BRAD. Born Oct. 5, 1960 in Lexington, MA. Attended Berklee Col. Debut 1990 OB in *Forbidden Broadway*.

ELLIS, LESLIE. Born Jul. 22, 1962 in Boston, MA. Graduate Carnegie-Mellon. Debut 1989 OB in *Up Against It*, followed by *The Rothschilds*.

ELLIS, WILLIAM. Born Dec. 5, 1929 near Cincinnati, OH. Graduate Goodman School, Columbia, NYU. Debut 1953 OB in *One Foot to the Sea*, followed by *Murder in the Cathedral, Hill of Beans, Rags to Reubens, Hidden Away in Stores, Today's Children, The Marriage Proposal, Much Ado about Nothing, Writers, A Doll's House, Legend of Sleepy Hollow, Yesterday in Warsaw*.

EMERY, LISA. Born Jan. 29 in Pittsburgh, PA. Graduate Hollins Col. Debut 1981 OB in *In Connecticut*, followed by *Talley & Son, Dalton's Back, Grownups!*, Bdwy in *Passion* (1983), *Burn This, Rumors*.

EMMET, ROBERT. Born Oct. 3, 1952 in Denver, CO. Graduate U. Wash. Debut 1976 OB in *The Mousetrap*, followed by *The Seagull, Blue Hotel, Miss Jairus, Hamlet, Deathwatch, Much Ado About Nothing, Songs and Ceremonies, Mass Appeal, Macbeth, Bell, Book and Candle, Comes the Happy Hour, The Gift, The Merchant of Venice, Arms and the Man, The Lady from the Sea, Two Gentlemen from Verona, Andromache, Hamlet, The Diaries of Adam and Eve*, Bdwy in *The Devil's Disciple*.

ENGEL, DAVID. Born Oct. 19, 1959 in Orange, CA. Attended U. Cal/Irvine. Bdwy debut 1983 in *La Cage aux Folles*, OB in *Forever Plaid*.

ENRIQUEZ, DAVID. Born Apr. 29, 1967 in Managua, Nicaragua. Bdwy debut 1990 in *Fiddler on the Roof*.

ERBE, KATHRYN. Born in 1965 in New York City. Graduate NYU. Bdwy debut 1990 in *Grapes of Wrath*, followed by *The Speed of Darkness*, OB in *The My House Play*.

ERDE, SARA. Born March 18, 1970 in NYC. Debut 1987 OB in *Roosters*, followed by *Dancing Feet, A Midsummer Night's Dream, Don Juan of Seville, Occasional Grace*.

ERWIN, BARBARA. Born June 30, 1937 in Boston, MA. Debut 1973 OB in *The Secret Life of Walter Mitty*, followed by *Broadway, One Way to Ulan Bator*, Bdwy in *Annie, Ballroom, Animals, Gypsy*.

ESSMANN, JEFFREY. Born Sept. 11, 1952 in Milwaukee, WI. Attended U. Wis./Madison, Marquette U., Goethe Inst., NYU. Debut 1986 OB in *Sills and Company*, followed by *Artificial Reality*.

ESTEY, SUELLEN. Born Nov. 21, in Mason City, IA. Graduate Stephens Col., Northwestern U. Debut 1970 OB in *Some Other Time*, followed by *June Moon, Buy Bonds Buster, Smile Smile Smile, Carousel, Lullaby of Broadway, I Can't Keep Running, The Guys in the Truck, Stop the World ..., Bittersuite—One More Time, Passionate Extremes, Sweeney Todd, Love in Two Countries*, Bdwy in *The Selling of the President* (1972), *Barnum, Sweethearts in Concert, Sweeney Todd* (1989).

EVANS, HARVEY. Born Jan. 7, 1941 in Cincinnati, OH. Bdwy debut 1957 in *New Girl in Town*, followed by *West Side Story, Redhead, Gypsy, Anyone Can Whistle, Hello Dolly!, George M!, Our Town, The Boy Friend, Follies, Barnum, La Cage aux Folles*, OB in *Sextet*.

EVANS, VENIDA. Born Sept. 2, 1947 in Ypsilanti, MI. Attended Fisk U. Debut 1981 OB in *Turbuckle*, followed by *Ladies, Dinah Washington Is Dead, Ground People, East Texas*, Bdwy in *Amen Corner* (1983).

EVERS, BRIAN. Born Feb. 14, 1942 in Miami, FL. Graduate Capital U., U. Miami. Debut 1979 OB in *How's the House?*, followed by *Details of the 16th Frame, Divine Fire, Silent Night Lonely Night, Uncommon Holidays, The Tamer Tamed, Death of a Buick, The Racket, Six Degrees of Separation*, Bdwy in *House of Blue Leaves, Six Degrees of Separation*.

Semina
De Laurentis

Ray
DeMattis

Sylvia
Dohi

Michael
Dolan

Illeana
Douglas

Jack
Doyle

David
Drake

Moira
Driscoll

Craig
Dudley

Laura
Duncan

Robert
DuSold

Margaret
Dyer

Rebecca
Ellens

Robert
Emmet

Barbara
Erwin

Brian
Evers

Marilyn J.
Farina

Michael
Feinstein

Clebert
Ford

Frances
Foster

Clement
Fowler

Elizabeth
Franz

Peter
Frechette

Betsy
Friday

Teri
Furr

Eddie L.
Furs

Lauren
Gaffney

Craig
Gahnz

Eileen
Galindo

Vincent
Gardenia

EWING, J. TIMOTHY (a.k.a. Tim). Born Apr. 3, 1954 in Evansville, IN. Graduate Okla. State U. Debut 1972 OB in *Colette Collage*, followed by *Promenade, Pacific Overtures, Good Times, Charley's Tale, Love in Two Countries.*

FABER, RON. Born Feb. 16, 1933 in Milwaukee, WI. Graduate Marquette U. Debut 1959 in *An Enemy of the People*, followed by *The Exception and the Rule, America Hurrah, They Put Handcuffs on Flowers, Dr. Selavy's Magic Theatre, Troilus and Cressida, The Beauty Part, Woyzeck, St. Joan of the Stockyards, Jungle of Cities, Scenes from Everyday Life, Mary Stuart, 3 by Pirandello, Times and Appetites of Toulouse-Lautrec, Hamlet, Johnstown Vindicator, Don Juan of Seville, Between the Acts, Baba Goya, Moving Targets, Arturo Ui*, Bdwy in *Medea* (1973), *First Monday in October.*

FACTORA, MARSHALL. Born Aug. 19 in the Philippines. Graduate U. St. Thomas, NYU. Debut 1990 OB in *The Wash.*

FALK, WILLY. Born Jul. 21 in New York City. Harvard, LAMDA graduate. Debut 1982 OB in *The Robber Bridegroom*, followed by *Pacific Overtures, The House in the Woods, Elizabeth and Essex*, Bdwy in *Marilyn: An American Fable, Starlight Express, Les Misérables, Miss Saigon.*

FANCY, RICHARD. Born Aug. 2, 1943 in Evanston, IL. Attended LAMDA. Debut 1973 OB in *The Creeps*, followed by *Kind Lady, Rites of Passage, A Limb of Snow, The Meeting, Child's Play, Our Own Family, Dance of Death.*

FARER, RHONDA (a.k.a. Ronnie). Born Oct. 19, 1951 in Colonia, NJ. Graduate Rider Col. Debut 1973 on Bdwy in *Rachel Lily Rosenbloom*, followed by *They're Playing Our Song*, OB in *The Dog beneath the Skin, Sally and Marsha, The Deep End, Tamara, Festival of One-Acts, Catch Me If I Fall.*

FARINA, MARILYN J. Born Apr. 9 1947 in New York City. Graduate Sacred Heart Col. Debut 1985 OB in *Nunsense.*

FARINA, MICHAEL J. Born Aug. 22, 1958 in the Bronx, NY. Attended NY Inst. of Tech., Mercy Col. Bdwy debut in *Fiddler on the Roof* (1990).

FAUGNO, RICHARD (Rick). Born Nov. 8, 1978 in New York City. Bdwy debut 1991 in *The Will Rogers Follies.*

FEINSTEIN, MICHAEL. Born in 1957 in Columbus, OH. Bdwy debut 1988 in *Michael Feinstein in Concert*, followed by *Voice and Piano.*

FELDSHUH, TOVAH. Born Dec. 28, 1953 in New York City. Graduate Sarah Lawrence Col., U. Minn. Bdwy debut 1973 in *Cyrano*, followed by *Dreyfus in Rehearsal, Rodgers and Hart, Yentl* for which she received a Theatre World Award, *Sarava, Lend Me a Tenor*, OB in *Yentl the Yeshiva Boy, Straws in the Wind, Three Sisters, She Stoops to Conquer, Springtime for Henry, The Time of Your Life, Children of the Sun, The Last of the Red Hot Lovers, Mistress of the Inn, A Fierce Attachment, Custody.*

FERGUSON, LYNNDA. Born in Denver, CO. Bdwy debut 1981 in *Bring Back Birdie*, followed by *Rumors*, OB in *Romeo and Juliet.*

FERLAND, DANIELLE. Born Jan. 31, 1971 in Derby, CT. Debut 1983 in *Sunday in the Park with George*, followed by *Paradise*, Bdwy in *Sunday in the Park with George* (1984), *Into the Woods* for which she received a Theatre World Award, *A Little Night Music* (NYCO/LC).

FERRARA, ANDY. Born Sept. 2, 1960 in Los Gatos, CA. Bdwy debut 1990 in *Peter Pan.*

FERRONE, RICHARD. Born May 7, 146 in Newton, MA. Graduate Holy Cross Col., Boston Law Col. Debut 1980 OB in *The Caine Mutiny Court-Martial*, followed by *Romeo and Juliet.*

FIELD, ROBIN. Born Apr. 13, 1947 in Los Angeles, CA. Attended San Bernardino Valley Col, Orange Coast Col. Debut 1967 OB in *Your Own Thing*, followed by *Look Me Up, Speed Gets the Poppys, Babes in Arms, Broadway A Hundred Years Ago, Daugherty & Field.*

FIERSTEIN, HARVEY. Born June 6, 1954 in Brooklyn, NY. Graduate Pratt Inst. Debut 1971 OB in *Pork*, followed by *International Stud, Figures in a Nursery, Haunted Host, Pouf Positive, Safe Sex*, Bdwy in *Torch Song Trilogy* for which he received a Theatre World Award, *Safe Sex.*

FINKEL, BARRY. Born Jul. 21, 1960 in Philadelphia, PA. Attended Temple U. AMDA. Debut 1986 OB in *Have I Got a Girl for You*, followed by *Cowboy, A Funny Thing Happened on the Way to the Forum*, Bdwy in *Late Nite Comic* (1987).

FITZGIBBON, JOHN. Born Sept. 13, 1946 in New York City. Graduate Fordham U. LAMDA. Debut 1967 in *Macbeth*, followed by *Macbird!, Screens, False Confessions, Julius Caesar, Gaugin in Tahiti, Moon Mysteries, Twelfth Night*, Bdwy in *The Incomparable Max* (1981).

FITZPATRICK, ALLEN. Born Jan. 31, 1955 in Boston, MA. Graduate U. Va. Debut 1977 OB in *Come Baçk Little Sheba*, followed by *Wonderful Town, The Rothschilds.*

FLAGG, LEON B. Born Oct. 22, in Milwaukee, WI. Graduate Sarah Lawrence Col. Debut 1987 OB in *She Stoops to Conquer*, followed by *The Lady and the Clarinet, Life on th Third Rail.*

FLEET, IAN. Born Mar. 6, 1957 in London, Eng. Graduate U. Bristol. Debut 1989 OB in *Equus*, followed by *The Elephant Man, Caligula, Dorian, Internal Affairs, Little Lies, Tonight at 8:30.*

FLEMING, ROBERT BARRY. Born Jan. 6, 1964 in Washington, DC. Graduate Temple U. Bdwy debut 1990 in *Stand-up Tragedy.*

FLETCHER, SUSANN. Born Sept. 7, 1955 in Wilmington, DE. Graduate Longwood Col. Bdwy debut 1980 in *The Best Little Whorehouse in Texas*, followed by *Raggedy Ann, Jerome Robbins' Broadway.*

FLYNN, SUSAN (formerly Susan Elizabeth Scott). Born Aug. 9 in Detroit, MI. Graduate U. Denver. Debut 1971 OB in *The Drunkard*, followed by *Mother, Company, Dames at Sea, Yiddle with a Fiddle, Broadway Jukebox*, Bdwy in *Music Is* (1976), *On the 20th Century, Fearless Frank, The 1940's Radio Hour.*

FORD, CLEBERT. Born Jan. 29, 1932 in Brooklyn, NY. Graduate CCNY, Boston U. Bdwy debut 1960 in *The Cool World*, followd by *Les Blancs, Ain't Supposed to Die a Natural Death, Via Galactica, Bubbling Brown Sugar, The Last Minstrel Show, Mule Bone*, OB in *Romeo and Juliet, The Blacks, Antony and Cleopatra, Ti-Jean and his Brothers, Ballad for Bimshire, Daddy, Gilbeau, Coriolanus, Before the Flood, The Lion and the Jewel, Branches from the Same Tree, Dreams deferred, Basin Street, 20 Year Friends, Celebration, Stories about the Old Days.*

FORLOW, TED. Born Apr. 29, 1931 in Independence, MO. Attended Baker U. Bdwy debut 1957 in *New Girl in Town*, followed by *Juno, Destry Rides Again, Subways Are for Sleeping, Can-Can, Wonderful Town, A Funny Thing Happened on the Way to the Forum, Milk and Honey, Carnival* (CC), *Man of La Mancha* (1965/1977), *Into the Light*, OB in *A Night at the Black Pig, Glory in the Glower, Perfect Analysis Given by a Parrot, Cat and the Fiddle, One Cannot Think of Everything, Man of Destiny, The Rothschilds.*

FORONDA, JOSEPH. Born Jan. 17, 1954 in Fairbanks, AK. Graduate San Jose State U. Bdwy debut 1990 in *Shogun.*

FORSYTHE, HENDERSON. Born Sept. 11, 1917 in Macon, MO. Attended U. Iowa. Debut 1956 OB in *The Iceman Cometh*, followed by *The Collection, The Room, A Slight Ache, Happiness Cage, Waiting for Godot, In Case of Accident, Not I, An Evening with the Poet Senator, Museum, How Far Is It to Babylon? Wild Life, Other Places, Cliffhanger, Broadcast Baby, After the Fall, Some Americans Abroad, Fridays*, Bdwy in *The Cellar and the Well* (1950), *Miss Lonelyhearts, Who's Afraid of Virginia Woolf?, Malcolm, Right Honourable Gentleman, Delicate Balance, Birthday Party, Harvey, Engagement Baby, Freedom of the City, Texas Trilogy, Best Little Whorehouse in Texas, Some Americans Abroad.*

FOSTER FRANCES. Born June 11 in Yonkers, NY. Bdwy debut 1955 in *The Wisteria Trees*, followed by *Nobody Loves an Albatross, Raisin in the Sun, The River Niger, First Breeze of Summer, Tap Dance Kid, Fences, Mule Bone*, OB in *Take a Giant Step, Edge of the City, Tammy and the Doctor, The Crucible, Happy Ending, Day of Absence, An Evening of One Acts, Man Better Man, Brotherhood, Akokawe, Rosalee Pritchett, Sty of the Blind Pig, Ballet Behind the Bridge, Good Woman of Setzuan* (LC), *Behold! Cometh the Vanderkellans, Origin, Boesman and Lena, Do Lord Remember Me, Henrietta, Welcome to Black River, House of Shadows, Miracle Worker, You Have Come Back, Ground People.*

FOWLER, CLEMENT. Born Dec. 27, 1924 in Detroit, MI. Graduate Wayne State U. Bdwy debut 1951 in *Legend of Lovers*, followed by *The Cold Wind and the Warm, Fragile Fox, The Sunshine Boys, Hamlet* (1964), OB in *The Eagle Has Two Heads, House Music, The Transfiguration of Benno Blimpie, The Inheritors, Paradise Lost, The Time of Your Life, Children of the Sun, Highest Standard of Living, Cymbeline, The Chairs.*

FOWLER, SCOTT. Born Mar. 22, 1967 in Medford, MA. Debut 1989 on Bdwy in *Jerome Robbins' Broadway.*

FRANCIS-JAMES, PETER. Born Sept 16, 1956 in Chicago, IL. Graduate RADA. Debut 1979 OB in *Julius Caesar*, followed by *Long Day's Journey into Night, Antigone, Richard II, Romeo and Juliet, Enrico IV, Cymbeline, Hamlet, Learned Ladies.*

FRANZ, ELIZABETH. Born June 18, 1941 in Akron, OH. Attended AADA. Debut 1965 in *In White America*, followed by *One Night Stands of a Noisey Passenger, The Real Inspector Hound, Augusta, Yesterday Is Over, Actor's Nightmare, Sister Mary Ignatius Explains It All, The Time of Your Life, Children of the Sun*, Bdwy in *Rosencrantz and Guildenstern Are Dead, The Cherry Orchard, Brighton Beach Memoirs, The Octette Bridge Club, Broadway Bound, The Cemetery Club, Getting Married.*

FRANZ, JOY. Born in 1944 in Modesto, CA. Graduate U. Mo. Debut 1969 OB in *Of Thee I Sing*, followed by *Jacques Brel Is Alive ..., Out of This World, Curtains, I Can't Keep Running in Place, Tomfoolery, Penelope, Bittersuite, Assassins*, Bdwy in *Sweet Charity, Lysistrata, A Little Night Music, Pippin, Musical Chairs, Into the Woods.*

FRASER, ALISON. Born Jul. 8, 1955 in Natick, MA. Attended Carnegie-Mellon, Boston Consv. Debut 1979 OB in *In Trousers*, followed by *March of the Falsettos, Beehive, Four One-Act Musicals, Tales of Tinseltown, Next Please! Up Against It*, Bdwy in *The Mystery of Edwin Drood (1986), Romance Romance, The Secret Garden.*

FRAZER, SUSANNA. Born Mar. 28 in New York City. Debut 1980 OB in *Kind Lady*, followed by *The Enchanted, A Doll's House, Scenes from American Life, Old Friends and Roommates, Something Old Something New, Times and Appetites of Toulouse-Lautrec, A Flash of Lightning, 5th of July, Yokohama Duty.*

FRECHETTE, PETER. Born Oct. 3, 1956 in Warwick, RI. Graduate U. RI. Debut OB 1979 in *The Hornbeam Maze*, followed by *Journey's End, In Cahoots, Harry Ruby's Songs My Mother Never Sang, Pontifications on Pigtails and Puberty, Scooter Thomas Makes it to the Top of the World, We're Home, Flora, the Red Menace, Eastern Standard, Hyde In Hollywood, Absent Friends*, Bdwy in *Eastern Standard* (1989) for which he received a Theatre World Award, *Our Country's Good.*

FREEMAN, MORGAN. Born June 1, 1937 in Memphis, TN. Attended LACC. Bdwy debut 1967 in *Hello Dolly!*, followed by *The Mighty Gents*, OB in *Ostrich Feathres, Niggerlovers, Exhibition, Black Visions, Cockfight, White Pelicans, Julius Caesar, Coriolanus, Mother Courage, The Connections, The World of Ben Caldwell, Buck, The Gospel at Colonus* (also Bdwy), *Medea and the Doll, Driving Miss Daisy, The Taming of the Shrew.*

FRENCH, ARTHUR. Born in New York City and attended Brooklyn Col. Debut 1962 OB in *Raisin' Hell in the Sun*, followed by *Ballad of Bimshire, Day of Absence, Happy Ending, Brotherhood, Perry's Mission, Rosalee Pritchett, Moonlight Arms, Dark Tower, Brownsville Raid, Nevis Mountain Dew, Julius Caesar, Friends, Court of Miracles, The Beautiful LaSalles, Blues for a Gospel Queen, Black Girl, Driving Miss Daisy, The Spring Thing, George Washington Slept Here*, Bdwy in *Ain't Supposed to Die a Natural Death, The Iceman Cometh, All God's Chillun Got Wings, The Resurrection of Lady Lester, You Can't Take It with You, Design for Living, Ma Rainey's Black Bottom, Mule Bone.*

FRID, JONATHAN. Born Dec. 1924 in Hamilton, Ont., Can. Graduate McMaster U., Yale, RADA. Debut 1959 OB in *The Golem*, followed by *Henry IV Parts 1 and 2, The Moon in the Yellow River, The Burning, Murder in the Cathedral, Fools and Fiends, Readers Theatre, Shakespearean Odyssey*, Bdwy in *Roar Like a Dove* (1964), *Arsenic and Old Lace* (1986).

FRIDAY, BETSY. Born Apr. 30, 1958 in Chapel Hill, NC. Graduate NC Schl. of Arts. Bdwy debut 1980 in *The Best Little Whorehouse n Texas*, followed by *Bring Back Birdie, The Secret Garden*, OB in *I Ought to Be in Pictures, Smile, Ace of Diamonds.*

FRIED, JONATHAN. Born Mar. 3, 1959 in Los Angeles, CA. Graduate Brown U., U. Cal/San Diego. Debut 1986 OB in *1951*, followed by *Dispatches from Hell, Richard III.*

FRIEDMAN, PETER. Born Apr. 24, 1949 in New York City. Debut 1971 OB in *James Joyce Memorial Theatre*, followed by *Big and Little, A Soldier's Play, Mr. and Mrs., And a Nightingale Sang, Dennis, The Common Pursuit, Marathon '88, The Heidi Chronicles*, Bdwy in *The Visit, Chemin de Fer, Love for Love, Rules of the Game, Piaf!, Execution of Justice, The Heidi Chronicles, Tenth Man.*

FURR, TERI. Born May 12, 1965 in Port Chester, NY. Graduate Syracuse U. Bdwy debut 1989 in *Gypsy* (1989/1991).

FURS, EDWARD L. Born July 23, 1957 in Brooklyn, NY. Graduate NYU. Debut 1986 OB in *Dance of Death*, followed by *Night Must Fall, Squaring the Circle, The Miser, Harpo, Family Portrait, Queen Christina, Chaste Maids in Cheapside, Measure for Measure.*

GABRIEL, SUSAN. Born Apr. 29 in Denver, CO. Graduate U. Utah, NYU. Debut 1984 OB in *Henry V*, followed by *Nest of the Woodgrouse, Talk Radio, Hannah Senesh, Hamlet* (1990), Bdwy in *Prelude to a Kiss* (1990).

GAFFNEY, LAUREN. Born OCt. 16, 1979 in Summit, NJ. Bdwy debut 1990 in *The Sound of Music* (LC), followed by OB's *Grownups!, The Good Times Are Killing Me.*

GAHNZ, CRAIG. Born Jul, 7, 1962 in Cochrane, WI. Graduate Luther Col. Bdwy debut 1990 in *Fiddler on the Roof.*

GAINES, BOYD. Born May 11, 1953 in Atlanta, GA. Graduate Juilliard. Debut 1978 OB in *Spring Awakening*, followed by *A Month in the Country* for which he received a Theatre World Award, BAM Theatre Co.'s *Winter's Tale, The Barbarians, and Johnny on a Spot, Vikings, Double Bass, The Maderati, The Heidi Chronicles*, Bdwy in *The Heidi Chronicles* (1989).

GALANTICH, TOM. Born in Brooklyn, NY. Debut 1985 OB in *On the 20th Century*, followed by *Mademoiselle Colombe*, Bdwy in *Into the Woods* (1989), *City of Angels.*

GALINDO, EILEEN. Born Dec. 5, 1956 in the Bronx, NY. Attended U. Miani. Debut 1989 OB in *Chinese Charade*, followed by *Ariano, In Miami as It Is in Heaven.*

GALINDO, RAMON. Born June 3 in San Francisco, CA. Graduate U. of Calif. Berkeley. Bdwy debut 1979 in *Carmelina*, followed by *Merlin, Cats, Song and Dance, Jerome Robbins' Broadway*, OB in *Funny Feet* (1987).

GALLAGHER, HELEN. Born in 1926 in Brooklyn, NY. Bdwy debut 1947 in *Seven Lively Arts*, followed by *Mr. Straus Goes to Boston, Billion Dollar Baby, Brigadoon, High Button Shoes, Touch and Go, Make a Wish, Pal Joey, Guys and Dolls, Finian's Rainbow, Oklahoma!, Pajama Game, Bus Stop, Portofino, Sweet Charity, Mame, Cry for Us All, No No Nanette, A Broadway Musical, Sugar Babies*, OB in *Hothouse, Tickles by Tucholsky, The Misanthrope, I Can't Keep Running in Place, Red Rover, Tallulah, The Flower Palace, Tallulah Tonight, Money Talks.*

GALLAGHER, MEGAN. Born Feb. 6, 1960 in Reading, PA. Graduate Juilliard. Debut 1983 OB in *Tartuffe*, followed by *Miss Julie, Come and Go, Play*, Bdwy in *A Few Good Men* (1989) for which she received a Theatre World Award.

GANUN, JOHN. Born Aug. 23, 1966 in Blissfield, MI. Graduate U. Mich. Bdwy debut 1991 in *The Will Rogers Follies.*

GARBER, VICTOR. Born Mar. 15, 1949 in London, Can. Debut 1973 OB in *Ghosts* for which he received a Theatre World Award, followed by *Joe's Opera, Cracks, Wenceslas Square, Love Letters, Assassins*, Bdwy in *Tartuffe, Deathtrap, Sweeney Todd, They're Playing Our Song, Little Me, Noises Off, You Never Can Tell, Devil's Disciple, Lend Me a Tenor.*

GARDENIA, VINCENT. Born Jan. 7, 1923 in Naples, It. Debut 1955 OB in *In April Once*, followed by *Man with the Golden Arm, Volpone, Brothers Karamazov, Power of Darkness, Machinal, Gallows Humor, Theatre of the Absurd, Lunatic View, Little Murders, Passing through from Exotic Places, Carpenters, Buried Inside Extra, Breaking Legs*, Bdwy in *The Visit* (1958), *Rashomon, The Cold Wind and the Warm, Only in America, The Wall, Daughter of Silence, Seidman & Son, Dr. Fish, The Prisoner of Second Avenue, God's Favorite, California Suite, Ballroom, Glengarry Glen Ross.*

GARDNER, ANN. Born in Iowa City, IA. Graduate Ill. Wesleyan Col. Bdwy debut 1960 in *The Sound of Music*, followed by *Canterbury Tales*, OB in *Yesterday in Warsaw.*

GARRETT, RUSSELL (formerly Giesenschlag). Born Jul. 8, 1959 in San Diego, CA. Attended San Diego State U. Bdwy debut 1982 in *Seven Brides for Seven Brothers*, followed by *42nd Street*, OB in *Girl Crazy, Pageant.*

GATTO, PETER. Born Jan. 24, 1946 in Brooklyn, NY. Graduate Brooklyn Col., Neighborhood Playhouse. Debut 1970 OB in *Edward II*, followed by *Bus Riley's Back in Town, Volpone, Sacraments, Chiaroscuro, Heroes, Beauty Part.*

GEHMAN, MARTHA. Born May 15, 1955 in New York City. Graduate Sarah Lawrence Col. Debut 1984 OB in *Cinders*, followed by *Day Room, Romeo and Juliet, Baba Goya, Love Diatribe.*

GELFER, STEVEN. Born Feb. 21, 1949 in Brooklyn, NY. Graduate NYU, Ind. U. Debut 1968 OB and Bdwy in *The Best Little Whorehouse in Texas*, followed by *Cats.*

GENEST, EDMOND. Born Oct. 27, 1943 in Boston, MA. Attended Suffolk U. Debut 1972 OB in *The Real Inspector Hound*, followed by *Second Prize: Two Months in Leningrad, Maneuvers, Pantomime, Scooncat*, Bdwy in *Dirty Linen/New Found Land, Whose Life Is It Anyway?, A Few Good Men.*

GENEVIERE, DEBORAH. Born Oct. 15, 1961 in Tokyo, Japan. Graduate SUNY/Stoneybrook. Bdwy debut 1988 in *Chess*, followed by *Shogun*, OB in *Wonderful Town.*

GEORGE, BEN. Born June 7, 1947 in Oxford, Eng. Attended Leeds Music Col. Debut 1984 OB in *Last of the Knucklemen*, Bdwy in *The Best Little Whorehouse in Texas* (1985), *Grand Hotel.*

GEORGIANA, TONI. Born Dec. 14, 1963 in Uniontown, PA. Attended Juilliard. Bdwy debut 1991 in *The Will Rogers Follies.*

GERACI, FRANK. Born Sept. 8, 1939 in Brooklyn, NY. Attended Yale. Debut 1961 OB in *Color of Darkness*, followed by *Mr. Grossman, Balm in Gilead, The Fantasticks, Tom Paine, End of All things Natural, Union Street, Uncle Vanya, Success Story, Hughie, Merchant of Venice, Three Zeks, Taming of the Shrew, The Lady from the Sea, Rivals, Deep Swimmer, The Imaginary Invalid, Candida, Uncle Vanya, Hedda Gabler, Serious Co., Berenice, The Philanderer, Hedda Gabler, All's Well That Ends Well, Three Sisters, A Midsummer Night's Dream, Medea, The Importance of Being Earnest, Major Barbara, Measure for Measure, The Fine Art of Finesse, Two Schnitzler One Acts*, Bdwy in *Love Suicide at Schofield Barracks* (1972).

GERACI, PAUL. Born June 2, 1963 in Chicago, IL. Attended Webster U. Bdwy debut 1987 in *Anything Goes*, followed by *Gypsy* (1989).

GERAGHTY, MARITA. Born Mar. 26, 1965 in Chicago, IL. Graduate U. Ill. Bdwy debut 1987 in *Coastal Disturbances*, followed by *The Night of the Iguana, The Heidi Chronicles.*

GERARD, DANNY. Born May 29, 1977 in New York City. Bdwy debut 1986 in *Into the Light*, followed by *Les Misérables, Lost in Yonkers*, OB in *Today I Am a Fountain Pen, Second Hurricane, Falsettoland.*

GERDES, GEORGE. Born Feb. 23, 1948 in New York City. Carnegie Tech graduate. Debut 1979 OB in *Modigliani*, followed by *The Idolmakers, The Doctor and the Devils, The Hit Parade, A Country for Old Men, Fool for Love, To Whom It May Concern, New Works '87*, Bdwy 1989 in *A Few Good Men.*

GERRITY, DAN. Born Dec. 21, 1957 in Red Bank, NJ. Attended SUNY/Albany, Neighborhood Playhouse. Debut 1987 OB in *Bouncers*, Bdwy in *Stand-up Tragedy* (1990).

GERSHENSON, SUE ANNE. Born Feb. 18, 1953 in Chicago, IL. Attended Ind. U. Debut 1976 OB in *Panama Hattie*, followed by *Carnival, Street Scene, The Rothschilds*, Bdwy in *Sunday in the Park with George* (1984).

GERUT, ROSALIE W. Born in Boston, MA Debut 1989 OB in *Songs of Paradise.*

GIBBS, SHEILA. Born Feb. 16, 1947 in New York City. Graduate NYU. Debut 1971 in *Two Gentlemen of Verona*, followed by *Runaways, Once on This Island*, OB in *Last Days of British Honduras, Poets from the Inside, Once on This Island.*

GIBSON, JULIA. Born June 8, 1962 in Norman, OK. Graduate U. Iowa, NYU. Debut 1987 OB in *A Midsummer Night's Dream*, followed by *Love's Labor's Lost, Crucible, The Man Who Fell in Love with His Wife, Learned Ladies.*

GIBSON, THOMAS. Born Jul. 3, 1962 in Charleston, SC. Graduate Juilliard. Debut 1985 OB in *Map of the World*, followed by *Twelfth Night, Bloody Poetry, Marathon '87, Two Gentlemen of Verona, Class 1 Acts, Macbeth, Marathon '88, Positive Me*, Bdwy in *Hay Fever* (1985), *The Miser.*

GILBERT, TONY. Born Mar. 22 in Roanoke, VA. Graduate UVA. Debut 1983 OB in *The Robber Bridegroom*, followed by *Sweeney Todd, Manhattan Class 1 Acts*, Bdwy in *Oliver!* (1984), *Sweeney Todd.*

GILPIN, JACK. Born May 31, 1951 in Boyce, VA. Harvard graduate. Debut 1976 OB in *Goodbye and Keep Cold*, followed by *Shay, The Soft Touch, Beyond Therapy, The Lady or the Tiger, The Middle Ages, The Rise of Daniel Rocket, No Happy Ending, Strange Behavior, The Foreigner, Marathon '86, The Spring Thing, Human Nature*, Bdwy in *Lunch Hour* (1980), *A Christmas Carol* (1990).

GIONSON, MEL DUANE. Born Feb. 23, 1954 in Honolulu, HI. Graduate U. HI. Debut 1979 OB in *Richard II*, followed by *Sunrise, Monkey Music, Behind Enemy Lines, Station J, Teahouse, A Midsummer Night's Dream, Empress of China, Chip Shot, Manoa Valley, Ghashiram, Shogun Macbeth, Life of the Land, Noiresque, Three Sisters, Lucky Come Hawaii, Henry IV Parts 1 & 2.*

GIOSA, SUE. Born Nov. 23, 1958 in Connecticut. Graduate Queens Col., RADA, LAMDA. Debut OB 1988 in *Tamara*, followed by *Breaking Legs.*

GIRARDEAU, FRANK. Born Oct. 19, 1942 in Beaumont, TX. Attended Rider Col. Debut 1972 OB in *22 Years*, followed by *The Soldier, Hughie, An American Story, El Hermano, Dumping Ground, Daddies, Accounts, Shadow Man, Marathon '84, Dennis, Marathon '89, Marathon '90.*

GLEASON, JAMES. Born Sept. 30, 1952 in NYC. Graduate Santa Fe. Col. Debut 1982 OB in *Guys in the Truck*, followed by *Corkscrews!, Patrick Pearse Motel, Taboo in Revue, Curse of the Starving Class, Signal Season, The Ambassador, Better Days*, Bdwy in *Guys in the Truck* (1983).

GLEASON, JOANNA. Born June 2, 1950 in Toronto, Can. Graduate UCLA. Bdwy debut 1977 in *I Love My Wife* for which she received a Theatre World Award, followed by *The Real Thing, Social Security, Into the Woods*, OB in *A Hell of a Town, Joe Egg, It's Only a Play, Eleemosynary.*

GLOVER, KEITH. Born Feb. 18, 1963 in Bessemer, AL. Graduate Bowling Green U. Debut OB in 1980 in *The Sign in Sidney Brustein's Window*, followed by *La Puta Vita Triology, A Raisin in the Sun, Master Harold and the Boys, Philoktetes, As You Like It.*

GLUSHAK, JOANNA. Born May 27, 1958 in New York City. Attended NYU. Debut 1983 OB in *Lenny and the Heartbreakers*, followed by *Lies and Legends, Miami, Unfinished Song, A Little Night Music* (NYCO), Bdwy in *Sunday in the Park with George* (1984), *Rags, Les Misérables.*

GOETHALS, ANGELA. Born May 20, 1977 in NYC. Bdwy debut 1987 in *Coastal Disturbance*, OB in *Positive Me, Approaching Zanzibar, The Good Times Are Killing Me.*

GOLDEN, ANNIE. Born Oct. 19, 1951 in Brooklyn, NY. Bdwy debut 1977 in *Hair*, followed by *Leader of the Pack*, OB in *Dementos, Dr. Selavy's Magic Theatre, A...My Name Is Alice, Little Shop of Horrors, Class of '86, Assassins.*

MERWIN GOLDSMITH. Born Aug. 7, 1937 in Detroit, MI. Graduate UCLA, Old Vic. Bdwy debut 1970 in *Minnie's Boys*, followed by *The Visit, Chemin de Fer, Rex, Leda Had a Little Swan, Trelawney of the Wells, Dirty Linen, The 1940's Radio Hour, Slab Boys, Me and My Girl*, OB in *The Naked Hamlet, Chickencoop Chinaman, Real Life Funnies, Wanted, Rubbers and Yanks, Chinchilla, Yours Anne, Big Apple Messenger, La Bohème, Learned Ladies.*

GOLDSTEIN, BERT. Born Jan 23, 1955 in Michigan City, IN. Graduate MacAlester Col. Debut 1987 OB in *Fire in th Basement*, followed by *Filthy Talk for Troubled Times.*

GOLDSTEIN, STEVEN. Born Oct. 22, 1963 in New York City. Graduate NYU. Debut 1987 OB in *Boys' Life*, followed by *Oh Hell, Three Sisters, Marathon '91*, Bdwy in *Our Town* (1988).

GOLDWYN, TONY. Born May 20, 1960 in Los Angeles, CA. Graduate Brandeis U., LAMDA. Debut 1985 OB in *Digby*, followed by *Messiah, The Sum of Us.*

GONZALEZ, CORDELIA. Born Aug. 11, 1958 in San Juan, PR. Graduate UPR, Yale. Debut 1985 OB in *Impact*, followed by *The Love of Don Perlimplin, Sabina and Lucrecia*, Bdwy in *Serious Money* (1988).

GOODMAN, LISA. Born in Detroit, MI. Attended U. Mich. Debut 1982 OB in *Talking With*, followed by *The First Warning, The Show-Off, Escape from Riverdale, Jesse's Land, State of the Union, The Wonder Years, Girl of the Golden West, Medea, O Sappho O Wilde!*

GOODSPEED, DON. Born Apr. 1, 1958 in Truro, NS, Can. Bdwy debut 1983 in *The Pirates of Penzance*, followed by *Into the Woods, Aspects of Love*, OB in *Diamonds, Charley's Tale.*

GOOR, CAROLYN. Born Oct. 11, 1960 in Paris, Fr. Debut 1983 OB in *The Jewish Gypsy*, followed by *Oy Mama Am I in Love, A Little Night Music, Singin' in the Rain*, Bdwy in *Jerome Robbins' Broadway.*

GORDON, CARL. Born Jan. 20, 1932 in Richmond, VA. Bdwy debut 1966 in *The Great White Hope*, followed by *Ain't Supposed to Die a Natural Death, The Piano Lesson*, OB in *Day of Absence, Happy Ending, The Strong Breed, Trials of Brother Jero, Kongi's Harvest, Welcome to Black River, Shark, Orrin and Sugar Mouth, A Love Play, The Great MacDaddy, In an Upstate Motel, Zooman and the Sign.*

GORDON, CLARKE. Born in Detroit, MI. Graduate Wayne State U. Debut 1949 OB in *The Son*, followed by *The Philistines, The Truth, Porch, China Fish, Them*, Bdwy in *Night Music* (1951), *Pal Joey* (1952), *The Vamp.*

GORDON-CLARK, SUSAN. Born Dec. 31, 1947 in Jackson, MS. Graduate Purdue U. Debut 1984 OB in *The Nunsense Story*, followed by *Chip Shot, Nunsense.*

GRAAE, JASON. Born May 15, 1958 in Chicago, IL. Graduate Cincinnati Consv. Debut 1981 OB in *Godspell*, followed by *Snoopy, Heaven on Earth, Promenade, Feathertop, Tales of Tinseltown, Living Color, Just So, Olympus on My Mind, Sitting Pretty in Concert, Babes in Arms, The Cat and the Fiddle, Forever Plaid, A Funny Thing Happened on the Way to the Forum, 50 Million Frenchmen.*

GRACE, EILEEN. Born July 25 in Pittsburgh, PA. Graduate Point Park Col. Bdwy debut in *42nd Street*, followed by *My One and Only, The Will Rogers Follies.*

Russell
Garrett

Martha
Geham

Paul
Geraci

Joanna
Gleason

Merwin
Goldsmith

Cordelia
González

Eileen
Grace

Kevin
Gray

Andrea
Green

Lawrence
Grenn

Lyn
Greene

Zach
Grenier

Sean G.
Griffin

Lisa
Griffith

Henry
Grossman

Donna
Haley

Andy
Halliday

Lauren
Hamilton

Roxanne
Hart

Ethan
Hawke

Lorey
Hayes

Anthony
Heald

Margaret
Hilton

Ron
Holgate

Tommy
Hollis

Celeste
Holm

John
Hoshko

Celia
Howard

Barnard
Hughes

Laura
Hughes

GRAFF, RANDY. Born May 23, 1955 in Brooklyn, NY. Graduate Wagner Col. Debut 1978 OB in *Pins and Needles*, followed by *Station Joy, A...My Name Is Alice, Once on a Summer's Day*, Bdwy in *Sarava, Grease, Les Misérables, City of Angels*.

GRAHAM, DEBORAH. Born Jan. 20, 1959 in Speedway, IN. Graduate U. Cinn. Debut 1982 OB in *Snoopy*, followed by *Romance! Romance!, A Funny Thing Happened on the Way to the Forum*, Bdwy in *Romance! Romance!* (1988).

GRAVES, RUTHANNA. Born Sept. 14, 1957 in Philadelphia, PA. Attended NYU. Debut 1980 OB in *Mother Courage*, followed by *Boogie Woogie Rumble, Blackamoor, Occasional Grace*, Bdwy in *Uptown It's Hot* (1986).

GRAY, DOLORES. Born June 7, 1924 in Hollywood, CA. Bdwy debut 1944 in *Seven Lively Arts*, followed by *Are You With It?, Annie Get Your Gun, Two on the Aisle, Carnival in Flanders, Destry Rides Again, Sherry!, 42nd Street*, OB in *Money Talks* (1990).

GRAY, KEVIN. Born Feb. 25, 1958 in Westport, CT. Graduate Duke U. Debut 1982 OB in *Lola*, followed by *Pacific Overtures, Family Snapshots, The Baker's Wife, The Knife, Magdalena in Concert*, Bdwy in *The Phantom of the Opera* (1989).

GRAY, SAM. Born July 18, 1923 in Chicago, IL. Graduate Columbia U. Bdwy debut 1955 in *Deadfall*, followed by *Six Fingers in a Five Finger Glove, Saturday Sunday Monday, Golda, A View from the Bridge*, OB in *Ascent of F-6, Family Portrait, One Tiger on a Hill, Shadow of Heroes, The Recruiting Officer, The Wild Duck, Jungle of Cities, 3 Acts of Recognition, Returnings, A Little Madness, The Danube, Dr. Cook's Garden, Child's Play, Kafka Father and Son, D, Dennis, Panache, Marathon '89, Bitter Friends, Arturo Ui, Blackout*.

GREEN, ANDREA. Born Oct. 31 in New York City. Graduate Queens Col./CUNY. Bdwy debut 1980 in *They're Playing Our Song*, followed by *Little Me*, OB in *And the World Goes 'Round, Yiddle with a Fiddle*.

GREEN, LAWRENCE. Born Jul. 18 in Boulder, CO. Graduate U. Wash., Juilliard. Debut 1988 OB in *King John*, followed by *Much Ado about Nothing, Hamlet, Black Eagles*.

GREENBERG, HELEN. Born Sept. 28, 1961 on Long Island, NY. Graduate NYU. Debut 1987 OB in *Words, Words, Words*, followed by *Double Blessing, Love Lemmings, Occasional Grace*.

GREENBERG, MITCHELL. Born Sept. 19, 1950 in Brooklyn, NY. Graduate Harpur Col., Neighborhood Playhouse. Debut 1979 OB in *Two Grown Men*, followed by *Scrambled Feet, A Christmas Carol, A Thurber Carnival, Isn't It Romantic?, Crazy Arnold, Yiddle with a Fiddle*, Bdwy in *A Day in Hollywood/A Night in the Ukraine* (1980), *Can-Can, Marilyn, Into the Light, 3 Penny Opera*.

GREENE, JAMES. Born Dec. 1, 1926 in Lawrence, MA. Graduate Emerson Col. OB in *The Iceman Cometh, American Gothic, The King and the Duke, The Hostage, Plays for Bleecker Street, Moon in the Yellow River, Misalliance, Government Inspector, Baba Goya*, LCRep 2 years, *You Can't Take It with You, School for Scandal, Wild Duck, Right You Are, The Show-Off, Pantagleize, Festival of Short Plays, Nourish the Beast, One Crack Out, Artichoke, Othello, Salt Lake City Skyline, Summer, Rope Dancers, Frugal Repast, Bella Figura, The Freak, Park Your Car in the Harvard Yard, Pigeons in the Walk, Endgame, Great Days, Playboy of the Western World, Brimstone and Treacle*, Bdwy *Romeo and Juliet, Girl on the Via Flaminia, Compulsion, Inherit the Wind, Shadow of a Gunman, Andersonville Trial, Night Life, School for Wives, Ring Round the Bathtub, Great God Brown, Don Juan, Foxfire, Play Memory, The Iceman Cometh, La Bete*.

GREENE, LYN. Born May 21, 1955 in Boston, MA. Graduate NYU, Juilliard. Debut 1984 OB in *Kid Purple*, followed by *Flora the Red Menace, Prisoner of Second Avenue, Assassins*.

GREENHILL, SUSAN. Born Mar. 19 in New York City. Graduate U. PA, Catholic U. Bdwy debut 1982 in *Crimes of the Heart*, OB in *Hooters, Our Lord of Lynchville, September in the Rain, Seascape with Sharks and Dancer, Young Playwrights Festival, Festival of One Acts, Murder of Crows, Marathon '89, Better Days*.

GREER, MICHAEL BARRY. Born Dec. 16, 1938 in San Francisco, CA. Graduate Cornell, Harvey, CUNY. OB in *Hay Fever, Comedy of Errors, The Motion of History, Cowboy Jack Street, Black Eagles*.

GREGG, CLARK. Born April 2, 1962 in Boston, MA. Graduate NYU. Debut 1987 OB in *Fun*, followed by *The Detective, Boy's Life, Three Sisters, The Old Boy*, Bdwy in *A Few Good Men* (1990).

GREGORY, MICHAEL SCOTT. Born Mar. 13, 1962 in Ft. Lauderdale, FL. Attended Atlantic Foundation. Bdwy debut 1981 in *Sophisticated Ladies*, followed by *Starlight Express, Jerome Robbins' Broadway*.

GRENIER, ZACH. Born Feb. 12, 1954 in Englewood, NJ. Graduate U. Mich., Boston U. Debut 1982 OB in *Baal*, followed by *Tomorrowland, Water Music, Morocco, The Cure, Birth of the Poet, Talk Radio, Marathon '90, Lilith, Arturo Ui*, Bdwy 1989 in *Mastergate*.

GRIFFIN, SEAN G. Born Oct. 14, 1942 in Limerick, Ire. Graduate Notre Dame U., U. Kan. Bdwy debut 1974 in *The National Health*, followed by *Poor Murder, Ah Wilderness!, Ned and Jack, The Queen and the Rebels, OB in March in Russia*.

GRIFFITH, LISA. Born June 18 in Honolulu, HI. Graduate Brandeis U., Trinity U. Debut 1977 in *The Homesickness of Capt. Rappaport*, followed by *The Kennedy Play, Chalkdust, Murder at the Vicarage, Ah, Wilderness!, Stud Silo, The Miser, Twelfth Night, Othello, The Apple Cart, Ladies Side, Measure for Measure*.

GROENENDAAL, CRIS. Born Feb. 17, 1948 in Erie, PA. Attended Allegheny Col., Exeter U., HB Studio. Bdwy debut 1979 in *Sweeney Todd*, followed by *Sunday in the Park with George, Brigadoon* (LC), *Desert Song* (LC), LC's *South Pacific* and *Sweeney Todd, Phantom of the Opera*, OB in *Francis, Sweethearts in Concert, Oh Boy, No No Nanette in Concert, Sitting Pretty, The Cat and the Fiddle*.

GROSSMAN, HENRY. Born Oct. 11, 1938 in New York City. Attended Actors Studio. Debut 1961 OB in *The Magistrate*, followed by *Galileo*, Bdwy 1989 in *Grand Hotel*.

GUIDALL, GEORGE. Born June 7, 1938 in Plainfield, NJ. Attended U. Buffalo, AADA. Bdwy debut 1969 in *Wrong Way Light Bulb*, followed by *Cold Storage, Café Crown*, OB in *Counsellor-at-Law, Taming of the Shrew, All's Well That Ends Well, The Art of Dining, Biography, After All, Henry V, The Time of the Cuckoo, Yours Anne, The Perfect Party, A Man for All Seasons, Morocco, Café Crown, Taking Stock*.

GUTTENBERG, STEVE. Born Aug. 24, 1958 in Massapequa, NY. Graduate UCLA. Bdwy debut 1991 in *Prelude to a Kiss*.

GUTTMAN, RONALD. Born Aug. 12, 1952 in Brussels, Belg. Graduate Brussels U. Debut 1986 OB in *Coastal Disturbances*, followed by *Modigliano*, Bdwy in *Coastal Disturbances* (1987).

HACK, STEVEN. Born Apr. 20, 1958 in St. Louis, MO. Attended Cal. Arts, AADA. Debut 1978 OB in *The Coolest Cat in Town*, followed by Bdwy in *Cats* (1982).

HADARY, JONATHAN. Born Oct. 11, 1948 in Chicago, IL. Attended Tufts U. Debut 1974 OB in *White Nights*, followed by *El Grande de Coca Cola, Songs from Pins and Needles, God Bless You Mr. Rosewater, Pushing 30, Scrambled Feet, Coming Attractions, Tom Foolery, Charley Bacon and Family, Road Show, 1-2-3-4-5, Wenceslas Square, Assassins*, Bdwy in *Gemini* (1977 also OB), *Torch Song Trilogy, As Is, Gypsy*.

HAFNER, JULIE J. Born June 4, 1952 in Dover, OH. Graduate Kent State U. Debut 1976 OB in *The Club*, followed by *Nunsense*, Bdwy in *Nine*.

HAGAN, JOHN. Born May 24, 1950 in New York City. Graduate NYU. Debut 1979 OB in *Disparate Acts*, followed by *Chang in a Void Moon, Two Kietzches in Love, Deep Sleep, Peter and Noel and Noel and Gertie, Dark Shadows, All That Fall, The River Runs Deep*.

HALEY, DONNA. Born Jan. 7, 1948 in Evanston, IL. Graduate Clarke Col., U. Mich. Debut 1978 OB in *Molière in Spite of Himself*, followed by *Old Man Joseph and his Family, Frankie and Johnny in the Clair de Lune, Spare Parts*, Bdwy in *Brighton Beach Memoirs* (1984).

HALL, CHARLES EDWARD. Born Nov. 12, 1951 in Frankfort, KY. Graduate Murray St. U. Debut 1977 OB in *Molly's Dream*, followed by *Sheridan Square, The Doctor in Spite of Himself, Loudspeaker, Action, The Tavern, Snow White, Radio City's Christmas Spectacular, As You Like It*.

HALLIDAY, ANDY. Born Mar. 31, 1953 in Orange, CT. Attended USIU/San Diego. Debut OB 1985 in *Vampire Lesbians of Sodom*, followed by *Times Square Angel, Psycho Beach Party, The Lady in Question, Red Scare on Sunset*.

HALSTON, JULIE. Born Dec. 7, 1954 in New York. Graduate Hofstra U. Debut OB 1985 in *Times Square Angel*, followed by *Vampire Lesbians of Sodom, Sleeping Beauty or Coma, The Dubliners, The Lady in Question, Money Talks, Red Scare on Sunset*.

HAMILTON, LAUREN. Born Nov. 10, 1959 in Boston, MA. Graduate Bard Col., Neighborhood Playhouse. Debut 1988 OB in *Famine Plays*, followed by *Tiny Dimes, Rodents and Radios, Hunger, Homo Sapien Shuffle, Famine Plays*.

HAMMER, BEN. Born Dec. 8, 1925 in Brooklyn, NY. Graduate Brooklyn Col. Bdwy debut 1955 in *The Great Sebastians*, followed by *The Diary of Anne Frank, The Tenth Man, Mother Courage, The Deputy, Royal Hunt of the Sun, Golda, Broadway Bound*, OB in *The Crucible, Murderous Angels, Richard III*.

HAMMER, MARK. Born Apr. 28, 1937 in San Jose, CA. Graduate Stanford, Catholic U. Debut 1966 OB in *Journey of the Fifth Horse*, followed by *Witness for the Prosecution, Cymbeline, Richard III, The Taming of the Shrew*, Bdwy in *Much Ado about Nothing* (1972).

HANAN, STEPHEN. Born Jan. 7, 1947 in Washington, DC. Graduate Harvard, LAMDA. Debut 1978 OB in *All's Well That Ends Well*, followed by *Taming of the Shrew, Rabboni*, Bdwy in *Pirates of Penzance* (1978), *Cats, Peter Pan*.

HANDLER, EVAN. Born Jan. 10, 1961 in New York City. Attended Juilliard. Debut 1979 OB in *Biography A Game*, followed by *Striker, Final Orders, Marathon '84, Found a Peanut, What's Wrong with This Picture? Bloodletters, Young Playwrights Festival, Human Nature, Six Degrees of Separation, Marathon '91*, Bdwy in *Solomon's Child* (1982), *Biloxi Blues, Brighton Beach Memoirs, Broadway Bound, Six Degrees of Separation, I Hate Hamlet*.

HANKET, ARTHUR. Born June 23, 1934 in Virginia. Graduate UVA, Fla. State U. Debut 1979 OB in *Cuchculain Cycle*, followed by *The Boys Next Door, In Perpetuity throughout the Universe, L'Illusion, White Collar, Heaven on Earth, One Act Festival, Kingfish, Love and Anger*.

HARDER, JAMES. Born Nov. 19, 1931 in New York City. Graduate Princeton U. Debut 1958 OB in *Bonds of Interest*, followed by *The Kitchen, Dulcy, Playboy of the Western World, The Athenian Touch, By Jupiter, Lend an Ear, On the Town, Isn't It Romantic, 50 Million Frenchmen, A Funny Thing Happened on the Way to the Forum*, Bdwy in *Very Good Eddie* (1975).

HARDING, JAN LESLIE. Born in 1956 in Cambridge, MA. Graduate Boston U. Debut 1980 in *Album*, followed by *Sunday Picnic, Buddies, The Lunch Girls, Marathon '86, Traps, Father Was a Peculiar Man*.

HARDY, MARK. Born Oct. 25, 1961 in Reidsville, NC. Graduate UNC/Greensboro. Debut 1990 OB in *The Rothschilds*, followed by *Juba*, Bdwy in *Les Misérables* (1990).

HARRIS, BAXTER. Born Nov. 18, 1940 in Columbus, KS. Attended U. Kan. Debut 1967 OB in *America Hurrah*, followed by *The Serpent, Battle of Angels, Down by the River..., Ferocious Kisses, The Three Sisters, The Dolphin Position, Broken Eggs, Paradise Lost, Ghosts, The Time of Your Life, The Madwoman of Chaillot, The Reckoning, Wicked Women Revue, More Than You Deserve, him, Pericles, Selma, Gradual Clearing, Children of the Sun, Marathon '90, Go to Ground*, Bdwy in *A Texas Trilogy* (1976), *Dracula, The Lady from Dubuque*.

HARRIS, JULIE. Born Dec. 2, 1925 in Grosse Pointe, MI. Yale Graduate. Bdwy debut 1945 in *It's a Gift*, followed by *Henry V, Oedipus, Playboy of the Western World, Alice in Wonderland, Macbeth, Sundown Beach* for which she received a Theatre World Award, *The Young and the Fair, Magnolia Alley, Montserrat, A Member of the Wedding, I Am a Camera, Mlle. Colombe, The Lark, Country Wife, Warm Peninsula, Little Moon of Alban, A Shot in the Dark, Marathon '33, Ready When You Are C.B., Hamlet* (CP), *Skyscraper, 40 Carats, And Miss Reardon Drinks a Little, Voices, The Last of Mrs. Lincoln, Au Pair Man, In Praise of Love, Belle of Amherst, Mixed Couples, Break a Leg, Lucifer's Child, A Christmas Carol*.

HARRIS, NIKI. Born Jul. 20, 1948 in Pittsburgh, PA. Graduate Duquesne U. Bdwy debut 1980 in *A Day in Hollywood/A Night in the Ukraine*, followed by *My One and Only, Grand Hotel*, OB in *Leave It to Jane, No No Nanette, Berkeley Square*.

HART, ROXANNE. Born in 1952 in Trenton, NJ. Attended Skidmore, Princton U. Bdwy debut 1977 in *Equus*, followed by *Loose Ends, Passion, Devil's Disciple*, OB in *Winter's Tale, Johnny On a Spot, The Purging, Hedda Gabler, Waiting for the Parade, La Brea Tarpits, Marathon '84, Digby, Lips Together, Teeth Apart*.

HARUM, EIVIND. Born May 24, 1944 in Stavanger, Norway. Attended Utah State U. Credits include *Sophie, Foxy, Baker Street, West Side Story* (1968), *A Chorus Line, Woman of the Year, Grand Hotel.*

HAWKE, ETHAN. Born in 1970 in Austin, TX. Debut 1991 OB in *Casanova.*

HAWTHORNE, NIGEL. Born Apr. 5, 1929 in Coventry, Eng. Bdwy debut 1974 in *As You Like It*, followed by *Shadowlands* (1990).

HAYES, LOREY. Born Oct. 12, 1956 in Wallace, NC. Graduate UNC Arts, U. Wisc. Debut 1975 OB in *For Colored Girls...*, followed by *The Michigan, Forty Deuce, Like Them That Dream, Special Interests, Giant on the Ceiling*, Bdwy in *Home* (1980), *Inacent Black.*

HAYS, REX. Born June 17, 1946 in Hollywood, CA. Graduate San Jose State U., Brandeis U. Bdwy debut 1975 in *Dance with Me*, followed by *Angel, King of Hearts, Evita, Onward Victoria!, Woman of the Year, La Cage aux Folles, Grand Hotel*, OB in *Charley's Tale.*

HEALD, ANTHONY. Born Aug. 25, 1944 in New Rochelle, NY. Graduate Mich. State U. Debut 1980 OB in *Glass Menagerie*, followed by *Misalliance* for which he received a Theatre World Award, *The Caretaker, The Fox, Quartermaine's Terms, The Philanthropist, Henry V, Digby, Principia Scriptoriae, Lisbon Traviata, Elliot Loves, Pygmalion, Lips Together Teeth Apart*, Bdwy in *Wake of Jamey Foster* (1982), *Marriage of Figaro, Anything Goes.*

HEARD, JOHN. Born Mar. 7, 1946 in Washington, DC. Graduate Clark U. Debut 1974 OB in *TheWager*, followed by *Macbeth, Hamlet, Fishing, G.R. Point* for which he received a Theatre World Award, *The Creditors, The Promise, Othello, Split, Chekhov Sketchbook, Love Letters, Marathon '91*, Bdwy in *Warp* (1973), *Total Abandon.*

HEINSOHN, ELISA. Born Oct. 11, 1962 in Butler, PA. Debut 1984 OB in *Oy Mama Am I in Love*, followed by *Scandal*, Bdwy in *42nd Street* (1985), *Smile, Phantom of the Opera.*

HELLER, ADAM. Born June 8, 1960 in Englewood, NJ. Graduate NYU. Debut 1984 OB in *Kuni-Leml*, followed by *The Special, Half a World Away, Encore!*, Bdwy in *Les Misérables* (1989).

HENDERSON, SUZANNE. Born May 21, 1960 in New Jersey. Attended U. Del. Debut 1981 OB in *City Suite*, Bdwy in *Grand Hotel* (1989).

HERBST, JEFF. Born Jan. 8, 1963 in Sioux Falls, SD. Graduate U. WI/Madison, Fla. State U. Debut 1988 OB in *On Tina Tuna Walk*, followed by *A Funny Thing Happened on the Way to the Forum*, Bdwy in *A Change in the Heir* (1990).

HERRERA, JOHN. Born Sept. 21, 1955 in Havana, Cuba. Graduate Loyola U. Bdwy debut 1979 in *Grease*, followed by *Evita, Camelot, The Mystery of Edwin Drood, Shogun*, OB in *La Bohème, Lies and Legends.*

HEUGHENS, TODD. Born Sept. 14, 1961 in Detroit, MI. Graduate U. Cinn. Bdwy debut 1990 in *Fiddler on the Roof.*

HIGGINS, JOHN MICHAEL. Born Feb. 12, 1963 in Boston, MA. Graduate Amherst Col. Debut 1986 in *National Lampoon's Class of '86*, followed by *Neddy, Self-torture and Strenuous Exercise, Trumps, Comic Safari, Maids of Honor*, Bdwy in *Mastergate* (1990), *La Bete.*

HILL, RALSTON. Born Apr. 24, 1927 in Cleveland, OH. Graduate Oberlin Col. OB in *The Changeling, Streets of New York, Valmouth, Carousel* (LC '65), *Beggar's Opera, Colette Collage*, Bdwy in *1776* (1969).

HILLIARD, RYAN. Born Jan. 20, 1945 in Ashtabula, OH. Graduate Kent State U. Debut 1971 OB in *Godspell*, followed by *The Bear, Under Milk Wood, The Madwoman of Chaillot, Behind a Mask*, One Act Festival, *What the Butler Saw.*

HILLNER, NANCY. Born June 7, 1949 in Wakefield, RI. Graduate U. Lowell. Bdwy debut 1975 in *Dance with Me*, followed by OB in *Nite Club Confidential, Trading Places, Nunsense, Puppetmaster of Lodz.*

HILTON, MARGARET. Born Jul. 20 in Marple, Cheshire, Eng. Graduate U. London, LAMDA. Debut 1979 OB in *Molly*, followed by *Stevie, Come Back to the Five & Dime Jimmy Dean, Pygmaiion in Concert, In Celebration, Joe Egg, The Film Society, Major Barbara*, Bdwy in *Rose* (1981), *Joe Egg* (1985).

HOFFMAN, PHILIP. Born May 12, 1954 in Chicago, IL. Graduate U. Ill. Bdwy debut 1981 in *The Moony Shapiro Songbook*, followed by *Is There Life after High School?, Baby, Into the Woods*, OB in *The Fabulous '50's, Isn't It Romantic, 1-2-3-4-5, Food and Shelter.*

HOFVENDAHL, STEVE. Born Sept. 1, 1956 in San Jose, CA. Graduate U. Santa Clara, Brandeis U. Debut 1986 OB in *A Lie of the Mind*, followed by *Ragged Trousered Philanthropists, The Miser, A Midsummer night's Dream, Light Shining in Buckinghamshire*, Bdwy 1989 in *Mastergate.*

HOGAN, JONATHAN. Born June 13, 1951 in Chicago, IL. Graduate Goodman Th. Debut 1972 OB in *The Hot l Baltimore*, followed by *The Mound Builders, Harry Outside, Cabin 12, 5th of July, Glorious Morning, Innocent Thoughts Harmless Intentions, Sunday Runners, Threads, Time Framed, Burn This!, The Balcony Scene*, Bdwy in *Comedians* (1976), *Otherwise Engaged, 5th of July, The Caine Mutiny Court-Martial, As Is, Burn This!, Taking Steps.*

HOLBROOK, HAL. Born Feb. 17, 1925 in Cleveland, OH. Graduate Denison U. Bdwy debut 1961 in *Do You Know the Milky Way?*, followed by *The Glass Menagerie, Mark Twain Tonight, The Apple Tree, I Never Sang for My Father, Man of La Mancha, Does a Tiger Wear a Necktie?* OB in *Henry IV, Richard II, Abe Lincoln in Illinois, Marco Millions, Incident at Vichy, Tartuffe, After the Fall, Lake of the Woods, Buried Inside Extra, The Country Girl, King Lear.*

HOLGATE, RONALD. Born May 26, 1937 in Aberdeen, SD. Attended Northwestern U., New Eng. Consv. Debut 1961 OB in *Hobo*, followed by *Hooray It's a Glorious Day, Blue Plate Special*, Bdwy in *A Funny Thing Happened on the Way to the Forum, Milk and Honey, 1776, Saturday Sunday Monday, The Grand Tour, Musical Chairs, 42nd Street, Lend Me a Tenor.*

HOLLIS, TOMMY. Born Mar. 27, 1954 in Jacksonville, TX. Attended Lon Morris Col., U. Houston. Debut 1985 OB in *Diamonds*, followed by *Secrets of the Lava Lamp, Paradise, Africanus Instructus, The Colored Museum*, Bdwy 1990 in *The Piano Lesson* for which he received a Theatre World Award.

HOLM, CELESTE. Born Apr. 29, 1919 in New York City. Attended UCLA, U. Chicago. Bdwy debut 1938 in *Glorianna*, followed by *The Time of Your Life, Another Sun, Return of the Vagabond, 8 O'Clock Tuesday, My Fair Ladies, Papa Is All, All the Comforts of Home, Damask Cheek, Oklahoma!, Bloomer Girl, She Stoops to Conquer, Affairs of State, Anna Christie, The King and I, His and Hers, Interlock, Third Best Sport, Invitation to a March, Mame, Candida, Habeus Corpus, The Utter Glory of Morrissey Hall, I Hate Hamlet*, OB in *A Month in the Country, Paris Was Yesterday, With Love and Laughter, A Christmas Carol.*

HOLTZMAN, MERRILL. Born Sept. 1, 1959. Bdwy debut 1989 in *Mastergate*, OB in *Chelsea Walls, Nebraska.*

HONDA, CAROL A. Born Nov. 20 in Kealakekus, HI. Graduate U. HI. Debut 1983 OB in *Yellor Fever*, followed by *Empress of China, Manoa Valley, Once Is Never Enough, Life of the Land, Rosie's Café, And the Soul Shall Dance, The Wash.*

HOODWIN, REBECCA. Born May 14, 1949 in Miami, FL. Graduate U. Fla. Bdwy debut 1973 in *The Pajama Game*, OB in *5th of July, Day Before Spring.*

HOPE, SHARON. Born in New York City. Graduate Baruch Col. Debut 1987 OB in *A Star Ain't Nothing But a Hole in Heaven*, followed by *Black Medea, Capital Cakewalk, The Trial.*

HOSHKO, JOHN. Born July 28, 1959 in Bethesda, MD. Graduate U. S. Cal. Bdwy debut 1989 in *Prince of Central Park*, OB in *Two by Two.*

HOSTETTER, CURT (formerly Curtis). Born Dec. 16, 1953 in Harrisburg, PA. Graduate Messiah Col. Debut 1977 OB in *My Life*, followed by *Romeo and Juliet, The Contrast, Hamlet, Richard III.*

HOTY, DEE. Born Aug. 16, 1952 in Lakewood, OH. Graduate Otterbein Col. Debut 1979 in *The Golden Apple* followed by *Ta-Dah!, Personals*, Bdwy in *The 5 O'Clock Girl* (1981), *Shakespeare Cabaret, City of Angels, The Will Rogers Follies.*

HOTY, TONY. Born Sept. 29, 1949 in Lakewood, OH. Attended Ithaca Col, U. W. VA. Debut 1974 OB in *Godspell* (also Bdwy 1976), followed by *Joseph and the Amazing Technicolor Dreamcoat, Robin Hood, Success and Succession*, Bdwy in *Gypsy* (1989).

HOWARD, CELIA. Born Aug. 23, 1937 in Oakland, CA. Graduate Stanford U. Debut OB in *Cat and the Canary* (1965), followed by *Whitsuntide, Last Summer at Blue Fish Cove, After the Rain, Midsummer.*

HOWARD, KEN. Born Mar. 28, 1944 in El Centro, CA. Graduate Yale. Bdwy debut 1968 in *Promises Promises*, followed by *1776* for which he received a Theatre World Award, *Child's Play, Seesaw, Little Black Sheep* (LC), *The Norman Conquests, 1600 Pennsylvania Avenue, Rumors, Love Letters.*

HOWES, SALLY ANN. Born July 20, 1934 in London, Eng. Has appeared in *My Fair Lady, Kwamina, Brigadoon, What Makes Sammy Run?, A Little Night Music* (NYCO).

HUDGINS, MARILYN. Born June 24 in Washington, DC. Graduate SBV Col., U. Redlands. Bdwy debut 1978 in *Hello Dolly!*, followed by *The Prince of Central Park* (1989), OB in *The Rothschilds.*

HUDSON, RODNEY. Born Oct. 14, 1948 in St. Louis, MO. Graduate U. S.E. Mo., U. S. Dak., U. Mich. Debut 1977 OB in *Agamemnon*, followed by *Indulgencies, Runaways, Dispatches, Alice in Concert, American Notes, Faith/Hope/Charity, Henry IV Parts 1 and 2.*

HUDSON, TRAVIS. Born Feb. 2 in Amarillo, TX. U. TX graduate. Bdwy debut in *New Faces of 1962*, followed by *Pousse Café, Very Good Eddie, The Grand Tour*, OB in *Triad, Tattooed Countess, Young Abe Lincoln, Get Thee to Canterbury, The Golden Apple, Annie Get Your Gun, Nunsense.*

HUFFMAN, CADY. Born Feb. 2, 1965 in Santa Barbara, CA. Debut 1983 OB in *They're Playing Our Song*, followed by *Festival of 1 Acts, Oh Hell!*, Bdwy 1985 in *La Cage aux Folles*, followed by *Big Deal, The Will Rogers Follies.*

HUFFMAN, FELICITY. Born Dec. 9, 1962 in Westchester, NY. Graduate NYU, AADA, RADA. Debut 1988 in *Boys' Life* followed by *Been Taken, Grotesque Lovesongs, Three Sisters*, Bdwy in *Speed-the-Plow* (1988).

HUGHES, BARNARD. Born Jul. 16, 1915 in Bedford Hills, NY. Attended Manhattan Col. Credits incude OB's *Rosmersholm, A Doll's House, Hogan's Goat, Lime, Older People, Hamlet, Merry Wives of Windsor, Pericles, Three Sisters, Translations, Prelude to a Kiss*, Bdwy in *The Ivy Green, Dinosaur Wharf, Teahouse of the August Moon, A Majority of One, Advise and Consent, The Advocate, Hamlet, I Was Dancing, Generations, How Now Dow Jones, Wrong Way Light Bulb, Sheep on the Runway, Abelard and Heloise, Much Ado about Nothing, Uncle Vanya, The Good Doctor, All over Town, Da, Angels Fall, End of the World, The Iceman Cometh, Prelude to a Kiss.*

HUGHES, LAURA. Born Jan. 28, 1959 in New York City. Graduate Neighborhood Playhouse. Debut 1980 OB in *The Diviners*, followed by *A Tale Told, Time Framed, Fables for Friends, Talley and Son, Kate's Diary, Playboy of the Western World.*

HULCE, TOM. Born Dec. 6, 1953 in Plymouth, MI. Graduate NC Schl. Arts. Bdwy debut 1975 in *Equus*, followed by *A Few Good Men*, OB in *A Memory of Two Mondays, Julius Caesar, Twelve Dreams, The Rise and Rise of Daniel Rocket, Haddock's Eyes.*

HULL, BRYAN. Born Sept. 12, 1937 in Amarillo, TX. Attended U. New Mex., Wayne State U. Bdwy debut 1976 in *Something's Afoot*, followed by *War and Peace*, OB in *Two Gentlemen of Verona, Here Be Dragons, The Fantasticks.*

HULSWIT, MART. Born May 24, 1940 in Maracaibo, Venz. Attended Hobart Col., AADA. Debut 1961 OB in *Romeo and Juliet*, followed by *Richard II, Merchant of Venice, The Tempest, King Lear, Macbeth, In Celebration, Summer People, Broadcast Baby*, Bdwy in *Present Laughter* (1983), *A Few Good Men.*

HUMES, LINDA H. Born Oct. 19, 1955 in New York City. Graduate SUNY/Stonybrook. Debut 1978 OB in *Antigone*, followed by *Spirit, Black and Female, Mitote.*

HUNT, HELEN. Born in Los Angeles, CA. Debut 1986 OB in *Been Taken*, followed by *The Taming of the Shrew*, Bdwy in *Our Town* (1989).

HURST, MELISSA. Born June 8, 1955 in Cleveland, OH. Graduate NYU. Debut 1980 OB in *Dark Ride*, followed by *A Walk on Lake Erie.*

HURT, MARY BETH. Born Sept. 26, 1948 in Marshalltown, IA. Attended U. Iowa, NYU. Debut 1972 OB in *More Than YouDeserve*, followed by *As You Like It, Trelawny of the Wells, The Cherry Orchard, Love for Love, A Member of the Wedding, Boy Meets Girl, Secret Service, Father's Day, Nest of the Wood Grouse, The Day Room, Secret Rapture, Othello*, Bdwy in *Crimes of the Heart* (1981), *The Misanthrope, Benefactors.*

HURT, WILLIAM. Born Mar. 20, 1950 in Washington, DC. Graduate Tufts U., Juilliard. Debut 1976 OB in *Henry V*, followed by *My Life, Ulysses in Traction, Lulu, 5th of July, The Runner Stumbles, Hamlet, Mary Stuart, Childe Byron, The Diviners, Richard II, The Great Grandson of Jedediah Kohler, A Midsummer Night's Dream, Hurlyburly, Joan of Arc at the Stake, Beside Herself*, Bdwy in *5th of July, Hurlyburly.* He received a 1978 Theatre World Award for his work that season with Circle Rep Theatre.

HUTCHISON, CHAD M. Born Apr. 28, 1980 in Indianapolis, IN. Bdwy debut 1990 in *Peter Pan.*

Linda H.
Humes

Timothy
Hutton

Linda
Igarashi

Paul
Jackel

Ernestine
Jackson

Leonard
Jackson

Max
Jacobs

Ruth
Jaroslow

Page
Johnson

Nancy
Johnston

Gordon G.
Jones

Jen
Jones

Rebecca
Judd

Raul
Julia

Laurie
Kennedy

Jack
Kenny

Linda
Kerns

Wiley
Kidd

Perry
King

Gretchen
Kingsley

Joseph
Kolinski

Mia
Korf

John
Kudan

Mary Ann
Lamb

Beverly
Lambert

Robert
Lambert

Zohra
Lampert

Jeffrey
Landman

Sofia
Landon

Nathan
Lane

HUTTON, TIMOTHY. Born Aug. 16, 1969 in Malibu, CA. Bdwy debut 1989 in *Love Letters*, followed by *Prelude to a Kiss*.

HYMAN, EARLE. Born Oct. 11, 1926 in Rocky Mount, NC. Attended New School, Am. Th. Wing. Bdwy debut 1943 in *Run Little Chillun*, followed by *Anna Lucasta, Climate of Eden, Merchant of Venice, Othello, Julius Caesar, The Tempest, No Time for Sergeants, Mr. Johnson*, for which he received a Theatre World Award, *St. Joan, Hamlet, Waiting for Godot, The Duchess of Malfi, Les Blancs, The Lady from Dubuque, Execution of Justice, Death of the King's Horseman*, OB in *The White Rose and the Red, Worlds of Shakespeare, Jonah, Life and Times of J. Walter Smintheus, Orrin, The Cherry Orchard, House Party, Carnival Dreams, Agamemnon, Othello, Julius Caesar, Coriolanus, Pygmalion*.

HYMAN, FRACASWELL. Born Jan. 4, 1958 in Wilson, NC. Debut 1981 OB in *An Evening with Joan Crawford*, followed by *Native Speech*, Bdwy in *Oh Kay!* (1990).

IGARISHI, LINDA. Born Nov. 4, 1966 in Los Angeles, CA. Graduate UCLA. Bdwy debut 1990 in *Shogun: The Musical*.

ISHII, LESLIE. Born Aug. 29, 1960 in Seattle, WA. Graduate U. Wash. Bdwy debut 1990 in *Shogun: The Musical*.

IVEY, DANA. Born Aug. 12 in Atlanta, GA. Graduate Rollins Col., LAMDA, Bdwy debut 1981 in *Macbeth* (LC), followed by *Present Laughter, Heartbreak House, Sunday in the Park with George, Pack of Lies, Marriage of Figaro*, OB in *A Call from the East, Vivien, Candida in Concert, Major Barbara in Concert, Quartermaine's Terms, Baby with the Bathwater, Driving Miss Daisy, Wenceslas Square, Love Letters, Hamlet, The Subject Was Roses*.

JACKEL, PAUL. Born June 30 in Winchester, MA. Graduate Harvard. Debut 1983 OB in *The Robber Bridegroom*, followed by *Side by Side by Sondheim, Gifts of the Magi*, Bdwy in *The Secret Garden* (1991).

JACKSON, DAVID. Born Dec. 4, 1948 in Philadelphia, PA. Bdwy debut 1980 in *Eubie!*, followed by *My One and Only, La Cage aux Folles, Grand Hotel*, OB in *Blackamoor*.

JACKSON, ERNESTINE. Born Sept. 18 in Corpus Christi, TX. Graduate Del Mar Col., Juilliard. Debut 1966 in *Show Boat* (LC), followed by *Finian's Rainbow, Hello Dolly!, Applause, Jesus Christ Superstar, Tricks, Raisin* for which she received a Theatre World Award, *Guys and Dolls, Bacchae*, OB in *Louis, Some Enchanted Evening, Money Notes, Jack and Jill, Black Girl, Brownstone, Sophie, Broadway Jukebox*.

JACKSON, GREG (a.k.a. Greg Vallee). Born Mar. 22, 1955 in NJ. Graduate Boston U. Debut 1980 OB in *Times Square*, followed by *A Loss of Roses, Ladies of the Odeon, Initiation Rites, Occasional Grace*.

JACKSON, LEONARD. Born Feb. 7, 1928 in Jacksonville, FL. Graduate Fiske U. Debut 1965 OB in *Troilus and Cressida*, followed by *Henry V, Happy Ending, Day of Absence, Who's Got His Own, Electronic Nigger and Others, Black Quartet, Five on the Blackhand Side, Boesman and Lena, Murderous Angels, Chickencoop Chinaman, Karl Marx Play, Prodigal Sister*, Bdwy in *The Great White Hope* (1968), *Lost in the Stars, Ma Rainey's Black Bottom, Mule Bone*.

JACOBS, MAX. Born Apr. 28, 1937 in Buffalo, NY. Graduate U. Ariz. Bdwy debut 1965 in *The Zulu and the Zayda*, OB in *Full Circle, The Working Man, Hallowed Halls, The Man in the Glass Booth, Different People, Different Rooms, Second Avenue, Othello, Birth of a Poet, Shaking the Foundation, Madonna & Mike, Romeo and Juliet*.

JACOBY, MARK. Born May 21, 1947 in Johnson City, TN. Graduate GA State U., FL State U., St. John's U. Debut 1984 OB in *Bells Are Ringing*, Bdwy in *Sweet Charity* for which he received a Theatre World Award, *Grand Hotel, The Phantom of the Opera*.

JAFFE, JOAN. Born Dec. 23, in Wilmington, DE. Attended Boston Consv., NYU. Debut 1960 OB in *Carousel*, followed by *The Boys from Syracuse, Once Upon a Mattress, Stage Door, Professionally Speaking, Young Rube, Charge It Please*, Bdwy in *Bajour* (1964), *Much Ado about Nothing*.

JAMES, KELLI. Born Mar. 18, 1959 in Council Bluffs, Iowa. Bdwy debut 1987 in *Les Misérables*.

JAMES, LAWRENCE. Born Jan. 8, 1935 in Gadsden. AL. Graduate Fordham U. Debut 1977 OB in *Cages*, followed by *Let Me Live, Black Eagles*.

JAMROG, JOSEPH. Born Dec. 21, 1932 in Flushing, NY. Graduate CCNY. Debut 1970 OB in *Nobody Hears a Broken Drum*, followed by *Tango, And Whose Little Boy Are You? When You Comin' Back, Red Ryder?, Drums at Yale, The Boy Friend, Love, Death Plays, Too Much Johnson, A Stitch in Time, Pantagleize, Final Hours, Returnings, Brass Birds Don't Sing, And Things That Go Bump in the Night, Fun, Henry Lumpur, I Am a Winner, Little Lies*, Bdwy in *The Miser* (1990).

JAROSLOW, RUTH. Born May 22 in Brooklyn, NY. Attended HB Studio. Debut 1964 OB in *That 5 A.M. Jazz*, followed by *Jonah, Fighting International Fat, Kretch*, Bdwy in *Mame, Fiddler on the Roof* (1964/77/81/90), *The Ritz*.

JARRETT, JERRY. Born Sept. 9, 1918 in Brooklyn, NY. Attended New Th. Schl. Bdwy debut 1948 in *At War with the Army*, followed by *Gentlemen Prefer Blonds, Stalag 17, Fiorello!, Fiddler on the Roof*, OB in *Waiting for Lefty, Nat Turner, Me Candido, That 5 A.m. Jazz, Valentines Day, Tickles by Tucholsky, Jazzbo Brown*.

JENNER, JAMES. Born Mar. 5, 1953 in Houston, TX. Attended U. Tex., LAMDA. Debut 1980 OB in *Kind Lady*, followed by *Station J, Yellow Fever, Comedy of Errors, Taster's Choice, Play Ball, Lucky Come Hawaii*.

JENNINGS, KEN. Born Oct. 10, 1947 in Jersey City, NJ. Graduate St. Peter's Col. Bdwy debut 1975 in *All God's Chillun Got Wings*, followed by *Sweeney Todd* for which he received a Theatre World Award, *Present Laughter, Grand Hotel*, OB in *Once on a Summer's Day, Mayor, Rabboni, Gifts of the Magi, Carmilla*.

JEROME, TIMOTHY. Born Dec. 29, 1943 in Los Angeles, CA. Graduate Ithaca Col. Bdwy debut 1969 in *Man of La Mancha*, followed by *The Rothschilds, Creation of the World..., Moony Shapiro Songbook, Cats, Me and My Girl, Grand Hotel*, OB in *Beggar's Opera, Pretzels, Civilization and Its Discontents, The Little Prince, Colette Collage, Room Service, Romance in Hard Times, Pretzels*

JETER, MICHAEL. Born Aug. 26, 1952 in Lawrenceburg, TN. Graduate Memphis State U. Bdwy debut 1978 in *Once in a Lifetime*, followed by *Grand Hotel*, OB in *The Master and Margarita, G.R. Point* for which he received a Theatre World Award, *Alice in Concert, El Bravo, Cloud 9, Greater Tuna, The Boys Next Door, Only Kidding*.

JILLETTE, PENN. Born in 1955 in Greenfield, MA. Debut 1985 OB in *Penn and Teller*, Bdwy 1987, 1991.

JOHNS, KURT. Born Feb. 28, 1954 in Cincinnati, OH. Graduate Cinn. Consv. Bdwy debut 1988 in *Chess*, followed by *Aspects of Love*.

JOHNSON, JEREMY. Born Oct. 2, 1933 in New Bedford, MA. Graduate CCNY, Columbia U. Debut 1975 OB in *Moby Dick*, followed by *Anna Christie, Harrison Texas, Romeo and Juliet*.

JOHNSON, PAGE. Born Aug. 25, 1930 in Welch, WV. Graduate Ithaca Col. Bdwy bow 1951 in *Romeo and Juliet*, followed by *Electra, Oedipus, Camino Real, In April Once* for which he received a Theatre World Award, *Red Roses for Me, The Lovers, Equus, You Can't Take It With You, Brush Arbor Revival*, OB in *The Enchanted, Guitar, 4 in 1, Journey of the Fifth Horse*, APA's *School for Scandal, The Tavern*, and *The Seagull, Odd Couple, Boys in the Band, Medea, Deathtrap, Best Little Whorehouse in Texas, Fool for Love, East Texas*.

JOHNSTON, NANCY. Born Jan. 15, 1949 in Statesville, NC. Graduate Carson Newman Col., UNC/Greensboro. Debut 1987 OB in *Olympus on My Mind*, followed by *Nunsense, Living Color*, Bdwy in *The Secret Garden* (1991).

JONES, CHERRY. Born Nov. 21, 1956 in Paris, TN. Graduate Carnegie-Mellon. Debut 1983 OB in *The Philanthropist*, followed by *he and she, The Ballad of Soapy Smith, The Importance of Being Earnest, I Am a Camera, Claptrap, Big Time, Light Shining in Buckinghamshire*, Bdwy in *Stepping Out* (1986), *Our Country's Good*.

JONES, GORDON. Born Nov. 1, 1941 in Urania, LA. Graduate La. Tech, U. Ark. Debut 1980 OB in *Room Service*, followed by *The Front Page, The Caine Mutiny Court-Martial, Panhandle, Caveat Emptor, Progress, The Italian Straw Hat, The Fantasticks, June Moon, The Little Foxes, In the Matter of J. Robert Oppenheimer, Unchanging Love*.

JONES, JAY AUBREY. Born Mar. 30, 1954 in Atlantic City, NJ. Graduate Syracuse U. Debut 1981 OB in *Sea Dream*, followed by *Divine Hysteria, Inacent Black and the Brothers, La Belle Helene*, Bdwy in *Cats* (1986).

JONES, JEN. Born Mar. 23, 1927 in Salt Lake City, UT. Debut 1960 OB in *Drums under the Window*, followed by *The Long Voyage Home, Diff'rent, Creditors, Look at Any Man, I Knock at the Door, Pictures in the Hallway, Grab Bag, Bo Bo, Oh Dad Poor Dad..., Henhouse, Uncle Vanya, Grandma's Play*, Bdwy in *Dr. Cook's Garden, But Seriously, Eccentricities of a Nightingale, The Music Man* (1980), *The Octette Bridge Club*.

JONES, SABRA. Born Mar. 22, 1951 in California. Debut 1982 OB in *Joan of Lorraine*, followed by *Inheritors, Paradise Lost, Ghosts, Clarence, Madwoman of Chaillot, Vivat! Vivat Regina!, Children of the Sun, Six Degrees of Separation*.

JOSHUA, LAWRENCE "LARRY." Born Feb. 12, 1954 in New York City. Debut 1979 OB in *Tooth of Crime*, followed by *Sunday Runners in the Rain, Middleman Out, Kid Champion, One Tiger to a Hill, Ground Zero Club, Savage in Limbo, Arturo Ui*.

JOSLYN, BETSY. Born Apr. 19, 1954 in Staten Island, NY. Graduate Wagner Col. Debut 1976 OB in *The Fantasticks*, followed by *Light up the Sky, Colette Collage*, Bdwy in *Sweeney Todd* (1979), *A Doll's Life*.

JOY, ROBERT. Born Aug. 17, 1951 in Montreal, Can. Graduate Oxford U. Debut 1978 OB in *The Diary o f Anne Frank*, followed by *Fables for Friends, Lydie Breeze, Sister Mary Ignatius Explains It All, Actor's Nightmare, What I Did Last Summer, The Death of von Richthofen, Lenny and the Heartbreakers, Found a Peanut, Field Day, Life and Limb, Hyde in Hollywood, The Taming of the Shrew*, Bdwy in *Hay Fever* (1985), *The Nerd*.

JOYCE, JOE. Born Nov. 22, 1957 in Pittsburgh, PA. Graduate Boston U. Debut 1981 OB in *Close Enough for Jazz*, followed by *Oh, Johnny!, They Came from Planet Mirth, Encore!, You Die at Recess, Forever Plaid, Pageant*.

JOYCE, STEPHEN. Born Mar. 7, 1933 in New York City. Attended Fordham U. Bdwy debut 1966 in *Those That Play the Clowns*, followed by *The Exercise, The Runner Stumbles, Devour the Snow, The Caine Mutiny Court-Martial*, OB in *Three Hand Reel, Galileo, St. Joan, Stephen D.* for which he received a Theatre World Award, *Fireworks, School for Wives, Savages, Scribes, Daisy, Maneuvers, Playboy of the Western World*.

JUDD, REBECCA. Born in Fresno, CA. Graduate U. Nev. Debut 1988 OB in *Dutchman*, followed by *Lost in the Stars, The Golden Apple*, Bdwy 1989 in *Sweeney Todd, The Secret Garden*.

JULIA, RAUL. Born Mar. 9, 1940 in San Juan, PR. Graduate U. PR. OB credits include *Macbeth, Titus Andronicus, Theatre in the Streets, Life Is a Dream, Blood Wedding, Ox Cart, No Exit, Memorandum, Frank Gagliano's City Scene, Your Own Thing, Persians, Castro Complex, Pinkville, Hamlet, King Lear, As You Like It, Emperor of Late Night Radio, Threepenny Opera, The Cherry Orchard, Taming of the Shrew, Othello, The Tempest, A Christmas Carol, Macbeth*, Bdwy in *The Cuban Thing, Indians, Two Gentlemen of Verona, Via Galactica, Where's Charley?, Dracula, Betrayal, Nine, Design for Living, Arms and the Man*.

KAGAN, DIANE. Born in Maplewood, NJ. Graduate Fla. State U. Debut 1963 OB in *Asylum*, followed by *Days and Nights of Beebee Fenstermaker, Death of a Well-Loved Boy, Mme. de Sade, Blue Boys, Alive and Well in Agentina, Little Black Sheep, The Family, Ladyhouse Blues, Scenes from Everyday Life, Marvelous Gray, Enrico IV, Five Women in a Chapel*, Bdwy in *Chinese Prime Minister* (1964), *Never Too Late, Any Wednesday, Venus Is, Tiger at the Gates, Vieux Carré*.

KAHN, GARY. Born Feb. 22, 1956 in the Bronx, NY. Graduate U. Miami, U. Tex. Debut OB 1982 in *All of the Above*. followed by Bdwy in *City of Angels* (1989).

KANDEL, PAUL. Born Feb. 15, 1951 in Queens, NY. Graduate Harpur Col. Debut 1977 OB in *Nightclub Cantata*, followed by *Two Grown Men, Scrambled Feet, The Taming of the Shrew, Lucky Stiff, 20 Fingers 20 Toes, Earth and Sky*.

KANE, DONNA. Born Aug. 12, 1962 in Beacon, NY. Graduate Mt. Holyoke Col. Debut 1985 OB in *Dames at Sea* for which she received a Theatre World Award, followed by *The Vinegar Tree, Johnny Pie and the Foolkiller, Babes in Arms, Young Rube, Go to Ground*, Bdwy in *Meet Me in St. Louis*.

KANTOR, KENNETH. Born Apr. 6, 1949 in the Bronx, NY. Graduate SUNY, Boston U. Debut 1974 OB in *Zorba*, followed by *Kiss Me kate, A Little Night Music, Buried Treasure, Sounds of Rodgers and Hammerstein, Shop on Main Street, kismet, The Fantasticks, Colette Collage, Philemon*, Bdwy in *The Grand Tour* (1979), *Brigadoon* (1980), *Mame* (1983), *The New Moon* (NYCO), *Me and My Girl*.

KARR, PATTI. Born Jul. 10 in St. Paul, MN. Attended TCU. Bdwy debut 1953 in *Maggie*, followed by *Carnival in Flanders, Pipe Dream, Bells Are Ringing, New Girl in Town, Body Beautiful, Bye Bye Birdie, New Faces of 1962, Come on Strong, Look to the Lilies, Different Times, Lysistrata, Seesaw, Irene, Pippin, A Broadway Musical, Got to Go Disco, Musical Chairs*, OB in *A Month of Sundays, Up Eden, Snapshot, Housewives Cantata, Something for the Boys, Baseball Wives, I Can Get It for You Wholesale.*

KAUFMAN, ERIC H. Born Sept. 11, 1961 in New York City. Attended U. Wis., NYU. Bdwy debut 1986 in *L'Chaim to Life*, followed by *Gypsy* (1989).

KAYE, JUDY. Born Oct. 11, 1948 in Phoenix, AZ. Attended UCLA, Ariz. State U. Bdwy debut 1977 in *Grease*, followed by *On the 20th Century* for which she received a Theatre World Award, *Moony Shapiro Songbook, Oh Brother!, Phantom of the Opera, The Pajama Game* (LC), OB in *Eileen in Concert, Can't Help Singing, Four to Make Two, Sweethearts in Concert, Love, No No Nanette in Concert, Magdalena in Concert, Babes in Arms, Desire Under the Elms, The Cat and the Fiddle.*

KEATING, CHARLES. Born Oct. 22, 1941 in London, Eng. Bdwy debut 1969 in *Arturo Ui*, followed by *The House of Atreus, Loot*, OB in *An Ounce of Prevention, A Man for All Seasons, There Is a Dream Dreaming Us, What the Butler Saw, Light Up the Sky, Pygmalion.*

KEATS, STEVEN. Born Feb. 6, 1945 in New York City. Attended Montclair State Col., Yale U. Debut 1970 OB in *One Flew over the Cuckoo's Nest*, followed by *We Bombed in New Haven*, Awake and *Sing, The Rose Tattoo, I'm Getting My Act Together..., Sunday Runners in the Rain, Who They Are and How It Is with Them, Other People's Money*, Bdwy in *Oh! Calcutta!* (1971).

KELLY-YOUNG, LEONARD. Born Sept. 29, 1948 in Chicago, IL. Attended Loop Jr. Col. Debut 1983 OB in *The Lady's Not for Burning*, followed by *Riverman.*

KENNEDY, LAURIE. Born Feb. 14, 1948 in Hollywood, CA. Graduate Sarah Lawrence Col. Debut 1974 OB in *End of Summer*, followed by *A Day in the Death of Joe Egg, Ladyhouse Blues, he and she, The Recruiting Officer, Isn't It Romantic, The Master Builder, Candida*, Bdwy in *Man and Superman* (1978) for which she received a Theatre World Award, *Major Barbara.*

KENNY, JACK. Born Mar. 9, 1958 in Chicago, IL. Attended Juilliard. Debut 1983 OB in *Pericles*, followed by *Tartuffe, Play and Other Plays, The Normal Heart, The Rise of David Levinsky, Festival of 1 Acts, Café Crown*, Bdwy in *Café Crown* (1989), *Fiddler on the Roof* (1990).

KERNS, LINDA. Born June 2, 1953 in Columbus, OH. Attended Temple U., AADA. Debut 1981 OB in *Crisp*, followed by *Henry 8th at the Grand Ole Opry, Smoke on the Mountain*, Bdwy in *Nine* (1982), *Big River.*

KERSHAW, WHITNEY. Born Apr. 10, 1962 in Orlando, FL. Attended Harkness/Joffrey Ballet Schools/Debut 1981 OB in *Francis*, Bdwy in *Cats.*

KHOURY, PAMELA. Born May 17, 1954 in Beirut, Lebanon. Graduate U. Tex. Bdwy debut 1980 in *West Side Story*, followed by *Oh Brother!, Jerome Robbins' Broadway*, OB in *Too Many Girls.*

KIDD, WILEY. Born Dec. 11, 1960 in Portsmouth, VA. Graduate Carnegie-Mellon. Bdwy debut in *Me and My Girl* (1987), followed by *Aspects of Love*, OB in *Mores.*

KIM, DANIEL DAE. Born Aug. 4, 1968 in Korea. Graduate Haverford Col. Debut 1991 OB in *Romeo and Juliet*, followed by *Letters from a Student Revolutionary.*

KING, PERRY. Born Apr. 30 in Alliance, OH. Yale Graduate. Debut 1972 OB in *Jesse James*, followed by *Knuckle, The Trouble with Europe*, Bdwy in *A Few Good Men* (1990).

KINGSLEY-WEIHE, GRETCHEN. Born Oct. 6, 1961 in Washington, DC. Attended Tulane U. Debut 1985 OB in *Mowgli*, followed by *This Could Be the Start*, Bdwy in *Les Misérables* (1987), *Sweeney Todd.*

KIRKLAND, SALLY. Born Oct. 31, 1944 in New York City. Attended Actors Studio. Bdwy debut 1961 in *Step on a Crack*, followed by *Bicycle Ride to Nevada, Marathon '33*, OB in *A Midsummer Night's Dream, Fitz, Bitch of Waverly Place, Tom Paine, Futz, Sweet Eros, Witness, One Night Stands of a Noisey Passenger, Justice Box, Delicate Champions, Where Has Tommy Flowers Gone?, Chickencoop Chinamen, Largo Desolato, Women Beware Women, Grotesque Lovesongs.*

KLEIN, LAUREN. Born Jan. 4, 1946 in Brooklyn, NY. Graduate Santa Fe Col. Debut 1983 OB in *Becoming Memories*, followed by *Zastrozzi, After the Fall, Twice Shy, What's Wrong with This Picture?*

KNAPP, SARAH. Born Jan. 20, 1959 in Kansas City, MO. Graduate AADA. Debut OB 1986 in *Gifts of the Magi*, followed by *The No Frills Revue, Nunsense, Gifts of the Magi, Manhattan Class One-Acts.*

KNELL, DANE. Born Sept. 27, 1932 in Winthrop, MA. Bdwy debut 1952 in *See the Jaguar*, followed by *Lettice and Lovage*, OB in *Ulster, Moon Dances, Court of Miracles, Gas Station, Zeks, She Stoops to Conquer, Modigliani.*

KOENIG, JACK. Born May 14, 1959 in Rockville Centre, NY. Graduate Columbia U. Debut OB 1991 in *Grand Finale.*

KOLINSKI, JOSEPH. Born June 26, 1953 in Detroit, MI. Attended U. Detroit. Bdwy debut 1980 in *Brigadoon* followed by *Dance a Little Closer, The Three Musketeers, Les Misérables*, OB in *Hijinks!, The Human Comedy* (also Bdwy).

KONG, PHILIP. Born Sept. 23, 1986 in Lattingtown, NY. Bdwy debut 1991 in *Miss Saigon.*

KORBICH, EDDIE. Born Nov. 6, 1960 in Washington, DC. Graduate Boston Consv. Debut 1985 OB in *A Little Night Music* followed by *Flora the Red Menace, No Frills Revue, The Last Musical Comedy, Godspell, Sweeney Todd* (also Bdwy 1989), *Assassins*, Bdwy in *Singin' in the Rain* (1985).

KOREY, ALIX (formerly Alexandra). Born May 14 in Brooklyn, NY. Graduate Columbia U. Debut 1976 OB in *Fiorello!*, followed by *Annie Get Your Gun, Jerry's Girls, Rosalie in Concert, America Kicks Up Its Heels, Gallery, Feathertop, Bittersuite, Romance in Hard Times, Songs You Might Have Missed*, Bdwy in *Hello Dolly!* (1978), *Show Boat* (1983).

KORF, MIA. Born Nov. 1, 1965 in Ithaca, NY. Attended Cornell U., Ithaca Col. Debut 1987 OB in *Two Gentlemen of Verona*, followed by *The Seagull, Godspell*, Young Playwrights '90.

KOSNICK, BRIAN. Born Nov. 20, 1955 in Cleveland, OH. Graduate Goodman Schl. Debut 1980 OB in *Edmond*, followed by *Taking in the Grave Outdoors, The Desk Set, Giant on the Ceiling.*

KRAKOWSKI, JANE. Born Oct. 11, 1968 in New Jersey. Debut 1984 OB in *American Passion*, followed by *Miami, A Little Night Music*, Bdwy in *Starlight Express* (1987), *Grand Hotel.*

KRISTIEN, DALE. Born May 18 in Washington, DC. Graduate Ithaca Col. Bdwy debut 1981 in *Camelot*, followed by *Show Boat, Radio City Music Specials, Phantom of the Opera.*

KUDAN, JOHN. Born Sept. 13, 1955 in White Plains, NY. Graduate Adelphi U. Debut 1985 OB in *Inside Out*, followed by *Oscar Wilde Solitaire, Titus Andronicus, An Ideal Husband, Nick Dad and the Elephant, O Sappho O Wilde!*

KUHN, BRUCE W. Born Dec. 7, 1955 in Davenport, IA. Graduate U. W. Va., U. Wash. Bdwy debut 1987 in *Les Misérables.*

KURTZ, SWOOSIE. Born Sept. 6 in Omaha, NE. Attended U. S. Cal., LAMDA. Debut 1968 OB in *The Firebugs*, followed by *The Effect of Gamma Rays..., Enter a Free Man, Children, Museum, Uncommon Women and Others, Wine Untouched, Summer, The Beach House, Six Degrees of Separation, Lips Together Teeth Apart*, Bdwy in *Ah Wilderness!* (1975), *Tartuffe, A History of the American Film, 5th of July, House of Blue Leaves.*

LaCHANZE. Born Dec. 16, 1961 in St. Augustine, FL. Attended Morgan State U., Philadelphia Col. Bdwy debut 1986 in *Uptown It's Hot*, followed by *Dreamgirls* (1987), *Once Upon This Island* for which she received a 1991 Theatre World Award, OB in *Once On This Island.*

LACONI, ROBERT. Born Apr. 23, 1954 in Akron, OH. Graduate Kent State U. Debut 1978 OB in *Gulliver's Travels*, followed by *A Book of Etiquette, cummings and goings, Let's Face It, Julius Caesar, Comedy of Errors, New Girl in Town, The Gambler, Based on a True Story, Picture of Dorian Gray, Let It Ride!*

LAGE, JORDAN. Born Feb. 17, 1963 in Palo Alto, CA. Graduate NYU. Debut 1988 OB in *Boy's Life*, followed by *Three Sisters, The Virgin Molly*, Bdwy in *Our Town* (1989).

LAHTI, CHRISTINE. Born Apr. 4, 1950 in Detroit, MI. Graduate U. Mich., HB Studio. Debut 1979 OB in *The Wood* for which she received a Theatre World Award, followed by *Landscape of the Body, The Country Girl, Little Murders*, Bdwy in *Loose Ends* (1980), *Division Street, Scenes and Revelations, Present Laughter, The Heidi Chronicles.*

LALLY, JAMES. Born Oct. 2, 1956 in Cleveland, OH. Attended Sarah Lawrence Col. Debut 1977 in *The Mandrake*, followed by *The Taming of the Shrew, All's Well That Ends Well, As You Like It, Murder in the Dummy's Tomb, Two Gentlemen of Verona, Guadelupe, The Way of the World.*

LAMB, MARY ANN. Born Jul. 4, 1959 in Seattle, WA. Attended Neighborhood Playhouse. Bdwy debut 1985 in *Song and Dance*, followed by *Starlight Express, Jerome Robbins' Broadway.*

LAMBERT, BEVERLY. Born May 20, 1956 in Stamford, CT. Graduate U. NH. Debut 1980 OB in *Plain and Fancy*, followed by *Sitting Pretty in Concert, The Fantasticks, A Little Night Music* (NYCO).

LAMBERT, ROBERT. Born Jul. 28, 1960 in Ypsilanti, MI. Graduate Wayne State U. Bdwy debut 1989 In *Gypsy* for which he received a Theatre World Award and return in 1991, OB in *Unfinished Song.*

LAMPERT, ZOHRA. Born May 13, 1936 in New York City. Attended U. Chicago. Bdwy debut 1956 in *Major Barbara*, followed by *Maybe Tuesday, Look We've Come Through, First Love, Mother Courage, Nathan Weinstein Mystic Conn., Lovers and Other Strangers, The Sign in Sidney Brustein's Window, Unexpected Guests*, OB in *Venus Observed, Diary of a Scoundrel, After the Fall, Marco Millions, Drinks before Dinner, Gifted Children, My Papa's Wine, Mr. Gogol and Mr. Preen.*

LANDER, JOHN-MICHAEL. Born Jan 17 in Hamilton, OH. Attended U. Cal./Irvine, Wright State U. Debut 1989 OB in *Adam and the Experts*, followed by *Custody.*

LANDIS, JEANETTE. Born Apr. 4 in England. Attended Nat. Theatre Schl. Bdwy debut 1966 in *Marat/deSade*, followed by *There's One in Every Marriage, Elizabeth I, Love for Love, Rules of the Game, Member of the Wedding* (1976), OB in *Cowardly Custard.*

LANDMAN, JEFFREY. Born Apr. 5 in East Amherst, NY. Bdwy debut 1989 in *Les Misérables*, OB in *Traveler in the Dark.*

LANDON, SOFIA. Born Jan. 24, 1949 in Montreal, Can. Attended Northwestern U. Debut 1971 OB in *Red White and Black*, followed by *Gypsy, Missouri Legend, Heartbreak House, Peg O' My Heart, Scenes and Revelations, The Hasty Heart, Blue Window, Flatbush Faithful, The Mud Angel.*

LANE, NATHAN. Born Feb. 3, 1956 in Jersey City, NJ. Debut 1978 OB in *A Midsummer Night's Dream*, followed by *Love, Measure for Measure, Claptrap, The Common Pursuit, In a Pig's Valise, Uncounted Blessings, The Film Society, The Lisbon Traviata, Bad Habits, Lips Together Teeth Apart*, Bdwy in *Present Laughter* (1982), *Merlin, Wind in the Willows, Some Americans Abroad.*

LANG, STEPHEN. Born Jul. 11, 1952 in New York City. Graduate Swarthmore Col. Debut 1975 OB in *Hamlet*, followed by *Henry V, Shadow of a Gunman, A Winter's Tale, Johnny on a Spot, Barbarians, Ah Men, Clownmaker, Hannah, Rosencrantz and Guildenstern Are Dead*, Bdwy in *St. Joan* (1977), *Death of a Salesman* (1984), *A Few Good Men, The Speed of Darkness.*

LANGE, ANNE. Born June 24, 1953 in Pipestone, MN. Attended Carnegie-Mellon U. Debut 1979 OB in *Rat's Nest*, followed by *Hunting Scenes from Lower Bavaria, Crossfire, Linda Her and the Fairy Garden, Little Footsteps*, Bdwy in *The Survivor* (1981), *The Heidi Chronicles.*

LANSING, ROBERT. Born June 5, 1929 in San Diego, CA. Bdwy debut 1951 in *Stalag 17*, followed by *Cyrano de Bergerac, Richard III, Charley's Aunt, The Lovers, Cue for Passion, The Great God Brown, Cut of the Axe, Finishing Touches*, OB in *The Father, The Cost of Living, The Line, Phaedra, Mi Vida Loca, The Sum of Us.*

LARSEN, LIZ. Born Jan. 16, 1959 in Philadelphia, PA. Attended Hofstra U., SUNY/Purchase. Bdwy debut 1981 in *Fiddler on the Roof*, followed by *Starmites, A Little Night Music* (NYCO), OB in *Kuni Leml, Hamlin, Personals, Starmites, Company, After These Messages, One Act Festival.*

LAUB, SANDRA. Born Dec. 15, 1956 in Bryn Mawr, PA. Graduate Northwestern U. Debut 1983 OB in *Richard III*, followed by Young Playwrights Festival, *Domestic Issues, Say Goodnight Gracie, Les Mouches, Three Sisters, Edward II, Intricate Aquaintances, The Relapse.*

LAURIA, DAN. Born Apr. 12, 1947 in Brooklyn, NY. Graduate S. Conn. State, U. Conn. Debut 1978 OB in *Game Plan*, followed by *All My Sons, Marlon Brando Sat Here, Home of the Brave, Collective Portraits, Dustoff, Niagara Falls, Punchy, Americans, Other People's Money.*

LAWLESS, WENDY. Born May 8, 1960 in Kansas City, MO. Attended Boston U., NYU. Debut 1989 OB in *Cymbeline*, followed by *La Vie en Rose, Midnight Rodeo, Pagan Day*, Bdwy in *The Heidi Chronicles* (1990).

Stephen
Lang

Wendy
Lawless

Darren
Lee

Kaiulani
Lee

John
Leguizamo

Johanna
Leister

Marcia
Lewis

Robert Sean
Leonard

Audra
Lindley

Lee
Lobenhofer

Emily
Loesser

Jeffery
Logan

Michael
Lombard

Jodi
Long

Chad
Lowe

Mary
Lum

Jason
Ma

Joan
MacIntosh

Lizbeth
Mackay

Bruce
MacVittie

Kristen
Mahon

John
Mahoney

Wendy
Makkena

Joel
Malina

Joshua
Malina

Yvonne
Marceau

Daniel
Markel

Jodie
Markell

Jamie
Marsh

Cynthia
Martells

LAWRENCE, SHARON. Born June 29, 1961 in Charlotte, NC. Attended UNC/Chapel Hill. Debut 1984 OB in *Panache*, followed by *Berlin in Light*, Bdwy in *Cabaret* (1987), *Fiddler on th Roof*.

LAYNE, MARY. Born June 20, 1950 in Colorado, TX. Attended Houston Baptist Col., U. Houston. Bdwy debut 1975 in *The Royal Family*, followed by *The Misanthrope, Shadowlands*, OB in *The Fox*.

LAZORE, MARK. Born Sept. 1, 1956 in Chicago, IL. Attended U. Ill. Debut 1987 OB in *Surviving in New York* followed by *Whatnot*, Bdwy in *Teddy and Alice* (1987).

LEA, BARBARA. Born Apr. 10, 1929 in Detroit, MI. Graduate Wellesley, San Fernando St. Col. Debut 1961 OB in *The Painted Days*, followed by *Do I Hear a Waltz?, Follies, The Music of Cole Porter*.

LEAVEL, BETH. Born Nov. 1, 1955 in Raleigh, NC. Graduate Meredith Col., UNC/Greensboro. Debut 1982 OB in *Applause*, followed by *Promises Promises, Broadway Jukebox, Unfinished Song*, Bdwy in *42nd Street* (1984).

LEE, DARREN. Born June 8, 1972 in Long Beach, CA. Bdwy debut 1990 in *Shogun*, followed by *Miss Saigon*.

LEE, JOY (a.k.a. Joie). Born in 1965 in Brooklyn, NY. Bdwy debut 1991 in *Mule Bone*.

LEE, LAIULANI. Born Feb. 28, 1950 in Princeton, NJ. Attended American U. Bdwy debut 1975 in *Kennedy's Children*, followed by *Macbeth, Pack of Lies*, OB in *Ballad of the Sad Café, Museum, Safe House, Days to Come, Othello, Strange Snow, Aristocrats, Rimers of Eldritch, Casanova*.

LEE, VICKI. Born Jan. 5 in Baltimore, MD. Graduate Fashion Inst. Bdwy debut 1990 in *Shogun: The Musical*.

LeFEVRE, ADAM. Born Aug. 11, 1950 in Albany, NY. Graduate Williams Col., U. Iowa. Debut 1981 OB in *Turnbuckle*, followed by *Badgers, Goose and Tomtom, In the Country, Submariners, Boys Next Door, Doctor's Dilemma*, Bdwy in *Devil's Disciple* (1988), *Our Country's Good*.

LEGUIZAMO, JOHN. Born Jul. 22, 1965. Attnded NYU. Debut 1987 OB in *La Puta Vida*, followed by *A Midsummer Night's Dream, Parting Gestures, She First Met Her Parents on the Subway, Mambo Mouth*.

LEIGHTON, JOHN. Born Dec. 30 on Staten Island, NY. Attended NYU, Columbia U. Debut 1954 OB in *Splendid Error*, followed by *Juno and the Paycock, A Christmas Carol, Quare Fellow, Brothers Karamazov, Montserrat, Othello, Merchant of Venice, Enter a Free Man, The Bone Ring, Romeo and Juliet*, Bdwy in *Of the Fields Lately* (1980).

LEISTER, JOHANNA. Born Sept. 5 in Orange, TX. Graduate Tex. Women's U. Debut 1972 OB in *The Rimers of Eldritch*, followed by *Mary Stuart, Twelfth Night, Spider's Web*, Bdwy in *Tartuffe* (1977), *Whose Life Is It Anyway?, Whodunnit, Dracula*.

LEONARD, ROBERT SEAN. Born Feb. 28, 1969 in Westwood, NJ. Debut 1985 OB in *Sally's Gone She Left Her Name*, followed by *Coming of Age in Soho, Beach House, Young Playwrights Festival, When She Danced, Romeo and Juliet*, Bdwy in *Brighton Beach Memoirs* (1985), *Breaking the Code, The Speed of Darkness*.

LESLIE, BETHEL. Born Aug. 3, 1929 in New York City. Bdwy debut 1944 in *Snafu*, followed by *Years Ago, Wisteria Trees, Goodbye My Fancy, Time of the Cuckoo, Mary Rose, Brass Ring, Inherit the Wind, Catch Me If You Can, But Seriously, Long Day's Journey into Night*, OB in *The Aunts, The March on Russia*.

LeSTRANGE, PHILIP. Born May 9, 1942 in the Bronx, NY. Graduate Catholic U., Fordham U. Debut 1970 OB in *Getting Married*, followed by *Erogenous Zones, The Quilling of Prue, The Front Page, Six Degrees of Separation*.

LEVINE, EARL AARON. Born Dec. 1, 1952 in Tallahassee, FL. Attended Temple U., Westchester State U. Bdwy debut 1982 in *Little Johnny Jones*, OB in *The Fantasticks*.

LEVINE, RICHARD S. Born Jul. 16, 1954 in Boston, MA. Graduate Juilliard. Debut 1978 OB in *Family Business*, followed by *Magic Time, It's Better with a Band, Emma, Mistress of the Inn, I Can Get It for You Wholesale*, Bdwy in *Dracula, Rock 'n' Roll: First 5000 Years, Rumors, Gypsy* (1991).

LEWIS, EDMUND. Born Feb. 12, 1959 in London, Eng. Attended Reading Blue Coat, RADA. Debut OB in *The Longboat*, followed by *A Most Secret War, Without Apologies, Up 'n' Under, Progress, Nightingale*.

LEWIS, MARCIA. Born Aug. 18, 1938 in Melrose, MA. Attended U. Cinn. OB in *The Impudent Wolf, Who's Who Baby, God Bless Coney, Let Yourself Go, Romance Language, When She Danced*, Bdwy in *The Time of Your Life, Hello Dolly!, Annie, Rags, Roza, Orpheus Descending, Gypsy* (1991).

LEWIS, VICKI. Born Mar. 17, 1969 in Cincinnati. OH. Graduate Cinn. Consv. Bdwy debut 1982 in *Do Black Patent Leather Shoes Really Refect Up?*, followed by *Wind in the Willows*, OB in *Snoopy, A Bundle of Nerves, Angry Housewives, 1-2-3-4-5, One Act Festival, The Love Talker, Buzzsaw Berkeley, Marathon '90, The Crucible, I Can Get It for You Wholesale*.

LICATO, FRANK. Born Apr. 20, 1952 in Brooklyn, NY. Attended Emerson Col. Debut 1974 OB in *Deathwatch*, followed by *Fever, American Music, Angel City, Killer's Head, Haunted Lives, The Taming of the Shrew*, New Voice Festival, *Jekyll in Chamber*.

LIMA, PAUL. Born Feb. 5, 1961 in Ithaca, NY. Graduate AADA. Debut 1987 OB in *Deathmarch*, followed by *Idiot's Delight, Fanny's First Play, The Archbishop's Ceiling, Threepenny Opera, The Knack, The Three Sisters, Romeo and Juliet*.

LINDERMAN, ED. Born May 21, 1947 in Chicago, IL. Attended Northwestern U., DePaul U., U. Ill., AMDA. Debut 1969 in *Weigh-In Weigh-Out!*, followed by *June Moon, Some Other Time, Broadway Jukebox*, Bdwy in *Fiddler on the Roof* (1971).

LINDLEY, AUDRA. Born Sept. 24, 1923 in Los Angeles, CA. Has appeared in *Comes the Revolution, Heads or Tails, Hear That Trumpet, The Young and the Fair, Venus Is, Spofford, Fire!*, OB in *Elba, About Face, Handy Dandy*.

LOBENHOFER, LEE. Born June 25, 1955 in Chicago, IL. Graduate U. Ill. Debut 1986 OB in *Rainbow*, followed by *I Married an Angel in Concert, Hans Christian Andersen, Bittersweet, Robin Hood, Lost in the Stars*, Bdwy in *Shogun* (1990), *Grand Hotel*.

LOCKWOOD, LISA. Born Feb. 13, 1958 in San Francisco, CA. Bdwy debut 1988 in *Phantom of the Opera*.

LOESSER, EMILY. Born June 2, 1965 in New York City. Graduate Northwestern U. Debut 1988 OB in *The Secret Garden*, followed by *Together Again for the First Time, The Witch, Follies, Yiddle with a Fiddle*, Bdwy in *The Sound of Music* (LC/90).

LOGAN, JEFFERY. Born Aug. 18, 1956 in Victorville, CA. Graduate UC/Berkeley. Bdwy debut 1986 in *Shakespeare on Broadway*, OB in *Related Retreats, Spinoza*.

LOMBARD, MICHAEL. Born Aug. 8, 1934 in Brooklyn, NY. Graduate Brooklyn Col., Boston U. OB in *King Lear, Merchant of Venice, Cages, Pinter Plays, La Turista, Elizabeth the Queen, Room Service, Mert and Phil, Side Street Scenes, Angelo's Wedding, Friends in High Places, What's Wrong with This Picture?*, Bdwy in *Poor Bitos* (1964), *The Devils, Gingerbread Lady, Bad Habits, Otherwise Engaged, Awake and Sing*.

LONG, JODI. Born in New York City. Graduate SUNY/Purchase. Bdwy debut 1963 in *Nowhere to Go But Up*, followed by *Loose Ends, Bacchae*, OB in *Fathers and Sons, Family Devotions, Rohwer, Tooth of the Crime, Dream of Kitamura, A Midsummer Night's Dream, Madame de Sade, The Wash*.

LONGWELL, KAREN. Born Feb. 7, 1955 in Ithaca, NY. Graduate Fredonia St. Col., Ithaca Col. Debut 1983 OB in *The Robber Bridegroom*, followed by *Very Warm for May, Radio City Christmas Spectacular*.

LOPEZ, PRISCILLA. Born Feb. 26, 1948 in the Bronx, NY. Bdwy debut 1966 in *Breakfast at Tiffany's*, followed by *Henry Sweet Henry, Lysistrata, Company, Her First Roman, Boy Friend, Pippin, A Chorus Line* (also OB), *Day in Hollywood/Night in the Ukraine, Nine*, OB in *What's a Nice Country Like You..., Key Exchange, Buck, Extremites, Non Pasquale, Be Happy for Me, Times and Appetites of oulouse-Lautrec, Marathon '88, Other People's Money*.

LOREN, JACIE. Born March 13, 1974 in New York City. Debut 1991 OB in *Romeo and Juliet*.

LORENZO. Born Sept. 22, 1925 in Beaumont, TX. Attended LACC. Debut OB in *Early Day*, followed by *Scenes from Richard III, Requiem for Romance, Fat Tuesday Blues, Trouble in Mind, Blackamoor, Mitote*.

LOUDON, DOROTHY. Born Sept. 17, 1933 in Boston, MA. Attended Emerson Col, Syracuse U. Debut 1961 OB in *World of Jules Feiffer*, Bdwy 1963 in *Nowhere to Go but Up* for which she received a Theatre World Award, followed by *Noel Coward's Sweet Potato, Fig Leaves Are Falling, Three Men on a Horse, The Women, Annie, Ballroom, West Side Waltz, Noises Off, Jerry's Girls*.

LOVE, VICTOR. Born Aug. 4, 1967 in Camp LeJeune, NC. Attended LACC, U. Wis. Bdwy debut 1989 in *A Few Good Men*, OB in *Richard II, Jonin'*.

LOWE, CHAD. Born Jan. 15, 1968 in Dayton, OH. Debut 1990 OB in *Grotesque Lovesongs*.

LUCKINBILL, LAURENCE. Born nov. 21, 1938 in Ft. Smith, AR. Graduate U. Ark., Catholic U. Bdwy debut 1962 in *A Man for All Seasons*, followed by *Beekman Place, Poor Murderers, A Meeting by the River, The Shadow Box, Chapter Two, Past Tense, Dancing in the End Zone*, OB in *Oedipus Rex, There's a Play Tonight, The Fantasticks, Tartuffe, Boys in the Band, Horseman, Pass By, Memory Bank, What the Butler Saw, Alpha Beta, A Prayer for My Daughter, Life of Galileo, The Memory Bank, Lyndon Johnson*.

LUDWIG, SALEM. Born Jul. 31, 1915 in Brooklyn, NY. Attended Brooklyn Col. Bdwy debut 1946 in *Miracle in the Mountains*, followed by *Camino Real, Enemy of the People, All You Need Is One Good Break, Inherit the Wind, Disenchanted, Rhinoceros, Three Sisters, The Zulu and the Zahda, Moonchildren, American Clock, A Month of Sundays*, OB in *The Brothers Karamazov, Victim, Troublemaker, Man of Destiny, Night of the Dunce, Corner of the Bed, Awake and Sing, Prodigal, Babylon, Burnt Flower Bed, Friends Too Numerous to Mention, After the Fall, What's Wrong with This Picture?, Spinoza*.

LUKAS, CARRENA. Born Dec. 8, 1965 in Oregon City, OR. Attended U.S. Intl. U., Nat. Shakespeare Consv. Debut 1989 OB in *Amulets Against the Dragon Forces*, followed by *The Cool Club*.

LUM, ALVIN. Born May 28, 1931 in Honolulu, HI. Attended U. HI. Debut 1969 OB in *In the Bar of a Tokyo Hotel*, followed by *Pursuit of Happiness, Monkey Music, Flowers and Household Gods, Station J, Double Dutch, Teahouse, Song for a Nisei Fisherman, Empress of China, Manos Valley, Hot Sake, Chu Chem* (also Bdwy), Bdwy in *Lovely Ladies Kind Gentlemen* (1970), *Two Gentlemen of Verona, City of Angels*.

LUM, MARY. Born July 26, 1948 in New York City. Graduate Hunter Col. Debut 1982 OB in *Hibakusha: Stories from Hiroshima*, followed by *Plaid on Both Sides, Full-Time Active, Autumn Dusk, Afternoon Shower, Food, Sister Sister, Daughters, Electra Speaks, Caucasian Chalk Circle, Julius Caesar, Eat a Bowl of Tea, Letters to a Student Revolutionary*.

LUZ, FRANC (a.k.a. Frank C.). Born Dec. 22 in Cambridge, MA. Attended New. Mex. State U. Debut 1974 OB in *The Rivals*, followed by *Fiorello!, Little Shop of Horrors*, Bdwy in *Whoopee!* (1979), *City of Angels*.

LYD-LYD, GASTON. Born Apr. 15, 1959 in New York City. Bdwy debut 1990 in *Jerome Robbins' Broadway*, followd by *Shogun: The Musical*.

LYLES, LESLIE. Born in Plainfield, NJ. Graduate Monmouth Col., Rutgers U. Debut 1981 OB in *Sea Marks*, followed by *Highest Standard of Living, Vanishing Act, I Am Who I Am, The Arbor, Terry by Terry, Marathon '88, Sleeping Dogs, Marathon '90, Young Playwrights '90, Nebraska, The My House Play, Life during Wartime*.

LYNG, NORA MAE. Born Jan. 27, 1951 in Jersey City, NJ. Debut 1981 OB in *Anything Goes*, followed by *Forbidden Broadway, Road to Hollywood, Tales of Tinseltown*, Festival of One Acts, Bdwy in *Wind in the Willows* (1983), *Cabaret* (1987).

LYNLEY, CAROL. Born Feb. 13, 1942 in New York City. Has appeared in *Anniversary Waltz, The Potting Shed* for which she received a Theatre World Award, *Blue Denim*, OB in *Answered the Flute, The Seagull: The Hamptons*.

MA, JASON. Born in Palo Alto, CA. Graduate UCLA. Bdwy debut 1989 in *Chu Chem*, followed by *Prince of Central Park, Shogun: The Musical, Miss Saigon*.

MacINTOSH, JOAN E. Born Nov. 25, 1945 in NJ. Graduate Beaver Col, NYU. Debut OB 1969 in *Dyonysus in '69*, followed by *Macbeth, The Beard, Tooth of Crime, Mother Courage, Marilyn Project, Seneca's Oedipus, St. Joan of the Stockyards, Wonderland in Concert, Dispatches, Endgame, Killings on the Last Line, Request Concert, 3 Acts of Recognition, Consequence, Whispers, Cymbeline, Night Sky, A Bright Room Called Day*, Bdwy in *Our Town* (1989), *Orpheus Descending*.

MacKAY, JOHN. Graduate CUNY. Bdwy debut 1960 in *Under the Yum Yum Tree*, followed by *A Gift of Time, A Man for All Seasons, The Lovers, Borstal Boy, The Miser*, OB in *Oedipus Cycle, Gilles de Rais, Marathon '89, 3 Poets*.

MACKAY, LIZBETH. Born Mar. 7 in Buffalo, NY. Graduate Adelphi U., Yale. Bdwy debut 1981 in *Crimes of the Heart* for which she received a Theatre World Award, followed by OB in *Kate's Diary, Tales of the Lost Formicans, Price of Fame, The Old Boy.*

MACKLIN, VALERIE. Born Apr. 25 in New York City. Graduate Hunter Col. Debut 1988 OB in *Struttin'*, followed by *A Funny Thing Happened on the Way to the Forum*, Bdwy in *Black and Blue* (1989).

MacPHERSON, LORI. Born July 23 in Albany, NY. Attended Skidmore Col. Bdwy debut 1988 in *The Phantom of the Opera.*

MacRAE, HEATHER. Born in New York City. Attended Colo. Women's Col. Bdwy debut 1968 in *Here's Where I Belong*, followed by *Hair, Coastal Disturbances*, OB in *The Hot l Baltimore, Coastal Disturbances, Falsettoland.*

MacVITTIE, BRUCE. Born Oct. 14, 1956 in Providence, RI. Graduate Boston U. Bdwy debut 1983 in *American Buffalo*, followed OB in *California Dog Fight, The Worker's Life, Cleveland and Half Way Back, Marathon '87, One of the Guys, Young Playwrights '90.*

MACY, W.H. Born Mar. 13, 1950 in Miami, FL. Graduate Goddard Col. Debut 1980 OB in *The Man in 605*, followed by *Twelfth Night, The Beaver Coat, A Call from the East, Sittin', Sunshine, The Dining Room, Speakeasy, Wild Life, Flirtations, Baby with the Bathwater, Prairie/Shawl, The Nice and the Nasty, Bodies, Rest and Motion, Oh Hell!, Marathon '90, Life during Wartime, Mr. Gogol and Mr. Preen*, Bdwy in *Our Town* (1989).

MAGUIRE, MICHAEL. Born Feb. 20, 1955 in Newport News, VA. Graduate Oberlin Col., U. Mich. Bdwy debut 1987 in *Les Misérables* for which he received a Theatre World Award, followed by *A Little Night Music* (NYCO).

MAHON, KRISTEN. Born Jan. 13, 1979 in Oceanside, NY. Bdwy debut 1989 in *Gypsy.*

MAHONEY, JOHN. Born June 20, 1940 in Manchester, Eng. Attended Quincy Col., W. W. Ill. U. Debut 1985 OB in *Orphans* for which he received a Theatre World Award, followed by *The Subject Was Roses*, Bdwy in *House of Blue Leaves* (1986).

MAILER, STEPHEN. Born Mar. 10, 1966 in New York City. Attended Middlebury Col., NYU. Debut OB 1989 in *For Dear Life*, followed by *What's Wrong with This Picture?*

MAKKENA, WENDY. Born in New York City. Attended Juilliard; danced with NYC Ballet. OB debut 1982 in *Divine Fire*, followed by *Wedding Presence, The Rivals, The Taming of the Shrew, Loman Family Picnic, The Birthday Party, Mountain Language, Prin, The American Plan*, Bdwy in *Pygmalion* (1987), *Lend Me a Tenor.*

MALINA, JOEL. Born June 1, 1964 in New York City. Yale graduate. Debut 1990 OB in *The Rothschilds*, followed by *Philemon.*

MALINA, JOSHUA. Born Jan. 17, 1966 in New York City. Yale graduate. Bdwy debut 1989 in *A Few Good Men.*

MALKOVICH, JOHN. Born Dec. 9, 1953 in Christopher, IL. Attended E. Ill. U., Ill. State U. Debut 1982 OB in *True West* for which he received a Theatre World Award, followed by *Balm in Gilead, Burn This!, States of Shock*, Bdwy in *Death of a Salesman, Burn This!*

MANDRACCHIA, CHARLES. Born Mar. 29, 1962 in Brooklyn, NY. Graduate Brooklyn Col. Debut OB 1987 in *Wish You Were Here*, followed by *Mr. Universe, Philoctetes, Pretty Faces*, Bdwy in *South Pacific, Kismet, Desert Song, Grand Hotel.*

MANIS, DAVID. Born Nov. 24, 1959 in Ann Arbor, MI. Graduate U. Wash. Debut 1983 OB in *Pericles*, followed by *Pieces of Eight, A New Way to Pay Old Debts, As You Like It, The Skin of Our Teeth, And They Dance Real Slow in Jackson, Rough Crossing, Starting Monday, Henry IV Parts 1 and 2.*

MANN, TERRENCE. Born in 1945 in Kentucky. Graduate NC Schl. of Arts. Bdwy debut 1980 in *Barnum*, followed by *Cats, Rags, Les Misérables, Jerome Robbins' Broadway*, OB in *A Night at the Fights, The Queen's Diamond, Assassins.*

MANTELLO, JOE. Born Dec. 27, 1962 in Rockford, IL. Debut 1986 OB in *Crackwalker*, followed by *Progress, Walking the Dead.*

MANZI, WARREN. Born July 1, 1955 in Laurence, MA. Graduate Holy Cross, Yale. Bdwy debut 1980 in *Amadeus*, OB in *Perfect Crime.*

MARCEAU, YVONNE. Born Jul. 13, 1950 in Chicago, IL. Graduate U. Utah. Bdwy debut 1989 in *Grand Hotel.*

MARCHAND, NANCY. Born June 19, 1928 in Buffalo, NY. Graduate Carnegie Tech. Debut 1951 in CC's *Taming of th Shrew*, followed by *Merchant of Venice, Much Ado About Nothing, Three Bags Full, After the Rain, The Alchemist, Yerma, Cyrano de Bergerac, Mary Stuart, Enemies, The Plough and the Stars, 40 Carats, And Miss Reardon Drinks a Little, Veronica's Room, Awake and Sing, Morning's at Seven, The Octette Bridge Club*, OB in *The Balcony, Children, Taken in Marriage, Sister Mary Ignatius Explains It All, Elecktra, The Cocktail Hour, Love Letters.*

MARDIROSIAN, TOM. Born Dec. 14, 1947 in Buffalo, NY. Graduate U. Buffalo. Debut 1976 OB in *Gemini*, followed by *Grand Magic, Losing Time, Passione, Success and Succession, Ground Zero Club, Cliffhanger, Cap and Bells, The Normal Heart, Measure for Measure, Largo Desolato, The Good Coach, Subfertile, The Taming of the Shrew*, Bdwy in *Happy End, Magic Show.*

MARINOS, PETER. Born Oct. 2, 1951 in Pontiac, MI. Graduate Mich. State U. Bdwy debut 1976 in *Chicago*, followed by *Evita, Zorba, The Secret Garden.*

MARKEL, DANIEL. Born Dec. 4, 1963 in Omaha, NE. Graduate Loyola Marymount, NYU. Debut 1987 OB in *Much Ado about Nothing*, followed by *Lulu, Sexual Perversity in Chicago*, Bdwy in *Prelude to a Kiss* (1991).

MARKELL, JODIE. Born Apr. 13, 1959 in Memphis, TN. Attended Northwestern U. Debut 1984 OB in *Balm in Gilead*, followed by *Carrying School Children, UBU, Sleeping Dogs, Machinal.*

MARKS, KENNETH. Born Feb. 17, 1954 in Harwick, PA. Graduate U. Penn., Lehigh U. Debut 1978 OB in *Clara Bow Loves Gary Cooper*, followed by *Canadian Gothic, Time and the Conways, Savoury Meringue, Thrombo, Fun, 1-2-3-4-5, Manhattan Class 1 Acts, A Bright Room Called Day.*

MARLEY, SUSANNE. Born Sept. 25, 1947 in Cleveland, OH. Graduate Ohio Wesleyan U. Debut 1985 OB in *Fool for Love*, followed by *Missouri Legend, Dutchman, Balm in Gilead, Other People's Money, White Collar, East Texas.*

MARSH, JAMIE. Born Sept. 17, 1966 in New York City. Attended HB Studio. Bdwy debut 1991 in *Lost in Yonkers.*

MARSHALL, LARRY. Born Apr. 3, 1944 in Spartanburg, SC. Attended Fordham U. New Eng. Consv. Bdwy debut in *Hair*, followed by *Two Gentlemen of Verona, A Midsummer Night's Dream, Rockabye Hamlet, Porgy and Bess, A Broadway Musical, Comin' Uptown, Oh Brother!, Big Deal, 3 Penny Opera*, OB in *Spell #7, Jus' Like Livin', The Haggadah, Lullabye and Goodnight, Alladin, In the House of the Blues, The Life.*

MARTELLS, CYNTHIA. Born Sept. 8, 1960 in London, Eng. Attended Rutgers U. Debut 1983 OB in *Under Heaven's Eye*, followed by *Lightning, Rules of Love, Thornwood, No No Nanette, Caucasian Chalk Circle, Young Playwrights '90.*

MARTIN, LEILA. Born Aug. 22, 1932 in New York City. Bdwy debut 1944 in *Peepshow*, followed by *Two on the Aisle, Wish You Were Here, Guys and Dolls, Best House in Naples, Henry Sweet Henry, The Wall, Visit to a Small Planet, The Rothschilds, 42nd Street, The Phantom of the Opera*, OB in *Ernest in Love, Beggar's Opera, King of the U.S., Philemon, Jerry's Girls.*

MARTIN, NAN. Born in Decatur, IL. Attended UCLA, Actors Studio. Bdwy debut 1950 in *A Story for a Sunday Evening*, followed by *The Constant Wife, J.B., The Great God Brown, Under the Yum Yum Tree, Summer Brave, Eccentricities of a Nightingale*, OB in *Saturday Night Kid, Sweet Confession, Lysistrata, Much Ado about Nothing, Phaedra, Merchant of Venice, Taming of the Shrew, Hamlet, The Old Boy.*

MARTINI, ROBERT LEE. Born July 30, 1960 in New York City. Graduate Wagner Col. Debut 1987 OB in *The Tavern*, followed by *Hamlet, Pericles, Measure for Measure.*

MASON, JACKIE. Born June 9, 1934 in Sheboygan, WI. Bdwy debut 1969 in *A Teaspoon Every Four Hours*, followed by *The World According to Me, Jackie Mason: Brand New.*

MASON, MARSHA. Born Apr. 3, 1942 in St. Louis, MO. Attended Webster Col. Debut 1967 OB in *Deer Park*, followed by *It's Called the Sugar Plum, Happy Birthday Wanda June, Richard III, Old Times, Love Letters, The Big Love, Lake No Bottom*, Bdwy in *The Good Doctor* (1973).

MASTERS, DAVID. Born Feb. 26, 1924 in St. Paul, MN. Graduate Wm. & Mary, NYU. Debut 1953 OB in *The Madwoman of Chaillot*, followed by *What Every Woman Knows, The Anatomist, The Big Knife, Measure for Measure*, Bdwy in *Fiddler on the Roof* (1967/76/90).

MASTRONE, FRANK. Born Nov. 1, 1960 in Bridgeport, CT. Graduate Central St. State U. Bdwy debut 1988 in *The Phantom of the Opera.*

MATAMOROS, DIEGO. Born Nov. 6, 1958 in Rio de Janeiro, Brazil. Attended LAMDA. Debut 1979 OB in *As You Like It*, followed by *Passion and Poetry, Spinoza.*

MATSUSAKA, TOM. Born Aug. 8 in Wahiawa, HI. Graduate Mich. State U. Bdwy debut 1968 in *Mame*, followed by *Ride the Winds, Pacific Overtures, South Pacific*, OB in *Agamemnon, Chu Chem, Jungle of Cities, Santa Anita '42, Extenuating Circumstances, Rohwer, Teahouse, Song of a Nisei Fisherman, Empress of China, Pacific Overtures* (1984), *Eat a Bowl of Tea, Shogun Macbeth, The Impostor, Privates on Parade, Lucky Come Hawaii.*

MATZ, JERRY. Born Nov. 15, 1935 in New York City. Graduate Syracuse U. Debut 1965 OB in *The Old Glory*, followed by *Hefetz, A Day Out of Time, A Mad World My Masters, The Rise of David Levinsky, The Last Danceman, Madrid Madrid*, Bdwy in *Ghetto* (1989), *Fiddler on the Roof* (1989).

MAUGANS, WAYNE. Born Sept. 26, 1964 in Harrisburg, PA. Graduate NYU. Debut 1990 OB in *Lusting after Pipino's Wife*, followed by *Ancient Boys.*

MAULDIN, MICHAEL. Born Dec. 17, 1957 in Panama City, FL. Graduate U. West Fla. Debut 1983 OB in *The Tempest*, followed by *The Three Sisters, All's Well That Ends Well, Othello, Tonight at 8:30.*

McALLEN, KATHLEEN ROWE. Born Nov. 30 in the Bay area, CA. Attended UCB. UCLA. Debut 1981 OB in *Joseph and the Amazing Technicolor Dreamcoat*, Bdwy in *Joseph and ...* (1982), followed by *Aspects of Love* for which she received a Theatre World Award.

McATEER, KATHRYN. Born Sept. 4, 1949 in Englewood, NJ. Graduate Montclair State Col. Debut 1983 OB in *Upstairs at O'Neal's*, followed by *Mayor, Take Me Along, Philemon*, Bdwy in *Mayor* (1985), *Into the Light.*

McCALL, KATHLEEN. Born Jan. 11 in Denver, CO. Graduate Moorhead State U., LAMDA. Debut 1986 OB in *Thanksgiving*, followed by *Acapella Hardcore, Class 1 Acts, Steel Magnolias*, Bdwy 1989 in *M. Butterfly, Theme and Variations.*

McCANN, CHRISTOPHER. Born Sept. 29, 1952 in New York City. Graduate NYU. Debut 1975 OB in *The Measures Taken*, followed by *Ghosts, Woyzeck, St. Joan of the Stockyards, Buried Child, Dwelling in Milk, Tongues, 3 Acts of Recognition, Don Juan, Michi's Blood, Five of Us, Richard III, The Golem, Kafka Father and Son, Flatbush Faithful, Black Market, King Lear, The Virgin Molly.*

McCARTY, CONAN. Born Sept. 16, 1955 in Lubbock, TX. Attended U.S. Cal., AADA/West. Debut 1980 OB in *Star Treatment*, followed by *Beyond Therapy, Henry IV Part 1, Titus Andronicus, The Man Who Shot Lincoln*, Bdwy in *Macbeth* (1988), *A Few Good Men.*

McCLARNON, KEVIN. Born Aug. 25, 1952 in Greenfield, IN. Graduate Butler U., LAMDA. Debut 1977 OB in *The Homecoming*, followed by *Heaven's Gate, A Winter's Tale, Johnny on a Spot, The Wedding, Between Daylight and Boonville, Macbeth, The Clownmaker, Cinders, The Ballad of Soapy Smith, Better Days.*

McCORD, LISA MERRILL. Born Mar. 3, 1962 in Louisville, KY. Graduate Syracuse U. Debut 1986 OB in *Two Gentlemen of Verona*, followed by *As You Like It, No No Nanette*, Bdwy in *Grand Hotel* (1990).

McCORMICK, MICHAEL. Born Jul. 24, 1951 in Gary, IN. Graduate Northwestern U. Bdwy debut 1964 in *Oliver!*, OB in *Coming Attractions, Tomfoolery, The Regard of Flight, Charlotte's Secret, Half a World Away, In a Pig's Valise, Arturo Ui.*

McCOURT, MALACHY. Born Sept. 20, 1931 in NYC. Debut 1958 OB in *Playboy of the Western World*, followed by *Plunkitt of Tammany Hall, Waiting for Godot, Shadow of a Gunman, Hostage, A Couple of Blaguards, Da, Mass Appeal, Remembrance*, Bdwy in *Mass Appeal (1983).*

McCRANE, PAUL. Born Jan. 19, 1961 in Philadelphia, PA. Debut 1977 OB in *Landscape of the Body*, followed by *Dispatches, Split, Hunting Scenes, Crossing Niagara, Hooters, Fables for Friends, Moonchildren, Right Behind the Flag, Human Nature, Six Degrees of Separation, The Country Girl*, Bdwy in *Runaways* (1978), *Curse of an Aching Heart, The Iceman Cometh* (1985).

McCUTCHEON, BILL. Born May 23, 1924 in Russell, KY. Attended Ohio U. Bdwy credits: *New Faces of 1956, DandelionWine, Out West of Eighth, My Daughter, Your Son, Over Here, West Side Story, The Front Page, The Man Who Came to Dinner, You Can't Take It with You, Anything Goes*, OB in *How to Steal an Election, Wet Paint, One's a Crowd, Shoestring Revue, Upstairs at the Downstairs, The Little Revue, The Marriage of Bette and Boo, Light Up the Sky.*

Leila
Martin

Robert
Martini

Marsha
Mason

Diego
Matamoros

Kathryn
McAteer

Christopher
McCann

Conan
McCarty

Lisa Merrill
McCord

Paul
McCrane

Ellen
McLaughlin

Barry
McNabb

Anna
McNeely

Frederica
Meister

Henry
Menendez

S. Epatha
Merkerson

George
Millenbach

Tammy
Minoff

Christopher
Mixon

David
Mogentale

Debra
Monk

Bruce
Moore

Dana
Moore

Daniel
Moran

Robin
Morse

Kathi
Moss

Alan
Muraoka

Donna
Murphy

Thomas
Nahrwold

Cheri
Nakamura

Ted
Neustadt

McFARLAND, ROBERT. Born May 7, 1931 in Omaha, NE. Graduate U. Mich., Columbia U. Debut 1978 OB in *The Taming of the Shrew*, followed by *When the War Was Over, Divine Fire, Ten Little Indians, The Male Animal, Comedy of Errors, Appointment with Death, The Education of One Miss February, Rule of Three, The Male Animal, Little Lies.*

McGILLIN, HOWARD. Born Nov. 5, 1953 in Los Angeles, CA. Graduate U. Cal./Santa Barbara. Debut 1984 OB in *La Bohème*, followed by Bdwy in *The Mystery of Edwin Drood* for which he received a Theatre World Award, *Sunday in the Park with George, Anything Goes, 50 Million Frenchmen in Concert.*

McGOVERN, ELIZABETH. Born July 18, 1961 in Evanston, IL. Attended Juilliard. Debut 1981 OB in *To Be Young Gifted and Black*, followed by *Hotel Play, My Sister in This House* for which she received a Theatre World Award, *Painting Churches, Hitch-Hikers, Map of the World, Two Gentlemen of Verona, Maids of Honor*, Bdwy in *Love Letters* (1989).

McGOWAN, TOM. Born Jul. 26, 1959 in Neptune, NJ. Graduate Yale, Hofstra U. Debut 1988 OB in *Coriolanus*, followed by *A Winter's Tale*, Bdwy in *La Bete* (1991).

McGUIRE, BIFF. Born Oct. 25, 1926 in New Haven, CT. Attended Mass. State Col. Bdwy in *Make Mine Manhattan, South Pacific, Dance Me a Song, The Time of Your Life, A View from the Bridge, The Greatest Man Alive, The Egghead, Triple Play, Happy Town, Beg Borrow or Steal, Finian's Rainbow, Beggar on Horseback, Father's Day, Trial of the Catonsville 9, A Streetcar Named Desire*, OB in *Present Tense, Marathon '91.*

McINTYRE, GERRY. Born May 31, 1962 in Grenada, West Indies. Graduate Montclair State Col. Debut 1985 OB in *Joan of Arc at the Stake*, followed by *Homeseekers, Once on This Island, Broadway Jukebox*, Bdwy in *Anything Goes* (1987).

McLAUGHLIN, ELLEN McGEHEE. Born Nov. 9, 1957 in Cambridge, MA. Graduate Yale. Debut 1991 OB in *A Bright Room Called Day.*

McLAUGHLIN, KAREN. Born Apr. 11 in Galesburg, IL. Graduate U. Wis. Debut 1976 OB in *Der Ring Gott Farblonjet*, followed by *Danton's Death, The Brothers Booth, Steeplechase, Jass, Wall to Wall Richard Rodgers, Spinoza.*

McNABB, BARRY. Born Aug. 26, 1960 in Toronto, Can. Graduate U. Ore. Bdwy debut 1986 in *Me and My Girl*, followed by *The Phantom of the Opera.*

McNEELY, ANNA. Born June 23, 1950 in Tower Hill, IL. Graduate McKendree Col. Bdwy debut 1982 in *Little Johnny Jones*, followed by *Cats, Gypsy.*

McROBBIE, PETER. Born Jan. 31, 1943 in Hawick, Scotland. Graduate Yale U. Debut 1976 OB in *The Wobblies*, followed by *The Devil's Disciple, Cinders, The Ballad of Soapy Smith, Rosmersholm, American Bagpipes, Richard III*, Bdwy in *Whose Life Is It Anyway?* (1979), *Macbeth* (1981), *The Mystery of Edwin Drood.*

MEIER, RON. Born Feb. 9, 1955 in Huntington, WV. Graduate Miami U. Bdwy debut 1983 in *Merlin*, followed by *Manhattan Showboat*, OB in *Spookhouse, Fiorello!, Pretty Faces.*

MEISLE, KATHRYN. Born June 7 in Appleton, WI. Graduate Smith Col, UNC/Chapel Hill. Debut 1988 OB in *Dandy Dick*, followed by *Cahoots, Twelfth Night, Othello.*

MEISNER, VICKI. Born Aug. 2, 1935 in New York City. Graduate Adelphi Col. Debut 1958 OB in *Blood Wedding*, followed by *The Prodigal, Shakuntala, Nathan the Wise, Decathlon, Afternoon in las Vegas, The Beauty Part.*

MEISTER, FREDERICA. Born Aug. 18, 1951 in San Francisco, CA. Graduate NYU. Debut 1978 OB in *Museum*, followed by *Dolphin Position, Waiting for the Parade, Dream of a Blacklisted Actor, No Damn Good, The Magic Act, Subfertile.*

MELIUS, NANCY. Born Nov. 20, 1964 in East Meadow, NY. Attended NYU. Debut 1989 OB in *Leave It to Jane*, Bdwy in *Gypsy* (1989).

MELLOR, STEPHEN. Born Oct. 17, 1954 in New Haven, CT. Graduate Boston U. Debut 1980 OB in *Paris Lights*, followed by *Coming Attractions, Plenty, Tooth of Crime, Shepard Sets, A Country Doctor, Harm's Way, Brightness Falling, Terminal Hip, Dead Mother*, Bdwy in *Big River.*

MENDILLO, STEPHEN. Born Oct. 9, 1942 in New Haven, CT. Graduate Colo. Col., Yale. Debut 1973 OB in *Nourish the Beast*, followed by *Gorky, Time Steps, The Marriage, Loot, Subject to Fits, Wedding Band, As You Like It, Fool for Love, Twelfth Night, Grotesque Lovesongs*, Bdwy in *National Health* (1974), *Ah Wilderness, A View from the Bridge, Wild Honey, Orpheus Descending.*

MENENDEZ, HENRY. Born Aug. 14, 1965 in Atlantic City, NJ. Graduate Boston Consv. Bdwy debut 1991 in *Miss Saigon.*

MEREDITH, LEE. Born Oct. 22, 1947 in River Edge, NJ. Graduate AADA. Bdwy debut 1969 in *A Teaspoon Every Four Hours*, followed by *The Sunshine Boys, Once in a Lifetime, Musical Chairs*, OB in *Hollywood Hotel, Life on the Third Rail.*

MEREDIZ, OLGA. Born Feb. 15, 1956 in Guantanamo, Cuba. Graduate Tulane U. Bdwy debut 1984 in *The Human Comedy*, OB in *El Bravo!, Women without Men, El Grande de Coca-Cola, The Blessing, The Lady from Havana.*

MERKERSON, S. EPATHA. Born Nov. 28, 1952 in Saginaw, MI. Graduate Wayne State U. Debut 1979 OB in *Spell #7*, followed by *Home, Puppetplay, Tintypes, Every Goodbye Ain't Gone, Hospice, The Harvesting, Moms, Lady Day at Emerson'a Bar and Grill*, Bdwy in *Tintypes* (1982), *The Piano Lesson.*

MERRITT, THERESA. Born Sept. 24, 1922 in Newport News, VA. Bdwy credits include *Carmen Jones, Golden Boy, Tambourines to Glory, Trumpets of the Lord, Don't Play Us Cheap, Division Street, The Wiz, Ma Rainey's Black Bottom, Mule Bone*, OB in *The Crucible, F. Jasmine Adams, Trouble in Mind, God's Trombones, Henry IV Part I.*

MILLENBACH, GEORGE. Born Aug. 24, 1953 in Toronto, Can. Graduate U. Toronto. Debut 1982 OB in *Cinderella*, followed by *As You Like It, A Cricket on the Hearth, Ceremony in Bohemia, The Lion in Winter, Little Lies, What the Butler Saw.*

MILLER, MARTHA. Born Aug. 30, 1929 in New Bedford, MA. Graduate Carnegie-Mellon U. Debut 1956 OB in *House of Connelly*, followed by *A Place without Morning, Julius Caesar, Major Barbara, In the Summer House, The Merry Wives of Windsor, Rimers of Eldritch, Heartbreak House, The Importance of Being Earnest, Who'll Save the Ploughboy?, The Fantod*, Bdwy in *Happy End* (1977), *Morning's at 7.*

MILLER, RUTH. Born June 25 in Chicago, IL. Graduate U. Chicago, Western Reserve. Debut 1980 OB in *Not Like Him*, followed by *The Truth, Lou Gehrig Did Not Die of Cancer*, Bdwy in *Come Back to the Five and Dime Jimmy Dean* (1982).

MINOFF, TAMMY. Born Oct. 4, 1979 in New York City. Debut 1988 OB in *The Traveling Man*, followed by *1-2-3-4-5*, Bdwy in *The Will Rogers Follies* (1991).

MITCHELL, ALETA. Born in Chicago. Graduate U. Iowa, Yale. Bdwy debut 1984 in *Ma Rainey's Black Bottom*, OB in *Approaching Zanzibar*, followed by *Night Sky.*

MITCHELL, BRIAN. Born Oct. 31, 1957 in Seattle, WA. Bdwy debut 1988 in *Mail* for which he received a Theatre World Award, followed by *Oh Kay!*

MITCHELL, JOHN CAMERON. Born Apr. 21, 1963 in El Paso, TX. Attended Northwestern U. Bdwy debut 1985 in *Big River*, followed by *Six Degrees of Separation, The Secret Garden*, OB in *Six Degrees of Separation.*

MIXON, CHRISTOPHER. Born in Orlando, FL. Graduate Warren Wilson Col., Rutgers U. Debut 1991 OB in *Candida.*

MOFFETT, D.W. Born Oct. 26, 1954 in Highland Park, IL. Graduate Stanford U. Debut 1984 OB in *Balm in Gilead*, followed by *The Normal Heart, How to Say Goodbye, The American Plan*, Bdwy in *The Real Thing* (1984), *The Boys of Winter.*

MOGENTALE, DAVID. Born Dec. 28, 1959 in Pittsburgh, PA. Graduate Auburn U. Debut 1987 OB in *The Signal Season of Dummy Hoy*, followed by *Killers.*

MONK, DEBRA. Born Feb. 27, 1949 in Middletown, OH. Graduate Frostburg State, S. Methodist U. Bdwy debut 1982 in *Pump Boys and Dinettes*, followed by *Prelude to a Kiss*, OB in Young Playwrights Festival, *A Narrow Bed, Oil City Symphony, Prelude to a Kiss, Assassins.*

MONTEVECCHI, LILIANE. Born Oct. 12, 1933 in Paris, Fr. With Roland Petit's Ballet, and Folies Bergère before her Bdwy debut in *Nine* (1982), followed by *Grand Hotel*, OB in her one-woman show *On the Boulevard.*

MOOR, BILL. Born Jul. 13, 1931 in Toledo, OH. Attended Northwestern, Denison U. Bdwy debut 1964 in *Blues for Mr. Charlie*, followed by *Great God Brown, Don Juan, The Visit, Chemin de Fer, Holiday, P.S. Your Cat Is Dead, Night of the Tribades, Water Engine, Plenty, Heartbreak House, The Iceman Cometh*, OB in *Dandy Dick, Love Nest, Days and Nights of Beebee Fenstermaker, The Collection, The Owl Answers, Long Christmas Dinner, Fortune and Men's Eyes, King Lear, Cry of Players, Boys in the Band, Alive and Well in Argentina, Rosmersholm, The Biko Inquest, A Winter's Tale, Johnny on a Spot, Barbarians, The Purging, Potsdam Quartet, Zones of the Spirit, The Marriage of Bette and Boo, Temptation, Devil's Disciple, Happy Days.*

MOORE, BRUCE. Born Feb. 5, 1962 in Gettysburg, PA. Graduate Cinn. Consv. Debut 1986 OB in *Olympus on My Mind*, followed by Bdwy in *Gypsy* (1989).

MOORE, CHARLOTTE. Born July 7, 1939 in Herrin, IL. Attended Smith Col. Bdwy debut 1972 in *Great God Brown*, followed by *Don Juan, The Visit, Chemin de Fer, Holiday, Love for Love, A Member of the Wedding, Morning's at 7, Meet Me in St. Louis*, OB in *Out of Our Father's House, A Lovely Sunday for Creve Coeur, Summer, Beside the Seaside, The Perfect Party.*

MOORE, CRISTA. Born Sept. 17 in Washington, DC. Attended Am. Ballet Th. Schl. Debut 1987 OB in *Birds of Paradise*, followed by Bdwy in *Gypsy* (1989) for which she received a Theatre World Award.

MOORE, DANA. Born in Sewickley, PA. Bdwy debut 1982 in *Sugar Babies*, followed by *Dancin', Copperfield, On Your Toes, Singin' in the Rain, Sweet Charity, Dangerous Games, A Chorus Line, The Will Rogers Follies.*

MOORE, MAUREEN. Born Aug. 12, 1951 in Wallingford, CT. Bdwy debut 1974 in *Gypsy*, followed by *The Moonie Shapiro Songbook, Do Black Patent Leather Shoes Really Reflect Up?, Amadeus, Big River, I Love My Wife, Song and Dance, Les Misérables, Amadeus, Jerome Robbins' Broadway, A Little Night Music (NYCO)*, OB in *Godspell, Unsung Cole, By Strouse.*

MORAN, DANIEL. Born Jul. 31, 1953 in Corcoran, CA. Graduate NYU. Debut 1980 OB in *True West*, followed by *The Vampires, Tongues and Savage Love, Life Is a Dream, The Filthy Rich. The Return of Pinocchio, Merchant of Venice, Festival of 1-Act Comedies.*

MOREAU, JENNIE. Born Nov. 19, 1960 in Lewisburg, PA. Graduate NC Schl. of Arts. Debut 1988 OB in *Tony 'n' Tina's Wedding*, followed by *Rimers of Eldritch, Eleemosynary* for which she received a Theatre World Award, *The Good Times Are Killing Me.*

MORFOGEN, GEORGE. Born Mar. 30, 1933 in New York City. Graduate Brown U., Yale. Debut 1957 OB in *The Trial of D. Karamazov*, followed by *Christmas Oratorio, Othello, Good Soldier Schweik, Cave Dwellers, Once in a Lifetime, Total Eclipse, Ice Age, Prince of Homburg, Biography: A Game, Mrs. Warren's Profession, Principia Scriptoriae, Tamara, Maggie and Misha, The Country Girl*, Bdwy in *The Fun Couple* (1962), *Kingdoms, Arms and the Man.*

MORITSUGU, KIKI. Born March 24, 1966 in Montreal, Can. Attended George Brown Col. Bdwy debut 1990 in *Shogun: The Musical.*

MORSE, ROBERT. Born May 18, 1931 in Newton, MA. Bdwy debut 1955 in *The Matchmaker*, followed by *Say Darling* for which he received a Theatre World Award, *Take Me Along, How to Succeed in Business ..., Sugar, So Long 174th Street, Tru*, OB in *More of Loesser, Eileen in Concert.*

MORSE, ROBIN. Born Jul. 8, 1963 in New York City. Bdwy debut 1981 in *Bring Back Birdie*, followed by *Brighton Beach Memoirs, Six Degrees of Separation*, OB in *Green Fields, Dec. 7th, Class I Acts, Eleemosynary, One Act Festival, Six Degrees of Separation.*

MOSS, KATHI. Born Oct. 22, 1945 in Dallas, TX. Graduate Barat Col., U. New Orleans. Debut 1972 OB in *Grease*, followed by *Country Cabaret, Hot Grog, Jack the Ripper Revue, The Perils of Pericles, Dr. Selavy's Magic Theatre, Walk on the Wild Side*, Bdwy in *Grease* (1972), *Nine, Grand Hotel.*

MULLINS, MELINDA. Born Apr. 20, 1958 in Clanton, AL. Graduate Mt. Holyoke Col, Juilliard. Bdwy debut 1987 in *Sherlock's Last Case*, followed by *Serious Money, Mastergate*, OB in *Macbeth.*

MURAKOSHI, SUZEN. Born May 20, 1958 in Honolulu, HI. Graduate U. HI. Debut 1980 OB in *Shining House*, followed by *Primary English Class, Much Ado about Nothing, A Silent Thunder*, Bdwy in *The King and I* (1984).

MURAOKA, ALAN. Born Aug. 10, 1962 in Los Angeles, CA. Graduate UCLA. Bdwy debut 1988 in *Mail*, followed by *Shogun: The Musical.*

MURCH, ROBERT. Born Apr. 17, 1935 in Jefferson Barracks, MO. Graduate Wash. U. Bdwy debut 1966 in *Hostile Witness*, followed by *The Harangues, Conduct Unbecoming, The Changing Room, Born Yesterday*, OB in *Charles Abbot & Son, She Stoops to Conquer, Transcendental Love, Julius Caesar, Hamlet, Making History, Twelfth Night.*

MURPHY, ALEC. Born Feb. 14, 1940 in Richmond, KY. Attended U. Ky, Am. Th. Wing. Debut 1965 OB in *The Wives*, followed by *In the Summerhouse, Suddenly Last Sumer, Little Lies, Woyzeck, Elizabeth the Queen*, Bdwy in *Man of La Mancha* (1969), *Street Scene* (LC).

MURPHY, DONNA. Born Mar. 7, 1959 in Corona, NY. Attended NYU. Bdwy debut 1979 in *They're Playing Our Song*, followed by *The Human Comedy, The Mystery of Edwin Drood*, OB in *Francis, Portable Pioneer and Prairie Show, Little Shop of Horrors, A...My Name Is Alice, Showing Off, Privates on Parade, Song of Singapore.*

MURTAGH, JAMES. Born Oct. 28, 1942 in Chicago, IL. Debut OB in *The Firebugs*, followed by *Highest Standard of Living, Marathon '87, Other People's Money, Marathon '88.*

MUSSER, LEWIS. Born Aug. 22, 1953 in Rocky Mount, NC. Attended UNC. Debut 1978 OB in *Rebel without a Cause*, followed by *Anna Christie, End as a Man, The Winter's Tale, A Midsummer Night's Dream, NYC Is Closed, Stud Silo, Measure for Measure.*

MUTNICK, ANDREW. Born in NYC. Graduate Colo. Col. Bdwy debut 1991 in *I Hate Hamlet.*

MYERS, LOU. Born Sept. 26, 1938 in Charleston, WV. Graduate W. Va. State Col., NYU. Debut 1975 OB in *First Breeze of Summer*, followed by *Fat Tuesday, Do Lord Remember Me, Paducah*, Bdwy in *First Breeze of Summer, Ma Rainey's Black Bottom, The Piano Lesson.*

NAHRWOLD, THOMAS. Born June 25, 1954 in Ft. Wayne, IN. Attended U.S. Intl. U., Am. Cons. Th. Bdwy debut 1982 in *84 Charing Cross Road*, followed by OB's *A Misummer Night's Dream, Bigfoot Stole My Wife, Resistance, The Foundation, The Almond Seller.*

NAKAHARA, RON. Born July 20, 1947 in Honolulu, HI. Attended U. HI., Tenri U. Debut 1981 OB in *Danton's Death*, followed by *Flowers and Household Gods, A Few Good Men, Rohwer, A Midsummer Night's Dream, Teahouse, Song for Nisei Fisherman, Eat a Bowl of Tea, Once Is Never Enough, Noiresque, Play Ball, Three Sisters, And the Soul Shall Dance, Earth and Sky.*

NAKAMURA, CHERI. Born Oct. 18, 1964 in Honolulu, HI. Graduate UCLA. Bdwy debut 1990 in *Shogun: The Musical*, OB in *Yokohama Duty.*

NAUFFTS, GOEFFREY. Born in Arlington, MA. Graduate NYU. Debut 1987 OB in *Moonchildren*, followed by *Stories from Home, Another Time Another Place, The Alarm, The Jerusalem Oratorio, The Survivor, Spring Awakening, The Summer Winds*, Bdwy in *A Few Good Men* (1989).

NAUGHTON, JAMES. Born Dec. 6, 1945 in Middletown, CT. Graduate Brown U., Yale. Debut 1971 OB in *Long Day's Journey into Night* for which he received a Theatre World Award, followed by *Drinks before Dinner, Losing Time*, Bdwy in *I Love My Wife, Whose Life Is It Anyway?, City of Angels.*

NEAL, KENNY. Born Oct. 14, 1957 in New Orleans, LA. Bdwy debut 1991 in *Mule Bone* for which he received a Theatre World Award.

NEENAN, MARIA. Born Jul. 14, 1965 in Boston, MA. Bdwy debut 1989 in *Jerome Robbins' Broadway.*

NELLIGAN, KATE. Born Mar. 16, 1951 in London, Can. Attended York U., Central Schl. Debut 1982 OB in *Plenty*, followed by *Virginia, Spoils of War* (also Bdwy), *Bad Habits*, Bdwy in *Plenty* (1983), *Moon for the Misbegotten, Serious Money, Love Letters.*

NELSON, MARI. Born Jul. 27, 1963 in Tacoma, WA. Graduate U. Wash., Juilliard. Debut 1989 OB in *Up Against It*, followed by *Twelfth Night*, Bdwy in *Six Degrees of Separation* (1990).

NELSON, MARK. Born Sept. 26, 1955 in Hackensack, NJ. Graduate Princeton U. Debut 1977 OB in *The Dybbuk*, followed by *Green Fields, The Keymaker, The Common Pursuit*, Bdwy in *Amadeus* (1981), *Brighton Beach Memoirs, Biloxi Blues, Broadway Bound, Rumors, A Few Good Men.*

NEUSTADT, TED. Born May 28, 1954 in Baltimore, MD. Graduate NYU, Fordham U. Debut 1990 OB in *Money Talks.*

NEWMAN, ROBERT. Born June 27, 1958 in Los Angeles, CA. Attended Cal. State U./ Northridge. Debut 1990 OB in *Quiet on the Set.*

NEWTON, JOHN. Born Nov. 2, 1925 in Grand Junction, CO. Graduate U. Wash. Debut 1951 OB in *Othello*, followed by *As You Like It, Candida, Candaules Commissioner, Sextet*, LCRep's *The Crucihble* and *A Streetcar Named Desire, The Rivals, The Subject Was Roses, The Brass Ring, Hadrian VII, The Best Little Whorehouse in Texas, A Midsummer Night's Dream, Night Games, A Frog in His Throat, Max and Maxie, The Lark, Measure for Measure*, Bdwy in *Weekend, First Monday in October, Present Laughter.*

NIELSEN, PAUL. Born Dec. 24 in Union, NJ. Graduate Rutgers U. Debut 1990 OB in *Light Up the Sky.*

NILES, BARBARA. Born in New York City. Graduate Boston U. Bdwy debut 1978 in *Jesus Christ Superstar*, followed by OB's *Berlin to Broadway, Cork Screws, Troopers, The Duel, Dime Store Diamonds, Let My People Come, Manhattan Madness, Madison Avenue, Grownups.*

NIVEN, KIP. Born May 27, 1945 in Kansas City, MO. Graduate Kan. U. Debut 1987 OB in *Company*, followed by *The Golden Apple, Two by Two*, Bdwy in *Chess* (1988).

NIXON, CYNTHIA. Born Apr. 9, 1966 in New York City. Debut 1980 in *The Philadelphia Story* (LC) for which she received a Theatre World Award, OB in *Lydie Breeze, Hurlyburly, Sally's Gone She Left Her Name, Lemon Sky, Cleveland and Half-Way Back, Alterations, Young Playwrights, Moonchildren, Romeo and Juliet, The Cherry Orchard, The Balcony Scene*, Bdwy in *The Real Thing* (1983), *Hurlyburly, The Heidi Chronicles.*

NOLEN, TIMOTHY. Born Jul. 9, 1941 in Rotan, TX. Graduate Trenton State Col., Manhattan School of Music. Debut in *Sweeney Todd* (1984) with NYC Opera. Bdwy in *Grind* (1985) followed by *Phantom of the Opera.*

NORMAN, JOHN. Born May 13, 1961 in Detroit, MI. Graduate Cinn. Consv. Bdwy debut 1987 in *Les Misérables.*

NORRIS, BRUCE. Born May 16, 1960 in Houston, TX. Graduate Northwestern U. Bdwy debut 1985 in *Biloxi Blues*, OB in *A Midsummer Night's Dream, Wenceslas Square, The Debutante Ball, What the Butler Saw, Life during Wartime.*

NUSSBAUM, MIKE. Born Dec. 28, 1923 in Chicago, IL. Attended U. Wis. Bdwy debut 1984 in *Glengarry Glen Ross*, followed by *House of Blue Leaves*, OB in *The Shawl, Principis Scriptoriae, Marathon '86, Little Murders, The Cherry Orchard, Mr. Gogol and Mr. Preen.*

NUTE, DON. Born Mar. 13, in Connellsville, PA. Attended Denver U. Debut OB 1965 in *The Trojan Women* followed by *Boys in the Band, Mad Theatre for Madmen, The Eleventh Dynasty, About Time, The Urban Crisis, Christmas Rappings, The Life of a Man, A Look at the Fifties, Aunt Millie.*

O'CONNELL, ELINORE. Born in Santa Ana, CA. Graduate CSU/Fullerton, UCLA. Bdwy debut 1990 in *Aspects of Love.*

O'CONNELL, PATRICIA. Born May 17 in New York City. Attended Am. Th. Wing. Debut 1958 OB in *The Saintliness of Margery Kemp*, followed by *Time Limit, An Evening's Frost, Mrs. Snow, Electric Ice, Survival of St. Joan, Rain, Rapists, Who Killed Richard Corey?, Misalliance, The Singular Life of Albert Nobbs, Come Back Little Sheba, Starting Monday*, Bdwy in *Criss-Crossing, Summer Brave, Break a Leg, The Man Who Came to Dinner, The Miser.*

O'HARE, MICHAEL. Born May 6, 1952 in Chicago, IL. Debut 1978 OB in Galileo, followed by *Shades of Brown*, Bdwy in *Players* (1978), *Man and Superman, A Few Good Men.*

O'KELLY, AIDEEN. Born in Dalkey, Ire. Member of Dublin's Abbey Theatre. Bdwy debut 1980 in *A Life*, followed by *Othello*, OB in *The Killing of Sister George, Man Enough, Resistance, Remembrance.*

O'LEARY, THOMAS JAMES. Born June 21, 1956 in Windsor Locks, CT. Graduate U. Conn. Bdwy debut 1991 in *Miss Saigon.*

OLIVER, ROCHELLE. Born Apr. 15, 1937 in New York City. Attended Brooklyn Col. Bdwy debut 1960 in *Toys in the Attic*, followed by *Harold, Who's Afraid of Virginia Woolf?, Happily Never After*, OB in *Brothers Karamazov, Jack Knife, Vincent, Stop You're Killing Me, Enclave, Bits and Pieces, Roads to Home, A Flower Palace, Fayebird.*

OLSEN, ROBERT. Born Dec. 11, 1959 in Kansas City, KS. Graduate Emporia State U. Debut 1990 OB in *Smoke on the Mountain.*

OLSON, MARCUS. Born Sept. 21, 1955 in Missoula, MT. Graduate Amherst Col. Debut 1986 OB in *Personals*, followed by *Where the Cookie Crumbles, Assassins.*

O'MALLEY, ETAIN. Born Aug. 8 in Dublin, Ire. Attended Vassar Col. Debut 1964 OB in *The Trojan Women*, followed by *Glad Tidings, God of Vengeance, A Difficult Borning, In the Garden, Sullivan and Gilbert, New Voice Festival*, Bdwy in *The Cherry Orchard* (1968), *The Cocktail Party, The Misanthrope, The Elephant Man, Kingdoms, The Queen and the Rebels, 84 Charing Cross Road.*

O'MARA, MOLLIE. Born Sept. 5, 1960 in Pittsburgh, PA. Attended Catholic U. Debut 1989 OB in *Rodents and Radios*, followed by *Crowbar, Famine Plays.*

O'MEARA, EVAN. Born Oct. 12, 1955 in Houston, TX. Graduate U. Tex., SMU. Debut 1986 OB in *One Fine Day*, followed by *The Racket, The Tempest, Big Fat and Ugly with a Moustache.*

O'REILLY, CIARAN. Born Mar. 13, 1959 in Ireland. Attended Carmelite Col., Julliard. Debut 1978 OB in *Playboy of the Western World*, followed by *Summer, Freedom of the City, Fannie, The Interrogation of Ambrose Fogarty, King Lear, Shadow of a Gunman, The Marry Month of May, I Do Not Like Thee, Dr. Fell, The Plough and the Stars, Yeats: A Celebration!, Philadelphia Here I Come!, Playboy of the Western World, Making History.*

O'SULLIVAN, ANNE. Born Feb. 6, 1952 in Limerick City, Ire. Debut 1977 OB in *Kid Champion*, followed by *Hello Out There, Fly Away Home, The Drunkard, Dennis, Three Sisters, Another Paradise, Living Quarters, Welcome to the Moon, The Dreamer Examines His Pillow, Mama Drama, Free Fall, The Magic Act, The Plough and the Stars, Marathon '88, Bobo's Guns, Marathon '90, Festival of 1 Acts, Marathon '91.*

O'SULLIVAN-MOORE, EMMETT. Born Oct. 3, 1919 in New Orleans, LA. Graduate La. State U. Debut 1982 OB in *Bottom of the Ninth*, followed by *Who'll Save the Plowboy?*, Marathon '90.

OSCAR, BRAD. Born Sept. 22, 1964 in Washington, DC. Graduate Boston U. Bdwy debut 1990 in *Aspects of Love.*

O'SHEA, MILO. Born June 2, 1926 in Dublin, Ire. Bdwy debut 1968 in *Staircase*, followed by *Dear World, Mrs. Warren's Profession, Comedians, A Touch of the Poet, Mass Appeal, Corpse, Meet Me in St. Louis*, OB in *Waiting for Godot, Mass Appeal, The Return of Herbert Bracewell, Educating Rita, Alive Alive Oh!*

OSTROW, RON. Born Dec. 9, 1960 in White Plains, NY. Graduate Ithaca Col. Bdwy debut 1989 in *A Few Good Men.*

OWENS, GORDON. Born Feb. 23, 1959 in Washington, DC. Attended UNC. Schl of Arts. Bdwy debut 1984 in *Dreamgirls*, followed by *A Chorus Line, Starlight Express, Miss Saigon.*

PALEY, PETRONIA. Born May 31 in Albany, GA. Graduate Howard U. Debut 1972 OB in *Us vs Nobody*, followed by *The Cherry Orchard, The Corner, Three Sisters, Frost of Renaissance, Long Time Since Yesterday, The Telltale Heart*, Bdwy in *The First Breeze of Summer* (1975).

PANARO, HUGH. Born Nov. 25 in Athens, Greece. Graduate CCNY. Debut 1964 OB in *The Comforter*, followed by *Consider the Lilies, A Christmas Carol, The Man with the Flower in His Mouth, King David and His Wives, 3 by Pirandello, Nymph Errant, The Tamer Tamed*, Bdwy in Phantom of the Opera (1990).

PAPPAS, EVAN. Born Aug. 21, 1958 in San Francisco, CA. Attended Cal. Jr. Col. Bdwy debut 1982 in *A Chorus Line*, OB in *I Can Get It for You Wholesale* (1991).

PARADY, RON. Born Mar. 12, 1940 in Columbus, OH. Graduate Ohio Wesleyan U., OH State U. Bdwy debut 1981 in *Candida*, followed by *Our Town, Prelude to a Kiss*, OB in *Uncle Vanya, The Father, The New Man, For Sale, Prelude to a Kiss.*

PARKER, ELLEN. Born Sept. 30, 1949 in Paris, Fr. Graduate Bard Col. Debut 1971 OB in *James Joyce Liquid Theatre*, followed by *Uncommon Women and Others, Dusa, Fish, Stas and Vi, A Day in the Life of the Czar, Fen, Isn't It Romantic? The Winter's Tale, Aunt Dan and Lemon, Cold Sweat, The Heidi Chronicles, Absent Friends*, Bdwy in *Equus, Strangers, Plenty.*

PARKER, MARY-LOUISE. Born Aug. 2, 1964 in Ft. Jackson, SC. Graduate NC Schl. of Arts. Debut 1989 OB in *The Art of Success*, followed by *Prelude to a Kiss*, Bdwy in *Prelude to a Kiss* for which she received a 1990 Theatre World Award.

PARKER, NATHANIEL. Born 1963 in London, Eng. Bdwy debut 1989 in *The Merchant of Venice.*

PARKER, SARAH JESSICA. Born March 25, 1965. Bdwy debut 1978 in *Annie*, OB in *The Innocents, One-Act Festival, To Gillian on Her 37th Birthday, The Heidi Chronicles, Substance of Fire.*

PARKS, KEN. Born Aug. 28, 1949 in Rockwood, TN. Graduate Kent State U. Debut 1991 OB in *A Funny Thing Happened on the Way to the Forum.*

PARRY, WILLIAM. Born Oct. 7, 1947 in Steubenville, OH. Graduate Mt. Union Col. Bdwy debut 1971 in *Jesus Christ Superstar*, followed by *Rockabye Hamlet, The Leaf People, Camelot* (1980), *Sunday in the Park with George, Into the Light*, OB in *Sgt. Pepper's Lonely Hearts Club Band, The Conjurer, Noah, The Misanthrope, Joseph and the Amazing Technicolor Dreamcoat, Agamemnon, Coolest Cat in Town, Dispatches, The Derby, The Knife, Cymbeline, Marathon '90, Assassins.*

| John
Newton | Cynthia
Nixon | Bruce
Norris | Elinore
O'Connell | Tom
O'Leary | Rochelle
Oliver |

| Anne
O'Sullivan | Brad
Oscar | Petronia
Paley | Hugh
Panaro | Marilyn
Pasekoff | Kelly
Patterson |

| Matthew
Pedersen | Elizabeth
Perry | Keith
Perry | Amy Jo
Phillips | Larry
Pine | Jacquelyn
Piro |

Anne
Pitoniak

Richard
Poe

Adina
Porter

W. Ellis
Porter

Jennifer
Prescott

Lonny
Price

David
Purdham

Lois
Raebeck

Victor
Raider-Wexler

Melissa
Randel

Ron
Randell

Reno

PARSONS, ESTELLE. Born Nov. 20, 1927 in Lynn, MA. Attended Boston U., Actors Studio. Bdwy debut 1956 in *Happy Hunting*, followed by *Whoop Up!, Beg Borrow or Steal, Mother Courage, Ready When You Are C.B., Malcolm, Seven Descents of Myrtle, And Miss Reardon Drinks a Little, The Norman Conquests, Ladies at the Alamo, Miss Margarida's Way, Pirates of Penzance*, OB in *Demi-Dozen, Pieces of 8, Threepenny Opera, Automobile Graveyard, Mrs. Dally Has a Lover* for which she received a 1963 Theatre World Award, *Next Time I'll Sing to You, Come to the Palace of Sin, In the Summer House, Monopoly, The East Wind, Galileo, Peer Gynt, Mahagonny, People Are Living There, Barbary Shore, Oh Glorious Tintinnabulation, Mert and Paul, Elizabeth and Essex, Dialogue for Lovers, New Moon in Concert, Orgasmo Adulto Escapes from the Zoo, The Unguided Missile, Baba Goya.*

PASEKOFF, MARILYN. Born Nov. 7, 1949 in Pittsburgh, PA. Graduate Boston U. Debut 1975 OB in *Godspell*, followed by *Maybe I'm Doing It Wrong, Professionally Speaking, Forbidden Broadway, Showing Off, Forbidden Broadway 1990, Forbidden Broadway 1991½*. Bdwy in *Godspell* (1976), *The Odd Couple* (1985).

PATINKIN, MANDY. Born Nov. 30, 1952 in Chicago, IL. Attended Juilliard. OB in *Henry IV*, followed by *Leave It to Beaver Is Dead, Rebel Women, Hamlet, Trelawny of the Wells, Savages, The Split, The Knife, Winter's Tale*, Bdwy in *The Shadow Box, Evita, Sunday in the Park with George, Mandy Patinkin in Concert, The Secret Garden.*

PATTERSON, KELLY. Born Feb. 22, 1964 in Midland, TX. Attended Southern Methodist U. Debut 1984 OB in *Up in Central Park*, followed by *Manhattan Serenade, Golden Apple*, Bdwy in *Sweet Charity* (1986), *Jerome Robbins' Broadway.*

PATTON, LUCILLE. Born in New York City. Attended Neighborhood Playhouse. Bdwy debut 1946 in *A Winter's Tale*, followed by *Topaze, Arms and the Man, Joy to the World, All You Need is One Good Break, Fifth Season, Heavenly Twins, Rhinoceros, Marathon 33, The Last Analysis, Dinner at 8, La Strada, Unlikely Heroes, Love Suicide at Schofield Barracks*, OB in *Ulysses in Nighttown, Failures, Three Sisters, Yes Yes No No, Tango, Mme. de Sade, Apple Pie, Follies, Yesterday Is Over, My Prince My King, I Am Who I Am, Double Game, Love in a Village, 1984, A Little Night Music, Cheri, Till the Eagle Hollers, Money Talks.*

PAUL, GUY. Born Sept. 12, 1949 in Milwaukee, WI. Attended U. Minn. Debut 1984 OB in *Flight of the Earls*, followed by *Frankenstein, The Underpants, Oresteia, Ever Afters, Oh Baby Oh Baby, Of Blessed Memory, Candida*, Bdwy in *Arms and the Man* (1985), *Wild Honey, Rumors.*

PEARLMAN, STEPHEN. Born Feb. 26, 1935 in New York City. Graduate Dartmouth Col. Bdwy debut 1964 in *Barefoot in the Park*, followed by *La Strada, Six Degrees of Separation*, OB in *Threepenny Opera, Time of the Key, Pimpernel, In White America, Viet Rock, Chocolates, Bloomers, Richie, Isn't It Romantic, Bloodletters, Light Up the Sky, Perfect Party, Come Blow Your Horn, A Shayna Maidel, Value of Names, Hyde in Hollywood, Six Degrees of Separation.*

PEARTHREE, PIPPA. Born Sept. 23, 1956 in Baltimore, MD. Attended NYU. Bdwy debut 1977 in *Grease*, followed by *Whose Life Is It Anyway? Taking Steps*, OB in *American Days, Hunting Scenes from Lower Bavaria, And I Ain't Finished Yet, The Dining Room, The Singular Life of Albert Nobbs, Hamlet, Aunt Dan and Lemon, Nightingale.*

PEDERSEN, MATTHEW. Born March 28, 1966 in Austin, TX. Bdwy debut 1990 in *A Chorus Line*, followed by *Miss Saigon.*

PEREZ, LUIS. Born July 28, 1959 in Atlanta, GA. With Joffrey Ballet before 1986 debut in *Brigadoon* (LC) followed by *Phantom of the Opera, Jerome Robbins' Broadway, Dangerous Games, Grand Hotel*, OB in *Wonderful Ice Cream Suit, Tango Apasionada.*

PEREZ, MIGUEL. Born Sept. 7, 1957 in San Jose, CA. Attended Nat. Shakespeare Consv. Debut 1986 OB in *Women Beware Women*, followed by *Don Juan of Seville, Cymbeline, Mountain Language, The Birthday Party, Hamlet, Henry IV Parts 1 and 2, Arturo Ui.*

PERLMAN, BONNIE. Born Sept. 9, 1953 in Baltimore, MD. Graduate NYU. Bdwy debut in *Prince of Central Park* (1989).

PERLMAN, RON. Born Apr. 13, 1950 in NYC. Graduate Lehman Col., U. Minn. Debut 1976 OB in *The Architect and the Emperor of Assyria*, followed by *Tartuffe, School for Buffoons, Measure for Measure, Hedda Gabler*, Bdwy in *Teibele and Her Demon* (1979), *A Few Good Men.*

PERRY, ELIZABETH. Born Oct. 18, 1937 in Pawtucket, RI. Attended RISU, Am. Th. Wing. Bdwy debut in *Inherit the Wind* (1956), followed by *The Women*, with APA in *The Misanthrope, Hamlet, Exit the King, Beckett*, and *Macbeth*, OB in *Royal Gambit, Here Be Dragons, Lady from the Sea, Heartbreak House, him, All the Way Home, The Frequency, Fefu and Her Friends, Out of the Broomcloset, Ruby Ruby Sam Sam, Did You See the Êlephant?, Last Stop Blue Jay Lane, A Difficult Borning, Presque Isle, Isn't It Romantic, The Chairs.*

PERRY, KEITH. Born Oct. 29, 1931 in Des Moines, Iowa. Graduate Rice U. Bdwy debut 1965 in *Pickwick*, followed by *I'm Solomon, Copperfield, City of Angels*, OB in *Epicene, the Silent Woman, Hope and Feathers, Ten Little Indians.*

PERRY, LYNNETTE. Born Sept. 29, 1963 in Bowling Green, OH. Graduate Cinn. Consv. Debut 1987 OB in *The Chosen*, followed by *Lucy's Lapses*, Bdwy in *Grand Hotel* (1989).

PETERSON, PATRICIA BEN. Born Sept. 11 in Portland, OR. Graduate Pacific Lutheran U. Debut 1985 OB in *Kuni Leml*, followed by *The Chosen, Grand Tour, Yiddle with a Fiddle*, Bdwy in *Into the Woods* (1989).

PETITTO, KEVIN. Born Oct. 15, 1963 in Moorestown, NJ. Graduate Rutgers U. Bdwy debut 1981 in *Bring Back Birdie*, followed by *Gypsy* (1990).

PETTIT, DODIE. Born Dec. 29 in Princeton, NJ. Attended Westminster Choir Col. Bdwy debut 1984 in *Cats*, followed by *The Phantom of the Opera.*

PEVSNER, DAVID. Born Dec. 31, 1958 in Skokie, IL. Graduate Carnegie-Mellon U. Debut 1985 OB in *A Flash of Lightning*, Bdwy in *Fiddler on the Roof* (1990).

PHILLIPS, AMY JO. Born Nov. 15, 1958 in Brooklyn, NY. Graduate Ithaca Col. Debut OB in *Little Shop of Horrors* (1986), followed by *Burnscape, Pretty Faces.*

PHILLIPS, ARTE. Born Feb. 13, 1959 in Astoria, Queens, NYC. Attended Baruch Col. Bdwy debut 1990 in *Grand Hotel.*

PHILLIPS, ETHAN. Born Feb. 8, 1950 in Rockville Center, NY. Graduate Boston U., Cornell U. Debut 1979 OB in *Modigliani*, followed by *Eccentricities of a Nightingale, Nature and Purpose of the Universe, The Beasts, Dumb Waiter, The Indian Wants the Bronx, Last of the Red Hot Lovers, Only Kidding, Almost Perfect, Theme and Variations, Marathon '91.*

PHILLIPS, KRIS. Born in China on Dec. 24, 1960. Attended Stanford U., Neighborhood Playhouse. Bdwy debut 1991 in *Miss Saigon.*

PIETROPINTO, ANGELA. Born Feb. 4 in New York City. Graduate NYU. OB credits include *Henry IV, Alice in Wonderland, Endgame, The Seagull, Jinx Bridge, The Mandrake, Marie and Bruce, Green Card Blues, 3 by Pirandello, The Broken Pitcher, Cymbeline, Romeo and Juliet, A Midsummer Night's Dream, Twelve Dreams, The Rivals, Cap and Bells, Thrombo, Lies My Father Told Me, Sorrows of Stephen, Between the Wars, The Hotel Play, Rain Some Fish No Elephants, Young Playwrights '90*, Bdwy in *The Suicide* (1980), *Eastern Standard.*

PILLARD, DAVID J. Born Sept. 27, 1958 in Hamilton, NY. Graduate Fordham U. Debut 1980 OB in *Twelfth Night*, followed by *Antigone.*

PINE, LARRY. Born Mar. 3, 1945 in Tucson, AZ. Graduate NYU. Debut 1967 OB in *Cyrano*, followed by *Alice in Wonderland, Mandrake, Aunt Dan and Lemon, The Taming of the Shrew, Better Days*, Bdwy in *End of the World* (1984).

PINKINS, TONYA. Born May 30, 1962 in Chicago, IL. Attended Carnegie-Mellon U. Bdwy debut 1981 in *Merrily We Roll Along*, OB in *Five Points, A Winter's Tale, An Ounce of Prevention, Just Say No, Mexican Hayride, Young Playwrights '90.*

PIONTEK, MICHAEL E. Born Jul. 31, 1956 in Canoga Park, CA. Graduate FSU. Bdwy debut 1987 in *Into the Woods*, followed by *3 Penny Opera, Grand Hotel*, OB in *Reckless, Florida Crackers.*

PIRO, JACQUELYN. Born Jan. 8, 1965 in Boston, MA. Graduate Boston U. Debut 1987 OB in *Company*, followed by Bdwy in *Les Misérables* (1990).

PITONIAK, ANNE. Born Mar. 30, 1922 in Westfield, MA. Attended UNC Women's Col. Debut 1982 OB in *Talking With*, followed by Young Playwrights Festival, *Phaedra, Steel Magnolias, Pygmalion*, Bdwy in *'night, Mother* (1983) for which she received a Theatre World Award, *The Octette Bridge Club.*

PLAYTEN, ALICE. Born Aug. 28, 1947 in New York City. Bdwy debut 1960 in *Gypsy*, followed by *Oliver!, Hello Dolly!, Henry Sweet Henry* for which she received a Theatre World Award, *George M!, Spoils of War, Rumors*, OB in *Promenade, The Last Sweet Days of Isaac, National Lampoon's Lemmings, Valentine's Day, Pirates of Penzance, Up from Paradise, A Visit, Sister Mary Ignatius Explains It All, An Actor's Nightmare, That's It Folks, 1-2-3-4-5, Spoils of War, Marathon '90.*

PLUMMER, AMANDA. Born Mar. 23, 1957 in New York City. Attended Middlebury Col., Neighborhood Playhouse. Debut 1978 OB in *Artichoke*, followed by *A Month in the Country, A Taste of Honey* for which she received a Theatre World Award, *Alice in Concert, A Stitch in Time, Life under Water, A Lie of the Mind, The Milk Train Doesn't Stop Here Anymore, Abundance*, Bdwy in *A Taste of Honey, Agnes of God, The Glass Menagerie, You Never Can Tell, Pygmalion* (1987).

PLUMMER, CHRISTOPHER. Born Dec. 13, 1929 in Toronto, Can. Bdwy debut 1954 in *Starcross Story*, followed by *Home Is the Hero, The Dark Is Light Enough* for which he received a Theatre World Award, *Medea, The Lark, Night of the Auk, J.B., Arturo Ui, The Royal Hunt of the Sun, Cyrano, The Good Doctor, Othello, Macbeth, A Christmas Carol*, OB in *Drinks Before Dinner.*

POE, RICHARD. Born Jan. 25, 1946 in Portola, CA. Graduate U. San Francisco, U. Cal./Davis. Debut 1971 OB in *Hamlet*, followed by *Seasons Greetings, Twelfth Night*, Bdwy in *Broadway* (1987), *M. Butterfly, Our Country's Good.*

POLETICK, ROBERT. Born Feb. 28, in Brooklyn, NY. Debut 1988 OB in *Brotherhood*, followed by *Beyond the Horizon, Hamlet, Holding Out, Them.*

POLITO, JON. Born Dec. 29, 1950 in Philadelphia, PA. Graduate Villanova U. Debut 1976 OB in *The Transfiguration of Benno Blimpie*, followed by *New Jerusalem, Emigres, A Winter's Tale, Johnny-on-a-Spot, Barbarians, The Wedding, Digby, Other People's Money, Road to Nirvana*, Bdwy in *American Buffalo* (1977), *Curse of an Aching Heart, Total Abandon, Death of a Salesman.*

PONAZECKI, JOE. Born Jan. 7, 1934 in Rochester, NY. Attended Rochester U., Columbia U. Bdwy debut 1959 in *Much Ado about Nothing*, followed by *Send Me No Flowers, A Call on Kuprin, Take Her She's Mine, Fiddler on the Roof, Xmas in Las Vegas, 3 Bags Full, Love in E Flat, 90 Day Mistress, Harvey, Trial of the Catonsville 9, The Country Girl, Freedom of the CIty, Summer Brave, Music Is, The Little Foxes, Prelude to a Kiss*, OB in *The Dragon, Muzeeka, Witness, All Is Bright, The Dog Ran Away, Dream of a Blacklisted Actor, Innocent Pleasures, The Dark at the Top of the Stairs, 36, After the Revolution, The Raspberry Picker, A Raisin in the Sun, Light Up the Sky, Marathon '80, One Act Festival.*

PEGGY POPE. Born May 15, 1929 in Montclair, NJ. Attended Smith Col. Bdwy in *Doctor's Dilemma, Volpone, Rose Tattoo, Harvey, School for Wives, Dr. Jazz*, OB in *Muzeeka, House of Blue Leaves, New Girl in Town, Romeo and Juliet.*

PORTER, ADINA. Born Feb. 18, 1963 in NYC. Attended SUNY/Purchase. Debut 1988 OB in *The Debutante Ball*, followed by *Inside Out, Tiny Mommie, Footsteps in the Rain, Jersey City.*

PORTER, W. ELLIS. Graduate Carnegie-Mellon U. Debut 1989 OB in *Romance in Hard Times*, Bdwy in *Miss Saigon* (1991).

POTTER, DON. Born Aug. 15, 1932 in Philadelphia, PA. Debut 1961 OB in *What a Killing*, followed by *Sunset, You're a Good Man Charlie Brown, One Cent Plain, The Ritz*, Bdwy in *Gypsy* (1974), *Snow White, Moose Murders, 42nd Street, Peter Pan.*

POTTER, JANE. Born June 15, 1966 in Milwaukee, WI. Graduate Syracuse U. Debut 1989 OB in *Nunsense*, followed by *Smoke on the Mountain.*

POWELL, MICHAEL WARREN. Born Jan. 22, 1937 in Martinsville, VA. Attended Goodman Theatre Schl. Debut 1954 OB in *Home Free!*, followed by *This Is the Rill Speaking, Balm in Gilead, The Gingham Dog, Thank You Miss Victoria, Futz, Tom Paine, Amulets against the Dragon Force, Dirty Talk, On the Wing, The Weather Outside, Prelude to a Kiss.*

PRENTICE, AMELIA. Born Sept. 14 in Toronto, Can. Graduate AADA, LAMDA. Bdwy debut 1987 in *Starlight Express*, OB in *Hooray for Hollywood, Lenny Bruce Revue, Broadway Jukebox.*

PRESCOTT, JENNIFER. Born Feb. 19, 1963 in Portland, OR. Graduate NYU, AMDA. Bdwy debut 1987 in *Starlight Express*, followed by *Fiddler on the Roof* (1990).

PRESTON, WILLIAM. Born Aug. 26, 1921 in Columbia, PA. Graduate Penn. State U. Debut 1972 OB in *We Bombed in New Haven*, followed by *Hedda Gabler, Whisper into My Good Ear, A Nestless Bird, Friends of Mine, Iphegenia in Aulis, Midsummer, The Fantasticks, Frozen Assets, The Golem, The Taming of the Shrew, His Master's Voice, Much Ado about Nothing, Hamlet, Winter Dreams, Palpitations, Rumor of Glory, Killers*, Bdwy in *Our Town.*

PRICE, LONNY. Born Mar. 9, 1959 in New York City. Attended Juilliard. Debut 1979 OB in *Class Enemy* for which he received a Theatre World Award, followed by *Up from Paradise, Rommel's Garden, Times and Appetites of Toulouse-Lautrec, Room Service, Come Blow Your Horn, The Immigrant, A Quiet End, Falsettoland*, Bdwy in *The Survivor* (1980), *Merrily We Roll Along, Master Harold and the Boys, The Time of Your Life, Children of the Sun, Rags, Broadway, Burn This!*

PRINCE, FAITH. Born Aug. 5, 1957 in Augusta, GA. Graduate U. Cinn. Debut OB 1981 in *Scrambled Feet*, followed by *Olympus on My Mind, Groucho, Living Color, Bad Habits, Falsettoland*, Bdwy in *Jerome Robbin's Broadway* (1989).

PRINCE, GINGER. Born June 3, 1945 in Stuart, FL. Attended Stephens Col. Debut 1987 OB in *Steel Magnolias*, followed by Bdwy in *Gypsy* (1989/91).

PRYCE, JONATHAN. Born June 1, 1947 in Wales, UK. Attended RADA. Bdwy debut 1976 in *Comedians* for which he received a Theatre World Award, followed by *Accidental Death of an Anarchist, Miss Saigon*.

PUGH, RICHARD WARREN. Born Oct. 20, 1950 in New York City. Graduate Tarkio Col. Bdwy debut 1979 in *Sweeney Todd*, followed by *The Music Man, The Five O'Clock Girl, Copperfield, Zorba* (1983), *Phantom of the Opera*, OB in *Chase a Rainbow*.

PURDHAM, DAVID. Born June 3, 1951 in San Antonio, TX. Graduate U. Md., U. Wash. Debut 1980 OB in *Journey's End*, followed by *Souvenirs, Once on a Summer's Day, Twelfth Night, Maneuvers, The Times and Appetites of Toulouse-Lautrec, The Winter's Tale, Rosencrantz and Guildenstern Are Dead, Absent Friends*, Bdwy in *Piaf* (1981).

QUINN, COLLEEN. Born Apr. 24 in Lindenhurst, NY. Debut 1988 OB in *Borderlines*, followed by *Keeping an Eye on Louie, Octoberfest, Dutchman, Beauty Marks, Midsummer*.

RAE, CHARLOTTE. Born Apr. 22, 1926 in Milwaukee, WI. Graduate Northwestern U. Bdwy debut 1952 in *Three Wishes for Jamie*, followed by *Li'l Abner, The Beauty Part, Pickwick, Morning Noon and Night, The Chinese*, OB in *Threepenny Opera, Littlest Revue, The Beggar's Opera, The New Tenant, Victims of Duty, Henry IV, Whiskey, Boom Boom Room, Happy Days*.

RAEBECK, LOIS. Born in West Chicago, IL. Graduate Purdue U. Debut 1986 OB in *Rule of Three*, followed by *Cork, Between Time and Timbuktu, The Women in the Family, All's Well That Ends Well, Necktie Breakfast*.

RAIDER-WEXLER, VICTOR. Born Dec. 31, 1943 in Toledo, OH. Attended U. Toledo. Debut 1976 OB in *The Prince of Homburg*, followed by *The Passion of Dracula, Ivanov, Brandy Before Breakfast, The Country Girl, Dream of a Blacklisted Actor, One Act Festival, Loveplay, Our Own Family, Candide*, Bdwy in *Best Friend* (1976), *Ma Rainey's Black Bottom, Gypsy* (1990).

RAINEY, DAVID. Born Jan. 30, 1960 in Tucson, AZ. Graduate E. N. Mex. U., Juilliard. Debut 1987 OB in *Richard II*, followed by *Henry IV Part I, Julius Caesar, Love's Labour's Lost, Boy Meets Girl, The Phantom Tollbooth, Black Eagles*.

RAITER, FRANK. Born Jan. 17, 1932 in Cloquet, MN. Yale graduate. Bdwy debut 1958 in *Cranks*, followed by *Dark at the Top of the Stairs, J.B., Camelot*, OB in *Soft Core Pornographer, The Winter's Tale, Twelfth Night, Tower of Evil, Endangered Species, A Bright Room Called Day, Learned Ladies*.

RAMOS, RICHARD RUSSELL. Born Aug. 23, 1941 in Seattle, WA. Graduate U. Minn. Bdwy debut 1968 in *House of Atreus*, followed by *Arturo Ui*, OB in *Adaptation, Screens, Lotta, The Tempest, A Midsummer Night's Dream, Gorky, The Seagull, Entertaining Mr. Sloane, Largo Desolato, Henry IV Parts I and 2*.

RAMSEY, BARRY. Born Sept. 6, 1963 in Birmingham, AL. Attended U. Ala. Bdwy debut 1990 in *Peter Pan*.

RAMSEY, KEVIN. Born Sept. 24, 1959 in New Orleans, LA. Graduate NYU. Bdwy debut in *Black and Blue* (1989), followed by *Oh Kay!* for which he received a Theatre World Award, OB in *Liberation Suite, Sweet Dreams, Prison Made Tuxedos, Staggerlee, Juba*.

RAND, RONALD. Born Oct. 13, 1958 in Coral Gables, FL. Graduate NYU, RADA. Debut 1978 OB in *Julius Caesar*, followed by *Vatzlav, The Closed Door, Cellmates, Full Circle*.

RANDEL, MELISSA. Born June 16, 1955 in Portland, ME. Graduate U. Cal./Irvine. Bdwy debut 1980 in *A Chorus Line*, OB in *Shooting Stars, Dark of the Moon*.

RANDELL, RON. Born Oct. 8, 1920 in Sydney, Aust. Attended St. Mary's Col. Bdwy debut 1949 in *The Browning Version*, followed by *Harlequinade, Candida, World of Suzie Wong, Sherlock Holmes, Mrs. Warren's Profession, Measure for Measure, Bent, The Troll Palace*, OB in *Holy Places, After You've Gone, Patrick Pease Motel, Maneuvers, King Lear*.

RANDOLPH, JOHN. Born June 1, 1915 in the Bronx, NY. Attended CCNY, Actors Studio. Bdwy debut 1937 in *Revolt of the Beavers*, followed by *The Emperor's New Clothes, Capt. Jinks, No More Peace, Coriolanus, Medicine Show, Hold on to Your Hats, Native Son, Command Decision, Come Back Little Sheba, Golden State, Peer Gynt, Paint Your Wagon, Seagulls over Sorrento, Grey-Eyed People, Room Service, All Summer Long, House of Flowers, The Visit, Mother Courage, The Sound of Music, Case of Libel, Conversation at Midnight, My Sweet Charlie, The American Clock, Broadway Bound, Prelude to a Kiss*, OB in *An Evening's Frost, The Peddler and the Dodo Bird, Our Town, Line, Baba Goya, Nourish the Beast, Back in the Race, The American Clock*.

RASCHE, DAVID. Born Aug. 7, 1944 in St. Louis, MO. Graduate Elmhurst Col, U. Chicago. Debut 1976 OB in *John*, followed by *Snow White, Isadora Duncan Sleeps with the Russian Navy, End of the War, A Sermon, Routed, Geniuses, Dolphin Position, To Gillian on Her 37th Birthday, Custom of the Country, The Country Girl, Marathon '91*, Bdwy in *Shadow Box* (1977), *Loose Ends, Lunch Hour, Speed-the-Plow, Mastergate, A Christmas Carol*.

RATHGEB, LAURA. Born Sept. 5, 1962 in Burlington, VT. Graduate St. Michael's Col. Debut 1987 OB in *Deep Swimmer*, followed by *The Imaginary Invalid, Electra, All's Well That Ends Well, She Stoops to Conquer, The Philanderer, Three Sisters, Midsummer Night's Dream, Importance of Being Earnest, Medea, The Fine Art of Finesse, Major Barbara*.

REBHORN, JAMES. Born Sept. 1, 1948 in Philadelphia, PA. Graduate Wittenberg U., Columbia U. Debut 1972 OB in *Blue Boys*, followed by *Are You Now or Have You Ever Been?*, Trouble with *Europe, Othello, Hunchback of Notre Dame, Period of Adjustment, The Freak, Half a Lifetime, Touch Black, To Gillian on Her 37th Birthday, Rain, The Hasty Heart, Husbandry, Isn't It Romantic?, Blind Date, Cold Sweat, Spoils of War, Marathon '88, Ice Cream with Hot Fudge, Life During Wartime*, Bdwy in *I'm Not Rappaport, Our Town* (1989).

REDFIELD, ADAM. Born Nov. 4, 1959 in New York City. Attended NYU. Debut 1977 OB in *Hamlet*, followed by *Androcles and the Lion, Twelfth Night, Reflected Glory, Movin' Up, The Unicorn, The Doctor's Dilemma, Young Playwrights Festival, Swan Song*, Bdwy (1980) in *A Life* for which he received a Theatre World Award, *Beethoven's Tenth, Execution of Justice, The Miser*.

REEHLING, JOYCE. Born Mar. 5, 1949 in Baltimore, MD. Graduate NC Schl. of Arts. Debut 1976 OB in *The Hot L Baltimore*, followed by *Who Killed Richard Cory?, Lulu, 5th of July, The Runner Stumbles, Life and/or Death, Back in the Race, Time Framed, Extremities, Hands of Its Enemy, Rcekless, Prelude to a Kiss*, Bdwy in *A Matter of Gravity* (1976), *5th of July, Prelude to a Kiss*.

REINGOLD, JACQUELYNE. Born Mar. 13, 1959 in New York City. Graduate Oberlin Col. Debut 1978 OB in A *Wrinkle in Time*, followed by *Marat/Sade, Unfettered Letters, Working One Acts, Mortality Project*.

REISSA, ELEANOR. Born May 11 in Brooklyn, NY. Graduate Brooklyn Col. Debut 1979 OB in *Rebecca the Rabbi's Daughter*, followed by *That's Not Funny That's Sick, The Rise of David Levinsky, Match Made in Heaven, Song for a Saturday, No No Nanette, Songs of Paradise, Those Were the Days*.

REMME, JOHN. Born Nov. 21 in Fargo, ND. Attended U. Minn. Debut 1972 in *One for the Money*, followed by *Anything Goes, The Rise of David Levinsky, Jubilee in Concert, The Firefly in Concert, Sweet Adeline in Concert, George White's Scandals in Concert, Tomfoolery, A Funny Thing Happened on the Way to the Forum*, Bdwy in *The Ritz* (1975), *The Royal Family, Can-Can, Alice in Wonderland, Teddy and Alice, Gypsy*.

RENO. Born Aug. 9, 1951 in New York City. Graduate Adelphi U., NYU. Debut 1989 OB in solo performance *Reno: In Rage and Rehab* followed by *Stop at Nothing, A Coupla Weirdos, A Bright Room Called Day*.

RESNIK, REGINA. Born Aug. 30, 1924 in New York City. Graduate Hunter Col. After a career as an internationally acclaimed operatic singer, she made her debut on Bdwy in *Cabaret* (1987), followed by *A Little Night Music* (NYCO/LC).

REYNOLDS, RICK. Born Dec. 13, 1951 in Wood Village, OR. Graduate Portland State U. Debut 1991 OB in his solo performance of *Only the Truth Is Funny*.

RHYS, WILLIAM. Born Jan. 2, 1945 in New York City. Graduate Wesleyan U. Bdwy debut 1969 with National Theatre of the Deaf, followed by *The Changing Room*, OB in *Birth, The Balcony, Romeo and Juliet*.

RICHARDS, CAROL. Born Dec. 26 in Aurora, IL. Graduate Northwestern U., Columbia U. Bdwy debut 1965 in *Half a Sixpence*, followed by *Mame, Last of the Red Hot Lovers, Company, Cats*.

RICHARDSON, LaTANYA. Born Oct. 21, 1949 in Atlanta, GA. Graduate Spelman Col. Debut 1976 OB in *Perdido*, followed by *Unfinished Women Cry in No Man's Land, Spell #7, The Trial of Dr. Beck, Charlotte's Web, Nonsectarian Conversations with the Dead, An Organdy Falsetto, Boogie Woogie and Booker T, Talented Tenth, Ma Rose, From the Mississippi Delta, Elliot Loves, Casanova*.

RIDDLE, GEORGE. Born May 21, 1937 in Auburn, IN. OB in *Eddie Fay, The Prodigal, Huui Huui, The Glorious Age, The Trail of Dr. Beck, Downriver, The Fantasticks*.

RIEBLING, TIA. Born July 21, 1954 in Pittsburgh, PA. Attended NYU, Carnegie Mellon U. Debut 1983 OB in *American Passion*, followed by *Preppies, Hamelin, Wish You Were Here*, Bdwy in *Smile* (1986), *Fiddler on the Roof* (1990).

RIEGEL, EDEN. Born Jan. 1, 1981 in Washington, DC. Bdwy debut 1989 in *Les Misérables*.

RIEGEL, SAM BRENT. Born Oct. 9, 1976 in Washington, DC. Debut 1990 in *The Sound of Music* (NYCO/LC), OB in *The Nerd, Where Have You Gone Joe DiMaggio?, Rube's All-Nite, Hard TImes at the Edge, I Can Get It for You Wholesale, 3 by Robert Shaffron*.

RIEGERT, PETER. Born Apr. 11, 1947 in New York City. Graduate U. Buffalo. Debut 1975 OB in *Dance with Me*, followed by *Sexual Perversity in Chicago, Sunday Runners, Isn't It Romantic, La Brea Tarpits, A Hell of a Town, Festival of One Acts, A Rosen by Any Other Name, The Birthday Party, Mountain Language, Road to Nirvana*, Bdwy in *The Nerd* (1987).

RIFKIN, ROGER. Born Dec. 29, 1954 in Brooklyn, NY. Attended Queens Col. Debut 1989 OB in *Wonderful Town*, followed by *Arsenic and Old Lace*.

RIFKIN, RON. Born Oct. 31, 1939 in New York City. Graduate NYU. Bdwy debut 1960 in *Come Blow Your Horn*, followed by *The Goodbye People, The Tenth Man*, OB in *Rosebloom, The Art of Dining, Temple, Substance of Fire*.

RIGOL, JOEY. Born Jan. 6, 1979 in Miami, FL. Debut 1988 OB in *The Chosen*, followed by *The Voyage of the Beagle, The Music Man, Stop the World, Sympathy*, Bdwy in *Les Misérables* (1989).

RILEY, ERIC. Born Mar. 22, 1955 in Albion, MI. Graduate U. Mich. Bdwy debut 1979 in *Ain't Misbehavin'*, folloed by *Dream Girls, Ain't Misbehavin'* (1988), *Once on This Island*, OB in *Once on This Island*.

RINEHART, ELAINE. Born Aug. 16, 1958 in San Antonio, TX. Graduate NC Schl. Arts. Debut 1975 OB in *Tenderloin*, followed by *Native Son, Joan of Lorraine, Dumping Ground, Fairweather Friends, The Color of the Evening Sky, The Best Little Whorehouse in Texas, The Wedding of the Siamese Twins, Festival of 1 Acts, Up 'n' Under, Crystal Clear, Black Market, Festival of 1-Act Comedies*.

RIVIN, LUCILLE. Born Mar. 25 in Brooklyn, NY. Graduate SUNY. Debut OB in *The Beggar*, followed by *Golden Leg, She First Met Her Parents on the Subway, The Seagull: The Hamptons*.

ROBARDS, JASON. Born July 26, 1922 in Chicago, IL. Attended AADA. Bdwy debut 1947 with D'Oyly Carte Co., followed by *Stalag 17, The Chase, Long Day's Journey into Night* for which he received a Theatre World Award, *The Disenchanted, Toys in the Attic, Big Fish Little Fish, A Thousand Clowns, Hughie, The Devils, We Bombed in New Haven, The Country Girl, Moon for the Misbegotten, A Touch of the Poet, You Can't Take It with You, The Iceman Cometh, A Month of Sundays, Ah Wilderness!, Long Day's Journey into Night* (1988), *A Christmas Carol*, OB in *American Gothic, The Iceman Cometh, After the Fall, But for Whom Charlie, Long Day's Journey into Night*.

ROBB, R.D. Born Mar. 31, 1972 in Philadelphia, PA. Bdwy debut 1980 in *Charlie and Algernon*, followed by *Oliver!, Les Misérables*.

LaTanya Richardson	Sam Brent Riegel	Jana Robbins	Tony Roberts	Tonia Rowe	David Roya
Stan Rubin	Patricia Ruck	Martin Rudy	Jeri Sager	John Salvatore	Janet Sarno
Carole Schweid	Ernie Scott	Kathrin King Segal	Christopher Shaw	Nicola Sheara	Keenan Shimizu
Sab Shimono	Barbara Spiegel	Robert Stanton	Jean Stapleton	Jack Stehlin	Helen Stenborg
Rose Stockton	Larry Storch	Jane Summerhays	George Takei	Ann Talman	Teller

ROBBINS, JANA. Born Apr. 18, 1947 in Johnstown, PA. Graduate Stephens Col. Bdwy debut 1974 in *Good News*, followed by *I Love My Wife, Crimes of the Heart, Romance/Romance, Gypsy*, OB in *Tickles by Tucholsky, Tip-Toes, All Night Strut, Colette Collage, Circus Gothic, Ad Hock*.

ROBERTS, LOUISE. Born in Philadelphia, PA. Graduate Carnegie-Mellon U. Bdwy debut in *Brighton Beach Memoirs*, followed by *Ah Wilderness!, Long Day's Journey into Night*, OB in *Epic Proportions, The Miser, A Shayna Maidel, The Cherry Orchard*.

ROBERTS, TONY. Born Oct. 22, 1939 in New York City. Graduate Northwestern U. Bdwy debut 1962 in *Something about a Soldier*, followed by *Take Her She's Mine, Last Analysis, Never Too Late, Barefoot in the Park, Don't Drink the Water, How Now Dow Jones, Play It Again Sam, Promises Promises, Sugar, Absurd Person Singular, Murder at the Howard Johnson's, They're Playing Our Song, Doubles, Brigadoon* (LC), *South Pacific* (LC), *Love Letters, Jerome Robbins' Broadway*, OB in *The Cradle Will Rock, Losing Time, The Good Parts, Time Framed*.

ROBERTSON, CLIFF. Born Sept. 9, 1925 in La Jolla, CA. Attended Antioch Col. Bdwy debut 1953 in *Late Love*, followed by *The Wisteria Trees, Orpheus Descending* for which he received a Theatre World Award, *Rosalie in Concert, Love Letters*.

ROBERTSON, SCOTT. Born Jan. 4, 1954 in Stamford, CT. Bdwy debut 1976 in *Grease*, followed by *The Pajama Game* (LC), OB in *Scrambled Feet, Applause, A Lady Needs a Change, A Baker's Audition, She Loves Me, Secrets of a Lava Lamp, Love in Two Countries*.

ROBINSON, HAL. Born in Bedford, IN. Graduate Ind. U. Debut 1972 OB in *Memphis Store-Bought Teeth*, followed by *From Berlin to Broadway, The Fantasticks, Promenade, The Baker's Wife, Yours Anne, Personals, And a Nightingale Sang*, Bdwy in *On Your Toes* (1983), *Broadway, Grand Hotel*.

ROBINSON, LANCE. Born June. 21, 1979 in Salisbury, MD. Bdwy debut 1989 in *Gypsy*, followed by *Shadowlands, The Will Rogers Follies*.

ROBINSON, PETER. Born Jan. 13, 1965 in New York City. Attended Queens Col. Debut 1990 OB in *Light Up the Sky*.

RODRIGUEZ, AL. Born May 29, 1960 in NYC. Graduate Syracuse U. Debut 1983 OB in *The Senorita from Tacna*, followed by *Savings, The Merchant of Venice, Death of Garcia Lorca, Don Juan of Seville, The English-Only Restaurant, Born to Rumba!*, Bdwy in *Open Admissions* (1984).

ROGERS, MICHAEL. Born Dec. 8, 1954 in Trinidad. Attended Long Island U., Yale. Debut 1974 OB in *Elena*, followed by *Chiaroscuro, Forty Deuce, Antigone, Julius Caesar, Insufficiant Evidence, Othello, Young Playwrights '90*.

ROSS, JAMIE. Born May 4, 1939 in Markinch, Scot. Attended RADA. Bdwy debut 1962 in *Little Moon of Alban*, followed by *Moon Beseiged, Ari, Different Times, Woman of the Year, La Cage aux Folles, 42nd Street, Gypsy* (1990), OB in *Penny Friend, Oh Coward!, Approaching Zanzibar*.

ROSSETTER, KATHRYN (a.k.a. Kathy). Born July 31 in Abington, PA. Graduate Gettysburg Col. Debut 1982 OB in *After the Fall*, followed by *The Incredibly Famous Willy Rivers, A Midsummer Night's Dream, How to Say Goodbye, The Good Coach, Love Lemmings*, Bdwy in *Death of a A Salesman* (1984).

ROWE, TONIA. Born Nov. 30, 1963 in Jersey City, NJ. Graduate Rutgers U. Debut 1987 OB in *Tiny Mommy* (Young Playwrights Festival), followed by *Love and Anger*.

ROYA, DAVID. Born Dec. 21, 1952 in New York City. Graduate Brooklyn Col. Debut 1966 OB in *Friends and Enemies*, followed by *The Have-Little*.

RUBIN, STAN. Born Jan. 7, 1938 in the Bronx, NY. Attended F.I.T. Debut 1974 OB in *You Can't Take It with You*, followed by *The Sign in Sidney Brustein's Window, A Slight Case of Murder, Witness for the Prosecution, Damn Yankees, Kiss Me Kate, The Gingerbread Lady, Pearls*, Bdwy in *Rags* (1986).

RUBINSTEIN, JOHN. Born Dec. 8, 1946 in Los Angeles. Attended UCLA. Bdwy debut 1972 in *Pippin*, for which he received a Theatre World Award, followed by *Children of a Lesser God, Fools, The Soldier's Tale, The Caine Mutiny Court-Martial, Hurlyburly, M. Butterly*, OB in *Rosencrantz and Guildenstern Are Dead, Urban Blight, Love Letters*.

RUCK, PATRICIA. Born Sept. 11, 1963 in Washington, DC. Attended Goucher Col. Bdwy debut 1986 in *Cats*.

RUCKER, BO. Born Aug. 17, 1948 in Tampa, FL. Debut 1978 OB in *Native Son* for which he received a Theatre World Award, followed by *Blues for Mr. Charlie, Streamers, Forty Deuce, Dustoff, Rosetta Street*, Bdwy in *Joe Turner's Come and Gone* (1988).

RUDY, MARTIN. Born Dec. 5, 1915 in Hartford, CT. Attended RADA. Bdwy in *Joan of Lorraine, To Dorothy A Son, The Man in the Glass Booth*, OB in *Modigliani*.

RUIVIVAR, FRANCIS. Born Dec. 21, 1960 in Hong Kong, China. Graduate Loretto Heights Col. Bdwy debut 1988 in *Chess*, followed by *Starlight Express, Shogun: The Musical* for which he received a Theatre World Award, *Miss Saigon*.

RUIZ, ANTHONY. Born Oct. 17, 1956 in New York City. Attended NYCC. Debut 1987 OB in *The Wonderful Ice Cream Suit*, followed by *Danny and the Deep Blue Sea, Born to Rumba!*

RULE, CHARLES. Born Aug. 4, 1928 in Springfield, MO. Bdwy debut 1951 in *Courtin' Time*, followed by *Happy Hunting, Oh Captain!, The Conquering Hero, Donnybrook, Bye Bye Birdie, Fiddler on the Roof, Henry Sweet Henry, Maggie Flynn, 1776, Cry for Us All, Gypsy, Goodtime Charley, On the 20th Century, Phantom of the Opera*, OB in *Family Portrait*.

RUPERT, MICHAEL. Born Oct. 23, 1951 in Denver, CO. Attended Pasadena Playhouse. Bdwy debut 1968 in *The Happy Time* for which he received a Theatre World Award, followed by *Pippin, Sweet Charity* (1986), *Mail, City of Angels*, OB in *Festival, Shakespeare's Cabaret, March of the Falsettos, Falsettoland*.

RUSH, JO ANNA (formerly Lehmann). Born Nov. 13, 1947 in Montclair, NJ. Bdwy debut 1986 in *Pousse Café*, followed by *Shirley MacLaine at the Palace*, OB in *Love Me Love My Children, Broadway Scandals of 1928, Options, Inside Out, O Sappho O Wilde*.

RYALL, WILLIAM. Born Sept. 18, 1954 in Binghamton, NY. Graduate AADA. Debut 1979 OB in *Canterbury Tales*, followed by *Elizabeth and Essex. He Who Gets Slapped, The Seagull, Tartuffe*, Bdwy in *Me and My Girl* (1986), *Grand Hotel*.

RYAN, STEVEN. Born June 19, 1947 in New York City. Graduate Boston U., U. Minn. Debut 1978 OB in *Winning Isn't Everything*, followed by *The Beethoven, September in the Rain, Romance Language, Love's Labour's Lost, Love and Anger*, Bdwy in *I'm Not Rappaport* (1986).

RYDER, AMY. Debut 1984 OB in *Options*, followed by *Falsies, Taboo in Revue, On Again, Songs in Blume, Friends and Music, Toulouse, Pretty Faces*.

SAGER, JERI. Born Nov. 15, 1960 in Wurzburg. Attended Mars Hill Col, Catholic U. Bdwy debut 1990 in *Fiddler on the Roof*.

ST. GEORGE, KATHY. Born Sept. 27, 1952 in Medford, MA. Graduate Salem State U. Bdwy debut 1981 in *Fiddler on the Roof* (also in 1990 revival).

SALINGER, MATT. Born Feb. 13, 1960 in Windsor, VT. Attended Princeton, Columbia U. graduate. Bdwy debut 1985 in *Dancing in the End Zone*, OB in *The Sum of Us* (1991).

SALLOWS, TRACY. Born Apr. 27, 1963 in Valley Stream, NY. Graduate SUNY/Purchase. Bdwy debut 1986 in *You Never Can Tell*, followed by *The Miser*.

SALONGA, LEA. Born Feb. 22, 1971 in Manila, PI. Attended Manila U. Bdwy debut 1991 in *Miss Saigon* for which she received a Theatre World Award.

SALVATORE, JOHN. Born Nov. 3, 1961 in Rockville Center, NY. Attended Adelphi U. Bdwy debut 1986 in *A Chorus Line*, OB in *Pageant*.

SAMUEL, PETER. Born Aug. 15, 1958 in Pana, IL. Graduate E. Ill U. Bdwy debut 1981 in *The First*, followed by *Joseph and the Amazing Technicolor Dreamcoat, Three Musketeers, Rags, Les Misérables, The Secret Garden*, OB in *The Human Comedy, 3 Guys Naked from the Waist Down, The Road to Hollywood, Elizabeth and Essex, Little Eyolf*.

SANTANA, MERLIN. Born March 14, 1976 in New York City. Debut 1988 OB in *Tapman*, followed by *Young Playwrights '90*.

SANTIAGO, SAUNDRA. Born Apr. 14, 1957 in New York City. Graduate U. Miami, SMU. Bdwy debut 1983 in *A View from the Bridge*, followed by OB's *Road to Nirvana* (1991).

SANTORO, MICHAEL. Born Nov. 23, 1957 in Brooklyn, NY. Attended Lee Strasberg Inst. Debut 1985 OB in *The Normal Heart*, followed by *Homesick, There Is an Angel in Las Vegas, Pokey, Who Collects the Pain?*

SARNO, JANET. Born Nov. 18, 1933 in Bridgeport, CT. Graduate SCTC, Yale U. Bdwy debut 1963 in *Dylan*, followed by *Equus, Knockout*, OB in *Six Characters in Search of an Author, Who's Happy Now, Closing Green, Fisher, Survival of St. Joan, The Orphan, Mama's Little Angels, Knuckle Sandwich, Marlon Brando Sat Here, Last Summer at Bluefish Cove, Brass Birds Don't Sing, Money Talke, Fayebird*.

SAVIN, RON LEE. Born Jul. 20, 1947 in Norfolk, VA. Graduate Coll. of Wm. & Mary. Debut 1981 OB in *Francis*, followed by *Greater Tuna, Road to Hollywood, Streetheat, One-Act Festival, The Fantasticks, Johnny Pye and the Fool Killer, Gifts of the Magi*.

SCANLAN, DICK. Born Apr. 14 in Washington, DC. Attended Carnegie-Mellon U., LAMDA. Debut 1986 OB in *Pageant*, followed by 1991 revival of *No No Nanette*.

SCHANUEL, GREG. Born Mar. 17, 1958 in Oakland, CA. Attended U. Pacific, NYU. Bdwy debut 1981 in *Can-Can*, followed by *Jerome Robbins' Broadway*, OB in *Mozez*.

SCHMITZ, PETER. Born Aug. 20, 1962 in St. Louis, MO. Graduate Yale, NYU. Debut 1987 OB in *Henry IV Part 1*, followed by *We the People, Blitzstein Project, Imperceptible Mutabilities, Henry IV Parts 1 and 2*.

SCHNEIDER, JOHN. Born Apr. 8, 1960 in Mt. Kisco, NY. Bdwy debut 1991 in *Grand Hotel*.

SCHNETZER, STEPHEN. Born June 11, 1948 in Boston, MA. Graduate U. Mass. Bdwy debut 1971 in *The Incomparable Max*, followed by *Filumena, A Talent for Murder*, OB in *Timon of Athens, Antony and Cleopatra, Julius Caesar, Fallen Angels, Miss Julie, Lisbon Traviata, One Act Festival, Romeo and Juliet*.

SCHULMAN, CRAIG. Born Mar. 1, 1956 in Weisbaden, W. Ger. Graduate SUNY/Oswego. Debut 1980 OB in *Pirates of Penzance*, Light Opera of Manhattan, Gilbert & Sullivan Players, Bdwy in *Les Misérables* (1990).

SCHULTZ, ARMAND. Born May 17, 1959 in Rochester, NY. Graduate Niagara U., Catholic U. Debut OB 1988 in *Crystal Clear*, followed by *Titus Andronicus, Tower of Evil, Richard III*.

SCHWARTZ, GARY. Born Nov. 20, 1964 in Englewood, NJ. Attended Hofstra U. Debut 1987 OB in *The Chosen*, followed by *What's a Nice Country Like You Doing in a State Like This?*, Bdwy in *Fiddler on the Roof* (1990).

SCHWEID, CAROLE. Born Oct. 5, 1946 in Newark, NJ. Graduate Boston U., Juilliard. Bdwy debut 1970 in *Minnie's Boys*, followed by *A Chorus Line, Street Scene*, OB in *Love Me Love My Children, Children of Adam, Comden and Green Review, Silk Stockings, Upstairs at O'Neal's, Durang Durang, Cradle Song, Funny Girl, The Beauty Part*.

SCOTT, ERNIE. Born Mar. 20 in New Brunswick, NJ. Attended Fisk, Rutgers, Kean, Trenton State. Debut 1980 OB in *Jam*, Bdwy in *Paul Robeson* (1988), followed by *The Piano Lesson*.

SEAMON, EDWARD. Born Apr. 15, 1937 in San Diego, CA. Attended San Diego State Col. Debut 1971 OB in *The Life and Times of J. Walter Smintheous*, followed by *The Contractor, The Family, Fishing, Feedlot, Cabin 12, Rear Column, Devour the Snow, Buried Child, Friends, Extenuating Circumstances, Confluence, Richard II, Great Grandson of Jedediah Kohler, Marvelous Gray, Time Framed, The Master Builder, Full Hookup, Fool for Love, The Harvesting, A Country for Old Men, Love's Labour's Lost, Caligula, The Mound Builders, Quiet in the Land, Talley and Son, Tomorrow's Monday, Ghosts, Of Mice and Men, Beside Herself, You Can't Think of Everything, Tales of the Lost Formicans, Love Diatribe*, Bdwy in *The Trip Back Down* (1977), *Devour the Snow, American Clock*.

SEFF, RICHARD. Born Sept. 23, 1927 in New York City. Attended NYU. Bdwy debut 1951 in *Darkness at Noon*, followed by *Herzl, Musical Comedy Murders*, OB in *Big Fish Little Fish, Modigliani, Childe Byron, Richard II, Time Framed, The Sea Gull, Only You, Countess Mitzi, Two Schnitzler One Acts*.

SEGAL, KATHRIN KING. Born Dec. 8, 1947 in Washington, DC. Debut 1969 OB in *Oh! Calcutta!*, followed by *The Drunkard, Alice in Wonderland, Pirates of Penzance, Portfolio Revue, Philemon, The Butter and Egg Man, The Art of Self-Defense, Camp Meeting, Festival of 1-Act Comedies*.

SELDES, MARIAN. Born Aug. 23, 1928 in New York City. Attended Neighborhood Playhouse. Bdwy debut 1947 in *Medea*, followed by *Crime and Punishment, That Lady, Tower Beyond Tragedy, Ondine, On High Ground, Come of Age, The Chalk Garden, The Milk Train Doesn't Stop Here Anymore, The Wall, A Gift of Time, A Delicate Balance, Before You Go, Father's Day, Equus, The Merchant, Deathtrap*, OB in *Different, Ginger Man, Mercy Street, Isadora Duncan Sleeps with the Russian Navy, Painting Churches, Gertrude Stein and Companion, Richard II, The Milk Train Doesn't Stop Here Anymore, A Bright Room Called Day*.

SERABIAN, LORRAINE. Born June 12, 1945 in NYC. Graduate Hofstra U. OB in *Sign of Jonah, Electra, Othello, Secret Life of Walter Mitty, Bugs and Veronica, Trojan Women, American Gothics, Gallows Humor, Company, Dorian, Deathtrap, Tonight at 8:30*, Bdwy in *Cabaret, Zorba*.

SERRANO, NESTOR. Born Nov. 5, 1955 in the Bronx, NY. Attended Queens Col. Debut 1983 OB in *Union City Thanksgiving*, followed by *Diamonds, Cuba and His Teddy Bear, Learned Ladies*.

SETRAKIAN, ED. Born Oct. 1, 1928 in Jenkinstown, WV. Graduate Concord Col., NYU. Debut 1966 OB in *Drums in the Night*, followed by *Othello, Coriolanus, Macbeth, Hamlet, Baal, Old Glory, Futz, Hey Rube, Seduced, Shout Across the River, American Days, Sheepskin, Inserts, Crossing the Bar, Boys Next Door, The Mensch*, Bdwy in *Days in the Trees* (1976), *St. Joan, The Best Little Whorehouse in Texas*.

SHAFER, PAMELA. Born Jan. 25, 1963 in Tiffin, OH. Graduate Point PK Col. Debut 1989 OB in *Gigi, Harriet the Spy, Ball*.

SHARKEY, SUSAN. Born Dec. 12 in New York City. Graduate U. Ariz. Debut 1968 OB in *Guns of Carrer*, followed by *Cuba Si, Playboy of the Western World, Good Woman of Setzuan, An Enemy of the People, People Are Living There, Narrow Road to the Deep North, Enemies, The Plough and the Stars, The Sea, The Sykovs, Catsplay, Ice, Cubistique, Frugal Repast, Summit Conference, The Maids, New Voice Festival*, Bdwy in *The American Clock* (1980).

SHAW, CHRISTOPHER. Born Oct. 4 in Pennsylvania. Attended NC Schl of Arts. Debut 1988 OB in *Romeo and Juliet*, followed by *Painted Rain, Psychoneurotic Phantasies, Angel in Las Vegas, Sunday Promenade, Boy's Play, Walking the Dead*.

SHEARA, NICOLA. Born May 23 in New York City. Graduate U. Syracuse. Debut 1975 OB in *Another Language*, followed by *Sananda Sez, All the Way Home, Inadmissible Evidence, Another Part of the Forest, Working One Acts, Undying Love*, Bdwy 1990 in *Grapes of Wrath*.

SHEEDY, ALLY. Born June 13, 1962 in New York City. Attended U. S. Cal. Debut 1991 OB in *Advice from a Caterpillar*.

SHELL, CLAUDIA. Born Sept. 11, 1959 in Passaic, NJ. Debut 1980 OB in *Jam*, Bdwy in *Merlin*, followed by *Cats*.

SHELLEY, CAROLE. Born Aug. 16, 1939 in London, Eng. Bdwy debut 1965 in *The Odd Couple*, followed by *The Astrakhan Coat, Loot, Noel Coward's Sweet Potato, Hay Fever, Absurd Person Singlar, The Norman Conquests, Elephant Man, The Misanthrope, Noises Off, Stepping Out, The Miser*, OB in *Little Murders, The Devil's Disciple, The Play's the Thing, Double Feature, Twelve Dreams, Pygmalion in Concert, A Christmas Carol, Jubilee in Concert, Waltz of the Toreadors, What the Butler Sw, Maggie and Misha*.

SHELTON, SLOANE. Born Mar. 17, 1934 in Asheville, NC. Attended Bates Col., RADA. Bdwy Debut 1967 in *The Imaginary Invalid*, followed by *A Touch of the Poet, Tonight at 8:30, I Never Sang for My Father, Sticks and Bones, The Runner Stumbles, Shadow Box, Passione, Open Admission, Orpheus Descending*, OB in *Androcles and the Lion, The Maids, Basic Training of Pavlo Hummel, Play and Other Plays, Julius Caesar, Chieftans, Passione, The Chinese Viewing Pavilion, Blood Relations, The Great Divide, Highest Standard of Living, The Flower Palace, April Snow, Nightingale*.

SHERMAN, BARRY. Born Nov. 10, 1962 in Fontana, CA. Attended Col. of Marin, Nat. Theatre Consv. Debut 1988 OB in *Rimers of Eldritch*, followed by *Kingfish, Love Diatribe, Chelsea Walls, The Summer Winds, Walking the Dead*.

SHEW, TIMOTHY. Born Feb. 7, 1959 in Grand Forks, ND. Graduate Millikin U., U. Mich. Debut 1987 OB in *The Knife*, Bdwy in *Les Misérables*.

SHIMIZU, KEENAN. Born Oct. 22, 1956 in New York City. Bdwy debut 1965 in *South Pacific*, followed by *The King and I*, OB in *Rashomon, The Year of the Dragon, The Catch, Peking Man, Flowers and Household Gods, Behind Enemy Lines, Station J, Rosie's Café, Boutique Living, Gonza the Lancer, Letters to a Student Revolutionary*.

SHIMONO, SAB. Born in Sacramento, CA. Graduate U. Cal. Bdwy debut 1965 in *South Pacific*, followed by *Mame, Lovely Ladies Kind Gentlemen, Pacific Overtures, Ride the Winds, Mame* (1983), OB in *Santa Anita, Yankee Dawg You Die, Chickencoop Chinaman, Year of the Dragon, Iago, Music Lesson, The Wash*.

SHULMAN, MICHAEL. Born Dec. 31, 1981 in New York City. Debut 1989 OB in *Gardenia*, followed by *Assassins*.

SIEGLER, BEN. Born Apr. 9, 1958 in Queens, NY. Attended HB Studio. Debut 1980 OB in *Innocent Thoughts Harmless Intentions*, followed by *Threads, Many Happy Returns, Snow Orchid, The Diviners, What I Did Last Summer, Time Framed, Gifted Children, Levitation, Elm Circle, Romance Language, Raw Youth, Voices in the Head, V & V Only, Bitter Friends, One of the Guys, Festival of 1-Act Comedies*, Bdwy in *Fifth of July*.

SILLIMAN, MAUREEN. Born Dec. 3 in New York City. Attended Hofstra U. Bdwy debut 1975 in *Shenandoah*, followed by *I Remember Mama, Is There Life after High School?*, OB in *Umbrellas of Cherbourg, Two Rooms, Macbeth, Blue Window, Three Postcards, Pictures in the Hall*.

SIMMONS, J.K. (formerly Jonathan) Born Jan. 9, 1955 in Detroit, MI. Graduate U. Mont. Debut 1987 OB in Birds of Paradise, followed by *Dirty Dick*, Bdwy in *A Change in the Heir* (1990), *A Few Good Men*.

SIMON, GERALD. Born Jul. 15, 1938 in Chicago, IL. Graduate Xavier U., Catholic U. Debut 1965 OB in *The Knack*, followed by *Dreams of Clytemnestra, Farm Bill, Pulp Alley, Terminal, Potters Field, Things That Almost Happen, Getting On, Queen for a Day, The Dream Cure*.

SLEZAK, VICTOR. Born Jul. 7, 1957 in Youngstown, OH. Debut 1979 OB in *Electra Myth*, followed by *Hasty Heart, Ghosts, Alice and Fred, Widow Claire, Miracle Worker, Talk Radio, Marathon '88, One Act Festival, Briar Patch, Marathon '90, Young Playwrights', Marathon '91*.

SLOAN, GARY. Born July 6, 1952 in New Castle, IN. Graduate Wheaton Col, SMU. Debut 1982 OB in *Faust*, followed by *Wild Oats, Balloon, Danton's Death, Hamlet, Big and Little, Love's Labour's Lost, King Lear*.

SMIAR, BRIAN. Born Aug. 27, 1937 in Cleveland, OH. Graduate Kent St. U., Emerson Col. Debut 1982 OB in *Edmond*, followed by *3 x 3, True to Life, Young Playwrights Festival, Marathon '90*.

SMITH, COTTER. Born May 29, 1949 in Washington, DC. Graduate Trinity Col. Debut 1980 OB in *The Blood Knot*, followed by *Death of a Miner, A Soldier's Play, El Salvador, Borderlines, Walking the Dead*.

SMITH, JENNIFER. Born Mar. 9, 1956 in Lubbock, TX. Graduate Tex. Tech. U. Debut 1981 OB in *Seesaw*, followed by *Suffragette, Henry the 8th and the Grand Old Opry, No Frills Revue, Whatnot, 1-2-3-4-5, You Die at Recess*, Bdwy in *La Cage aux Folles* (1981), *A Change in the Heir*.

SMITH, NICK. Born Jan. 13, 1932 in Philadelphia, PA. Attended Boston U. Debut 1963 OB in *The Blacks*, followed by *Man Is Man, The Connection, Blood Knot, No Place to Be Somebody, Androcles and the Lion, So Nice They Named It Twice, In the Recovery Lounge, Liberty Call, Raisin in the Sun, Boogie Woogie and Booker T., The Balm Years*.

SMITH, REX. Born Sept. 19, 1955 in Jacksonville, FL. Bdwy debut 1978 in *Grease*, followed by *The Pirates of Penzance* for which he received a Theatre World Award, *The Human Comedy, Grand Hotel*, OB in *Brownstone, Common Pursuit*.

SMITH-CAMERON, J. Born Sept. 7 in Louisville, KY. Attended Fla. State U. Bdwy debut 1982 in *Crimes of the Heart*, followed by *Wild Honey, Lend Me A Tenor, Our Country's Good*, OB in *Asian Shade, The Knack, Second Prize: 2 Weeks in Leningrad, Great Divide, Voice of the Turtle, Women of Manhattan, Alice and Fred, Mi Vida Loca*.

SOLO, WILLIAM. Born Mar. 16, 1948 in Worcester, MA. Graduate U. Mass. Bdwy debut 1987 in *Les Misérables*.

SPAISMAN, ZIPORA. Born Jan. 2, 1920 in Lublin, Poland. Debut 1955 OB in *Lonesome Ship*, followed by *In My Father's Court, Thousand and One Nights, Eleventh Inheritor, Enchanting Melody, Fifth Commandment, Bronx Express, Melody Lingers On, Yoshke Muzikant, Stempenyu, Generations of Green Fields, Shop, A Play for the Devil, Broome St. America, Flowering Peach, Riverside Drive, Big Winner, The Land of Dreams, Father's Inheritance*.

SPERBERG, FRITZ. Born Jul. 20 in Borger, TX. Graduate Trinity U. Debut 1979 OB in *Getting Out*, followed by *Battery, The Sea Gull*, Bdwy in *Loose Ends* (1979), *Macbeth* (LC), *A Few Good Men*.

SPEREDAKOS, JOHN. Born Aug. 11, 1962 in New York City. Graduate Muhlenberg Col., Rutgers U. Debut 1983 OB in *Canaries and Sitting Ducks*, followed by *On Tina Tuna Walk, Life and Limb, Crossin' the Line, Food and Shelter*.

SPIEGEL, BARBARA. Born Mar. 12 in New York City. Debut 1969 in LCREP's *Camino Real, Operation Sidewinder* and *Beggar on Horseback*, OB in *The Disintegration of James Cherry, Feast for Fleas, Museum, Powder, The Bleachers, Nightshift, Cassatt, Rope Dancers, Friends Too Numerous to Mention, Rope Dancers, Bronx Dreams, Green Fields, Festival of 1-Acts, What's Wrong with This Picture?*

SPIEGEL, HOWARD. Born Mar. 30, 1954 in Brooklyn, NY. Attended Queens Col. Debut 1989 OB in *Only Kidding*, for which he received a Theatre World Award.

SPIELBERG, ROBIN. Born Nov. 20, 1962 in New Jersey. Attended Mich. State U., NYU. Debut 1988 OB in *Boys' Life*, followed by *Marathon '90, Three Sisters*.

SPIEWAK, TAMARA ROBIN. Born Feb. 20, 1980 in Bridgeport, CT. Bdwy debut 1990 in *Les Misérables*.

SPINDELL, AHVI. Born June 26, 1954 in Boston, MA. Attended Ithaca Col., U. NH, Juilliard. Bdwy debut 1977 in *Something Old Something New*, followed by *Ghetto*, OB in *Antony and Cleopatra, Forty Deuce, Alexandria, Emma, The Art of Finesse*.

SPIVEY, TOM. Born Jan. 28, 1951 in Richmond, VA. Graduate Wm. & Mary, Penn State. Debut 1989 OB in *The Thirteenth Chair*, followed by *The Rover*.

SPOLAN, TOM. Born Jul. 14, 1947 in New York City. Graduate Adelphi U. Debut 1982 OB in *Yellow Fever*, followed by *Savage in Limbo*.

SPORE, RICHARD. Born March 23, 1948 in Chicago, IL. Debut 1982 OB in *The Frances Farmer Story*, followed by *Counselor-at-Law, Troilus and Cressida, Motions of History, Henry IV*.

STADLEN, LEWIS J. Born Mar. 7, 1947 in Brooklyn, NY. Attended Stella Adler Studio. Bdwy debut 1970 in *Minnie's Boys* for which he received a Theatre World Award, followed by *The Sunshine Boys, Candide, The Odd Couple*, OB in *The Happiness Cage, Heaven on Earth, Barb-a-Que, Don Juan and Non Don Juan, Olympus on My Mind, 1-2-3-4-5, S.J. Perelman in Person, The My House Play*.

STAHL, MARY LEIGH. Born Aug. 29, 1946 in Madison, WI. Graduate Jacksonville State U. Debut 1974 OB in *Circus*, followed by *Dragons, Sullivan and Gilbert, The World of Sholem Aleichem*, Bdwy in *The Phantom of the Opera* (1988).

STANLEY, DOROTHY. Born Nov. 18 in Hartford, CT. Graduate Ithaca Col., Carnegie-Mellon U. Debut 1978 OB in *Gay Divorce*, followed by *Dames at Sea*, Bdwy in *Sugar Babies* (1980), *Annie, 42nd Street, Broadway, Jerome Robbins' Broadway*.

STANLEY, GORDON. Born Dec. 20, 1951 in Boston, MA. Graduate Brown U., Temple U. Debut 1977 OB in *Lyrical and Satirical*, followed by *Allegro, Elizabeth and Essex, Red, Hot and Blue, Two on the Isles, Moby Dick, Johnny Pye and the Foolkiller, Golden Apple, Gifts of the Magi, Big Fat and Ugly with a Moustache*, Bdwy in *Onward Victoria* (1980), *Joseph and the Amazing Technicolor Dreamcoat, Into the Light, Teddy and Alice*.

STANTON, ROBERT. Born Mar. 8, 1963 in San Antonio, TX. Graduate George Mason U., NYU. Debut 1985 OB in *Measure for Measure*, followed by *Rum and Coke, Cheapside, Highest Standard of Living, One Act Festival, Best Half-Foot Forward, Sure Thing, Emily, Ubu, Casanova*.

STAPLETON, JEAN. Born Jan. 19, 1923 in New York City. Attended Hunter Col., Am. Th. Wing. Bdwy debut 1953 in *In the Summer House*, followed by *Damn Yankees, Bells Are Ringing, Juno, Rhinoceros, Funny Girl, Arsenic and Old Lace*, OB in *Mountain Language/The Birthday Party, Learned Ladies*.

STAPLETON, MAUREEN. Born June 21, 1925 in Troy, NY. Bdwy debut 1946 in *Playboy of the Western World*, followed by *Antony and Cleopatra, Detective Story, The Bird Cage, The Rose Tattoo* for which she received a Theatre World Award, *The Emperor's Clothes, The Crucible, Richard III, The Seagull, 27 Wagons Full of Cotton, Orpheus Descending, The Cold Wind and the Warm, Toys in the Attic, The Glass Menagerie* (1965/1975), *Plaza Suite, Norman Is That You?, Gingerbread Lady, The Country Girl, The Secret Affairs of Mildred Wild, The Gin Game, The Little Foxes* (1981), *A Christmas Carol*.

Evan
Thompson

Lauren
Thompson

Peter
Toran

Christine
Toy

Glenn
Turner

Margaret
Tyzack

Tracey
Ullman

Joe
Urla

Jennifer
Van Dyck

Harley
Venton

Susan
Wands

Stuart
Warmflash

Denzel
Washington

Sharon
Washington

Sam
Waterston

Terri
White

Scott
Whitehurst

Debra
Whitfield

Kathy
Wilhelm

Ray
Wills

Lori
Wilner

Walter
Willison

Mary Louise
Wilson

William
Wise

John
Wojda

Jenny
Woo

Richard
Woods

Shanelle
Workman

Stephen
Wright

Monya
Wyatt

STEHLIN, JACK. Born June 21, 1936 in Allentown, PA. Graduate Juilliard. Debut 1984 OB in *Henry V* followed by *Gravity Shoes, Julius Caesar, Romeo and Juliet, Phaedra Britannica, Don Juan of Seville, Uncle Vanya, Henry IV Part 1, Life on Earth, Danton's Death, Casanova.*

STEINBACH, VICTOR. Born Jan. 1, 1944 in USSR. Graduate Leningrad-Gorky Schl. Debut 1986 OB in *House of Shadows*, followed by *My Life in Art, Maggie and Misha.*

STENBORG, HELEN. Born Jan. 24, 1925 in Minneapolis, MN. Attended Hunter Col. OB in *A Doll's House, Say Nothing, Rosmersholm, Rimers of Eldritch, Trial of the Catonsville 9, The Hot l Baltimore, Pericles, Elephant in the House, A Tribute to Lili Lamont, Museum, 5th of July, In the Recovery Lounge, The Chisholm Trail, Time Framed, Levitation, Enter a Free Man, Talley and Son, Tomorrow's Monday, Niedecker, Heaven on Earth, Daytrips,* Bdwy in *Sheep on the Runway* (1970), *Da, A Life.*

STEPHENSON, DON. Born Sept. 10, 1964 in Chattanooga, TN. Graduate U. Tenn. Debut 1986 OB in *Southern Lights*, followed by *Hypothetic, The Tavern, Young Rube, A Charles Dickens Christmas, Follies.*

STERNER, STEVE. Born May 5, 1951 in New York City. Attended CCNY. Bdwy debut 1980 in *Clothes for a Summer Hotel*, followed by *Oh Brother!*, OB in *Lovesong, Vagabond Stars, The Fabulous '50s, My Heart Is in the East, Mandrake, The Special, Let It Ride!, Encore!, Yiddle with a Fiddle.*

STEVENS, WESLEY. Born Apr. 6, 1948 in Evansville, IN. Graduate U. Va., Ohio St. U. Debut 1978 OB in *Othello*, followed by *The Importance of Being Earnest, Candida, Platanov, But Mostly Because It's Raining, Comedy of Errors, Measure for Measure.*

STILLMAN, ROBERT. Born Dec. 2, 1954 in NYC. Graduate Princeton U. Debut 1981 OB in *The Haggadah*, followed by *Street Scene, Lola, No Frills Revue,* Bdwy in *Grand Hotel* (1989).

STOCKTON, ROSE. Born in Urbane, OH. Graduate Antioch Col. Debut 1983 OB in *Prime Time* followed by *The 3 Zeks, Arms and the Man, Antigone, Two Gentlemen of Verona, The Rivals, The Imaginary Invalid, Candida, The Diaries of Adam and Eve.*

STONEBURNER, SAM. Born Feb. 24, 1934 in Fairfax, VA. Graduate Georgetown U., AADA. Debut 1960 OB in *Ernest in Love*, followed by *Foreplay, Anyone Can Whistle, Twilight Cantata, Six Degrees of Separation,* Bdwy in *Different Times* (1972), *Bent, Macbeth* (1981), *The First, Six Degrees of Separation.*

STORCH, LARRY. Born Jan. 8, 1923 in New York City. Bdwy debut 1958 in *Who Was That Lady I Saw You With?*, followed by *Porgy and Bess* (1983), *Arsenic and Old Lace,* OB in *The Littlest Revue* (1956), *Breaking Legs.*

STORK, RENEE. Born Nov. 11, 1962 in St. Louis, MO. Attended NCSA, ABT. Debut 1989 on Bdwy in *Jerome Robbins' Broadway.*

STOVALL, COUNT. Born Jan. 15, 1946 in Los Angeles, CA. Graduate U. Cal. Debut 1973 OB in *He's Got a Jones*, followed by *In White America, Rashomon, Sidnee Poet Heroical, A Photo, Julius Caesar, Coriolanus, Spell # 7, The Jail Diary of Albie Sachs, To Make a Poet Black, Transcendental Blues, Edward II, Children of the Sun, Shades of Brown, American Dreams, Pantomime, Stovall, The Telltale Heart,* Bdwy in *Inacent Black* (1981), *The Philadelphia Story.*

STRAM, HENRY. Born Sept. 10, 1954 in Lafayette, IN. Attended Juilliard. Debut 1978 OB in *King Lear*, followed by *Shout and Twist, The Cradle Will Rock, Prison-made Tuxedos, Cinderella/Cendrillon, The Making of Americans, Black Sea Follies, Eddie Goes to Poetry City, A Bright Room Called Day.*

STROMAN, GUY. Born Sept. 11, 1951 in Terrell, TX. Graduate Tex. Christian U. Bdwy debut 1979 in *Peter Pan*, followed by *Annie*, OB in *After the Rain, Jerome Moross Revue, Close Your Eyes, Juno and the Paycock, Glory Hallelujah!, To Whom It May Concern, Aldersgate '88, Forever Plaid.*

STUART, IAN. Born May 25, 1940 in London, Eng. Debut 1971 OB in *Misalliance*, followed by *Count Dracula, Jack the Ripper Review, The Accrington Pals, The Foreigner, The Doctor's Dilemma, Romeo and Juliet,* Bdwy in *Caesar and Cleopatra* (1977), *Run for Your Life.*

SULLIVAN, JO. Born Aug. 2 in Mounds, IL. Attended Columbia U. Bdwy debut 1950 in *Let's Make an Opera*, followed by *Carousel, A Most Happy Fella, Wonderful Town, Show Boat, Perfectly Frank,* OB in *Threepenny Opera, Together Again, Follies.*

SUMMERHAYS, JANE. Born Oct. 11 in Salt Lake City, UT. Graduate U. Utah, Catholic U. Debut 1980 OB in *Paris Lights*, followed by *On Approval, One Act Festival, Taking Steps,* Bdwy in *Sugar Babies* (1980), *A Chorus Line, Me and My Girl, Lend Me a Tenor.*

SUROVY, NICOLAS. Born June 30, 1944 in Los Angeles, CA. Attended Northwestern U., Neighborhood Playhouse. Debut 1964 OB in *Helen* for which he received a Theatre World Award, followed by *Sisters of Mercy, Cloud 9, Breaking Legs,* Bdwy in *The Merchant* (1977), *Crucifer of Blood, Major Barbara, You Can't Take It With you, The Night of the Iguana.*

SUTTON, DOLORES. Born in New York City. NYU graduate. Bdwy debut 1962 in *Rhinoceros*, followed by *General Seeger*, OB in *Man with the Golden Arm, Machinal, Career, Brecht on Brecht, To Be Young Gifted and Black, The Web and the Rock, My Prince My King, Our Own Family, What's Wrong with This Picture?*

TADKEN, NEIL. Born Apr. 25, 1960 in New York City. Graduate Occidental Col., Cornell U. Debut 1989 OB in *Pericles Prince of Tyre*, followed by *The Rover.*

TAFLER, JEAN. Born Nov. 18, 1957 in Schenectady, NY. Graduate Hofstra U. Debut 1981 OB in *Mandragola*, followed by *Lady Windermere's Fan, Richard II, Towards Zero, The Cotton Web, A Lady Named Joe, Guadeloupe, Brass Jackal, Philemon.*

TAKEI, GEORGE. Born Apr. 20, 1939 in Los Angeles, CA. Graduate UCLA. Debut 1962 OB in *Fly Blackbird*, followed by *Year of the Dragon, The Wash.*

TALMAN, ANN. Born Sept. 13, 1957 in Welch, WV. Graduate Penn. St. U. Debut 1980 OB in *What's So Beautiful about a Sunset over Prairie Avenue?*, followed by *Louisiana Summer, Winterplay, Prairie Avenue, Broken Eggs, Octoberfest, We're Home, Yours Anne, Songs on a Shipwrecked Sofa, House Arrest, One Act Festival, Some Americans Abroad,* Bdwy in *The Little Foxes* (1981), *House of Blue Leaves, Some Americans Abroad, Better Days.*

TALYN, OLGA. Born Dec. 5 in West Ger. Attended Syracuse U., U. Buffalo. Debut 1975 OB in *The Proposition*, followed by *Corral, Tales of Tinseltown, Shop on Main Street,* Bdwy in *A Doll's House, The Phantom of the Opera.*

TANKERSLEY, MARK. Born Aug. 23, 1958 in Houston, TX. Attended Houston Baptist U., Juilliard. Debut 1985 OB in *Life Is a Dream*, followed by *Macbeth, Picture of Dorian Gray, The Island of Dr. Moreau.*

TASSIN, CHRISTEN. Born Jan. 2, 1979 in Spartanburg, SC. Bdwy debut 1989 in *Gypsy.*

TATUM, MARIANNE. Born Feb. 18, 1951 in Houston, TX. Attended Manhattan Schl. of Music. Debut 1971 OB in *Ruddigore*, followed by *The Gilded Cage, Charley's Tale, Passionate Extremes,* Bdwy in *Barnum* (1980) for which she received a Theatre World Award, *The Three Musketeers, The Sound of Music.*

TAYLOR, DREW. Born Mar. 9, 1955 in Milwaukee, WI. Attended AADA. Debut 1985 OB in *She Loves Me*, followed by *Kiss Me Kate,* Bdwy in *The Secret Garden* (1991).

TAYLOR, MYRA. Born July 9, 1960 in Ft. Motte, SC. Graduate Yale U. Debut 1985 OB in *Dennis*, followed by *The Tempest, Black Girl, Marathon '86, Phantasie, Walking the Dead,* Bdwy in *A Streetcar Named Desire* (1988), *Mule Bone.*

TAYLOR, REGINA. Born Aug. 22, 1960 in Dallas, TX. Graduate SMU. Debut 1983 OB in *Young Playwrights Festival*, followed by *As You Like It, Macbeth, Map of the World, The Box, Dr. Faustus, L'Illusion, New Anatomies, Machinal,* Bdwy in *Shakespeare on Broadway* (1987).

TAYLOR, SCOTT. Born June 29, 1962 in Milan, TN. Attended Miss. State U. Bdwy in *Wind in the Willows* (1985), followed by *Cats.*

TAYLOR-MORRIS, MAXINE. Born June 26 in New York City. Graduate NYU. Debut 1977 OB in *Counsellor-at-Law*, followed by *Manny, The Devil's Disciple, Fallen Angels, Billy Liar, Uncle Vanya, What the Butler Saw, The Subject Was Roses, Goodnight Grandpa, The Thirteenth Chair, Comedy of Errors, Second Avenue, One Act Festival, Midsummer.*

TELEMAQUE, CHI-EN. Born Jan. 11, 1961 in New York City. Graduate NYU, LAMDA. Bdwy debut 1990 in *Shogun: The Musical.*

TELLER. Born in 1948 in Philadelphia, PA. Graduate Amherst Col. Debut 1985 OB in *Penn & Teller,* Bdwy in same (1987), followed by *Refrigerator Tour.*

TERRY, SUSAN. Born May 30, 1953 in New Haven, CT. Graduate U. NH. Bdwy debut 1979 in *Evita*, followed by *Zorba*, OB in *Insert Foot, Follies in Concert, Forbidden Broadway, A Little Night Music* (NYCO/LC).

THOMAS, JOHN NORMAN. Born May 13, 1961 in Detroit, MI. Graduate Cinn. Consv. Bdwy debut 1987 in *Les Misérables*, followed by *The Merchant of Venice.*

THOMAS, RAYMOND ANTHONY. Born Dec. 19, 1956 in Kentwood, LA. Graduate U. Tex/El Paso. Debut 1981 OB in *Escape to Freedom*, followed by *The Sun Gets Blue, Blues for Mr. Charlie, The Hunchback of Notre Dame, Ground People, The Weather Outside, One-Act Festival, Caucasian Chalk Circle, The Virgin Molly, Black Eagles.*

THOME, DAVID. Born Jul. 24, 1951 in Salt Lake City, UT. Bdwy debut 1971 in *No No Nanette*, followed by *Different Times, Good News, Rodgers and Hart, A Chorus Line, Dancin', Dreamgirls* (1981/1987), *Peter Pan* (1990).

THOMPSON, EVAN. Born Sept. 3, 1931 in New York City. Graduate U. Cal. Bdwy debut 1969 in *Jimmy*, followed by *1776, City of Angels*, OB in *Mahagonny, Treasure Island, Knitters in the Sun, Half-Life, Fasnacht Dau, Importance of Being Earnest, Under the Gaslight, Henry V, The Fantasticks, Walk the Dog Willie, Macbeth, 1984, Leave It to Me, Earth and Sky.*

THOMPSON, JENN. Born Dec. 13, 1967 in New York City. Debut 1975 OB in *The Wooing of Lady Sunday*, followed by *Cowboy Jack Street, The Wobblies, Looice, One Time One Place, You're a Good Man Charlie Brown, I Ought to Be in Pictures,* Bdwy in *Annie* (1978).

THOMPSON, LAUREN. Born in 1950; attended Penn. St. U., Pittsburgh Playhouse. Bdwy debut 1979 in *Dracula*, followed by *A Life, Peter Pan* (1990), OB in *The Wedding of the Siamese Twins.*

THORSON, LINDA. Born June 18, 1947 in Toronto, Can. Graduate RADA. Bdwy debut 1982 in *Steaming* for which she received a Theatre World Award, followed by *Noises Off, Zoya's Apartment, Getting Married.*

TIMMERMAN, ALEC. Born Aug. 23, 1963 in Philadelphia, PA. Attended Temple U. Bdwy debut 1987 in *Anything Goes*, followed by *Gypsy, The Secret Garden,* OB in *Oy, Mama Am I in Love.*

TOBIE, ELLEN. Born March 26 in Chambersburg, PA. Graduate Ohio Wesleyan U. , Wayne St. U. Debut 1981 OB in *The Chisholm Trail Went Through Here*, followed by *Welded, Talking With, The Entertainer, Equal Wrights, Remembrance.*

TOLIN, MEG. Born Nov. 11, 1966 in Wheatridge, CO. Attended Ind. U. Bdwy debut 1990 in *Grand Hotel.*

John
Wylie

Courtney
Wyn

Peter
Yoshida

Christina
Youngman

Greg
Zerkle

Lizabeth
Zindell

TOMEI, MARISA. Born Dec. 4, 1964 in Brooklyn, NY. Attended Boston U., NYU. Debut 1986 OB in *Daughters* for which she received a Theatre World Award, followed by *Class I Act, Evening Star, What the Butler Saw, Marathon '88, Sharon and Billy, Chelsea Walls, The Summer Winds.*

TOMPOS, DOUG. Born Jan. 27, 1962 in Columbus, OH. Graduate Syracuse U., LAMDA. Debut 1985 OB in *Very Warm for May*, followed by *A Midsummer Night's Dream, Mighty Fine Music, Muzeeka, Wish You Were Here, Vampire Lesbians of Sodom*, Bdwy in *City of Angels.*

TONER, THOMAS. Born May 25, 1928 in Homestead, PA. Graduate UCLA. Bdwy debut 1973 in *Tricks*, followed by *The Good Doctor, All Over Town, The Elephant Man, California Suite, A Texas Trilogy, The Inspector General, Me and My Girl, The Secret Garden*, OB in *Pericles, The Merry Wives of Windsor, A Midsummer Night's Dream, Richard III, My Early Years, Life and Limb, Measure for Measure, Little Footsteps.*

TORAN, PETER. Born Jul. 16, 1955 in McLean, VA. Graduate Tufts U. Debut 1980 OB in *Romeo and Juliet*, followed by *It's Wilde!, The Marquis, Mr. Universe, Full Circle.*

TOY, CHRISTINE. Born Dec. 26, 1959 in Scarsdale, NY. Graduate Sarah Lawrence Col. Debut 1982 OB in *Oh Johnny!*, followed by *Pacific Overtures, Genesis, Festival of 1-Act Comedies.*

TRUE, BETSY. Born Apr. 19, 1960 in Cincinnati, OH. Graduate Boston Conv. Bdwy debut 1989 in *Les Misérables.*

TSOUTSOUVAS, SAM. Born Aug. 20, 1948 in Santa Barbara, CA. Attended U. Cal., Juilliard. Debut 1969 OB in *Peer Gynt*, followed by *Twelfth Night, Timon of Athens, Cymbeline, School for Scandal, The Hostage, Women Beware Women, Lower Depths, Emigre, Hello Dali, The Merchant of Venice, The Leader, The Bald Soprano, The Taming of the Shrew, Gus & Al, Tamara, The Man Who Shot Lincoln, Puppetmaster of Lodz, Richard III*, Bdwy in *Three Sisters, Measure for Measure, Beggar's Opera, Scapin, Dracula, Our Country's Good.*

TSUJI, ANN M. Born Jul. 3, 1961 in Yokohama, Japan. Graduate U. Rochester, Ohio U. Debut 1987 OB in *Rosie's Café*, followed by *Madame de Sade, Boutique Living and Disposable Icons, Lucky Come Hawaii.*

TUCCI, MARIA. Born June 19, 1941 in Florence, It. Attended Actors Studio. Bdwy debut 1963 in *The Milk Train Doesn't Stop Here Anymore*, followed by *The Rose Tattoo, The Little Foxes, The Cuban Thing, The Great White Hope, School for Wives, Lesson from Aloes, Kingdoms, Requiem for a Heavyweight, The Night of the Iguana*, OB in *Corruption in the Palace of Justice, Five Evenings, Trojan Women, White Devil, Horseman Pass By, Yerma, Shepherd of Avenue B, The Gathering, A Man for All Seasons, Love Letters, Substance of Fire.*

TUCCI, MICHAEL. Born Apr. 15, 1946 in New York City. Graduate Post Col. Debut 1974 OB in *Godspell*, followed by *Jules Feiffer's Hold Me!, Drinks Before Dinner, Philemon*, Bdwy in *Grease* (1975), *Spokesong.*

TURNER, GLENN. Born Sept. 21, 1957 in Atlanta, GA. Bdwy debut 1984 in *My One and Only*, followed by *A Chorus Line, Grand Hotel.*

TURPIN, BAHNI. Born June 4 in Pontiac, MI. Attended Howard U., NYU. Debut 1990 OB in *Ground People*, followed by *Who Collects the Pain?*

TURTURRO, JOHN. Born Feb. 28, 1957 in Brooklyn, NY. Graduate SUNY/New Paltz, La. U. Debut 1984 OB in *Danny and the Deep Blue Sea*, for which he received a Theatre World Award, followed by *Men without Dates, Chaos and Hard Times, Steel on Steel, Tooth of Crime, Of Mice and Men, Jamie's Gang, Marathon '86, The Bald Soprano/The Leader, La Puta Vita Trilogy, Italian American Reconciliation, Arturo Ui*, Bdwy in *Death of a Salesman* (1984).

TWAINE, MICHAEL. Born Nov. 1, 1936 in Lawrence, NY. Graduate Ohio St. U. Bdwy debut 1956 in *Mr. Roberts*, OB in *Kill the One-Eyed Man, The Duchess of Malfi, Recess, The Empire Builders, Pictures at an Exhibition, Holy Heist, The Seagull: The Hamptons, As You Like It.*

TYRRELL, JOHN. Born Nov. 24, 1951 in Perth Amboy, NJ. Graduate Marquette U., Neighborhood Playhouse. Bdwy debut 1976 in *Equus*, followed by *The Merchant, The Miser.*

TYZACK, MARGARET. Born Sept. 9, 1931 in London, Eng. Attended RADA. Debut 1975 OB in *Summerfolk*, followed by *Tom and Viv*, Bdwy in *All's Well That Ends Well* (1983), *Lettice and Lovage.*

ULLMAN, TRACEY. Born in Hackbridge, Eng. NY debut 1990 in *The Taming of the Shrew* (NYSF), and Bdwy in *The Big Love* (1991) for which she received a Theatre World Award.

URLA, JOE. Born Dec. 25, 1958 in Pontiac, MI. Graduate U. Mich., Yale U. Debut 1985 OB in *Measure for Measure*, followed by *Henry V, Principia Scriptoriae* for which he received a Theatre World Award, *Our Own Family, Return of Pinocchio, The Boys Next Door, Maids of Honor, The Way of the World.*

VANCE, COURTNEY B. Born Mar. 12, 1960 in Detroit, MI. Harvard graduate. Bdwy debut 1987 in *Fences* for which he received a Theatre World Award, followed by *Six Degrees of Separation*, OB in *Temptation, Six Degrees of Separation.*

VAN DYCK, JENNIFER. Born Dec. 23, 1962 in St. Andrews, Scotland. Graduate Brown U. Debut OB 1988 in *Gus and Al*, followed by *Marathon '88, Secret Rapture, Earth and Sky*, Bdwy in *Secret Rapture.*

VARGAS, OVIDIO. Born Nov. 30, 1959 in Brooklyn, NY. Graduate Boston Conv. Debut OB in *Yes Dear* followed by *Wonderful Town, Salon, Blood on Blood, Greed, Eastern Standard.*

VENNEMA, JOHN C. Born Aug. 24, 1948 in Houston, TX. Graduate Princeton U., LAMDA. Bdwy debut 1976 in *The Royal Family*, followed by *The Elephant Man, Otherwise Engaged*, OB in *Loot, Statements after an Arrest, The Biko Inquest, No End of Blame, In Celebration, Custom of the Counrty, The Basement, A Slight Ache, Young Playwrights Festival, Dandy Dick, Nasty Little Secrets, Mountain, Light Up the Sky.*

VENNER, TRACY. Born in 1968 in Boulder, CO. Attended Stephens Col. Bdwy debut 1989 in *Gypsy.*

VENTON, HARLEY. Born Dec. 28, 1952 in Thunder Bay, Can. Graduate U. ND, M. Minn. Bdwy debut 1981 in *Crimes of the Heart*, followed by *The Circle*, OB in *What Is This Thing?, Father's Day, Advice from a Caterpillar.*

VERICA, TOM. Born in Philadelphia, PA. Debut 1989 OB in *Blue Window*, followed by *The Welcoming*, Bdwy in *Prelude to a Kiss* (1990), *Half-Life.*

VIVIANO, SAL. Born Jul. 12, 1960 in Detroit, MI. Graduate E. Ill. U. Debut 1984 OB in *The Three Musketeers*, followed by *Romance/Romance*, OB in *Miami* (1986), *Hot Times and Suicide, Romance/Romance, Broadway Jukebox, Catch Me if I Fall.*

VON BARGEN, DANIEL. Born June 5, 1950 in Cincinnati, OH. Graduate Purdue U. Debut 1981 OB in *Missing Persons*, followed by *Macbeth*, Bdwy debut in *Mastergate* (1989) for which he received a Theatre World Award.

WAARA, SCOTT. Born June 5, 1957 in Chicago, IL. Graduate SMU. Debut 1982 OB in *The Rise of Daniel Rocket*, followed by *The Dining Room, Johnny Pye and the Foolkiller, Gifts of the Magi, Falsettoland, 50 Million Frenchmen*, Bdwy in *The Wind in the Willows* (1985), *Welcome to the Club, City of Angels.*

WAGNER, HANK. Born Mar. 12, 1969 in New York City. Graduate London Central Schl. Debut 1990 OB in *Measure for Measure*, followed by *Cork, The Fine Art of Finesse, Two Schnitzler One-Acts.*

WALKEN, CHRISTOPHER. Born Mar. 31, 1943 in Astoria, NY. Attended Hofstra U. Bdwy debut 1958 in *J.B.*, followed by *High Spirits, Baker Street, The Lion in Winter, Measure for Measure, The Rose Tattoo* for which he received a Theatre World Award, *The Unknown Soldier and His Wife, Rosencrantz and Guildenstern Are Dead, Scenes from American Life, Cymbeline, Enemies, The Plough and the Stars, Merchant of Venice, The Tempest, Troilus and Cressida, Macbeth, Sweet Bird of Youth*, OB in *Best Foot Forward* (1962), *Iphigenia in Aulis, Lemon Sky, Kid Champion, The Seagull, Cinders, Hurlyburly, House of Blue Leaves, Love Letters, Coriolanus, Othello.*

WALKER, RAY. Born Aug. 13, 1963 in St. Johnsbury, VT. Graduate NYU. Debut 1985 OB in *Christmas Spectacular*, followed by *Merrily We Roll Along*, Bdwy 1988 in *Les Misérables.*

WALLACE, LEE. Born Jul. 15, 1930 in New York City. Attended NYU. Debut 1966 OB in *Journey of the Fifth Horse*, followed by *Saturday Night, An Evening with Garcia Lorca, Macbeth, Booth Is Back in Town, Awake and Sing, Shepherd of Avenue B, Basic Training of Pavlo Hummel, Curtains, Elephants, Goodnight Grandpa, Jesse's Land, The Sunshine Boys, Taking Stock*, Bdwy in *Secret Affairs of Mildred Wild, Molly, Zalmen or the Madness of God, Some of My Best Friends, Grind, The Cemetery Club.*

WALLER, KENNETH. Born Apr. 12, 1945 in Atlanta, GA. Graduate Piedmont Col. Debut 1976 OB in *Boys from Syracuse*, Bdwy in *Sarava* (1979), *Onward Victoria, Me and My Girl, Phantom of the Opera*.

WALSH, ELIZABETH. Born Oct. 12, in Puerto Rico. Graduate U. Wis., U. Mass. Debut 1987 OB in *Mademoiselle Colombe*, followed by *She Love Me, Frankie, Love in Two Countries*.

WALSH, NANCY. Born Jan. 5, 1965 in Greenfield, MA. Graduate U. Conn., SMU. Debut 1991 OB in *Sabina and Lucretia*.

WALTERS, WILLIAM R. Born Sept. 6, 1936 in East Chicago, IN. Graduate St. Joseph's Col. Debut OB in *Tropicana*, followed by *Senor Discretion, Kiss Me Quick Before the Lava Reaches the Village, A Dopey Fairy Tale, Let It Ride!*

WALTON, JIM. Born Jul. 31, 1955 in Tachikawa, Japan. Graduate U. Cinn. Debut 1979 OB in *Big Bad Burlesque*, followed by *Scrambled Feet, Stardust, Sweeney Todd, Closer Than Ever, Life on theThird Rail, And the World Goes 'Round*, Bdwy in *Perfectly Frank* (1980), *Merrily We Roll Along, 42nd Street, Stardust, Sweeney Todd*.

WANDS, SUSAN. Born Oct. 20 in Denver, CO. Graduate U. Wash. Debut 1985 OB in *Whining and Dining*, followed by *And They Dance Real Slow in Jackson, Henry IV Parts 1 & 2*.

WARD, DOUGLAS TURNER. Born May 5, 1930 in Burnside, LA. Attended U. Mich. Bdwy debut 1959 in *Raisin in the Sun*, followed by *One Flew over the Cuckoo's Nest, Last Breeze of Summer*, OB in *The Iceman Cometh, The Blacks, Pullman Car Hiawatha, Bloodknot, Happy Ending, Day of Absence, Kongi's Harvest, Ceremonies in Dark Old Men, The Harangues, The Reckoning, Frederick Douglas through His Own Words, River Niger, The Brownsville Raid, The Offering, Old Phantoms, The Michigan, About Heaven and Earth, Louie and Ophelia, Lifetimes, The Little Tommy Parker Celebrated Minstrel Show*.

WARDEN, YVONNE. Born Jan. 16, 1928 in NYC. Attended UCLA, NYU. Debut 1967 OB in *Trials of Brother Jero*, followed by *The Strong Breed, Macbeth, Waiting for Godot, Welfare, Where Have All the Dreamers Gone, Calalou, Masque and Dasha, Black Girl, Prince, Mitote*.

WARING, WENDY. Born Dec. 7, 1960 in Melrose, MA. Attended Emerson Col., NYU. Debut 1987 OB in *Wish You Were Here*, Bdwy in *Legs Diamond* (1988), *The Will Rogers Follies*.

WARMFLASH, STUART. Born June 27, 1949 in New York City. Graduate NYU. Debut 1970 OB in *The Lady from Maxim's*, followed by *Secret Service, Boy Meets Girl, Let Me Finish!*

WARNER, AMY. Born June 29, 1951 in Minneapolis, MN. Graduate Principia Col. Debut 1982 OB in *Faust*, followed by *Ghost Sonata, Wild Oats, Big Little Scenes, Hamlet, George Dandin, The Underpants, As the Wind Rocks the Wagon, Three Little Plays about Sex*.

WASHINGTON, DENZEL. Born Dec. 28, 1954 in Mt. Vernon, NY. Graduate Fordham U. debut 1975 OB in *The Emperor Jones*, followed by *Othello, Coriolanus, Mighty Gents, Becket, Spell #7, Ceremonies in Dark Old Men, One Tiger to a Hill, A Soldier's Play, Every Goodbye Ain't Gone, Richard III*, Bdwy 1988 in *Checkmates*.

WASHINGTON, SHARON. Born Sept. 12, 1959 in New York City. Graduate Dartmouth Col, Yale U. Debut 1988 OB in *Coriolanus* followed by *Cymbeline, Richard III, The Balcony, Caucasian Chalk Circle*.

WATERSTON, SAM. Born Nov. 15, 1940 in Cambridge, MA. Yale graduate. Bdwy debut 1963 in *Oh Dad Poor Dad …*, followed by *First One Asleep Whistle, Halfway Up the Tree, Indians, Hay Fever, Much Ado about Nothing, A Meeting by the River, Lunch Hour, Benefactors, A Walk in the Woods*, OB in *As You Like It, A Thistle in My Bed, The Knack, Ritz, Biscuit, La Turista, Posterity for Sale, Ergo, Muzeeka, Red Cross, Henry IV, Spitting Image, I Met a Man, Brass Butterfly, Trial of the Catonsville 9, Cymbeline, Hamlet, The Tempest, A Doll's House, Measure for Measure, Chez Vous, Waiting for Godot, Gardenia, The Three Sisters, An Evening of Primo Levi*.

WEBER, JAKE. Born Mar. 12, 1963 in London, Eng. Graduate Middlebury Col, Juilliard. Debut 1988 OB in *Road*, followed by *Twelfth Night, Maids of Honor, Richard III, The Big Funk, Othello*.

WEISS, JEFF. Born in 1940 in Allentown, PA. Debut 1986 OB in Hamlet, followed by *The Front Page* (LC), *Casanova*, Bdwy in *Macbeth* (1988), *Our Town, Mastergate*.

WELBY, DONNAH. Born May 4, 1952 in Scranton, PA. Graduate Catholic U. Debut 1981 OB in *Between Friends*, followed by *Double Inconstancy, The Taming of the Shrew, The Contrast, Macbeth, Electra, All's Well That Ends Well, Hot I Baltimore, The Philanderer, Three Sisters, The Importance of Being Earnest, A Midsummer Night's Dream, Between Friends, The Fine Art of Finesse*.

WELDON, CHARLES. Born June 1, 1940 in Wetumka, OK. Bdwy debut 1969 in *Big Time Buck White*, followed by *River Niger*, OB in *Ride a Black Horse, Long Time Coming, Jamimma, In The Deepest Part of Sleep, Brownsville Raid, The Great MacDaddy, The Offering, Colored People's Time, Raisin in the Sun, Lifetimes, Jonquil, Burner's Frolic, The Little Tommy Parker Celebrated Minstrel Show*.

WELLS, CRAIG. Born Jul. 2, 1955 in Newark, NJ. Graduate Albion Col. Debut 1985 OB in *Forbidden Broadway*, followed by *The Best of Forbidden Broadway, Closer Than Ever, Colette Collage*, Bdwy in *Chess* (1988).

WESTENBERG, ROBERT. Born Oct. 26, 1953 in Miami Beach, FL. Graduate U. Cal/Fresno. Debut 1981 OB in *Henry IV Part 1*, followed by *Hamlet, The Death of von Richthofen*, Bdwy in *Zorba* (1983) for which he received a Theatre World Award, *Sunday in the Park with George, Into the Woods, Les Misérables*.

WHITE, ALICE. Born Jan. 6, 1945 in Washington, DC. Graduate Oberlin Col. Debut 1977 OB in *The Passion of Dracula*, followed by *La Belle au bois, Zoology, Snow Leopards, Fridays, Candida*.

WHITE, JULIE. Born June 4, 1962 in San Diego, CA. Attended Fordham U. Debut 1988 OB in *Lucky Stiff*, followed by *Just Say No, Early One Evening at the Rainbow Bar and Grill, The Stick Wife, Marathon '91*.

WHITE, PATRICK. Born Sept. 9, 1963 in Albany, NY. Graduate AADA. Debut 1988 OB in *Male Animal*, followed by *After the Rain, Take the Waking Slow*.

WHITE, TERRI. Born Jan. 24, 1953 in Palo Alto, CA. Attended USIU. Debut 1976 OB in *The Club*, followed by *Juba*, Bdwy in *Barnum* (1980), *Ain't Misbehavin', Welcome to the Club*.

WHITEHEAD, MARILYN. Born Jul. 30, 1959 in Vero Beach, FL. Graduate Fla. St. Col. Debut 1989 OB in *Give My Regards to Broadway*, followed by *The Fantasticks*.

WHITEHURST, SCOTT. Born Dec. 24, 1962 in Indianapolis, IN. Graduate Columbia U., Rutgers U. Debut 1991 OB in *Black Eagles*.

WHITFIELD, DEBRA. Born Jul. 1, 1957 in Charlotte, NC. Graduate Ohio St. U., Kent St. U. Debut 1983 OB in *Brandy before Breakfast*, followed by *Dr. Jekyll and Mr. Hyde, Bravo, Appointment with Death, Hound of the Baskervilles, The Land Is Bright, Black Coffee, On the Move, Measure for Measure*.

WHITFORD, BRADLEY. Born in Madison, WI. Graduate Wesleyan U., Juilliard. Debut 1985 OB in *Curse of the Starving Class*, followed by *Measure for Measure, Romeo and Juliet, Tower of Evil*, Bdwy in *A Few Good Men* (1989).

WHITMORE, JAMES. Born Oct. 1, 1922 in White Plains, NY. Attended Yale U. Bdwy debut in *Command Decision* (1947), followed by *A Case of Libel, Inquest, Will Rogers U.S.A., Bully, Almost an Eagle*, OB in *Elba, About Face, Handy Dandy*.

WILHELM, KATHY. Born Jul. 7, 1967 in Tokyo, Japan. With Oakland Ballet before Bdwy debut in *Shogun: the Musical* (1990).

WILLIAMS, VAN. Born Apr. 10, 1925 in Pharr, TX. Attended U. Tex., Yale U. Bdwy debut 1951 in *Richard II*, followed by *St. Joan, Dial "M" for Murder, Little Moon of Alban, No Time for Sergeants, The Teahouse of the August Moon*.

WILLISON, WALTER. Born June 24, 1947 in Monterey Park, CA. Bdwy debut 1970 in *Norman Is That You?*, followed by *Two by Two* for which he received a Theatre World Award, *Wild and Wonderful, A Celebration of Richard Rodgers, Pippin, A Tribute to Joshua Logan, A Tribute to George Abbott, Grand Hotel*, OB in *South Pacific in Concert, They Say It's Wonderful, Broadway Scandals of 1928* and *Options*, both of which he wrote, *Aldersgate 88*.

WILLS, RAY. Born Sept. 14, 1960 in Santa Monica, CA. Graduate Wichita St. U., Brandeis U. Debut 1988 OB in *Side by Side by Sondheim*, followed by *Kiss Me Quick, The Grand Tour, The Cardigans, The Rothschilds*.

WILKOF, LEE. Born June 25, 1951 in Canton, OH. Graduate U. Cinn. Debut 1977 OB in *Present Tense*, followed by *Little Shop of Horrors, Holding Patterns, Angry Housewives, Assassins*, Bdwy in *Sweet Charity* (1986), *The Front Page*.

WILLIAMS, ELLIS. Born June 28, 1951 in Brunswick., GA. Graduate Boston U. Debut 1977 OB in *Intimation*, followed by *Spell #7, Mother Courage, Ties That Bind, Kid Purple, The Boys Next Door*, Bdwy in *The Basic Training of Pavlo Hummel, Pirates of Penzance, Solomon's Child, Trio, Requiem for a Heavyweight, Once on This Island*.

WILLIAMSON, NICOL. Born Sept. 14, 1938 n Hamilton, Scotland, Bdwy debut 1965 in *Inadmissible Evidence*, followed by *Plaza Suite, Hamlet, Uncle Vanya, Macbeth, The Real Thing, I Hate Hamlet*, OB in *Nicol Williamson's Late Show, Inadmissible Evidence, The Entertainer*.

WILLIFORD, LOU. Born Aug. 14, 1957 in Dallas, TX. Graduate Trinity U. Debut 1990 OB in *The Brass Jackal*, followed by Bdwy in *Fiddler on the Roof* (1990).

WILNER, LORI. Born Jul. 17, 1959 in New York City. Graduate SUNY/Binghamton. OB in *I Never Sang for My Father*, followed by *Hair, School Daze, Poor Murderer, Cricket on the Hearth, Hannah Senesh, Those Were the Days*.

WILSON, CHANDRA. Born Aug. 27, 1969 in Houston, TX. Graduate NYU. Debut 1991 OB in *The Good Times Are Killing Me* for which she received a Theatre World Award.

WILSON, MARY LOUISE. Born Nov. 12, 1936 in New Haven, CT. Graduate Northwestern U. Bdwy debut 1963 in *Hot Spot*, followed by *Flora the Red Menace, Criss-Crossing, Promises Promises, The Women, The Gypsy, The Royal Family, The Importance of Being Earnest, Philadelphia Story, Fools, Alice in Wonderland, The Odd Couple, Prelude to a Kiss*, OB in *Our Town, Upstairs at the Downstairs, Threepenny Opera, A Great Career, Whispers on the Wind, Beggar's Opera, Buried Child, Sister Mary Ignatius Explains It All, Actor's Nightmare, Baby with the Bathwater, Musical Comedy Murders of 1940, Macbeth*.

WILSON, TYRONE. Born Feb. 23, 1959 in Lumberton, NC. Graduate Middlebury Col., Yale U. Debut 1988 OB in *Julius Caesar*, followed by *Water Music, The Vigil, A Lesson from Aloes, Macbeth, The Country Doctor, Walking the Dead*, Bdwy in *Lettice and Lovage* (1990).

WINANT, BRUCE. Born Apr. 9, 1957 in Santa Monica, CA. Graduate U.S. Intl. U. Bdwy debut 1991 in *Miss Saigon*.

WING, VIRGINIA. Born Nov. 9 in Marks, MS. Graduate Miss. Col. Debut 1989 OB in *Two by Two*, followed by *Food and Shelter*.

WINSON, SUZI. Born Feb. 28, 1962 in New York City. Bdwy debut 1980 in *Brigadoon*, followed by OB in *Moondance, Nunsense*.

WINSTON, LEE. Born Mar. 14, 1941 in Great Bend, KS. Graduate U. Kan. Debut 1966 OB in *The Drunkard*, followed by *Little Mahagony, The Good Soldier Schweik, Adopted Moon, Miss Waters to You, Christmas Bride, The Elephant Piece*. Bdwy in *Showboat* (1966), *1600 Pennsylvania Avenue*.

WISE, WILLIAM. Born May 11 in Chicago, IL. Attended Bradley U., Northwestern U. Debut 1970 OB in *Adaptation/Next*, followed by *Him, Hot l Baltimore, Just the Immediate Family, 36, For the Use of the Hall, Orphans, Working Theatre Festival, Copperhead, Early One Evening at the Rainbow Bar & Grill, Special Interests, Theme and Variations, Marathon '91*.

WISOFF, JILL. Born April 27 in Queens, NY. Graduate Bennington Col. Debut 1990 OB in *Money Talks*.

WOJDA, JOHN. Born Feb. 19, 1957 in Detroit, MI. Attended U. Mich. Bdwy debut 1982 in *Macbeth*, followed by *The Merchant of Venice*, OB in *The Merchant of Venice, Natural Disasters, The Coming of Mr. Pine, Henry IV Parts 1 and 2*.

WOLF, KELLY. Born Jan. 9, 1964 in Nashville, TN. Graduate Interlochen Arts Acad. Debut 1983 OB in *Ah Wilderness*, followed by *Marathon '86, Young Playwrights Festival, Bloody Poetry, The Summer Winds*.

WOO, JENNY. Born Feb. 7, 1970 in Los Angeles, CA. Attended UCLA. Bdwy debut 1990 in *Shogun: The Musical*.

WOODARD, CHARLAINE. Born Dec. 29 in Albany, NY. Graduate Goodman Theatre, SUNY. Debut 1975 OB in *Don't Bother Me I Can't Cope*, followed by *Dementos, Under Fire, A...My Name Is Alice, Twelfth Night, Hang on to the Good Times, Paradise, Twelfth Night* (CP), *Caucasian Chalk Circle*, Bdwy in *Hair* (1977), *Ain't Misbehavin'* (1978/1988).

WOODS, ALLIE. Born Sept. 28 in Houston, TX. Graduate Tex. St. U. Debut 1989 OB in *Forbidden City*, followed by Bdwy in *Mule Bone* (1991).

WOODS, RICHARD. Born May 9, 1923 in Buffalo, NY. Graduate Ithaca Col. Bdwy in *Beg Borrow or Steal, Capt. Brassbound's Conversion, Sail Away, Coco, Last of Mrs. Lincoln, Gigi, Sherlock Holmes, Murder Among Friends, Royal Family, Deathtrap, Man and Superman, Man Who Came to Dinner, The Father, Present Laughter, Alice in Wonderland, You Can't Take It with You, Design for Living, Smile*, OB in *The Crucible, Summer and Smoke, American Gothic, Four-in-One, My Heart's in the Highlands, Eastward in Eden, Long Gallery, Year Boston Won the Pennant, In the Matter of J. Robert Oppenheimer*, with APA in *You Can't Take It with You, War and Peace, School for Scandal, Right you Are, Wild Duck, Pantagleize, Exit the King, Cherry Orchard, Cock-a-doodle Dandy*, and *Hamlet, Crimes and Dreams, Marathon '84, Much Ado about Nothing, Sitting Pretty in Concert, The Cat and the Fiddle, The Old Boy*.

WOODSON, JOHN. Born May 12, 1950 in Des Moines, IA. Attended NC Schl. of Arts. Debut 1990 OB in *King Lear*.

WOPAT, TOM. Born in 1950 in Lodi, WI. Attended U. Wis. Debut 1978 OB in *A Bistro Car on the CNR*, followed by *Oklahoma!, The Robber Bridegroom, Olympus on My Mind*, Bdwy in *I Love My Wife* (1979), *City of Angels*.

WORKMAN, JASON. Born Oct. 9, 1962 in Omaha, Neb. Attended U. Ky., Goodman School. Bdwy debut 1989 in *Meet Me in St. Louis* for which he received a Theatre World Award, OB in *Haunted Host*.

WORKMAN, SHANELLE. Born Aug. 3, 1978 in Fairfax, VA. Bdwy debut 1988 in *Les Misérables*.

WORTH, PENNY. Born Mar. 2, 1950 in London, Eng. Attended Sorbonne/Paris. Bdwy debut 1970 in *Coco*, followed by *Irene, Annie, Grand Hotel*.

WORTH, WENDY. Born Jan. 12 in Morristown, NJ. Attended Pima Col. Bdwy debut 1974 in *Irene*, OB in *Dazy* (1987) followed by *Let It Ride!*

WRIGHT, STEPHEN. Born July 26 in Chester, SC. Graduate Wofford Col., Neighborhood Playhouse. Bdwy debut 1977 in *Fiddler on the Roof*, followed by 1981/1990 revivals.

WROE, CRAIG. Born Apr. 8, 1958 in Los Angeles, CA. Graduate Loyola U., Catholic U. Debut 1989 OB in *The Tempest*, followed by *Othello, Measure for Measure*.

WYATT, MONA. Born Jan. 31 in Ft. Monmouth, NJ. Attended Shenandoah Consv. Debut 1984 in *Radio City Christmas Spectacular*, followed OB in *Manhattan Serenade*, Bdwy in *Oh Kay!* (1990)

WYCHE, MIMI. Born Dec. 2, 1955 in Greenville, SC. Graduate Stanford U. Debut 1986 OB in *Once on a Summer's Day*, followed by *Senor Discretion, Juan Darien, The Golden Apple*, Bdwy in *Cats* (1988).

WYLIE, JOHN. Born Dec. 14, 1925 in Peacock, TX. Graduate No. Tex. St. U. Debut 1987 OB in *Lucky Spot*, followed by Bdwy in *Born Yesterday* (1989), *Grand Hotel*.

WYMAN, NICHOLAS. Born May 18, 1950 in Portland, ME. Graduate Harvard U. Bdwy debut 1975 in *Very Good Eddie*, followed by *Grease, The Magic Show, On the 20th Century, Whoopee!, My Fair Lady* (1981), *Doubles, Musical Comedy Murders of 1940, Phantom of the Opera*, OB in *Paris Lights, When We Dead Awaken, Charlotte Sweet, Kennedy at Colonus, Once on a Summer's Day, Angry Housewives*.

WYN, COURTNEY. Born Apr. 27, 1969 in Ft. Worth, TX. Attended Southwestern U. Bdwy debut 1990 in *Peter Pan*.

XIFO, RAY. Born Sept. 3, 1942 in Newark, NJ. Graduate Don Bosco Col. Debut 1974 OB in *The Tempest*, followed by *Frogs, My Uncle Sam, Shlemiel the First*, Bdwy in *City of Angels* (1989).

YEOMAN, JO ANN. Born Mar. 19, 1948 in Phoenix, AZ. Graduate Ariz. St. U., Purdue U. Debut 1974 OB in *The Boy Friend*, followed by *Texas Starlight, Ba Ta Clan, A Christmas Carol*.

YOSHIDA, PETER. Born May 28, 1945 in Chicago, IL. Graduate U. Ill., Princeton, AADA. Debut 1965 OB in *Coriolanus*, followed by *Troilus and Cressida, Santa Anita '42, Pursuit of Happiness, Servant of Two Masters, The Peking Man, Monkey Magic, Station J., Double Dutch, Prime Time, Occasional Grace, The Longest Walk, Rashomon, A Midsummer Night's Dream, Mikado Amas, Tropical Tree, Yokohama Duty*.

YOUNGMAN, CHRISTINA. Born Sept. 14, 1963 in Philadelphia, PA. Attended Point Park Col. Debut 1983 OB in *Emperor of My Baby's Heart*, followed by *Carouselle des Folles*, Bdwy in *Starlight Express* (1987), *Largely New York, The Will Rogers Follies*.

ZAGNIT, STUART. Born Mar. 28 in New Brunswick, NJ. Graduate Montclair St. Col. Debut 1978 OB in *The Wager*, followed by *Manhattan Transference, Women in Tune, Enter Laughing, Kuni Leml, Tattermalion, Golden Land, Little Shop of Horrors, Lucky Stiff, Grand Tour, Majestic Kid, Made in Heaven, Encore!*

ZALOOM, JOE. Born July 30, 1944 in Utica, NY. Graduate Catholic U. Bdwy debut 1972 in *Capt. Brassbound's Conversion*, followed by *Kingdoms*, OB in *Nature and the Purpose of the Universe, Plot Counter Plot, Midsummer Night's Dream, Madrid Madrid, Much Ado about Nothing, Cymbeline, Tamara, The Taming of the Shrew*.

ZALOOM, PAUL. Born Dec. 14, 1951 in Brooklyn, NY. Graduate Goddard Col. Debut 1979 OB in *Fruit of Zaloom*, followed by *Crazy as Zaloom, Return of the Creature from the Blue Zaloom, Theatre of Trash, House of Horrors, My Civilization*.

ZARISH, JANET. Born Apr. 21, 1954 in Chicago, IL. Graduate Juilliard. Debut 1981 OB in *The Villager*, followed by *Playing with Fire, Royal Bob, Enemy of the People, Midsummer Night's Dream, Festival of 1-Acts, Other People's Money, Human Nature*.

ZELLER, MARK. Born Apr. 20, 1932 in New York City. Attended NYU. Bdwy debut 1956 in *Shangri-La*, followed by *Happy Hunting, Wonderful Town* (CC), *Saratoga, Ari, Chu Chem, Fiddler on the Roof* (1990), OB in *Candle in the Wind, Margaret's Bed, Freud, Kuni Leml, Lies My Father Told Me, Big Block Party, Chu Chem*.

ZEMON, TOM. Born Jan. 13, 1964 in Hartford, CT. Graduate U. Hartford. Bdwy debut 1988 in *Les Misérables*.

ZERKLE, GREG. Born Aug. 19, 1957 in Wisconsin. Graduate U. Wis., U. Wash. Debut 1986 OB in *Sherlock Holmes and the Redheaded League*, followed by *Bittersuite, Juba*, Bdwy in *Into the Woods* (1988), *Grand Hotel*.

ZIEMBA, KAREN. Born Nov. 12 in St. Joseph, MO. Graduate U. Akron. Debut 1981 OB in *Seesaw*, followed by *I Married an Angel, Sing for Your Supper, 50 Million Frenchmen, And the World Goes Round*.

ZIEN, CHIP. Born Mar. 20, 1947 in Milwaukee, WI. Attended U. Penn. OB in *You're a Good Man, Charlie Brown*, followed by *Kadish, How to Succeed ..., Dear Mr. G., Tuscaloosa's Calling, Hot l Baltimore, El Grande de Coca Cola, Split, Real Life Funnies, March of the Falsettos, Isn't It Romantic, Diamonds, Falsettoland*, Bdwy in *All Over Town* (1974), *The Suicide, Into the Woods, Grand Hotel*.

ZINDEL, LIZABETH. Born Oct. 30, 1976 in New York City. Debut 1989 OB in *Essence of Margrovia*, followed by *Last Night, Come Again, Common Clay, David's Mother, Night Sky*.

ZORICH, LOUIS. Born Feb. 12, 1924 in Chicago, IL. Attended Roosevelt U. OB in *Six Characters in Search of an Author, Crimes and Crimes, Henry V, Thracian Horses, All Women Are One, Good Soldier Schweik, Shadow of Heroes, To Clothe the Naked, Sundet, A Memory of Two Mondays, They Knew What They Wanted, The Gathering, True West, The Tempest, Come Dog Come Night, Henry IV Parts 1 and 2*, Bdwy in *Becket, Moby Dick, The Odd Couple, Hadrian VII, Moonchildren, Fun City, Goodtime Charley, Herzl, Death of a Salesman* (1984), *Arms and the Man, The Marriage of Figaro*.

Eve Arden

Pearl Bailey

Ina Balin

Barbara Baxley

Joan Bennett

Coral Browne

OBITUARIES

(June 1, 1990–May 31, 1991)

LAMAR ALFORD, 46, stage actor-singer, an original cast member of the 1971 musical *Godspell*, died March 29, 1991 in Atlanta, GA, of undisclosed cause. He appeared also in *Your Arms Too Short to Box with God*. Later he founded the King Players at Morehouse College in Atlanta. Surviving are two brothers and two sisters.

EVE ARDEN, 83, California-born stage, screen, radio and TV actress, died on November 12, 1990 of heart disease at her home in Beverly Hills. One of film's most popular supporting players, she received an "Oscar" nomination for her role in *Mildred Pierce*, and later won an Emmy Award for her hit TV series, *Our Miss Brooks*. She made her Broadway debut in 1934 in *Ziegfeld Follies*, followed by appearances in *Very Warm for May*, *Two for the Show*, *Let's Face It*, *Over 21*, *Auntie Mame*, and *Hello, Dolly!* Survivors include two sons and two daughters.

MONROE ARNOLD, 64, stage, screen and TV actor, died on February 1, 1991 of a heart attack at his home in Queens, NY. He appeared Off-Broadway in the 1959 revival of *Leave It to Jane* and *The Days and Nights of Beebee Fenstermaker*, and on Broadway in *Enter Laughing*. He is survived by his brother.

HOWARD ASHMAN, 40, Baltimore-born lyricist, librettist, playwright, and director, who wrote and staged the 1982 Off-Broadway musical version of *Little Shop of Horrors*, died of AIDS on March 14, 1991 in Manhattan. With his collaborator, Alan Menken, he also wrote a musical version of *God Bless You Mr. Rosewater* for Off-Broadway and songs for the 1989 Disney animated feature *The Little Mermaid*, winning an "Oscar" for the song "Under the Sea." For Broadway he wrote the book and lyrics for *Smile* with composer Marvin Hamlisch. Surviving are his companion, a sister, and his mother.

JOSEPH ATTLES, 88, actor, died on October 29, 1990 in his native Charleston, SC, of prostate cancer. He made his Broadway debut in *Blackbirds* of 1928, followed by *John Henry*, *Porgy and Bess*, *Kwamina*, *Tambourines to Glory*, *The Last of Mrs. Lincoln*, and *Bubbling Brown Sugar*. His Off-Broadway appearances include *Jerico-Jim Crow*, *Cabin in the Sky*, *Prodigal Son*, *Day of Absence*, *Cry of Players*, *King Lear*, *Duplex*, and *Do Lord Remember Me*. No immediate survivors.

PEARL BAILEY, 72, Virginia-born stage, screen, and TV actress-singer, famous for her unique, casual singing style, died on August 17, 1990 in Philadelphia after collapsing at a local hotel. She had a long history of heart ailments. Her Broadway debut was in *St. Louis Woman* (1946), followed by *Arms and the Girl*, *House of Flowers*, and *Hello, Dolly!* She is survived by her husband, drummer Louis Belson, Jr., two children, and two sisters.

INA BALIN, 52, Brooklyn-born stage, screen, and TV actress, who helped evacuate hundreds of Vietnamese orphans at the end of the Vietnam War, died on June 20, 1990 in New Haven, CT, of pulmonary hypertension. She made her Broadway debut in *Compulsion* in 1957 followed by *A Majority of One*, for which she received a Theatre World Award. Off-Broadway she appeared in *Face to Face*.

BARBARA BAXLEY, 39, California-born stage, screen, and TV actress, was found dead in her New York apartment on June 7, 1990 of an apparent heart attack. She made her Broadway debut in 1948 in *Private Lives*, followed by *Out West of Eighth*, *Peter Pan*, *I Am a Camera*, *Bus Stop*, *Camino Real*, *Frogs of Spring*, *Oh Men! Oh Women!*, *The Flowering Peach*, *Period of Adjustment*, *She Loves Me*, *Three Sisters*, *Plaza Suite*, *Me Jack You Jill*, *Best Friend*, and *Whodunnit*. Her Off-Broadway credits include *Brecht on Brecht*, *Measure for Measure*, *To Be Young Gifted and Black*, *Oh Pioneers*, *Are You Now or Have You Ever Been?*, and *Isn't It Romantic?* No reported survivors.

JILL BENNETT, 59, British stage, screen, and TV actress, died on October 4, 1990 in London of undisclosed causes. In addition to her work on the London stage she appeared in New York in *The Night of the Ball*, *Lily of Little India*, *Time Present*, and *Three Months Gone*. No reported survivors.

JOAN BENNETT, 80, New Jersey-born stage and TV actress, and top movie star in the 1930s and '40s, died on December 7, 1990 in White Plains, NY, of a heart attack. She made her Broadway debut in *Jarnegan* in 1928 and later appeared on the New York stage in *The Pirate*, *Love Me Little*, and *Never Too Late*. She is survived by her fourth husband, David Wilde, and four daughters.

HERBERT BERGHOF, 81, Vienna-born stage and screen actor, director, and teacher, died November 5, 1990 of heart failure in his Manhattan home. In 1945 he founded HB Studio in New York and later the HB Playwrights Foundation in Chelsea. As an actor his New York stage credits include *Nathan the Wise*, *King Lear*, *Ghosts*, *Hedda Gabler*, *The Lady from the Sea*, *Tovarich*, *The Deep Blue Sea*, *The Andersonville Trial*, and *In the Matter of J. Robert Oppenheimer*. He directed *Waiting for Godot*, *Infernal Machine*, *This Side of Paradise*, *Poor Murderer*, and *Charlotte*, among others. He is survived by his wife, actress Uta Hagen, a stepdaughter, and a granddaughter.

LEONARD BERNSTEIN, 72, Massachusetts-born composer, conductor, and one of th century's most noted figures in the world of music, died on October 14, 1990 of progressive lung failure in his Manhattan home. For the Broadway stage he wrote the music for *On the Town*, *Peter Pan* (1950), *Trouble in Tahiti*, *The Lark*, *Wonderful Town*, *Candide*, *West Side Story*, and *1600 Pennsylvania Avenue*. He is survived by a son and two daughters.

EDWARD BINNS, 74, Philadelphia-born stage, screen, and TV actor, died on December 4, 1991 of a heart attack in Brewster, NY, while driving to his Warren, CT, home with his wife, actress Elizabeth Franz. His New York stage credits include *Command Decision*, *Sundown Beach*, *Detective Story*, *The Lark*, *A View from the Bridge*, *Caligula*, and *Ghosts*. In addition to his wife he is survived by three daughters, a brother, and five granddaughters.

KATHARINE BLAKE, 62, South Africa-born stage and TV actress, and writer, died on March 1, 1991 in London of undisclosed causes. On Broadway she appeared with Laurence Olivier and Vivien Leigh in *Antony and Cleopatra* and *Caesar and Cleopatra*. She is survived by two daughters.

LILIAN BOND, 83, London-born stage and screen actress, died on January 25, 1991 of a heart attack in Reseda, CA. Her Broadway credits include *Stepping Out* (1929), *Luana*, *Free for All*, *Three and One*, *Little Shot*, *All Men Are Alike*, as well as various productions of the *Ziegfeld Follies* and the *Earl Carroll Vanities*. She is survived by a niece, a stepson, and a stepdaughter.

STANLEY BROCK, 59, Brooklyn-born stage, screen, and TV actor-comedian, died on January 25, 1991 in Los Angeles of a heart attack. He appeared on Broadway in *We Interrupt This Program* and *Troilus and Cressida*, and Off-Broadway in *Scuba Duba* and *20th Century Tar*. He was a regular on the daytime TV serial *Days of Our Lives*. Two brothers survive.

JOHN BROCKMEYER, 50, Ohio-born actor, best known for his work with the Ridiculous Theatrical Company, died on December 16, 1990 of AIDS, in Columbus, OH. His appearances with the company include *Bluebeard*, *The Enchanted Pig*, *Stage Blood*, *Der Ring Got Farbonjet*, and *Corn*. His last appearance was in *Don't Remind Me* (1988) at La Mama. He is survived by his parents, two brothers, and four sisters.

CORAL BROWNE, 77, Australia-born stage, screen, and TV actress, died on May 29, 1991 of breast cancer at her home in Los Angeles. New York stage appearances include *Basalik*, *Tamburlaine the Great*, *Macbeth*, *Troilus and Cressida*, *The Rehearsal*, and *The Right Honourable Gentleman*. She is survived by her husband, actor Vincent Price.

MIRIAM BURTON (HOLMAN), 64, New York City-born Broadway and opera singer-actress, died of respiratory failure in the Bronx on February 2, 1991. Her New York stage credits include *Run Little Chillun*, *House of Flowers*, *Ballad of Bimshire*, *Waltz of the Toreadors*, and *The Sunshine Boys*. She is survived by a daughter, her father, a brother, and a sister.

Barbara
Cason

Tom
Clancy

Roderick
Cook

Robert
Cummings

Don
Draper

Irene
Dunne

VINCENT CARISTI, 42, Brooklyn-born stage and TV actor-playwright, died September 20, 1990 in New York City of cancer. Off-Broadway he acted in and co-wrote *Tracers*, winning three Drama Desk Awards in 1985. An earlier 1980 staging in Los Angeles won him the L.A. Drama Critics Award. He is survived by his parents and two sisters.

THOMAS A. CARLIN, 62, Chicago-born stage, screen, and TV actor, died May 6, 1991 of heart failure at his home in New Rochelle, NY. His Broadway credits include *Time Limit!*, *Holiday for Lovers*, *Man in the Dog Suit*, *A Cook for Mr. General*, *Great Day in the Morning*, *A Thousand Clowns*, *The Deputy*, and *Players*. He appeared Off-Broadway in *Thieves Carnival*, *Brecht on Brecht*, *Summer*, and *Pigeons on the Walk*. He is survived by his wife, actress Frances Sternhagen, six children, a brother, and two grandchildren.

BARBARA CASON, 61, Memphis-born stage, screen and TV actress, died June 18, 1990 of a heart attack at her home in the Hollywood Hills area of Los Angeles. She made her 1967 Broadway debut in *Marat/Sade* (1967), followed by *Jimmy Shine* and *Night Watch*. Off-Braodway she appeared in *Firebugs*, *Spitting Image*, *Enemy of the People*, *Oh Coward!*, and *The Sea Gull*. She is survived by her husband, actor Dennis Patrick.

DALTON CATHEY, 44, stage and TV actor, died of AIDS December 31, 1990 in Los Angeles. Broadway credits include *Dracula*, *Major Barbara*, and *Macbeth*. He founded the Livingroom Theatre in Los Angeles. Surviving are his parents and a brother.

TOM CLANCY, 67, Irish actor-singer, best known as a member of The Clancy Brothers, died of stomach cancer on November 7, 1990 in Cork, Ireland. On Broadway he appeared in *King Lear*, *Under Milk Wood*, *A Touch of the Poet*, and *A Moon for the Misbegotten*, and Off-Broadway in *Winkelberg*, *Ulysses in Nighttown*, *Guests of the Nation*, and *Pygmalion*. In addition to his two brothers-partners, Paddy and Liam, he is survived by his wife, two daughters, and four sisters.

RODERICK COOK, 58, British-born stage, screen, and TV actor, died August 17, 1990 in Los Angeles of an apparent heart attack. He was perhaps best known for creating and performing the revue *Oh Coward!* which played Off-Broadway in 1972 and on Broadway in 1986, winning him a Tony Award nomination. His other Broadway credits are *Kean* (debut, 1961), *Roar Like a Dove*, *The Girl Who Came to Supper*, *Noel Coward's Sweet Potato*, *The Man Who Came to Dinner*, *Woman of the Year*, *Eileen*. He appeared Off-Broadway in *A Scent of Flowers*, *Sweethearts in Concert*, and *Jubilee in Concert*. His stepfather survives.

JOHN EDWARD CRAVEN, 83, New york City-born stage and screen actor, died in his sleep on May 17, 1991 in Studio City, CA. His Broadway appearances include *Wonder Boy*, *Wild Waves*, *Little Ol' Boy*, *Sailor Beware*, *The Ragged Edge*, *Star Spangled*, *Fulton of Oak Falls*, *Great Lady*, *Without Warning*, and *Tortilla Flat*. He is survived by his wife, a son, and three grandchildren.

ROBERT CUMMINGS, 82, Missouri-born stage, screen, and TV actor, died December 2, 1990 of kidney failure and complications of pneumonia in Woodland Hills, CA. Best known for his film and TV work, he appeared in over 100 movies and starred in the popular 1950's sit-com *The Bob Cummings Show*. He made his Broadway bow in 1931 in *The Roof*, billed as Blade Stanhope Conway, followed by roles in *Earl Carroll's Vanities* and *Ziegfeld Follies* (as Brice Hutchens), *Strange Orchestra* (as Robert C. Conway), and finally under his screen name in 1951's *Faithfully Yours* and *The Wayward Stork*. He is survived by his fifth wife, three sons, four daughters and nine grandchildren.

BOBBY DALE, 92, former stage and screen actor-dancer, died May 21, 1991 in Woodland Hills, CA, of myocardial infarction. He appeared on Broadway in *Sinbad*, *Bombo*, *Padlocks of 1927*, and the first edition of the *George White Scandals*. Later he became a prop-maker. His brother survives.

NICHOLAS DANTE (born Conrado Morales in Manhattan), 49, dancer and playwright, died May 21, 1991 in New York City of AIDS. He co-wrote the book for *A Chorus Line*, winning the Pulitzer Prize and the Tony Award. As a dancer he appeared in such shows as *Applause*, *Smith*, *Ambassador*, and *I'm Solomon*. He is survived by his mother.

WILLIAM DeACUTIS, 33, Connecticut-born stage, screen, and TV actor, died of brain lymphoma in Los Angeles on May 5, 1991. He appeared Off-Broadway in *The Normal Heart*, *Talk Radio*, and *Spring Awakening*. He is survived by his companion and a brother.

GEORGE T. DELACORTE, 97, philanthropist and founder of Dell Publishing, died on May 4, 1991 in New York of natural causes. Among his several gifts to the city is the Delacorte Theatre in Central Park for summer productions of the New York Shakespeare Festival. He is survived by his second wife, two sons, three daughters, a sister and a brother.

DON DRAPER, 62, stage, screen, and TV actor, died December 17, 1990 in Los Angeles of AIDS. He appeared on Broadway in *Advise and Consent*, *Madame Will You Walk*, *Coriolanus*, and *Eye for an Eye*, and Off-Broadway in such plays as *The Importance of Being Earnest* and *Nightride*. He is survived by two brothers.

IRENE DUNNE (née Irene Marie Dunn), 91, Kentucky-born stage and screen actress, and one of the leading film stars of the 1930's and '40's, died September 4, 1990 of heart failure at her home in the Holmby Hills section of Los Angeles. She made her Broadway debut in *The Clinging Vine* in 1923, followed by *Lollipop*, *Sweetheart Time*, *Yours Truly*, *Luckee Girl*, and *She's My Baby*. She played Magnolia in the 1929 road company of *Show Boat*, later repeating the role in the 1936 film version. Following her movie career she was named delegate to the United Nations 12th General Assembly. She is survived by her daughter and two grandchildren.

Valerie French

Jack Gilford

George Gobel

Rex Harrison

Wilfred Hyde White

Dean Jagger

RONNIE DYSON, 40, Brooklyn-born actor-singer, died November 10, 1990 in Philadelphia, PA of acute heart problems following degenerative liver and respiratory ailments. He introduced the song "Aquarius" in the original Off-Broadway production of *Hair*, later repeating his performance when the show moved to Broadway. He also had a small role in the 1979 film version of the show. No reported survivors.

TOM EYEN, 50, Ohio-born playwright and lyricist, died May 26, 1991 in Palm Beach, FL, of a heart attack. He won a Tony Award for writing the book of the 1981 musical *Dreamgirls*, and received a Grammy Award for writing the lyrics. He is survived by his mother, three brothers and two sisters.

VALERIE FRENCH (née Harrison), 59, London-born stage, screen, and TV actress, died November 3, 1990 in her Manhattan home. Her Broadway credits include *Inadmissible Evidence*, *Help Stamp Out Marriage!*, *The Mother Lover*, and the 1981 revival of *A Taste of Honey*. She appeared Off-Broadway in *Tea Party*, *The Basement*, and *Fallen Angels*. No immediate survivors. She was the widow of actor Thayer David.

JACK GILFORD (Jacob Gellman), 81, New York City-born stage, screen and TV character actor, died June 4, 1990 of stomach cancer in New York. He made his Broadway debut in 1940 in *Meet the People*, followed by *They Should Have Stood in Bed*, *Count Me In*, *The Live Wire*, *Alive and Kicking*, *Once Over Lightly*, *The Diary of Anne Frank*, *Romanoff and Juliet*, *The Tenth Man*, *A Funny Thing Happened on the Way to the Forum*, *Cabaret*, *Three Men on a Horse*, *No No Nanette*, *The Sunshine Boys*, *Sly Fox*, *Supporting Cast*, and *The World of Sholom Aleichem*. He appeared Off-Broadway in *Three Sisters*. Survived by his wife, a daughter, and two sons.

GEORGE GOBEL, 71, stage, screen, and TV actor-comedian, best known for his 1950's television series, *The George Gobel Show*, died February 24, 1991 in Encino, CA, of complications following bypass surgery on the major artery of his left leg. He appeared on Broadway in *Three Men on a Horse*, *Let It Ride!*, and *The Odd Couple*. Surviving are his wife, a son, two daughters, and three grandchildren.

DEL GREEN, 52, Idaho-born stage actress, died October 8, 1990 after a brief illness. She made her Broadway debut in 1967 in *Illya Darling*, followed by *Love-Suicide at Schofield Barracks*, *How to Succeed in Business Without Really Trying*, and Off-Broadway in *Archy and Mehitabel*, *Slight Ache*, and *Bittersuite*.

STANLEY GREEN, 67, musical theatre historian and author, died December 12, 1990 in Brooklyn, NY of complications from leukemia. His books include *The World of Musical Comedy*, *Starring Fred Astaire*, *Encyclopedia of the Musical Theatre* and *Broadway Musicals Show by Show*. He is survived by his wife, daughter, and son.

GRAHAM GREENE, 86, British novelist and playwright, one of the most notable writers of the 20th century, died April 3, 1991 of a blood disease, in Vevey, Switzerland. Although best known for such novels as *The Power and the Glory*, *Our Man in Havana*, and *The Comedians*, he also authored the plays *The Living Room*, *The Potting Shed*, *The Heart of the Matter* (from his novel), *Carving a Statue*, *The Complaisant Lover*, and an adaptation of *The Power and the Glory*. He is survived by his son and daughter.

FRANK HAMILTON, 66, stage, screen and TV actor, died April 25, 1991 of prostate cancer in Los Angeles. His Broadway credits include *The Visit*, *The Skin of Our Teeth*, *Inherit the Wind*, *Da*, *Major Barbara*, *Brigadoon*, and *The Corn Is Green*. He is survived by his wife, mother, a son, and two daughters.

SIR REX HARRISON (Reginald Carey Harrison), 82, British stage, screen, and TV actor, died June 2, 1990 of pancreatic cancer in his Manhattan home. One of the most sophisticated performers, he scored his greatest success playing Professor Henry Higgins in the 1956 Broadway musical *My Fair Lady*, winning the "Tony" Award and later the "Oscar" when he repeated the role in the 1964 film version. His Broadway debut was *Sweet Aloes* in 1936, followed by *Anne of the Thousand Days*, *Bell Book and Candle*, *Venus Observed*, *Love of Four Colonels*, *Fighting Cock*, *Emperor Henry IV*, *In Praise of Love*, *Caesar and Cleopatra*, *The Kingfisher*, *Heartbreak House*, *Aren't We All?*, and *The Circle* which ended its run a few days before his death. He is survived by his sixth wife and two sons, one of whom, Noel, is an actor.

WILFRID HYDE-WHITE, 87, British stage, screen, and TV actor, died May 6, 1991 of congestive heart failure in Woodland Hills, CA. In addition to his many roles on the London stage he appeared on Broadway in *Under the Counter* (his debut in 1947), *Antony and Cleopatra*, *The Reluctant Debutante*, *Caesar and Cleopatra*, and *The Jockey Club Stakes* for which he received a "Tony" Award nomination. He is survived by his second wife, actress Ethel Drew, two sons, one of whom, Alex, is an actor, a daughter, and four grandchildren.

DEAN JAGGER, 87, Ohio-born stage, screen, and TV star, who became one of Hollywood's leading character actors, winning an "Oscar" for his role in *Twelve O'Clock High*, died in his sleep on February 5, 1991 in his home in Santa Monica, CA. He had been suffering from heart disease. On Broadway he appeared in *Tobacco Road*, *They Shall Not Die*, *Missouri Legend*, *Everywhere I Roam*, *Brown Danube*, *Farm of Three Echoes*, *The Unconquered*, and *Doctor Social*. He is survived by his third wife, a daughter, two stepsons, and a sister.

Lisa
Kirk

Will
Kuluva

Glenn
Langan

Marcella
Markham

Keye
Luke

Mary
Martin

LAWRENCE KASHA, 57, New York-born producer, director, and former actor, died of brain cancer September 29, 1990 in Los Angeles. As an actor he appeared on Broadway in *Brigadoon* and *Finian's Rainbow*. He began producing with the Off-Broadway revue *Parade* before his Broadway debut with *She Loves Me*. He directed the 1962 Off-Broadway revival of *Anything Goes*, as well as several national companies of such shows as *Funny Girl*, *Camelot*, and *Li'l Abner*. His other Broadway producing credits include *Hadrian VII*, *Applause* (for which he won a "Tony" Award), *Seesaw*, *Woman of the Year*, and *Seven Brides for Seven Brothers*. He is survived by his brother, composer Al Kasha.

SHEPPARD KERMAN, 62, actor and playwright, died on April 15, 1991 in Manhasset, NY of lung cancer. As an actor he appeared on Broadway in *The Prescott Proposals*, *Tonight in Samarkand*, *The Great Sebastians*, and *The Sound of Music*. He wrote *Cut of the Axe* for Broadway, and *Mister Simian* for Off-Broadway, winning an "Obie" Award for the latter. He is survived by his wife, Ilona Murai, a dancer, a daughter, and two sisters.

LISA KIRK, 62, Pennsylvania-born stage actress and cabaret performer, best known for her roles in *Allegro* and *Kiss Me Kate*, died November 11, 1990 in New York of lung cancer. She made her Broadway debut in 1945 in *Goodnight Ladies*, and also appeared in *Here's Love*, *Mack and Mabel*, *Me Jack You Jill*, and the 1984 revival of *Design for Living*. She is survived by her husband, lyricist-producer Robert Wells.

BERRY KROEGER, 78, stage, screen, radio, and TV character actor, died January 4, 1991 of kidney failure in Los Angeles. Following his 1943 Broadway debut in *The World's Full of Girls*, he appeared in *The Tempest*, *Therese*, *Joan of Lorraine*, *Julius Caesar*, *Reclining Figure* and *Shangri-La*. He is survived by his wife and sister.

WILL KULUVA, 73, Kansas City-born stage, screen, and TV actor, died November 6, 1990 of an embolism while on a Caribbean cruise. His Broadway credits include *Hold on to Your Hats*, *Steps Leading Up*, *The Wanhope Building*, *Open House*, *A Tragedian in Spite of Himself*, *The Wedding*, *The Bear*, *On the Harmfulness of Tobacco*, *The Alchemist*, *Richard III*, *That Lady*, *Gods of the Mountain*, *Arms and the Man*, *Darkness at Noon*, *The Shrike*, *My Three Angels*, *The Doctor's Dilemma*, *A Very Special Baby* and *Clerambard*. He is survived by a daughter.

GLENN LANGAN, 73, Denver-born stage, screen, and TV actor, died January 19, 1991 in Los Angeles of cancer. His Broadway credits include *Glamour Preferred*, *A Kiss for Cinderella*, and *Fancy Meeting You Again*. He is survived by his wife, actress Adele Jergens, and his son.

BOB LESLIE, 64, stage and screen actor and writer, died in Los Angeles, on February 4, 1991 of undisclosed causes. He appeared on Broadway in *Mr. Wonderful* and *Ziegfeld Follies* (1957). Surviving are three sons, a daughter, and his mother.

EDWIN LESTER, 95, New York-born producer, founder and general director of the Los Angeles Civic Light Opera and the San Francisco Civic Light Opera, died December 13, 1990 in Beverly Hills of cardiac arrest. He was responsible for bringing many Broadway hits to Los Angeles including *The King and I*, *Gypsy*, and *Hello, Dolly!* In turn several of his productions eventually went to Broadway including *Song of Norway*, *Kismet*, *Peter Pan*, and *Gigi*. No immediate survivors.

HERMAN LEVIN, 83, Philadelphia-born Broadway producer responsible for the original production of *My Fair Lady*, died December 27, 1990 in New York of undisclosed causes. Other credits include *Call Me Mister*, *No Exit*, *Bonanza Bound*, *Richard III*, *Gentlemen Prefer Blondes*, *Bless You All*, *The Girl Who Came to Supper*, *The Great White Hope*, *Lovely Ladies, Kind Gentlemen*, and the 1976 revival of *My Fair Lady*. He is survived by a daughter.

MARTA LINDEN, 87, stage actress, died December 13, 1990 of pneumonia in Manhattan. Following her 1946 Broadway debut in *Present Laughter*, she appeared in *The Men We Marry*, *Cry of the Peacock*, *The Curious Savage*, and *The Starcross Story*. She is survived by her daughter, three granddaughters, and one great-granddaughter.

JANE LLOYD-JONES, 69, stage actress, died March 11, 1991 of a stroke in Kingston, NY. She appeared on Broadway in *The Shop at Sly Corner* and *The Gray-Eyed People*, and Off-Broadway in *No Exit*, *The Daughters of Atrius* and *Macbeth*. She is survived by her husband, writer-actor Heywood Hale Broun.

LAWRENCE LOTT, 40, Colorado-born stage, screen, and TV actor, died January 24, 1991 in Greeley, CO, of AIDS. He appeared Off-Broadway in *Bingo*, *Heartbreak House*, *Two Noble Kinsmen*, and *The Normal Heart*. His parents survive.

KEYE LUKE, 86, China-born stage, screen, and TV actor, one of the most notable Asian-American performers, died January 12, 1991 in Whittier CA following a stroke. His numerous film credits include several appearances as Charlie Chan's Number 1 Son. He was also a regular on the hit TV series *Kung Fu*. He appeared in the 1958 Broadway musical *Flower Drum Song*, in which he sang "The Other Generation" with Juanita Hall. Survivors include a daughter.

RUSSELL MARKERT, 91, New Jersey-born dancer-choreographer and founder of the Radio City Music Hall Rockettes, died December 1, 1990 in Waterbury, CT. For Broadway he choreographed such shows as *Just a Minute*, *Americana*, *New Americana*, *Keep It Clean*, *Here Goes the Bride*, and *George White's Scandals*. From 1932 to 1971 he staged and choreographed the Rockettes' numbers. No reported survivors.

MARCELLA MARKHAM, 68, Brooklyn-born stage and TV actress, died February 24, 1991 in New York of breast cancer. She appeared on Broadway in *Vickie*, *Flamingo Road*, *The Threepenny Opera*, *Are You Now or Have You Ever Been?*, and *A Conflict of Interest*. Survived by her second husband, a son, and a grandson.

ROBERT MAROFF, 57, Brooklyn-born stage, screen, and TV actor-director, died April 9, 1991 of prostate cancer in Pennington, NJ. He appeared Off-Broadway in *Short Eyes* in 1974. Survived by his sister, and a brother.

MARY MARTIN, 76, Texas-born stage, screen, and TV actress-singer, one of the most acclaimed stars of the American musical theatre, died November 4, 1990 in Rancho Mirage, CA, of cancer. She became a star with her 1938 Broadway debut, singing "My Heart Belongs to Daddy" in *Leave It to Me*, followed by *One Touch of Venus*, *Lute Song*, *South Pacific*, *Kind Sir*, *Peter Pan* (a "Tony" Award winning performance she repeated memorably for TV), *The Skin of Our Teeth*, *The Sound of Music* ("Tony" Award), *Jennie*, *I Do! I Do!*, and *Do You Turn Somersaults?* She is survived by her son, actor Larry Hagman, her daughter and six grandchildren.

EMILY McLAUGHLIN, 61, stage, and TV actress, best known for her continuing role in the daytime serial *General Hospital*, died of cancer April 26, 1991 in Los Angeles. Her New York stage appearances include *The Frogs of Spring* and *The Lovers*. She is survived by a daughter and a son.

TOD MILLER, 46, Illinois-born stage actor and choreographer, died December 14, 1990 in New York of a brain tumor. Following his 1967 Broadway debut in *Mame*, he appeared in *Here's Where I Belong*, *Cabaret*, *Canterbury Tales*, *Promises Promises*, *Goodtime Charley*. Survived by his wife, actress Virginia Seidel, and a son, Garrett.

PEGGY MONDO, 50, Connecticut-born stage, screen, and TV actress, who appeared in both the Broadway and film versions of *The Music Man*, died February 19, 1991 of a heart attack in Los Angeles. She is survived by her husband and three brothers.

Gilbert
Price

Anne
Revere

Raymond
St. Jacques

Natalie
Schafer

Mario
Siletti

Danny
Thomas

CARLOS MONTALBAN, 87, Spanish stage, screen, and TV actor, perhaps best known to audiences for his El Exigente/Savarin TV commercials, died March 28, 1991. He appeared on the New York stage in *Me Candido!* in 1956. Surviving are his brother, actor Ricardo Montalban, his wife, and a sister.

ADA MOORE, 64, Chicago-born stage actress and singer, who appeared as Gladiola in the original 1954 production of *House of Flowers*, died of cancer January 11, 1991 in Brooklyn. She is survived by her husband.

HERMES PAN (Panagiotopolous), 80, Memphis-born stage and screen dancer-choreographer, died September 19, 1990 in Beverly Hills, CA, of an apparent stroke. He was best known for his many film collaborations with Fred Astaire. From 1927 to 1930 he was a chorus dancer in several Broadway musicals, including *Top Speed*, in which he danced with Ginger Rogers. He is survived by a sister.

GILBERT PRICE, 48, New York-born stage actor-singer, died January 2, 1991 in Vienna of undisclosed causes. For his work on Broadway he earned four "Tony" Award nominations for *Lost in the Stars*, *The Night That Made America Famous*, *1600 Pennsylvania Aveune*, and *Timbuktu*. He also appeared on Broadway in *The Roar of the Greasepaint—The Smell of the Crowd*, and Off-Broadway in *Fly Blackbird*, *Jerico-Jim Crow* for which he received a Theatre World Award, *Promenade*, *Slow Dance on the Killing Ground*, *Six*, *Melodrama Play*, *The Crucifixion*, and *Throw Down*. He is survived by his father and a sister.

GAVIN REED, 59, British stage, screen, and TV actor, died in Portland, ME, of respiratory failure on December 3, 1990. He had collapsed on stage during a production of *Loot* at the Portland Stage Company a few weeks earlier. He appeared Off-Broadway in *The Taming of the Shrew*, *French without Tears*, *Potsdam Quartet*, *Two Fish in the Sky*, and on Broadway in *Scapino*, *Some of My Best Friends*, and *Run for Your Wife*. He is survived by a brother.

ANNE REVERE, 87, Manhattan-born stage, screen, and TV actress, one of film's notable supporting players, who won an "Oscar" for her role in *National Velvet*, died December 18, 1990 of pneumonia at her home in Locust Valley, NY. Following her 1931 Broadway debut in *The Great Barrington*, she appeared in *The Lady with a Lamp*, *Wild Waves*, *Double Door*, *The Children's Hour*, *As You Like It*, *The Three Sisters*, *4 Twelves are 48*, *Cue for Passion*, *Jolly's Progress*, and *Toys in the Attic*, for which she won a "Tony" Award. Off-Broadway she was in *Night of the Dunce*. She is survived by a sister.

MARTIN RITT, 76, Manhattan-born stage, screen and TV actor-turned-director, died December 8, 1990 in Santa Monica, CA of cardiac disease. Prior to becoming one of Hollywood's foremost directors, he acted on the New York stage in such productions as *Golden Boy*, *Gentle People*, *Two on an Island*, *No for an Answer*, *Criminals*, *They Should Have Stood in Bed*, *The Eve of St. Mark*, *Winged Victory*, *Men of Distinction*, *Maya*, and *The Flowering Peach*. His Broadway directorial credits include *Yellow Jack*, *Mr. Peebles and Mr. Hooker*, *Set My People Free*, *The Man*, *Cry of the Peacock*, *A Memory of Two Mondays*, and *A View from the Bridge*. He is survived by his wife, a daughter, and a son.

MEGHAN ROBINSON, 35, stage actress and founding member of Theatre-in-Limbo, died November 18, 1990 in Manhattan of AIDS-related cancer. She appeared for the company in *The Lady in Question*, *Psycho Beach Party*, *Vampire Lesbians of Sodom*, and *Times Square Angel*. She is survived by her companion and her father, sister and brother.

TOM ROSQUI, 62, Oakland-born stage, screen, and TV actor, died April 11, 1991 in Los Angeles of cancer. He appeared with LCRep in *Danton's Death*, *Condemned of Altona*, *Country Wife*, *Caucasian Chalk Circle*, *Alchemist*, *Yerma*, *East Wind*, and *A Streetcar Named Desire*, Off-Broadway in *Collision Course*, *Day of Absence*, *Brotherhood*, *What the Butler Saw*, *Waiting for Godot*, and *Whiskey*, and on Broadway in *Unlikely Heroes* and *The Lincoln Mask*. He is survived by a son, a stepson, and a stepdaughter.

RAYMOND ST. JACQUES (James Arthur Johnson), 60, Connecticut-born stage, film and TV actor, died August 27, 1990 in Los Angeles of cancer of the lymph glands. Following his Off-Broadway debut in *High Name Today*, he appeared in *Romeo and Juliet*, *The Cool World*, *Henry V*, *Night Life*, *Seventh Heaven*, and *The Blacks*. He is survived by his mother.

BERNARD SAUER, 67, Argentina-born stage actor and president of the Hebrew Actors Union, died of a heart attack in New York on February 13, 1991. His New York stage credits include *Let's Sing Yiddish*, *Light Lively and Yiddish*, and *Sing Israel Sing*. He is survived by four sisters and a brother.

NATALIE SCHAFER, 90, New Jersey-born stage, screen and TV actress, perhaps best known for her role as Mrs. Howell on the 1960's sit-com *Gilligan's Island*, died April 10, 1991 of cancer at her home in Beverly Hills, CA. Following her 1927 Broadway debut in *Trigger*, she appeared in *March Hares*, *These Few Ashes*, *Nut Farm*, *Rhapsody*, *Great Barrington*, *Perfectly Scandalous*, *New York to Cherbourg*, *So Many Paths*, *Lady Precious Stream*, *Susan and God*, *Lady in the Dark*, *Doughgirls*, *A Joy Forever*, *Forward*, *Romanoff and Juliet*, *The Highest Tree* and *The Killing of Sister George*. Off-Broadway her credits include *Six Characters in Search of an Author* and *The Circle*. No immediate survivors.

ATHENE SEYLER, 101, stage and screen actress, died on September 12, 1990 in her native London. In addition to her work on the London stage she appeared in New York in *The Gift Horse*, *The Country Wife*, *Transit of Venus*, *These Few Ashes*, *The Last Enemy*, *Marriage à la Mode*, *The Last of the Ladies*, *The Cherry Orchard*, *Watch on the Rhine*, *Harvey*, and *The Chances*. She is survived by her daughter and four grandchildren.

NORRIS M. SHIMABUKU, 44, stage actor, died in his sleep April 10, 1991 in his Manhattan home. For the Pan Asian Repertory Theater he appeared in such plays as *The Imposter*, *Lucky Come Hawaii*, *Shogun Macbeth*, and *The man Who Turned into a Stick*. He also appeared in the New York Shakespeare Festival's production of *Henry IV, Parts 1 and 2*. He is survived by his mother, two sisters and a brother.

MARIO SILETTI, 65, New York City-born stage actor, teacher, and co-founder of the National Shakespeare Conservatory, died January 7, 1991 in New York of pneumonia. In addition to teaching at the Stella Adler Studio for 25 years he acted Off-Broadway in *Out of This World*, *Queen After Death*, *Little Mary Sunshine*, *He Who Gets Slapped*, and *The Alchemist*. His Broadway debut was in *School for Wives* in 1971. He is survived by his companion and two brothers.

DANNY THOMAS (Amos Jacobs), 79, Michigan-born stage, screen, and TV actor-singer, died February 7, 1991 in Los Angeles following a heart attack. He won his greatest fame on television starring in the successful sit-com *Make Room for Daddy/The Danny Thomas Show*. He appeared on Broadway in the 1950 production *Untitled Revue*. He is survived by his wife and three children, including actress Marlo Thomas and producer Tony Thomas, and five grandchildren.

MARJORIE WARFIELD, 88, Philadelphia-born stage, radio and silent screen actress, died April 15, 1991 in Los Angeles of pneumonia. She appeared on Broadway in *It Never Rains*, *Pagan Lady* and *Legal Murder*, and Off-Broadway in *Barefoot in the Park*, and *A Flea in Her Ear*. She is survived by her daughter, a sister, and two grandchildren.

DAVID WHITE, 74, stage, screen, and TV actor, best known for his role as Larry Tate in the hit sit-com *Bewitched*, died November 26, 1990 in Hollywood of a heart attack. He appeared on Broadway in *Leaf and Bough*, *Affairs of State*, *The Bird Cage*, *Anniversary Waltz*, and *One Foot in the Door*. He is survived by a daughter.

VIOLET WINTON, 90, stage actress, who performed the "Varsity Drag" number in the original Broadway production of *Good News*, died February 8, 1991 in Miami. She is survived by a son.

RAYMOND WOOD, 43, stage actor and playwright, died in New York of AIDS on July 20, 1990. He starred in the 1975 Off-Broadway musical *Boy Meets Boy*. Surviving are his father, and a sister.

INDEX

212

216

220

237

Rifkin, Ron, 98, 194
Rigby, Cathy, 21
Rigdon, Kevin, 89, 102
Rigert, Peter, 85
Riggs, Jacquelyn, 120
Rigol, Joey, 15, 41, 194
Riley, Eric, 10, 194
Riley, Lizza, 131
Riley-Normile, Betsy, 66
Rinaldi, Philip, 10, 62, 71, 97
Rinehart, Elaine, 68, 194
Rinehart, Susanna, 146
Ring Round the Moon, 61
Ring, David, 92
Ringham, Nancy, 119
Ringwald, Molly, 167
Rios, Jorge, 52
Risenhoover, Max, 80
Rispoli, Michael, 85
Risser, Patricia M., 154
Ritchie, Lynn, 79
Ritchie, Michael F., 89
Ritt, Martin, 207
Rittenhouse, Terrell, 51
Rivas, Fernando, 58
Rivera, Chita, 124
Rivera, Elan, 75
Rivera, Gloria, 50
Rivera, James, 110
Rivera, José M., 142
Rivera, René, 94
Riverman, 64
Rivers, Gwynne, 86
Rivers, Voza, 121
Riverside Shakespeare Company, 100
Rivin, Lucille, 64, 194
Rivkin, Gigi, 76
Rizzo, Karen, 79
Rizzo, Mark, 53
Roach, Bruce, 139
Roach, Kevin D., 158
Roach, Kevin Joseph, 85
Roach, Max, 149
Road to Mecca, The, 168
Road to Nirvana, 85
Roar Of The Greasepaint-The Smell Of The Crowd, The, 142
Roark, Jonathan, 134
Robards, Jason, 20, 166, 194
Robb, Lou, 136
Robbins, Carrie, 87
Robbins, Elizabeth, 139
Robbins, Erin, 110
Robbins, Jana, 34, 196
Robbins, Jerome, 17, 21, 34, 110, 168-169, 173, 175-176, 178-179, 181, 185, 187-188, 190-191, 193, 196-197, 199
Robbins, Mark, 139
Roberson, Ken, 11
Robert, Maggie, 156
Roberts, Angela, 100
Roberts, Chris, 125
Roberts, Eric, 167
Roberts, Gary, 150
Roberts, Heather, 69
Roberts, Jackie Mari, 69

Roberts, Judith, 118
Roberts, Lance, 149
Roberts, Leslie, 51, 73
Roberts, Louise, 135, 196
Roberts, Sarah, 84, 121
Roberts, Tony, 73, 110, 196
Robertson, Barbara E., 127
Robertson, Cliff, 166, 196
Robertson, Joel, 41
Robertson, Lanie, 144
Robertson, Scott, 72, 128, 196
Robertson, Suzanne, 86
Robin, Michael, 83
Robins, Laila, 104
Robinson, Bruce Taylor, 77
Robinson, Cindy, 21
Robinson, Darryl, 158
Robinson, Diane, 122
Robinson, Dorothy Marie, 120
Robinson, Edward G., 19
Robinson, Hal, 40, 196
Robinson, Kathy, 143
Robinson, Lance, 16, 37, 196
Robinson, Max, 101, 128
Robinson, Meghan, 207
Robinson, Muriel, 57
Robinson, Pepsi, 72
Robinson, Peter, 21, 101, 120, 196
Robinson, Robin Francis, 74
Robinson, Robin, 34
Robinson, Sloane, 123
Robinson, Valerie D., 134
Robison, Blake, 146
Robison, Terry, 66
Roblin, Jennifer, 9
Roby, Elizabeth, 50
Roche, Elisa De La, 77
Rochon, Valerie Jerusha, 121
Rock & Roll, 62, 123
Rock, Kevin, 97
Rockwell, Sam, 64, 79
Roderick, Connie, 24
Roderick, Ray, 38, 63
Rodgers, Bruce L., 120
Rodgers, Gaby, 166
Rodgers, Richard, 11, 25, 57, 63, 110, 116, 128, 190, 201
Rodgers, Terrence Charles, 153
Rodriguez, Al D., 77, 99
Rodriguez, Dianne, 149
Rodriguez, E.J., 127
Rodriguez, Johanna, 117
Rodriguez, Steven, 68
Rodriguez, Valente, 136
Rodriquez, Joseph W., 131
Roebling, Paul, 166
Roehrman, Todd, 123
Roesch, William, 118
Roffe, Al, 77
Rogers, David, 108, 132
Rogers, Diana, 113
Rogers, Erica, 121
Rogers, Irma, 32
Rogers, Ken Leigh, 11
Rogers, Laura, 61
Rogers, Mary, 37, 97
Rogers, Michael, 97, 196
Rogers, Reg, 156

Rogers, Wayne, 121
Rogerson, Gus, 14, 79
Rogness, Peter, 59
Rohan, Brian, 79
Roht, Ken, 51
Roker, Roxie, 72
Rollins, Jack, 74
Rolph, Marti, 167
Romano, Kate, 140
Romanov, Joe, 134
Romans, Bruce Marshall, 80
Rome, Harold, 82
Romeo And Juliet, 64, 67, 93, 100, 105, 158-159
Romeo, John, 66
Romeo, Marc, 48
Romick, James, 42
Rooker, Michael, 90
Room Of One's Own, A, 70
Rooney, Deborah, 79
Rooney, Mickey, 167
Roos, Caspar, 140
Root, The, 125
Roper, Randle, 148
Rosa, Dennis, 139
Rosales, Rachel, 7
Rosario, Carmen, 60
Rosario, Willie, 10
Rosato, Mary Lou, 158
Rose, Danny, 51
Rose, Hugh A., 16
Rose, Isabel, 105
Rose, L. Arthur, 142
Rose, Lloyd, 150
Rose, Reva, 166
Rose, Richard, 34, 56, 64, 159
Rose, Robin Pearson, 140
Roselin, Stephan, 101, 129
Roseman, Ralph, 16, 39, 76
Rosen, Louis, 127
Rosen, Madelon, 13, 58, 61, 72, 74, 99
Rosenberg, D.C., 59, 87
Rosenberg, Michael, 103
Rosenberg, Sandy, 112
Rosenblat, Barbara, 33
Rosenblum, M. Edgar, 135
Rosenfeld, Jyll, 9
Rosenfeld, Moishe, 13
Rosenfield, Lois, 54
Rosentel, Robert W., 121
Rosenthal, Karine, 158
Rosenthal, Mark, 130
Rosetta Street, 64
Rosetti-Finn, Dianne, 61
Rosqui, Tom, 136, 207
Ross, Audrey, 51, 70, 78
Ross, Carolyn, 148
Ross, Ian, 149
Ross, J. Michael, 149
Ross, Marion, 150
Ross, Marty, 17
Ross, Michael, 130, 149
Ross, Pamela, 53
Ross, Sandra, 72
Ross, Stanley Ralph, 124
Ross, Stuart, 46, 60, 65
Ross, Tavis, 141, 149

Rosset, Caca, 92
Rossetter, Kathryn, 73, 148, 196
Rossi, Angelo Del, 142
Rossini, Gioacchino, 13
Rossomme, Richard, 119
Rosten, Tracy, 106
Rotella, Mary, 110
Roth, Ann, 85
Roth, Ari, 117
Roth, Frank, 133
Roth, Mark, 137
Roth, Michael, 90
Roth, Tisha, 152
Rothaar, Michael, 116
Rothenberg, David, 28, 48, 51-53, 55, 60-61, 65-67, 72-73, 80, 83
Rothenberg, Josh, 52, 65
Rothhaar, Michael, 116
Rothman, Carole, 102
Rothman, Jane, 145
Rothman, Stephen, 119, 125
Rothschild, Lloyd, 144
Rothschilds, The, 47, 49
Roudis, John, 74
Rough Crossing, 152
Roundabout Theatre Company, 101
Rounds, Danny, 107
Rounds, David, 167
Rousseau, Brenda, 65
Routh, Marc, 27, 77
Routman, Steve, 129, 152
Routolo, Robert, 8, 121-122
Routt, Jean, 135
Roven, Glen, 32
Rover, The, 63
Rovere, Jodi Ginniver, 159
Rowe, Darby, 93
Rowe, Rick, 84
Rowe, Spencer, 142
Rowe, Stephen, 130
Rowe, Tonia, 95, 196
Rowell, Jody, 135
Rowen, Glenn, 7
Roy, Richard, 92
Roya, David, 81, 196
Royal Family, The, 119
Rubano, John, 147
Rube's All-Night, 63
Rubenstein, Arthur B., 121
Rubenstein, John, 62
Rubenstein, Murray, 118, 148
Rubin, Arthur, 21
Rubin, Cyma, 63
Rubin, John Gould, 123
Rubin, Leon, 64
Rubin, Rich, 73
Rubin, Stan, 34, 196
Rubin, Steven, 130, 140
Rubinek, Saul, 95
Rubino, Giselle, 149
Rubinstein, John, 98, 164, 167, 196
Rucker, Bo, 64, 167, 196
Rucker, Larry, 140
Ruckman, David, 101, 129
Rudman, Bill, 129
Rudnick, Paul, 29

241

242